READING PROCESS AND PRACTICE

With a chapter on whole language
by
Dorothy Watson and Paul Crowley
University of Missouri—Columbia

and a chapter on reading in the content areas
by
Marilyn Wilson
Michigan State University

and a concluding chapter
by
Dorothy Watson
University of Missouri—Columbia

READING PROCESS AND PRACTICE

FROM SOCIO-PSYCHOLINGUISTICS TO WHOLE LANGUAGE

Constance Weaver

Western Michigan University

Heinemann Educational Books
Portsmouth, NH

HEINEMANN EDUCATIONAL BOOKS, INC.
70 Court Street   Portsmouth, NH 03801
Offices and agents throughout the world

Acknowledgments begin on page *xxii*.

Library of Congress Cataloging-in-Publication Data

Weaver, Constance.
  Reading process and practice.

  Rev. ed. of: Psycholinguistics and reading. c1980.
  Bibliography: p.
  Includes index.
  1. Reading. 2. Psycholinguistics. 3. Language
awareness in children. I. Weaver, Constance.
Psycholinguistics and reading. II. Title.
LB1050.22.W43 1987   428.4   87-12114
ISBN 0-435-08444-5

Printed in the United States of America

10 9 8 7 6 5 4

For my son John
without whom this book
and my life
would be much less lively

And psycholinguistics can help to assert the right of children to learn to read with the aid of people rather than procedures.
—Frank Smith

Contents

List of Activities

Preface

And reading itself, as a psycho-physiological process, is almost as good as a miracle.

          —Edmund Burke Huey

As experienced teachers know all too well, there is no magic formula for teaching reading. But some approaches and procedures are more defensible than others, given what we know about the process of reading. The purpose of this book is to help preservice and practicing teachers better understand that process and better grasp some of the implications for teaching. The book is intended particularly for those with little or no prior study in the nature of the reading process. Thus the style of the text and also most entries in the end-of-chapter bibliographies are generally directed toward newcomers to the field, though references in the text itself can often provide a valuable starting point for more in-depth study.

  The basic thesis of this book is that reading is not a passive process by which we soak up words and information from the page, but an active process by which we predict, sample, and confirm or correct our hypotheses about the written text. Suppose, for example, that you are reading the sentence ''The cruel giant fell into the . . . .'' What do you know about the word that follows *the*? First, you know it is likely to be a noun, a ''thing'' or substance (or a word that modifies an upcoming noun). Second, you know that this word probably denotes something that one can fall into. Using your lifetime of knowledge and experience, and without even seeing the word, you can narrow it down to a few likely possibilities: *water, well, lake, pond, hole, vat*, and so forth—but probably not *chair, glass*, or *dog*, much less *crowded, investigate*, or *cleverly*. Having narrowed the possibilities, you would need to look at only one or two of the letters, or at only parts of some of the letters, in order to identify the word. And you could confirm (or correct) your tentative identification by seeing if that word made sense with the following context. Such, in fact, is what proficient readers normally do.

  In brief, then, this example illustrates the ''psycholinguistic'' nature of the reading process, the fact that reading involves a transaction between the mind of the reader and the language of the text. Equally important, this transaction occurs within a particular social and sociolinguistic context: for example, the expectations about reading that children bring with them to the classroom form one kind of social "context," as do the classroom itself and the expectations of the teacher. These and many other social factors contribute to making reading not only a *psycholinguistic* process, but a *socio-psycholinguistic* process of incredible complexity. It is this process and some of the implications for teaching that are explored in the pages that follow. Psycholinguistic aspects of the reading process receive the most attention explicitly, but various social and sociolinguistic factors affecting reading and learning to read are implicit throughout the book, particularly in the last six chapters.

As indicated, one of the most important observations about reading is that it is an active process: the reader must actively construct meaning, rather than passively soak it up from the page. I have endeavored to encourage such active, participatory reading of this book itself, in several ways:

1. By including "Questions for Journals and Discussion," some of which can be profitably discussed prior to reading the chapter.
2. By including a number of end-of-chapter activities that anticipate the following chapter.
3. By including numerous participatory activities in the chapters that focus on the reading process.

I myself often lead classes through several of the activities within a chapter before assigning the chapter to be read, and I would encourage teachers to consider doing likewise. The "List of Activities" in the front of the book should assist in locating such activities. Another way to encourage purposeful reading is to ask students to respond to some of the "Questions for Journals and Discussion" before reading the chapter, either in a journal or in classroom discussion—or both. Chapter 9 on reading in the content areas includes a number of valuable suggestions that can be used to encourage active reading and understanding of this text.

This text was originally intended as a second edition of my earlier *Psycholinguistics and Reading: From Process to Practice* (1980), but it grew far beyond the scope of the original edition—so much so, that we decided to give it a new title, *Reading Process and Practice: From Socio-Psycholinguistics to Whole Language.* Unlike the earlier text, this one is not divided into two parts, the first dealing with the reading process and the second dealing with implications and applications for the teaching of reading. Though the differing emphases remain, they no longer seem so neatly divisible. This is partly because topics occur and reoccur throughout the book: the teaching of phonics and the use of context in reading are two topics dealt with repeatedly, particularly in the early chapters but also in most later chapters. A whole-language approach and research on the effectiveness of differing approaches to beginning reading are two topics that also reoccur, particularly in the later chapters but also in earlier ones. Such incremental repetition resembles the "spiral curriculum" advocated by Jerome Bruner in *The Process of Education* (1960): a topic is addressed repeatedly, at increasingly higher levels of sophistication, each time deepening the learner's understanding.

Another reason for not separating the book into parts is that I firmly believe that our understanding of the reading process and our understanding of effective approaches to the teaching of reading enhance one another: the whole is somehow greater than the mere sum of the parts. Thus the totality of this book is something like a fabric, with various threads—such as phonics, or a whole-language approach—woven throughout. Remove any of the major threads, or divide the whole into parts, and you have destroyed the basic nature of the whole cloth.

Of course this book differs from *Psycholinguistics and Reading* not only in overall form, but most crucially in content. Chapter 1 and Chapters 3 through 6 are similar to the originals, though with considerable clarifying and updating. Chapter 2 has been almost completely rewritten, to clarify the nature of schemas and transactions in reading, and to focus more clearly on contrasting models of the reading process. Chapter 7 on miscue analysis has become Chapter 10, with considerable revision. Chapters 8 and 9 and the grammatical appendix of the original have been omitted to make room for four new chapters: Chapter 7, on the acquisition of literacy; Chapter 8, on a whole-language approach to the teaching of reading; Chapter 9, on reading in the content areas; and Chapter 11, on preventing reading difficulties and assisting readers with special needs. The text concludes with Chapter 12, a coda titled "Coming Whole Circle." The Table of Contents further suggests the nature of these changes. In addition to revising and adding chapters, I have included appendices and more bibliographies that should be useful to teachers and students, and enhanced many of the sets of end-of-chapter activities. Also, I think the text organization offers flexibility: one might, for example, cover Chapters 1 and 2, then go to Chapter 7 before returning to Chapter 3. All of these changes should, I think, make this book even more teachable than its predecessor.

Those who lament the loss of something from *Psycholinguistics and Reading* are hereby granted permission to photocopy those materials for educational use. However, I cannot be legally responsible for your photocopying anything that includes copyrighted material for which I originally obtained permission; that responsibility must be yours. Permission is also hereby granted for photocopying the blank miscue analysis forms in Chapter 10.

I scarcely know where to begin in thanking the various people who have contributed, directly and indirectly, to this text. In addition to those individuals acknowledged in *Psycholinguistics and Reading*, I would thank, of course, my many students whose experiences and questions have further challenged my thinking, and the students and colleagues elsewhere who have expressed appreciation for the first text and made suggestions for improving it.

Many who have used the text will also be grateful, I think, for the wonderful new chapters contributed by others: the chapter on whole language, contributed by Dorothy Watson and Paul Crowley of the University of Missouri-Columbia; the conclusion, contributed by Dorothy Watson; and the chapter on reading in the content areas, contributed by Marilyn Wilson of Michigan State University. As I use this text myself, I know I will continue to be thankful for their fine contributions. I particularly want to thank also those who have read and commented on part or all of the text: Sharon Rich, current editor of the *Canadian Journal of English Language Arts*, and Kathryn Mitchell Pierce, of Webster University. Having read the entire manuscript, Kathryn made several suggestions that have clearly enhanced the book. But of course, I alone bear responsibility for the remaining limitations of the text, and it cannot be assumed that any of the contributors or readers necessarily agrees with everything I have said.

Thanks to financial support from my university, in May of 1986 I had the privilege of attending the Fourth International Conference on the Teaching of English, held in Ottawa, Ontario. It was, quite simply, the most professionally rewarding conference I have ever attended. There I met a number of people, literally from around the globe, who generously shared their expertise and their research. Among the many teachers and scholars who contributed to this book, then, are many people with whom I became acquainted at this conference: Jon Cook (and through him, Libby Charnock), David Doake, Lee Dobson, Henrietta Dombey (and through her, Katharine Perera), Warwick Elley, Martha King (and through her, Marie Clay), Julie Kniskern, Moira McKenzie, Adrian Peetoom (and through him, Jane Baskwill and Margaret Phinney), Sharon Rich, and Charles Temple. Together, these individuals have made major contributions to this text.

Continuing to pervade this new book is the work of other prominent scholars and friends: Yetta and Ken Goodman, Dorothy Watson, Jerry Harste, Carolyn Burke, Don Graves, Lucy Calkins, and Frank Smith. I have been fortunate to serve with several of these people on the Reading Commission of the National Council of Teachers of English. Other Commission members I want particularly to thank for their influence and assistance are Paul Crowley, Bob Carey, Karl Koenke, Judith Langer, Gordon Pradl, and Margaret Stevenson. I particularly thank these people not only for their contributions to this text but for the model they provide in their humanistic approach to education.

Others in the reading field who have contributed materials and ideas include Diane DeFord, Lynn Rhodes, Terry Smith, Marie Carbo, and Sue Miller. Even professionals in other fields have helped: these include Lon Jones, Gary Ruoff, and Jeanne Hartenstein. My thanks to them all, as well as to colleagues—Maryellen Hains, Nancy Stone, Anne Szalkowski—and students—Lisa Black, Richonda Radom—who have contributed materials new to this book.

I particularly appreciate those who helped with research and with preparing the final manuscript: Barbara Myers, Kathy Neidlinger, Susan Heyse, and John Weaver. They lightened the burden considerably. So did the Honors College at Western Michigan University, by awarding Kathy Neidlinger a scholarship to assist me.

I am grateful also for two fellowships from the Faculty Research and Creative Activities Fund of Western Michigan University, one to study "Parallels Between New Paradigms in Science and in Reading and Literary Theories" and one to study "Reading as a Whole Brain Process." These fellowships enabled me to pursue research that has contributed substantially to Chapters 2, 7, and 11, thus considerably enhancing the quality of the book.

The people at Heinemann have been wonderful to work with. I particularly appreciate the wisdom, humor, patience, and support of Philippa Stratton, Editor-in-Chief. When the task of finishing this manuscript seemed hopeless, she was always there to make it seem possible again. In addition, I would like to thank Donna Bouvier of Heinemann, for overseeing the production of this text; Claire

McKean, Joanne Davidson, and Michael Hodges of G&H SOHO, for carrying out the details of production; and Winifred M. Davis, for her careful and helpful editing of the text. I would also like to thank Nancy Sheridan of Heinemann for her invaluable assistance with the Acknowledgments.

In *Psycholinguistics and Reading*, I expressed gratitude to my friend and former teacher, Owen Thomas, who ''had faith in me long before I learned to have faith in myself.'' But long before he became my mentor, my mother encouraged me to a degree that I have only begun to realize. There was no such word as ''impossible'' in her vocabulary; she led me to believe that anything I wanted to do, I could do. And I have. So this book is not only for my son but for my mother, who believed in me long, long before anyone else. Thank you.

Acknowledgments

We are grateful to the publishers and individuals below for granting permission to reprint material from previously published works.

Epigraph

Page vii: From *Psycholinguistics and Reading* by Frank Smith. Copyright © 1985 by Frank Smith. Reprinted by permission of the author.

Chapter 1

Page 1: From "Understanding the Hypothesis, It's the Teacher That Makes the Difference" by Jerome C. Harste, in *Reading Horizons* (1977), quarterly journal, College of Education, Western Michigan University, Kalamazoo, Michigan.

Page 3: From *Psychology of Language* by David S. Palermo. Copyright © 1978 by Scott, Foresman and Company. Reprinted by permission.

Pages 5–7: From *A Camel in the Sea* by Lee Garrett Goetz. Copyright © 1966 by McGraw-Hill Book Company. Reprinted by permission.

Pages 11–13: From "Validating the Construct to Theoretical Orientation in Reading Instruction" by Diane DeFord in *Reading Research Quarterly*, Spring 1985. Reprinted with permission of Diane DeFord and the International Reading Association.

Chapter 2

Figure 2.5: Reproduced by Special Permission of *Playboy* Magazine: Copyright © 1975 by *Playboy*.

Page 28: From *Reading House Series: Comprehension and Vocabulary*, Random House 1980. Used by permission.

Page 29: Bloome, David, and Green, Judith. "Looking at Reading Instruction: Sociolinguistic and Ethnographic Approaches." In *Contexts of Reading*, edited by Carolyn N. Hedley and Anthony N. Baratta. Norwood, NJ: ABLEX, 1985, pp. 167–184.

Page 43: Reprinted with permission of Scribner Educational Publishers, a Division of Macmillan, Inc. from Book A of *Lippincott Basic Reading* by Charles C. Walcutt and Glenn McCracken. Copyright © 1975 by Macmillan, Inc.

Pages 50–51: From "Cultural Schemata and Reading Comprehension" by Ralph E. Reynolds, Marsha A. Taylor, Margaret S. Steffensen, Larry L. Shirey and Richard C. Anderson, in *Reading Research Quarterly*, Vol. 17, No. 3. Reprinted with permission of Ralph E. Reynolds and the International Reading Association.

Chapter 3

Page 54: From *Understanding Reading: A Psycholinguistic Analysis of Reading and Learning to Read* by Frank Smith. Copyright © 1985 by Frank Smith. Reprinted by permission of the author.

Figure 3.4: From "The Utility of Phonic Generalizations in the Primary Grades" by T. Clymer in *The Reading Teacher*, January, 1963. Reprinted with permission of T. Clymer and the International Reading Association.

Pages 74–75: From *To Help Children Read: Mastery Performance Modules for Teachers in Training* by Frank B. May. Copyright © 1973 by Charles E. Merrill Publishing Company. Reprinted by permission.

Chapter 4

Page 84: From *Comprehension and Learning: A Conceptual Framework for Teachers* by Frank Smith. Copyright © 1985 by Frank Smith. Reprinted by permission of the author.

Pages 86–87: From "Literacy in the Classroom" by John R. Bormuth in *Help for the Reading Teacher: New Directions in Research*, ed. William D. Page. Copyright © 1975 by the National Council of Teachers of English. Reprinted with permission.

Page 93: From "Poison" in *Someone Like You* by Roald Dahl. Copyright © 1950 by Roald Dahl. Reprinted by permission of Alfred A. Knopf, Inc.

Pages 97–99: "Jimmy Hayes and Muriel" from *The Complete Works of O. Henry.* Copyright © 1937 by Garden City Publishing Company Inc. Used by permission of the publisher.

Pages 101–2: From "Phonics Revisited" by A. Sterl Artley in *Language Arts* 54 (February 1977). Copyright © 1977 by the National Council of Teachers of English. Reprinted with permission.

Pages 102–3: From "Using Context: Before or After?" by Constance Weaver in *Language Arts* 54 (November/December 1977). Copyright © 1977 by the National Council of Teachers of English. Reprinted by permission.

Pages 105–6: From "Theoretically Based Studies of Patterns of Miscues in Oral Reading Performance" by Kenneth S. Goodman. Wayne State University, 1973. Reprinted by permission of the author.

Pages 107–8: From *Dandelion Wine* by Ray Bradbury. Reprinted by permission of Don Congdon Associates, Inc. Copyright © 1953 by Gourmet Inc.; renewed 1981 by Ray Bradbury.

Chapter 5

Page 113: From "The Law and Reading Instruction" by Robert J. Harper and Gary Kilarr in *Language Arts* 54 (November/December 1977). Copyright © 1977 by the National Council of Teachers of English. Reprinted by permission.

Page 114: Excerpt from *Little Circus Dog* by Jene Barr. Copyright © 1949 by Albert Whitman & Company. Reprinted by permission.

Page 119: From *Bristle Face* by Zachary Ball. Copyright © 1962 by Kelly R. Masters. Reprinted by permission of Holiday House.

Page 120: From *Manchild in the Promised Land* by Claude Brown, New York: Macmillan Publishing Co., Inc. Copyright © Claude Brown 1965. Reprinted by permission.

Page 120: From *The Power and the Glory* by Graham Greene. Copyright © 1940 by Graham Greene. Copyright © renewed 1968 by Graham Greene. All rights reserved. Reprinted by permission of Viking Penguin, Inc.

Page 123: From *Theoretically Based Studies of Patterns of Miscues in Oral Reading Performance* by Kenneth S. Goodman. Wayne State University, 1973. Reprinted by permission of the author.

Page 123: From "What We Know About Reading" by Kenneth S. Goodman in *Findings of Research in Miscue Analysis*, ed. P. David Allen and Dorothy J. Watson. Copyright © 1976 by the National Council of Teachers of English. Reprinted by permission.

Pages 126, 131: Reprinted by permission of Dodd, Mead & Company, Inc. from *Morris Has a Cold* by Bernard Wiseman. Copyright © 1978 by Bernard Wiseman.

Page 127: From *The New York Times*, May 5, 1970. Copyright © 1970 by The New York Times Company. Reprinted by permission.

Pages 128–29: From *The Glorious Conspiracy* by Joanne Williamson. Copyright © 1961 by Alfred A. Knopf, Inc. Reprinted by permission.

Page 130: From *The Macmillan Reading Program*. Albert J. Harris and Mae Knight Clark, Senior Authors: *A Magic Box* and *Opening Doors*. Copyright © 1965 by Macmillan Publishing Company. Reprinted by permission.

Pages 131–32: From "Dialect Barriers to Reading Comprehension Revisited," by Kenneth S. Goodman and Catherine Buck in *The Reading Teacher* (October 1973). Reprinted with permission of the authors and the International Reading Association.

Page 133: From *English in Black and White* by Robbins Burling. Copyright © 1973 by Holt, Rinehart and Winston, Inc. Reprinted by permission.

Chapter 6

Page 137: From ''Orthography in a Theory of Reading Instruction'' by Kenneth Goodman in *Elementary English* 49 (December 1972). Copyright © 1972 by the National Council of Teachers of English. Reprinted by permission.

Page 141: Reprinted by permission of Dodd, Mead & Company, Inc. from *Morris Has a Cold* by Bernard Wiseman. Copyright © 1978 by Bernard Wiseman.

Page 158: From *Teaching Reading: A Phonic/Linguistic Approach to Developmental Reading* by Charles C. Walcutt, Joan Lamport, Robert Dykstra, and Glenn McCracken. Copyright © 1974 by Macmillan Publishing Company. Reprinted by permission.

Pages 158–59: From *Learning to Read: The Great Debate* by Jeanne Chall. Copyright © 1967, 1983 by McGraw-Hill. Reprinted by permission.

Page 164: From *English Language Arts I-VI*, the official policy statement of the Direction Générale de Dévelopement Pédagogique, Ministère de l'Éducation for the Province of Quebec. Reprinted by permission.

Pages 167–68: From *Becoming a Nation of Readers*, prepared by Richard C. Anderson et al., 1985. Published by the U.S. Department of Education.

Pages 168–70: From ''Validating the Construct to Theoretical Orientation in Reading Instruction'' by Diane DeFord in *Reading Research Quarterly*, Spring 1985. Reprinted with permission of Diane DeFord and the International Reading Association.

Chapter 7

Figures 7.2, 7.3, 7.4 (top), 7.10, 7.11: Charles Temple, Ruth Nathan, Nancy Burris, and Frances Temple, *The Beginnings of Writing, Second Edition* (Boston: Allyn & Bacon, 1987). Reprinted by permission.

Figure 7.4 (bottom): From ''Emergent Writers in a Grade One Classroom'' by Lee N. Dobson in *Reading-Canada-Lecture* 4 (Fall 1986). Reprinted by permission.

Figures 7.5, 7.8, 7.9: From ''Emergent Writers in a Grade One Classroom'' by Lee N. Dobson. Paper presented at the Fourth International Conference on the Teaching of English, Ottawa, Ontario, May 15, 1986. Reprinted by permission.

Figure 7.7: From ''Invented Spelling in the Open Classroom'' by Carol Chomsky in *Word* 27 (1971). Reprinted by permission.

Figures 7.12, 7.13: From ''Literacy: Reading, Writing, and Other Essentials'' by Diane E. DeFord in *Language Arts* 58 (September 1981). Reprinted by permission of the National Council of Teachers of English.

Figure 7.14: From ''Beginning Reading and Writing Through Singing: A Natural Approach'' by Sheila Fitzgerald in *Highway One* 7, ii (Spring 1984). Reprinted by permission of the author and the Canadian Council of Teachers of English.

Figure 7.15: From *Reading, Writing and Caring* (Cochrane, Cochrane, Scalena, & Buchanan 1984). Reprinted by permission.

Figure 7.16: From "Helping Children Become More Responsible for Their Own Writing" by Mary Ellen Giacobbe in *LiveWire* first issue (1984). Reprinted by permission of the National Council of Teachers of English.

Figure 7.18: Diagram on "The Gradual Release of Responsibility Model of Instruction" in "Changing the Face of Reading Instruction" by P. David Pearson in *The Reading Teacher* 38 (April 1985). Reprinted by permission of the author.

Page 211: From "What Teachers Can Learn From 'Natural Readers'" by Anne D. Forester in *The Reading Teacher* (November 1977). Used by permission of the International Reading Association.

Pages 213, 216–17: From *Becoming a Nation of Readers* prepared by Richard C. Anderson et al., 1985. Published by the U.S. Department of Education.

Pages 213–15: From August 1986 letter by Margaret Phinney detailing results of a four-year informal research study at Bridgetown Regional Elementary School in Nova Scotia.

Page 226: From *Children's Writing and Language Growth* by Ronald L. Cramer. Copyright © 1978 by Merrill Publishing Company, Columbus, Ohio. Reprinted by permission of the publisher.

Chapter 8

Pages 236–37: "What's in the Sack" (text only) from *Where the Sidewalk Ends* by Shel Silverstein. Copyright © 1974 by Snake Eye Music, Inc. Reprinted by permission of Harper & Row, Publishers, Inc.

Page 252: From *One At a Time* by David McCord. Copyright © 1952 by David McCord. By permission of Little, Brown and Company.

Page 262: From *The House of Sixty Fathers* by Meindert DeJong. Copyright © 1956 by Meindert DeJong. Reprinted by permission of Harper & Row, Publishers, Inc.

Pages 271–72: Excerpt by Gary Kilarr and Gayle Jennings. New South Wales Department of Education, 1983. Reprinted by permission.

Chapter 9

Pages 287–89, 299: From *Teaching Reading Comprehension* by P. David Pearson and Dale D. Johnson. Copyright © 1978 by Holt, Rinehart and Winston. Reprinted by permission.

Page 309: From *Julie of the Wolves* by Jean Craighead George. Copyright © 1972 by Jean Craighead George. Reprinted by permission of Harper & Row, Publishers, Inc.

Pages 313–14: From "Experiencing History Through Literature: Integrated Activities for *Johnny Tremain*" by Jan Caudell, Denise DeVries, Peggy Garthe, and Jeane Wilson in *Another Day, Another Pineapple* (Fall 1980). Edited by Jan Caudell and Constance Weaver. Western Michigan University, Department of English. Reprinted by permission.

Chapter 10

Page 321: From ''Testing in Reading: A General Critique'' by Kenneth S. Goodman in *Accountability and Reading Instruction*, ed. Robert B. Ruddell. Copyright © 1973 by the National Council of Teachers of English. Reprinted by permission.

Pages 323–24: From *To Help Children Read: Mastery Performance Modules for Teachers in Training* by Frank B. May. Copyright © 1973 by Charles E. Merrill Publishing Company. Reprinted by permission.

Page 324: From ''Theoretically Based Studies of Patterns of Miscues in Oral Reading Performance'' by Kenneth S. Goodman. Wayne State University, 1973. Reprinted by permission of the author.

Page 327: From ''An Analysis of Published Informal Reading Inventories'' by Larry A. Harris and Jerome A. Niles in *Reading Horizons* 22 (Spring 1982). Reprinted by permission.

Pages 335, 356: From *Reading Miscue Inventory: Alternative Procedures* by Y. Goodman, D. Watson, and C. Burke. New York: Richard C. Owen Publishers, Inc. Reprinted by permission.

Pages 337–38: Reprinted by permission of Dodd, Mead & Company, Inc. from *Morris Has a Cold* by Bernard Wiseman. Copyright © 1978 by Bernard Wiseman.

Pages 345–46: ''Jimmy Hayes and Muriel'' from *The Complete Works of O. Henry*. Copyright © 1937 by Garden City Publishing Company, Inc. Used by permission of the publisher.

Pages 349–50, 358–62: From *A Camel in the Sea* by Lee Garrett Goetz. Copyright © 1966 by McGraw-Hill Book Company. Reprinted by permission.

Chapter 11

Figure 11.1: Chart of ''Elements of Reading Style Identified by the Reading Style Inventory'' by Marie Carbo from *Reading Style Inventory Manual* 1981. Reprinted by permission of Marie Carbo, Director of Research & Staff Development, Learning Research Associates, Roslyn, NY.

Figure 11.2: M. Carbo/R. Dunn/K. Dunn, *Teaching Students to Read Through Their Individual Learning Styles*, 1986, pp. 61-62. Reprinted by permission of Prentice-Hall, Inc., Englewood Cliffs, New Jersey.

Figures 11.3, 11.4, 11.5, 11.6: Charts on identifying modality strengths by Marie Carbo. Copyright © 1986 by Marie Carbo. From *Teaching Students to Read Through Their Individual Learning Styles* by M. Carbo, R. Dunn, and K. Dunn. Prentice-Hall, 1986. Reprinted by permission of Marie Carbo, Director of Research & Staff Development, Learning Research Associates, Roslyn, NY.

Page 376: From ''Case Study of Jimmy'' by Marie Carbo from her 1986 Reading Styles Seminar. Copyright © Marie Carbo, 1981. Reprinted by permission of Marie Carbo, Director of Research & Staff Development, Learning Research Associates, Roslyn, NY.

Page 385: From ''Concept of Word: A Developmental Phenomenon in the Beginning Reading and Writing Processes'' by Darrell Morris in *Langue Arts* 58 (September 1981). Reprinted by permission of the National Council of Teachers of English.

Page 388: From "After Decoding: What?" by Carol Chomsky in *Language Arts* 53 (March 1976). Copyright © 1976 by the National Council of Teachers of English. Reprinted by permission of the publisher.

Pages 389–90: From *Whole Language Principles and Practices in Reading Development with Special Emphasis on Reading Recovery* by David Doake. Viewing guide accompanying videotape filmed at the 1985 Reading for the Love of It conference in Toronto. Used by permission of Scholastic-TAB.

Page 391: Gilles, Carol; Bixby, Mary; Crowley, Paul; Crenshaw, Shirley; Heinrichs, Margaret; Reynolds, Frances; and Pyle, Donelle. *Whole Language Strategies for Secondary Students*. New York: Richard C. Owen Publishers, 1987. Reprinted by permission.

Appendix A

Page 415–21: From *The Practical Princess and Other Liberating Fairy Tales* by Jay Williams. Copyright © 1978 by Jay Williams. Reprinted by permission of Scholastic, Inc.

1

What Are Your Beliefs About Reading?

Our findings suggest that both teachers and learners hold particular and identifiable theoretical orientations about reading which in turn significantly affect expectations, goals, behavior, and outcomes at all levels.

—Jerome Harste

QUESTIONS FOR JOURNALS AND DISCUSSION

1. What is reading? That is, what do people do when they read?

2. How do we learn to read? (This question invites more than one kind of answer.)

3. How do you think good readers implicitly define reading? What do they *do* when they read, and how does this differ from what poor readers do?

4. How is a teacher likely to teach children to read if he or she believes that reading means, first of all, identifying the words on the page? If he or she believes that reading means, most importantly, getting the essential meaning of the text or constructing meaning from the text?

5. At this point, how do *you* think children should be taught to read?

THE IMPORTANCE OF A DEFINITION

What is reading anyway? Here are some answers from children (Harste 1978, p. 92):

"It's filling out workbooks."
"Pronouncing the letters."
"It's when you put sounds together."
"Reading is learning hard words."
"Reading is like think . . . you know, it's understanding the story."
"It's when you find out things."

1

There is considerable variation in these definitions. One emphasizes a medium of instruction, the workbook; others emphasize words or parts of words; and still others emphasize meaning. Of course, children do not often stop to define reading. Nevertheless, their approach to the task of reading is guided by what they think reading is.

Where do children get such definitions of reading? Often they simply infer them from what is emphasized during reading instruction. If the teacher spends a lot of time teaching correspondences between letters and sounds, at least some children will conclude that reading means pronouncing letters or sounding out words. If the teacher spends a lot of time teaching children to recognize words as wholes, at least some children will conclude that reading means identifying words or knowing a lot of words. Whatever the instructional approach, it is likely to affect at least some children's implicit definitions of reading and hence their strategies for dealing with the written text. And ironically, those children who are least successful at reading may be the very ones who try hardest to do just what the teacher emphasizes. They concentrate on just these one or two strategies rather than on the several strategies that must be integrated in order to read successfully.

The instructional approach is crucial, then, if we want to help children develop productive reading strategies. But again, the instructional approach reflects a definition of reading, whether that definition be consciously formulated or only implicit.

Children's success at reading reflects their reading strategies; their reading strategies typically reflect their implicit definitions of reading; children's definitions of reading often reflect the instructional approach; and the instructional approach reflects a definition of reading, whether implicit or explicit. In fact, the instructional approach may reflect a definition quite different from that consciously espoused by the teacher or the textbook.

The vital question, then, is *what* approach, and *whose* definition? If the teacher has only a vague notion of how people read and learn to read, he or she may in effect adopt the definition implicit in a given reading program, perhaps a basal reading series. In that case, the guiding definition may reflect more the publisher's knowledge of what will sell than scholars' and educators' knowledge of how people read and learn to read.

Fortunately, teachers can have far more influence on the instructional approach than they often realize. Armed with a viable definition of reading and an understanding of some of the instructional implications of this definition, teachers can use almost *any* reading materials to help children develop productive reading strategies. The teacher is the key.

One of the primary purposes of this book, then, is to help teachers become knowledgeable enough to foster good reading strategies in children, perhaps despite the approach of the reading materials provided by the schools.

CHARACTERIZING READING AND READING INSTRUCTION

As people become increasingly knowledgeable about the reading process, they typically modify their definitions of reading. But first it is important to determine where one stands. The remainder of this chapter consists mainly of three activities intended to help you determine your own views of reading and reading instruction.

Activity 1. First, please read the following paragraph from David Palermo's excellent *Psychology of Language* (1978, p. 38):

> At least four theoretical variants of the interpretive semantic theory have appeared in the literature since Chomsky first grappled with the problem of semantics. In the late 1960s, alternatives were offered by Lakoff (1968), McCawley (1968), and Ross (1967). Their arguments centered around the idea that it is not possible to separate the semantic and syntactic components of the grammar. According to these linguists, there is no single base phrase marker but, rather, sentence generation begins with the semantic component and subsequent interaction between lexical insertion and transformational rules leads eventually to the surface structure and the application of the phonological component. Thus, the focus of linguistic inquiry should give at least equal billing to the semantic component rather than merely relegating semantics to a role of interpreting the syntactic component. The generative semanticists, as these linguists have come to be called, have argued that the underlying structures in standard theory are too concrete. Once the presuppositions and implications of sentences are analyzed in more detail, it becomes necessary to postulate more abstract underlying structures which make the deep structures of sentences deeper and more complex. Ross (1974), for example, shows how a simple causative sentence such as ''Dr. Grusel is sharpening the spurs'' involves more than seven underlying sentence forms or propositions encompassed within its meaning including, for example, the presuppositions that Dr. Grusel and the spurs exist.

Were you able to read the paragraph, as requested? It should be interesting to discuss your response with others who have tried to read this same paragraph.

Activity 2. Probably the most effective way of determining how a person goes about the task of reading is to examine his or her reading miscues. In order for you to do this more readily, it should help to have some terms defined. Kenneth Goodman coined the term ''miscue'' in the 1960s to describe any departure the reader makes from the actual words of the text (e.g., K. Goodman 1965). For example, if a reader substitutes one word for another, adds or omits a word, or reorganizes a sequence of words, he or she has made a miscue. Goodman's purpose in coining this term ''miscue'' was twofold. First, he wanted to get away from the notion that every departure from the words of the text is necessarily bad, something to be considered an error. Second, he wanted to emphasize how such departures from the text indicate which language cue systems the reader is using and not using, at least at that particular moment; the pattern of miscues thus suggests the reader's strengths as well as weaknesses, as we shall see in more detail later.

There are three major cue systems within the language of a text:

Syntactic cues:	that is, grammatical cues like word order, function words,[1] and word endings
Semantic cues:	that is, meaning cues from each sentence and from the developing whole, as one progresses through the entire text
Grapho/phonemic cues:	that is, letter/sound cues, the correspondences between letters (graphemes) and sounds (phonemes)

Never does a miscue show attention to only one of these language cue systems. The following are some of the "purest" examples I have found, and even in these cases, the reader has paid attention to more than one language cue:

truck
"The little monkey had it."   Attention to syntactic cues. The reader seems also to have attended to a picture cue.

. . . to see if there was any   Attention to semantic cues, with some attention to grapho/phonemic cues.
afraid
danger. He heard the . . .

expert
Every day except Friday, . . .   Attention to grapho/phonemic cues, but also attention to preceding grammar.

Given these definitions and examples, compare David's miscues with Tony's, in the following two transcripts of a selection they each read aloud. In each case, do the miscues suggest that the child is using implicit knowledge of *syntactic cues* (grammar) to predict words that are grammatically acceptable in context? Do the miscues suggest that the child is using *semantic cues* (meaning) to predict words that are meaningful in context? Do the miscues suggest that the child is using *grapho/phonemic cues* (letter/sound correspondences) to pronounce or sound out words? Which child would you say better integrates the language cues into effective reading strategies? What do you think each child's implicit definition of reading is? Again, discuss this activity with others, if possible.

The following key indicates how to interpret the major markings in the transcripts below:

may
Substitution   They did not have books. . . .
   (A word written over another word indicates a substitution.)

Omission   . . . they dove into (the) waves.

(A circle around a word or group of words indicates an omission.)

Insertion   . . . splashing ^high^ and spraying the water. . . .

(A carat points to whatever is inserted.)

Correction   . . . in the shade of a tall |palm tree. ©twee

(The © indicates that the miscue was corrected, and the underlining indicates what portion of the text was repeated as the reader made the correction.)

Multiple attempt   How lucky he was to live in a Somali village. . . . (2 Sammon / 1 Sam—)

(Multiple attempts at a word are numbered consecutively.)

Partial word   Mohamed loved to go swimming in the sea. (Mo—)

(One or more letters followed by a hyphen indicate that the reader uttered what he or she apparently considered only part of a word, judging by the reader's intonation.)

The reading selection is adapted from Lee Garrett Goetz, *A Camel in the Sea* (New York: McGraw-Hill, 1966), pp. 11–14. This particular adaptation is from *Fiesta*, one of the Houghton Mifflin readers (1971). The line divisions differ in the two transcripts because the story was typed differently for each child. The line numbers are indicated at the left, in each case.

a. David's Miscues

1   Mohamed (mo-hah′med) loved to go swim-

2   ming in the sea. How lucky he was to live in a

3   Somali (so-mah′lee) |village right on the Indian (*Sami* / ©willage on the right hand or)

4   Ocean! The sandy shore rang with the happy

5   shouts (and cries) of the village boys and girls. ©

6   They liked to race one another into the surf,

7   splashing and spraying the water into (a) white

8   dancing foam before they dove into (the) waves.

9   Mohamed and his young *younger* sister, Āsha (ie'shuh),

10   spent all the time they could in the cool, clean

11   ~~sea~~ *swimming* swimming and playing water games. *in the water* They

12   were good swimmers because their mother*s* had taught them.

13   Every day except Friday, Mohamed went to

14   school with the other village boys. The class

15   was outdoors, and the children sat on little

16   benches in front of the teacher in the shade of

17   a tall palm *twee* *may* tree. They did not have books, so

18   the boys repeated everything the teacher said,

19   over and over *again* until they knew their lessons by

20   heart. The girls of the village did not go to school,

21   for the people thought that school was not as

22   important for girls as it was for boys.

b. Tony's Miscues

1   *Mo—* Mohamed (mo-hah'med) loved to go swimming in the sea.

2   How lucky he was to live in a Somali (so-mah'lee) village *2 sammon* *1 Sam—*

3   right on the Indian Ocean! The sandy shore rang with the happy

4   *souts* shouts and cries of the village boys and girls. They liked

5   to race one another into the surf, splashing *high* and spraying

6   the water into a white dancing foam before they dove into the *drase*

7   waves. Mohamed and his young sister, Āsha (ie'shuh), *Mola* *yūng* *Asla*

8   (spent all the time they could in the cool, clean sea,)

9   swimming and playing water games. They were good swimmers

10   because their mother had taught them.

11   Every day except Friday, Mohamed went to school with the *expert* *Molda*

12   other village boys. The class was outdoors, and the children *nother vi'ner*

13   sat on little benches in front of the teacher in the shade *beaches* *frose* *shape*

14   of a tall palm tree. They did not have books, so the boys

15   repeated everything the teacher said, over and over, until *ramped*

16   they knew their lessons by heart. The girls of the village *other classrooms hurt* *vengil*

17   did not go to school, for the people thought that school was

18   not as important for girls as it was for boys. *imprentice* *to*

Activity 3. Having tried to read a paragraph for which you may not have had much background, and having compared the miscues of two children, you should be able to select or formulate a definition of reading that accords with your beliefs at the present time. Below are some definitions and characterizations of reading and the reading process, arranged more or less from simple to complex. Which one or ones come closest to expressing your own opinion? If none of these is satisfactory, formulate your own. Then, as you finish each of the first six chapters, return to your chosen definition and, if necessary, modify it in accordance with your increased understanding of the reading process.

a. Reading means getting meaning from certain combinations of letters. Teach the child what each letter stands for and he can read. (Flesch 1955, p. 10)

   Johnny must learn, once and for all, that words are written by putting down letters from left to right, and that they are read in the same direction. (Flesch 1955, p. 31)

b. Reading is a precise process. It involves exact, detailed, sequential perception and identification of letters, words, spelling patterns and larger language units. (view denounced in K. Goodman 1967, p. 126)

c. The [structural] linguist's concept of reading is not the concept commonly held by the classroom teacher and the reading specialist—that reading is getting meaning from the print on a page. The [structural] linguist conceives the reading act as that of turning the stimulus of the graphic shapes on a surface back into speech. The shapes represent speech; meaning is not found in the marks but in the speech which the marks represent. (Strickland 1964, p. 10)

   In order to comprehend what he reads, the reader turns the visual stimulus of written language back into speech—overtly if he is inexperienced and immature, subliminally if he is a rapid, experienced reader. (Strickland 1964, pp. 13–14)

d. Printing is a visual means of representing the sounds which are language. Meaning is in these sounds. We want to equip the child to turn the written word into a spoken word (whether he actually utters it or not) so he will hear what it says, that is, get its meaning. . . . we have never found anybody who did not think that the purpose of reading was to get the meaning. The only possible defense of skipping sound and going directly from print to meaning would be that printed words are directly meaningful—that the printed word *green* means the color, but this is not so. It is the spoken word *green* that designates the color, while the printed word designates the sound of the spoken word. Various [structural] linguistics specialists have recently been stressing this fact. (McCracken and Walcutt, Teacher's Edition for Book E, 1970, p. xiv)

e. Corresponding to the auditory analysis of sentences the skill of reading can be viewed as the ability to extract from a *visual* signal the underlying structure of sentences. (Bever and Bower 1966, p. 20)

f. Reading is a psycholinguistic guessing game. It involves an interaction between thought and language. Efficient reading does not result from precise perception and identification of all elements, but from skill in selecting the fewest, most productive cues necessary to produce guesses which are right the first time. The ability to anticipate that which has not been seen, of course, is vital in reading, just as the ability to anticipate what has not yet been heard is vital in listening. (K. Goodman 1967, p. 127)

g. Reading is the active process of reconstructing meaning from language represented by graphic symbols (letters), just as listening is the active process of reconstructing meaning from the sound symbols (phonemes) of oral language. (Smith, Goodman, and Meredith 1970, p. 247)

h. When the light rays from the printed page hit the retinal cells of the eyes, signals are sent along the optic nerve to the visual centers of the brain. This is not yet reading. The mind must function in the process, the signals must be interpreted, and the reader must give significance to what he reads. He must bring *meaning* to the graphic symbol. (Dechant 1970, p. 12)

i. The reader brings to the text his past experience and present personality. Under the magnetism of the ordered symbols of the text, he marshals his resources and crystallizes out from the stuff of memory, thought, and feeling a new order, a new experience, which he sees as the poem [not necessarily what we think of as a poem, but *any* literary work created by a reader in the process of reading a text]. This becomes part of the ongoing stream of his life experience, to be reflected on from any angle important to him as a human being. (Rosenblatt 1978, p. 12)

ACTIVITIES AND PROJECTS FOR FURTHER EXPLORATION

1. Compare the following four sketches of children in first grade classrooms (King and Watson 1983, p. 70). Try to decide which of the above definitions of reading might underlie each of the approaches implicitly illustrated. Which of the children do you think will become the better reader(s)? Why? Discuss.

   Jamie sits looking at a list of words: fat, pat, bat, sat, cat, hat. . . . Later she sees, "The fat cat sat on the bat. Pat the fat cat."

   Josie is waiting her turn in a group whose members are reading aloud a story in which the words "green," "table," and "wood" appear ten times each. Later she will do skill exercises in her workbook.

   Harold looks at a page with *spwn, baul, rig, shout, cheer*, and *txcks* on it. Later he will write a story using the symbols he has learned in school.

   Hildy sits on the floor and reads along with her friends and teacher a story the class has just written. Later she will write a letter to a friend about the book she has just finished reading.

2. Interview some children and/or teachers about their views of reading. (If you don't have ready access to either children or teachers, perhaps you can interview students planning to become teachers.) Ask questions similar to those below, modifying the language of the question as appropriate for the individual. Ask

follow-up questions when the opportunity arises. Here are some possible questions, adapted from Harste 1978 and from Burke 1980, as reported in Y. Goodman, Watson, and Burke 1987):

    a. What do you think reading is? What do people do when they read something?

    b. When you are reading and come to something you don't know, what do you do? (After receiving a response, you might ask a follow-up question: Do you ever do anything else?)

    c. Who is a good reader you know?

    d. What makes _____ a good reader?

    e. Do you think _____ ever comes to something he/she doesn't know? (After receiving a response, ask: Suppose _____ does come to something he/she doesn't know. What do you think _____ would do?)

    f. If you knew someone was having trouble reading, how would you help that person?

    g. What would a/your teacher do to help that person?

    h. How did you learn to read?

    i. What would you like to do better as a reader?

    j. Do you think you are a good reader? Why?

In addition to questions like some of these, you might ask some (or all) of the questions in activity 4 below—depending, of course, on whom you are interviewing.

3. If possible, observe several teachers during reading instruction. What kinds of direct instruction do they give? How do they respond to children's miscues? How do the activities in which children are involved differ from one room to another? Why? Try to decide what each teacher's implicit definition of reading must be. Later, ask each teacher how he or she would define reading and how reading should be taught. Compare these interview results with what you observed and what you inferred from the observation. In each case, does the teacher's definition of reading seem consistent with his or her teaching practices? Discuss.

    If in carrying out this activity you discover teachers with widely differing instructional approaches and/or definitions of reading, it might be particularly interesting to try a further project with some students from the most diverse teachers. With the teachers' permission, interview some of the poorest and some of the best readers from each class. If possible, tape record the interviews for later study. Ask the kinds of questions suggested in activity 2 above, and/or some of the questions in activity 5 below, rephrased as appropriate for the children.

4. In an article reviewing thirty years of inquiry into students' perceptions of reading, Johns (1986) mentions, among others, a study of 1,655 students from grades 1 to 8. The students were asked three questions: (1) "What is reading?" (2) "What do you do when you read?" and (3) "If someone didn't know how to read, what would you tell him/her that he/she would need to learn?" Johns points out that students often know more than they reveal in such brief inter-

views. In fact, many of the students' responses had to be classified as "meaning-less"—no response, "I don't know," or a vague, circular, or irrelevant response; in many cases, such responses may have indicated that the student did not understand what the question might mean. In any case, in responding to the question "What is reading?," fewer than 20 percent of the students made any reference to getting meaning through reading (the percentage was higher with the older students, and lower with the younger ones). Most of the students described reading as decoding (e.g., sounding words out), or as an activity involving a textbook and occurring in a classroom or school environment (Johns and Ellis 1976, as reported in Johns 1986, p. 36). What do you think accounts for this low percentage of children who define reading as having to do with the getting of meaning? What do you think of the apparently high percentage of children who describe reading only as something occurring in school? Is this a matter for concern? Why or why not? Discuss.

5. To explore further your own views of reading and reading instruction, respond to the following questionnaire; you might also use it during the interviews suggested above. For each question, circle the one best answer that reflects the strength of your agreement or disagreement: SA means "strongly agree," while SD means "strongly disagree." This questionnaire is the DeFord Theoretical Orientation to Reading Profile (TORP), included and discussed in DeFord 1985:

1. A child needs to be able to verbalize the rules of phonics in order to assure proficiency in processing new words.

   1 2 3 4 5
   SA   SD

2. An increase in reading errors is usually related to a decrease in comprehension.

   1 2 3 4 5
   SA   SD

3. Dividing words into syllables according to rules is a helpful instructional practice for reading new words.

   1 2 3 4 5
   SA   SD

4. Fluency and expression are necessary components of reading that indicate good comprehension.

   1 2 3 4 5
   SA   SD

5. Materials for early reading should be written in natural language without concern for short, simple words and sentences.

   1 2 3 4 5
   SA   SD

6. When children do not know a word, they should be instructed to sound out its parts.

   1 2 3 4 5
   SA   SD

7. It is a good practice to allow children to edit what is written into their own dialect when learning to read.

   1 2 3 4 5
   SA   SD

8. The use of a glossary or dictionary is necessary in determining the meaning and pronunciation of new words.

   1 2 3 4 5
   SA   SD

9. Reversals (e.g., saying "saw" for "was") are significant problems in the teaching of reading.

   1 2 3 4 5
   SA   SD

10. It is a good practice to correct a child as soon as an oral reading mistake is made.

1	2	3	4	5
SA				SD

11. It is important for a word to be repeated a number of times after it has been introduced to insure that it will become a part of sight vocabulary.

1	2	3	4	5
SA				SD

12. Paying close attention to punctuation marks is necessary to understanding story content.

1	2	3	4	5
SA				SD

13. It is a sign of an ineffective reader when words and phrases are repeated.

1	2	3	4	5
SA				SD

14. Being able to label words according to grammatical function (nouns, etc.) is useful in proficient reading.

1	2	3	4	5
SA				SD

15. When coming to a word that's unknown, the reader should be encouraged to guess upon meaning and go on.

1	2	3	4	5
SA				SD

16. Young readers need to be introduced to the root form of words (run, long) before they are asked to read inflected forms (running, longest).

1	2	3	4	5
SA				SD

17. It is not necessary for a child to know the letters of the alphabet in order to learn to read.

1	2	3	4	5
SA				SD

18. Flashcard drills with sightwords is an unnecessary form of practice in reading instruction.

1	2	3	4	5
SA				SD

19. Ability to use accent patterns in multisyllable words (pho′ to graph, pho to′ gra phy, and pho to gra′ phic) should be developed as part of reading instruction.

1	2	3	4	5
SA				SD

20. Controlling text through consistent spelling patterns (The fat cat ran back. The fat cat sat on a hat) is a means by which children can best learn to read.

1	2	3	4	5
SA				SD

21. Formal instruction in reading is necessary to insure the adequate development of all the skills used in reading.

1	2	3	4	5
SA				SD

22. Phonic analysis is the most important form of analysis used when meeting new words.

1	2	3	4	5
SA				SD

23. Children's initial encounters with print should focus on meaning, not upon exact graphic representation.

1	2	3	4	5
SA				SD

24. Word shapes (word configuration) should be taught in reading to aid in word recognition.

1	2	3	4	5
SA				SD

25. It is important to teach skills in relation to other skills.

1	2	3	4	5
SA				SD

26. If a child says "house" for the written word "home," the response should be left uncorrected.

1	2	3	4	5
SA				SD

27. It is not necessary to introduce new words before they appear in the reading text.

1	2	3	4	5
SA				SD

28. Some problems in reading are caused by readers dropping the inflectional endings from words (e.g., jump*s*, jump*ed*).

1	2	3	4	5
SA				SD

READINGS FOR FURTHER EXPLORATION

Harste, Jerome C. Fall 1977. Understanding the Hypothesis, It's the Teacher That Makes the Difference: Part I. *Reading Horizons* 18: 32–43. Indicates that the teacher's definition of reading and approach to reading may be crucial in reading instruction.

DeFord, Diane, and Jerome C. Harste. September 1982. Child Language Research and Curriculum. *Language Arts* 59: 590–600. Presents illuminating examples of how children's beliefs about reading are affected by teachers' actions: how children "learn" what teachers may not have intended to teach, with the result that the children internalize limited and limiting views of reading and writing.

Downing, John. December 1969. How Children Think about Reading. *The Reading Teacher* 23: 217–30. Discusses five-year-olds' understanding of reading and of key terms used in reading instruction.

Johns, Jerry L. 1986. Students' Perceptions of Reading: Thirty Years of Inquiry. *Metalinguistic Awareness and Beginning Literacy.* Ed. D. B. Yaden, Jr., and S. Templeton. Portsmouth, N.H.: Heinemann, 31–40. An excellent article summarizing research on children's perceptions of reading (see activity 4, above).

Goodman, Yetta. November 1974. I Never Read Such a Long Story Before. *English Journal* 63: 65–71. In examining the miscues of one particular student, Goodman makes several important points about the reading process and reading instruction. This oldie-but-goodie is highly recommended by my students.

Barr, Rebecca. January 1975. Processes Underlying the Learning of Printed Words. *Elementary School Journal* 75: 258–68. Summarizes research concerning the relation between instructional methods and reading miscues.

2

How Does Language Mean, and Why Does It Matter in the Teaching of Reading?

Normal reading seems to begin, proceed, and end in meaning, and the source of meaningfulness must be the prior knowledge in the reader's head. Nothing is comprehended if it does not reflect or elaborate on what the reader already knows.

—Frank Smith

QUESTIONS FOR JOURNALS AND DISCUSSION

1. How do sentences mean?

2. What kinds of context are involved in determining the meanings of words?

3. What are schemas, and how/why are they important in comprehending language?

4. What does it mean to say that meaning arises in the transaction between reader and text? What are some of the implications for teaching?

5. How do various social and situational contexts affect the reading transaction? Again, what are some of the implications for teaching?

6. What kinds of grammatical cues signal and facilitate the transactions among words in a sentence?

7. What are surface structure and deep structure, and how are these concepts important in understanding the reading process?

8. What is a part-to-whole, bottom-up, surface-deep, outside-in view of reading and the teaching of reading? How does this contrast with a whole-to-part, top-down, deep-to-surface, inside-out view?

9. Which approaches to reading instruction reflect the former view of reading, and which reflect the latter?

10. Why is it inadequate to say that reading and learning to read mean identifying words and getting their meaning?

11.   In your present opinion, is it important that beginning reading instruction reflect what we know about how language is comprehended? If not, why not? If so, what might be some of the practical implications for the teaching of reading?

COMPREHENDING AND LEARNING TO READ

You may never have given much thought to *how* words, sentences, and texts mean. In your daily life, you understand much of what you hear and read, while other things you doubtless do not understand. However, you may seldom have reflected upon the how or why of comprehension; you may never have constructed from your own experience a theory about how language means. It is important for teachers of reading to have such a theory, however, in order to approach the teaching of reading in a manner that accords with what is known about how language means.

Of course everyone agrees that the ultimate purpose of reading is to arrive at meaning, but there are differing views about what is involved in learning to read. Most reading instruction is based, implicitly if not explicitly, on one of the three following views:

View 1   Learning to read means learning to pronounce words.
View 2   Learning to read means learning to identify words and get their meaning.
View 3   Learning to read means learning to bring meaning *to* a text in order to get meaning *from* it.

The first view seems based on the assumption that once words are pronounced, meaning will take care of itself. The second implicitly assumes that once the meaning of individual words is determined, the meaning of the whole (paragraph, text) will take care of itself. In sharp contrast, the third view assumes that meaning results not necessarily from the precise identification of every word in a sentence, but from the constant interplay between the mind of the reader and the language of the text. The latter is a *psycholinguistic* view, as will be explained below.

Many people would of course find the first definition unsatisfactory, incomplete: it is not enough to pronounce the words. If readers cannot also get meaning, we tend to feel that they are not really reading. This, indeed, may have been your response to the paragraph on generative semantics (activity 1 in Chapter 1). You may have been able to pronounce most of the words, yet felt that such word identification did not really constitute reading.

While rejecting as inadequate the view that learning to read means learning to pronounce words, many people unthinkingly adopt the second view, because they assume that reading itself means identifying words and getting their meaning. The implication, of course, is that the meaning of the whole sentence and text will automatically follow from the meaningful identification of words. Since this view seems to underlie most of the reading approaches currently used in the United States, it is important to examine this assumption that meaning is built up from smaller parts to increasingly larger wholes.

THE MEANING OF WORDS AND SENTENCES: A FIRST LOOK

Since the mid-1900s, many psychologists and linguists have turned to the investigation of how people learn their native language and how they produce and comprehend sentences. There naturally arose a hybrid discipline called *psycholinguistics* (from *psyche*, meaning 'mind,' and *linguistics*, meaning 'the study of language'). Since the early 1970s when a psycholinguistic view of reading was first popularized through the books of Frank Smith (*Understanding Reading*, 1971; *Psycholinguistics and Reading*, 1973) and the miscue research of Kenneth Goodman and his colleagues (K. Goodman, *Theoretically Based Studies . . .* , 1973), scholars in related disciplines have come to essentially the same conclusions about how language means.

Such scholarly research by socio-psycholinguists, schema theorists, semioticians, literary theorists, and reading educators simply confirms what we ourselves might conclude from thoughtful observation of how we and others comprehend. So—let us work inductively, together building a theory of comprehension.

To begin, please take a moment to write five to ten sentences using the word *run*. Try to create sentences in which *run* has different meanings.

The following are some of my sentences:

1. Can you run the store for an hour?
2. Can you run the word processor?
3. Can you run the 500-yard dash?
4. Can you run in the next election?
5. Can you run next year's marathon?

6. I helped Samuel with his milk run.
7. They'll print 5,000 copies in the first run.
8. Sherry has a run in her hose.
9. There was a run on snow shovels yesterday morning.
10. It was a long run.

Doubtless you have thought of several additional meanings of *run*.

Now the question is, in these and other sentences, how does the reader (or listener) know what *run* means? One of my small "pocket" dictionaries lists nearly forty meanings for the word *run*; one of my desk dictionaries lists over eighty definitions. Can readers arbitrarily take one of the meanings of *run* from their mental dictionaries and apply it to the word *run* in these sentences? Clearly the answer is no. More often than not, meaningless sentences would result.

From even this simple example, then, it should be obvious that we do not simply add together the meanings of individual words to get the meaning of a sentence. To determine the meanings of the words, we use context of various sorts:

1. *Grammatical context within the sentence.* In the first five example sentences above, *run* occurs in a context that signals its use as a verb. The grammatical context partially delimits the meaning of *run*.

2. *Semantic context within the sentence.* In "run the store" we know that *run* means something like 'manage'; in "run the word processor," we know that *run* means something like 'operate'; in "his milk run," we know that *run* means something like 'route,' and so forth. Interestingly, in the sentences where *run* is a verb, the precise meaning is determined by a noun that comes after it, rather than before.

3. *Situational, pragmatic context.* A sentence like "It was a long run" has several possible meanings, depending on the context in which it is uttered or written. In the context of stockings, *run* would refer to a tear (notice that the meaning and pronunciation of *tear* depends on its context, too). In the context of a dog kennel, *run* would mean an enclosure. In the context of fishing, *run* would mean migrating fish. In the context of skiing, *run* would mean a downhill path or route. In the context of theater, "It was a long run" would mean that the play was performed for a long period of time. And so forth. Situational context can be either verbal or nonverbal or both, as you can readily imagine from the preceding examples.

4. *Schematic context.* This refers to knowledge in our heads: a mental *schema* (plural, *schemata* or *schemas*) is simply an organized "chunk" of knowledge or experience. (The Latin plural *schemata* is often used, but I will use the Anglicized plural here.) If we did not have mental schemas, we could not make practical use of the other kinds of context mentioned. That is, if we did not have an intuitive sense of grammar, we could not use grammatical context to limit a word's possible meanings to those that are appropriate for the verb function of the word (as in examples 1 through 5) or to limit the word's possible meanings to those that are appropriate for the noun function (as in examples 6 through 10). This process of grammatically delimiting a word's possible meanings is so automatic that we are often not aware of it, but it nevertheless occurs—and is made possible by our grammatical schemas.

Since our schemas develop as we transact with the external world, we may often lack appropriate schemas for understanding what we hear or read. For example, if you take your dog to be boarded at a kennel while you're on vacation, then return home and reassuringly tell your children "Gretchen's okay, she's got a long run," this sentence may make no sense to the children. They may not be able to make use of the *verbal* situational context unless they have experienced the *nonverbal*—that is, unless they have actually seen the enclosure called a "dog run" at a kennel. Thus the children's schemas may be inadequate for making sense of what you've said.

From the examples and discussion so far, we can make several preliminary observations about how words and sentences mean:

1. First, it is clear that we do not simply add together the meanings of the individual words in a sentence to get the meaning of the whole. This is because we cannot know what a word means until we see it in context. Oddly enough, the supposedly "simplest" words like *in, on, at,* and *by* typically have about fifteen to thirty meanings listed in a desk dictionary. In isolation, words have only *potential* meanings, a range of meanings that a dictionary attempts to characterize (e.g., Halliday 1978). It is only when used in context (of various sorts) that one or more of these meanings is "actualized."

2. Second, it is clear that without knowledge in our heads, our schemas, we could not make use of the information provided by other kinds of context: grammatical, semantic, situational.

3. These observations strongly suggest that meaning does not arise from part to whole but in some much more complex way. Bizarre as it sounds, we are able to grasp the meanings of individual words only when we see how they interrelate with each other, so meaning arises from whole to part more than from part to whole.

Thus as a first approximation, I would like to offer the following summary of how sentences mean:

> The meaning of a sentence arises or develops by means of transactions among words whose meanings are not identifiable except in context, where context includes grammar, semantics, and situation. It is the readers' and listeners' schemas that enable them to make use of these various kinds of context to comprehend language.

The truth of this observation should become clearer as the chapter progresses.

The use of context in identifying words will be further discussed in Chapter 4. The heart of the present chapter will develop the concepts of schemas and transactions, of deep structure and surface structure, of contrasting views of language processing and reading, and then briefly sketch differing approaches to teaching children to read, showing which approaches do and which do not reflect what we know about how language means. These ideas too will be further developed in subsequent chapters.

SCHEMAS: WHAT ARE THEY?

In recent years, those interested in how the mind operates have postulated the existence of cognitive schemas. A *schema* is simply an organized "chunk" of knowledge and experience, often accompanied by feelings (e.g., Anderson et al. 1977; Adams and Collins 1979; Rumelhart 1980; Iran-Nejad 1980; and Iran-Nejad and Ortony 1984).

To get some idea of what a schema is and how it operates in our daily lives, let us explore for a moment our schemas for restaurants (the idea comes from Pearson and Johnson 1978). What are some of the different kinds of restaurants you can think of—not specific restaurants or even restaurant chains, but categories into which these might be organized? A preliminary list might include truck stops and greasy spoons, fast food restaurants, cafeterias, ethnic restaurants, family restaurants, and fancy/expensive/gourmet restaurants. In addition, I have a concept for what might be called a cocktail restaurant: it's something in between a family restaurant and a fancy restaurant, a place where you go for drinks, a nice-but-not-too-expensive meal, and entertainment on Friday or Saturday night—without the kids. Figure 2.1 shows these categories in a hierarchic, "branching tree" diagram. You might add the additional categories you have thought of.

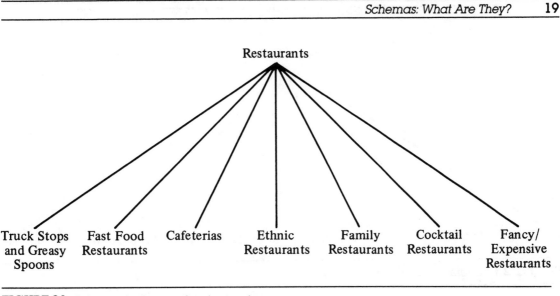

FIGURE 2.1 *Schema for types of restaurants*

Notice that it is difficult to say exactly how ''big'' or ''little'' a schema is. We have an ethnic restaurant schema that is part of a general restaurant schema, but the ethnic restaurant schema can be further subdivided into schemas for Italian restaurants, Mexican restaurants, Chinese restaurants, and so forth; your schemas for ethnic restaurants will depend a lot on where you live and what cities and countries you have visited, and Figure 2.2 can be expanded to add several more ethnic restaurants. On the other hand, our original category, ''restaurants,'' is part of a

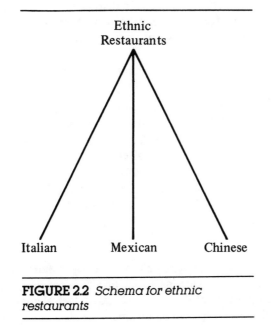

FIGURE 2.2 *Schema for ethnic restaurants*

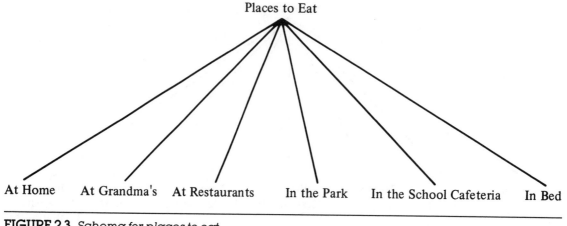

FIGURE 2.3 *Schema for places to eat*

larger schema, "places to eat." Other places to eat might be at home, at Grandma's, in the park, in the school cafeteria, or even in bed; Figure 2.3 is only a beginning of the possibilities. Obviously our schemas for these various places to eat will differ from one another.

Most if not all of these categories are what Arthur Koestler (1969) called *holons*: each is simultaneously a whole, with its own subparts, and yet a part of something else. "Ethnic restaurants" has its own subcategories yet is itself a subcategory of "restaurants," and so forth.

Now how are categories related to schemas? A schema is the organized knowledge we have about the category. Let's compare, for instance, our schema for fast food restaurants with our schema for fancy/expensive restaurants. Some of the obvious differences are given below; doubtless you can add others.

Schema for Fast Food Restaurants	*Schema for Fancy/Expensive Restaurants*
limited menu, often consisting of hamburgers plus a few other items	generally a wide selection of foods, often including European cuisine
order food across a counter	order food from waitress or waiter (often the latter)
pay before receiving your food	pay after eating
eat quickly	eat slowly, with food served in several courses
use paper napkins and plastic utensils	use cloth napkins and silverware

Notice that cutting across the *category schemas* for types of restaurants are what we might call *operational schemas* for selecting food, ordering, paying, and eating (see Figure 2.4). From these operational schemas, we can select elements that together will uniquely characterize each type of restaurant.

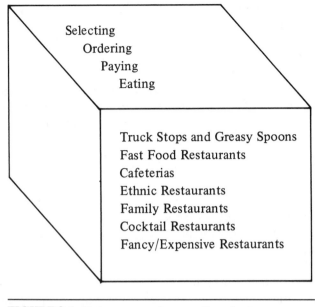

Selecting
  Ordering
    Paying
      Eating

Truck Stops and Greasy Spoons
Fast Food Restaurants
Cafeterias
Ethnic Restaurants
Family Restaurants
Cocktail Restaurants
Fancy/Expensive Restaurants

FIGURE 2.4 *Category and operational schemas*

The distinctions within these operational schemas can be amazingly subtle. For example, take the schema of paying for the food. In a fast food restaurant (at least where I live), you often pay for the food before receiving it. In a cafeteria, you pay for the food after receiving it, but still before eating it. In drugstore counter restaurants (not included in the previous list), you receive the check as soon as you are served, and may be asked to pay for the food then. In family restaurants, you often receive the check as soon as you are served, but you pay as you leave. In cocktail restaurants, you usually do not receive the check until after you have finished eating and have had an after-dinner drink or cup of coffee—or at least have been invited to do so. Your waitress or waiter may take the check to the cashier for you, or you may pay on the way out. In a fancy restaurant, of course, the waitress or waiter (traditionally a waiter) will present the check on a platter or in a menulike booklet and take the check to the cashier for you.

A moment's reflection will reveal the importance of schemas in our daily lives. Suppose someone has a well-developed schema for fast food restaurants and for family restaurants, but has never been to a fancy restaurant before. If a child, this person will surely be unprepared to endure the lengthy wait for one course after another, or the interminable adult discussions, or being repeatedly admonished to sit still and keep quiet. What happened to the playground outside? To the video games? Even as an adult, a person may not know what to do with the "extra" silverware and may not realize that the reason the check is served on a tray or platter is so that the diners can put their money on it for the waitress or waiter to take. As for wine tasting—what's that? One of my students related her father's first experience in a fancy restaurant. The waiter opened a bottle of wine and handed her father the cork to sniff. Not knowing what was expected, he looked at the cork and said, "Yup, that's a cork all right." Another student admitted that when first confronted with a finger bowl at a gourmet restaurant, she drank the water. Obviously their schemas for fancy restaurants did not include what to do in situations like these.

Can you think of examples when your own cognitive schemas were obviously not adequate to the situation? Can you remember times when you tried to understand an explanation or a lecture, a textbook or a library book, and found your schemas inadequate? What are some of the implications for teaching?

SCHEMAS IN READING

To explore the importance of schemas in the reading process, read one or the other of the following paragraphs once, without rereading. Then write a brief summary of what you have read.

> *Passage 1: Cost or Other Basis* (on the topic of capital gains and losses)
> In general, the cost or other basis is the cost of the property plus purchase commissions, improvements, and minus depreciation, amortization, and depletion. If you inherited the property or got it as a gift, in a tax-free exchange, involuntary conversion, or "wash sale" of stock, you may not be able to use the actual cash cost as the basis. If you do not use cash cost, attach an explanation of your basis.
>
> —Internal Revenue Service, 1985 booklet on *1040*
> *Federal Income Tax Forms and Instructions*

> *Passage 2: Dissipative Structures* (based on Prigogine & Stengers 1984)
> Ilya Prigogine has demonstrated that when an "open system," one which exchanges matter and/or energy with its environment, has reached a state of maximum entropy, its molecules are in a state of equilibrium. Spontaneously, small fluctuations can increase in amplitude, bringing the system into a "far-from-equilibrium" state. Perhaps it is the instability of subatomic "particles" (events) on the microscopic level that causes fluctuations on the so-called macroscopic level of molecules. At any rate, strongly fluctuating molecules in a far-from-equilibrium state are highly unstable. Responding to internal and/or external influences, they may either degenerate into chaos or reorganize at a higher level of complexity.
>
> —Constance Weaver, 1985, "Parallels Between New Paradigms
> in Science and in Reading and Literary Theories"

Now check your summary with the original. Did you leave out any important ideas? Distort any ideas? Or can't you even tell? Many of us simply have schemas inadequate for this task. Because we do not already know something about capital gains and losses or dissipative structures, we cannot understand much of what we read, and therefore we find it difficult to summarize the passage or even to evaluate our summary afterwards. We simply have no cognitive schemas for these topics.

Now let's take a slightly different situation. Again, read the following passage and then summarize it in writing without looking back. Check your summary with the original.

> The procedure is actually quite simple. First you arrange things into different groups. Of course one pile may be sufficient depending on how much there is to do. If you have to go somewhere else due to lack of facilities that is the next step, otherwise you are pretty well set. It is important not to overdo things. That is, it is better to do too few things at once than too many. In the short run this may not seem important but complications can easily arise. A mistake can be expensive as well. At first the whole procedure will seem complicated. Soon however, it will become just another facet of life. It is difficult to foresee any end to the necessity for this task in the immediate future, but then one never can tell. After the procedure is completed one arranges the materials into different groups again. Then they can be put into their appropriate places. Eventually they will be used once more and the whole cycle will then have to be repeated. However, that is a part of life.
>
> —John D. Bransford and Nancy S. McCarrell, 1974, ''A Sketch of a Cognitive Approach to Comprehension''

Many people find that their summaries are inadequate, not because they can't understand the passage but because they can't place the operations described within a context that makes sense to them. They understand the passage as they read, but recall relatively little.

Now try this latter experiment with someone else, but tell the person beforehand that the passage is about washing clothes. Compare the two summaries. Is the other person's more complete? Did this person include anything about washing clothes that was not explicitly stated in the passage? Often people will mention sorting the clothes into light colors and dark, or going to a laundromat if you don't have a washing machine at home. Clearly these ideas can be inferred from the passage, but only if you know that the passage is about washing clothes—and if you know something about that process. Only when we have cognitive schemas adequate to what we are reading and only when these schemas are somehow activated will we have much understanding and recall of what we hear or read.

This issue of activating one's schemas is crucial, as the recently popular terms *metalinguistic awareness, metacognition*, and *metacomprehension* suggest. Basically these terms refer to being aware that you have such strategies, and being able to use them consciously. For instance, having metalinguistic awareness means you are aware that you have linguistic knowledge (schemas) that you can use in listening and reading, as for example in predicting that a noun will come soon after the word *the*. Being aware that you have such knowledge, you can use it consciously when necessary. Here, in contrast, is an example of a college student who seemed unaware that she had cognitive strategies to monitor her own comprehension; at any rate, she had apparently not learned to use those strategies effectively in reading her textbooks. This student had just flunked her last introductory psychology exam (Santa 1981, p. 168; italics mine):

> She had the proper "good student facade"; she underlined essential points in her text and had an adequate set of lecture notes. She also claimed to spend a considerable amount of time studying. After having her [the student] reread a short selection from her psychology text, I was somewhat amazed that she could not even answer the simplest question. Thinking she might have a poor memory, I asked her several other questions allowing her to look back in her text for the appropriate answer. Still, she had no success. *What is interesting is that she was very surprised that she had comprehended so little.* She had assumed she had understood without ever testing her assumption and *appeared totally oblivious to strategies which might help her monitor her own comprehension.*

Thus we might say that not only was she neglecting to activate whatever schemas she might have had relevant to the understanding of psychology, she was even unaware of having strategies or schemas that might enable her to determine whether or not she was comprehending. Obviously readers need to mobilize such self-monitoring schemas as well as schemas relevant to the content of what they are reading.

SCHEMAS AND TRANSACTIONS

This discussion of schemas leads naturally into discussion of the concept of *transaction*. To gain experientially an understanding of this concept, read the following poem as many times as you wish. Then write down what you think the poem says.

To Pat

On the day you died
my lover caught a fish
a big-mouthed bass
nineteen inches long
four and a half pounds strong
they measured it.

They measured it,
stretching the tape to match
 its length,
piercing its mouth to heft
 its bulk.
They measured, examined,
 praised it.

"Fish, dear fish," he said,
"you are too beautiful to eat.
I will put you back."

But it was too late.
Like you, the fish could not
     be revived.
He died in the kitchen sink.

And now I have eaten
of his sweet flesh,
the communion denied me
by the church of your people.

It is finished.

Typically, people will give different responses to the poem. One student suggested that the author—or at least the "I" of the poem—had been in love with Pat, but that the church had kept them from marrying. Another student, in a similar vein, suggested that the writer couldn't have Pat because he was a priest. Some people have interpreted "On the day you died" metaphorically: on the day you died to me, the day our friendship or romance ended. Others have taken the line literally, as describing the physical death of the person addressed. Some students take the line about communion as referring to sexual communion. Others interpret the line as referring to the taking of the sacraments in church; for some of these students, this interpretation seems to be fostered by the knowledge that certain churches forbid nonmembers to take communion. Still other students have taken that line as signaling both meanings, sexual and religious communion. Some students have seen religious elements in various parts of the poem after reading the last line. Others, not knowing that Christ's last words on the cross were "It is finished," have seen no religious elements at all. Often, of course, students have modified their opinion of what the poem says during the social give-and-take of classroom discussion. (For discussions of how literary meaning can be developed through social interaction, see Rosenblatt 1938; Bleich 1975; and Fish 1980.)

Clearly each reader has brought to bear his or her own schemas in grappling with the poem—including a schema for interpreting poetry, which often goes something like this: "There must be a deep meaning here that I don't immediately get. It probably has to do with sex and/or religion." An interesting commentary on the experience students have had with reading poetry in school, is it not? Notice, too, that although I have asked students to tell just what the poem "said," not what they thought it "meant," most students have not separated the two. This is similar to what we shall see in a later chapter: that after a very brief interval, readers typically cannot distinguish between what they've actually read and what is a logical inference from what they have read—as you may have observed with people who summarized the "washing clothes" passage knowing what it's supposed to be about. As readers internalize what they have read, recall and inference and interpretation become inseparable. (Again, you might consider the implications for teaching and learning.)

Clearly each person's experience of the poem above, and of everything else we read as well, is influenced by the person's own schemas, the person's knowledge and experience and feelings. Recognition of this fact is, however, a sharp departure from an earlier (and in some quarters, a still-popular) concept of comprehension. For a long time after the introduction of Shannon's revolutionary concepts of information theory (Shannon 1948), it was thought that a message would travel pure and unchanged from sender to receiver, provided the channel—the medium through which the message was transmitted—did not contain "noise," that is, something that would distort the message. Shannon's basic concept can be represented as follows:

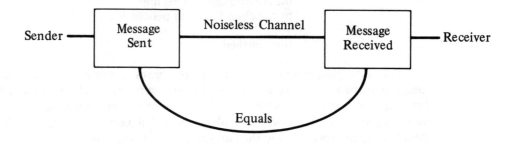

Now we understand, however, that in human communication the message received is *never* identical to the message sent, whether the communication is oral or written. This is true not particularly because there is noise in the channel, though there may be. Rather, the message received is inevitably different from the message sent because the receiver—the reader or listener—brings to bear his or her schemas in interpreting the message. The speaker or writer tries to encode a message in language, but because no two people's experiences, thoughts, and feelings are ever identical, the message received is never quite identical to the message sent. This view can be represented as follows:

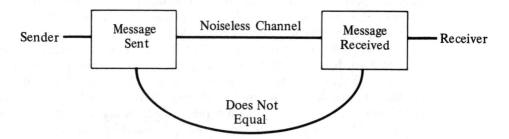

From the listener's or reader's point of view, then, meaning is not in the spoken or written word, the text itself. Rather, meaning arises during a transaction between the words and the listener or reader.

The person who has stimulated widespread understanding of this concept and term is Louise Rosenblatt (e.g., 1938, 1964, 1978), who borrowed and popularized the concept of *transaction* introduced by Dewey and Bentley (1949). To clarify the concept of transaction, Rosenblatt (1978) defines some key terms:

The Reader is the person seeking to make meaning by transacting with (actively reading) a text, of whatever kind.

The Text is the collection of word symbols and patterns on the page, the physical object you hold in your hand as you read.

The Poem is the literary work created as the reader transacts with the text. ("Poem" refers metaphorically to *any* literary work—not just a poem in the usual sense, but a short story, novel, play.)

The crucial point is that meaning is not in the text itself, whether the text be literary or otherwise. Rather, meaning arises during the transaction between reader and text. Thus reading is a process, a transaction between reader and text in a given situational context, an event during which meaning evolves.

To elaborate: the writer has, let us say, a novel in his or her head (though much of the novel typically develops as one writes). The writer chooses word symbols and patterns to represent that novel, usually knowing full well that from the text thus created, the reader will create his or her own novel. No two novels, so created, will ever be alike. The novel I created from the text *Katherine* (by Anya Seton) at age fifteen is not the same novel I created upon re-transacting with the text at thirty-five, and certainly the novel you create will never be the same as either of mine. We bring different life experiences, different schemas, to the word symbols and patterns of the text.

These schemas depend in part on a variety of social factors: our ethnic and socioeconomic background, our age and educational attainment, and so forth, as succinctly illustrated in the cartoon in Figure 2.5. In addition, the activation of

"But it's only a word!"

FIGURE 2.5 *More contrasting schemas*

schemas is influenced by our interpretation of the social context in the here-and-now, the situational context. For example: A child may read to identify words correctly in school, because he or she has learned that correct word identification is what's expected. When reading for pleasure, however, the child may read for meaning. In taking multiple-choice "reading comprehension" tests, the child may read merely to locate the phrase in the paragraph(s) that corresponds with the phrase in one of the answers. Elsewhere, the child may again read for meaning. A personal example comes readily to mind. When my son was in fourth grade, he had vocabulary tests of the matching type: match the word to the definition. One of the words for study was *assumption*, defined as "an assuming." I tried to find a more suitable definition in our dictionaries at home, but with little luck; finally, I concluded that the best way to help my son understand the word was with examples from his own life. John's reply, however, was typical of the student who has learned to play the academic game. "Oh, don't worry," he said. "On the test, I'll just match *ass*'s" (the first three letters of *assumption* and *assuming*). Obviously the situational context of the classroom did not demand genuine understanding.

An example of how social and situational factors intersect may help to illuminate both. Various researchers seeking to determine why inner-city children typically score lower on reading achievement tests than children from affluent suburbs have discovered, not surprisingly, that one difference is that inner-city children less frequently have schemas that would facilitate comprehension of the passages in such tests. The passages are often based on experiences, knowledge, and/or vocabulary that they do not have. More interesting, though, is that many children from non-mainstream cultures (e.g., black inner-city youth) apparently bring a different mind-set to the testing task itself. Though many children have learned that in responding to questions on a so-called comprehension test you're not supposed to draw upon prior knowledge but only to use information in the passage at hand, many inner-city youth do not operate upon this principle; rather, they answer test questions by using what they know (Nix and Schwarz 1979).

Bloome and Green (1985) provide an interesting example, with an even more interesting commentary. The passage and question below were taken from a reading workbook, *Reading House Series* (1980, p. 71). The question, of course, is multiple-choice:

> Bill Benson looked only once at his homework assignment. Immediately, he started moaning to his seatmate, Candy Caries, about its length. As he shuffled out of the room after the bell, he couldn't help but remark to his teacher that the room was too stuffy to work in. The teacher only smiled and shook her head at Bill's complaints.
>
> Faced with the possibility of running an errand for his parents, Bill is likely to say _____
>
> A. "Do I have to go? Why don't you ask Uncle Joe this time?"
> B. "Sure I'll go! Should I walk or take the bus?"
> C. "Okay, Dad. I'll go right after I finish my homework."
> D. "I'm way ahead of you, Pop! I took care of it already."

According to Bloome and Green (1985), one ninth grader explained why he chose option C (a "wrong" answer) instead of A (the "right" answer) by pointing out that Bill Benson had no intention of doing his homework or of going to the store, but that confronting his father—which is the situation in option A—would probably result in punishment. Thus, the student chose C, which superficially indicates compliance, but which may allow Bill to procrastinate indefinitely. Bloome and Green comment (1985, p. 180):

> In answering the question, the student used his own background knowledge as a frame for interpreting the story and the question. However, when high-achieving students from the same grade, school, and background were given the same passage and questions, they gave the answer designated correct by the teacher's guide. In brief, one of the strategies some students may need to learn is to suppress their own background knowledge and assume the interpretive frame of the school.

Bloome and Green thus explain the problem as one of an interpretive "frame," adding that "Differences in interpretive frames may be the result of cultural differences, economic differences, personal experience differences, and so on" (p. 179). Thus *social context* (background of the student) may intersect with *situational context* (testing situation) in such a way as to result in apparent failure to comprehend. Ironically, however, students like the one described above are doing precisely what readers must do in order to read "real" texts effectively: they are bringing their prior experience and knowledge to the task of making sense of what they read.

Reading, then, is not merely a psycholinguistic process, involving a transaction between the mind of the reader and the language of the text. Rather, reading is a socio-psycholinguistic process, because the reader-text transaction occurs within a social and situational context (see, for example, the longitudinal Bristol study documented in Wells 1986). More accurately, there are a variety of social and situational factors, a variety of contexts, that affect the activation of one's schemas and the outcomes of the reader-text transaction. That is, there are a variety of social and situational factors that influence how the person reads and what the reader understands (see, for example, Carey, Harste, and Smith 1981, and Bloome 1985). Figure 2.6 is an attempt to capture the complexity of these relationships. While I have generally followed the practice of my *Psycholinguistics and Reading* (1980) in referring to reading as a "psycholinguistic" process, it should be remembered that in fact reading is a *socio*-psycholinguistic process of incredible complexity.

TRANSACTIONS WITHIN THE LANGUAGE OF THE TEXT: GRAMMATICAL SIGNALS

The reader-text transaction that takes place within an immediate situational context and broader social context is by no means the only transaction taking place during the reading process. In particular, there are also numerous transactions, on various levels, within the language of the text itself.

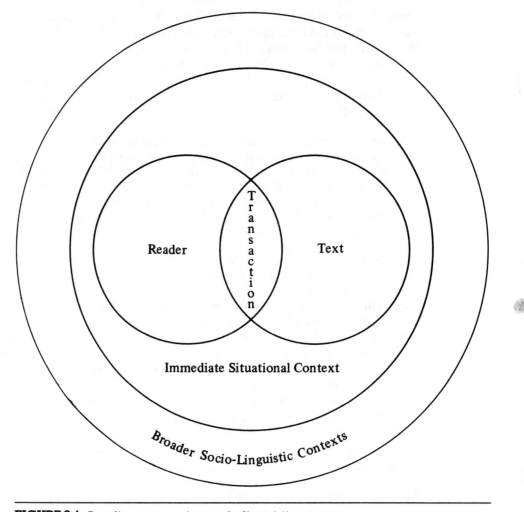

FIGURE 2.6 *Reading as a socio-psycholinguistic process*

Some of these transactions are signaled by grammatical cues: word endings, function words, and/or word order. Take, for example, word endings. The ending *-ed* indicates past action, as in "She *chaired* the meeting." The ending *-er* indicates one who does something, as in "Cindy is a top-notch *runner*." The ending *-en* denotes an action, as in "Bleach will *whiten* your clothes." And *-ly* indicates the manner in which an action is carried out, as in "She examined it *closely*." What, however, do these same endings indicate in the following sentences?

1. The *exhausted* doctor slept all day.
2. I can't run any *faster*.

3. The tomato is *rotten*.
4. Her cocker spaniel is very *friendly*.

Here, the *-ed* indicates a condition or state, the *-er* indicates the manner of an action, the *-en* indicates a condition or quality, and the *-ly* indicates a quality or characteristic. Our knowledge of words and the endings they can take, plus our recognition of how the italicized words are functioning in the above sentences, tells us that this time the endings are functioning differently than before. Both the meaning and the part of speech are different, as readers intuitively know.

Thus although word endings do help to signal the meanings of words and the kinds of semantic and syntactic transactions into which they can enter, nevertheless we often do not know the meaning of an ending until we see it in the word to which it is attached—and in some cases, not until we see how that word is used in the sentence. For example, in addition to its use as an adjective, *exhausted* can be a verb, as in "The recent demand for computers *exhausted* all our supply." Thus, in isolation, *exhausted* has the potential to be either a verb or an adjective.

Function words are another major grammatical signal, for they glue together the content words—the nouns and pronouns, verbs, adjectives, and adverbs that carry most of the meaning of a sentence. Thus the major function words or signal words are noun determiners (ND), including articles; verb auxiliaries (VA); prepositions (P); and conjunctions (C). Note the examples of function words below.

After it *had* rained *for an* hour, *the* young people gave up *their* idea
  C   VA   P ND   ND   ND
of camping out. Instead they rented *a* room *at a* motel where they
P   ND   P ND
could swim *in a* pool *and* eat *by the* poolside.
VA   P ND   C   P ND

Like word endings, such function words serve as useful but not infallible signals of what is coming next in a sentence. The word *this*, for example, usually works as a noun determiner, to signal that a noun is coming up in a sentence, as in "*This* problem is difficult." However, the word *this* can also work as a pronoun taking the place of a noun, as in "I can't understand *this*." Somewhat similarly, the words *will* and *can* commonly work as verb auxiliaries, to signal that a verb is coming up, as in "Terry *will* do it" and "Maryellen *can* come." However, both words sometimes function as nouns, as in "She has an iron *will*" and "He couldn't open the *can*." Thus although function words help to signal the relations among words, we don't always know whether something is even a function word or not until we see how it fits with the other words in a sentence.

Even when we know something is a function word, we cannot tell its precise meaning in isolation. Take, for example, the preposition *by* in the following sentences. In each case what does it mean, and *how do you know?*

1. That was prescribed *by* Dr. Lucy.
2. Charlie sat down *by* Dr. Lucy.
3. Woodstock went *by* plane.
4. *By* the way, how old do you think Snoopy is?
5. *By* Snoopy's calculations, it ought to work.

The fact that *by* is a preposition tells us little about how it relates to the other words in a sentence. It is actually the other words that give *by* a specific meaning, rather than the other way around. *By* acquires meaning by transacting with the other words in the sentence.

In fact, the meaning of the function words and often the precise function words themselves can be predicted from the content words. Try again to read the sentence about giving up camping, as reproduced below. You will probably find that you can supply most of the missing words, getting at least the gist if not always the actual word of the original:

> _____ it ___ rained ___ _ hour, ___ young people gave up ____ idea _ camping out. Instead they rented _ room _ _ motel where they _____ swim _ _ pool ___ eat _ _ poolside.

If indeed you could read the passage with little trouble and supply most if not all of the missing words, what might this suggest about the importance of function words in signaling grammar and thus meaning? Clearly function words are useful in signaling the relations among words, but they may not be nearly so vital as is commonly supposed. (For a similar activity from which this conclusion may likewise be drawn, see the Kent State passage in Chapter 5, page 127.)

Word order is more reliable than either word endings or function words in signaling the relationships among words. Compare, for example, the following pairs of sentences:

1. Snoopy kissed Lucy.
   Lucy kissed Snoopy.
2. Dog bites man.
   Man bites dog.
3. Wendy loves Greg.
   Greg loves Wendy.
4. Cook the roast.
   Roast the cook.

In each case, our knowledge of English word order tells us that the first word indicates the doer of the action, while the third indicates the recipient of the action. The two sentences in each pair contain the same words, but the differing word order signals different relations, different transactions among the words. Note that the sentence ''Roast the cook'' may sound either cannibalistic or nonsensical to some readers, while other readers may have a schema that allows for an interpretation like the following: "Have a ceremony in which we honor the cook by seeming to dishonor him or her."

So far, then, it should be clear that word endings, function words, and word order all help us determine the meanings of words and the relations among the words in a sentence. On the other hand, we have seen that word endings are not infallible clues to word function or meaning, and that function words are also limited in their usefulness: what appears to be a function word may not always be working as one; the meanings of some function words (particularly the prepositions) can by no means be determined out of context; and in any case, many function words are often dispensable in a given context, being themselves predictable from the nouns, verbs, adjectives, and adverbs. These limitations leave us with word order as the best clue to word relationships. However, we shall see in the next section that even word order is often not adequate to signal the basic relations among the words of a sentence.

SURFACE VERSUS DEEP STRUCTURE

The grammatical clues of word endings, function words, and word order are surface structure clues—that is, clues that are visible to the eye. As adult speakers of the language, we perceive many kinds of relationships that are not signaled, or not signaled adequately, by the visible surface structure. These cues are part of the *deep structure*, a term coined by Noam Chomsky in the early 1960s to denote those relationships among words that are intuitively clear to a native speaker of the language, but that are not overtly signaled in the flow of language itself (see, for example, N. Chomsky 1965).

Chomsky emphasized deep, underlying relationships that he considered grammatical. Take, for example, the following pair of sentences:

The operation was performed by a new surgeon.
The operation was performed by a new technique.

The two sentences have the same grammatical surface structure, but they mean in different ways. On the surface, "operation" is the subject, "was performed" is the verb phrase, and "by a new surgeon" and "by a new technique" are both prepositional phrases; the surface grammar is essentially the same. However, we know that in the first sentence it is the surgeon who performed the operation; "surgeon" is the agent or doer of the action and hence the "deep" subject, as we can demonstrate by turning the sentence around and making it active: "A new surgeon performed the operation." We also know that the parallel word in the second sentence, "technique," is not the doer of the action or the deep subject: it would not make sense to say "A new technique performed the operation." The deep subject is, in fact, unspecified. For all we know, the operation may have been performed by a butcher. Or the operation may be of a totally different kind, having nothing to do with surgery.

Structurally ambiguous sentences provide further evidence that surface structure, including word order, is not always adequate to signal deep structure, the underlying relationships among words. Take, for example, the following sentences. What do they mean?

Visiting relatives can be a nuisance.
They asked the police to stop drinking.

The surface grammar of the first sentence gives us no clue to the deep grammar, to *who* is doing the visiting. Does the sentence mean that relatives who visit can be a nuisance? Or does it mean that the act of going to visit relatives can be a nuisance? In the second sentence above, the surface grammar similarly gives no clue as to the deep subject of *drinking*: are the police to stop other people from drinking, or are they themselves to cease drinking? The surface grammar, including word order, is insufficient to make the meaning or the deep grammar clear.

In context, however, such sentences are usually understood. In fact, we understand the deep grammar precisely because we understand the meaning of the sentences, given a particular situational context. Thus Chomsky's insistence on the importance of the deep structure *grammar* (as opposed to meaning) no longer seems as important as it once did. Historically, however, Chomsky's distinction between surface and deep grammar was of tremendous significance, paving the way for the widespread recognition that meaning does not lie in language itself but rather arises during the transaction between reader and text.

Modernizing Chomsky's definitions of surface and deep structure, then, we can say that *surface structure* is the visible or audible text, the squiggles and vibrations that are interpreted as words and word patterns—including the grammatical signals of word endings, function words, and word order. The *deep structure* is the underlying relationships that are perceived by, or rather constructed by, the reader or listener, on the basis of his or her prior knowledge and experience—schemas, in other words. Surface structure is what you see, or hear. Deep structure is what you don't see or hear, but nevertheless understand.

Figure 2.7 summarizes these aspects of language and language processing in a surface–deep structure continuum. As the previous discussion suggests, however, we do *not* simply go from surface to deep structure in interpreting sentences. For

SURFACE STRUCTURE Visible—Supplied by the Text			DEEP STRUCTURE Invisible—Supplied by the Reader		
Vibrations in the air or squiggles on the page	Words on the page	Surface grammar (word endings, function words, word order)	Possible word meanings	Relational meanings among words in sentences	Listener's or reader's schemas

FIGURE 2.7 *Surface-deep structure continuum. Language processing occurs in both directions, surface to deep and deep to surface, and is still much more complex than that reflected here.*

example, if you have ever listened to someone speak a language that you do not know, you may have found that you could not even tell when one word ended and another began; the spoken words may have seemed little more than noises. For someone who has no acquaintance with written language, written words probably look like little more than scribbles or hieroglyphics; such, in fact, is our own experience when first encountering a radically different writing system. What enables us to make sense of language is our schemas, including our schemas about the structure of the language in question and, for written language, our schemas about the nature of print in that language. Thus language processing goes as much or more from deep to surface structure as the other way around.

To solidify our understanding of how sentences mean, let us work through one more set of examples, considering how syntactic and semantic context, situational context, and schemas all play a role. First, quickly define the words *chair, white, run, close*, and *love*, in your head or on paper. Now see if your definitions are appropriate for these contexts:

1. Get Shirley to *chair* the meeting.
2. Separate the *white* from the yolk.
3. Angie can *run* the outfit.
4. That was a *close* call.
5. I *love* you.

In the first sentence, surface grammar is enough to signal the meaning. That is, *chair* coming immediately after *to* must be a verb, and for most of us that verb has only one possible meaning: to take charge of, to preside over. In the second sentence, *the* indicates that *white* is a noun, but we don't know much about that noun *white* until we see it in context with *yolk*; here, we must have recourse to semantic cues within the sentence. In the third sentence, *can* clearly signals that *run* is a verb, but what does that verb mean? And what does the noun *outfit* mean? The two words can be understood only in transaction with each other.

In the fourth sentence, grammatical context indicates that *close* is an adjective rather than a verb and *call* is a noun rather than a verb, but what about the meaning of the phrase "a close call"? We need to know more about the situational context in which the sentence occurs. Is the speaker/writer describing a baseball game? Or a near-accident? Or what?

On the surface, the word *love* in "I love you" appears clear enough: it is a verb, with *I* as subject and *you* as object. The transaction among the words is clear, but what does it mean to the person who hears or reads it? To one who does not know English, the sentence will mean nothing at all, unless the nonverbal context makes it clear. To those who know the language, it will still have different meanings under different circumstances and for different individuals. Under some circumstances, one may interpret the words "I love you" to be merely a verbal enticement to sexual gratification, while under other circumstances one may interpret the same words as an expression of lifelong devotion. It all depends upon the situation and the schemas, the deepest of deep structures that the individual brings to bear.

These examples again illustrate what we have already seen: that comprehension is not a one-way process from surface structure to deep structure. Indeed, as we interpret what we hear or read, we in effect impose deep structure on surface structure. Our prior knowledge and experience determine our understanding of the relations among the words in a sentence—or our inability to understand what a sentence means. Perhaps more surprising, however, is the fact that our entire system of knowledge and belief can affect even our perception of individual words and parts of words. While reading a story to my son, I once made the following miscue:

older

The other seals knew better.

In the context of the story, the other seals were in fact older. However, my students have insisted that this miscue was caused not so much by the preceding context of the story as by my unwarranted assumption that to be older is to be wiser. Probably they are right.

CONTRASTING MODELS OF READING

We began this chapter by discussing contrasting views of learning to read, views that seem related to contrasting views of reading itself and, still more generally, of how language means. Let us consider one more example before bringing the discussion full circle, back to the point at which we began.

Developing a Model of Our Own

It will help you develop your own model or theory of language comprehension and reading if, once again, you participate wholeheartedly in the activity suggested. Read the following paragraph silently, not worrying about how the words are pronounced. Just see if you can get some sense of what the passage is about, rereading the passage as necessary. Incidentally, the seeming nonsense words are actually "lost words" that have been revived for the occasion:

> The blonke was maily, like all the others. Unlike the other blonkes, however, it had spiss crinet completely covering its fairney cloots and concealing, just below one of them, a small wam.
>
> This particular blonke was quite drumly—lennow, in fact, and almost samded. When yerden, it did not quetch like the other blonkes, or even blore. The others blored very readily.
>
> It was probably his bellytimber that had made the one blonke so drumly. The bellytimber was quite kexy, had a strong shawk, and was apparently venenated. There was only one thing to do with the venenated bellytimber: givel it in the flosh. This would be much better than to sparple it in the wong, since the blonkes that were not drumly could icchen in the wong, but not in the flosh.

Were you able to get any sense from the passage at all? Much to my initial surprise, I have found that people typically *do* get some meaning on a first or second reading. Typically they get the impression that the blonke is an animal of some sort, one who is obviously different from the others of his kind. Often, students comment that something seems to be wrong with this particular blonke. Can you see how they might get that impression? See if that impression becomes more obvious as you reread the passage knowing that a *blonke* is a large, powerful horse, and that *drumly* means something like 'sluggish.' As you reread the last paragraph, do you get any idea as to what might be wrong with the blonke, what might have made him so sluggish?

Upon rereading that paragraph, you may have concluded, rightly, that the blonke's *bellytimber* is a good clue to the problem. What do you suppose bellytimber is? And what do you suppose *venenated* means? Often, I have found, readers are able to get the general drift: that bellytimber is food, and that something is wrong with the food—it is spoiled or poisoned. Correct! Now please reread the entire "story" again, knowing the meanings of these key words *blonke, drumly, bellytimber*, and *venenated*. In general terms, what do you suppose is being recommended in the last two sentences, and why? You will surely find that you do *not* need to know the meanings of the "nonsense" words in those two sentences in order to get the general drift of the meaning.[1]

Why? Because, of course, you are using your schemas. You are using your knowledge of real-life situations to conclude that somehow the poisoned food must be put in a place where the other blonkes can't get to it, so that they won't get sick too. Frankly, I still find it amazing that we can get so much meaning with so many of the key words unknown, yet this illustrates what children who become voracious readers do all the time. They read materials that are supposedly far beyond their ability to comprehend, but because they use their schemas and all kinds of context cues within what they are reading, they get most of the essential meaning of stories even when they do not already "know" many of the words. I distinctly recall, for example, that when my son was much younger, I found him reading a book based on the Flintstone characters Pebbles and Bam-Bam, wherein the two children went on some kind of space adventure. A quick glance at the book convinced me that *many* of the words would be beyond his previous acquaintance, words he had never even heard of, much less seen in print. Nevertheless, he enjoyed the book thoroughly.

Unfortunately, we may deny children such satisfying experiences with books if we assume that first and foremost, reading means identifying the words and getting their meaning. It is all too common to assume that word identification precedes comprehension, whereas in fact it is clear that in large part language comprehension is the other way around: because, or if, we are getting the meaning of the whole, we can then grasp the meanings of the individual words. The words have meaning only as they transact with one another, within the context of the emerging whole.

Thus we have two contrasting models of reading and language comprehension: one which assumes that language is processed from part to whole, and the other which asserts that language processing occurs just as much or more from whole to part. Let me contrast these views in somewhat more detail.

"Person-on-the-street" or "commonsense" model

These are my idiosyncratic terms for the view that simply assumes, typically without reflection, that *of course* we read and comprehend by working from smaller parts to increasingly larger parts: by sounding out words and thus identifying them, by combining the meanings of individual words to get the meaning of a sentence, by combining the meanings of sentences to get the meaning of the whole text. Another way of saying we process language from part to whole is to say that we read (and listen) in a bottom-up direction, starting with the smallest units and moving to increasingly larger parts. According to this "commonsense" view, we thus process language from surface structure to deep, from outside in; that is, not only is language processed from smaller units to larger, but the meaning comes from the text to the reader. For those of us who are visually oriented, it may help to list some of these characteristics of this "commonsense" model (see Figure 2.8, a).

Reading proceeds from

part-to-whole (letters to words to sentences)

bottom-up (another way of saying part-to-whole)

surface-to-deep structure (from what's on the page to what's in our heads, from text to reader)

outside-in (another way of saying from text to reader)

Socio-psycholinguistic, transactional model[2]

A socio-psycholinguistic view recognizes, of course, that there is some part-to-whole, bottom-up, surface-deep, outside-in processing involved in reading. After all, if it weren't for those squiggles on the page, we simply wouldn't be reading! However, sociolinguistic and psycholinguistic research confirms what we have just been experiencing and concluding for ourselves: that reading is to an amazing degree a matter of whole-to-part, top-to-bottom, deep-to-surface, inside-out processing. As we shall continue to see in later chapters, it is the reader's schemas, expectations, and reading strategies that determine how the parts will be perceived and what meanings will be assigned to them. The meaning does not come from the page to the reader but rather emerges as the reader transacts with the text. Again, a list may help (see also Figure 2.8, b).

According to a socio-psycholinguistic model of reading, reading proceeds

not only from part-to-whole, but from whole-to-part

not only from bottom-up but from top-down

not only from surface-to-deep structure but from deep-to-surface

not only from outside-in but from inside-out

To counteract the simplistic, "commonsense" view of reading, psycholinguists tend to emphasize, of course, the whole-to-part nature of language processing and the active role of the reader. Reading is a transaction between the mind (schemas) of the reader and the language of the text, in a particular situational and social context. Thus reading means bringing meaning to a text in order to get meaning from it.

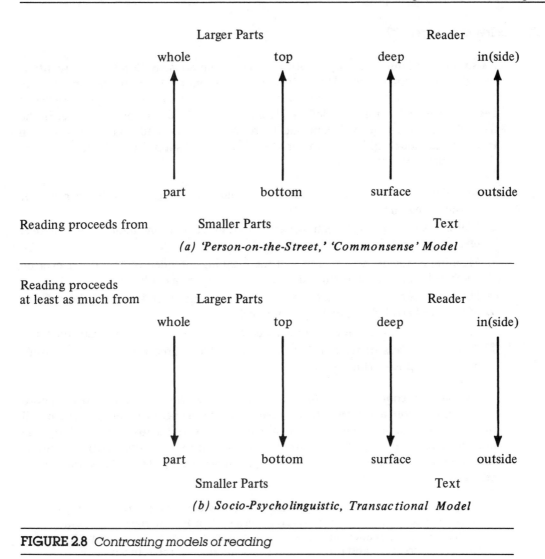

(a) *'Person-on-the-Street,' 'Commonsense' Model*

(b) *Socio-Psycholinguistic, Transactional Model*

FIGURE 2.8 *Contrasting models of reading*

Viewing These Contrasting Models in a Larger Perspective

You may find it useful to enrich your understanding of these contrasting models of reading by reading the first two sections of Chapter 7; the first major section on learning to talk provides background for understanding the second major section, titled "Contrasting Paradigms in Language and Literacy Learning." There, the "commonsense" model of reading is discussed as part of a mechanistic paradigm of teaching and learning, while the "socio-psycholinguistic" view is discussed as part of a larger transactional paradigm.

Which Model Is "Correct"?

As so often in human history, another of our "commonsense" notions of reality is seriously deficient (Geertz 1983). Ironically, it should take even the stereotypical person-on-the-street only a little reflection upon his or her own reading experience to begin to reject what I have called the "commonsense" view as too simplistic. In the following chapters we will continue to refine our own understanding, our own theories and models of the reading process. However, it should already be clear from the activities in this chapter that

1. In isolation, most words do not have a single meaning but rather a range of possible meanings.
2. Words take on specific meanings as they transact with one another in sentence, text, social, and situational contexts.
3. Meaning is not in the text, nor will the meaning intended by the writer ever be perceived (or rather, constructed) exactly the same by a reader.
4. Readers make sense of texts by bringing to bear their schemas, their entire lifetime of knowledge, experience, and feelings.
5. Meaning emerges as readers transact with a text in a specific situational context.
6. Thus the process of reading is to a considerable degree whole-to-part, top-to-bottom, deep-to-surface, inside-out.

Actually, of course, it is far too simplistic to say even that reading proceeds both from part to whole and from whole to part. During the act of reading, there are all kinds of transactions taking place, within and among and across levels of language and understanding. Elsewhere, I have tried to express this complexity somewhat poetically, suggesting that the meaning which arises during the reader's transaction with a text

> may be viewed as an ever-fluctuating dance that occurs more or less simultaneously on and across various levels: letters, words, sentences, schemata; writer, text, and reader; text/reader and context; the present reader with other readers, past and present; and so forth; all connected in a multidimensional holarchy, an interlocking network or web of meaning, a synchronous dance. . . . (Weaver 1985, p. 313)

In the face of such complexity, how can we fail to marvel at the human capacity to process language?

CONTRASTING APPROACHES TO THE TEACHING OF READING

For those readers who like an overview of what is to follow, or for those who have no acquaintance with different approaches to reading instruction, it seems useful at this point to sketch the major approaches to the teaching of reading and to suggest how they reflect contrasting models of the reading process. Other readers may prefer to go directly to Chapters 3 through 6, or even to go directly to the first two major sections of Chapter 7, before returning to this section.

What follows, then, is a brief sketch of six approaches to reading instruction: a phonics approach, a so-called linguistic approach, a sight word approach, a basal reader approach, a language experience approach, and a whole-language approach. The first four of these approaches reflect the so-called "commonsense" view, a view that tends to focus on words and/or parts of words as initial units of instruction. The latter two approaches reflect a socio-psycholinguistic view, focusing first on meaning. Those who work mainly with older students will doubtless recognize vestiges of one or more of these approaches in the materials designed for their students. The reader is hereby warned, however, that these sketches are gross simplifications, designed expressly to highlight the similarities and differences among the approaches.

Approaches That Reflect a "Commonsense" Model of Reading

Those approaches most obviously reflecting the simplistic "commonsense" view are the phonics approach, the so-called linguistic approach, and the sight word approach. Elements of these approaches are reflected in the more common basal reader approach, which also tends to reflect the "commonsense" view of reading.

A phonics approach

Advocates of a phonics approach are concerned about helping beginners become independent readers as soon as possible. They feel the best way to do this is to help children learn letter/sound correspondences so that they can sound out or "decode" words. Typically, children are taught not only basic letter/sound correspondences but *rules* for sounding out words. This approach was especially popular from about 1890 through the 1920s, when it was gradually superseded by a sight word approach. The most extreme advocates of a phonics approach obviously believe that learning to read means learning to pronounce the words. As Rudolf Flesch put it, "Reading means getting meaning from certain combinations of letters. Teach the child what each letter stands for and he can read" (Flesch 1955, p. 10). Like Flesch, most proponents of a phonics approach seem to think that once words are identified, meaning will take care of itself. They emphasize rapid and fluent "decoding" rather than comprehension. Today, many "reading readiness" programs focus heavily on phonics.

A "linguistic" approach

The so-called linguistic approach is based upon the tenets of structural linguists, whose view of language and language learning was prominent in the 1950s. Unfortunately, the term "linguistic" was appropriated to describe the reading approach advocated by this one school of linguistic thought, now largely superseded by other views. Those who advocate this particular approach are generally concerned with helping children internalize regular patterns of spelling/sound correspondence. In one respect this approach differs sharply from a phonics approach. Whereas a phonics approach emphasizes the direct teaching and conscious learning of rules, the "linguistic" approach advocates exposing children to regularly spelled words from which the children can unconsciously infer the common spelling/sound patterns. A typical sentence from an early lesson in a linguistic reader might be something like "Nan can fan Dan."

The founder of this approach was Leonard Bloomfield, more widely known as the founder of structural linguistics itself. Although Bloomfield first advocated his "linguistic" approach to reading in the early 1940s, it did not become embodied in a text of any kind until the early 1960s, when Bloomfield and Barnhart's *Let's Read* finally appeared. Their linguistic or "spelling-pattern" approach was embodied in several reading series of the late 1960s and early 1970s. While the approach reflects a psycholinguistic philosophy in its emphasis on learning spelling/sound patterns unconsciously, without direct instruction (see Chapter 7), this linguistic approach is like the phonics approach in assuming that learning to read means learning to pronounce the words, and that once words are identified, meaning will take care of itself. (See the "linguistic" definitions of reading in activity 3 at the end of Chapter 1.)

A sight word or "look-say" approach

Those who advocate a sight word approach, in contrast to phonics, claim to be concerned that meaning be emphasized from the very outset of reading instruction. They stress helping children develop a stock of words that the children can recognize on sight. Thus instead of stressing letter/sound correspondences and phonics "rules," teachers might use flash cards and other devices to help children learn to recognize basic words like *I, and*, and *the*. Advocates of a sight word approach argue that if children can begin with a stock of about one hundred basic sight words, they will be able to read about half the words in any text they might ordinarily encounter.

This approach was widely used from about 1930 until about the mid-1960s, when it became increasingly intertwined with (or infiltrated by) a phonics approach. Although prominent advocates of the sight word approach (e.g., William Gray 1948, 1960) have expressed concern with meaning, actual classroom instruction has tended to focus heavily on the recognition of words. Thus the sight word approach also seems to assume that once words are identified, meaning will take care of itself. The sight word or "look-say" approach differs from a phonics approach in focusing on whole words rather than on parts of words, but both seem more concerned with word recognition than with meaning.

A basal reader approach

In the late 1960s and early 1970s, the development of basal reading series became a multimillion dollar business. Today's basal reading series typically include pupil texts with a variety of reading selections for grades K–6 or K–8, accompanied by teacher's manuals, pupil workbooks, tests, and often an array of supplementary materials. These basal reading series typically reflect all three of the aforementioned approaches, in varying degrees. They typically reflect a phonics approach by explicitly teaching letter/sound correspondences and phonics rules. They may reflect a sight word approach in at least three ways: by explicitly teaching "basic" sight words, by encouraging teachers to pre-teach new vocabulary before the children read a selection, and by simplifying the language of the reading selections, often to the point that the selections are difficult to read precisely *because* the language is so unnatural (see Chapter 9 for a brief discussion of such simplification). Some of the basal reading series reflect a so-called linguistic approach in that the selections are written so as to contain a high degree of phonic regularity. My favorite example is the first "story" in the first preprimer of *Lippincott's Basic Reading* (Book A, 1975):

Pam and the Pup

Pam ran up the ramp.
Up the ramp ran the pup.
The pup and Pam nap.

Surely the eclectic basal reader approach is preferable to a phonics, linguistic, or sight word approach alone, yet it shares their same basic focus on the word. Stemming from a simplistic "commonsense" view of reading, virtually all basal readers focus at the outset on skills for identifying words rather than on strategies for constructing meaning from the text. Even comprehension itself is taught as a set of hierarchical, part-to-whole skills. And now that it is becoming increasingly recognized that meaning does *not* take care of itself once words are identified, the basal reading series have incorporated still more instruction in skills: this time, skills for developing "higher order reasoning." But this skills approach still reflects the part-to-whole, text-to-reader approach, which we have begun to see as an inadequate reflection of how people actually read—even beginners.

Approaches That Reflect a Socio-Psycholinguistic Model of Reading

Currently the approaches that reflect a socio-psycholinguistic view of reading are the language experience approach and a whole-language approach, the latter often being explained as more a philosophy than an approach per se. These two approaches are not necessarily separate: language experience activities are often part of a whole-language approach to reading and the language arts.

A language experience approach

Today, the approach known as "language experience" (commonly abbreviated LEA) is associated with the name of Roach Van Allen (see his *Language Experiences in Education*, 1976). Those who advocate a language experience approach are concerned with helping beginners learn to bring their own knowledge and experience to bear in constructing meaning from the printed word. The importance of relating oral language to written language and of relating reading to writing is emphasized in the motto "Anything I can say, I can write; anything I can write, I can read."

Thus the teacher begins with the language and experiences of the children—not only the experiences they may have had individually, but experiences they have had together, in raising guinea pigs, studying dinosaurs, taking a field trip to the zoo. With an individual child, the teacher typically writes a word or sentence that the child has dictated under a picture that the child has drawn—or, later, takes the child's dictation for a longer story. With a group, the children typically compose together a story, poem, report, or "all about" list ("all about" planets, for example), perhaps with each child contributing a line; the teacher writes what the children dictate on the chalkboard or on chart paper.

The teacher reads the group composition and teacher and children then read and reread what the children have composed, until the children can read the lines alone and then begin to associate written words with their own spoken words. At this point, the teacher may begin to help children focus on recognizing individual words, so that they will more readily develop a stock of sight words. The teacher may also use the children's dictated composition to focus on important letter/sound patterns, such as initial consonants and final rhyming elements. Thus the teacher uses the children's own language and composition to teach the sight words, letter/sound correspondences, and other "skills" that are typically taught out of context in the approaches that reflect the "commonsense" view of reading.

It should be noted that in some people's view, the teacher can and should be much more active in helping children shape their group writings. The teacher helps children not only brainstorm for ideas but select ideas and details and order and shape them, then perhaps even revise and edit the composition. Through such "shared writing" experiences, the children not only learn what good writers do, but learn to expect printed books to be well-crafted; thus the reading/writing connection is reinforced.

The language experience approach and philosophically related approaches have had several peaks of popularity: from about 1909 to 1918; in the late 1920s and early 1930s; and again from about the mid-1960s into the early 1970s. The language experience approach seems to assume that learning to read means learning to construct meaning from a text, and that in order to construct meaning, we must *bring* meaning *to* what we read.

A whole-language approach

Like advocates of the language experience approach, those who advocate a whole-language approach emphasize the importance of approaching reading and writing by building upon the language and experiences of the child. This means several things:

1. Children are expected to learn to read and write as they learned to talk—gradually, naturally, with a minimum of direct instruction, and with encouragement rather than the discouragement of constant corrections (see Chapter 7).
2. Learning is emphasized more than teaching: the teacher makes detailed observations of the children's needs, then guides their development accordingly.

3. Children read and write every day—and they are never asked to read artificially simplified or contrived language, or to write something that does not have a "real" purpose and audience.

4. Reading, writing, and oral language are not considered separate components of the curriculum, or merely ends in themselves; rather, they permeate everything the children are doing in science, social studies, and the so-called creative arts— drawing and painting, music, drama.

5. There is no division between first "learning to read" and later "reading to learn," as there is in the code-emphasis, sight words, and basal reading approaches. From the very beginning, children are presented with and encouraged to compose *whole* texts—real language written for real purposes and a real audience.

Thus in a whole-language approach, letter/sound relationships and sight words will not be taught as prerequisites to reading. Rather, children learn them through repeated exposure to songs and rhymes, stories, and signs and labels for objects in the classroom. While whole-language teachers may draw upon aurally familiar materials to help children learn sight words and gain a firmer grasp of letter/sound relationships, as language experience teachers do, such teachers are quick to point out that much of this kind of word and letter/sound knowledge will develop naturally, without direct instruction, through repeated exposure to materials that children can already "read." This assumption is based upon the observation that this is the way children learn the sound patterns and syntax of their language in the first place: by listening to it spoken and formulating their own unconscious hypotheses about its structure.

In order for children to learn letter/sound patterns and other conventions of print without much direct instruction, they must be exposed to a wide variety of natural, meaningful print. This is one of the main reasons for not asking children to deal with the bits and pieces of language typically found in workbook exercises and standardized tests. It is also one of the main reasons for avoiding the artificiality of controlled-vocabulary materials with sentences like the famous "See Spot run!" What child (or adult) ever uttered a sentence like that? Equally to be avoided are texts with artificial limitations on the letter/sound patterns, as advocated in the so-called linguistic approach (see, for example, the "story" in the section on basal readers above). Basal reading series tend to "simplify" the language of beginning reading materials in one or both ways, but whole-language teachers point out that such artificial restrictions actually make the texts more difficult to read, and nearly impossible for children to use in order to develop their own concepts about print and how it works. Thus whole-language advocates insist that from the very beginning— ideally from infancy, but certainly long before "formal" reading instruction— children must be exposed to meaningful print written in natural language.

In the last decade, a whole-language approach has been gaining in popularity around the globe. For at least twice that long, many teachers and schools in Great Britain have used what has come to be known as a whole-language approach, though the term has only recently begun to be popular there. In New Zealand, parts of Australia, and some of the provinces of Canada, whole language has become the official policy and approach (see, for example, Ken Goodman's *What's Whole in Whole Language?* 1986). In the past five to ten years, a whole-language movement has been increasing in the United States, encouraged by socio-psycholinguists and other like-minded theorists, by outstanding educators and teacher educators, by publishers of professional books (most notably Heinemann, for elementary education), by publishers and distributors of Big Books for whole-class use (see Chapters 7 and 8), and most of all by classroom teachers committed to a whole-language philosophy of literacy and learning.

RELATING APPROACHES TO TEACHING READING WITH MODELS OF THE READING PROCESS

As just explained, there are at least these half dozen approaches to the teaching of reading: phonics, "linguistic," sight word, basal reader, language experience, and whole language. Oddly enough, however, not only the public in general but even many educators tend to reduce the approaches to two simple alternatives: phonics or sight word (also known as "look-say"). If you're not a phonics advocate, then you're assumed to be an advocate of a sight word approach, and vice versa. For many people, including the "person-on-the-street," the entire world of reading instruction is divided into just these two parts. See Figure 2.9.

In her influential book *Learning to Read: The Great Debate* (1967), Jeanne Chall divided beginning reading approaches into two similar but more inclusive categories: *code-emphasis* and *meaning-emphasis*. By a code-emphasis approach she meant an approach that initially emphasizes breaking the alphabetic code, that

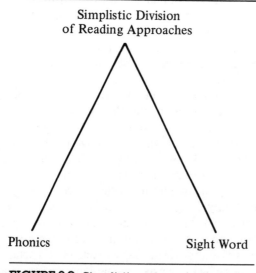

FIGURE 2.9 *Simplistic categorization of reading approaches*

emphasizes learning correspondences between letters and sounds. The phonics approach and the linguistic or ''spelling-pattern'' approach are both code-emphasis approaches. By a meaning-emphasis approach, Chall meant one that initially emphasizes getting meaning. In her scheme, the sight word approach and the language experience approach were both considered meaning-emphasis approaches. The more recent whole-language approach would also fall within this second of her categories. In Chall's 1983 update of the original 1967 book, she includes a third category, a *combined ''eclectic'' approach*, which is roughly the same as what I have characterized as a basal reader approach (*The Great Debate*, revised updated 1983 edition, p. 33).

I mention the simplistic ''phonics or sight word'' view because it is such a common misconception that one must be prepared to encounter it. Chall's original characterization of approaches as either code-emphasis or meaning-emphasis I mention because it is so well known among educators that it too may be encountered, not only in the strictly professional literature but in documents intended for the interested non-educator: an example is the recent much-publicized *Becoming a Nation of Readers* (Anderson et al., 1985), which Jeanne Chall had a hand in shaping.

By now it must be obvious, however, that I would divide the universe of reading approaches in a significantly different way. As I see it, the phonics, ''linguistic,'' sight word, and basal reader approaches all reflect the simplistic ''commonsense'' view that reading proceeds from part-to-whole, bottom-up, and from surface-to-deep structure, outside-in, text-to-reader. And these approaches all typically focus on identifying *words*, as if meaning will magically take care of itself once words are identified. See Figure 2.10. In contrast, I see language experience and whole lan-

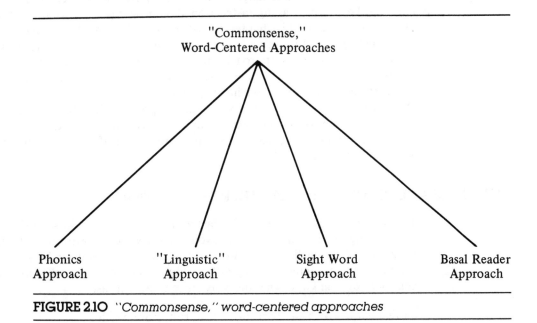

FIGURE 2.10 *"Commonsense," word-centered approaches*

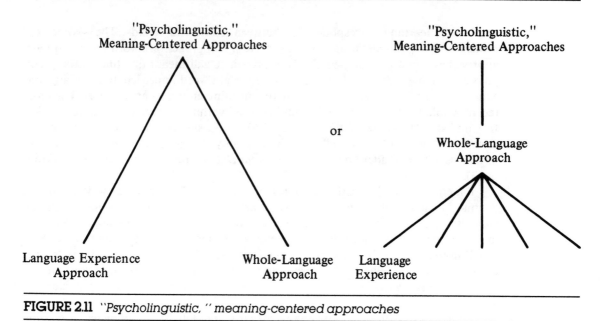

FIGURE 2.11 *"Psycholinguistic," meaning-centered approaches*

guage as the only genuine meaning-emphasis approaches. They are psycholinguistic in nature, emphasizing the fact that meaning is not "in" the text itself but rather develops (or fails to develop!) during an active transaction between reader and text. Thus these approaches emphasize the fact that to a great extent, reading involves whole-to-part, top-down, deep-to-surface, inside-out processing. That is, the language experience and whole-language approaches are the only current ones which assume that beginning reading instruction should be based on what we discovered about reading earlier in this chapter, namely that reading involves bringing meaning to a text in order to get meaning from it. See Figure 2.11. Furthermore, it is neither phonics nor a whole word approach but instead such holistic approaches as these that most often match the learning styles of beginning readers and of older, underachieving readers—as we shall see in Chapter 11.

Since the word-emphasis approaches are so popular, however, it seems wise to turn our attention next to the perception and identification of words, suggesting that some of the commonly accepted notions about word identification are in fact myths. This we shall do in Chapter 3.

ACTIVITIES AND PROJECTS FOR FURTHER EXPLORATION

1. To further explore the role of schemas and the various kinds of context in determining the meanings of words, you might try the following activity. Drawing from the following list of ten words, plus any others you might want to add, compose several sentences using at least two of the words in each sentence. Then consider *how* you know what the words mean, in each case.

   baste, coat, cook, hose, part, rag, roast, run, store, wash

8. We might run short of food.

9. I had a run in with my boss.

10. He gave her a run for her money.

Note that in most of these cases, *run* or *ran* is followed by another word that functions along with it, as a single unit: *ran up, ran over, run over, run out, run short, run in*, and maybe *run for*. No wonder idioms are difficult for children and foreigners to learn!

If possible, try out these or some other idioms with early elementary children and/or people who have learned English as a second language. Find out whether they can read the words of the sentences and, if so, whether they can explain the idiomatic meaning. What you may find is that they have difficulty reading the words, precisely because they are not getting the meaning!

An interesting and useful source of idioms is Maxine Tull Boatner and John Edward Gates's *A Dictionary of American Idioms*, updated by Adam Makkai (Woodbury, N.Y.: Barron's Educational Series, 1975). There are some delightful books of idioms that attempt to capture children's humorous misinterpretations of common idioms. Two of these are by Fred Gwynne: *The King Who Rained* and *Chocolate Moose* (New York: Windmill Books and E. P. Dutton, 1970 and 1979 respectively). Upper elementary children typically enjoy creating such books of their own.

3. Read the story "Petronella," by Jay Williams, included as Appendix A at the back of the book. Then jot down what you remember about the story, particularly those things you consider important. Now compose a list of questions that you might ask others about the story. Discuss your notes and your questions with others, noting in particular how your responses differ. What accounts for such differences? Discuss the implications for education—and keep these notes and your questions for later discussion.

4. To further explore the importance of readers' schemas, read the following letter written by a teenager to his friend. Then write down a one-or-two-sentence summary of the third paragraph, without looking back at the letter. If possible, compare your responses with others'.

Dear Joe,

I bet you're surprised to be hearing from your old friend Sam. It's been a long time since you moved away so I thought I'd drop you a line to catch you up on what's going on around here. Things haven't changed much. The weather's been really bad but we've only been let out of school a couple days. Everybody in the family is O.K., and my cousin is still asking about you. School has been going O.K. but I did get in some trouble last week.

It started out as a typical Thursday. Typical that is until lunchtime; at that point things started to get interesting. But don't let me get ahead of myself. I'll start at the beginning. Renee, my sister, and I were almost late for school. Renee had trouble getting her chores done and I couldn't leave without her. We barely caught our ride and made it to school just as the tardy bell rang.

Classes went at their usual slow pace through the morning, so at noon I was really ready for lunch. I got in line behind Bubba. As usual the line was moving pretty slow and we were all getting pretty restless. For a little action Bubba turned around and said, "Hey, Sam! What you doin' man? You so ugly that when the doctor delivered you he slapped your face!" Everyone laughed, but they laughed even harder when I shot back, "Oh, yeah? Well, you so ugly the doctor turned around and slapped your momma!" It got even wilder when Bubba said, "Well man, at least my daddy ain't no girlscout!" We really got into it then. After a while more people got involved—4, 5, then 6. It was a riot! People helping out anyone who seemed to be getting the worst of the deal. All of a sudden Mr. Reynolds the gym teacher came over to try to quiet things down. The next thing we knew we were all in the office. The principal made us stay after school for a week; he's so straight! On top of that, he sent word home that he wanted to talk to our folks in his office Monday afternoon. Boy! Did I get it when I got home. That's the third notice I've gotten this semester. As we were leaving the principal's office, I ran into Bubba again. We decided we'd finish where we left off, but this time we would wait until we were off the school grounds.

Well, I have to run now. I've got to take out the trash before Mom gets home. Write soon and let me know what's going on with you.

Later,
Sam

When you summarized the third paragraph, did you say, in one way or another, that the teenagers had gotten into a fight, a physical confrontation? Or did you think that the battle was merely verbal, not physical? If the latter, you're right. What Sam was describing to his friend Joe was an instance of "sounding" or "playing the dozens," a form of ritual insult found especially among black males. When black and white eighth grade students tried to recall the letter and responded to questions about its content, the white students (who were from an agricultural area) tended to describe the events as "horrible," described the two participants as angry, and generally recalled the event as a fight: "Soon there was a riot all the kids were fighting"; "Me and Bubba agreed to finish our fight later, off the school grounds." The black students, in contrast, more often recognized that the participants were just joking, just having fun. In fact, when told that white students tended to interpret the letter as being about a fight instead of an

instance of "sounding," one of the black stu⁀
"What's the matter? Can't they read?" (Rey
the implications for education.

5. As you may have concluded from the p
students' schemas, "where they are com⁀
assignments and when we interpret thei⁀
interviewed ten inner-city high school s⁀
test questions. The investigators fou⁀
different system of assumptions thar⁀
them to answers which were often
from their perspective. As Reynolds et ⁀

> The research on cultural schemata has in⁀
> minority children. Standardized tests, basa⁀
> tent area texts lean heavily on the conventiona⁀
> is inherent in the words and structure of a discourse. ᴡ⁀⁀⁀ ⁀⁀⁀⁀⁀ ᴋnowl-
> edge is required, it is assumed to be knowledge common to children from
> every background. When new information is introduced, it is assumed to
> be as accessible to one child as to the next. The question that naturally
> arises is whether children from different subcultures can generally be as-
> sumed to bring to bear a common schema.

(1982, p. 356)

Discuss in light of your own experience, as a student and/or a teacher. If possible, administer to one or more students a standardized reading test of the multiple-choice variety. Then interview the student to find out how he or she went about answering the questions and why the student chose the responses given. Discuss.

6. Return to the "blonke" passage earlier in the chapter. This time, do the following things:

   a. Read the passage aloud. Did you have much difficulty pronouncing the strange words? If so, why? If not, why not? Were you consciously applying phonics rules in pronouncing the words? If not, what enabled you to pronounce them with little difficulty? Consider the implications for the teaching of phonics rules.

   b. Answer the following typical kinds of comprehension questions about the passage, without checking the meanings of the strange words:

      1. *Literal*: Where was the small wam?
      2. *Translation*: What is "drumly"?
      3. *Inference*: Why weren't the other blonkes drumly?
      4. *Reorganization*: In what way(s) was the drumly blonke like/unlike the others?
      5. *Evaluation*: If bellytimber is venenated, is it wise to givel it in the flosh? Why or why not?

Did you have serious difficulty answering the questions? If in fact you had little difficulty, even not knowing many of the words, what does this suggest about comprehension and/or about the typical kinds of "comprehension" questions found in workbooks and on standardized tests?

7. Sometimes an approach to reading can be inferred from trade books. Particularly interesting in this regard are the "Bright and Early" books published by Random House. Compare, for example, the following three books: Al Perkins's *Hand, Hand, Fingers, Thumb* (1969); Theo. Le Sieg's (Dr. Seuss's) *In a People House* (1972); and Stan and Jan Berenstain's *Bears in the Night* (1971). What reading approach or approaches seem to be reflected in each of these books?

8. In order to become better acquainted with some of the approaches reflected in various reading materials, you might compare the following series. Some of these are currently out of print, but they are historically interesting and may be available in your college or university library:

Lippincott's Basic Reading, 4th ed. 1975. Philadelphia: J. B. Lippincott. A complete basal reading series based on what its authors call a "phonic/linguistic" approach.

Houghton Mifflin Readers, Boston: Houghton Mifflin or the *Holt Basic Reading System*, New York: Holt, Rinehart. Use the latest available editions. In recent years, these series have typified what I have characterized as the basal reader approach.

Reading Unlimited: Scott, Foresman Systems, Revised, 1976. Glenview, Ill.: Scott, Foresman. This was the most psycholinguistically oriented of the comprehensive basal reading series available in the late 1970s.

Sounds of Language, 2d ed. 1972–1974. New York: Holt, Rinehart. This set of readers by Bill Martin and Peggy Brogan reflects a whole-language philosophy. There are no workbooks, no tests, no accompanying manuals, but only a teacher's edition section in the teacher's version of the books—which may be, alas, why the books are currently out of print!

Impressions. 1984. Holt, Rinehart. Published by Holt, Rinehart of Canada but available from the New York office of Holt as well, this series is advertised as a whole-language series. In addition to the anthologies of readings, there are the typical teacher's manuals and pupil workbooks.

See Chapter 8 for two other Canadian whole-language series and a British series.

READINGS FOR FURTHER EXPLORATION

The following are recommended for further insights into the nature of the reading process:

Smith, Frank. 1975. Two Faces of Language. *Comprehension and Learning: A Conceptual Framework for Teachers*. New York: Holt, Rinehart, 83–117. The first parts of the chapter (to the top of p. 95) are highly recommended as a complement to the discussion here.

————. 1985. *Reading Without Nonsense*. 2d ed. New York: Teachers College Press. This book constitutes an excellent introduction to the reading process.

The following articles are recommended for insights into the "socio" aspect of socio-psycholinguistics:

Anderson, Billie V., and John G. Barnitz. November 1984. Cross-Cultural Schemata and Reading Comprehension Instruction. *Journal of Reading* 28: 102–8. Provides interesting examples of how cultural background affects readers' comprehension and recall of information. Suggests some ways that teachers can adapt their instruction and evaluation for culturally different students.

Bloome, David. February 1985. Reading as a Social Process. *Language Arts* 62: 134–42. Describes three dimensions of reading as a social process: first, all reading events involve a social context; second, reading is a cultural activity; third, reading is a socio-cognitive process. Presents some implications for teaching.

The following articles are recommended for further discussion of contrasting models of the reading process:

Goodman, Kenneth S. September 1979. The Know-More and the Know-Nothing Movements in Reading: A Personal Response. *Language Arts* 56: 657–63. Goodman contrasts the socio-psycholinguistic model of reading with what I have called the "person-on-the street" or "commonsense" model.

Smith, Frank. 1979. Conflicting Approaches to Reading Research and Instruction. *Theory and Practice of Early Reading* 2, Ed. L. B. Resnick and P. A. Weaver. Hillsdale, N.J.: Erlbaum. 31–42. This article is much more difficult reading than the Goodman article above, but worth the effort.

The following books are recommended as introductions to different approaches to the teaching of reading:

Walcutt, Charles Child, Joan Lamport, and Glenn McCracken. 1974. *Teaching Reading: A Phonic/Linguistic Approach to Developmental Reading*. New York: Macmillan. An excellent introduction to the philosophy and practice of these combined approaches.

Hall, MaryAnne. 1976. *Teaching Reading as a Language Experience*. 2d ed. Columbus, Ohio: Charles E. Merrill Publishing. An excellent introduction to the language experience approach.

Goodman, Kenneth. 1986. *What's Whole in Whole Language?* Richmond Hill, Ontario: Scholastic-TAB. Available from Heinemann in the U.S. This is an excellent introduction to the whole-language philosophy.

3

How Are Words Perceived?

Words may be identified when their individual letters are separately indistinguishable.

—Frank Smith

QUESTIONS FOR JOURNALS AND DISCUSSION

1. How do the eyes function in visual perception?

2. What does it mean to say that visual perception is more a function of the brain than of the eye?

3. Do we normally process words letter by letter, from left to right?

4. Which parts of words are more useful in word identification: the consonants, or the vowels? The beginnings, the middles, or the ends?

5. How useful are phonics rules? How necessary is it for children to learn phonics rules?

6. Why/how can children internalize "phonics" knowledge (knowledge of letter/sound relationships) without formally studying phonics rules?

THE EYES AND THE BRAIN

When children have difficulty reading, it is common practice to have their eyes checked. This is wise, because various kinds of eye malfunction can indeed make reading more difficult. In most cases, however, appropriately prescribed glasses will be adequate to compensate for problems with the eyes themselves. There are few children whose reading problems can be attributed to irremediable difficulties with the eyes. This is because visual perception is only partly a function of the eyes. Perhaps your experience on the super-highways illustrates this point. Have you ever "seen" the words on a road sign, yet passed the sign before you were able to determine what the words were? Perhaps you were a little slow in looking at the sign, or perhaps you have nearsighted eyes that were a little slow in picking up the visual image. Nevertheless, the crucial problem was not in the eyes, but in the brain: your brain simply did not have enough time to process the visual image before it disappeared from sight.

The preceding illustration suggests that visual perception is not merely a function of the eyes, but a function of the brain. In this text we are concerned with one particular kind of visual perception, the perception of words. We will be concerned with *both* aspects of word perception: with ocular and sensory processing, and with the actual identification of words.[1] However, such division is merely a convenient fiction, as this and the next two chapters should make increasingly clear. Visual perception is an *active* process, and what the eye processes is in large part determined by what the brain directs it to look for, as well as the knowledge that the brain brings *to* the visual task. We use our prior knowledge and experience to guide even the most elementary aspects of visual processing.

After discussing the ocular and sensory processing of words, we will turn to several activities which should help you better understand how words are perceived.

OCULAR AND SENSORY PROCESSING

It was noted previously that the eye registers a visual image. Strictly speaking, however, this statement is not accurate. As the psycholinguist Frank Smith explains, "What goes into the open eyes is a diffuse and continual bombardment of electromagnetic radiation, minute waves of light energy that vary only in frequency, amplitude, and spatial and temporal patterning. The rays of light that impinge on the eye do not in themselves carry the color and form and texture and movement that we see." Rather, these are constructions of the brain (F. Smith 1978, pp. 26–27). So, too, in reading: the eye itself receives waves of light energy that are transmitted to the brain as a series of neural impulses. Initially, the written symbols may be perceived as sets of bars, slits, edges, curves, angles, and breaks (Gough 1972, p. 332; see also F. Smith 1978, chaps. 8 and 9). The brain may then construct the words of the text from these bars, curves, angles, or whatever.

How, then, do the eyes (the ocular part of the system) pick up these waves of light energy that are transformed into words? In 1879, the Frenchman Emile Javal discovered that the eyes move along a line of print with a series of jerky movements which he called *saccades*, meaning 'jerks.' It is difficult if not impossible to become aware of one's own saccades, for the eyes *seem* to move along a line of print with a smooth, continuous motion. Nevertheless, they do not: they move in a sequence of tiny leaps or jerks.

There is no useful vision during the eye movements themselves, as you can demonstrate by looking into a mirror with your head held still and moving your eyes from left to right between two imaginary points. As you will discover, you cannot see your eyes in motion. Neither can you read with your eyes in motion (Anderson and Dearborn 1952, p. 101).

The saccades, or eye movements, take up only a small fraction of total reading time—about 10 percent of the time in rapid reading and about 5 percent of the time in slow reading (Anderson and Dearborn 1952, p. 107). The rest of the time is taken up by eye *fixations*, or pauses. It is during these fixations that the eye receives the stimuli which are transformed into visual images in the brain.

Various aspects of visual processing have been studied in the laboratory, usually with the help of a *tachistoscope*. In simple terms, a tachistoscope is a device for presenting visual information for very short periods of time—say as little as 10 milliseconds (10 thousandths of a second, or 1 hundredth of a second). With the use of the tachistoscope, it has been found that successive letters or words can be perceived from a visual presentation as short as one-tenth of a second (see Huey 1908, p. 65). Further, it has been found that as many as four or five words can be perceived in a single fixation (see F. Smith 1971, p. 92). Such statistics represent the *maximal efficiency* of the ocular and sensory systems.

Usually, however, reading proceeds much more slowly. The average adult reader makes about four eye fixations per second and identifies about one word per fixation. This gives an average adult reading speed of 240 words per minute (see Carroll 1970, p. 292; Anderson and Dearborn 1952, p. 177; and Dechant 1970, p. 16). Many readers have a slightly higher rate, up to about 300 words per minute. This means either that they average slightly more than four fixations per second, or that they average slightly more than one word per fixation, or both.

These various measurements indicate that there is a considerable discrepancy between what the ocular and the sensory systems are capable of doing, and what they typically do in reading. The crucial differences are summarized in Figure 3.1. From these comparisons it should be obvious that, for most people, the ocular and sensory systems do not operate at maximal efficiency in normal reading. The eyes can handle about 960 to 1200 words per minute, yet most of us read at an average speed of about 240 to 300 words per minute. Apparently most of us read at this slower rate because that is a comfortable speed for comprehending.

Of course, readers need to learn to vary their reading rate according to the material and their purpose for reading. To some extent we all do this, yet many of us

Maximal Ocular and Sensory Efficiency	Typical Ocular and Sensory Functioning in Reading
An eye fixation of 1/10 second is enough for identifying a letter or word.	Eye fixations are normally about 1/4 second long.
We can identify four or five words in a normal eye fixation of about 1/4 second.	Readers typically process about one word in a normal eye fixation of about 1/4 second.
We can visually process about 960 to 1200 words per minute.	Most of us read at an average rate of about 240 to 300 words per minute.

FIGURE 3.1 *Ocular and sensory processing*

could benefit from instruction and practice. We need to learn, for example, that it's okay to read a novel rapidly and without necessarily trying to remember all the details: there is no need to read a novel at a rate of only 240 to 300 words per minute unless we really want to. Then, too, we need to learn to skim and scan informational material, selecting only those parts of the text that are relevant to the particular purpose at hand. In general, these seem to be the purposes of so-called speed reading courses.

While recognizing the widespread need for this kind of instruction, one should be wary of the simplistic notion that to improve a person's reading, all we have to do is improve his or her reading rate. If a person reads much slower than the average, this may mean that he or she has difficulty getting meaning from the text. The slow reading speed may be more a *symptom* of reading difficulty than a cause. In such cases, it may not help much to get readers to identify words faster; indeed, this may not even be possible.

What *will* help is various strategies for helping readers learn to bring meaning to a text in order to get meaning from it. This approach will actually make word identification faster and more accurate, as the next section begins to show.

HOW WE PERCEIVE WORDS

The brain does not just passively interpret the data relayed through the eyes. In fact, the brain is in large measure independent of the eye. In normal vision, the picture that the eye registers is upside down, but the brain rights it. And as Frank Smith observes,

> In a number of perceptual experiments, many men and animals have been fitted with special spectacles which completely distort the information received by the eye, switching top to bottom, or left to right, or distorting form or color. But within a very short while the brain "adapts" and the perceived world reverts to its normal appearance. No further distortion is perceived until the trick spectacles are removed, whereupon the "normal" pattern of stimulation produces a topsy-turvy percept which persists until the brain readapts. (F. Smith 1971, p. 89)

For more details, see Kohler 1962. As you will probably conclude, the brain performs equally marvelous feats in normal reading.

Before investigating what cues within words are especially important in word perception, it seems wise to deal with the typical notion that words are processed in serial fashion, letter by letter, from left to right.

Activity 1. First, try the following exercise on formulating phonics rules. In each of the words below, one letter is printed in boldface type. Determine how each boldfaced letter should be pronounced, and what part of the word signals the pronunciation of the boldfaced letter. In other words, try to formulate a *rule* for producing the correct pronunciation of the boldfaced letters. You will need at least one rule for each of the three sets:

a.	hat	hate
	hatter	hater
	pet	Pete
	petted	Peter
	bit	bite
	bitter	biting
	mop	mope
	mopping	moping
	cut	cute
	cutter	cuter
b.	wrap	war
	wren	wet
	wring	win
	wrong	won
c.	car	cent
	care	cereal
	coat	cite
	cough	city
	cube	cyclone
	cut	cyst

DISCUSSION. For the first column of words in set *a*, you may have formulated a rule something like this: a vowel is short when it is followed by just a single consonant, or when it is followed by a double consonant plus an ending of some sort. For the second column of words in set *a*, you may have formulated a rule something like the following: a vowel is long when it is followed by a silent *e*, or when it is followed by a single consonant plus an ending of some sort. Complicated, yes? The words in set *b* should have been easier to deal with, and you may have formulated a rather simple rule such as this: when a word begins with a *w* followed by an *r*, the *w* is not pronounced; otherwise, it is pronounced as a /w/. (The slashes indicate that we are talking about a sound rather than a letter.) For the words in set *c*, you might have formulated a rule something like this: when *c* is followed by *a*, *o*, or *u*, it is pronounced /k/; when *c* is followed by *e*, *i*, or *y*, it is pronounced /s/.

Doubtless these are not the only rules possible, nor are they necessarily the best rules. But note that in each case *the pronunciation of the boldfaced letter is determined not by what precedes, but by what follows.* We could not possibly pronounce the listed words correctly if we processed and pronounced them merely letter by letter, from left to right. Furthermore, most of these words are not exotic words that we encounter only once or twice in a lifetime; most are relatively common words that we encounter fairly often. As Venezky put it in *The Structure of English Orthography*, "a person who attempts to scan left to right, letter by letter, pronouncing as he goes, could not correctly read most English words'' (1970, p. 129).

Activity 2. Activity 1 leaves open the possibility that we might process each letter separately, even if not left to right. To test this possibility, try replicating the following experiment from p. 100 of Edmund Huey's *The Psychology and Pedagogy of Reading* (1968; first published in 1908). For this experiment, you will need either a stop watch or a watch or clock with a second hand. Figure 3.2 contains a column of letters, a column of four-letter words, and a column of eight-letter words. Time yourself or someone else reading the column of letters as rapidly as possible, either simply identifying each letter mentally or pronouncing it aloud. Repeat the same procedure for the column of four-letter words and the column of eight-letter words.

y	pool	analysis
w	rugs	habitual
u	mark	occupied
s	send	inherent
q	list	probable
o	more	summoned
m	pick	devotion
k	stab	remarked
i	neck	overcome
g	your	resolute
e	dice	elements
c	font	conclude
a	earl	numbered
z	whit	struggle
x	ants	division
v	role	research
t	sink	original
r	rust	involved
p	ware	obstacle
n	fuss	relative
l	tick	physical
j	rasp	pastness
h	mold	lacteals
f	hive	sameness
d	four	distract

FIGURE 3.2 *Huey's list of letters and words*

D<small>ISCUSSION.</small> Even though you may have stumbled over some unfamiliar words, you probably found that it did not take nearly four times as long to read the column of four-letter words as it took to read the column of single letters. Nor, surely, did it take eight times as long to read the column of eight-letter words. Huey's four experimental subjects read the columns aloud, averaging 15.7 seconds for the isolated letters, 17.3 seconds for the four-letter words, and 19.6 seconds for the eight-letter words (Huey 1968, p. 101). When I first tried the experiment, I read the columns silently. It took me 7 seconds for the single letters, 7 seconds for the four-letter words, and almost 8 seconds for the eight-letter words. Clearly, fluent readers do not process words letter by letter. Just as we do not comprehend sentences merely by combining the meanings of individual words, so we do not perceive words merely by combining the perceptions of individual letters.

———————

Activity 3. We have now demonstrated that we do not simply read words from left to right, and that we do not identify each of the letters in a word prior to identifying the word itself. This leaves open three major possibilities. On the one hand, we might process just part of the visual information from all or most of the letters in a word. On the other hand, we might process all or most of the visual information from just some of the letters in a word. Or we might process just some of the visual information from some of the letters. To test the first possibility, try to identify the mutilated words in Figure 3.3.

D<small>ISCUSSION.</small> You may have tried to determine individual letters in order to decide upon some of the words.[2] But for most words, you were probably able to identify the word as a whole, without consciously identifying the separate letters, and by using only some of the visual information normally available from each letter.

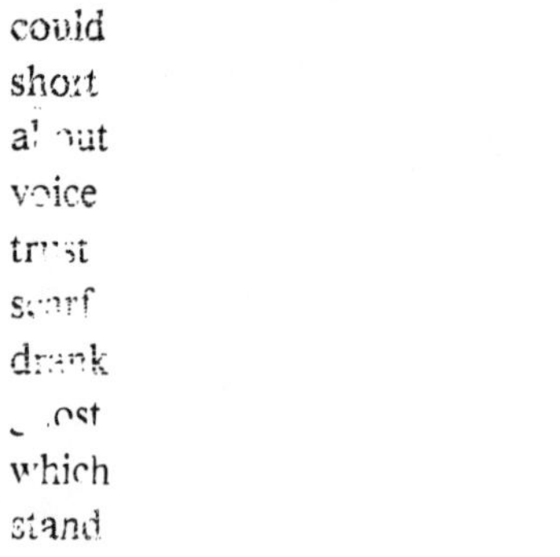

———————

could
short
a out
voice
trust
scarf
drank
ost
which
stand

———————

FIGURE 3.3 *Mutilated words*

Word Perception in Review

From the foregoing activities we can draw several generalizations about word recognition in fluent reading:

1. We do not simply process a word from left to right.
2. We do not separately identify each of the letters in a word prior to identifying the word itself.
3. It may be that we process just part of the visual information from all or most of the letters in a word; certainly this *can* be done. On the other hand, it may be that we process all or most of the visual information from just some of the letters in a word. Or we may process just some of the visual information from some of the letters.

The next section points out that certain letters and certain parts of letters are particularly useful in word identification. Hence the last of the possibilities in number 3 above seems most likely, namely that we identify words by processing just *part* of the visual information from *some* of the letters in a word. This is particularly likely when the word occurs in a context that narrows down the reasonable possibilities. Consider, for example, the following sentence:

Johnny put on his pajamas and jumped into b-d.

Surely we do not need to see the vowel letter or even all the parts of *b* and *d* to know that the last word is *bed*.

Given this example, it may not be surprising that words can be identified under conditions which make it impossible to identify individual letters. As long ago as the turn of the century, Erdmann and Dodge determined: (1) that words can be recognized when lying too far from the eyes' fixation point to permit recognition of individual letters; (2) that words can be recognized when they are constructed of letters so small that the letters cannot be singly identified; and (3) that words can be recognized from distances at which the letters, exposed singly, cannot be recognized (see Huey 1968, pp. 73–74). Similarly, it has been found that words can be identified at illuminations (lighting conditions) which do not permit the identification of single letters. In one experiment, it was found that even first graders could identify familiar three-letter words at lower light intensities than they needed for identifying single letters (see F. Smith 1971, p. 141).

To get an idea of what these experiments are like, suppose that two letters are flashed upon a screen in front of you and that you are told these letters form an English word. Suppose too that you cannot identify either of the letters with certainty, but you can see enough features to determine that the first letter must be *a* or *e*, and that the second letter must be *f* or *t*. Since this limits the possible combinations to *af*, *at*, *ef*, and *et*, you can readily identify the word as *at*. Because only one of the possible combinations forms a word in standard written English, you can identify the word without being able to identify either letter by itself (see F. Smith 1978, p. 125).

A similar thing happens when you play the travel game of locating first one letter of the alphabet and then the next on roadsigns as you travel down the highway. If you have ever played this game with a young child just learning to read, you may have realized that your tremendous advantage is the fact that you identify the words *first*, and then "recognize" the letter you are looking for. The child who knows letters of the alphabet but few words must, of course, look for the individual letters. Your ability to recognize whole words aids your "perception" of individual letters.

In a similar vein, some rather startling experiments indicate that a person can get some sense of a word's meaning without consciously being able to identify it. McKean (1985) mentions, for example, the work of Anthony Marcel at Cambridge, England. Using a tachistoscope to flash words on a screen for an extremely brief period of time, Marcel noted that his volunteer readers were able to get some sense of the meaning of the word, even though they hadn't seen the word long enough to identify it. For example: If the word on the screen was "queen," people would guess it as "king," or when the target word was "yellow" they would guess it as "blue." Odd as it sounds, the people in the experiment retained a nonconscious impression of a word's meaning not only without knowing its identity, but even when the visual exposure was so brief that they weren't sure they had seen any word at all. Recent experiments into chemical changes in the brain have confirmed more generally that people make decisions before they are conscious of having done so.

At this point, we can see in more detail what it means to say that we bring meaning *to* the written page in order to get meaning *from* it. We bring not only our knowledge of the world and our intuitive knowledge of grammar, but even an internalized knowledge of letter and sound patterns. Consider, for a moment, the following list of words. Which ones look like English words? Which ones do not?

glung	rpet	cratn	drepm
tsont	dremp	terp	stont
pret	lgung	crant	tepr

Without ever having been told, we know what is possible in English, and what is not. For example, we know that *glung* and *dremp* are possible, while *lgung* and *drepm* are not (see Gibson, Shurcliff, and Yonas 1970, p. 59; Gibson 1972, p. 13). Just as we do not consciously think of how sentences are structured as we speak, so we do not consciously think of how words are structured as we listen or read. Nevertheless, even before learning to read, we have acquired an internalized knowledge of sound patterns, and we quickly begin to acquire a similar internalized knowledge of letter patterns. Thus our internalized knowledge of letter patterns enables us to identify words from only a fraction of the visual information available.

Edmund Huey's 1908 conclusion still serves to summarize much of what is known about word perception (1968, pp. 111–112):

> Even in the more pronounced cases of letter consciousness, . . . it is perfectly certain that words are not perceived by a successive recognition of letter after letter, or even by any simultaneous recognition of all the letters *as such*. By whatever cues the recognition may be set off, it is certainly a recognition of word-wholes, except when even these recognition units are sub-

sumed under the recognition of a still larger unit. The only question is as to what parts are especially operative as cues in setting off this recognition.

It is to precisely this question that we will turn our attention in the next section.

PARTS OF WORDS AT WORK

The following three activities are designed to help you determine which parts of words are highly useful and which parts less useful in cueing the recognition of words. However, it must be admitted that the experiments are highly unscientific. There has been no strict control over vocabulary or sentence length and structure, and, most importantly, the words are presented in context rather than in isolation. But these experiments are more fun and easier to carry out than the more scientific kinds of experiments on isolated words, and in most cases your conclusions are likely to be the same.[3]

Activity 1. You will need a stop watch, or a watch or clock with a second hand, to time yourself or someone else reading the following two sets of sentences, which constitute the beginning of a little story:

a. *Vowels absent*

–nc– –p–n – t–m– th–r– w–s – h–nds–m– y––ng w–lf
n–m–d L–b–. L–b– l–v–d w–th h–s m–th–r –nd f–th–r
–t th– –dg– –f – d––p, d–rk w––ds. –v–r d–– L–b–
w–nt t– h–nt –t th– n–rth –dg– –f th– w––ds, n––r
th– l–ttl– v–ll–g– –f C–l––s.

b. *Consonants absent*

–o–e–i–e– a–– –o–o –ou–– –i–– –a– a –i–e–e– o––
–a––e– o– –i– –i–e, –o––i–– i– ––e –ie––s –ea– ––e
–oo–– o– –i––i–– –e––ie– i– ––e ––i––e–. A– o––e–
–i–e–, –o–o –i––– –e –u––y e–ou–– –o –i–– a ––u––,
–ui–y ––i–– ––a– –a– –i–o–eye– i–– –a–e––– a–– –––aye–
–oo –a– ––o– –o–e.

DISCUSSION. After this experiment, it should be obvious that consonants are more important than vowels in cueing word recognition. This can be explained, at least in part, by two simple factors. First, there are considerably more consonants than vowels in English, and hence the consonants are more distinctive, more able to narrow down the number of possible alternatives that any given word could be. Second, the consonants occur more frequently than the vowels; that is, in most cases there are more consonants per word. Given these factors, it is hardly surprising to find that consonants are more useful in cueing word recognition. Indeed, written Arabic omits the vowels altogether, except in beginners' books (Gibson and Levin 1975, p. 524).

Activity 2. This activity is related to the first. Again, time yourself or someone else reading the following two sets of sentences, a continuation of our ongoing story:

  a. Bottoms absent

    One day as Lobo was skirting the edge of the forest, he came upon a little girl in a red hood. Her cheeks were so rosy and her arms so nudgy that Lobo knew she would be delicious. "Where are you going, little girl?" he asked. "Oh," she replied, "I'm taking this basket of goodies to my grandmother on the other side of the woods. Grandma isn't feeling very well."

  b. Tops absent

    Lobo thought for a moment. He could hardly wait to devour this scrumptious child, but then again he was hungry enough to eat the grandmother too. "Which house does your grandmother live in?" asked the wolf. "In the house by the three big oak trees," said Red Riding Hood (for that is what she was called). "She lives there all by herself."

DISCUSSION. Which paragraph took longer to read? Which part seems to be more important in cueing word recognition: the tops of words, or the bottoms? Most people conclude that the tops are more important, and this is indeed what research suggests. If you have not already figured out why, then look at the following list of the letters in our alphabet. How many ascend above the top line? How many descend below the bottom line?

        a b c d e f g h i j k l m n o p q r s t u v w x y z

As you can readily see, almost twice as many ascend above the top line, making them visually more prominent. Note, too, that more than half of the consonants either ascend above the top line or descend below the bottom line, while none of the vowels do either (with the exception of *y*, which is only sometimes a vowel). Hence consonants are not only more numerous and more frequently occurring than vowels, but many are also more prominent visually.

Activity 3. Again, time yourself or someone else reading the following passages, in order to determine the relative importance of the beginnings, middles, and ends of words:

a. *Middles absent*

"W–at a mar–––ous oppo–––nity!" th–––ht L–bo. He t–ld t–e c––ld to s–op a–d p–ck fl–––rs f–r h–r gran–––ther on t–e w–y th–––gh t–e w––ds, t–en t–ok o–f on a s––rt c–t t–at o–ly t–e wo––es k–ow a––ut. S–on he ar–––ed at t–e grand–––her's co–––ge. "I–'s me, Gr–––ma," L–bo s–id in a t–ny v––ce, as he kn–––ed on t–e d–or. He pu––ed t–e d––r o–en a–d w–nt in.

b. *Ends absent*

Lob– wen– strai––– to th– grandmoth––'– be– an– gobb–––– he– up. He donn–– he– ca– an– gow– an– clim––– int– be–, feel––– non– to– wel– hims–––. By th– tim– Litt–– Re– Ridi–– Hoo– ha– arri–––, howe–––, he ha– overc––– hi– atta–– of indigest––– and wa– rea–– fo– dess–––. He answe––– Red'– kno–– in an ol–, crack–– voi––: "Com– in, dea–. Jus– com– on in."

c. *Beginnings absent*

–obo –as so –––enous –hat he ––dn't –ait –or ––ttle –ed ––ding –ood to –sk –er "–––ndma" –ow –he –as or –o ––ing –er –he ––sket of –––dies. He ––rew –ack –he ––vers, ––mped –ut of –ed, –nd –an –ver to –he ––ild. –he –––eamed –nd –an, –ut it –as –oo –ate. –obo –––bled –er up. –––erwards he –at by –he –––eside –––king –––ndma's –ipe, –––aming of ––icy ––ttle ––rls.

DISCUSSION. Once again, which set of sentences took longest to read? Which took the shortest time to read? From this experiment, you have probably concluded that the beginnings of words are more important in word identification than the middles or the ends, and this is certainly what research suggests. Various kinds of research also indicate, quite clearly, that the ends are more important than the middles. If your results suggested otherwise, it was probably due to the flaws in the design of this particular experiment.

Again, we may ask the reasons for these common observations. First, it seems that the beginnings and ends of words are important just because they are visually prominent, being either preceded or followed by white space. Second, the beginnings of words are particularly important because we read the words of a text more or less from left to right. In addition, the beginnings of words are less predictable than the ends, and therefore more necessary. The ends are more predictable than the beginnings because they often consist of grammatical endings, many of which are predictable from context (see the second activity at the end of this chapter). Thus endings are less important cues to word recognition than beginnings, because endings are more predictable. On the other hand, endings are more important than middles, partly because they often do carry grammatical information. For a discussion of many of the experiments that give rise to such observations, see Chapter 5 of Anderson and Dearborn 1952.

It is interesting to note that children pay increasing attention to the beginnings and ends of words as they become more proficient at reading. In one study, for example, the spaces between words were filled in with a symbol created by superimposing an *x* on a *c* (*see&Spot&run*). Groups of children in the first and second grade read such a "filled" version of a story, as well as an "unfilled" or normal version of a story. The filled version took significantly longer to read, but the difference was most noticeable for the better readers. The poorer, slower readers were affected relatively little by the filled-in text (Hochberg 1970, pp. 87–88). Since the poorer and slower readers were not much affected by the lack of spaces between words, it seems that these readers had not yet learned to pay particular attention to the beginnings and ends of words (see Brown 1970, pp. 169–170). And this, in fact, might be one reason why these children *were* the less proficient readers.

Parts of Words in Review

Which parts of words are particularly important in cueing word recognition? We have found that:

1. Consonants are more important than vowels.
2. Beginnings of words are more important than middles and ends, and ends are more important than middles.
3. Some people may be relatively nonproficient readers at least in part because they have not yet learned to attend to the parts of words that provide the most useful information.

It seems evident that proficient readers do not identify words by first identifying the letters in the word; normal reading proceeds far too fast for this. Instead, we select some of the information from some of the letters in order to arrive at an identification of the whole word. And we do this by bringing to bear not only our unconscious knowledge of which parts of letters and words are particularly useful, but also our internalized knowledge of letter and sound patterns. We use a minimal amount of visual information and a maximal amount of nonvisual information. Thus the brain does not passively interpret data gathered by the eyes. On the contrary, the brain tells the eyes what data to gather, which parts of words to attend to. Visual perception is in fact more a function of the brain than of the eye.

An anecdote may help to solidify this point. Bateman reports the following (1974, p. 662):

> At a meeting several years ago, an opthalmologist presented a paper on the eye and reading. After the introduction he came to the podium and stood silently for a moment. Slowly and deliberately he delivered his paper—

"Ladies and gentlemen, there are no important relationships between the eye and reading. Thank you." And he returned to his seat.

An exaggeration, but . . . one containing much truth.

PHONICS KNOWLEDGE AND PHONICS INSTRUCTION

In many phonics programs, about two-thirds of the rules taught are concerned with vowel letters and their sounds. But since vowels are so much less important than consonants in word recognition, you may have wondered about the need for teaching such a number of vowel rules, or even about the need for teaching consonant rules. How much phonics should be taught and how it should be taught is an issue that we will continue to explore in the next several chapters. The following activities and discussion are but a beginning in that exploration.

Activity 1. First, pronounce the following lists of words:

a. longer	singer	finger	ranger
longest	wringer	anger	stranger
stronger	hanger	dangle	danger
strongest			manger

b. phone	uphill	father	fathead
sphere	uphold	other	outhouse
graph			

c. thesis	the	there
theory	this	then
theater	these	thence
thinks	that	thenceforth
thought	those	thus
thin	they	therefore
thick	them	though
thirsty	their(s)	than

Presumably you had no difficulty pronouncing these words. But examine the words more carefully. How did you pronounce the *ng* in the words of set *a* above? Did your pronunciation differ somewhat from column to column? Try to formulate a phonics rule or set of related rules which would enable someone to pronounce correctly the *ng* in the *longer, singer, finger,* and *ranger* columns. Then do the same kind of thing with the *ph* and *th* in set *b,* and with the *th* in set *c.* In each case, try to formulate a phonics rule or set of rules that would enable someone to pronounce these letters correctly.

Discussion. Let us deal first with the words in set *a.* You probably pronounced the *ng* in the *longer* column as an "ng" sound plus a "g" sound;

together, these two sounds can be symbolized as /ŋg/. You probably pronounced the *ng* in the *singer* column simply as /ŋ/, unless your dialect happens to dictate an /ŋg/ pronunciation here too. In the *finger* column, you probably pronounced the *ng* as /ŋg/; and in the *ranger* column, you probably pronounced the *ng* as /n/ plus a "j" sound, which can be symbolized as /ǰ/. For convenience, these pronunciations might be recapitulated as follows:

/ŋg/	/ŋ/	/ŋg/	/nǰ/
longer	singer	finger	ranger

Now the question is, what rules govern these pronunciations? I myself am not completely certain, but the following rules are the best my students and I have been able to formulate:

1. When the base word is an adjective (like *long*), pronounce the *ng* as /ŋg/.

2. When the base word is a verb (like *sing*), pronounce the *ng* as /ŋ/, in most dialects.

3. When the base word is a noun of Germanic origin (as in *finger*), pronounce the *ng* as /ŋg/.

4. When the base word is a noun of Romance origin (like *ranger*), pronounce the *ng* as /nǰ/.

These rules will correctly account for the pronunciation of *ng* in most words that end in *nge(r)*. Note, however, that *range* could be considered a verb as well as a noun, and could thus be assigned to category (2). Further specification of the rules would be necessary to avoid this consequence.

Now then, what about the rules for sets *b* and *c*? By comparison, these rules are relatively simple. The following will more or less take care of set *b*:

1. When the word is a compound word divided between *p* and *h* (as in *uphill*), pronounce the *p* and *h* separately, as /p/ plus /h/. Otherwise, pronounce *ph* as /f/.

2. When the word is a compound word divided between *t* and *h* (as in *fathead*), pronounce the *t* and *h* separately as /t/ plus /h/. Otherwise, pronounce *th* as a single sound. (Actually this still does not tell us how to pronounce the unit *th*, because there are two so-called "th" sounds, as in *thin* and *the*, respectively.)

In order to formulate any halfway simple rule for the *th* units in set *c*, we would have to specify that we are talking about *th* in the initial position, at the beginning of a word. Then our rules might look something like this:

1. When a word begins with *th*, pronounce it as a "soft" *th* /θ/ if the word is a noun, a verb, or an adjective (as in the first column of set *c*).

2. When a word begins with *th*, pronounce it as a "hard" *th* /ð/ if the word
    is a pronoun, noun determiner, adverb, conjunctive adverb, or subor-
    dinating conjunction (as in the second and third columns of set *c*).

There are a few exceptions, like *through, throughout*, and *thither* (which,
according to the rule, ought to be pronounced with a "hard" /ð/ sound).
For the most part, however, these two rules will accurately predict the
pronunciation of *th* at the beginnings of words.

If you are beginning to think that spelling/sound correspondences are
very complicated, you are absolutely right. Imagine telling a child that you
pronounce *ng* one way if the word is a noun of Germanic origin, but another
way if the word is a noun of Romance origin. Or imagine telling a child that
in order to decide on the pronunciation of *ph* and *th* within a word, you have
to decide first whether it is a compound word or not. One hardly needs the
phonics rule if one already knows whether or not the word is made up of two
smaller words. And it is equally ridiculous to try to decide on a word's
grammatical category in order to determine how to pronounce initial *th*; if
one knows the word's grammatical category, one presumably knows the
word itself and thus how to pronounce it.

Detailed investigations into the nature of our spelling system have dis-
closed that there are far more correspondences between spelling and sound
than detractors of the spelling system have supposed. On the other hand,
such investigations have also revealed what we have begun to see for
ourselves: that the conditions governing such spelling/sound correspondences are often far more complex than is generally recognized (see Venezky
1970, both items, and Venezky 1967). Nor is this complexity confined to
words that are used primarily by adults rather than children. In one of the
more extensive studies, Berdiansky and her associates tried to establish a set
of rules to account for the spelling/sound correspondences in over 6000 one-
syllable and two-syllable words among 9000 different words in the comprehension vocabularies of six- to nine-year-old children. The researchers
discovered that their 6092 words involved 211 separate spelling/sound correspondences, 211 correspondences between a letter or two letters functioning together (like *qu*) and a sound. Of these 211 correspondences, 166
occurred in at least 10 words out of the set of 6092 words; 45 correspondences occurred in fewer than 10 words (Berdiansky et al. 1969, p. 11; see
F. Smith 1978, pp. 139–140).

The foregoing sets of words and rules should convince you that it is not
possible to teach the more complex letter/sound correspondences or
"rules" to children. But what of the simpler correspondences and rules, the
kinds typically taught in phonics programs?

The fact is, many of these "rules" do not work very well. There are too
many exceptions (the vowel rules are especially unreliable). These conclusions were made painfully obvious through a series of studies (Clymer 1963;
Emans 1967; Bailey 1967; and Burmeister 1968). See, for example, Figure
3.4, Clymer's chart on the utility of forty-five phonics generalizations.

*Generalizations	Number of Words Conforming	Number of Exceptions	Percent of Utility
1. When there are two vowels side by side, the long sound of the first one is heard and the second is usually silent.	309 (bead)†	377 (chief)†	45
2. When a vowel is in the middle of a one-syllable word, the vowel is short.	408	249	62
middle letter	191 (dress)	84 (scold)	69
one of the middle two letters in a word of four letters	191 (rest)	135 (told)	59
one vowel *within* a word of more than four letters	26 (splash)	30 (fight)	46
3. If the only vowel letter is at the end of a word, the letter usually stands for a long sound.	23 (he)	8 (to)	74
4. When there are two vowels, one of which is final *e*, the first vowel is long and the *e* is silent.	180 (bone)	108 (done)	63
* 5. The *r* gives the preceding vowel a sound that is neither long nor short.	484 (horn)	134 (wire)	78
6. The first vowel is usually long and the second silent in the diagraphs *ai, ea, oa,* and *ui.*	179	92	66
ai	43 (nail)	24 (said)	64
ea	101 (bead)	51 (head)	66
oa	34 (boat)	1 (cupboard)	97
ui	1 (suit)	16 (build)	6

*Generalizations marked with an asterisk were found "useful" according to the criteria.

†Words in parentheses are examples—either of words that conform or of exceptions, depending on the column.

SOURCE: Clymer, T. "The Utility of Phonic Generalizations in the Primary Grades." *The Reading Teacher* 16 (January 1963): 252–58.

FIGURE 3.4 *The utility of forty-five phonic generalizations*

*Generalizations	Number of Words Conforming	Number of Exceptions	Percent of Utility
7. In the phonogram *ie*, the *i* is silent and the *e* has a long sound.	8 (field)	39 (friend)	17
* 8. Words having double *e* usually have the long *e* sound.	85 (seem)	2 (been)	98
9. When words end with silent *e*, the preceding *a* or *i* is long.	164 (cake)	108 (have)	60
*10. In *ay* the *y* is silent and gives *a* its long sound.	36 (play)	10 (always)	78
11. When the letter *i* is followed by the letters *gh*, the *i* usually stands for its long sound and the *gh* is silent.	22 (high)	9 (neighbor)	71
12. When *a* follows *w* in a word, it usually has the sound *a* as in *was*.	15 (watch)	32 (swam)	32
13. When *e* is followed by *w*, the vowel sound is the same as represented by *oo*.	9 (blew)	17 (sew)	35
14. The two letters *ow* make the long *o* sound.	50 (own)	35 (down)	59
15. *W* is sometimes a vowel and follows the vowel digraph rule.	50 (crow)	75 (threw)	40
*16. When *y* is the final letter in a word, it usually has a vowel sound.	169 (dry)	32 (tray)	84
17. When *y* is used as a vowel in words, it sometimes has the sound of long *i*.	29 (fly)	170 (funny)	15
18. The letter *a* has the same sound (ȯ) when followed by *l*, *w*, and *u*.	61 (all)	65 (canal)	48

FIGURE 3.4 *Continued*

*Generalizations	Conforming	Exceptions	Utility
19. When *a* is followed by *r* and final *e*, we expect to hear the sound heard in *care*.	9 (dare)	1 (are)	90
*20. When *c* and *h* are next to each other, they make only one sound.	103 (peach)	0	100
*21. *Ch* is usually pronounced as it is in *kitchen, catch,* and *chair,* not like *sh*.	99 (catch)	5 (machine)	95
*22. When *c* is followed by *e* or *i*, the sound of *s* is likely to be heard.	66 (cent)	3 (ocean)	96
*23. When the letter *c* is followed by *o* or *a*, the sound of *k* is likely to be heard.	143 (camp)	0	100
24. The letter *g* often has a sound similar to that of *j* in *jump* when it precedes the letter *i* or *e*.	49 (engine)	28 (give)	64
*25. When *ght* is seen in a word, *gh* is silent.	30 (fight)	0	100
26. When a word begins *kn,* the *k* is silent.	10 (knife)	0	100
27. When a word begins with *wr*, the *w* is silent.	8 (write)	0	100
*28. When two of the same consonants are side by side, only one is heard.	334 (carry)	3 (suggest)	99
*29. When a word ends in *ck,* it has the same last sound as in *look*.	46 (brick)	0	100
*30. In most two-syllable words, the first syllable is accented.	828 (famous)	143 (polite)	85
*31. If *a, in, re, ex, de,* or *be* is the first syllable in a word, it is usually unaccented.	86 (belong)	13 (insect)	87
*32. In most two-syllable words that end in a consonant followed by *y,* the first syllable is accented and the last is unaccented.	101 (baby)	4 (supply)	96

FIGURE 3.4 *Continued*

*Generalizations	Conforming	Exceptions	Utility
33. One vowel letter in an accented syllable has its short sound.	547 (city)	356 (lady)	61
34. When *y* or *ey* is seen in the last syllable that is not accented, the long sound of *e* is heard.	0	157 (baby)	0
35. When *ture* is the final syllable in a word, it is unaccented.	4 (picture)	0	100
36. When *tion* is the final syllable in a word, it is unaccented.	5 (station)	0	100
37. In many two- and three-syllable words, the final *e* lengthens the vowel in the last syllable.	52 (invite)	62 (gasoline)	46
38. If the first vowel sound in a word is followed by two consonants, the first syllable usually ends with the first of the two consonants.	404 (bullet)	159 (singer)	72
39. If the first vowel sound in a word is followed by a single consonant, that consonant usually begins the second syllable.	190 (over)	237 (oven)	44
*40. If the last syllable of a word ends in *le*, the consonant preceding the *le* usually begins the last syllable.	62 (tumble)	2 (buckle)	97
*41. When the first vowel element in a word is followed by *th, ch,* or *sh,* these symbols are not broken when the word is divided into syllables and may go with either the first or second syllables.	30 (dishes)	0	100
42. In a word of more than one syllable, the letter *v* usually goes with the preceding vowel to form a syllable.	53 (cover)	29 (clover)	73

FIGURE 3.4 Continued

*Generalizations	Number of Words Conforming	Number of Exceptions	Percent of Utility
43. When a word has only one vowel letter, the vowel sound is likely to be short.	433 (hid)	322 (kind)	57
*44. When there is one *e* in a word that ends in a consonant, the *e* usually has a short sound.	85 (leg)	27 (blew)	76
*45. When the last syllable is the sound *r,* it is unaccented.	188 (butter)	9 (appear)	95

FIGURE 3.4 *Continued*

As Frank May and Susan Eliot conclude in *To Help Children Read* (1978), only a few phonics rules are consistent enough or cover enough words to meet these criteria (p. 38):

1. The "*c* rule." When *c* comes just before *a, o,* or *u,* it usually has the hard sound heard in *cat, cot,* and *cut.* Otherwise, it usually has the soft sound heard in *cent, city,* and *bicycle.*

2. The "*g* rule." (Similar to the "*c* rule.") When *g* comes at the end of words or just before *a, o,* or *u,* it usually has the hard sound heard in *tag, game, go,* and *gush.* Otherwise, it usually has the soft sound heard in *gem, giant* and *gym.* (Some important exceptions are *get, give, begin* and *girl.*)

3. The VC pattern. This pattern is seen in words such as *an, can, candy,* and *dinner.* As a verbal generalization it might be stated as follows: In either a word or a syllable, a single vowel letter followed by a consonant letter, digraph, or blend usually represents a short vowel sound. (Some teachers find it easier for children to remember the pattern rather than the rule. Note that C stands for either a consonant letter, consonant digraph, or consonant blend, e.g., *bat, bath, bask.*)

4. The VV (vowel digraph) pattern. This pattern is seen in words such as *eat, beater, peach, see, feed, bait, float,* and *play.* As a verbal generalization it might be stated like this: In a word or syllable containing a vowel digraph, the first letter in the digraph usually represents the long vowel sound and the second letter is usually silent. ("When two vowel letters go walking, the first one does the talking.") According to Clymer (1963), this generalization is quite reliable for *ee, oa,* and *ay* (*fee, coat, tray*) and works about two-thirds of the time for *ea* and *ai* (*seat, bait*), but is not reliable for other vowel digraphs such as *ei, ie,* or *oo* (*eight, chief, boot*). And, of course, it is not valid for diphthongs represented by *oi, oy, ou,* and *ow* (*oil, boy, out, cow*).

5. The VCE (final *e*) pattern. This pattern is seen in words such as *ice, nice, ate, plate, paste, flute, vote*, and *clothe*. As a generalization it might be stated this way: In one-syllable words containing two vowel letters, one of which is a final *e*, the first vowel letter usually represents a long vowel sound, and the final *e* is silent.

6. The CV pattern. This pattern is seen in words or syllables such as *he, she, go, my, cry, hotel, going*, and *flying*. As a generalization it could be stated like this: When there is only one vowel letter in a word or syllable and it comes at the end of the word or syllable, it usually represents the long vowel sound.

7. The "*r* rule." This rule applies to words like *far, fare, girl, fur, her*, and *here*. As a generalization it might be stated as follows: The letter *r* usually modifies the short or long sound of the preceding vowel letter. For instance, the word *car* does *not* illustrate the VC pattern seen in the word *cat*; nor does *fir* represent the VC pattern seen in *fit*. The word *care* usually doesn't illustrate the VCE pattern seen in the word *cape* (although in some dialects it does). Likewise, the word *fair* usually doesn't illustrate the VV pattern seen in *wait*.

The following activity should help you consider whether children need to learn consciously even such generalizations and "rules" as the ones May has listed.

Activity 2. Read the following paragraph aloud, as smoothly as possible:

> Corandic is an emurient grof with many fribs; it granks from corite, an olg which cargs like lange. Corite grinkles several other tarances, which garkers excarp by glarcking the corite and starping it in tranker-clarped storbs. The tarances starp a chark which is exparged with worters, branking a slorp. This slorp is garped through several other coruses, finally frasting a pragety, blickant crankle: coranda. Coranda is a cargurt, grinkling corandic and borigen. The corandic is nacerated from the borigen by means of loracity. Thus garkers finally thrap a glick, bracht, glupous grapant, corandic, which granks in many starps.

DISCUSSION. You were no doubt able to pronounce most of the words in the paragraph. But did you *consciously* apply any phonics rules? If so, which ones? If not, how did you know or decide how to pronounce the words? Once having recovered from the shock of seeing so many nonwords, most people are able to read the paragraph rather well, and without consciously applying many (if any) phonics rules. They have simply internalized enough knowledge of spelling/sound correspondences to be able to pronounce most of the words with little trouble. In fact, I have found that most adult readers who once had phonics instruction cannot verbalize many (if any) of the rules, whereas most adult readers who have never had phonics instruction can apply phonics rules anyway.

The same is true of most children: though they cannot remember abstract phonics terms and rules, nevertheless they can apply such rules unconsciously in their reading. Tovey demonstrated this in a study of children from grades 2 to 6, with five children from each grade. Though their teachers indicated that the children had learned terms like *consonant, consonant blend, consonant digraph, vowel, long vowel, short vowel, vowel digraph*, and *diphthong*, the children's responses suggested otherwise. The only term acceptably defined by over half of the children was *silent letter*. More than half of the terms were acceptably defined by only 20 percent or fewer children. Interestingly, Tovey notes that second graders produced only two acceptable responses to questions about terms, and that sixth graders seemed relatively less able to deal with phonics terms than children in grades 3 through 5—probably, I would assume, because upper elementary students do not typically receive phonics instruction. However, all the children did much better on a phonics test which required them to pronounce nonsense words and to deal with the kinds of elements listed above (plus others) in reading actual text. On this test, all the scores were 55 percent or above, with the percentage rising steadily from 55 percent at grade 2 to 79 percent at grade 6 (actually, fourth graders broke the gradually rising pattern temporarily with 83 percent). The children were able to make use of phonics knowledge that they were not conscious of, that they could not verbalize. Tovey concludes that "Instruction which requires children to deal constantly with the abstract or technical language related to phonics does not warrant the time and effort often expended. This time might better be spent reading" (Tovey 1980, p. 437).

Certainly there is a correlation between rapid decoding and comprehension, especially in timed tests (see, for example, Perfetti & Hogaboam 1975; Stanovich 1980; and Allen 1985). However, it does not necessarily follow that children must be *taught* phonics rules in order to decode rapidly. Since children can *apply* phonics rules even though they cannot define the terms or verbalize the rules, much of the current phonics instruction surely goes beyond what is needed, as is pointed out even by phonics advocates. (See, for example, the discussion of phonics in *Becoming a Nation of Readers* [Anderson et al. 1985, p. 38], and see my fuller discussion of this report's treatment of phonics in Chapter 7.) It is not necessary for children to consciously learn phonics rules, just as you probably never learned the "rules" for pronouncing *ng* or *th*. Yes, children need to know basic letter/sound correspondences, and they may need some guidance in establishing such correlations between letters and sounds. However, most children need far less explicit phonics instruction than is commonly supposed. With a little guided observation, children can internalize the most useful correspondences and patterns well enough to apply them: correspondences like the basic relationships between consonant letters and sounds, for example, and patterns like the final *-ate* in words like *ate, date, late, mate, rate* (as suggested by structural linguists; see Chapter 2). Such instruction will help children unconsciously formulate their own "rule" for pronouncing similarly patterned words. But consciously learning a lot of terms and rules seems highly unnecessary. We do not expect toddlers to *consciously* learn rules for putting sounds together in order to form words, and neither need we expect young school-age children to consciously learn rules for taking words apart and putting them back together again.

To those steeped in phonics, it must be startling to think that we can learn spelling/sound correspondences without consciously studying phonics rules. Nevertheless, there is considerable evidence to substantiate this point. For one thing, most adults of my generation never studied phonics at all. However, they can demonstrate ''phonics'' knowledge by reading words like those in the ''Corandic'' passage in activity 2. So can most children. In fact, children who learn to read before attending school usually demonstrate this kind of internalized knowledge, even if no one has called much attention to letter/sound correspondences and spelling/sound patterns. Although phonics *knowledge* (understanding of letter/sound relationships) is necessary for fluent reading, heavy phonics *instruction* is not.

This phenomenon of ''overteach'' became obvious to me when my then seven-year-old son was working on a phonics exercise that involved words beginning with consonant clusters. Suspecting that he did not know several of the words on his worksheet, I asked him to read me the list. He proceeded to do so, with only a few hesitations. The ensuing conversation went essentially like this:

Me: ''How did you read all those words?''
John: ''Well, some I knew, and some I just tried.''
Me: ''On the ones you just tried, did you try to use any rule?''
John: ''In school, the rule is just try to sound it out the best you can.''
Me: ''But did you try to use any specific rule you've been taught, like thinking 'That could be a silent *e*, so the *a* before it might be a long *a*'?''
John: ''No, because sometimes the rules don't work anyway. I just tried saying the words.''

The irony, of course, is that having taught the children certain phonics rules from the basal reading series, the teacher then had to teach the children not to apply the rules but just to ''sound it out the best you can.'' And given the unreliability of many of the common phonics rules, and the difficulty of knowing *which* rule to apply, this was doubtless good advice.

Phonics in Review

Several points were introduced in this preliminary discussion of the teaching of phonics:

1. Since vowels are relatively unimportant in identifying words, it seems unnecessary to teach numerous vowel rules, as most phonics programs do.
2. Spelling/sound correspondences are often very complex and not easily reducible to rules that can or should be taught.
3. Only a few of the frequently taught rules are both consistent and comprehensive—that is, applicable to a considerable number of words.

4. Even most of these rules probably do not need to be explicitly taught to whole classes of children, since most children can and will internalize spelling/sound patterns just by reading a lot and/or with minimal guidance in observing correspondences and patterns.

5. Thus most children probably do not need nearly as much phonics instruction as they are typically receiving in today's phonics programs and basal reading series.

Most of these points will be further developed and supported in subsequent chapters.

Meanwhile, here is one further point to consider. Activity 1 at the end of Chapter 1 included from King and Watson (1983, p. 70) four sketches of children in first grade classrooms: one child being taught by what is probably a combined phonics/linguistics approach, one being taught by a sight word approach, one being taught through the Initial Teaching Alphabet (see activity 3 at the end of this chapter), and one being taught by a language experience/whole-language approach. Are all of these children going to become readers, King and Watson ask? Their answer: it is quite likely. But they suggest that some children may learn to read *in spite of* the instructional program rather than because of it.

If children are taught by a phonics method and they in fact learn to read, it seems logical to assume that they learned to read *because of* the phonics instruction. But this is not necessarily so. The fact that the rooster crows and the sun then comes up does not mean that the rooster's crowing causes the sun to rise, even though primitive societies and young children in our own society have assumed the former causes the latter. The fact that parents buy their son or daughter a typewriter does not necessarily mean that the student will get better grades because of the typewriter, though a typewriter ad a few years ago would have had us believe in the cause-effect relationship. And the fact that children who have been exposed to a phonics approach learn to read does not necessarily mean that they learned to read *because of* that approach, though people unaware of the nature of the reading process and what is involved in learning to read are of course inclined to make that assumption.

In determining how children best learn to read, Marie Carbo points out that "what works is not always phonics, and, in fact, for young children, what works *best* in reading may seldom be intensive phonic instruction" (Carbo "What Works . . . ," 1987). Carbo has concluded that a small percentage of children really *need* phonics instruction to become good readers. However, most children fall into other categories: "those who are capable of learning phonics, but who *do not need* it to become good readers, and children who are *unable* to master phonics" (Carbo, "Ten Myths . . . ," 1987).

One reason that most children are able—perhaps *best* able—to learn to read without intensive phonics instruction is, as we have begun to see, that learning to read involves much more than learning to sound out words. It involves learning to bring one's own schemas to the task of transacting with the text, and it involves learning to use and coordinate all three language cue systems: syntactic, semantic, and grapho/phonemic. If children try to read by merely sounding out words, merely using grapho/phonemic cues, they may never learn to read effectively. Even word identification itself, a seemingly "low-level skill," will suffer, as we shall see in Chapter 4.

How is it, then, that children can learn to read with, or perhaps in spite of, an approach that focuses mainly on the grapho/phonemic cues? Because children have a natural, innate tendency to create meaning by transacting with their environment. Because they are often surrounded by meaningful print in their daily lives. Because many of them naturally transfer to the reading of print the strategies they have learned to use in making sense of spoken language. And because they have a tremendous capacity for forming their own hypotheses about how language works, a capacity clearly exemplified in the infant and preschool years as they learn to speak more and more like adults. These points will be explored further in Chapter 7.

ACTIVITIES AND PROJECTS FOR FURTHER EXPLORATION

1. In a *Time* magazine article reporting on a "government" study concluding that one in eight Americans cannot read, the suggestion is made that

    the American school system is partly to blame. In many elementary
    schools, reading time is devoted to "See Jane run" readers and dull
    word-drill workbooks. Another pedagogical problem: children fre-
    quently are force-fed new words by the "look and say" method, which
    requires recognition of whole words, rather than the more flexible and
    effective technique of phonics, or sounding out words, phoneme by pho-
    neme. (*Time*, 5 May 1986)

    Comment on this quote in light of the discussion of reading approaches in Chapter 2 and the discussion of phonics in the present chapter.

2. To test for yourself the assertion that grammatical endings are often predictable when a word occurs in context, try to provide the endings missing from the following sentences (the same sentences from which the consonants were earlier omitted). As before, the dash indicates an omitted letter:

    Sometime- all Lobo could find was a wizen-- old farm-- and his wife,
    work--- in the field- near the wood- or pick--- berri-- in the thicket. At
    other time-, Lobo might be luck- enough to find a plump, juic- child that
    had disobey-- its parent- and stray-- too far from home.

    Did you find it easy to provide the grammatical endings? What do you think of the notion that we should teach grammatical endings to children in order to help them identify words?

3. If you are not familiar with the symbols of the Initial Teaching Alphabet, try the following experiment (or try it with someone else who is not familiar with the ITA). First, try to decide what sounds are probably represented by the following symbols:

    æ   ʊ   ω   ie   th   ʒ   ʃh   dʒ   ŋ

Now, simply read the paragraph below. This is an alternative conclusion to our story about the wolf and Red Riding Hood:

the littl girl taested delifhous
but loeboe hardly had tiem tw
enjoi fhe flaevor befoer somwun
nakt at fhe doer. fhe wwlf
skrambld bak intw bed and sed,
"Cum on in. just oepen fhe doer."
in stroed a big wwdsman. hee
recogniesd fhe wwlf at wuns,
and loeboe berly had tiem tw
jump out ov bed and thrw a
windoe befoer fhe wwdsman's aks
fel. tw fhis dae, loeboe has never
gon bak tw fhe south edz ov fhe
wwds. hee staes nir hoem,
settlirj for weezend oeld farmers
and fher wievs.

What words caused particular difficulty, and why? On the whole, were you able to read the preceding paragraph fairly easily, even if you did not know what sound each of the symbols represents? If so, how were you able to read the passage without knowing all the letter/sound relationships?

4. To continue exploring the idea that the use of context can reduce our need for visual information during normal reading, have someone try to supply the words which are missing from the following, our story about the wolf and Red Riding Hood. The first letter of each missing word is provided as a clue, along with dashes to represent the missing letters:

Once upon a t--- there was a handsome y---- wolf named Lobo. Lobo l---- with his mother and f----- at the edge of a d---, dark woods. Every day L--- went to hunt at t-- north edge of the w----, near the little village o- Calais. Sometimes all Lobo c---- find was a wizened o-- farmer and his wife, w------ in the fields near t-- woods or picking berries i- the thicket. At other t----, Lobo might be lucky e----- to find a plump, j---- child that had disobeyed i-- parents and strayed too f-- from home.

One day a- Lobo was skirting the e--- of the forest, he c--- upon a little girl i- a red hood. Her c----- were so rosy and h-- arms so pudgy that L--- knew she would be d--------. "Where are you going, l----- girl?" he asked. "Oh," s-- replied, "I'm taking this b----- of goodies to my g---------- on the other side o- the woods. Grandma isn't f------ very well."

Lobo thought f-- a moment. He could h----- wait to devour this s---------- child, but then again h- was hungry enough to e-- the grandmother too. "Which h---- does your grandmother live i-?" asked the wolf. "In t-- house by the three b-- oak trees," said Red R----- Hood (for that is w--- she was called). "She l---- there all by herself."

"W--- a marvelous opportunity!" thought L---. He told the child t- stop and pick flowers f-- her grandmother on the w-- through the woods, then t--- off on a short c-- that only the wolves k--- about. Soon he arrived a- the grandmother's cottage. "It's m-, Grandma," Lobo said in a t--- voice, as he knocked o- the door. He pulled t-- door open and went i-.

Lobo went straight to t-- grandmother's bed and gobbled h-- up. He donned her c-- and gown and climbed i--- bed, feeling none too w--- himself. By the time L----- Red Riding Hood had a------, however, he had overcome h-- attack of indigestion and w-- ready for dessert. He a------- Red's knock in an o--, cracked voice: "Come in, d---. Just come on in."

L--- was so ravenous that h- didn't wait for Little R-- Riding Hood to ask h-- "grandma" how she was o- to bring her the b----- of goodies. He threw b--- the covers, jumped out o- bed, and ran over t- the child. She screamed a-- ran, but it was t-- late. Lobo gobbled her u-. Afterwards he sat b- the fireside smoking grandma's p---, dreaming of juicy little g----.

Which kinds of missing words were easier to supply: content words, or function words? Was it possible to get the essential meaning, even without being able to supply all the words?

5. In order to better anticipate and participate in the discussion of Chapter 4, you might try the following activities:

a. Cut a slit in a piece of paper so that the slit will expose just one of the following lines at a time. Then find someone to be your experimental subject. Tell the person you are going to expose some lines of print one at a time, each for only a fraction of a second. The person is to try to focus attention on the middle of the line and then to write down in order all of the print seen, after which you will then expose another line. Try, of course, to expose each line for the same amount of time as the others, ideally only long enough for one eye fixation (about a quarter of a second!). See if the person is able to recall more print from some lines than from others. What do you think accounts for any observed differences in how many letters are recalled?

QLH WCGMZK PGTXW NBFJMSV

BAX GORPLE CHURK FRENTLY

ANGRY GROW TAXES BOY UGLY

SILLY WINDOWS HIT THE BOX

FUNNY CLOWNS MAKE ME LAUGH

b. Have some of your friends, or some children, brainstorm for words that might reasonably come next in a sentence that begins

The cruel giant fell into the . . .

Encourage your brainstormers to be imaginative. (Some of my students have suggested such responses as *witches' cauldron, septic tank*, and *flour bin*, to mention only a few.) When you are satisfied with the brainstorming, then tell the brainstormers that following the word or words they have supplied come the words ". . . and drowned." Which of the suggested alternatives can you now eliminate as extremely unlikely? Discuss what enabled/encouraged your brainstormers to make the predictions they did, and what enabled them to eliminate certain alternatives. What does this activity suggest about the kinds of contexts we use in reading?

c. Try activity 5 in Chapter 4 (p. 108).

READINGS FOR FURTHER EXPLORATION

Carbo, Marie. February 1987. Reading Styles Research: "What Works" Isn't Always Phonics. *Phi Delta Kappan* 68:431–35. Explains that the vast majority of young children are not strong in the auditory and analytic processing abilities needed to learn phonics. Further indicates that neither phonics nor the whole word approach appears to be the best for most children.

Artley, A. Sterl. February 1977. Phonics Revisited. *Language Arts* 54: 121–26. Convincingly puts phonics into an appropriate perspective.

McKee, Paul. 1975. *Primer for Parents.* 3rd ed. Boston: Houghton Mifflin. By introducing a strange set of symbols for us to read, this little booklet gives adults some sense of what it might be like to be a beginning reader. The booklet suggests that beginning reading instruction should stress the use of consonants and context as cues to word recognition.

Smith, Frank. 1973. The Efficiency of Phonics. *Psycholinguistics and Reading.* Ed. F. Smith. New York: Holt, Rinehart, 84–90. A convincing discussion of why it would be highly inefficient to rely on phonics as the sole method of teaching reading or the sole method of identifying words that are not immediately recognized on sight.

————. 1978. The Fallacy of Phonics. *Reading Without Nonsense.* New York: Teachers College Press, 51–70. This section is similar to Smith's discussion of phonics in the above-cited book, but more thorough.

Gibson, Eleanor J., and Harry Levin. 1975. *The Psychology of Reading.* Cambridge, Mass.: MIT Press, 119–25. As this summary reveals, there is considerable experimental evidence that many first graders may not be able to hear the separate sounds (phonemes) within words. The entire chapter on "Language Development" is very interesting, though much of it is too technical for the beginner.

Teach Reading Old-Fashioned Way? 19 Apr. 1982. *U.S. News and World Report*: 69–70. This brief article presents interviews with people whose views on phonics contrast sharply: Rudolf Flesch, author of *Why Johnny* Still *Can't Read* and Stanley Sharp, author of *The REAL Reason Why Johnny Still Can't Read*.

Sebasta, Sam. May 1981. Why Rudolph Can't Read. *Language Arts* 58: 545–48. Tongue-in-cheek story about his "son" Rudolph, whom he and his wife unsuccessfully tried to teach to read by following Rudolf Flesch's prescriptions.

___4___

How Does Context Aid in Word Identification?

The art of becoming a fluent reader lies in learning to rely less and less on information from the eyes.

—Frank Smith

QUESTIONS FOR JOURNALS AND DISCUSSION

1. What are the various kinds of context that can aid in word identification?
2. Are words easier to identify in isolation, or in context?
3. What does it mean to say that the more nonvisual information a reader can use, the less visual information he or she needs?
4. How do good and poor readers typically differ in their use of context?
5. How are the language cue systems (syntactic, semantic, grapho/phonemic) related to reading strategies?
6. What characterizes the effective and efficient reader?
7. How much phonics should be taught? When, why, and how?
8. Given what is known about the reading process, what are some objections to the sight word, phonics, and basal reader approaches?

THE VARIETIES OF CONTEXT: AN OVERVIEW

In the preceding chapter, we saw that our knowledge of letter patterns aids in word identification. To convince yourself further, glance quickly at the column of pseudowords on the left below, then write down as many as you can remember. Next, do the same with the column of pseudowords on the right (Miller, Bruner, and

Postman, 1954, p. 133):

RICANING	YRULPZOC
VERNALIT	OZHGPMTJ
MOISSANT	DLEGQMNW
POKERSON	GFUJXZAQ
FAVORIAL	WXPAUJVB

The pseudowords on the left are obviously much easier to perceive and recall, simply because their letter patterns are a much closer approximation to normal English.

Given our internalized knowledge of letter patterns, it should not be surprising that we can identify a word in about as much time as it takes to identify a single letter. Indeed, we have already seen this in the experiment with Huey's lists of letters and words. And we shall now see that just as we can identify a related group of letters in about the same length of time as it takes to identify a single letter, so we can identify a related group of words in about the same length of time as it takes to identify a single word. Research shows, in fact, that during a normal eye fixation of about one-fourth second, we can identify about four or five unrelated letters, or about ten or twelve letters organized into two or three unrelated words, or about twenty to twenty-five letters organized into a sequence of four or five related words (see, for example, F. Smith 1973, p. 56, and F. Smith 1975, p. 58). Hence during a normal eye fixation, we might be able to identify a sequence like *lgibh*, a sequence like *know boys that*, or a sequence like *that girl knew many boys*. Our perceptual span increases as does the relatedness of the units being identified:

4 or 5 unrelated letters	lgibh
10 to 12 letters, organized into 2 or 3 unrelated words	knew boys that
20 to 25 letters, organized into 4 or 5 related words	that girl knew many boys

We can identify more letters when they are organized into words, and more words when they are organized into a related phrase or sentence.

In phrases and sentences, we have basically two kinds of context to aid in word identification: syntactic context and semantic context. *Syntactic context* consists of the signals provided by word endings, function words, and word order (see Chapter 2). *Semantic context* consists of the meaningful relations among the words. In short, *syntax* means grammar, and *semantics* means meaning.

To see how grammar and meaning aid in the identification and recall of words, look for a moment at the following four strings of words. Which string would be easiest to process? Which would be hardest? Why?

1. Furry wildcats fight furious battles.
2. Furry jewelers create distressed stains.
3. Furry fight furious wildcats battles.
4. Furry create distressed jewelers stains.

As you might suspect, the first string is typically easiest to process, because it has both grammar and meaning: that is, it preserves normal word order, and it makes reasonable sense. The fourth string is typically hardest to process, because it has neither grammar nor meaning: the string does not preserve normal word order, and it does not make sense. Processing is easier when we have either normal word order (string 2) or some semblance of meaning (string 3). (For details, see Marks and Miller 1964, pp. 1–5.)

Various laboratory experiments indicate that *both* grammar and meaning aid in the identification and recall of words. Both syntactic context and semantic context are important, as you probably concluded from some of the activities in the preceding chapter.

Another revealing activity is the so-called *cloze test*, a widely known and widely respected method for assessing a reader's comprehension and his or her use of reading strategies. The "standard" cloze test typically requires supplying every fifth word of a text, as in the following example from Bormuth (1975, p. 70). Try to fill each blank space with whatever you think was omitted from the original text (in some cases a number or a part of a hyphenated word has been omitted). As you fill in the blanks, try to be conscious of how you are using context, of what kinds of context you are using:

The Beaver

Indians call beavers the "little men of the woods."

But they (1)_____ really so very little.

(2)_____ beavers grow to be (3)_____ or four

feet long (4)_____ weigh from 30 to (5)_____

pounds. These "little men (6)_____ the woods" are

busy (7)_____ of the time. That (8)_____ why

we sometimes say, "(9)_____ busy as a beaver."

(10)_____ know how to build (11)_____ that

can hold water. (12)_____ use their two front

(13)_____ to do some of (14)_____ work. Cutting

down a (15)_____ with their four sharp-(16)_____

teeth is easy. A (17)_____ can cut down a (18)_____

four inches thick in (19)_____ 15 minutes.

At the outset you probably found that to fill in the blanks you had to use both the grammar and the meaning of the preceding part of the sentence. In the first sentence where a blank occurs, *But they* _____ . . . , the word *they* suggests that a verb will be coming next; this is grammatical context, or syntax. The word *but* suggests that this second sentence will in some way contradict the first, and that the verb should therefore contain a negative marker; this is meaning context, or semantics. Putting both kinds of information together (and some other information as well), we are likely to supply the word *aren't: But they* aren't *really so very little*. This word seems to fit syntactically and semantically with what comes after the blank as well as with what comes before.[1]

In some cases, following context is even more essential than in the first example. Look, for instance, at the sentence *That* _____ *why we sometimes say,* "_____ *busy as a beaver*." The word *that* can function as a noun determiner rather than a noun, as in *That fact explains why we sometimes say, "as busy as a beaver*." If we did not look ahead, we might supply the wrong kind of word in the blank following the word *that*. And we need to see "*busy as a beaver*" to know that the word in the second blank should be *as*.

As we began to see in Chapter 2, ''context'' is far more inclusive than most people realize. Most globally, we can and do use our entire personal ''context'' of knowledge and experience, our schemas (including our entire social context, our background), to help us identify and sometimes misidentify words. Second, we use aspects of the situational context, verbal and/or nonverbal: an amusing example of a situationally caused miscue is from the sign in a church parking lot that one boy misread for a long time as ''Angel parking.'' For simplicity, I would include under situational context various aspects of the sociolinguistic context, also. The classroom setting, for example, is a powerful sociolinguistic context, giving rise to particular kinds of assumptions and expectations on the part of both teachers and students. An example would be the expectation that many of my students bring to reading the poem ''To Pat'' (Chapter 2) in class, namely that there must be some ''deep,'' hidden meaning in the poem, a meaning that they probably aren't seeing clearly. Like the ''context'' within the reader, the sociolinguistic context can both aid and thwart word identification.

In addition to using these kinds of contexts that are outside or beyond the text, we of course use context within the text in identifying words. First, we use context before and after the sentence being read, but within the same reading selection. Second, we use context before and after the word being identified, but within the same sentence. Figure 4.1 summarizes all these major kinds of contexts, while suggesting two major ways of subdividing them: context within the text versus context beyond the text, and context within the sentence versus context beyond the sentence.

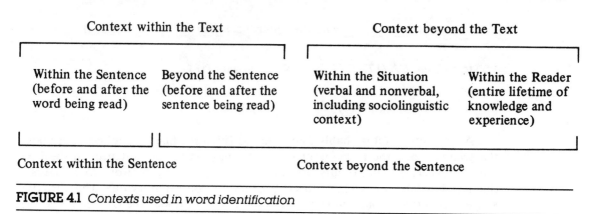

Context within the Text		Context beyond the Text	
Within the Sentence (before and after the word being read)	Beyond the Sentence (before and after the sentence being read)	Within the Situation (verbal and nonverbal, including sociolinguistic context)	Within the Reader (entire lifetime of knowledge and experience)
Context within the Sentence		Context beyond the Sentence	

FIGURE 4.1 *Contexts used in word identification*

Since the various kinds of contexts beyond the sentence tend especially to blend together, the following discussion will reflect this latter division.

CONTEXT WITHIN THE SENTENCE

You may be most aware of context within the sentence. Yet even this kind of context has various aspects. On the one hand, we use both syntactic context and semantic context, both grammar and meaning. On the other hand, we use both preceding context and following context, both what comes before and what comes after the word being identified. Figure 4.2 summarizes these kinds of contexts in a grid, showing how each kind helps us identify the word *water* in *The cruel giant fell into the water and drowned.* The word *the* indicates that the next word must be a noun or noun modifier, while the word *fell* suggests that the word after *the* should indicate

	Preceding Context	*Following Context*
Syntactic Context	Preceding syntactic context indicates the word is a noun or a noun modifier.	Following syntactic context confirms that the word is a noun.
	The cruel giant fell into the water and drowned.	
Semantic Context	Preceding semantic context suggests the word should indicate something into which one can fall.	Following semantic context shows that the word should indicate something in which one can drown.

FIGURE 4.2 *Context within the sentence*

something into which one can fall. The word *drowned* confirms that the word in question must indeed be a noun; further, *drowned* shows that the word should indicate something in which one can drown. The word in question could be *water, lake, pond, river, ocean, well*, or *moat*, but there may not be many other likely alternatives. The various kinds of contexts within the sentence have helped us narrow the alternatives to such a point that we need to use only a small amount of visual information from the word itself to identify the word in question as *water*.

In looking at the sentence about the cruel giant (Figure 4.2), you may have thought, ''That's silly. I already know the word *water*. I don't need to use context in order to identify that word.'' And no doubt that is true. Nevertheless, the identification of words proceeds much faster and more efficiently when we are using the context provided by connected text. The fact is that fluent readers use context so automatically that they are rarely conscious of doing so. We become aware of our reliance on context mainly when we come to a word whose meaning we do not know, or when we make a miscue because of our reliance on preceding context.

To understand better this automatic use of context, read aloud the following sentences, without looking them over beforehand:

1. Can you read rapidly?
2. There was a strong wind blowing.
3. He wound the string up tightly.
4. I looked up and read the sign.
5. Her dress had a tear in it.
6. I saw a tear in her eye.
7. She looked at the minute printing on the label.
8. He made her a bow and arrow.

Each sentence contains a word that has, potentially, more than one pronunciation. In sentences 1–4, the preceding syntactic context was enough to signal the appropriate pronunciation of *read, wind, wound*, and *read*. In sentence 5, we needed the preceding semantic context to tell us that *tear* should rhyme with *dare* rather than with *dear*. In sentences 6–8, we needed following semantic context to signal the appropriate pronunciation of *tear, minute*, and *bow*. In short, we use preceding context to predict what is coming next, and we use following context to confirm or correct our predictions. This use of following context is facilitated by the fact that our eyes typically register about four words beyond the word we are focusing upon.[2] If we do not use following context to help identify a word correctly in the first place, we use following context to tell us when we have made a miscue. Thus if you incorrectly pronounced *bow* to rhyme with *now* in sentence 8, you surely recognized the miscue when you noticed the word *arrow*.

Although such sentences as these are somewhat atypical, they do help us understand the nature of proficient reading. We do not normally rely just on *grapho/phonemics*, our knowledge of letter/sound relations. Rather, we use context to reduce our reliance on grapho/phonemic cues. Or, to rephrase the matter, we use nonvisual information to reduce our dependence on visual information.

It should come as no surprise, then, that beginning readers and nonproficient readers can often read words better in context than in isolation. Here are some examples from first and second graders. On the left is the word misread in isolation, with the miscue indicated above the word. On the right is a sentence in which the same child read the word correctly:

has
his   . . . said his father.

hot
not   His father said, "You are not old enough for that."

want
went   The next day Hap and his mother and father went to the fair.

which
with   "Hap can come with me."

wig
wag   All morning Peter tried to make the turtle wag its tail.

now
know   "I know you would," said his mother. . . .

don't
didn't   But she didn't bring it back to Peter.

our
your   "Come on, Lassie," said Peter. "Wag your tail."

tall
tail   He wanted the turtle to wag its tail.

made
named   Peter named his fish Lassie.

Such examples are quite typical, as a study by Kenneth Goodman indicates. In context, his first grade group correctly read 62 percent of the words that they had missed in isolation; his second graders correctly read 75 percent of the words they had missed in isolation; and his third graders correctly read 82 percent of the words they had missed in isolation (K. Goodman 1965, p. 640).

A related study revealed that words are easier to recognize in familiar contexts than in relatively unfamiliar contexts. Even the function words tended to cause more recognition problems in the B sentences than in the A sentences following, for the less proficient beginning readers tested (Reid 1958, p. 297):

Group A

You must do your best work.
I can see his face in the darkness.

Group B

You must not go back on your word.
No man can do more than his best.

We went back to the deep mud.	Darkness was upon the face of the deep.
Can you give me more words to read?	We must not give up when work is hard.

The best readers had no trouble with either set of sentences, but the less proficient readers had difficulty with many of the words in what was, to them, an unfamiliar context. Murphy's study (1986) produced similar results.

Similarly, others have found that beginning readers may know color names like *brown* and *green*, but not be able to recognize these words when they are used in names like *Mr. Brown* and *Green Street*. Or the word *had* may be recognizable in a sentence where it indicates possession (as in *I had a dog*), but unrecognizable in a sentence where it indicates past perfect aspect (as in *He had left already*).

My favorite example of such difficulty comes from my son John. Early in his first grade year, we visited Chicago's Field Museum of Natural History. As we were looking at the bird exhibits, my husband excitedly called John's attention to a display of Weaver birds. "Look, John. What kind of bird is this?" he asked, pointing to the identifying label. But in such an unfamiliar and unexpected context, our son could not recognize his own last name.

We can now begin to assess the wisdom of a sight word approach to reading. It has sometimes been assumed that if only children had a large enough stock of sight words, they could read. But we have seen that children can often read in context words that they cannot read in isolation, and that they can often read in familiar context words that they cannot read in unfamiliar contexts. *Thus instead of helping children build up a stock of sight words in order to read, perhaps we should help children read in order to build up a stock of sight words.*

It should be noted that this is not necessarily the *fastest* method of developing a stock of sight words, as various research studies suggest. For example: In a study by Ehri and Wilce, first graders practiced reading ten unfamiliar function words (like *might, which, enough*). Half of the children studied the words in actual sentences, while the other half studied the words in lists and then listened to sentences comprised of the words. It turned out that the children who studied the words in lists could recognize the words in isolation faster and more accurately. However, the children who studied the words in sentences had a better understanding of the syntactic and semantic properties of the words (Ehri and Wilce 1980). To the extent that this study is typical, it may mean that children who read words in sentences rather than study them in lists or on flash cards may be slower to learn to recognize the words in isolation. But when do children need to recognize words in isolation anyway, other than in school? In the "real" world, words typically occur in contexts of one or more kinds: in sentences, on labels, on signs. If indeed children do learn to develop a stock of sight words somewhat more slowly through reading itself, so be it. The compensation is that children typically have much greater understanding of what the words mean, because they are reading for meaning, not to identify words. They are using and further refining the strategies characteristic of proficient readers.

This approach to learning words is, in fact, a cornerstone of the whole-language and language experience approaches, as we shall see in Chapters 7 and 8.

CONTEXT BEYOND THE SENTENCE

As proficient adult readers, we are often conscious of using context to determine the *meaning* of words we do not know. One of my more interesting experiences was with the word *desiccant*. I could pronounce the word with no difficulty, but without context I would have had no idea what it meant. The word was printed on the outside of a little packet that came inside a bag of potato chips, and the manufacturers obligingly indicated that this packet of desiccant was included to absorb moisture and keep the chips fresh. Thanks to this explanation, I realized that the desiccant was not something to be thrown away as soon as the bag of chips was opened.

Writers are not always so obliging, yet often the preceding or following context gives a clue to the meaning of an unfamiliar word. Consider, for example, the context leading up to the word *fragile* and the word *melancholy*, below:

> The teacups were delicate, easily broken. So *fragile* that Ellen hardly dared grasp the handle.

> It was a gloomy day, more depressing than any that Margo had ever known. She lay motionless in bed, listless and *melancholy*.

Here, the preceding context indicates the meaning of *fragile* rather clearly, and at least supplies an appropriate connotation for *melancholy*. Note also that a reader would be able to get the essential meaning from these contexts, whether or not the words were pronounced "correctly." As a matter of fact, I knew the meaning of *melancholy* for years before I finally learned that my mental pronunciation of the word was incorrect (among other things, I incorrectly syllabicated and stressed the word: me•LAN•cho•ly).

If the context of preceding sentences is not enough to make the meaning of a word clear, often the context of following sentences will come to the rescue. This is what happened when I first encountered the word "scofflaw." When I read the headline "Scofflaw off to a Bad Start," I thought *flaw* must be the base word, so I mentally pronounced the word like this: /SKO•fla/. I could not even syllabicate or pronounce it correctly until I had read most of the article. It was the third paragraph that finally triggered my understanding:

> Cooper had ignored 780 parking tickets between 1973 and 1977. He was identified by a computer in 1977 as the city's worst traffic scofflaw. It took nearly a year for police to find him.[3]

In this case, I used following context to correct my tentative stab at the word. Once I realized that a "scofflaw" is someone who scoffs at the law, I was able to syllabicate and pronounce the word correctly.

In a similar vein, Yetta Goodman cites as an interesting and instructionally useful example the concept of the word *krait* in Roald Dahl's short story "Poison" (1950). Goodman has excerpted the following sentences from the story (Y. Goodman 1976b, p.101). Stop after each sentence and ask yourself what mental picture you have of the krait:

"A krait! Oh, oh! Where'd it bite you?"

"It's on my stomach. Lying there asleep."

"Then out of the corner of my eye I saw this krait sliding over my pajamas. Small, about ten inches."

They hang around people's houses and they go for warm places.

The bite is quite deadly, except sometimes when you catch it at once; and they kill a fair number of people each year in Bengal, mostly in the villages.

I was going to be ready to cut the bitten place and try to suck the venom out.

"Shall we draw the sheet back quick and brush it off before it has time to strike?"

"It is not safe," he continued, "because a snake is cold-blooded and anesthetic does not work so well or so quick with such animals."

Obviously the author builds suspense by only gradually providing the information necessary to identify the krait as a snake. Note, too, that how quickly a person understands this fact will depend largely upon how much that person knows about snakes. If one knew nothing about snakes, one might have to read even the last of the sentences above to realize what a krait is. Context within the selection must be supplemented by personal context, the sum total of one's knowledge and experience.

So far we have talked about determining the *meaning* of words that one might not have understood without context. However, beginning and less proficient readers actually use context to identify (that is, to name) words that are in their speaking vocabulary but that they do not immediately recognize in print. We have already illustrated, with a wealth of examples, the fact that such readers use context within the sentence to identify words that they do not always identify correctly in isolation. However, it is also true that such readers use context in preceding and following sentences. Perhaps most remarkable is the fact that readers can use the context of following sentences to correct the miscues they themselves have made. Again, an example from my own son comes readily to mind. He was having unusual difficulty with a story I had asked him to read (there are certain disadvantages to being a professor's son). The boy in the story was named Hap. While at a local fair, he noticed someone who was jumping high as he walked along. The boy's father explained that the person was able to jump so high because of the pack on his back. Here are the following four sentences of the story, along with my son's miscues on the word gas:

gams
"The pack has a kind of gas in it.

gangs
The gas is very light.

It helps the boy to jump high.''

gangs

"What kind of gas is it?'' asked Hap.

As you might suspect, my son was getting little meaning from this passage. But on the next page of the story, Hap's father explained to him that the gas is called helium. This explanation apparently triggered my son's understanding, because the next time he came to the word *gas* his face lit up and he said "I got that wrong on the other page. It was *gas* all the time.'' In this case, the meaning of the word was familiar to the reader, but he did not recognize the word in print until the context of following sentences triggered his own personal context, his prior knowledge of helium and its effects.

Of course sometimes prior knowledge will lead us astray, as with the third grader who made the following miscue in a story about Henry Ford:

Henry felt that everyone should be able to own a car,

not just the wealthy people. In 1903 he started the Ford

more

Motor Company. His cars cost much less than other cars

had before.

Then there was the sixth grade boy who seemed to have read his own role expectations into the following sentences written with the first person "I":

Ⓒa *pilot*

Sometimes I'm in a ballet costume, dancing on a stage.

psychiatrist waiting   Ⓒ*littles*

Or I'm a secretary, writing important letters.

He knows that boys are still more likely to become pilots or psychiatrists than to become ballet dancers or secretaries.

One more example of how making good use of one's schemas can actually cause miscues in word identification comes from the fourth grade son of one of my students. Reading one of the "Encyclopedia Brown" stories about a fictional ten-year-old "Sherlock Holmes in sneakers," David kept making miscues on the nickname "Encyclopedia," saying things like "Enkeycalapia," "Encaspeelas," and "Incapinkia." The mother was surprised by these miscues, since she thought he was familiar with the word "Encyclopedia." To test her belief, she wrote three sentences for the boy to read, two in which the word "Encyclopedia" meant what it typically does, and one in which the word was used as a boy's nickname. She asked her son to read these three sentences:

> If you want to find out about Abe Lincoln you can look in the Encyclopedia.
>
> I read in the Encyclopedia all about World War I.
>
> Bob and Danny went to Encyclopedia's house to see if he could play.

This time, David read "Encyclopedia" correctly in all three sentences, but he was convinced he had misread it in the third sentence. In that context, the word "Encyclopedia" simply did not make sense to him. "I got that wrong," he said. "Is it 'Encaplesia'?" Though again the reader has been led astray by his own prior knowledge, David's problem with "Encyclopedia" illustrates once more what is usually a productive and in fact crucial reading strategy: using everything you know (or think you know) to try to make sense out of what you read.

Such miscues will not always be corrected, of course, but far more often than we realize, even young readers are capable of noticing when they have made a miscue. They may not express their realization overtly, as my son John did with the miscues on *gas*. Still, we ourselves must realize that children can and will do a lot of self-correcting, internally if not out loud. And we must give them opportunity and encouragement to correct their own miscues.

With children who already read for meaning, almost all we have to do is encourage them to detect and correct miscues that seriously disrupt sense, and then avoid correcting them ourselves or letting other children correct them. With children who do not already read for meaning, our task is of course more difficult: we must help them learn to read for meaning before we can expect them to detect and correct miscues that do not make sense. Or perhaps the two kinds of learning go hand in hand. In any case, such self-correction—at least silent, internal self-correction of miscues that seriously disrupt meaning—should be an important goal of reading instruction at every level. Otherwise, students may have difficulty becoming independent readers, able to read silently and without assistance. Instead of relying just on grapho/phonemics and on us, children need to learn to make use of all the various kinds of contexts at their disposal. They must learn to use context within and beyond the sentence, in order to identify words and get meaning most effectively and efficiently.

LANGUAGE CUES AND READING STRATEGIES

The major *language cues* are syntactic, semantic, and grapho/phonemic. Our intuitive knowledge of syntax, our grammatical schemas, enables us to use word endings, function words, and word order as cues to word identification. These syntactic cues are supplemented by semantic cues, the meaning relations among words and sentences in the text we are reading. In addition, we bring to bear various situational cues and our entire store of personal knowledge and experience. We use not only the syntactic and semantic cues available in the text and the situation, but also our entire experience with language and with life. Of course, reading could not exist without the grapho/phonemic cues, the letters and words on the page and our intuitive knowledge of letter/sound relations and patterns. However, our reading would be both inefficient and ineffective if we relied just on grapho/phonemic cues. As Paul Kolers has written, "reading is only incidentally visual" (Kolers 1969). At this point, such an outrageous statement should begin to make sense.

Figure 4.3 indicates how language cues give rise to reading strategies. Of course during normal reading, all kinds of processing are going on simultaneously. But in order to understand some of this complexity, it may help, temporarily, to think of reading as a matter of identifying words. In order to identify a word, proficient readers first use syntactic and semantic knowledge and cues to *predict* what is coming next. We do not necessarily predict a specific word, but at least we subconsciously narrow down the possibilities. Thus there is a limited number of words that might reasonably come after the second *the* in *The cruel giant fell into the* _____. After mentally restricting the possibilities, we normally look at the word itself—that is, we use grapho/phonemic cues. But because prediction has narrowed down the number of reasonable alternatives, we need to use only a minimum of visual information to tentatively identify the word. In the sentence about the giant, we would need to process only two or three consonant letters or parts of them in order to decide that the word is *water* rather than one of the other reasonable possibilities. As proficient readers, we merely sample the grapho/phonemic cues, even though we have the impression that we've "seen" the entire word. Finally, we use following syntactic and semantic cues to confirm our tentative identification of the word, or to correct if we have made a miscue that does not fit with the following context. The word *water* fits not only with the preceding context but with the following context in *The cruel giant fell into the water and drowned.* Hence we would confirm our identification of the word in question. Figure 4.3

LANGUAGE CUES	READING STRATEGIES			Other Kinds of Contexts (including situational and context in the text)
	Predict	Sample	Confirm/Correct	
Syntactic	✓		✓	
Semantic	✓		✓	
Grapho/Phonemic		✓		

Reader's Schemas (including intuitive knowledge of grammar and of conventions of print)

FIGURE 4.3 *Language cues and reading strategies*

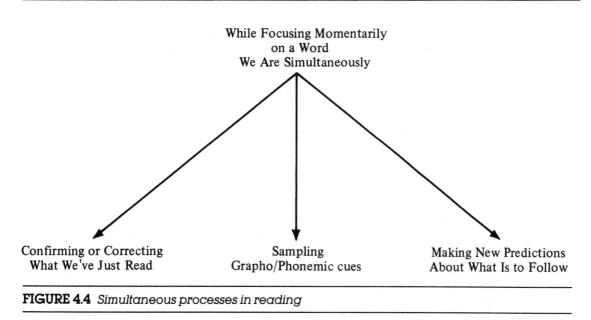

FIGURE 4.4 *Simultaneous processes in reading*

depicts this relationship between language cues and reading strategies, suggesting in addition the use of other contextual cues and the fact that it is our schemas that enable us to make use of the cues provided by text and situation. Figure 4.4 attempts to suggest the simultaneity of these strategies: at one and the same time, we are sampling new grapho/phonemic cues, confirming or correcting what we've just read, and making new predictions about what is to follow. "Each [system and strategy] follows the others but at the same time precedes them, always moving toward constructing a text and making meaning" (Y. Goodman, Watson, and Burke 1987, p. 33).

READING PROFICIENCY AND THE USE OF CONTEXT

Almost by definition, we can say that good readers are ones who use context efficiently, to reduce their reliance on visual cues and grapho/phonemic knowledge. The following excerpt from a miscue analysis illustrates such use of context. The symbols have the same meaning as before: a carat points to an insertion, a circle indicates an omission, $\sim$ indicates a reversal, and one or more words written above the text indicate a substitution. Each miscue or set of related miscues is numbered to facilitate discussion, but the reader's corrections are not marked. Try to read the text as this sixth grader did, complete with all his miscues. If your first reading tends to be jerky, read the paragraphs again, more smoothly. The passage is from an O. Henry story, "Jimmy Hayes and Muriel" (Porter 1936, p. 670).

After a hearty supper Hayes joined the smokers about *around*①

*at all*②
the fire. His appearance did not settle all the questions in

the minds of his brother rangers. They saw simply a loose, ③

young ④

lank youth with tow-colored sunburned hair and a berry-

ingenious ⑤

brown, ingenuous face that wore a quizzical, good-

natured smile.

"Fellows," said the new ranger, "I'm goin' to interduce

⑥   much about ⑦

you to a lady friend of mine. Ain't ever heard anybody

⑦   a ⑧

call her a beauty, but you'll all admit she's got some fine

points about her. Come along, Muriel!"

⑨

He held open the front of his blue flannel shirt. Out of

⑨   toad ⑩

it crawled a horned frog. A bright red ribbon was tied

the ⑪

jauntily around its spiky neck. It crawled to its owner's

it ⑫

knee and sat there motionless.

's ⑬

"This here Muriel," said Hayes, with an oratorical wave

⑬. She's ⑬

of his hand, "has got qualities. She never talks back, she

⑭

always stays at home, and she's satisfied with one red

dress for everyday and Sunday, too."

d ⑮

"Look at that blame insect!" said one of the rangers

toads ⑯

with a grin. "I've seen plenty of them horny frogs, but I

never knew anybody to have one for a(side)partner. Does *(17)*

the blame thing know you from anybody else?''

her *(18)*
"Take it over there and see," said Hayes.

Almost all the boy's miscues fit the context: the preceding syntactic and semantic context, and the following syntactic and semantic context. The reader brought knowledge and meaning *to* the text, and constructed meaning *from* it.

Linguists generally agree that children have mastered the basic grammatical signals and patterns before entering school, so it should not be surprising that many beginners automatically make use of syntatic context as they read. In one study with first graders, Rose-Marie Weber sought to determine what percentage of miscues were acceptable with preceding syntax only, and what percentage were acceptable with following syntax as well. The following examples illustrate the two types of miscues:

Acceptable only with preceding *syntax*	*and* Spot can help Dick.
Acceptable with both preceding *and following syntax*	*hear* Spot can help Dick.

The miscue "and" for *can* is syntactically acceptable up to that point in the sentence, but not beyond it. However, "hear" for *help* is syntactically acceptable with the following context as well (though of course it does change the meaning).

Weber found that about 90 percent of these first graders' miscues were acceptable with the preceding syntax. This startling percentage was true for the low proficiency group as well as for the high proficiency group. Furthermore, 72 percent of the high group's miscues and 63 percent of the low group's miscues were acceptable with the following syntax as well. The major difference between groups was in the *correction* of miscues that did not fit with the following syntactic context (miscues like "and" for *can* in *Spot can help Dick*). The high group corrected 85 percent of these, while the low group corrected only 42 percent (Weber 1970, pp. 153, 160, and 161). Thus a major difference between proficient and nonproficient readers lies in the correction of miscues that are unacceptable with the following syntactic context.

We have focused just on the use of syntactic context. However, the broad conclusions are equally applicable to the use of semantic context as well. Beginning readers can indeed use context as a means of word identification, and many tend to do so, especially if they are already well acquainted with books and the joys of being read to. But we have seen that other readers make much less use of context, and that these readers tend to be among the less proficient, the least able either to identify words or to get meaning.

In many if not most cases, then, nonproficient readers are those who make inadequate use of context in identifying words and getting meaning. They over-attend to grapho/phonemic cues and underattend to syntactic and semantic cues. In his extensive study of reading miscues, Kenneth Goodman found that the miscues of low proficiency eighth and tenth graders frequently looked and sounded more like the text word than the miscues of high proficiency readers (K. Goodman 1973, *Theoretically Based Studies*, pp. 51, 53). But often this careful attention to grapho/phonemic cues produced nonwords (like ''souts'' and ''ramped'') or words that did not fit the context. Such overreliance on grapho/phonemics actually hindered word identification.

Doubtless an underreliance on context is not the only cause of reading difficulty, but it is certainly a major cause, given today's greater instructional emphasis on phonics and sight words. In fact, I would go so far as to hypothesize the following as a typical continuum of reading proficiency (the term ''interpretation'' is used to suggest that the essence of a word may be understood, even when the word is not identified ''correctly''):

1. Highly effective readers use preceding syntactic and semantic context to predict what is coming next (that is, to reduce the number of reasonable alternatives). In addition, they use following syntactic and semantic context to confirm their tentative interpretation of a word or to correct this interpretation if it does not fit with the following context.

2. Moderately effective readers use preceding syntactic and semantic context to predict what is coming next, but they are less successful in using following context to correct inappropriate interpretations.

3. Somewhat effective readers use preceding syntactic context to predict, but they are not so successful in using preceding semantic context to predict a word that is appropriate to the meaning. Such readers make little or no use of following context to confirm or correct their tentative interpretation of a word.

Obviously such statements involve some degree of overgeneralization and over-simplification, but research suggests that they contain much truth. See, for example, Allen and Watson's *Findings of Research in Miscue Analysis: Classroom Implications* (1976), which reports on ten years of research into reading miscues. See also Carey's *Findings of Research in Miscue Analysis: Ten Years Later* (forthcoming).

We know now that reading does not proceed by grapho/phonemics alone. Rather, proficient reading involves the use of context to predict what is coming next; the selective sampling of grapho/phonemic cues to interpret tentatively the word in question; and the use of following context to confirm or correct this tentative interpretation. Thus reading involves the constant interplay of *all* the language cue systems: grapho/phonemic, syntactic, and semantic. Let us reexamine phonics from this perspective.

PHONICS REVISITED

Without realizing it, teachers may unintentionally teach children to read as if each word stood isolated and alone, in a word list. This can happen if the teacher emphasizes just the use of phonics and structural analysis[4] to identify words that are not immediately recognized on sight. If the teacher typically says "Sound it out" whenever a child stumbles over a word, the teacher may inadvertently convey the unfortunate notion that letters and their sounds are the most important or only cues to use in reading. This can all too easily happen when the instructional materials emphasize phonics.

We have already seen several other problems with phonics, in Chapter 3: (1) since vowels are relatively unimportant in identifying words, it seems unnecessary to teach numerous vowel rules, as many phonics programs do; (2) spelling/sound correspondences are often very complex and not easily reducible to rules that can or should be taught; (3) only a few of the frequently taught rules are both consistent and comprehensive—that is, applicable to a considerable number of words; and (4) even most of these rules do not need to be explicitly taught to whole classes of children, since most children can and will internalize spelling/sound patterns just by reading and writing a lot, and/or with minimal guidance. In the long run, however, the most crucial problem with phonics instruction may be this: that a heavy instructional emphasis on phonics encourages readers to use just one language cue system, the grapho/phonemic. And sole reliance on grapho/phonemics makes the task of reading inordinately difficult, if not impossible.

Thus if beginning reading instruction emphasizes just phonics, only those children who intuitively use context to make sense of a text will be using all the resources that a successful reader needs to draw upon. Those who do just what they are taught will be in serious trouble. This is why I feel that teaching phonics alone is something like "teaching" a baby to walk by tying up one foot, and tying behind the child the arms needed for balance. It's as if we were to say, "Okay, we're going to make this task as difficult as possible. If you can learn to do it under these conditions, then and only then will we let you use the resources that the successful walker/reader uses." An imperfect analogy? Yes. An exaggeration? Yes, again. And yet, I think, not so very far from the mark.

At this point, we may well ask just how much phonics should be taught. There is no one answer appropriate to all situations, but many important observations and guidelines are provided in A. Sterl. Artley's "Phonics Revisited" (1977), from which the title of this section is borrowed. Artley makes several major points, including some which have already been touched upon in the preceding chapters of the present text. In particular, Artley makes the following observations about phonics:

1. First, phonics must be taught not as a method of reading, but as one cue system that is important in reading.
2. Context should be the first cue to word identification (or more properly, to meaning).

3. Where a choice must be made from among several words that would reasonably fit the given context, phonics knowledge becomes an invaluable aid.

4. However, "sounding out" a word is cumbersome, time-consuming, and unnecessary. By using context, we can identify words with only minimal attention to grapho/phonemic cues.

5. Children should be taught the basic symbol/sound relations for consonants: the single consonants; consonant digraphs (*ch, th,* etc.); and consonant clusters (*st, bl,* etc.).

6. It is much less important to teach symbol/sound relations for vowels, since they are much less useful in word identification. Furthermore, in about four out of every five words met in early reading, a vowel letter will indicate either the typical "long" or "short" vowel sound, or the unstressed schwa (an "uh" sound). Therefore, "if a teacher feels impelled to deal with vowel letters and sounds, the reader could be taught the long and short vowel symbol/sound relations, and, on coming to a new word, to try both sounds to discover which pronunciation makes a known word, which fits, and which makes sense in its contextual setting" (p. 125).

An example may help to clarify the latter point. Artley suggests that instead of teaching children the silent *e* rule, we should just teach them the long and short vowel sounds and have children use context to decide which sound is appropriate in any given case. Thus if a child comes to the visually unfamiliar word *tame* in normal reading, he or she would not have to remember and apply the appropriate rule. In a sentence like *The lion was very tame*, the correct pronunciation should be obvious from the preceding context, assuming the reader is aurally familiar with the word *tame*.

In concluding his fine article, Artley quotes from Heilman (1972, p. 280): "'In the final analysis, the *optimum* amount of phonics instruction for every child is the *minimum* that he needs to become an independent reader.'" And, as we have suggested, this minimum is much less than commonly supposed, because grapho/phonemics is only one of the three language cue systems available to the reader. Instead of learning a multiplicity of letter/sound correspondences and phonics "rules," children need to learn to minimize their use of grapho/phonemic cues. Or as Frank Smith puts it, "The art of becoming a fluent reader lies in learning to rely less and less on information from the eyes" (F. Smith 1975, p. 50).

The message, then, seems clear: we should help children learn to use context *first*.

There are at least two important implications of this statement. One is that we should use context to introduce letter/sound relations and "new" words. Another implication is that we should help children learn to use context to *predict* what is coming next, *before* sampling the available grapho/phonemic cues. Such use of context will reduce their need for visual information.

In beginning reading instruction, both objectives can be approached almost at the same time. Suppose, for example, that you wanted to teach the letter *s* and its basic sound. You could begin by saying, "I'm going to put a sentence on the board:

Mary saw a snake. Do you hear the "sssss" sound at the beginning of the word *snake*? Okay, can you think of another word that makes sense here and that also begins with a "sssss" sound? *Mary saw a . . .* what?" In the process of learning a specific letter/sound correspondence, the children are also learning to attend to syntactic context (the word must be a noun) and to semantic context (the word must designate something that can be observed), while at the same time bringing to bear the totality of their personal knowledge and experience (Weaver 1977, p. 883).

The following would be a more overt way of emphasizing the need to use context *first*. Before children can read anything at all, they can be asked to finish a sentence like *Rain came in when Sally opened the _____*. One obvious response is "window"; another is "door." Later, children can be asked to finish a sentence when the initial consonant of the last word narrows down the reasonable possibilities: *Rain came in when Sally opened the w _____*, or *Rain came in when Sally opened the d_____*. Activities such as this would help children learn to use a maximum of nonvisual information and a minimum of visual information as they read.

In trying such activities with young children, teachers should remember that it may be difficult if not impossible for some children to hear and identify the separate sounds in words. Teaching such things may help many kindergarteners and first graders, but it is unrealistic and unreasonable to expect every child to master what has been taught. Some will simply not be ready to profit from such instruction. The best "phonics" instruction may in fact stem from encouraging children to write, sounding out words as best they can. This approach to developing literacy is discussed in Chapter 7.

There are at least two dangers of too much direct phonics instruction, particularly in the earliest years of instruction. One is that we tend to expect children to master what we have taught, and this is an unrealistic expectation for at least some children: the mere fact that such rules can be formulated and "taught" does not mean that children necessarily can—or should—learn them. Furthermore, some of the children who seem unable to learn phonics rules are quite able to comprehend what they read. I am reminded of an anecdote told by Barbara Vitale (1985), author of *Unicorns Are Real*, a book on "right-brained" approaches to learning. As I remember the story, a second grade girl was sent to the remedial reading teacher because she could not do her phonics exercises. The remedial reading teacher was reluctant to work with the child because she found that the girl was compehending on a fifth grade level. The classroom teacher insisted, however, so the reading teacher complied. The result: the girl learned to do the phonics exercises, but her comprehension regressed to second grade level.

This example illustrates the second major danger of too much phonics instruction, namely that the child will inappropriately center on grapho/phonemic cues, assuming that reading means sounding out or pronouncing the words. Even if we were to be satisfied with mere word identification rather than the getting of meaning, it is quite clear that such word identification can best be accomplished through the use of *all three* kinds of language cues: syntactic, semantic, and grapho/phonemic.

When they come to school, children are already experienced in using syntactic and semantic cues to understand what they hear: they bring a wealth of knowledge and experience to the task of reading. Perhaps it seems logical, then, to *teach* the one thing they do not know: letters and their sounds. However, some children may find phonics instruction too abstract and meaningless, while many others may fail to use their syntactic and semantic knowledge if they are not explicitly helped and encouraged to do so. Therefore, we must help children learn to use their prior knowledge to get meaning from the text.

Indeed, an emphasis on semantic cues to word identification is particularly appropriate for young children, since they tend to center their attention on one cue system and strategy. Although beginning readers *can* use all the cue systems to some extent, they may have trouble using them simultaneously (see, for example, K. Goodman 1973, *Theoretically Based Studies*, p. 215). Canney makes a similar observation about poor readers: while proficient readers "seem to integrate, almost unconsciously, the various skills we teach into an effective method of reading, . . . the poor readers seem to learn the skills separately, yet do not integrate them into an effective strategy for processing print" (Canney 1977, p. 10). In effect, Canney's generalization is an indictment against the "eclectic" skills approach of most basal reading systems.

Teachers must help children coordinate the language cue systems, to use simultaneously the productive reading strategies of predicting, sampling, and confirming/ correcting their tentative identifications of words. But because there will be some children who necessarily center their attention on one cue system and strategy, we had better give careful thought to what should be emphasized. A heavy emphasis on letter/sound correspondences and "phonics" may produce readers who are not proficient either at identifying words or at getting meaning. Again, it seems wise to focus on context and meaning first, before giving much attention to grapho/ phonemics. Paradoxically, meaning is both an aid to word identification and the ultimate goal of reading itself.

CONTEXT IN REVIEW

Following is a brief summary of the major points covered in this chapter:

1. Proficient readers use four major kinds of contexts: context within each sentence; context beyond the sentence but within the selection; the situational and sociolinguistic context, both verbal and nonverbal (discussed somewhat more thoroughly in Chapter 2); and their entire personal context of knowledge and experience.

2. Words are easier to identify in context than in isolation. In fact, beginning and less proficient readers can often identify words in context that they cannot identify in isolation.

3. Language cues are related to reading strategies. To identify words, we use preceding syntactic and semantic cues to predict what might be coming next (that

is, to narrow down the reasonable alternatives); we sample grapho/phonemic cues to make tentative identifications of words; and we use following syntactic and semantic context to confirm or correct these tentative identifications. Such strategies are essential to proficient reading.

4. The most effective and efficient readers are those who use a maximum of nonvisual information (context) and a minimum of visual information (grapho/phonemics).

In the course of the discussion, I mentioned objections to three of the major reading approaches presented in Chapter 2. The *sight word approach* is objectionable because it puts the cart before the horse: it assumes that children cannot read until they know a number of words on sight. We have seen, however, that children can often read in context words that they cannot identify in isolation. Hence it may be more sensible to help children read aurally familiar material in order gradually to build up a stock of sight words, rather than vice versa. The *phonics approach* is objectionable for a variety of reasons discussed here and in Chapter 3. The most compelling objection is that overreliance on grapho/phonemics will lead to inefficient and ineffective reading: indeed, poor readers typically need to pay *less* attention to grapho/phonemics, and more attention to context (see, for example, Tony's miscues in activity 2 within Chapter 1. The *linguistic approach* is similarly objectionable because of its exclusive focus on developing spelling/sound knowledge. All three of these approaches are woefully incomplete.

On the face of it, a *basal reader approach* would seem much better, because it typically deals with sight words, phonics, *and* context. The problem, however, is that instruction all too often fails to emphasize the integration of the various skills that are taught. Many children will integrate the language cues more or less automatically, of course, but others may never learn that in order to read effectively they must predict, sample, and confirm/correct their tentative identification of words. It is these children who are shortchanged the most by a basal reader approach.

ACTIVITIES AND PROJECTS FOR FURTHER EXPLORATION

1. Look again at David's and Tony's miscues in activity 2 within Chapter 1. What language cues and reading strategies does each child seem to have been using? Ask yourself the same question about the miscues recorded here. Examples (a) through (e) are from second graders; the others are from older readers (sixth, eighth, and tenth graders). The source is K. Goodman 1973, *Theoretically Based Studies*, pp. 210–11, 230–31, 250, 258, and 310).

   to get down.
   a. Here is something you can do.
   I have not help the little kitten will we want little kitten to play ?
   b. I am not too little to help with little things, am I?

   truck
   c. "The little monkey had it."

d. . . . a voice calling *him*, somewhere above.

e. . . . it was enough to wake *up* the dead.

f. Billy knew that fawns were always very shy.
    know   *fun* *was*   *sky*

g. I leaned over the crib, pointing a finger . . .
    liked   *a crab potted*

h. Billy was so pleased by the hunter's words.
    proud

i. . . . to see if there was any danger. He heard the . . .
    afraid

j. . . . stop driving until we can see Los Angeles.

k. . . . I went over to his bed.

l. . . . when the children begin assuming *the* control of the country.

m. . . . the door of Harry's room. . . .
    to   *bedroom*

n. . . . a pair of pyjamas with blue, *and* brown *with* and white stripes.

2. The following is similar to the "Blonke" passage in Chapter 2, except this time you may have much less of an idea what the passage "means." To demonstrate that you, as a typical reader, use syntactic cues like word endings, function words, and word order, reread the "corandic" passage reprinted here, and then answer the comprehension questions that follow. How is it that you are able to answer such questions? And what does this experience suggest about the kinds of "comprehension" questions typical of standardized tests?

> Corandic is an emurient grof with many fribs; it granks from corite, an olg which cargs like lange. Corite grinkles several other tarances, which garkers excarp by glarcking the corite and starping it in tranker-clarped storbs. The tarances starp a chark which is exparged with worters, branking a slorp. This slorp is garped through several other coruscles, finally frasting a pragety, blickant crankle: coranda. Coranda is a cargurt, grinkling corandic and borigen. The corandic is nacerated from the borigen by means of loracity. Thus garkers finally thrap a glick, bracht, glupous grapant, corandic, which granks in many starps.

> What is corandic?
> What does corandic grank from?

How do garkers excarp the tarances from the corite?
What does the slorp finally frast?
What is coranda?
How is the corandic nacerated from the borigen?
What do the garkers finally thrap?

3. To determine for yourself whether words are easier to read in context or in isolation, first choose a reader to work with, either a beginning reader (late first grade, or second grade) or a poor reader of any age. Then choose a reading selection that should be appropriate for this reader: not easy, but not terribly difficult either. The selection should be about 250 words long or longer (except for the youngest readers, who may find this too much). It might be wise to photocopy the selection for your later convenience in analysis and discussion.

Once you have chosen the reading selection, type from this selection a list of about 50 words for the person to read (fewer, if the reader is a nonproficient beginner). One possibility would be to make a list of all the different function words in the selection. Another possibility is simply to choose every fifth word (avoiding duplications).

Have the reader read the list of words and then read the entire selection. Instead of trying to take notes on the reader's miscues as he or she reads, just tape record the session for later study.

To facilitate discussion, you will need to mark each of the miscues on the word list and each of the miscues the reader made on the reading selection itself. For the most part, the marking symbols introduced in Chapter 1 should be adequate.

Consider such questions as the following:

   a. On the whole, did the reader seem to be using context to predict what was coming next? What examples support your conclusion?

   b. Did the person read in context any of the words that he or she missed in isolation? If so, what are some examples? How or why might the context have helped?

   c. Did the person read in isolation any words that he or she later missed in context? If so, what are some examples? Why do you suppose these words were read correctly in isolation but not in context?

   d. On the whole, would you conclude that words are easier to read in isolation, or in context?

4. Even words that are central to a passage can often be determined from context. What word or words would you put in the blanks below? Essentially the same item belongs in each blank. The paragraph is from Ray Bradbury's *Dandelion Wine* (1957, p. 34):

Somehow the people who made _____ knew what boys needed and wanted. They put marshmallows and coiled springs in the soles and they wove the rest out of grasses bleached and fired in the wilderness. Somewhere deep in the soft loam of the _____ the thin hard sinews of the buck deer were hidden. The people that made the _____ must have watched a lot of winds blow the trees and a lot of rivers going down to the lakes. Whatever it was, it was in the _____, and it was summer.[5]

You might try finding or creating similar passages to use with children.

5. We can often get the meaning of a word from context (even though we may never pronounce the word correctly). Try it:

   a. First, jot down a definition for the following words: *deng, tolchock, veck,* and *viddy.* Just make up a definition that seems reasonable.

   b. Now see if you can tell what the words mean, as used in this sentence from Anthony Burgess's novel *A Clockwork Orange* (1963): "Our pockets were full of *deng*, so there was no real need . . . to *tolchock* some old *veck* in an alley and *viddy* him swim in his blood while we counted the takings. . . . " (pp. 1–2). Discuss what cues enable you to determine what the words mean.

   c. Try essentially the same procedure again. Write down a definition for these words:

creech	malenky	razrez
droogs	messel	skorry
glazzies	millicents	spatted
goloss	poogly	zoobies

   Do you notice yourself using any fairly consistent principle for determining what the words might mean? Discuss.

   d. Now read the first chapter of *A Clockwork Orange.* In each case, how do you finally determine what the word means?

6. Many children who tend to deal with each word as if it stood in isolation will make habitual confusions of one sort or another. They may confuse *then* with *than, the* with *they, and* with *can,* and so forth. The solution is not to drill students on these words in isolation, but to help them learn to use context to disentangle the confusion. You can begin with passages in which both grammar and meaning strongly signal the word intended. For example, if a person commonly reads "can" for *and* and vice versa, you might construct a passage beginning as follows:

   Jim called to ask his friends Bob *and* Mike, "*Can* you come to the fort today?" Bob answered, "Yes, we *can*. But let's go get some pop *and* cookies to take with us.

You might even initially omit the problem words and ask the reader to supply whichever one is appropriate in context (in this case, *can* or *and*).

   As an activity, then, create several passages that might be used to help readers overcome habitual confusions between pairs of words like those listed above. You might first create a passage where only one of the words is appropriate, and create a companion passage for the other word. You might then create a passage that includes blanks where the two words belong. Finally, you might create a passage like the one above, where both words are explicitly included. It would be better yet to find appropriate passages from children's literature and blank out the relevant words, since artificially constructed passages tend not to have the supportive language and meaningful context that make it possible for readers to supply or read the troublesome words. If possible, then, try these passages with readers who habitually confuse the words.

For various kinds of strategy lessons to use with middle grade children and older, see Y. Goodman and C. Burke, *Reading Strategies: Focus on Comprehension* (New York: Richard C. Owen, 1980).

7. As indicated earlier in the chapter, the ''Beaver'' activity is an example of what's known as the *cloze* procedure. The ''basic'' cloze procedure, first developed by Wilson Taylor in 1953, involves supplying every fifth word, on the assumption that about one of every five words in a text can be predicted from context. Various modifications of the cloze procedure can be useful in helping students learn to use all the language cue systems. Accordingly, you might prepare some mini-lessons, using one or more of the following suggestions:

a. Omit the last word of a sentence, if it is highly predictable—or include just the first letter of the last word. This is particularly useful with beginning readers.

b. Omit inflectional endings, to help readers recognize their own syntactic knowledge.

c. Omit function words, to help readers realize their ability to predict these words from the content words, word order, and context.

d. Omit key concept-carrying words (as in the passage from Bradbury in activity 4 above), to help readers see how words can be understood from context.

e. Omit every fifth word (or whatever) and have students read just for meaning, not to fill in the words, in order to help them see that comprehension is ordinarily possible without identifying all the words.

f. For less confident readers, omit only words and sentences that are highly predictable, to assure success.

You might use a variety of materials: songs, poems, and stories; content-area textbooks; newspapers and magazines; and anything else that might be suitable. Whatever the variations and materials used, however, it is important for students to read through the entire cloze activity before filling in any of the missing parts. This should help them see the value of using following context to identify and/or get the meaning of difficult words. It is crucial for students to discuss their answers to a cloze exercise. They need the opportunity to share and compare their responses with those of other students, and the challenge of defending their choices or rejecting them in favor of something better. Of course you should accept any/all responses that reasonably fit in each blank, not just the word originally omitted.

A useful reference is Eugene Jongsma's *Cloze Instruction Research: A Second Look* (Newark, Del.: International Reading Association, 1980). Jongsma reviews the 1970 through 1980 research on the use of cloze as a teaching technique, identifying weaknesses and suggesting directions for the future.

8. Sometimes people who are convinced that heavy phonics instruction is not necessary for helping most children read will still defend phonics instruction on the grounds that it is important in helping children spell. Try this as a class activity, and compare your results. Have someone dictate the following words to the rest of the class. Compare spellings. Then discuss what your chances are of spelling the words correctly, using phonics alone. What would you conclude about the importance of phonics in learning to spell correctly?

   a. *Real words: homonyms* (don't define these or use them in a sentence)

      sun
      brake
      rowed
      mete

   b. *Nonsense words*

      keak
      pite
      wraim
      /ne' dər le/[6]

   c. *Real words that most people do not know*

      coriaceous /kôr' ē ā shəs/
      deraign /di rān'/
      escharotic /es' kə rät' ik/
      gaudeamus /gou' dā ä mōōs/
      isochronal /ī säk' rə nªl/
      mesophyte /mes' o fīt/
      piceous /pis' ē əs/

   (I often give this "spelling test" at the end of class and ask that students look up in a large "desk" dictionary before the next class the words in group *c*. Subsequent discussion on the difficulty of locating these words proves most illuminating.)

9. To help you formulate your own position on the teaching of phonics, brainstorm all the reasons you can think of that are commonly given for and against the teaching of phonics. Compile a class list from your individual lists, and discuss.

10. In preparation for Chapter 5, locate in a dictionary ten words you can pronounce without looking at the pronunciation given, but whose meaning you do not know. What does this suggest about the importance of saying the words right? Discuss. (Incidentally, my own list of ten words is as follows: *anopheles, arcuate, autochthonous, barratry, kieselguhr, lutetium, maduro, mephitic, pyronine, scarious*.)

11. Again in preparation for Chapter 5, examine the "dialect" miscues that a college student made in reading the passage below. The passage is from the dialect reader *Friends*, by Joan Baratz and William Stewart (1970, pp. 24–30). What do you think caused the reader to make these miscues? Discuss.

One morning Ollie and Leroy was getting ready to

go to school. Leroy, he put on one of Ollie socks

'cause he lost his. Ollie say, "Boy, give me_{back}my

sock" but Leroy_{he}wouldn't give it to him. Leroy

say "It's my sock." But Ollie know_{knew}it wasn't

'cause it wasn't even the same color as Leroy_{'s}

other sock. Ollie kept on begging and begging

Leroy for the sock. But Leroy still wouldn't

give it to him. Ollie hit Leroy. And they got to_{into}

fighting._{a fight} Leroy hit Ollie in the nose and it start_{ed}

to bleeding. Then, Ollie got real mad and hit Leroy

on the arm as hard as he could. Leroy hollered real

loud. Big Momma must have heard them fighting 'cause

she come_{came}running in the room and she stop the fight.

She say "All right, who start_{ed}this mess?" Ollie say

Leroy start it and Leroy say Ollie start it.

Big Momma say, "I done told you about fighting

before. Since don't nobody know who start this

mess I'm just going to whip both of you."

Incidentally, I have typed this just the way it was typed by the student who carried out the experiment with her college friend. My student made two dialect miscues in reading and typing the passage! Compare this version with the one on p. 134–35 and see if you can locate the miscues.

READINGS FOR FURTHER EXPLORATION

Allington, Richard L., and Anne McGill-Franzen. April 1980. Word Identification Errors in Isolation and in Context: Apples vs. Oranges. *The Reading Teacher* 33: 795–800. The authors found that good and poor readers both read words better in context than in isolation; that poor readers were helped most by context, since good readers did relatively well under both conditions; and that readers tended to miscue on different words in context than in isolation. Because of the latter observation, the authors concluded that a child's performance on word lists is not a good predictor of which words might be missed in context.

Smith, Frank. 1978, 1985. *Reading Without Nonsense.* New York: Teachers College Press. Smith's second chapter, "Reading—From Behind the Eyes," is an excellent complement to the discussion here.

Goodman, Kenneth S., E. Brooks Smith, Robert Meredith, and Yetta M. Goodman. Reading and Writing: A Psycholinguistic View. *Language and Thinking in School: A Whole-Language Curriculum.* 3rd ed. New York: Richard C. Owen, 265–83. This chapter is also an excellent complement to the present discussion. Also highly recommended is the subsequent chapter, "Learning and Teaching Reading: Strategies for Comprehension," pp. 284–302.

Smith, Frank. 1975. Between Eye and Brain. *Comprehension and Learning: A Conceptual Framework for Teachers.* New York: Holt, Rinehart and Winston, 49–61. Though somewhat technical in places, this is a fine discussion of the role of visual and nonvisual information in reading.

Weaver, Constance. November/December 1977. Using Context: Before or After? *Language Arts* 54: 880–86. Discusses the role of context in normal reading and provides some suggestions for helping children learn to use context more effectively.

Dahl, Patricia R., and S. Jay Samuels. March 1977. Teaching Children to Read Using Hypothesis/Test Strategies. *The Reading Teacher* 30: 603–06. Reports on a program in which children were taught to use context first.

Bortnick, Robert, and Genevieve S. Lopardo. January 1973. An Instructional Application of the Cloze Procedure. *Journal of Reading* 16: 296–300. Presents some practical suggestions for using the cloze procedure to help readers make better use of context.

5

Why Is a Word-Identification View of Reading Inappropriate?

The major folklore of reading instruction relates to the "theory" that reading is considered an exact process. In other words, the reader is expected to read everything exactly as printed on the page in order to understand the message of the author. In general the consuming public, legislatures, courts and too many educators hold to this theory. It is like the theory of the world being flat during the time of Columbus.

—Harper and Kilarr

QUESTIONS FOR JOURNALS AND DISCUSSION

1. Why is the quantity of a person's miscues not necessarily an adequate measure of his or her reading ability?

2. How do good readers' miscues typically differ from poor readers' miscues? That is, what are some of the qualitative differences?

3. About how long is surface structure held in short-term memory? What happens to information when it is "rechunked" into long-term memory?

4. How can we demonstrate that proficient readers impose deep structure on surface structure?

5. Why are dialect miscues usually "good" miscues?

6. What good is it to get the surface structure (words) if you do not get the deep structure (meaning)? Conversely, what need is there to get every detail of the surface structure, if you do get the deep structure?

7. Why is a word-identification view of reading inappropriate?

MISCUES AND READING PROFICIENCY

By focusing on word identification, the last two chapters demonstrated (1) that even in isolation, words can be identified from only a fraction of the visual information normally available to us; and (2) that in normal reading, we use syntactic and semantic context to reduce even further our need for visual information. Thus the focus upon word identification has shown the importance of the knowledge and information that the proficient reader brings *to* the written text. Now, however, it is time to reexamine the common notion that reading is first and foremost a matter of identifying words.

Let us begin by examining Anne's miscues on the following reading selection. Which miscues fit with the context? Which ones do not? The selection is from Jene Barr's *Little Circus Dog* (1949):

Now the band began to play. Then the lions roared.

about ①
Peter the pony ran around the ring. Bill the circus boy

Ⓒ *let* ②   *Everyone* ③
⌊led Penny the elephant into the circus ring. Everybody

forgot to eat popcorn. They forgot to drink soda pop.

A ④
They forgot to wave balloons. The circus man made a bow.

Trixie ran into the middle of the ring. She sat and

went ⑤
waited. Carlo the clown ran up to Trixie. Trixie jumped

on ⑥   *the* ⑦
up and sat in his hand. Carlo put Trixie on a box. Trixie

stood on her hind legs. Then she jumped onto Carlo's head.

Every –
Trixie looked very funny sitting on Carlo's head. Every-

one ⑧
body laughed.

In every case, the miscue fits both the syntactic context and the semantic context. That is, the miscue results in a grammatical sentence that preserves the essential meaning of the original. Such miscues are typical of a good reader, one who ordinarily gets meaning from what is read. And in fact, Anne recalled almost every detail of the passage. She was a first grader.

Oddly enough, by some standards the foregoing passage might be considered too difficult for this particular child. In order to determine where to place a child within a given basal reading series, it is common to have the child read passages from several of the basal readers to determine the child's *independent, instructional,* and *frustration* levels within that series. Material at the independent level is supposed to be suitable for the child's unaided reading; material at the instructional level is supposed to be suitable for instructional use with that child; and material at the frustration level is considered simply too difficult for that child to read.

The time-honored Betts criteria for determining these levels are as follows (Betts 1946):

Reading Level	*Words Decoded*	*Questions Answered*
Independent	99%	90%
Instructional	95%	75%
Frustration	Below 90%	50%

More recently, there has been somewhat greater variation. Most of the twelve IRIs (informal reading inventories) reviewed by Harris and Niles (1982) suggested percentages within these ranges:

Independent	97–99%	80–90%
Instructional	90–97%	60–80%
Frustration	Below 90%	50–60%

However, this neat chart masks the extremes that are found in some of the IRIs. In most cases, these percentages seem to be arbitrarily determined. Worse yet, the word recognition score is often considered more important than the comprehension score, reflecting the typical emphasis on word-perfect reading (May and Eliot 1978, p. 144).

If we compute the word recognition score for the child whose miscues were just noted, we see that this passage from *Little Circus Dog* is too difficult for her to read without instructional help, according to the preceding word recognition criteria. Anne pronounced only 92 percent of the words without error, which puts this selection at her instructional level, according to today's typical criteria.

Doubtless some children who read 8 percent of the words inaccurately in a given selection will consider that selection too difficult to read independently, particularly if their miscues reflect a loss of meaning and particularly if they have learned that word-perfect reading is the expected goal. But Anne's miscues suggest that she was making use of prior context to predict what was coming next; she was bringing meaning to the text in order to get meaning from it. Since following context confirmed the appropriateness of the miscues, she left most of them uncorrected. She was reading not to identify words, but to get meaning.

The same is true of Jay, the sixth grader whose miscues on the O. Henry passage we examined in Chapter 4. Jay made 18 miscues but corrected only 3 of them: miscue numbers 4, 9, and 17. With the exception of miscue 4, all of Jay's miscues fit with both the preceding and the following grammar and meaning. Furthermore, both Anne and Jay read their respective passages fluently and confidently, and both recalled almost every detail of what they had read.

Is it reasonable, then, to conclude that Anne cannot read *Little Circus Dog* independently because she correctly identified only 92 percent of the words in a sample passage? Or that Jay cannot read "Jimmy Hayes and Muriel" independently because he correctly identified only 91 percent of the words in a sample passage?

These examples surely ought to make us question the notion that reading means identifying words. Over and over again, miscue analysis shows that the *crucial* difference between good readers and poor readers is not the quantity of their miscues, but the *quality*. Almost all readers make some use of semantic and especially syntactic cues, but the very poorest readers tend to read almost one word at a time, as if each word stood in a list rather than in a sentence. They painfully sound words out, often producing a nonword or a real word that is inappropriate to the meaning of the text. Or they choose a grapho/phonemically similar word from their stock of sight words, again often producing a word whose meaning is inappropriate. Because they concentrate too much on surface structure (the words), they are not very proficient at getting either the surface structure or the deep structure (the meaning). In contrast, the best readers tend to read for meaning rather than for words; they use only as much surface structure as necessary to get the deep structure.

GETTING THE WORDS

There are at least two basic objections to thinking of reading as involving the precise identification of words. One objection is that getting the words does not necessarily result in getting the meaning. The other is that getting the meaning is usually possible without getting all the words.

We have already seen some evidence for both of these objections. In Chapter 2 we began to see the inadequacy of the notion that once words are identified, sentence meaning will take care of itself. In Chapters 3 and 4 the various activities should have suggested that readers can get the essential meaning of a text without identifying all the words, an observation which is supported by our examination of Anne's and Jay's miscues. Our own experience as readers, too, typically supports the notion that the meaning of a text can be understood without identifying all the words.

It was shown in Chapter 4 that the use of context facilitates word identification, so that getting the meaning helps us to get the words. We also saw that less proficient readers may have difficulty recognizing familiar words in unfamiliar contexts, but even when they can recognize the individual words, both nonproficient and proficient readers may have difficulty getting the meaning of the whole sentence.

Comprehension can be thwarted by a variety of factors. Consider, for example, the following sentences. What might cause a problem with comprehension, even when the words are identified correctly?

1. She had a cramp in the calf of her leg.
2. Harley will chair the meeting.
3. Mom and Dad are playing bridge tonight.

4. He can't cut the mustard.
5. We should be proud of our flag.
6. They fed her dog biscuits.
7. The mayor asked the police to stop drinking.

The word *calf* may be a problem in sentence 1, if readers are familiar only with the animal type of calf. The word *chair* may be a problem in sentence 2, if readers are familiar only with its use as a noun. The word *bridge* may be a problem in sentence 3, if readers are not familiar with the card game: are Mom and Dad playing "London Bridge Is Falling Down," or what? In sentence 4, readers familiar with the word *mustard* may nevertheless fail to understand the idiomatic expression *cut the mustard*. And in sentence 5, readers may not understand that the sentence is supposed to be metaphorical rather than literal: it is not really the flag itself that we are to be proud of, but that for which the flag stands. In sentences 6 and 7, the problem is that the sentences are syntactically ambiguous. Did they feed biscuits to her dog, or did they feed dog biscuits to her? And are the police supposed to stop their own drinking, or are they supposed to stop others from drinking? (The last two examples are from Brause 1977, p. 41.)

When children are reading aloud, it is all too easy to assume that if they identify the words correctly, they are getting the meaning. This is often not the case. Some children do not read for meaning in the first place; they simply try to identify the words. Even good readers may fail to get the meaning if they lack experience with the words, the expressions, or the ideas. Consider your own experience reading technical literature like the generative semantics passage in Chapter 1 or the capital gains or dissipative structures passage in Chapter 2. You too may sometimes find it possible to identify the words of a sentence without getting the meaning.

Still other kinds of evidence support the point that getting the words does not necessarily result in getting the meaning. For example: Given two synonymous sentences, one may be harder to comprehend than the other, and perhaps impossible for some readers to comprehend. This fact is obvious when the two sentences contain words of differing sophistication, as in *They have a high death rate* versus *They have a high mortality rate*. Different syntactic patterns can also be a factor. Consider the following pairs of sentences. In each pair, which sentence would be somewhat harder for most readers to comprehend? Why?

That Bob didn't know his way around was obvious.
It was obvious that Bob didn't know his way around.

He gave the son who lives in California all his stamps.
He gave all his stamps to the son who lives in California.

Jimmy, who plays with me every day, is my best friend.
Jimmy plays with me every day, and he is my best friend.

Various kinds of studies suggest that in each pair the first sentence would typically be harder to comprehend. The first sentence places a greater burden upon short-term memory: it requires us to hold a fairly lengthy construction in mind while processing something else. Take, for example, the third sentence pair, about Jimmy. With the first sentence of the pair, we must hold the adjective clause in memory while trying to find out the main point about Jimmy: that he is my best friend. The second sentence about Jimmy is really two sentences, grammatically. It is easier to comprehend because we can process first one independent clause and then the other.

The following pairs of sentences also illustrate the fact that two sentences may not be equally easy to comprehend, even though they are synonymous and contain the same or nearly the same words. In each pair, which sentence would be somewhat harder to comprehend? Why?

> They took a Thanksgiving turkey to the woman down the street.
> They took a Thanksgiving turkey to the woman who lives down the street.
>
> They thought Sam should know the truth.
> They thought that Sam should know the truth.
>
> He didn't remember having done it himself.
> He didn't remember that he had done it himself.
>
> Ask Mary what to feed the dog.
> Ask Mary what you should feed the dog.

In each pair, the first sentence would be harder for most people to comprehend because it is less explicit in signaling the underlying relations among the words. Note that the harder sentence in each pair is the shorter one, not the longer. The longer versions may be easier because they contain syntactic markers (like *who* and *that*) to help signal the deep structure, the meaning.

In a particular context, of course, a "difficult" sentence might be easy to comprehend, or an "easy" sentence might become difficult. But given two synonymous sentences in isolation, with the same or nearly the same words, one sentence may still be harder to comprehend than the other. Less proficient readers may have trouble even identifying the words, particularly in the structurally difficult sentences. But even those readers who have no trouble with word identification will find it somewhat more difficult to process sentences which place a considerable burden on short-term memory or which are not very explicit in signaling underlying relations. When structure is a deterrent rather than a help, even relatively proficient readers may sometimes get the words but not the meaning.

The difficulty of getting the meaning is perhaps most humorously illustrated by some of the early attempts at computer translation of sentences. In the mid- to late 1950s and early 1960s, American scientists were trying to catch up with Russian space technology. In order to test the feasibility of translating Russian technical literature by computer, linguists first tried word-by-word translation of sentences into Russian and then back into English. But even when the computer was programmed to choose word meanings that were compatible with each other, the retranslations were unsatisfactory. Whether fictitious or real, the following examples illustrate the early difficulties with computer translation (taken from Malmstrom et al. 1965):

Input sentence	*Output sentence*
Mary suspended for youthful prank.	Mary hung for juvenile delinquency.
The spirit is willing but the flesh is weak.	The liquor is good but the meat is rotten.

Even though not strictly translating word for word, the computer programs were not adequate to preserve the meaning of the original. Small wonder, then, that as early as 1956, "it became obvious that a mere word-for-word translation was so poor as to be nearly worthless" (Yngve 1962, p. 71).

So it is with reading: word-by-word reading and word identification are inadequate. And one of the reasons is that getting the words does not necessarily result in getting the meaning.

GETTING THE MEANING

Word-by-word reading is inappropriate as well as inadequate, in part because context aids in word identification and in part because getting the essential meaning of a sentence is usually possible without getting all the words. We will deal first with the latter observation, then discuss how surface structure is lost from short-term memory as deep structure is "chunked" into long-term memory.

Even proficient readers make miscues, because they are constantly trying to predict what will come next. It may help you realize how much the reader contributes to the task of reading if you think about how you read storybooks to children. If you are like most adults, you may often change the syntax and vocabulary to something more comprehensible and familiar to the child.

To further explore how proficient readers alter the surface structure of a text, you might try the following experiment with someone you consider to be a reasonably proficient reader. Without giving any hint of your purpose, have him or her read the following passage aloud, while you take careful note of any miscues that are made. The passage is from Zachary Ball's *Bristle Face* (1962, p. 75), discussed in Rigg (1978, p. 287):

> He nodded. "Some good mud cats in there. That bluff you speak of, I denned me a bear in the rocks up there oncet."
> "A bear! When was that? Lately?"
> He chuckled. "Naw, that was way back yonder, when I was a boy, no older'n you. Ain't been no bear around here for sixty year, about. That was the last one ever I heard of hereabouts."

For those whose dialect is different from this rural mountain speech, "sixty years" for *sixty year* is a common miscue. As I checked this quote for accuracy, I first read

"I ever" for *ever I*, changing the syntactic pattern to one more common in my speech. Your reader may have made other miscues that preserve the deep structure but change the surface structure to a more familiar pattern.

A second dialect passage may again help demonstrate the fact that we do not necessarily have to get all the words right in order to get the meaning. If possible, try this passage on yet another reader, someone who does not know your purpose. The passage is from Claude Brown's *Manchild in the Promised Land* (1965, p. 39):

> "Seem like nobody can't make him understand. I talk to him, I yell at him, I whip his ass, but it don't do no good. His daddy preach to him, he yell at him, he beat him so bad sometimes, I gotta run in the kitchen and git that big knife at him to stop him from killin' that boy. You think that might break him outta those devilish ways he got? Child, that scamp'll look Jesus dead in the eye when he standin' on a mountain of Bibles and swear to God in heaven he ain't gon do it no more. The next day, or even the next minute, that little lyin' Negro done gone and did it again—and got a mouthful-a lies when he git caught."

Among the numerous possible dialect miscues here, the more common are "he's got" for *he got*, and "he's standin'" for *he standin'*. Another is "gonna" for *gon*, which should be pronounced with a nasalized vowel and no final consonant. You may also find that your reader adds third person singular verb endings, saying, for example, "seems" for *seem*, "yells" for *yell*, and "beats" for *beat*. With miscues such as these, the reader has gotten the meaning without getting all the words entirely "right." Indeed, it is *because* the reader has gotten the meaning that he or she makes such miscues.

The Loss of Surface Structure

As the dialect passages suggest, an author's surface structure can be partially lost through "translation." The reader grasps the author's meaning, but expresses it in his or her alternative surface structure.

What about the loss of surface structure when the passage conforms more closely to standard written English? The following exercise should help you answer that question. Read through the following passage twice, trying to fix it verbatim in your mind. Then write the sentences as you remember them, without looking back at the original. The passage is from Graham Greene's *The Power and the Glory* (1940, p. 139):

> The young men and women walked round and round the plaza in the hot electric night: the men one way, the girls another, never speaking to each other. In the northern sky the lightning flapped. It was like a religious ceremony which had lost all meaning, but at which they still wore their best clothes.

You may have found that you could not recall all of the passage after just two readings; this is indeed typical. But in trying to recall as much as possible, you probably preserved the essential meaning, making only or mostly superficial changes in surface structure. Among the more common changes are these:

"around" for *round*	"flashed" for *flapped*
"women" for *girls*	"that" for *which*
"the other" for *another*	"to which" for *at which*

In addition, it is common to find the first sentence divided into two sentences, or even three:

> The young men and women walked round and round the plaza in the hot electric night. The men went one way and the girls another. They never spoke to each other.

Obviously the wording and sentence structure may be changed in several other ways while still preserving the essential meaning. Most of the deep structure is retained, but some of the surface structure is lost.

There is perhaps no definitive answer to the question of precisely how fast surface structure is lost, but an experiment by Sachs sheds some light on this question. The experimental subjects were told that as they listened to short passages, each passage would be interrupted and a sentence from somewhere in the passage would be more or less repeated. The subjects were to decide whether the sentence had been repeated word for word, whether it had been repeated with some change in meaning, or whether it had been repeated with some change in syntactic form. Sachs notes, for example, that after eighty syllables of interpolated material, seven of the eight subjects recognized the difference in *meaning* between the following two sentences:

> *Original*
> There he met an archaeologist, Howard Carter, who urged him to join in the search for the tomb of King Tut.

> *"Repeated"*
> There he met an archaeologist, Howard Carter, and urged him to join in the search for the tomb of King Tut.

Though signaled by only a one-word difference, the meaning change in the "repetition" was relatively easy to detect. But with a second "repetition," only one of the eight experimental subjects recognized the difference in syntactic *form* between the original sentence and the following:

> *"Repeated"*
> There he met an archaeologist, Howard Carter, who urged that he join in the search for the tomb of King Tut.

The change from *urged him to join in* to *urged that he join in* went relatively unnoticed. Slight differences from the original sentence tended to be recognized if they affected the meaning, but not if they affected the form alone. After about one-half second, the subjects' recall of surface structure was no longer reliable (Sachs 1967).

As deep structure is chunked into increasingly larger units for storage in long-term memory, surface structure is lost from short-term memory.

The Storage of Deep Structure

Much of what we hear or read either is immediately forgotten or is integrated with our previous experiences and beliefs. We often forget what we have heard or read, or else remember only the broad gist, often in garbled and distorted form. I once experienced this phenomenon in trying to cite an experiment in a letter I was writing to the editor of our local newspaper. At first I could not locate the source of my information, so I decided to take a chance and rely on memory. Here is what I wrote:

> I am reminded of an experiment in which a Russian investigator tried teaching a young child the word for ''doll.'' The child still had not learned the word after the investigator had repeated it a thousand times. But when he introduced the word in the context of a game, the child learned the word within ten minutes.

About two weeks after my letter to the editor was published, I finally ran across the discussion of this experiment in a book I had read a year before. Sure enough, I had gotten most of the details wrong, yet reported the general gist of the discussion.[3]

How is it that we move from a specific surface structure to a generalized and often distorted representation of deep structure? There is no simple answer, but psycholinguistic research does suggest certain interesting possibilities.

We know that surface structure is stored in what is called *short-term memory* and that this working memory can hold only about five to nine chunks of information at a time. With verbal information, the upper limit seems to be around five chunks: we can hold in memory about five unrelated letters, or four or five related words, or even three or four related and familiar phrases or short sentences (see Miller 1956, pp. 90–95). Short-term memory accepts a new chunk of information about every quarter second; this may explain why our eye fixations are normally about one-quarter second long. As short-term memory accepts more chunks of information, the information is either lost or rechunked into larger units for processing into long-term memory. Our so-called *long-term memory* accepts a new chunk of information about every three to five seconds.

There is a fair amount of evidence to suggest that the clause is the major syntactic unit into which verbal material is initially rechunked, and the major unit from which meaning is initially determined. Some of the evidence comes from laboratory experiments, while other evidence comes from studies of reading miscues.

One of the more interesting experiments involved pairs of sentences like this:

> Now that artists are working in oil, prints are rare.
> Now that artists are working fewer hours, oil prints are rare.

Each subject listened to one or the other of these sentences and was then asked whether or not the word *oil* occurred in the sentence heard. Those who heard the first sentence took longer to respond. Note that the word *oil* was four words from the end of the sentence in each case. But with the first sentence, the word *oil* occurred not in the clause just heard, but in the preceding one. Those who heard the first sentence seem to have mentally closed off that first clause, making it harder for them to acknowledge that they had indeed heard the word *oil* (Caplan 1972). Though the experiment is hardly conclusive, it at least suggests that verbal material is rechunked into clausal units as it is processed into long-term memory.

Further evidence comes from the accumulation of the first ten years' research into reading miscues. As Kenneth Goodman notes, the clause seems to be a more significant unit than the sentence. Readers sometimes change sentence boundaries, making one sentence into two, two sentences into one, or shifting a dependent clause from one sentence to another. In virtually all cases, however, the clause boundaries remain intact. Consider the following examples (from K. Goodman 1973, *Theoretically Based Studies*, pp. 141 and 236, and K. S. Goodman 1976, "What We Know about Reading," pp. 60–61):

Text	*Reader*
It must have been around midnight when I drove home, and as I approached the gates of the bungalow I switched off the headlamps of the car . . .	It must have been around midnight when I drove home. As I approached the gates of the bungalow I switched off the headlamps of the car . . .
The boys fished. Then they cooked their catch.	The boys fished and then they cooked their catch.
Then Billy and his father built a summer house. They covered it . . .	When Billy and his father built a summer house, they covered it . . .
It must have been around midnight when I drove home . . .	It must have been around midnight. When I drove home . . .
It was fun to go to school. When he wasn't in school he skated with his friends.	It was fun to go to school when he wasn't in school. He skated with his friends.

Such shifts in sentence organization usually cause no change in meaning, but even where there is a meaning change, the clause boundaries remain intact. Such examples suggest that the clause is a significant unit in the rechunking of verbal information into increasingly larger and more global units.

As we process clauses, we apparently extract the underlying propositions for storage in long-term memory. Consider the following example:

The ants in the kitchen ate the sweet jelly which was on the table.

The sentence contains two clauses and four underlying "propositions" (simple, basic statements):

The ants were in the kitchen.
The jelly was on the table.
The jelly was sweet.
The ants ate the jelly.

As you might suspect, the proposition we are most likely to retain in memory is the major one, expressed by the main surface structure subject, verb, and direct object: *The ants ate the jelly.* It is possible to retain more propositions from the original sentence, however, and Bransford and his associates have discovered some interesting things about the way we combine related propositions when we store them in memory.

Bransford and Franks first took the four propositions just cited and incorporated them in a set of six sentences: two sentences that included only one of the propositions above, two that included two of the propositions, and two that included three of the propositions. The following are examples:

> The ants were in the kitchen.   (one proposition)
> The ants ate the sweet jelly. (two propositions)
> The ants ate the sweet jelly which was on the table.   (three propositions)

After listening to the set of six sentences (and to three other similar sets), subjects were presented with additional sentences and asked which ones they had heard before. The additional set contained some of the sentences actually heard, as well as some other sentences embodying one, two, or three of the original propositions. In addition, subjects were presented with a sentence embodying all four of the original propositions: *The ants in the kitchen ate the sweet jelly which was on the table.* People were most confident that they had heard the sentence including all four of the propositions, even though they had never heard this sentence at all. They were less confident of having heard the three-proposition sentences, still less confident of the two-proposition sentences, and least confident of the one-proposition sentences (Bransford and Franks 1971). From the six sentences they had actually heard, these people seem to have determined the four underlying propositions and integrated them into a coherent whole.

This and subsequent experiments are powerful evidence for the view that the mind actively constructs meaning from what is heard and read (see, for example, the summaries in Palermo 1978, pp. 161–67).

At first, such experiments were undertaken with adults. More recent studies show much the same results with children (for example, Blachowicz 1977–78 and Pearson 1974–75). Blachowicz worked with children ranging from second grade through seventh grade, as well as with adults. She presented her subjects with ten short, written paragraphs, such as:

> The birds sat on the branch.
> A hawk flew over it.
> The birds were robins.

Less than five minutes after the original paragraphs were taken away from the readers, they were given a set of forty sentences, with four related to each of the original ten paragraphs. The task was to indicate whether the sentence had or had not been read before. There was a strong tendency for all subjects to "recognize" not only sentences they had actually read, but also sentences that reflected a reasonable inference from what was actually read. In the preceding example, subjects claimed to have read not only *The birds sat on the branch*, but also *A hawk flew over the birds* (Blachowicz 1977–78). The readers' mental construct of the paragraph included more than what they had read. They used their real world knowledge to supplement and interpret the information actually presented.

Meaning in Review

We have come a long way from the starting point of this section, the observation that it is usually possible to get the essential meaning of a sentence without getting all the words. This suggests, of course, that it may be inappropriate for teachers to insist that precise identification of every word is necessary if one is to get the meaning. And this suggestion is further supported, somewhat indirectly, by the fact that we lose the details of surface structure within about one-half second anyway: our memory for the precise words and constructions is no longer very reliable. We have determined the underlying propositions and chunked the information into a more global mental representation, losing at least some of the surface structure in the process. Koestler (1969) offers a succinct example of how the spoken word resolves itself into increasingly more abstract mental representations for the listener, just as the written word does for the reader:

> You watch a television play. The exact words of each actor are forgotten by the time he speaks his next line, and only their meaning remains; the next morning you can only remember the sequence of scenes which constituted the story; after a month, all you remember is that it was about a gangster on the run or about two men and a woman on a desert island. (p. 201)

In a few months, you may not remember the movie at all, yet it has somehow affected your available gangster-movie schema or your love-triangle schema.

THE (UN)IMPORTANCE OF WORD IDENTIFICATION

In the commonsense view, words stand for things. It is rare for a "thing" to be designated by one and only one word, however. Look, for example, at the italicized words and phrases in the following sentences:

> "Here, *Daisy*."
> "Don't let *the dog* in."
> "Look at *'er* go!"
> "*She's a handsome animal*."

All of these expressions and more could be used to designate a particular dog. Usually more than one word or expression can be used to designate an entity; more than one word can be used to express an action; and so forth. As speakers and writers, we choose whichever word best suits our immediate purpose. And as listeners and readers, we may well substitute a contextually equivalent word or expression for that of the original.

One example is Jay's substitution of "toad" for *frog* in the O. Henry story "Jimmy Hayes and Muriel":

toad
Out of it crawled a horned frog.

toads
I've seen plenty of them horny frogs . . .

Though Jay's term was different, it still designated the same entity: Muriel. Like me, Jay had probably heard of horned toads but not of horned frogs. Instead of reflecting a loss of meaning, his substitution showed that he got the essential meaning of the author but translated it into something that made more sense to him.[4]

Especially common is the substitution of an appropriate pronoun for the noun to which it refers, as was done by a second grader reading the following passage from Bernard Wiseman's *Morris Has a Cold* (1978):

Boris said,

"Beds do not jump.

Beds do not run.

Beds just stand still."

"Why?" asked Morris.
they
"Are beds lazy?"

In this context, it was perfectly reasonable to substitute the pronoun "they" for the repeated noun *beds*. Jay made a similar miscue, substituting one pronoun for another:

her
"Take it over there and see," said Hayes.

In context, "her" made perfectly good sense, because Muriel was female.

It is mainly proficient readers who make substitutions like these. The percentage of miscues involving pronouns and function words tends to *increase* as one becomes a more proficient reader (see K. Goodman 1973, *Theoretically Based Studies*, pp. 165–66 and p. 184). Insofar as they serve to signal relations between words, pronouns are like function words. And we can often supply many of the function words ourselves, if we are getting the essential meaning. That is, the content words, word order, and the total context are often adequate to signal many of the relations among the words in a sentence. To test this, try to fill in the function words missing from the following paragraph (the original is from the *New York Times*, May 5, 1970, p. 17):

███crack███rifle volley cut ███suddenly still air. It appeared ██go on,
███solid volley, ███perhaps ██full minute ███little longer.
    Some ██students dived███ground, crawling ███grass ██terror.
Others stood shocked ██half crouched, apparently believing ███troops were
firing███ ██air. Some ███rifle barrels ███pointing upward.
    ███top ██hill ██corner ██Taylor Hall, ██student crumpled
over, spun sideways ███fell ███ground, shot ██head.
    ███firing stopped, ██slim girl, wearing ██cowboy shirt ██faded
jeans, ██lying face down ███road ███edge ███parking lot, blood
pouring ██ ██the macadam, ███10 feet ███reporter.

People usually find they can supply reasonable function words, often the precise one that was omitted from the original.[5] Just as words can often be identified from only part of the visual information normally available, sentences can often be understood from fewer than the total number of words normally available. We are able to recreate part of the surface structure from our understanding of the deep structure.

If meaning is the goal of reading, we hardly need to insist that every word be identified accurately. Instead of demanding an accurate rendition of the surface structure, we might better call for a reasonable interpretation of the deep structure.

Some will argue that there are times when it is vital to read every word accurately, and this is probably true. In savoring a poem, for example, one often dwells on the significance of virtually every word. And surface accuracy may be important, in getting the deep structure of warranties and guarantees, application forms, recipes and other directions, or legal contracts. But even with such materials, surface accuracy is not as important or as helpful as commonly supposed. The proof of this is in our everyday experience. Many of us have had the frustrating experience of being able to read all the words in a set of directions or a contract, yet been unable to determine precisely what was meant. We are often able to get the surface structure, yet unable to get the deep structure—the intended meaning.

An experience of my own seems pertinent; a few years ago I was asked to render an expert linguistic opinion in a court case involving a life insurance claim. The deceased had died piloting his own plane. The linguistic question involved the following exclusion clause in the insurance policy, and in particular the word *passenger*. The insured person was not covered by the policy

> While engaged in or taking part in aeronautics and/or aviation of any de-
> scription or resulting from being in any aircraft except while a passenger in
> an aircraft previously tried, tested, and approved.

The insurance company claimed that the word *passenger* excluded the pilot of a plane, and hence the man was not covered by the policy at the time of his death. The family claimed that the man *was* covered at the time of his death, because the pilot of a plane is also one of its passengers. Both parties agreed on the word, but not on the meaning of the word. And it was a crucial $50,000 difference.[6]

Once again the conclusion seems clear: what is important is not necessarily the surface structure, but the deep structure. The proficient reader reads more for meaning than for surface detail.

MISCUES REVISITED

It is true, of course, that many proficient readers make relatively few miscues of any sort. However, the most *crucial* difference between good readers and poor readers is not the quantity of their miscues, but the *quality*.

Poor readers' miscues show more attention to grapho/phonemic cues than to meaning (e.g., Feldman and Feldman's 1983 study of elementary-level "learning disabled" students). In contrast, good readers' miscues typically preserve meaning, fitting both the preceding and the following syntactic and semantic context. For another example, try to read the next passage as the sixth grader Billy originally did, complete with all his miscues. After one or two attempts, you will probably find that you can read the passage fluently and with expression, since most of the miscues fit the given context. The passage is from Joanne Williamson's *The Glorious Conspiracy* (1961, pp. 17–18):

Tŭlly ①

Life went on as usual. Mr. Tully beat me more often

and more cruelly than Mr. Coffin had (done.) ② But I was

used to that now. And there were ways a poor boy could

find of having a bit of fun once in a while—like daring

the other apprentices to steal (a bit ©) of ③ from the shops and

watching to see if they got caught. If they did get

caught, they would be hanged at Gallows Mill, so that was

a real dare. Or one could throw bits of garbage in the way

of gentlemen in wigs and hide around the corner to see

them slip and fall (down) ④. There wasn't much time for

such sports, so we made the most of what time we had. *though* ⑤

My granddad had become pretty sick about this time.

He had the lung fever. He had had it a long while, but ⑥

now it was beginning to be bad, and Aunt Bet was begin-

ning to look frightened. I began to be scared, too, hearing

him cough so much and seeing him look so pale and ill.

And when I got through work at eight or nine of the *o'clock* ⑦

clock, I took to hanging about the streets, tired and hun-

gry as I was, hiding out of the way of the watchmen, so ⑧

as not to go home till I had to. I knew this made Aunt Bet

even more frightened; and that made me ashamed and

even more anxious not to go home. *to* ⑨

One night after I had scrubbed down Mr. Tully's fish

house and come out into the street, I saw a man come out ⑩

of a chandler's shop. I knew who he was—Mr. Watson, ⑪

a ropemaker and an excellent workman, so everyone said.

to see him ⑫

I didn't want him to see me, for I meant to tell Aunt Bet

that I had been kept late, and go looking for mischief. ⑬

him go by. ⑭

So I hid in a doorway and watched for him to go by.

It is interesting that most of these miscues involve the omission, insertion, or substitution of function words. Since function words are the most predictable part of a sentence, good readers are especially likely to make miscues involving them.

More generally, good readers tend to predict what is coming next. The good readers' miscues usually preserve the essential meaning of the text, and hence they often go uncorrected. However, good readers generally do correct (at least silently) those miscues which are not confirmed by the following context. In contrast, the poorest readers tend to deal with each word almost as if it existed in isolation, paying some attention to syntactic cues but hardly reading for meaning. Hence there is nothing that prompts them to correct their miscues.

Even beginning readers can be good readers, proficient at predicting what is coming next and correcting those miscues that do not make sense in context. The following miscues were made by a boy with only two months of reading instruction. In context each miscue preserves the sense of the original. The sentences are from Mae Knight Clark's *Opening Doors* (1965) and *A Magic Box* (1965):

> *the*
> Get a ball, Mary.

> Who rides with Mike?

> *can ride*
> Mary rides with Mike.

> Mary said, "Play ball, Jeff.
>   *ball*
> Mike and I want to play."

> Mike said, "I can't ride.
>   *Mary and Jeff*
> I can't play with Jeff and Mary.
> *but*
>   I can play ball."

> Velvet will go (on) up the tree.

Though the child has departed somewhat from the surface structure of the original sentences, he has retained the deep structure. In some cases his surface structure is even more explicit in reflecting the deep structure.

All of these examples suggest that having understood the deep structure of a sentence, proficient readers sometimes express it partially in their own words and language patterns. This is demonstrated particularly by miscues that reflect immature language patterns, such as the following one:

sticked
Morris stuck out his tongue.

Fortunately, many teachers are more amused than distressed by such miscues, realizing that the child has understood the meaning of the original.

DIALECT MISCUES

Dialect miscues, on the other hand, are seldom treated with such indulgence. We tend to think that the words on a page must be reproduced in the sound patterns and grammatical patterns of standard English as we know it. Your experience with the dialect passages earlier in this chapter should have helped you see the fallacy of this assumption, though. We saw that in reading a passage like that from *Manchild in the Promised Land*, speakers of a so-called standard dialect will often *add* some of the surface grammatical markers that would be normal for their dialect. Similarly, speakers of other dialects may read a passage written in standard English and *omit* some of the surface grammatical markers that are not always present in their dialect. What we often fail to realize is that such dialect translation would not be possible unless the reader had understood the deep structure of the author's sentence. Actively transacting with the text, the reader has simply expressed it in his or her own surface structure.

Teachers are most disturbed by miscues that reflect a partially different grammatical system: "we was" for *we were*, "he don't have none" for *he doesn't have any*, and so forth. But such miscues as these are relatively rare. The more common grammatical miscues involve just pieces of words, the grammatical endings. Kenneth Goodman and his associates have found, for example, that among inner-city black children, the following are the most common dialect-related miscues that appear to involve grammar. Most of these miscues involve grammatical elements (adapted from K. Goodman and C. Buck 1973, p. 9).[7]

Absence of past tense marker
"look" for *looked*, "call" for *called*, "wreck" for *wrecked*, "love" for *loved*, "pound" for *pounded*, "help" for *helped*, "use" for *used*, "run" for *ran*, "have" for *had*, "keep" for *kept*, "do" for *did*

Absence of plural noun marker
"*thing*" for *things*, "work" for *works*, "story" for *stories*, "prize" for *prizes*

Absence of third person singular verb marker
"*look*" for *looks*, "work" for *works*, "hide" for *hides*

Absence of possessive noun or pronoun marker
"*Freddie*" for *Freddie's*, "Mr. Vine" for *Mr. Vine's*, "one" for *one's*, "it" for *its*

Substitution and omission of forms of *to be*
"was" for *were*, "is" for *are*, "we" for *we're*, "he be talking" for *he'd been talking*

Hypercorrections (the use of two grammatical markers of the same type)
"likeded" for *liked*, "helpeded" for *helped*, "stoppeded" for *stopped*

More recently, Kenneth and Yetta Goodman and their associates have completed a massive study (1978) of miscues among second, fourth, and sixth graders who speak a nonmainstream dialect or who speak English as a second language. The dialect groups were downeast Maine, Mississippi black, Appalachian, and Hawaiian Pidgin. The second-language groups were Texas Spanish, Hawaiian Samoan, Arabic, and Navajo. The most common kind of grammatical miscue, for both the dialect speakers and the English-as-a-Second-Language speakers, was again the absence of grammatical inflections on the ends of words.

From this impressive study in which they examined not only the children's miscues but also their comprehension, the Goodmans concluded that there is "no evidence that inability to cope with Book English is a general problem for any group" (1978, p. 3-5). The students' dialect or language influence is evident in their reading, "but it is not in itself a barrier to comprehension" (p. 3-22).

With oral reading, then, we do not ordinarily need to be concerned about the absence or use of such features as those cited by Goodman and Buck. Such miscues typically reflect not a lack of understanding, but only an alternative surface structure common in the reader's everyday speech. Having understood the deep structure, the reader simply expresses it in an alternative oral form. Such a process is reflected in Figure 5.1.

This model indicates that when reading aloud, our understanding is usually ahead of our voice, as was suggested in Chapter 4. Unless we are having unusual difficulty, we get the meaning *before* speaking the words, rather than vice versa.

Given this fact as well as the specific research into dialect miscues and English-as-a-Second-Language (ESL) miscues, the Goodmans point out that special reading materials are not needed for *any* of the low-status dialect groups studied, nor is special methodology needed (p. 8-5). What *is* needed, however, is a positive attitude toward reading miscues in general and toward dialect and ESL miscues in particular.

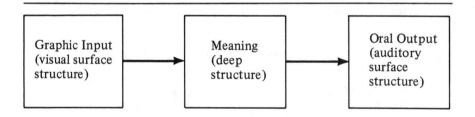

FIGURE 5.1 *A simplified model of proficient oral reading*

This point can hardly be emphasized enough. In a survey in which 94 Midwestern elementary teachers rated miscues as acceptable or unacceptable, Tovey (1979) found that when miscues were syntactically and semantically appropriate in the teacher's dialect, only 16 percent of the teachers would not accept the miscues. However, when the miscues reflected translation into the reader's dialect, 60 percent of the teachers would not accept the miscues. An earlier study by Cunningham produced similar results (1977). Teachers, then, must have the knowledge, the experience, and the *attitudes* which will enable them to recognize and accept miscues that merely reflect an alternative spoken dialect. This is essentially one of the conclusions that can be drawn from the famed Ann Arbor decision of 1979, in which a group of black children won their court suit charging that the school had failed to take their home language into account in teaching them to read (see *Ann Arbor Decision*, p. 9 in particular).

In his excellent book on the Black English dialect, Robbins Burling offers some particularly pertinent remarks (1973, pp. 158–59):

> What should a teacher do when her children make such "mistakes"? She may be willing to accept the idea that children should be permitted to read aloud in their own natural pronunciation, but grammatical changes [or apparent grammatical changes] seem far more dramatic. To most teachers they look like out-and-out errors and they seem to warrant correction. Nevertheless, these "errors" give far better evidence of comprehension than would more literal and "accurate" recitation of the words. Word-for-word recitation may amount to no more than parroting. It may be no different from reading a word list in which the words have no relation to one another. Conversion to nonstandard forms, so long as the meaning is preserved, amounts to a kind of translation that would be quite impossible if the child did not understand. If reading with comprehension is our goal, then these "errors" prove that we have been successful.

At least some research indicates that it is the *best* readers who produce the most dialect-based miscues (B. Hunt 1974–75), supporting the observation that good readers tend to express the author's deep structure in a surface structure which is partially their own. They are less concerned with surface detail than with meaning.

THE READING PROCESS IN REVIEW

Reading is commonly viewed as first and foremost a matter of identifying words. In this chapter, however, we have seen a number of reasons for challenging that view:

Getting the words of a sentence does not necessarily result in getting the meaning.

Within about half a second or less, we have already begun to forget some of the details of sentence surface structure. What we "remember" is not necessarily the words or their grammatical organization, but the meaning. We determine the underlying propositions from the clauses of the text and construct a global representation of the meaning. This mental representation is influenced and even distorted by our prior knowledge, beliefs, and experiences.

All readers make some miscues, but good and poor readers differ in the quality of their miscues. The miscues of poor readers often suggest that they are attending mainly to surface structure, although even poor readers usually show some concern for meaning. The miscues of good readers usually suggest that they are attending mainly to deep structure.

Getting the meaning is usually possible without identifying all the words.

Thus there seems to be little justification for the common or "commonsense" view that precise word identification is a necessary prerequisite to understanding.

It is true, of course, that many proficient readers will make no more than one or two miscues per hundred words, at most: there does tend to be *some* correlation between accurate word identification and good comprehension. However, this correlation is not nearly so strong as most people suppose. For one thing, many nonproficient readers can reproduce surface structure (identify the words) with reasonable accuracy, even though they get little meaning from what they read. And a surprising number of readers can make numerous miscues and still get the essential meaning of the text. Remember, too, that no two people will ever "get" exactly the same meaning anyway; the meaning depends in part on the schemas that the reader brings to his or her transaction with the text. Thus accurate word identification is not an appropriate criterion for measuring reading ability. Reading is not an exact process, and we should not define or measure it as if it were. The proficient *and efficient* reader uses only as much surface structure as necessary to get to deep structure.

As Harper and Kilarr have so incisively put it, the view that precise word identification is necessary for understanding "is like the theory of the world being flat during the time of Columbus" (1977, p. 918).

ACTIVITIES AND PROJECTS FOR FURTHER EXPLORATION

1. The passage below is from Joan Baratz and William Stewart's dialect reader *Friends* (1970, pp. 24–30).[8]

> One morning Ollie and Leroy was getting ready to go to school. Leroy he put on one of Ollie sock 'cause he lost his. Ollie say, "Boy give me my sock" but Leroy wouldn't give it to him. Leroy say, "It's my sock." But Ollie know it wasn't 'cause it wasn't even the same color as Leroy other sock. Ollie kept on begging and begging Leroy for the sock. But Leroy still wouldn't give it to him. Ollie hit Leroy. And they got to fighting. Leroy hit Ollie in the nose and it start to bleeding. Then, Ollie got real mad and hit Leroy on his arm as hard as he could. Leroy hollered real loud. Big Momma must of heard them fighting 'cause she come running in the room and she stop the fight. She say, "All right, who start this mess?" Ollie say Leroy start it and Leroy say Ollie start it. Big Momma

say, "I done told you about fighting before. Since don't nobody know who start this mess I'm just going to whip both of you."

It might be interesting to try one or both of the following activities with this passage:

a. Have one or more persons read the first four sentences of the passage twice, then try to write down exactly what they have read. Look to see what changes they have made in the authors' surface structure. Have they translated some of the patterns of the text into the patterns of their own dialect?

b. Have one or more persons read the passage aloud; if possible, try it with both children and adults. Listen to hear what dialect miscues they make. Again, have they translated some of the patterns of the text into the patterns of their own dialect?

2. To compare proficient reading with nonproficient reading, try our blacked-out *New York Times* passage (p. 127) with both good and poor readers of about junior high age or beyond. First, be certain that each person can identify all of the content words in the selection; if necessary, read these words for the person one or more times. Then ask the person to write in the missing function words (you may want to use a photocopy of the passage for this purpose). Are the good and poor readers equally able to supply reasonable possibilities for the missing words? If not, what does this suggest about their differing approaches to the task of reading?

3. If you know of any teachers with widely differing instructional approaches and/ or definitions of reading, it might be interesting to compare their reactions to Anne's miscues (p. 114) or Jay's (pp. 97–99) or Billy's (pp. 128–29), or all of them. Does the teacher think most of these miscues are "serious," a matter for concern? If not, why not? If so, what kind of instructional help would the teacher recommend? Compare the responses from the different teachers.

4. This group activity emphasizes that the same ideas can be expressed in different ways. Working separately, each participant should first follow the directions below. The sentence-combining activity is from R. O'Donnell and K. Hunt, as printed in Fagan et al. 1975, p. 201; see also Hunt's 1970 monograph, pp. 64–65. Once you have all completed this part of the activity, compare your results. Did you indeed find different ways to express the same ideas? What are some of the possible implications for reading?

Aluminum

Directions: Read the passage all the way through. You will notice that the sentences are short and choppy. Study the passage, and then rewrite it in a better way. You may combine sentences, change the order of words, and omit words that are repeated too many times. But try not to leave out any of the information.

Aluminum is a metal. It is abundant. It has many uses. It comes from bauxite. Bauxite is an ore. Bauxite looks like clay. Bauxite contains aluminum. It contains several other substances. Workmen extract these other substances from the bauxite. They grind the bauxite. They put it in tanks. Pressure is in the tanks. The other substances form a mass. They remove the mass. They use filters. A liquid remains. They put it through several other processes. It finally yields a chemical. The chemical is powdery. It is white. The chemical is alumina. It is a mixture. It contains aluminum. It contains oxygen. Workmen separate the aluminum from the oxygen. They use electricity. They finally produce a metal. The metal is light. It has a luster. The luster is bright. The luster is silvery. This metal comes in many forms.

READINGS FOR FURTHER EXPLORATION

Goodman, Yetta. November 1974. I Never Read Such a Long Story Before. *English Journal* 63: 65–71. Highly recommended by my students, this is "must" reading for teachers at all levels.

Allen, P. David. 1976. Implications for Reading Instruction. *Findings of Research in Miscue Analysis: Classroom Implications*. Ed. P. D. Allen and D. J. Watson. Urbana, Ill.: ERIC Clearinghouse on Reading and Communication Skills and the National Council of Teachers of English, 107–12. More "must" reading. In only a few pages, Allen has provided a number of valuable suggestions for teachers.

D'Angelo, Karen. January 1982. Correction Behavior: Implications for Reading Instruction. *The Reading Teacher* 35: 395–98. Discusses research demonstrating that good readers consistently correct higher percentages of miscues than poor readers. Provides nine suggestions for teachers who want to encourage corrections during reading.

Adams, Marilyn Jager. January 1978. Beginning Reading: Theory and Practice. *Language Arts* 55: 19–25. A discussion of the difficulty of determining the underlying syntax and hence the meaning of word groups and phrases.

Davison, Alice, and Robert N. Kantor. 1982. On the Failure of Readability Formulas to Define Readable Texts: A Case Study from Adaptations. *Reading Research Quarterly* 17, ii: 187–209. Though the article itself is not easy to read, it has marvelous examples of how the supposedly easier-to-read adaptations of children's literature that are typically found in basal readers are, in fact, more difficult to comprehend because connections between ideas are missing.

Harber, Jean R. 1981. The Effect of Cultural and Linguistic Differences on Reading Performance. *The Social Psychology of Reading*, 1. Ed. J. R. Edwards, 173–92. Silver Springs, Md.: Institute of Modern Languages. An excellent review article.

Troutman, Denise E., and Julia S. Falk. 1982. Speaking Black English and Reading—Is There a Problem of Interference? *Journal of Negro Education* 51, ii: 123–32. Another excellent discussion of the relationship between Black English, reading, and the teaching of reading.

6

How Is a Socio-Psycholinguistic View of Reading Relevant to Reading Instruction?

A viable theory of reading instruction has to be based on an articulated theory of the reading process.

—Kenneth Goodman

QUESTIONS FOR JOURNALS AND DISCUSSION

1. How do socio-psycholinguistic definitions of reading typically differ from other definitions?

2. How can we demonstrate that for the proficient reader, comprehension is usually ahead of the voice in reading aloud, and that it is not necessary to decode either to overt sound or to "silent speech" in order to get meaning?

3. What are some of the problems with a word-centered approach to reading instruction?

4. What is the difference between reading *skills* and reading *strategies*?

5. How might we differentiate two different word-emphasis approaches, a *subskills* approach and a *skills* approach?

6. What are some of the weaknesses of a skills approach, and how can a typical basal reader lesson be improved to minimize these weaknesses?

7. Why are skills and subskills approaches so popular, and what are some questions we might ask before assuming that these approaches are the best?

8. How is a socio-psycholinguistically based whole-language approach being implemented in the schools?

READING DEFINITIONS REVISITED

The most successful reading instruction is likely to be that which is based on a solid understanding of the reading process itself and to be an approach which promotes rather than thwarts the acquisition of good reading strategies. Therefore, this chapter will review the nature of the reading process and continue discussing some of the implications for reading instruction.

Just as there is no single definition of deep and surface structure, so there is no single socio-psycholinguistic definition of reading. However, it may help to review the major differences between a socio-psycholinguistic view of reading and some of the other common views. Here, then, are three different characterizations of the reading process:

Reading means pronouncing words. That is, reading means going from visible surface structure (written words) to audible surface structure (spoken words).

Reading means identifying words and getting their meaning. That is, reading means going from visible surface structure to deep structure (meaning).

Reading means bringing meaning *to* a text in order to get meaning from it. That is, reading means actively transacting with a text to create meaning. It means using one's schemas and the situational and sociolinguistic context—in short, using all kinds of deep structure—in order to create meaning from surface structure.

The first definition is clearly incompatible with a socio-psycholinguistic view, since it emphasizes the recognition of words rather than the getting of meaning; indeed, it says nothing whatsoever about meaning. The second definition mentions getting meaning but is also inadequate. It implies that sentence meaning can be derived from individual word meanings, whereas the reverse is more often the case: our general understanding of the whole sentence, the context, helps us determine the meaning of the individual words (see Chapters 2 and 5). Further, the definition would remain unsatisfactory even if we were to eliminate this problem by saying "Reading means identifying words *and getting the meaning of the sentence.*" There are three basic problems with this reformulated definition. First, it implies that precise word identification is necessary in order to get meaning, which is ordinarily not so. Second, this definition says nothing about what readers bring *to* a text. It gives no hint of the fact that proficient readers use contexts of all sorts, including their entire store of knowledge and experience, in order to construct meaning as they read. Third, it erroneously implies that meaning resides in the text itself.

The first two definitions reflect what I call an *ink blotter* or *sponge* view of reading. They imply that readers are essentially passive, and that reading is entirely a one-way process, originating in the text and ending in the reader. The reader merely soaks up the words and meanings signaled by the marks on the page. A socio-psycholinguistic view of reading contrasts sharply with this view (see Figure 6.1). Psycholinguists and sociolinguists emphasize the fact that meaning does not reside within the words on the page. If we are to *get* meaning from a text, we must actively create meaning, and to do so we must bring meaning *to* what we read. Hence reading is not a one-way process, but a two-way transaction between the mind of the reader and the language of the text. *The proficient and efficient reader uses nonvisual information (context of all sorts) plus the fewest, most productive visual cues to get deep structure.*

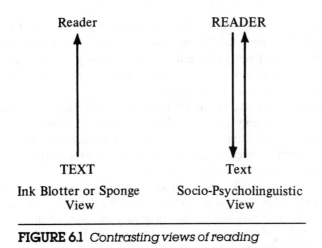

FIGURE 6.1 *Contrasting views of reading*

Some of the major tenets of a psycholinguistic view of reading are as follows:

Constructing meaning is more important than identifying words. Indeed, precise identification of all the words is not usually necessary for getting the meaning.

Reading involves the use of all three language cue systems: syntactic, semantic, and grapho/phonemic. It is both inefficient and ineffective to rely just on the grapho/phonemic system, to deal with each word as if it stood in isolation. Indeed, readers who make effective use of nonvisual information can greatly reduce their need for visual information.

Reading is an active process, a deliberate search for meaning. And indeed, readers cannot get meaning from a text unless they bring meaning to it.

Most socio-psycholinguistic definitions of reading emphasize one or more of these points.

THE (UN)IMPORTANCE OF SOUND IN A SOCIO-PSYCHOLINGUISTIC MODEL

This section is especially for those who have always thought that as readers, we must not only identify all the words, but pronounce them—either aloud or in our heads. The word identification view of reading seems to have gained support from the theory that we necessarily go from the written word to the spoken word and *then* to meaning as we read, a view promulgated by certain structural linguists and by various educators who have followed in their footsteps. Consider, for example, the following statement (Strickland 1964, p. 10):

> The linguist conceives the reading act as that of turning the stimulus of the graphic shapes on a surface back into speech. The shapes represent speech; meaning is not found in the marks but in the speech which the marks represent.

Similar definitions can be found in Soffietti 1955 (p. 69), Bloomfield and Barnhart 1961 (p. 31), and McCracken and Walcutt 1970 (p. xiv). Of course these theorists recognize that there is such a thing as silent reading, but they argue that even in silent reading we to some degree say the words to ourselves. That is, we go from the written word to "silent speech" and then to meaning.

This view has lent credence to the idea that we must identify all the words in order to get meaning. Although for most of us some form of silent speech does often accompany silent reading, the getting of meaning usually *precedes* overt speech and presumably silent speech as well, when we are reading. Hence there is no need to turn written words into spoken words.

Obviously there are varying degrees of silent speech. At one extreme, we have speech which is nearly audible or semi-audible. At the other extreme, we have some sort of articulatory or auditory imagery—perhaps some sort of mental "echo" of the spoken word (Edfeldt 1960, p. 77; Conrad 1972, p. 207).

Before we look at some of the relevant laboratory experiments, you may want to investigate the role of silent speech for yourself. Here is an easy experiment. Read the following words: *wound, lead*, and *tears*. Did you mentally pronounce the words? Most people do, even though there is no way to predict a "correct" pronunciation out of context. Such evidence is informal, of course, but it does strongly suggest that reading is usually accompanied by some form of silent speech.

Another experiment you might try is to ask someone to cross out all the *e*'s in a paragraph or two of prose. Do not tell the person what you are investigating, but have him or her cross out the *e*'s as rapidly as possible. When your subject is through look carefully for the *e*'s that have been missed. Has the person missed more silent *e*'s (as in *hope*) than pronounced *e*'s (as in *seat*)? If so, what does this suggest about the role of silent speech in visual processing?

In a similar laboratory experiment, silent *e*'s were missed nearly four times as often as pronounced *e*'s (Corcoran 1966, p. 658). In a second experiment, *e*'s were systematically omitted from a text and the subject was asked to detect the absence of *e*. Once again, significantly more silent *e*'s were undetected (Corcoran 1967, pp. 851–52). This seems to be fairly strong evidence, then, that most of us commonly "hear," in some sense, the words that we are reading.

An interesting experiment with deaf subjects suggests that reading is often accompanied by some degree of activity in the speech muscles. Though such activity may be invisible to the eye, it can be measured by determining the electrical charge of the muscles: the greater the muscle activity, the greater the electrical charge. Because the deaf people in this experiment communicated through sign language, the experimenter measured the electrical charge in the muscles of the *hands*, rather than in the speech muscles. A control group, people who had no hearing difficulty, showed hand muscle activity in only 31 percent of the tests of abstract thinking, including reading. The deaf subjects showed hand muscle activity in 84 percent of these tests. That is, reading seemed to be accompanied by movement in their speech muscles (Max 1937, p. 335). People who speak "normally" also show a tendency toward some speech muscle activity while reading (Edfeldt 1960, pp. 151–52).

Both common experience and laboratory research suggest, then, that silent reading is often accompanied by some form of silent speech. Silent speech appears to be most evident when our attention is called to individual words and parts of words, as in most of the experiments just mentioned (and in most instructional programs). But the crucial question is whether or not silent speech is a necessary *prelude* to understanding.

The evidence suggests the contrary, that understanding normally precedes vocalization as we are reading aloud. And it seems only logical that the same would be true for silent reading.

Some of the evidence comes from reading miscues. We have seen, for example, that good readers may translate the language of a text into alternative dialect patterns as they read aloud. Similarly the reader's understanding seems to have been ahead of his voice in the following examples:

not getting anything

I'm getting nothing for Christmas.   [a line from a song]

mean inside

"No, no," said Boris. "I don't mean outside."

ⓒ *didn't do*

Boris growled, "That's because you did it the wrong way."

[The reader started to say, "You didn't do it right."]

In each example, the reader grasped the meaning of the original and "translated" it into his own words. Clearly, understanding preceded the overt act of speech.

Such translation is possible in part because our eyes are typically ahead of the word we are focusing on. We can measure this phenomenon by seeing how far the eyes are ahead of the voice when someone is reading aloud. Simply obscure the person's sight of the page (say, by putting your hand over it), and then ask the person what additional words he or she can report. Here are the additional words reported from five trials with a person who was reading a science fiction story:

> but rather because of
> from the galactic rim
> none completely satisfactory
> of the universe
> but as the ship leaves

The shortest stretch of words is *of the universe*, a grammatically complete unit. These examples suggest what research in fact shows: that a reader's *eye-voice span* (EVS) is influenced not only by the difficulty of the material being read, but also by the syntactic structure of whatever follows the word focused upon. The EVS ordinarily extends to the end of the largest grammatical unit possible. On the average, the eyes are about four words ahead of the voice. This helps explain how our understanding can precede overt or silent speech.

Evidence from earlier chapters also suggests that understanding normally comes before vocalization, not after. We have seen, for example, that it is not until we know the word or the structure of the word that we know how to pronounce the *t* and *h* in *father* and *fathead*, or the *p* and *h* in *graph* and *uphill*. With the italicized words in the sentences below, the situation is similar. To see this for yourself, read the sentences aloud:

> She had an ugly *wound* on her cheek.
> The elephant can *lead* the parade.
> Big *tears* rolled down her cheeks.
> Have you *wound* up the string?
> It's made of *lead*.
> Did you see the *tears* in his pants?

We do not know how to pronounce these words until we know something about their meaning. In the case of *wound* and *lead*, we must know their grammatical category; in the case of *tears*, we must know even more specific information about the word. Comprehension must come *before* overt or silent speech.

We have seen, then, that silent reading is often accompanied by some form of silent speech. But we have also seen that silent speech does not seem to be necessary for comprehension, since understanding normally precedes overt speech and presumably covert speech as well. Furthermore, it has been discovered that good readers show less use of silent speech than poorer readers (see, for example, Edfeldt 1960, pp. 153–54; Cleland 1971, pp. 139–40; Bever and Bower 1966, pp. 13–14, 23–24).

It is mostly when we are having difficulty comprehending what we are reading that we engage in silent speech, particularly in the more obvious kinds (like forming the words with our lips or even mumbling them semi-audibly). So instead of being necessary to comprehension, silent speech may often be a sign of comprehension difficulty. The fastest and best readers seem to make the least use of silent speech.

This is not to suggest, of course, that we should avoid associating written words with their spoken counterparts as we help children learn to read. Can you imagine trying to teach a child the meaning of *the, of, pretty, enjoy*, and thousands of other words, without speaking the words aloud? This would be an unnecessarily difficult task. No, of course I am not suggesting that the spoken word has no place in reading instruction. Indeed, I would argue precisely the opposite: that beginning reading instruction should help children associate aurally familiar materials with their written counterparts. But once they know some of the written words, even beginners can go directly from print to meaning. It is not *necessary* to pronounce the words, even mentally, as we read.

APPROACHES TO READING INSTRUCTION REVISITED

Most of the major approaches to beginning reading instruction have one basic element in common: they typically focus on the identification of words. This is true of (1) the sight word approach, which emphasizes the development of a stock of words that can be immediately recognized; (2) the phonics approach, which emphasizes the sounding-out of words; (3) the so-called linguistic approach, which emphasizes the internalizing of regular patterns of spelling/sound correspondence; and (4) the basal reader approach, which initially emphasizes a variety of skills for identifying words.

Even if reading *did* necessarily involve the precise identification of all the words, there would be a major problem with these word-centered approaches. Although supposedly recognizing the importance of context, even the sight word approach and the basal reader approach often encourage children initially to "attack" words as if they stood in isolation.[1] When they cannot recognize a word immediately on sight, children are encouraged to try to pronounce the word, using their knowledge of letter/sound correspondences and, if relevant, their knowledge of bases and affixes (their "structural analysis" skills). Often, they are encouraged to use context only if this procedure has failed, or only as a check on their tentative identification of the word. For identifying words, then, the following sequence is often recommended:

1. Memory for word form: see if you can recognize the word.
2. Word analysis skills: try to pronounce the word, using your knowledge of letter/sound correspondences, plus your knowledge of bases and affixes (if relevant).
3. Context: if the word analysis skills have not worked, use context to get at least the gist of the word, if not the word itself.

Since the resurgence of interest in phonics during the late 1960s, context has often been recommended only as a last resort.[2] We have seen, however, that using context as a last resort is neither efficient nor effective. The proficient reader uses context *first*, to predict what is coming next. By using both preceding syntactic and preceding semantic contexts, the reader is able to reduce his or her dependence upon visual information. On the whole, this makes word identification not only easier but more accurate. Thus to make reading more efficient and effective, we should recommend the following sequence instead of the one just listed:

1. Context: use your entire store of knowledge and experience plus the preceding context in order to predict what might be coming next.
2. The word itself: using only as many visual cues as necessary to confirm or modify your prediction, make a tentative identification of the word.
3. Context: use the following context to confirm or correct your tentative identification of the word.

Such a procedure would certainly help children become proficient readers. Proficient readers predict what is coming next and then confirm or correct their predictions in accordance with what follows.

But remember that proficient reading does not necessarily involve the precise identification of every word in a text, and proficient readers do not necessarily correct those miscues which fit with the context. Hence the second major problem with the various word-centered or word-identification models of reading: they focus on the identification of words, rather than the getting of meaning. Though supposedly a means to an end, word identification becomes an end in itself. And, as we have seen, this is inappropriate for several reasons:

1. Getting the words does not necessarily result in getting the meaning.
2. Within a very short time, we no longer remember surface structure anyway. We "remember" not the precise words or even necessarily the exact ideas of the author, but our own mental construct of what we have read.
3. Good readers read for meaning rather than for the precise identification of all the words.
4. Getting the meaning is usually possible without identifying all the words.

These facts suggest, then, the inadequacy of a word-centered approach to reading instruction. For one thing, such approaches are inefficient: they make reading as difficult as possible, by encouraging children to deal with each word as if it stood in isolation. As a result, even word identification suffers. Further, a word-identification approach distorts the nature of the reading process, inaccurately implying that precise identification of all the words is necessary for getting meaning. As a result, all too many children come to assume that reading means simply identifying words. The supposed means to comprehension becomes an end in itself, and in fact *the* end, for some children. This happens, of course, when children center on the word attack *skills* explicitly taught and fail to use, intuitively, the *strategies* for predicting/ sampling/confirming and correcting that they long ago learned to use in comprehending others' speech.

To clarify, it may help to contrast how teachers from different approaches might respond to children's miscues. Suppose that while reading a story about Jane's father fixing their TV antenna, a child comes to the sentence *Jane's father was on the house.* Now what if the child says "horse" for *house*? Given a sight word approach, a teacher might say "Look at that word again. You know that word." Given a phonics approach, the teacher might say "Look at that word again. There isn't any *r* in it, is there? And what sound does the *ou* make?" In both cases, the teacher is focusing attention on the word *as if* it stood in isolation; both are word-centered approaches. Given a socio-psycholinguistic viewpoint, however, the teacher might say "Think for a moment. Where was Jane's father, anyway? Where did he climb to in order to get to the TV antenna? Then what would make sense here?" In other words, a psycholinguistically oriented teacher would emphasize using one's schemas and all relevant contexts, in order to predict what would logically come next. If the child had read "roof" for *house*, such a teacher would not have expected the child to correct the miscue.

In this example (adapted from Weaver 1977), the phonics-oriented teacher has emphasized a *skill* for identifying a word, whereas the psycholinguistically oriented teacher has emphasized a *strategy* for getting meaning.

This difference between *skills* and *strategies* is a crucial one. Most approaches to reading and most reading instruction in the U.S. today emphasize the development of reading *skills*. Though some of these are "comprehension skills," a great deal of attention is paid to skills for pronouncing and/or identifying words. In contrast,

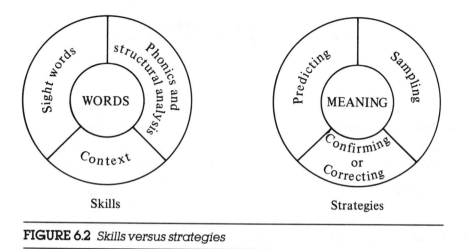

FIGURE 6.2 *Skills versus strategies*

most socio-psycholinguists emphasize the development of *strategies* for getting meaning from connected text. Figure 6.2 illustrates this difference. In the word-centered skills approaches, children are taught to use their stock of sight words, their phonics and structural analysis skills, and (often last if at all) their understanding of context in order to identify words. Concern with comprehension typically comes later, after the selection has been read. But in a meaning-centered strategies approach, children are actually taught to use their developing comprehension of a text in order to help them identify the words. They are taught to use context of all sorts to *predict* what will come next; to *sample* the visual display, using a minimum of grapho/phonemic cues to confirm or modify their prediction and to tentatively interpret a word; and to use following context to *confirm* or *correct* this tentative interpretation. As the term ''interpretation'' suggests, creating meaning from the text is more important than identifying all the words. It is assumed that no two readers of the same text will create identical meanings, and that in transacting with the text, each reader will create both a deep and a surface structure that is in some ways uniquely his or her own. Meaning is the beginning and the end of reading, and the means as well. This socio-psycholinguistic view of reading is a major part of the philosophy that underlies the language experience and whole-language approaches.

THE BASAL READER "SKILLS" APPROACH—AND HOW IT MIGHT BE IMPROVED

My division of reading approaches into word-centered and meaning-centered has, of course, obscured differences that proponents of the word-centered approaches might want to highlight. Word-centered approaches are often divided into *subskills* approaches versus *skills* approaches: the former, particularly phonics, concentrate on the very smallest units of language, while the latter go beyond a preoccupation with mere word identification to a concern for meaning (see Figure 6.3). The basal reader approach is, of course, a skills approach, for it attends to comprehension as well as

WORD-EMPHASIS APPROACHES

Subskills Approaches

focus on (sub) skills for pronouncing
and identifying words

particularly a
phonics approach

Skills Approaches

focus on skills—not only skills for identifying
words but also comprehension "skills"

particularly a
basal reader approach

FIGURE 6.3 *Subskills and skills approaches*

to word identification. However, several points should be noted about the typical
basal reader attention to comprehension:

1. There is typically a concern for pre-teaching vocabulary, which may sometimes be
   important. However, such pre-teaching often does not draw sufficiently upon
   readers' prior knowledge; also, the pre-teaching of vocabulary and concepts can
   inadvertently discourage readers from developing their ability to understand new
   words through context.

2. The suggestions for pre-reading discussion often are not as adequate as they
   might be for activating readers' schemas and thus enhancing comprehension.

3. Often, the majority of the post-reading questions focus on recall of details rather
   than on understanding of the characters' motivations and feelings and how these
   are reflected in the development of the plot. Thus the questions seem designed
   more to see whether the students have read and remembered the words of the
   story than to genuinely engage them in comprehending and appreciating what
   they have read. (See, for example, Durkin's 1981 study of "Reading Comprehension Instruction in Five Basal Reading Series." The preponderance of literal
   questions "in search of a single answer" helps explain why, as Durkin had found
   earlier (1978–79), teachers tend to ask such questions predominantly.)

As an example, let us consider a basal reader lesson for "Petronella," by Jay
Williams (Appendix A). This story is included in the book *Weavers*, the first of the
intermediate level readers in the Houghton Mifflin Reading Series (1983). The
teacher's manual provides first a summary of the story and then a list of glossary
words. In the subsequent section on "Motivation and Silent Reading," the teacher is
advised to write the word *enchanter* on the chalkboard and pronounce it, then ask a
volunteer to define it, and finally define it for the students if no one knows an
acceptable definition. Students are next to be advised that the story they are about to
read is a fairy tale, but one somewhat different from the ordinary; as they read, the

students are to think about how this story differs from typical fairy tales. Finally, the teacher is advised to have the students read the title and the author's name silently, then to have a volunteer read these aloud. From this point, students are apparently on their own, until faced with post-reading questions. Only 6 out of 17 of these questions are labeled as literal—fortunately a relatively low percentage, but still probably more than necessary, particularly since most of these literal questions are not used as stepping stones to more challenging and interesting questions.

Perhaps the easiest way to demonstrate the weaknesses of this approach is to suggest how a psycholinguistically aware teacher might depart from the suggestions in the teacher's manual, translating the typical "skills" approach to vocabulary and comprehension into an approach that more effectively encourages reading for meaning and for personal engagement with the story. Following this lesson is a discussion of various features of it, along with a recapitulation of how the imaginary teacher's lesson departs from that of the basal reading series. The idea for using this story comes from Charles Temple (Temple and Burns 1986), as do some of the discussion questions.

SCENE: A fifth grade classroom. The teacher has decided to use the story "Petronella" with the whole class, then later do additional reading strategy work with children who seem to need it. The children's desks are pulled together in pairs so that they can share books, and the less competent readers are paired with someone who can help them if necessary. The teacher's name is Ms. Matthews.

Ms. M.: The story we're going to read today is a modern fairy tale. Before we open our books, let's review what we know about fairy tales. Where and when do they usually take place?

Class: Long ago and far away.

Ms. M.: Right. What do we know about typical plots and characters?

Class: Well, often there's some kind of test or challenge, like in "The Princess and the Pea."
Yes, and the events often come in threes, like in "The Fisherman and His Wife" or "The Three Billy Goats Gruff" or "Rumplestiltskin."
There's often a mean stepmother, or a stupid father, or a younger brother who's kinda innocent but succeeds where his older brothers have failed.
Or just some simple kid who succeeds, like Jack [and the Beanstalk].
Or a simple girl, like Cinderella, who beats out her nasty sisters to wear the glass slipper and win the prince.
Yeah, or a prince who wins a princess, like in "Cinderella" or "Sleeping Beauty."

Ms. M.: What are princes and princesses usually like?

Class: The prince is handsome. Yeah, and the princess is beautiful. And they live happily ever after.

Ms. M.: Does anybody typically help the main character get what he or she wants?

Class: Yeah, sometimes. There's the fairy godmother in "Cinderella." And the giant's wife in "Jack and the Beanstalk."

Ms. M.:   Okay, good. Would you say these stories are realistic?

Class: No.

Ms. M.:   Why not?

Class: 'Cause there's usually some kind of magic going on. Things that couldn't really happen.
Yeah, like a wolf dressing up in a woman's clothes.
Or fairy godmothers and magic fish and magic beans and little men like Rumplestiltskin.

Ms. M.:   Okay, good. Do you know any names for kinds of people who do magical things?

Class: Fairy godmothers.
Magicians.
Witches.
Wizards [this from someone who plays "Dungeons and Dragons"].

Ms. M.:   Right. Another word is *enchanter* [she writes this on the chalkboard]. Usually an enchanter casts spells of different kinds. There's an enchanter in the story we're going to read.

Class: Hurray! Maybe he can cast a spell to give us pizza for lunch!

Ms. M.:   Okay! What do we know about how fairy tales usually end?

Class: "And everybody lived happily ever after."

Ms. M.:   Yes, good. Okay, let's review what we've discussed.
[As discussion has progressed, Ms. Matthews has been writing the main points on the chalkboard. She now reviews these.]
Okay, open your books to page 43. What's the title of this modern fairy tale?

Class: "Petronella."

Ms. M.:   Yes. Does the title give you any hints as to what the story might be about?

Class: Well, probably someone named "Petronella."
Sounds like "Cinderella."
Maybe it's a poor kid like Cinderella.

Ms. M.:   Okay, good. We haven't read any stories by Jay Williams before, so knowing the author's name doesn't tell us much. We could look at his biographical sketch, but let's skip that for now. What about the picture? Judging from this picture, what do you think is going to happen?

Class: Looks like a dragon with a paintbrush and paint.
Maybe somebody's going to go slay a dragon.

Ms. M.:   Well, let's read and see. First let's look just at the opening sentence: "In the kingdom of Skyclear Mountain, three princes were always born to the king and queen." Do you have any more ideas about who the story is going to be about or what's going to happen?

Class: Well, it might be about their three princes. Maybe the youngest one goes on a quest or outsmarts his older brothers somehow.
Yeah, but maybe it's going to be different this time.

Ms. M.:   What do you mean?

Class: Well, maybe there aren't going to be three princes.
                Maybe there will be only two. Or four.
                Yeah, or maybe the king and queen will have girls instead.
_Ms. M._: What makes you think things might be different this time?
Class: Well, it says "always." The king and queen "always" have three
                princes. "Always" makes you think somehow that things are
                going to change.
_Ms. M._: Okay, let me read you the rest of the paragraph and see what you
                think. Just listen; don't try to read along.
                [Ms. Matthew reads]:

> The oldest prince was always called Michael, the middle
> prince was always called George, and the youngest was al-
> ways called Peter. When they were grown, they always went
> out to seek their fortunes. What happened to the oldest
> prince and the middle prince no one ever knew. But the
> youngest prince always rescued a princess, brought her home,
> and in time ruled over the kingdom. That was the way it had
> always been. And so far as anyone knew, that was the way it
> would always be.

_Ms. M._: Okay, now what do you think? Are there going to be three
                princes? Or what?
Class: No. Nope. No way. [a chorus of denials]
_Ms. M._: Why not?
Class: Well, it keeps saying _this_ "always" happens or _that_ "always"
                happens.
                So you know it's going to be different this time.
                Yeah. From those last two sentences, you just know it's going to
                be different.
_Ms. M._: Yes, you're right. Look at the last sentence on p. 43: "Until
                now." That was the way it always was, until now. Any idea how
                things might be different now?
Class: Like Rob said: maybe there will be more kids.
                Or not as many.
                Or maybe they won't have any kids at all. Maybe they'll adopt a
                dragon!
_Ms. M._: Let's read on and find out. Read the next paragraph silently, and
                then look up when you're done. Read _just_ the next paragraph.
                . . . Okay, now that everybody's done, would someone care to
                read the paragraph aloud? Okay, Mark, go ahead.
                [Mark is by no means the most fluent reader in the class, but Ms.
                Matthews has helped the children learn to be respectful of each
                other's efforts, to listen for and praise each other's good miscues
                on the rare occasions when they read aloud in small groups, and
                never to interrupt a reader by yelling out a word. Thus Mark has
                gained some confidence in his reading and is occasionally willing
                to risk reading in front of the others, especially when he has had a
                chance to read ahead silently.]

Mark: "Now was the time of King Peter the twenty-sixth

of
and Queen Blossom. An oldest prince was

then
born, and a middle prince. But the youngest

~~prince~~ turned out to be a girl.''

Ms. M.:   Very good, Mark. Class, what do you think might happen, now that the youngest prince has turned out to be a girl?

Class: The king won't like it.
            The queen will be jealous of her, like Sleeping Beauty's stepmother.
            They'll disown her, give her away to some poor woman to raise.
            Yeah, and then she'll grow up and find out she's really a princess.
            And come back and rule the kingdom, 'cause her older brothers have been killed.

Ms. M.:   Well, let's read on. Go ahead and read through the paragraph that ends at the top of page 45, then look up to let me know you're done. [They all read the following:]

> "Well," said the king gloomily, "we can't call her Peter. We'll have to call her Petronella. And what's to be done about it, I'm sure I don't know."
>   There was nothing to be done. The years passed, and the time came for the princes to go out and seek their fortunes. Michael and George said good-bye to the king and queen and mounted their horses. Then out came Petronella. She was dressed in traveling clothes, with her bag packed and a sword by her side.

Ms. M.:   What kind of girl do you think Petronella is? What's she like?
Class: Not the type that plays with dolls.
            She probably wears blue jeans.
            Yeah. And plays with the boys. [Someone snickers.]
            Doesn't sound like a princess to me.
Ms. M.:   What do you think she's going to do, all dressed up in traveling clothes?
Class: She's going to seek her fortune too.
            Maybe she'll go looking for a prince.
Ms. M.:   What makes you think so?
Class: They said the youngest prince always goes out to look for a princess.
            Well, Petronella is the youngest, but she's a princess, not a prince. So, maybe she's going to look for a prince.
Ms. M.:   Any other ideas?
Class: Maybe she's going to go on some other kind of quest.
            Maybe she'll kill a dragon and become king of some other land.
            Not king, you dope. Queen.
Ms. M.:   Well, let's read and find out. Read through the paragraph that ends at

the top of page 46, and raise your hand so I can tell you're through. While you wait for others to finish, jot down your ideas about what's going to happen in the story.
[They read the following:]

> "If you think," she said, "that I'm going to sit at home, you are mistaken. I'm going to seek my fortune too."
> "Impossible!" said the king.
> "What will people say?" cried the queen.
> "Look," said Prince Michael. "Be reasonable, Pet. Stay home. Sooner or later a prince will turn up here."
> Petronella smiled. She was a tall, handsome girl with flaming red hair, and when she smiled in that particular way, it meant she was trying to keep her temper.
> "I'm going with you," she said. "I'll find a prince if I have to rescue one from something myself. And that's that."

At this point, Ms. Matthews encourages most of the class to finish the story silently. She tells them that when they have finished, they should brainstorm and make a list of fun activities to do individually or in groups, as a follow-up to the "Petronella" story. Figure 6.4 indicates some of the possibilities, translated into adult language. While most of the class are reading silently and brainstorming, Ms.

---

1. Write about what happens when Petronella arrives home with the enchanter. That is, write a sequel to the story.
2. Pretend that Petronella took the prince home with her, instead of the enchanter. Write a sequel.
3. Write diary entries from the viewpoint of Petronella, maybe when she was a child, or when she is going on her quest to find and rescue the prince.
4. Write a story about the prince and what happens to him.
5. Write a different story about a modern girl like Petronella, or a story about a boy who doesn't fit our stereotype of the macho male. Maybe make our own books, with illustrations.
6. Write dialogue for a play retelling the story of Petronella, and then act out the play. Maybe put on the play for other classes. Or videotape the play.
7. Make a mural of one of the important scenes from "Petronella." Display it on the wall outside our classroom.
8. Read some library books with non-traditional protagonists. Do TV "commercials" for the books we've read; maybe videotape. Or write ads for our books. Maybe make a display of some of these books for the glass case by the principal's office.
9. Make a book of enchanters' spells.
10. Have Ms. Matthews take us on a guided visualization of Petronella's three tasks (see Appendix A).

FIGURE 6.4 *"Petronella" activities*

Matthews continues the prediction procedure with a small group who need to develop their predicting and comprehension-monitoring strategies. She stops at crucial points to ask what the students think is going to happen next and why they think so, then later asks which of their predictions were confirmed and disconfirmed and how they knew. Students are expected to justify their responses with specific references to the text. (If you have not already read the ''Petronella'' story in Appendix A, you might follow this procedure yourself as you read the rest of the story: stop at each line of asterisks, ask yourself the kinds of questions Ms. Matthews might ask about what will happen next and why, and then read to see whether or to what degree you were right.) Obviously such a procedure encourages readers to become actively involved with the story, to use their own schemas, and to predict, sample, and confirm/correct as they read, all at the story level.

When the students have all finished reading ''Petronella,'' the teacher turns to the list of questions she has prepared. First, she has prepared an outline of the major events in the story—a ''story grammar''—and then she has developed questions keyed to these points, as well as some going beyond. Basically assuming that the students will understand the literal content of the story and knowing that she can always backtrack to literal questions if necessary, Ms. Matthews has selected carefully from among the questions accompanying the selection in the Teacher's Manual. She has used literal questions only when they lead into more thought-provoking ones, and she has added a generous number of inferential, interpretive, and evaluative questions not in the Teacher's Manual. The questions with an asterisk are the same as or similar to questions in the TM.

PETRONELLA IS BORN

*1. How do you think King Peter felt when he found out that his youngest child was a girl? How do you think you would have felt?

DEPARTS TO FIND A PRINCE

2. When Petronella left to find a prince, what do you think she really wanted? What makes you think this?

ENCOUNTERS MAN AT CROSSROADS

3. What did Petronella ask the old man at the crossroads? *How was her question different from her brothers' questions? Why do you think she was the first to ask the old man the question that would free him?

SEES PRINCE AT THE ENCHANTER'S

4. What do you think Petronella thought of the prince when she first saw him? What makes you think this?

ASKS TO WORK FOR ALBION IN ORDER TO FREE PRINCE

*5. Why do you think Petronella goes through with rescuing the prince, even though she's not much impressed with him?

COMPLETES THE TASKS SUCCESSFULLY

6. How did Petronella quiet the hounds? The horses? The hawks? Do you think a prince would have handled the situation in the same way? Why or why not?

FLEES WITH PRINCE	7. How do you think Petronella felt when she and the prince were fleeing from the enchanter? Was she glad to have rescued the prince? What makes you think as you do?
STOPS TO FREE ALBION	8. Why do you think Petronella stopped to free Albion from the ring? How is her behavior here similar to her behavior at other points in the story?
TAKES ALBION HOME	9. Do you think Petronella made a wise decision in abandoning the prince and taking the enchanter home with her? Why or why not? *What do you think will happen when Petronella returns home with the enchanter? *Do you think she will rule the kingdom of Skyclear Mountain?

Additional questions:

10. Is Petronella more like a typical (stereotypical) princess, or more like a prince? How does she differ from both stereotypes? (These questions may need to be preceded by ones focusing on stereotypes of male and female roles, particularly with respect to princes and princesses.)

11. How is the story ''Petronella'' like a typical fairy tale? How is it different from a typical fairy tale?

12. For girls: If you were Petronella, would you have rescued the prince? Would you have liked to be Petronella? Why or why not?
    For boys: If you were the enchanter, would you have wanted to marry Petronella? Why or why not?

Although Ms. Matthews may call on children to give evidence from the text to support their recollections and interpretations, many of her questions focus more on bringing to bear what children already know about human behavior and male/female roles and stereotypes.

Let us look briefly at the major ways in which Ms. Matthews has used and departed from the suggestions in the Teacher's Manual as she led the class in reading and discussing ''Petronella.''

1. The Teacher's Manual suggests some activities for vocabulary development to precede the reading of the story. Wanting students to learn to use context and their own schemas to cope with most unfamiliar words, Ms. Matthews postpones this kind of activity until after the reading. Then, she has the students most likely to need vocabulary and concept development work in a group to puzzle out the meanings of problem words together. The following day she will discuss these ''vocabulary'' words with the group or perhaps with the whole class, now that this group has worked out its own definitions.

2. As previously mentioned, the Teacher's Manual includes a section titled "Motivation and Silent Reading." It is suggested that the teacher write the word *enchanter* on the chalkboard and define it, if none of the students can; then, the teacher is to tell students that they are going to read a fairy tale that is somewhat different from other fairy tales they've heard or read. According to the Teacher's Manual, students are to think about how this tale differs from a typical fairy tale, as they will discuss these differences after reading the story. Ms. Matthews's approach is virtually the opposite. She begins by *eliciting* what the children already know about fairy tales, to help them draw upon and develop their schemas. She *elicits* other words for those who perform magic and then, having recalled and developed the concept, she offers the specific word that is new to many of them: *enchanter*. Finally, she refrains from telling them that this fairy tale is atypical; she wants the class to pick up on the cues in the text to *predict* that it will be different, then read to confirm that prediction.

3. Once the title and author's name have been read aloud, the TM suggests having children read silently. While silent reading is the major part of the total curriculum, Ms. Matthews also knows it is particularly helpful to less competent readers for her to occasionally lead the class as well as smaller groups of students through what is sometimes called a "Directed Reading-Thinking Activity" (DRTA); see Stauffer (1960) and Stauffer and Cramer (1968). Basically this technique involves predicting what will come next and citing evidence to justify those predictions; reading to confirm, reject, or modify predictions; making and justifying new predictions; and so forth. By occasionally leading the class through such an activity, Ms. Matthews reinforces the importance of transacting actively with a text.

4. In preparing questions to discuss with the students after the reading of the story, Ms. Matthews chooses carefully from among those in the Teacher's Manual, omitting many of the recall questions and adding others that she thinks are more interesting and challenging. She is aware, of course, of such popular "taxonomies" of reading comprehension as Barrett's, which divides comprehension and comprehension questions into bits and pieces labeled *literal recognition* or *recall* (reading the lines), *inference* (reading between the lines), and *evaluation* and *appreciation* (reading beyond the lines) (Barrett, in R. Smith and T. Barrett 1974, pp. 53–57). However, she is also aware of the limitations of such schemes.

For one thing, the division of questions into such neat types does not correspond with how people comprehend. For example, students may make inferences and/or draw upon their own schemas in answering questions which are thought to be literal recall questions, and of course this kind of *active* processing of text is to be encouraged rather than discouraged. For instance, the question about how Petronella quieted the hounds, horses, and hawks (question 6) is more or less literal. Though it can be answered either by reference to Petronella's actions (she kept the dogs company, talking to them and stroking them) or by reference to the quality she exhibited in doing so (her bravery), in either case an answer is provided in the text. However, the students might answer by drawing *inferences* from the text and/or by using their own *schemas*: for example, "She quieted the dogs by being nice to them" or "After a minute, the dogs could tell she wasn't scared of them, so they quieted down." Neither answer comes directly from the text. While it is sometimes important for students to be able to justify their responses by appropriate reference to the text read, it would be unfortunate indeed if the teacher rejected the latter two responses just because they aren't found directly stated in the text.

Another problem with such a breakdown of comprehension questions is that reading for minute details often becomes treated as more important than reading for understanding. The following is a poignant example from Estes and Johnstone (1977, p. 895):

> Last Christmas, the first author read to his students a story by Truman Capote called, "A Christmas Memory." It is beautiful and poignant, as affecting as any story one could choose. Many of the students cried at the end. Their teacher looked at the questions following the story—he cried.
>
> 1. To what uses is the dilapidated baby carriage put in the various scenes?
> 2. What evidence is there in the story that the setting, a rural town, is located in the southern area of our country?

Perhaps the most serious problem with such hierarchies of comprehension is the assumption that literal recall questions must precede the supposedly more complex kinds of questions, and even that less competent readers should be asked only the "easier" recall kinds of questions. This, Ms. Matthews knows, is sheer nonsense. In fact, students who tend not to remember details well can often demonstrate highly sophisticated thinking in response to the more probing kinds of questions.

Given such objections to dividing comprehension into different types of questions that only purport to reflect separable reading/thinking skills, Ms. Matthews has developed her own guidelines for asking questions about literature:

1. As a general rule, don't ask literal recall questions unless they are a springboard to more challenging questions. For example, the question about how Petronella quieted the hounds, horses, and hawks is followed by the question "Do you think a prince would have handled the situation in the same way? Why or why not?"

2. Ask questions that focus on the motivation and feelings of the characters. The literal question "What did so-and-so do when . . .?" leads into questions like "Why do you think so-and-so did this?" and "How do you think so-and-so felt when . . .?"

3. Ask questions that involve students in evaluating the actions of the characters. "Do you think so-and-so did the best/right thing when . . .?"

4. Ask questions that invite students to project themselves into the story and to imagine themselves in similar situations: "How do you think *you* would have felt if . . .?" or "How do you think you would feel if . . .?" "What would you have done when . . .?" or "What would you do if . . .?"

These recommended kinds of questions do in fact involve students in remembering "literal" information, drawing inferences, and so forth; they simply do not make artificial divisions among the kinds of comprehension involved. Students responding to thoughtful questions about a reading selection will of necessity be analyzing and synthesizing and comparing information, drawing upon their schemas as well as the text to make inferences and evaluations, to hypothesize, and to weigh alternatives. In short, such questions will stimulate the kinds of thinking that Piaget said characterize formal operational "adult" thought. Though his research suggested that such thought patterns did not typically develop until early or pre-adolescence, many people have come to realize that in real life, as opposed to artificial testing situations, children do not necessarily exhibit the cognitive limitations that Piaget found among younger children (see Donaldson 1978, for example). It is abundantly clear that asking thought-provoking questions about literature from a very early age is one way that teachers can "naturally" stimulate the development of sophisticated forms of thought.

In summary, Ms. Matthews's modification of the basal reader lesson has enabled her to encourage the students to:

1. Activate relevant schemas before reading a selection.
2. Use schemas and all available cues to make predictions, then sample the text, and keep confirming and revising predictions as the selection develops (the DRTA, Directed Reading-Thinking Activity).
3. Transact with the story in ways that will help them develop their reasoning ability (the discussion questions).
4. Use context as well as schemas to focus on getting meaning at the sentence and word levels (since most "vocabulary" words were not pre-taught).
5. Prepare for additional activities that "extend" the story and the children's interest in it.

Thus Ms. Matthews has helped her students strengthen their reading and critical thinking abilities.

Having demonstrated some of the inadequacies of the typical "skills" approach in a basal reader by contrasting the directions in the teacher's manual with the way a psycholinguistically knowledgeable teacher might lead the lesson, we will turn our attention in the next section to a discussion of why skills and subskills approaches are so popular, despite their inadequacies.

WHY SKILLS AND SUBSKILLS APPROACHES ARE SO POPULAR

Given that the skills and subskills approaches are so out of line with what we know about the reading process, one may well wonder why they are so popular. One reason is their ease of construction and ease of use. Frank Smith offers this perceptive comment (1979, p. 37):

> The outside-in perspective [that underlies skills and subskills approaches] is a boon to instructional program developers who need to decompose complex tasks into series of discrete and simple steps so that teaching can be

standardized and made amenable to technology. To achieve this simplification, a few contemporary reading programs claim to teach only "subskills" of reading, relieving the teacher of anxiety about the total skill of which the subskills are a part.

Ease of program development is surely one factor contributing to the popularity of such programs, as is the fact that adults seem to be absolved of responsibility if the child cannot learn to read from the carefully sequenced set of lessons. And, as Smith also points out, such programs "are conceptually simple and lend themselves easily to measurement, manipulation, and control"; in addition, they are "frequently successful—within their own limited range of objectives," and by testing what has been directly taught (or at least assigned in the workbooks), "they have the great advantage of being able to demonstrate their success" (Smith 1979, p. 36).

My own list of suggested reasons for the popularity of skills and subskills approaches is similar. Among the more important are these:

1. They reflect the "commonsense" view of the person-on-the-street, someone who has never given much thought to how people actually read. Most people—including many educators, administrators, and boards of education—simply take it for granted that *of course* you have to identify all the words in order to read well, that *of course* it makes sense to work upwards gradually, from smaller units like letter/sound correspondences and words to larger units like sentences and paragraphs and eventually whole texts. In short, most people are unaware that reading is not simply a bottom-up process of extracting meaning that is "in" the text.

2. In the late 1960s there was a movement toward competency-based education and the use of minimal performance objectives, followed by an emphasis on educational "accountability": that is, schools and teachers are increasingly expected to be "accountable" for students' learning. If we are to measure students' learning in order to hold teachers and schools accountable, it of course seems easier and more "objective" to use standardized tests that can be machine scored. Clearly it is easier with such tests to assess children's ability to identify words or to master phonics rules than to assess their ability to comprehend what they have read. And even when such tests do attempt and purport to measure comprehension, they often are all too similar to the kinds of "tests" on our *blonke* and *corandic* passages: that is, tests that measure one's ability to manipulate language more than one's ability to comprehend—or tests that assess one's prior knowledge (see activity 6 in Chapter 2 (pp. 51–52) and activity 2 in Chapter 4 (pp. 106–107). Nevertheless, performance on such tests is often a major way that children's reading ability, and teachers' competence, is assessed. Again this form of assessment stems, I think, not only from practical considerations and an unrealistic view of "objectivity," but also—perhaps mainly—from an inadequate conception of the reading process and of how people learn. And unfortunately the means of assessment tends to determine what and how children will be taught to read. Naturally everyone wants the children to do well on the tests by which they and the teachers and the schools will be evaluated.

3. A third reason for the popularity of word-emphasis, skills approaches is that in the late 1960s and early 1970s, a considerable body of research was interpreted as favoring a phonics approach to teaching reading. Particularly influential were the *27 USOE Comparative First Grade Studies* conducted during 1965–66, as discussed in Bond and Dykstra 1967.

In a later summary of his conclusions favoring phonics, Dykstra says:

The evidence clearly demonstrates that children who receive early intensive instruction in phonics develop superior word recognition skills in the early stages of reading and tend to maintain their superiority at least through the third grade. These same pupils tend to do somewhat better than pupils enrolled in meaning-emphasis (delayed gradual phonics) programs in reading comprehension at the end of the first grade. (Dykstra 1974, p. 397)

Dykstra goes on to say that through grade 3, children who have received early intensive instruction in phonics are "at least as capable" in reading comprehension as those whose instruction has been characterized by a delayed and more gradual introduction to phonics. He then concludes with the seeming voice of authority:

We can summarize the results of sixty years of research dealing with beginning reading instruction by stating that early systematic instruction in phonics provides the child with the skills necessary to become an independent reader at an earlier age than is likely if phonics instruction is delayed and less systematic. As a consequence of his early success in "learning to read," the child can more quickly go about the job of "reading to learn." (Dykstra 1974, p. 397)

Obviously in Dykstra's mind, there is only one conclusion to be drawn from the USOE studies.

Much the same conclusion was drawn by Jeanne Chall in her influential book *Learning to Read: The Great Debate* (1967), which was perhaps *the* major factor that led publishers to include more phonics in the basal reading series of the 1970s. Yet Chall herself admits the ambiguity and the limitations of the studies she attempted to synthesize:

Since previous summaries based on practically the same body of experimental research had arrived at conflicting conclusions, I knew before starting that a major problem was how to read the research. . . .
As I had suspected beforehand, practically none of the studies specified all these [the aforementioned] conditions. Most did not indicate how the experimental and control groups were selected, how much time was allotted to various aspects of reading, how the teachers were selected, whether the quality of the teaching was comparable in both groups, or even whether the teachers followed the methods under study. Even more important, most studies did not specify clearly what a "method" involved, but instead merely assigned labels (e.g., "phonics"), expecting the reader to understand what was meant.

Many of the early studies did not use standard measures of outcomes or statistical tests of significance to determine whether the various results obtained could have been attributable to chance differences.

(Chall 1967, pp. 100–101)

Unfortunately, this honest admission of the limitations of her attempt to synthesize the research comparing various methods of teaching beginning reading was lost as her study became more and more publicized, eventually being accepted as "gospel."

In Chall's 1983 update of *The Great Debate*, she says that between 1967 and 1981, there was scarcely any research to either support or challenge her earlier conclusion: "The hope that coordinated studies would avoid uncertainties in [earlier] results did not materialize" (Chall 1983a, p. 7). She does admit, however, that several reviews of the studies she earlier examined did *not*, in fact, conclude that code-emphasis approaches (typically phonics) were superior to meaning-emphasis approaches. Chall writes:

Yet many of the summaries of the USOE studies, and particularly the interpretations of their findings, contradicted this [her] conclusion. Only a few indicated that the results showed an advantage for a heavier code-emphasis. Several, in fact, concluded that the USOE findings contradicted those of *The Great Debate*. This would mean that the USOE studies pointed to a meaning-emphasis as the advantageous approach. Yet this was not reported either. Indeed, most reviewers seemed to conclude that the 27 USOE studies found no method superior to any other. Superior results, if any, were attributed to the teacher.

(1983a, p. 6)

Thus although Chall and some other, later interpreters of the USOE studies construed them as demonstrating the advantage of a heavier code-emphasis approach, this was by no means the universal conclusion.

Another important point about these studies that were interpreted as showing the superiority of a code-emphasis approach (typically phonics) to a meaning-emphasis approach is this: most of the so-called meaning emphasis approaches focused on sight word recognition, so that what was compared was most often a phonics approach with a sight word approach. In other words, one word-emphasis approach was compared with another. A few of the classrooms in the study used a language experience approach, but none used what is now known as a whole-language approach. And in a recent reanalysis of the Bond and Dykstra data, a well-known European scholar concludes that those approaches that came closest to being "whole language" actually produced the best results of the various approaches compared (Grundin 1985, p. 265).

On the one hand, then, we are confronted with the fact that the conclusions of scholars like Chall and Dykstra have had a profound influence on the basal reading series used today: these series typically include much more emphasis on phonics than did the basal series of the early 1960s. On the other hand, we are left with doubts and questions such as these:

1. When phonics advocates claim that a substantial amount of phonics instruction enables children to read "independently" at an earlier age, what do they really mean? That children are able to sound out words sooner? That they are able to read for meaning sooner? Or . . .?

2. When phonics advocates claim that early emphasis on phonics facilitates comprehension in the early grades, what do they really mean? That is, what is really being tested in the tests that purport to assess comprehension? To what extent are such comprehension tests merely tests of a reader's ability to identify words or to locate the answers to recall questions in a paragraph they may not even understand?

3. How does a word-emphasis approach like the current basal reader approach, with typically a heavy emphasis on phonics, actually compare with today's most widespread meaning-emphasis approach, the whole-language approach? Is either one clearly superior in enabling children to identify words? To comprehend? How long do these advantages appear to persist?

4. Are there advantages to a whole-language approach that might make it preferable to a basal reader approach with its typical emphasis on phonics, even *if* it turns out that children in a whole-language classroom are initially slower in developing a stock of sight words and/or skills for sounding out and "attacking" words?

Most of these are among the issues that will be addressed in Chapter 7.

READING INSTRUCTION REVISITED

Though not all of the above questions can be answered definitively, there are an increasing number of teachers, professional organizations, states and (in Canada) provinces, and even countries that are moving toward teaching and toward positions about teaching that are more psycholinguistically based and more whole-language oriented. I mention psycholinguistics particularly because that was the title and the focus of *Psycholinguistics and Reading*, the precursor of this book, but in fact the new trends in reading instruction are based upon the work of scholars and educators in a variety of related fields, including sociolinguistics, the hybrid field socio-psycholinguistics, semiotics, schema theory, a transactional reader-response theory of literature, cognitive psychology, and ethnography. It is also based on the classroom experience of whole-language teachers and teacher-scholars, many of whom have recently been sharing their teaching practices with others through publications (see, for example, Butler and Turbill 1984; Hansen, Newkirk, and Graves 1985; Newman's book on whole-language teaching, 1985; and Ken Goodman's overview, *What's Whole in Whole Language?* 1986). My discussion of the reading process, reading research, and the teaching of reading reflects this broader base, even though I have avoided much of the terminology.

    This broader base is similarly reflected in an increasing number of position and philosophy statements made by professional organizations and state and province officials. In *Psycholinguistics and Reading*, I quoted at some length a psycholinguistically influenced definition of reading from Michigan, my own state. I am delighted now to be able to cite excerpts from an updated position paper developed by the Michigan Reading Association in cooperation with the Michigan Department of Education, a position paper that is being used as a basis for revising the state assessment test in reading.

A comparison of the old and new definitions of reading clearly shows the influence of our increased understanding of the reading process:

Old definition
Reading must be defined not as the process of transforming visual configurations into sound, which is a widely held conventional view of reading, but the *process of transforming the visual representation of language into meaning*. Thus, if one is reading, an idea is being transferred from the written page to the reader's mind.[3]

New definition
Reading is the process of constructing meaning through the dynamic interaction [transaction] among the reader's existing knowledge, the information suggested by the written language, and the context of the reading situation. ("Reading Redefined," p. 5)

Notice that the old definition assumes that meaning resides in the text: the reader's responsibility is to determine that meaning. The new definition, in contrast, recognizes the fact that meaning does not reside in the text but rather develops during the transaction between reader and text and is influenced by various aspects of the reading situation. What a difference! Though it will not be easy to develop a statewide reading assessment test that acknowledges the contribution of the reader and the context to reading comprehension, it is a giant step forward that reading educators and state officials are even trying to do so. (Those interested in Michigan's new definition of reading, goals and objectives, and efforts to revise the statewide reading assessment test can write for more information to Elaine Weber, Michigan Department of Education, P.O. Box 3008, Lansing, Michigan 48909.)

This is only one example of how teachers and teacher educators, working together, can have an influence upon official policy and practice at a major administrative level, in this case the state level. In addition to position and philosophy statements, we find curriculum guides at various levels that reflect a more psycholinguistically oriented view (again, the term "psycholinguistically oriented" is to be broadly construed to include the various related disciplines that have contributed to our current understanding of reading). One such guide is the publication *A Guide to Curriculum Planning in Reading*, published by the Wisconsin Department of Public Instruction, 1986 (my thanks to Sue Miller of Gilmore Middle School in Racine, Wisconsin for sending me a copy). Like the Michigan position paper, this guide talks about reading as an interactive process involving a complex relationship among reader, text, and context; in both documents, "interaction" seems to mean essentially the same as what we have called the reading *transaction*, using the term popularized by Rosenblatt (1978). Particularly interesting is a chart on the development of word analysis skills. The "phonics" skills include attention to only beginning and ending consonants, consonant blends and digraphs, and short and long vowels. Also, students are to be taught "integrated strategies," not just phonics, for identifying words in context (Cook 1986, p. 39). The teacher:

Teaches integration of phonics, structural, and contextual analysis

Models *what, how, when,* and *why* for each skill [might be interpreted as demonstrating how to predict, sample, confirm/correct]

Teaches and guides independence in use of word analysis strategy in oral and written context [again, mentions word analysis *in context*]

The student:

Identifies words by use in sentences [context again]

Uses integrated strategies to pronounce unfamiliar words in context [predicting, sampling, confirming/correcting]

Begins to apply decoding skills flexibly

On the one hand, it is unfortunate that some of what I have suggested in brackets is not spelled out more explicitly in the curriculum guide, because teachers with no background in the reading process may not interpret such a guide as I have suggested. On the other hand, teachers "in the know" will surely read it much as I have, and be pleased to find support for their attempt to put phonics in appropriate perspective, as relating to only one language cue and strategy.

Obviously the Michigan position paper and the Wisconsin curriculum guide are but two examples of the kinds of changes underway in the United States, as a result of our increased understanding of how people read.

In Canada, educators and administrators have in many cases developed philosophy and position statements and curriculum guides that reflect to a considerably greater degree our current understanding of how children learn, how the development of reading and writing parallels the acquisition of oral language, how all the language arts interrelate and stimulate one another, and how literacy development and content area learning go hand in hand. The province of Alberta, for example, has prepared an innovative curriculum guide for senior high school language arts (Iveson 1982; for a copy of the guide, I am indebted to Margaret Stevenson, Supervisor of Language Arts for the Edmonton Public Schools). Of particular interest is the fact that the goals of the program are not fragmented into goals for reading, literature, writing, speaking, listening, and viewing, though there are separate discussions on these; furthermore, there is one integrative set of goals for grades 1 through 12. The basic principles upon which these goals are based are as follows (each is of course elaborated with resulting implications; see pp. 4–5 of the guide):

1. A language arts program should emphasize lifelong applications of language arts skills.
2. Language use reflects the interrelatedness of the processes of listening, speaking, reading, writing and viewing.

3. Language variation is an integral part of language use.

4. Experience and language are closely interwoven in all learning situations. On the one hand, experiences expand students' language by providing them with new meanings and by modifying and enlarging previously acquired ones. On the other hand, as students gain in their ability to understand and use language, they can enter into, comprehend and react to a variety of experiences.

5. Language expansion occurs primarily through active involvement in language situations.

6. Language is used to communicate understandings, ideas and feelings, to assist social and personal development and to mediate thought processes.

7. Language functions throughout the entire curriculum.

8. In the early years, a child's thinking and language ability develop in his own dialect.

9. In the high school years, more emphasis should be placed on the recognition of quality and flexibility in the use of language.

10. Through talk the students learn to organize their environment, interpret their experiences, and communicate with others. As they mature they continue to use talk for these purposes as well as to check their understandings against those of others and to build up an objective view of reality.

11. Through writing the student can learn to clarify thought, emotion and experience, and to share ideas, emotions and experiences with others.

12. Various mass media have their own characteristic ways of presenting ideas.

13. Literature is an integral part of language learning.

Note that in this entire statement of philosophical principles, not one refers to reading alone. Reading is never isolated from the other language arts nor from the purposes of human communication.

The "General Language Arts Objectives for Grades 1–12" include only one objective that makes any reference to phonics. This objective reads as follows (p. 8):

Production and reception of sounds and printed words

This objective refers to the ability of students to hear and produce the sounds in words and to recognize and write words. It represents the phonics component of the objectives. Together with the next objective, it suggests that relationships between sounds and printed sentences are made in the context of the full meaning of individual sentences and larger pieces of writing. These two objectives underscore the need for developing in students a "sense" or a "feeling" for what sentences and stories are.

What a difference between this "phonics" objective and the detailed lists of phonics skills that basal reading series and curriculum guides typically suggest as necessary for reading! Obviously, the educational administration has placed the province of Alberta squarely in a whole-language approach, where phonics is taught minimally, in context, and through writing as well as reading.

One more example from Canada must suffice to illustrate the growing movement toward a psycholinguistically based, whole-language approach to literacy. *English-Language Arts I-VI* is the official policy statement of the Direction Générale de Dévelopement Pédagogique, Ministère de l'Éducation for the Province of Quebec. It mandates a "whole language, child-centered, integrated approach," as explained in a series of theoretical assumptions and instructional principles. Ken Goodman (*What's Whole . . .* 1986, p. 61) quotes the following examples:

> *Theoretical assumption*: language learning is an active developmental process which occurs over a period of time.
> *Instructional principle*: children need time to internalize the process by actively engaging in the process of speaking, listening, reading, and writing.

> *Theoretical assumption*: language arts must occur and flourish in literate environments where language users are free to discover and to realize their intentions.
> *Instructional principle*: children need to be encouraged to take risks and need to experience varied opportunities for language use.

Again the emphasis is on a broadly humanistic approach to literacy, not on a narrowly defined skills approach that characterizes so much of beginning literacy instruction in the United States.

The development of an official whole-language philosophy at the province level, in provinces such as Alberta and Quebec, has enabled educators to put pressure on publishers to produce basal reading series that are more whole-language oriented than those typically published in the United States. As of the mid-1980s, there are three such series that are particularly notable: the *Networks* series, by Nelson Canada; the *Unicorn* series, by McGraw-Hill Ryerson; and the *Impressions* series, by Holt, Rinehart and Winston of Canada. As of this writing, the latter series is available from Holt, Rinehart in New York as well as from the Canadian publisher. In Great Britain, *Journeys into Literacy* is available from Schofield and Sims Ltd. See the "List of Useful Addresses" in Appendix B.

In some cases the shift to a more psycholinguistically based, whole-language program at least appears to be occurring top-down, mandated by the educational establishment, as in the case of Quebec—and the country of New Zealand. Such mandates are not likely to be effective, of course, unless teachers are educated in a whole-language philosophy, so extensive in-service education must be provided. New Zealand has developed a teacher in-service course that Australia has adapted to its own needs. First developed in South Australia, the National Early Literacy Inservice Course is now available to teachers throughout that country. The course consists of ten workshops (approximately one and a half hours each) dealing with Young Children Learning Language, Observing Children Reading, Interpreting Running Records, Matching Children with Books, Encouraging Reading Development, The Writing Process, Children's Writing Development, Encouraging Writing Development, Teaching Writing, and Making Programming Decisions (English Language Curriculum Services Unit, 1985). The brochure describing this in-service program indicates that it is not intended as a prescriptive course, and involvement of teachers in the ELIC course should be voluntary.

Such voluntary reeducation is more likely to bring about lasting change than official statements and mandated curricula. In fact, significant changes are most often occurring in the classrooms of individual teachers, among teachers banded together to support one another, within individual schools and school systems, and then ultimately, perhaps, at a state or province level, often with the help and sometimes the initiative of teacher educators. Thus the lines of influence are really multidirectional, involving teachers, teacher educators, researchers, and administrators, with parents a supportive element as well. In the United States, many teachers have established local support groups, and there is now a national network of such TAWL groups (TAWL stands for Teachers Applying Whole Language; see Appendix B: "Lists of Useful Addresses"). CAWL (Children And Whole Language) and CEL (Child-centered, Experience-based Learning) are other established support groups. There is also a whole-language newsletter, *Teachers Networking*, published by Richard C. Owen; in Canada, a *Whole Language Newsletter* is available from Scholastic-TAB (again, see the list of addresses). The whole-language support groups and whole-language newsletters both reflect the growing trend in the United States and especially Canada for professionally informed and dedicated teachers to implement a whole-language curriculum based on what is known about reading, learning, and literacy development.

In the next chapter, we will extend the rationale for a whole-language approach, and in Chapter 8 we will suggest some of the ways that teachers can implement a whole-language philosophy.

ACTIVITIES AND PROJECTS FOR FURTHER EXPLORATION

1. In his 1973 book *Psycholinguistics and Reading*, Frank Smith published an essay titled "Twelve Easy Ways to Make Learning to Read Difficult, and One Difficult Way to Make It Easy." In 1977, Estes and Johnstone published a take-off on Smith's article, titled "Twelve Easy Ways to Make Readers Hate Reading (and One Difficult Way to Make Them Love It)." Similar tongue-in-cheek rules can be inferred from Allen's article "Implications for Reading Instruction," 1976 (full references on page 167). Here are some statements taken or adapted from these articles, along with some "real" rules for teaching reading. For each "rule," decide whether it is one that teachers should follow or one that they should not, and why. Discuss, as some of these "rules" will surely generate controversy even among those who have adopted a "psycholinguistic" view of reading. To facilitate discussion, you might make three lists, one a list of rules that are definite "no-nos," one a list of rules that are definite "yeses," and one a list of rules that are debatable or that depend upon how one interprets the rule.

   1. Fail children who do not read up to grade level.
   2. Don't correct children's miscues; rather, allow (encourage, help) them learn

to detect when their miscues don't make sense, and to correct those miscues themselves.

3. Use only basal readers for reading instruction.

4. Follow the lesson plan in the basal reader, without any deviations.

5. Don't worry about precise word identification, as long as meaning is preserved.

6. Assess children's reading by determining their reading strategies and their ability to comprehend a variety of reading materials.

7. Emphasize strategies for getting meaning rather than skills for identifying words.

8. Define reading ability as scores on a standardized test.

9. Assume that young children must learn to read before they can read to learn.

10. Provide many opportunities for children to read.

11. Encourage the avoidance of errors.

12. Don't be concerned about the quantity of miscues, as long as they preserve meaning.

13. Emphasize the strengths that a reader brings to the reading task.

14. Integrate reading with all other content areas; combine learning to read with reading to learn.

15. For vocabulary development, have children copy definitions from the dictionary.

16. Help children learn to establish their own purposes for reading.

17. Emphasize the teaching of skills for identifying words, even if this leaves no time for actual reading.

18. Ensure that phonics rules are learned and consciously applied to sound out problem words.

19. Have children read aloud in groups, round robin.

20. Make word-perfect reading the prime objective.

21. Don't skip over stories in the basal, and do not switch children from one basal series to another.

22. Teach letters or words one at a time, making sure each new letter or word is learned before moving on.

23. Insist on careful reading for detail.

24. Don't let children guess at words.

25. Make sure children understand the importance of reading and the seriousness of falling behind.

26. Don't let children proceed without correcting their errors; correct the errors for them if necessary.

27. Spend most of your "reading" time preparing children for standardized tests (tests of phonics knowledge, sight word knowledge, and multiple-choice comprehension).

28. Identify and give special attention to problem readers as soon as possible.

29. Make it a primary goal to create "independent" readers as early as possible.
30. Make it a primary goal to help children develop a love of reading as early as possible.

After completing this activity, you might read the articles mentioned above to see what they have to say about the "rules" discussed.

Smith, Frank. 1973. Twelve Easy Ways to Make Learning to Read Difficult, and One Difficult Way to Make It Easy. *Psycholinguistics and Reading*. Ed. F. Smith. New York: Holt, Rinehart and Winston, 183–96.

Estes, Thomas H., and Julie P. Johnstone. November/December 1977. Twelve Easy Ways to Make Readers Hate Reading (and One Difficult Way to Make Them Love It). *Language Arts* 54: 891–97.

Allen, P. David. 1976. Implications for Reading Instruction. *Findings of Research in Miscue Analysis: Classroom Implications*. Ed. P. D. Allen and D. J. Watson. Urbana, Ill.: ERIC Clearinghouse on Reading and Communication Skills and the National Council of Teachers of English, 107–12.

2. Below are ten statements from *Becoming a Nation of Readers* (Anderson et al. 1985). Some of the statements are ones with which psycholinguistics and whole-language advocates would heartily agree. Others are statements that, for one reason or another, would make psycholinguists and whole-language advocates cringe. Locate the statements that would disturb psycholinguists and whole-language advocates and *explain* why they would find at least part of the statement disturbing. It seems to me that most psycholinguists and whole-language teachers would find something disturbing in about half of these statements, give or take a couple either way. In other words, there's definitely room for individual interpretation here, as is appropriate in a text emphasizing the fact that reading is a unique transaction between the individual reader and the text.

   It may be valuable to do this activity now, before reading Chapter 7, and then again after reading that chapter, to see if your responses have changed.

   1. "While there is more consensus about reading than in the past, there are still important issues about which reasonable people disagree" (p.4).
   2. "First, like the performance of a symphony, reading is a holistic act. In other words, while reading can be analyzed into subskills such as discriminating letters and identifying words, performing the subskills one at a time does not constitute reading" (p.7).
   3. "The meaning constructed from the same text can vary greatly among people because of differences in the knowledge they possess. . . . Research reveals that children are not good at drawing on their prior knowledge, especially in school settings" (p.10).
   4. "Research suggests that, no matter which strategies are used to introduce them to reading, the children who earn the best scores on reading comprehension tests in second grade are the ones who made the most progress in fast and accurate word identification in the first grade" (p. 10).

5. "Immature readers are sometimes unable to focus on meaning during reading because they have such a low level of decoding skill" (p. 12).

6. "Increasing the proportion of children who read widely and with evident satisfaction ought to be as much a goal of reading instruction as increasing the number who are competent readers" (p. 15).

7. "Many of the tasks assigned to children in the name of reading are drudgery" (p. 15).

8. "A good rule of thumb is that the most useful form of practice is doing the whole skill of reading—that is, reading meaningful text for the purpose of understanding the message it contains" (p. 17).

9. "Thus, the issue is no longer, as it was several decades ago, whether children should be taught phonics. The issues now are specific ones of just how it should be done" (p. 37).

10. "Once the basic relationships have been taught, the best way to get children to refine and extend their knowledge of letter-sound correspondences is through repeated opportunities to read" (p. 38).

3. Respond again to the DeFord Theoretical Orientation to Reading Profile (TORP) included at the end of Chapter 1 (DeFord 1985), and compare your responses now with those before. For each question, circle the one best answer that reflects the strength of your agreement or disagreement; SA means "strongly agree," while SD means "strongly disagree." In what respects have your views changed, if any?

1. A child needs to be able to verbalize the rules of phonics in order to assure proficiency in processing new words.

  1 2 3 4 5
  SA   SD

2. An increase in reading errors is usually related to a decrease in comprehension.

  1 2 3 4 5
  SA   SD

3. Dividing words into syllables according to rules is a helpful instructional practice for reading new words.

  1 2 3 4 5
  SA   SD

4. Fluency and expression are necessary components of reading that indicate good comprehension.

  1 2 3 4 5
  SA   SD

5. Materials for early reading should be written in natural language without concern for short, simple words and sentences.

  1 2 3 4 5
  SA   SD

6. When children do not know a word, they should be instructed to sound out its parts.

  1 2 3 4 5
  SA   SD

7. It is a good practice to allow children to edit what is written into their own dialect when learning to read.

  1 2 3 4 5
  SA   SD

8. The use of a glossary or dictionary is necessary in determining the meaning and pronunciation of new words.

  1 2 3 4 5
  SA   SD

9. Reversals (e.g., saying "saw" for "was") are significant problems in the teaching of reading.

1	2	3	4	5
SA				SD

10. It is a good practice to correct a child as soon as an oral reading mistake is made.

1	2	3	4	5
SA				SD

11. It is important for a word to be repeated a number of times after it has been introduced to insure that it will become a part of sight vocabulary.

1	2	3	4	5
SA				SD

12. Paying close attention to punctuation marks is necessary to understanding story content.

1	2	3	4	5
SA				SD

13. It is a sign of an ineffective reader when words and phrases are repeated.

1	2	3	4	5
SA				SD

14. Being able to label words according to grammatical function (nouns, etc.) is useful in proficient reading.

1	2	3	4	5
SA				SD

15. When coming to a word that's unknown, the reader should be encouraged to guess upon meaning and go on.

1	2	3	4	5
SA				SD

16. Young readers need to be introduced to the root form of words (run, long) before they are asked to read inflected forms (running, longest).

1	2	3	4	5
SA				SD

17. It is not necessary for a child to know the letters of the alphabet in order to learn to read.

1	2	3	4	5
SA				SD

18. Flashcard drills with sightwords is an unnecessary form of practice in reading instruction.

1	2	3	4	5
SA				SD

19. Ability to use accent patterns in multisyllable words (pho′ to graph, pho to′ gra phy, and pho to gra′ phic) should be developed as part of reading instruction.

1	2	3	4	5
SA				SD

20. Controlling text through consistent spelling patterns (The fat cat ran back. The fat cat sat on a hat) is a means by which children can best learn to read.

1	2	3	4	5
SA				SD

21. Formal instruction in reading is necessary to insure the adequate development of all the skills used in reading.

1	2	3	4	5
SA				SD

22. Phonic analysis is the most important form of analysis used when meeting new words.

1	2	3	4	5
SA				SD

23. Children's initial encounters with print should focus on meaning, not upon exact graphic representation.

1	2	3	4	5
SA				SD

24. Word shapes (word configuration) should be taught in reading to aid in word recognition.

1	2	3	4	5
SA				SD

25. It is important to teach skills in relation to other skills.

1	2	3	4	5
SA				SD

26. If a child says "house" for the written word "home," the response should be left uncorrected.

1	2	3	4	5
SA				SD

27. It is not necessary to introduce new words before they appear in the reading text.

1	2	3	4	5
SA				SD

28. Some problems in reading are caused by readers dropping the inflectional endings from words (e.g., jump*s*, jump*ed*)

1	2	3	4	5
SA				SD

4. The points listed below can be used as a basis for journal entries, for class discussion, or for a comprehensive essay over the first six chapters of the book. (Question 6 can best be discussed after also reading Chapter 7.) Recently I have been using such questions both for in-class review and as the basis of an out-of-class midterm exam. Since I have been generally delighted with the results of the written exams, I am including my directions to students here, in case they will be useful to someone else. Here, then, is my current essay exam:

Essay Exam

Length: I have generally found that excellent essays run ten to twelve typewritten double-spaced pages, or slightly more.

Format: While it is acceptable to answer the questions one by one as in an ordinary essay test, I *strongly* encourage one of the following formats:

Letter: Write a letter to someone with whom you would like to share what you have been learning about the reading process and implications for reading instruction. This can be anyone you choose: a parent or family member, a former teacher, a friend who has recently begun teaching, a principal who has interviewed you for a job, the local board of education (assuming or pretending that you already have a job)—*anyone*, real or imaginary.

"Creative": Recently I have received some delightful exams written in a variety of creative formats. One person wrote a dialogue between himself and a friend who was interviewing for a teaching job; another wrote a dialogue between herself and a Martian who needed to know how to teach his people to read English; another wrote an extended diary entry from the point of view of a three-year-old (you'd need to read Chapter 7 before doing this one). Still another person wrote her exam as a takeoff on Charles Dickens's *A Christmas Carol* (complete, of course, with a Ghost of Phonics Past), and this essay has been published in *The Michigan Reading Journal* (M. Peterson 1987). These should give you ideas for creative possibilities of your own.

Style: By focusing on a specific audience and/or by writing "creatively," you should be able to avoid a stuffy, textbooky style. In fact, I'd suggest that you put this book away while writing. To make your writing come alive, and to be convincing, you will need to use a wealth of *examples* to illustrate your points. I suggest you use examples from your own experience and/or make up examples rather than use ones from the text, as this will suggest that you have actively transacted with this text and created meanings of your own. Your essay should sound like *you*, not like me!

Content: As you know, the commonsense, person-on-the-street notion of how we read seems to be that we combine letters to form words, then combine the meanings of words to get the meanings of sentences, and so forth. In short, many people who have never studied the reading process seem to think of it as strictly a bottom-up process, proceeding from smaller units to larger. This view of course affects the kind of reading instruction they provide as teachers and administrators and the kind of instruction they expect as parents.

Certainly there is some bottom-up processing involved; after all, without those squiggles on the page we would not even be reading (in the usual sense) at all. However, as you now know, this commonsense bottom-up view of the reading process is a grossly oversimplified view, apparently more inaccurate than accurate.

All of this is by way of preamble: *What I would like you to demonstrate in your essay is how socio-psycholinguistic research (broadly interpreted) demonstrates the "commonsense" view to be inadequate/inaccurate and what some of the possible implications are for reading instruction.*

I will expect you to cover the following points, though not necessarily in this order. In fact, I suggest that you let your essay flow as it will from one idea to another rather than try to follow this sequence rigidly, just being ultimately certain that these points are covered. The index in the back of the book may be useful in locating information to review, but your essay should not sound like the language of the text! The points to cover, then, are these—plus any others that seem important to you personally:

1. The top-down, transactive aspects of the reading process (discuss schemas, transactions, deep/surface structure).

2. Why/how reading is actually more a nonvisual process than a visual one (discuss the various kinds of contexts and how we use these to identify words and get meaning).

3. How the strategies and miscues of good readers often differ from the strategies and miscues of poorer readers, and what kinds of instructional help poorer readers may need.

4. Reasons for downplaying phonics instruction, and how we can help children acquire phonics *knowledge* (an understanding of letter/sound relationships) without teaching them phonics rules.

5. Why psycholinguists believe that a word-centered approach to reading instruction (phonics or "linguistic," sight word or basal reader approach) is inappropriate.

6. How a whole-language approach to reading (and writing) instruction is supported not only by what we know about the reading process itself, but by what

we know about how children initially learn language—and how children learn in general. (Omit, if we haven't yet discussed the issues in Chapter 7.)

7. How and why a socio-psycholinguistic definition of reading contrasts with a "commonsense" definition (this can be a starting point or a summary, or both).

Clearly some of these items invite you to go somewhat beyond what has been explicitly discussed in the preceding chapters, to draw inferences and suggest implications of your own.

5. Compare and critique two reading series. Take notes on each, considering such factors as the following:

1. *Philosophy* (for example, explicit and/or implicit view of the reading process).

2. *Content* (for example, variety of lifestyles, ethnic backgrounds, and roles; variety, quality, and appropriateness of the literature and other reading selections).

3. *Readability* (not just according to readability formulas, but considering such factors as clarity of presentation, background schemas required, style, interest, and so forth).

4. Treatment of *phonics, vocabulary development, comprehension*, and *strategies for getting meaning*.

5. *Testing* methods and materials.

6. Other *auxiliary materials* (such as workbooks, Big Books, games).

7. *Format, and adaptability* for use with children of varying needs.

Be sure, of course, to apply what you have learned from this text as you take notes on the strengths and weaknesses of each series.

Then write an essay in which you discuss the two series, suggesting which is better in what respects. Give a wealth of examples to illustrate your points, and write so that your essay will make sense to someone who has never examined either of the series. (In my experience, excellent essays again tend to run at least ten to twelve double-spaced pages.)

READINGS FOR FURTHER EXPLORATION

I highly recommend the three readings cited immediately above in activity 1; these are excellent supplements to this chapter.

Cooper, Charles R., and Anthony R. Petrosky. December 1976. A Psycholinguistic View of the Fluent Reading Process. *Journal of Reading*: 184–207. This oldie-but-goodie is still an excellent summary of fluent reading, showing how our understanding of the reading process can be implemented in a developmental reading program for secondary students.

Smith, Frank. 1973. Decoding: The Great Fallacy. *Psycholinguistics and Reading*. Ed. F. Smith. New York: Holt, Rinehart and Winston, 70–83. Provides good follow-up to our discussion of whether people decode written words to spoken words and then to meaning.

Goodman, Yetta, and Dorothy J. Watson. November/December 1977. A Reading Program to Live With: Focus on Comprehension. *Language Arts* 54: 868–79. Suggests ways to implement a psycholinguistic understanding of reading in the classroom.

Atwell, Margaret A., and Lynn K. Rhodes. May 1984. Strategy Lessons as Alternatives to Skills Lessons in Reading. *Journal of Reading* 27: 700–705. Offers valuable suggestions for focusing on strategies rather than minute skills.

McIntosh, Margaret E. April 1985. What Do Practitioners Need to Know About Current Inference Research? *The Reading Teacher* 38: 755–61. Points out that much of what children learn in the first few years of life is learned through the inferences they make, yet ironically when children enter school, they're usually not asked to draw inferences from their readings because inference is considered too difficult a task, one typically not introduced in the scope and sequence charts of basal readers until fifth or sixth grade.

Farrar, Mary Thomas. October 1984. Asking Better Questions. *The Reading Teacher* 38: 10–15. Demonstrates that both recall and inference can be approached through various kinds of questions, some more demanding than others. Suggests that the use of factual questions be followed by questions that deal with reasons, forming an integrated sequence of questions.

Pearson, P. David. April 1985. Changing the Face of Reading Comprehension Instruction. *The Reading Teacher* 38: 724–38. Points out, among other things, that according to the most recent data from the National Assessment of Educational Progress (1981), our nation's 13-year-olds and 17-year-olds did not fare well on test items requiring inferential and interpretive comprehension. Pearson discusses recent theory and research on comprehension, elucidating six recommended changes in the way we teach comprehension.

Christenbury, Leila, and Patricia P. Kelly. 1983. *Questioning: A Path to Critical Thinking*. Urbana, Ill.: ERIC/RCS and the National Council of Teachers of English. Intended to help upper elementary and secondary school teachers increase their students' critical thinking skills, this booklet discusses the theory and techniques behind the use of questioning to evoke prior knowledge and to further inquiry.

Goodman, Kenneth S. September 1979. The Know-More and the Know-Nothing Movements in Reading: A Personal Response. *Language Arts* 56: 657–63. Goodman contrasts the socio-psycholinguistic model of reading with what I have called the "person-on-the-street" or "commonsense" model.

Smith, Frank. 1979. Conflicting Approaches to Reading Research and Instruction. *Theory and Practice of Early Reading* 2. Ed. L. B. Resnick and P. A. Weaver.

Hillsdale, N.J.: Erlbaum, 31–42. This article is much more difficult reading than the Goodman article above, but worth the effort.

Goodman, Kenneth S. April 1986. Basal Readers: A Call for Action. *Language Arts* 63: 358–63. An excellent discussion of recent improvements in basal readers and a critique of them, suggesting what we might do to bring about much-needed improvements.

7

How Does the Acquisition of Literacy Parallel the Acquisition of Oral Language?

Teachers, like the parents and teachers of pre-school children, need to perceive children, not as deficient, but emerging over a period of time as competent in their communicative attempts.

—Janet Black

QUESTIONS FOR JOURNALS AND DISCUSSION

1. How do children learn to talk?

2. How does a mechanistic view of reality and of education contrast with an organic view? How does a transactional view both resemble the organic view and differ from it?

3. What tend to be some naturally occurring stages in learning to spell? In learning to read? How are these two parallel?

4. How are learning to write and to read "naturally" similar to learning to talk?

5. How can we teach transactionally, so as to encourage children's natural writing/reading development?

6. How can we best develop a nation of readers?

AN OVERVIEW

In effect, this chapter develops much of the theoretical base upon which a whole-language approach rests. The section on "Learning to Talk" briefly demonstrates how, in learning to speak, children develop their own increasingly sophisticated rules for structuring language. We do not teach them language mechanistically, bit by bit, from smaller parts to larger; rather they learn language by transacting with a language-rich environment. This view of language acquisition is then placed within a larger framework in the second major section, "Contrasting Paradigms in Language and Literacy Learning."

At the risk of overemphasizing spelling, which is only a minor aspect of writing, the next section on "Learning to Write" focuses heavily on children's natural development of increasingly more sophisticated spelling rules, in order to demonstrate one of the major ways in which the natural acquisition of literacy is like the initial acquisition of language. The next section deals with increasingly sophisticated concepts of the reading process, again highlighting the parallels between learning to talk and learning to read and write. Thus one of the major rationales for a whole-language approach is that it makes the acquisition of literacy as natural a process as learning to talk.

Before turning in Chapter 8 to what typifies a whole-language approach and how a whole-language philosophy can be implemented in the classroom, however, it seems wise to ask to what extent research supports the adoption of a whole-language approach. This we shall do in the process of discussing the report *Becoming a Nation of Readers*. This section discusses the report's conclusions about whole-language teaching and about phonics, then turns to "new" research that supports a whole-language approach. Finally, it is suggested that empirical research alone should never be the sole basis for accepting or rejecting any approach: rather, the choice of approaches should also—perhaps more importantly—be based upon what is known about how children learn, how children learn language, and of course how people read. This brings the chapter full circle and prepares the way for Chapter 8.

LEARNING TO TALK

Since learning to read and write "naturally" in many respects parallels the ways in which a child learns to talk, it is useful to compare the two processes.

How, then, does a child learn to talk? Imagine this scene: A young mother greets her husband enthusiastically as they sit down to dinner. "Guess what, dear? I've found this marvelous program for teaching Johnny to talk. It's called 'Getting Back to Basics: Teaching Your Child to Talk.' It's a great program. It starts first with the basic sounds, like /d/ and /æ/—you know, like in *dog* and *apple*. First you teach the child to say these sounds in isolation and then to blend them together. Why, in a couple of weeks Johnny might be able to say 'daddy.'"

Her husband looks at her dubiously. "Then what?"

"Well, then you teach him to put words together to make sentences. It's simple. You work from the smallest parts to larger and larger parts, until he can say whole sentences. It's just a matter of teaching him the rules."

"Sounds like a lot of nonsense to me," her husband frowns, winding his spaghetti onto his fork. "That's certainly not how my nephews are learning to talk. You must be kidding."

The father is right, of course, in implying that no one ever learned to talk this way. We do not *teach* children to talk, in any direct fashion. That is, we do not tell them abstract rules to follow in order to create words and sentences appropriately. Take, for example, the "rule" for formulating the past tense of regular verbs. What *sound* do we add in changing *like* to *liked*? A /t/ sound. What *sound* do we add in changing *love* to *loved*? A /d/ sound. What *sounds* do we add in changing *hate* to *hated*? A vowel sound plus a /d/, something close to /id/. There is a completely regular rule operating here: when a word ends in a /t/ or /d/ sound, we add /id/; when the word ends in any other unvoiced consonant, we add /t/; and when the word ends in any other voiced sound, consonant or vowel, we add /d/ (an unvoiced sound is one made without the vocal chords vibrating; a voiced sound is one made with the vocal chords vibrating). But how many adults even know this rule? And if we did, how could we possibly teach it to children?

We have clear evidence, however, that children learn this as a *rule*: they do not simply learn to imitate adult past tense forms. How do we know this? Because at a certain stage of language development (often occurring around ages 2 to 3), the child will begin to apply this rule to irregular verbs as well as to regular ones. The child who formerly said "I ate it" and "Mommy bought it" (apparently having learned *ate* and *bought* through imitation) will now begin to say "I eated it" or "I ated it," "Mommy buyed it" or "Mommy boughted it"—the child adding the regular past tense ending either to the base form or to the irregular past tense form. A similar thing happens, of course, with nouns that form their plurals by irregular means in English. The child who formerly said "men" to refer to more than one man will now begin saying "mans" or "mens" (see, for example, Cazden 1972, pp. 44–45).

Clearly the child has not learned these regularized forms like *eated, ated, buyed, boughted, mans*, and *mens* either through direct instruction by adults or through imitating them. Nor is it highly likely that the young child learns such forms from peers, since children begin using such forms even when they have had scarcely any contact with other children. Instead, it appears that on the basis of the language forms the child hears, he or she abstracts the pattern at an unconscious level. Neither the adults nor the child could tell you the rule, but the child learns it and is able to apply it systematically—not only to regular verbs but to verbs that in fact are not regular, like *eat* and *buy*, and even to nonsense words like *rick* or *zib* (Berko 1958).

Powerful evidence of the child's own rule-forming capacity comes from observation of the stages children typically go through in the way they form negative sentences. Each set of sentences below reflects an increasingly more sophisticated stage, an increasingly more sophisticated rule for making sentences negative. See if you yourself can verbalize the rule for each stage:

Stage One

No money.
No a boy bed.
Not a teddy bear.
Not . . . fit.
Wear mitten no.

Stage Two

That no fish school.
That no Mommy.
He no bite you.
I no want envelope.

This not ice cream.
They not hot.
I not crying.
He not taking the walls down.

Stage Three

I didn't did it.
You didn't caught me.
I didn't caught it.

Stage Four

You didn't eat supper with us.
I didn't see something.
Paul didn't laugh.

These examples are from Klima and Bellugi-Klima (1966, pp. 192–96), with the stages simplified somewhat for the sake of the adults trying to determine the rules that are operating for the children at each stage.

At Stage One, the rule is simply "Put *no* or *not* at the beginning of the entire utterance, or add *no* at the end." This is the simplest rule for making a sentence negative. The Stage Two rule (typically not immediately clear to adults) is simply to put *no* or *not* between the subject and predicate parts of the sentence. In Stage Three, the rule is "Add the appropriate present or past tense form of *do* to carry the negative *n't* and put this before the verb, when the verb doesn't already have an auxiliary (a 'helper' verb)." Since a tense marker is not removed from the main verb in this stage, the child produces Stage Three verb phrases like *didn't did* and *didn't caught*. Finally, in Stage Four, the child's rule is identical to the adult's, and the tense marker is removed from the main verb when the appropriate form of *do* is added.

If these rules seem hard to grasp, much less to figure out for yourself, then you are certainly in a position to appreciate the task that the child accomplishes in learning to talk. Clearly the child does not merely imitate the language he or she hears. While imitation certainly plays a part, the child goes far beyond imitation in formulating more and more sophisticated rules for creating sentences in the native language. Eventually the child formulates rules comparable to those of the adults in the environment.

Thus one of the most important observations about language acquisition is that *we do not directly **teach** children how to talk. They **learn** to talk, by transacting with us in a language-rich environment.* We do not teach the rules of language because we ourselves do not consciously know most of them, because children could not understand the rules if we did know and try to teach them, and—most important of all—because children do not need to have the rules taught explicitly. They formulate increasingly more sophisticated rules themselves, unconsciously and without direct instruction, until their rules are like the adult rules that neither they nor the adults can verbalize! All of the basic rules of language structure are ordinarily mastered before children enter school.

If we do not and cannot teach children how to talk, how do and can we facilitate learning to talk? There are several ways.

First of all, we expose them to a *language-rich environment.* This means several things:

1. We model adult language for children. Though we simplify our sentence structure and our vocabulary, focusing on the here-and-now, we do not usually speak in

unnatural kinds of language patterns. (When people deliberately imitate children's "baby talk," this does appear to retard a child's growth in using adult language patterns.)

2. We use language in naturalistic, real-life contexts, such as: in the process of feeding the baby, changing the baby's diapers, and so forth; in the process of acquainting the baby with his/her environment ("That's a dog," "Here's a ball"); in the process of reciting nursery rhymes, reading to the baby, and engaging in other literacy events.

3. We illustrate a variety of language functions, language used for a variety of purposes (Halliday 1975, p. 28):

    Instrumental language for getting things, for satisfying needs ("I want . . .," "May I . . .?")

    Regulatory language for controlling others ("Don't do that!" "Go away!" "Let's do this!")

    Interactional language for maintaining personal relationships (Names, greetings, etc.)

    Personal language for expressing personality or individuality ("I like reading stories," "I like milk")

    Imaginative language for creating a fantasy world ("Once upon a time," "Once there was a lonely monster")

    Informative language for conveying information (Reports, observations about the experienced world)

    Heuristic language for finding things out, for wondering, for hypothesizing ("Why?" "What for?" "What makes it go?" "I wonder what would happen if . . .?")

4. As the foregoing observations suggest, we provide *whole language*—real language used for real purposes in natural contexts—from which children can abstract the patterns of the language. When we use single words like "Look," "Daddy," "Milk," or "No," these words are in a context where the situation makes our meaning clear. We do not speak to children in single sounds or in single words isolated from meaningful contexts. Nor do we recite sequences of sounds or lists of words for children to learn.

Second, and equally important, we have appropriate expectations regarding children's language development, and we respond appropriately to their attempts to communicate. Among other things, this means that:

1. We expect success. We assume that children will eventually learn to talk like adults, and we rarely try to push them into a higher stage of development (at least until they begin school, when they are sometimes sent to a speech therapist because of immature pronunciation). We do not expect failure, nor do we penalize children for not being "on schedule."

2. We focus on the child's meaning, rather than on the form of the utterance. Until children approach school age, at the earliest, they are not usually corrected for

immature grammar ("That no fish school") or for immature phonology ("Dass gweat" for "That's great"). Young children are typically corrected only for inappropriate meaning (calling a horse a dog) or for social inappropriateness (using so-called four-letter words at Grandma's house) (Slobin 1971, pp. 58–59). For the most part, we accept the child's utterances without correction. That is, we attend to the *deep structure*, the meaning, assuming that the surface structure will gradually come to resemble that of adults in the language community. Only rarely is this expectation not fulfilled.

3. We provide feedback to the child in his or her attempts to communicate. When the child's meaning is not clear, we may be unable to respond appropriately, thus indirectly encouraging the child to expand his or her utterances in the direction of the adult forms. When we do understand the child, we ourselves may expand the utterance, modeling a fuller adult form. Thus when the child says "Mommy home" her father may reply "Yes, Mommy's coming home." Simply responding to the child's meaning seems to be even more effective in stimulating the child's language growth. Thus the father might respond by saying "Yes, now we can all go out for supper."

Briefly summarized, then, here are some of the most important observations about how children learn language, how they learn to talk:

1. Adults do not, indeed cannot, teach the rules of language structure directly.
2. Rather, children internalize rules for themselves, by transacting with others in a language-rich environment, an environment in which *whole* language is used for real purposes.
3. Children's focus of attention moves from the *whole* (the idea they are trying to communicate) to the *parts*; gradually they are able to articulate more and more parts to convey that whole—by using more content words, more grammatical markers (inflectional endings and function words), and more and more complex sentence structures.
4. We expect that the child will eventually succeed in learning to talk like the adults in his or her language environment.
5. Accepting the fact that the acquisition of language is a process that will take several years (indeed, a lifetime), we do not usually correct the form of young children's utterances. In fact, we welcome new kinds of errors—such as *eated* and *buyed*—as evidence that children are making progress in acquiring language. We do not expect surface structure perfection for years—if ever.

Two particularly good discussions of child language acquisition are found in Lindfors 1980 and Genishi and Dyson 1984.

CONTRASTING PARADIGMS IN LANGUAGE AND LITERACY LEARNING

As indicated above, a massive amount of research into the nature of language acquisition reveals that children learn language by *transacting* with their environment.

This transactional paradigm of language learning contrasts sharply with the mechanistic paradigm, the mechanistic set of assumptions upon which so much of our school instruction is based. At the two extremes are a mechanistic paradigm and an organic paradigm. Drawing heavily upon an organic paradigm, the transactional paradigm transcends both extremes.

In order to acquire some perspective, a context in which to understand the contrasting approaches to the teaching of reading, it is important to understand these contrasting paradigms, these differing sets of assumptions about the nature of human knowledge and the nature of learning.

First, the mechanistic paradigm. This paradigm has dominated thought in the Western world for the last three to four centuries, since the French philosopher Descartes compared the world to a clock, a machine that could be understood by tearing it down part-by-part and then reassembling it from smaller parts to larger. This view was reinforced in the seventeenth century by the empiricism of the English philosopher John Locke, according to whom the mind at birth was a *tabula rasa*, a blank tablet open to impressions from the external world but not in any way directing the acquisition of knowledge. In this century, the mechanistic paradigm has been advanced particularly by behavioral psychologists, most notably B. F. Skinner, who similarly suggest that the learner is relatively passive, subject to direction from without.

Unfortunately, this mechanistic paradigm has had, and continues to have, a profound and often negative effect upon education, particularly the education of younger children. Some of the educational assumptions that logically follow from this mechanistic view of reality are:

1. The learner is passive, a receptacle into which the teacher pours information.
2. Children will learn only what they are directly taught.
3. Knowledge is constructed "bottom up" from elemental "building blocks," from the smallest parts to increasingly larger wholes. The whole is merely the sum of the parts.
4. Errors reflect a learner's failure to learn and/or apply what has been taught. Therefore, errors are bad. (Alternatively, if rarely, the learner's errors might be assumed to result from the teacher's failure to teach appropriately.)
5. What's important is the measurable *product*, the information learned or the skills acquired. Therefore, instructional attention is focused on the product.

As we have seen, each of these assumptions runs counter to what we know about how people read and about how children learn language. We know that:

1. Children engaging in language and literacy learning are active; they bring their prior knowledge and experience to the task, and they formulate increasingly sophisticated rules *for and by themselves*. Just as they developed tacit rules for making verbs past tense and for making sentences negative, so they can learn and apply letter/sound generalizations for themselves, without needing to verbalize "phonics" rules.

2. Children do not learn merely what they are directly taught. Before attending school, they acquire the essentials of the phonological, morphological, and syntactic structure of English, all without explicit instruction. Explicit attempts at early language instruction usually fail, in fact—see activity 2 at the end of this chapter. Similarly, it is often true that schoolchildren learn *least* well that which they are directly taught, since they often have no personal investment in such learning.

3. Knowledge is not simply constructed "bottom up" from elemental "building blocks," from smaller to increasingly larger wholes. We do not teach children sounds, then isolated words, then the stringing together of words to make sentences. Similarly, the most inefficient way of reading is to sound out words, to try to identify and determine the meanings of words without regard to context, and then to combine the meanings of the words. In neither language nor literacy learning can one build from the smallest parts to increasingly larger wholes. Rather, the whole is achieved by working at least as much "top down," by drawing upon one's entire lifetime of knowledge, experience, and cognitive strategies for making meaning.

4. Errors often reflect simply the stage of a learner's development; if any "failure" is involved, it may be the teacher's failure to understand and accept "where the child is at," and to develop learning experiences based on that understanding.

5. What's important is the process: for example, the process of *learning* to talk and to read and write, and of course the processes of talking, reading, and writing themselves. Focusing instructional attention on the process of learning will, paradoxically, produce the best products.

These latter assumptions strongly reflect an organic paradigm, which flourished during the Renaissance and again during the Romantic period, but which lay relatively dormant most of the time between the era of Descartes and the early twentieth century. Oddly enough, it is one of the "hard" sciences, quantum physics (concerned with the nature of the reality that comprises the atom), which has stimulated the revival of the organic paradigm in this century. With considerable impetus from cognitive psychologists like Lev Vygotsky and Jerome Bruner and transformational linguists like Noam Chomsky and his intellectual descendants, this paradigm has emphasized the learner's contribution to learning. Thus Chomsky, for example, hypothesized that humans have an innate language-learning capacity and that there are features of human language that are "universal" because we all share the same language-learning and language-creating abilities (N. Chomsky 1968).

Most recently there has been an emphasis on the transactional nature of learning. In fact, quantum physics supports a transactional paradigm even more strongly than an organic one (Weaver 1985). Drawing heavily upon the organic paradigm, the transactional paradigm emphasizes not only the fact that the learner is active in learning, but the fact that the environment is crucial too, and can either enhance or impede learning. As indicated, I think we as parents intuitively and implicitly reflect this paradigm as we interact with—or rather *transact* with—young children learning to talk.

Mechanistic Paradigm	*Transactional Paradigm*	*Organic Paradigm*
ENVIRONMENT→learner OUTSIDE———→in	LEARNER◄—►ENVIRONMENT INSIDE———→OUTSIDE	LEARNER—►environment INSIDE———►out
Learner is passive.	Learner is active, formulating hypotheses by transacting with the environment.	Learner is active, formulating increasingly more sophisticated hypotheses about the environment.
Teacher is active, dispensing information.	Teacher is a facilitator, creating an environment and structuring activities that provide the learner with opportunities to direct his or her own learning.	Teacher is passive, simply observing children's growth.
Complex processes (like reading) can best be taught by building up from the smallest parts to increasingly larger wholes.	Complex processes (like reading) can best be learned if the teacher assists the learner in moving from whole to part and in seeing parts in the context of the whole.	Complex processes (like reading) can best be learned from whole to part.
Learners' errors reflect their failure to learn and/or apply what was taught (or, perhaps, the teacher's failure to teach).	Learners' errors reflect their current stage of development and provide teachers with information that will assist them in planning appropriate learning activities.	Learners' errors reflect their current stage of development.
Emphasis is on product of instruction.	Emphasis is on process, with the result that better products are produced.	Emphasis is on process of learning.

FIGURE 7.1 *Contrasting paradigms*

Figure 7.1 contrasts these three paradigms as they apply to education: the mechanistic, which is contradicted by our everyday experience as well as by most learning theories today; the organic, which is likewise a lopsided and incomplete view, though according more with naturalistic observations of how learning occurs; and the transactional, which is supported by the work of learning theorists like Jean Piaget (see Gorman 1972) and by research into the acquisition of language and literacy as well (see Harste, Woodward, and Burke 1984).

In education, surely the organic paradigm presented here is something of a "straw man," an extreme existing more on paper than in reality. The real contest is between the mechanistic paradigm and the transactional paradigm. Steeped in the mechanistic paradigm that has pervaded our entire society for so long, many people advocate a mechanistic approach to teaching and learning, often simply unaware of the research that supports a transactional view instead (see, for example, Goodman and Goodman 1979, and Teale 1982).

In previous chapters, we have seen ample evidence that reading itself is a transaction between the reader and the text. Here, we have seen that the process of learning a language is similarly a transaction, between the child and others in a language-rich environment. Before turning our attention to the process of learning to read, we shall examine in the next section the process of learning to write. It too is a transaction, a process in which children reveal increasingly sophisticated "rules" for representing oral language in written symbols.

LEARNING TO WRITE

Have you ever seen children scribble something that looks vaguely like adults' cursive writing, then proceed to tell what the "writing" says? Figure 7.2 shows a "grocery" list" from Susie, age 3, who dictated the meaning of the words to her mother.

This "scribble writing" tends to be the earliest kind. The child knows that marks like these *mean* something; she understands that writing is symbolic, standing for something else.

SCRIBBLE WRITING
Age 3

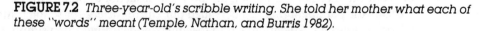

FIGURE 7.2 *Three-year-old's scribble writing. She told her mother what each of these "words" meant (Temple, Nathan, and Burris 1982).*

PREPHONEMIC STAGE
Age 4

Kindergartener

FIGURE 7.3 *Four-year-old and kindergartener in prephonemic stage: the letters do not represent sounds (Temple, Nathan, and Burris 1982).*

Soon, letterlike marks may appear randomly in the child's drawings/writings. Then, at a slightly more sophisticated stage, the child will begin using real letters, almost always capitals, to represent language. Sometimes the child will proudly produce a string of letters and then ask an adult what it says. (Hence the title of Marie Clay's book *What Did I Write?*) I remember my son doing this with large plastic blocks. He would create a totally unpronounceable string of letters and then ask me what it said. Moving slightly beyond this stage, the child will "translate" the string of letters into spoken words, but the letters will have no phonemic resemblance to the words read by the child. In both of these cases, the child is in what might be called the *prephonemic stage*, since the child's letters do not yet represent sounds. Figure 7.3 presents examples.

The next stage is sometimes called the *early phonemic* stage. Each word is typically represented by one or at most two letters, usually the first consonant and the last consonant (if, of course, the word begins and ends with consonant sounds). The examples in Figure 7.4 illustrate this stage.

Children in transition between this stage and the next will sometimes represent each syllable in a word with a letter. Figure 7.5 illustrates this pattern.

EARLY PHONEMIC STAGE
Age 5

RCRBKD

Our car broke down.

Kindergartener

MBEWWMLnt

My Baby was with me last night.

First Grader

INOU

I know you.

FIGURE 7.4 *Children in the early phonemic stage. Notice the letter-name spelling of U for ''you'' in the last example. The first two examples are from Temple, Nathan, and Burris, 1982; the latter is from Dobson, Fall 1986.*

EARLY PHONEMIC STAGE
First Grader
The child represents
each syllable with letters.

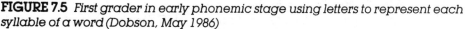

There was a beautiful house.

FIGURE 7.5 *First grader in early phonemic stage using letters to represent each syllable of a word (Dobson, May 1986)*

The next major stage is the *letter-name stage*. Children are still using the phonemic principle: letters are used to represent sounds. But children now usually represent more than just one or two sounds in the word; also, vowel sounds are represented as well as consonant sounds. In this stage it becomes increasingly obvious that although these young spellers typically know the *names* of many of the letters of the alphabet, they do not necessarily know which letters are conventionally used to represent certain sounds. Thus they rely on what they know: when searching for a letter to represent a given sound, they choose the letter whose *name* sounds most like the sound they're trying to represent. Figure 7.6 presents most of the more unusual-looking spellings that result from this logical strategy. As in learning to talk, the children are apparently formulating their own rules about spelling. The examples in Figures 7.7 through 7.9 illustrate some of the spellings typical of the letter-name stage. Of course some of the spellings will typically be inexplicable by *any* of the principles discussed!

As children move toward the next stage, their spellings show increased influence of the standard spellings they have encountered in books, in stores and restaurants, in the classroom, and elsewhere in the environment; the spelling *blue* in Figure 7.10 is an example.

Consonant patterns reflecting the letter-name strategy

Y for the /w/ sound, as in *we* and *went*. The *name* of the letter Y begins with a /w/ sound.

> *Examples:* YUTS for *once*   YENT or YET for *went*
> YOZ for *was*   YEEL for *whale*

V for the /ð/ sound, as in *the* and *mother*. The name of the letter V sounds a lot like the /ð/ sound in these words, and the sounds are made similarly. Thus V is sometimes used to represent the /ð/ sound.

> *Examples:* IHOVR for *each other*   VE for *the*   VA for *they*
> Note that in the former case, *each other,* a young child may actually pronounce the *th* as a /v/ sound, so this fact alone might account for the V used here. However, /v/ for *th* at the beginning of a word is not common; the sound is likely to be /ð/ or /d/. Thus we might expect initial *th* in such words to be spelled as V, if the child pronounces such words as /ð/ and is using a letter-name strategy, or as D, if the child pronounces these words with a /d/ and is using a letter-name strategy.

H for the /č/ sound, as in *chip*. The *name* of the letter H, "aitch," ends in a /č/ sound.

> *Examples:* BRENH for *branch*   WHT for *watched*
> NHR for *nature*   IHOVR for *each other*

H for the /š/ sound, as in *ship*. The *name* of the letter H, "aitch," ends in a /č/ sound, but the /č/ sound itself consists of two sounds run together, /t/ plus /š/. Thus the name "aitch" actually ends in the /š/ sound.

> *Examples:* FEHEG for *fishing*   HE for *she*
> Of course the /š/ sound is often represented by the letter S also, since the sounds are so similar.
> *Examples:* SOS for *shoes*   SES for *she's*

At the beginning of a word, CH is often used for /t/, when an /r/ follows. The /č/ sound actually consists of a /t/ sound followed by a /š/ sound, so again there is logic to the choice.

> *Examples:* CHRAN for *train*   CHRIBLS for *troubles*   CHRAY for *tray*

At the beginning of a word, J is often used for /d/, when an /r/ follows. The /ǰ/ sound actually consists of a /d/ sound followed by a /ž/ sound (the first consonant in *azure*). Again, the choice is logical.

> *Examples:* JRIV for *drive*   JRAGN for *dragon*
> JRAN for *drain*   JREMS for *dreams*

FIGURE 7.6 *Typical letter-name spellings. The examples are taken mostly from Read (1975), the pioneering study of children's letter-name spellings. Other examples are from C. Chomsky (1979); Temple, Nathan, and Burris (1982); and Dobson (May 1986).*

Other consonant patterns typical of the letter-name stage

The letters representing the nasal sounds /n/, /m/, and /ŋ/ (as in *think* or *finger*) are typically omitted before consonants.

Examples: MOSTR for *monster* NUBRS for *numbers* AGRE for *angry*
PLAT for *plant* ATTEPT for *attempt* SEK for *sink*
AD for *and* STAPS for *stamps* THEKCE for *thanks*
CAT for *can't*

The consonants /l/, /r/, /n/, and /m/ tend to "swallow up" the vowel associated with them in an unaccented syllable, particularly at the ends of words. Thus the vowel letter is often omitted before or after /l/ or before /r/, /n/, or /m/ in such syllables.

Examples: SPESHL for *special* BRATHR for *brother* OPN for *open*
LITL for *little* FETHR for *feather* WAGN for *wagon*
CANDL for *candle* GRANMOTR EVN for *even*
GOBL for *gobble* for *grandmother* CRAN for *crayon*
SOPR for *supper*

FRM for *from*

Vowel patterns reflecting the letter-name strategy

A for the /e/ sound, as in *bet*. The *name* of the letter A (eh-ee) begins with an /e/-like sound. Thus A is frequently used to represent the /e/ sound.

Examples: PAN for *pen* PRTAND for *pretend*
FALL for *fell* DAVL for *devil*

E for the /i/ sound, as in *bit*. The *name* of the letter E (ih-ee) begins with an /i/-like sound. Thus E is sometimes used to represent the /i/ sound.

Examples: SEP for *ship* FES for *fish*
FLEPR for *Flipper* WEL for *will*

I for the /ɔ/ sound, as in *clock*. The *name* of the letter I (ah-ee) begins with an /ɔ/-like sound. Thus an I is occasionally used to represent the /ɔ/ sound.

Examples: GIT for *got* CLICK for *clock* DIKTR for *doctor* IR for *are*

O for the stressed /ə/ sound, as in *mud*. The *name* of the letter O (uh-oh) begins with an /ə/-like sound. Thus an O is occasionally used to represent the stressed /ə/ sound.

Examples: MOD for *mud* SOPR for *supper*
JOPT for *jumped* HOGZ for *hugs*

FIGURE 7.6 *Continued*

KUTZ A LADE YET FEH
EG AD HE KOT FLEPR

Once a lady went fishing and she caught Flipper.

FIGURE 7.7 *Four-year-old in the early letter-name stage (C. Chomsky 1971, p. 509)*

LETTER-NAME STAGE
First Grader

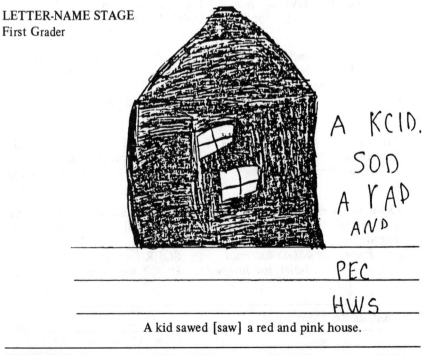

A KCID.
SOD
A RAD
AND

PEC

HWS

A kid sawed [saw] a red and pink house.

FIGURE 7.8 *First grader in the letter-name stage (Dobson, May 1986)*

LETTER-NAME STAGE (late)
First Grader

I:yeNt:toot: The
yeeL The yeeL
yos a gtod yeeL
keeeNd

I went to the whale. The whale was a good whale.
The end.

FIGURE 7.9 *First grader in the late letter-name stage (the use of Y for /w/ shows the letter-name strategy, while the use of double vowel letters shows the influence of environmental print). (Dobson, May 1986.)*

When children have fully entered what some have called the *transitional stage* (I have used the labels of Temple, Nathan, and Burris 1982), their spellings show the influence of standard print by incorporating not only some correct spellings that could not be attained through a letter-name strategy but also some spellings that show overgeneralization of the patterns found in print. Like the young child overgeneralizing the past-tense rule and creating forms like *eated* and *buyed* in the spoken language, the child becoming acquainted with print will overgeneralize some of the patterns of written language, such as the "rule" that a final *e* may be used to signal that a preceding vowel is long. In Figure 7.11, note not only the correct spellings that suggest the influence of children's reading but also the transitional spellings that reflect the overapplication of patterns found in print.

Last, of course, is the final stage that none of us ever completely attains: conventional, standard spelling. It takes most children many years of reading and

LETTER-NAME STAGE (late)
Age 5

He had a blue cloth. It turned into a bird.

FIGURE 7.10 *Five-year-old in the late letter-name stage. Some of the spellings show the influence of environmental print (Temple, Nathan, and Burris 1982).*

writing before they will spell even most (not all) words "correctly" in a rough draft, just as it takes most children several years before their speech is sufficiently "correct" as to approximate adult norms of pronunciation and grammar.

These major stages of spelling development are nicely summarized in a chart from Temple, Nathan, and Burris (1982, p. 103); for slightly different treatments of spelling stages, see Bissex 1980; Henderson and Beers 1980; and Ferreiro and Teberosky 1982.

Prephonemic	*Early Phonemic*	*Letter-Name*	*Transitional*	*Standard*
MPRMRHM	J	GAGIN	DRAGUN	DRAGON
BDRNMPH	P	PRD	PURD	PURRED
Brian	Angela	Chris	Joyce	Lorraine
Kindergarten	Kindergarten	1st Grade	2nd Grade	2nd Grade

While these examples are from different children, they might well have been from the same child at different stages of development. Cramer gives one such example of a child whose spontaneous spellings changed over the course of her first-grade year, as a result of transactions with a print-rich environment (Cramer 1978, p. 107):

TRANSITIONAL STAGE
First Grader

Elaine

At my house i have some
dayseses they are flowrs
they growe in the spreing
i pike them in the
spreing the rain mak the
flowrs growe and in the
somre they all droy up
and more flowrs
growe bak and they
have naw levs and
i peke them agan.

Elaine

I have a ducke. I can drcke
wottre. She has baby ducklings.
Theye foloe her in a strat line.
Theye leve ina barine.
Thoye are yellow. Theye can
tack a bathe and The
un is out. and we play a
lot with Theme.

FIGURE 7.11 *A first grader in the transitional stage of spelling (Temple, Nathan, and Burris 1982)*

October	lfnt
December	elfnt
February	elphnt
June	elephant

In these various stages of spelling development, children seem to formulate increasingly sophisticated rules for how to spell words. For the stages from prephonemic through transitional, these unconscious rules might be something like this:

Prephonemic: To spell a word, just put down some letters; the longer a word is, the more letters you should write.

Early phonemic: To spell a word, use letters to represent the first sound of a word, and maybe the last sound.

Letter-name: To spell a word, write letters for at least three of the sounds in the word (if there are three or more), and represent vowels as well as consonants. Use letters whose name sounds like the sound you're trying to represent. (This principle is operant in the early phonemic stage also, but it is not so obvious, simply because children are only representing one or two sounds per word.)

Transitional: To spell a word, use what you remember from seeing the word in print. If you don't remember how a word is spelled, try using the "rules" for spelling that you've observed in print (e.g., final *e* to make a preceding vowel long, two vowel letters to represent a long vowel sound).

Clearly children's spelling development progresses along a continuum rather than in neat stages; also, children's spellings will typically include some renditions that simply cannot be understood as exemplifying any of these "rules." Viewing their spelling strategies as reflecting a series of increasingly sophisticated rules helps us to understand and appreciate their spelling growth, but talking about "stages" creates some dangers that we must be careful to avoid. First, we must not assume that every child will progress through such stages of growth. To conclude that something is wrong with any child who does not progress in this way would be nonsense. Second, having identified major trends in spelling development, we must not try to hasten children's progress from one stage to another (as teachers all too often did in the wake of Piaget's delineation of cognitive stages of development). As Donald Graves says (1982, p. 28): "It is natural to want children to progress. But our anxieties about child growth lead us to take control of the writing away from children. . . . When children feel in control of their writing their dedication is such that they violate the child labour laws. We could never assign what they choose to do."

With this warning, then, let us proceed to consider what has been revealed by more than a decade of research into children's development in spelling. The following are some important generalizations that can be made about such spelling growth:

1. First, it is clear that children who learn to spell "naturally" in the home or at school do so for the same reasons why they learned to talk: they write, and thus gradually learn to spell, out of a strong desire to express themselves, to communicate, and finally to achieve control over their environment.

2. Second, such children develop an increasingly sophisticated sequence of rules for representing words in print. These rules are not taught by adults but develop naturally, through repeated transactions with a language-rich environment and as a result of feedback from adults and peers who are focusing on the message they are trying to convey.

3. Third, children's attention moves from the whole (the idea they are trying to express) to increasingly greater focus on the parts, as their rules for representing words and their ability to represent them become increasingly more complex.

4. Fourth, adults enable children to progress through these stages of development not by correcting their spellings or expecting standard spelling from the outset, but by focusing on the message that the children are trying to convey, by providing a print-rich environment from which children can obtain concepts about the nature of written language and from which they can absorb the correct spellings of many words and can abstract some of the spelling patterns that are common in the language.

For stimulating children's writing growth, the importance of surrounding children with "real" language can readily be seen by contrasting writing samples from three different classrooms: a phonics classroom, where the reading materials apparently emphasized basic letter/sound correspondences (the "Nan can fan Dan" sort of reading fare); a skills classroom, where beginning reading instruction focused on the development of sight vocabulary using flash cards and simple stories made up of these words; and a whole-language classroom, where the children read and wrote various kinds of "real" materials, such as stories, songs, poems, informational material. According to DeFord (1981), about a third of the children in the phonics classroom and about three-fourths of those in the skills ("look-say") classroom produced the limited kinds of writing illustrated for each group in Figure 7.12. DeFord implies that the majority of children in the whole-language classroom produced writing more like Jason's in Figure 7.13, with variety and individuality. Given such examples, there can be little doubt that a print-restricted environment inhibits children's writing growth, whereas a print-rich environment facilitates it.

Of course one might logically ask such questions as "Will the children ever learn standard spelling this way? Will they ever learn the conventions of written language, such as punctuation? When we talk about learning to write and spell and punctuate 'naturally,' does this reflect an 'organic' view of growth, in which the teacher does little but observe children's progress? Or does the teacher actively transact with the children to facilitate their writing growth?" Clearly these could be paralleled by similar questions about reading: "Will children ever learn phonics generalizations, if they aren't directly taught? And what is the role of the teacher, if not to teach the 'rules' of reading directly?"

Regarding the development of spelling, Cramer (1978, p. 106) summarizes relevant research undertaken by himself and others:

> Research conducted by Cramer and by Stauffer and Hammond has shown that first grade children whose language arts program emphasized writing and wide reading became superior spellers within six months. Furthermore, a follow-up study by Stauffer and Hammond showed that these same chil-

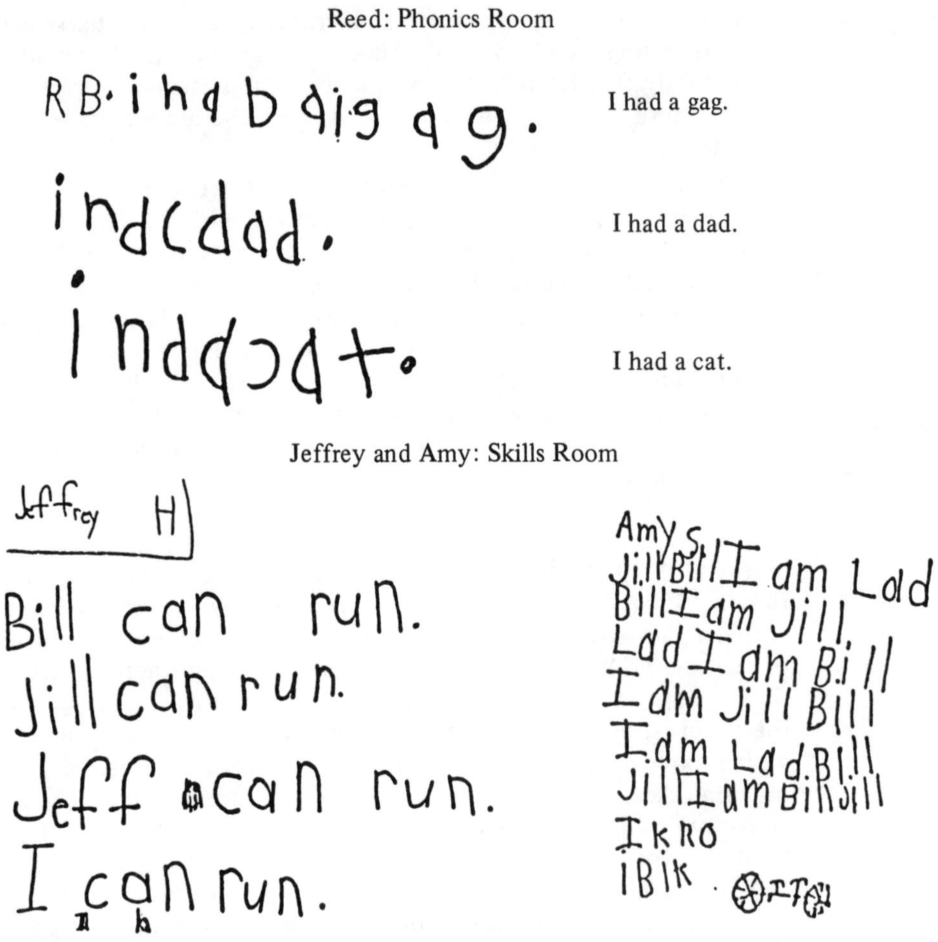

Reed: Phonics Room

RB·ihɑbɑigɑg.   I had a gag.

ihɑcdɑd.   I had a dad.

ihɑdɑt.   I had a cat.

Jeffrey and Amy: Skills Room

Jeffrey   H)

Bill can run.
Jill can run.
Jeff can run.
I can run.

Amy
JillBill I am Lad
Bill I am Jill
Lad I am Bill
I am Jill Bill
I am Lad Bill
Jill I am Bill Jill
I k Ro
IBik.

FIGURE 7.12 *Typical writing of children in classrooms where phonics (top) and sight word recognition (bottom) were emphasized (DeFord 1981)*

dren maintained their spelling superiority throughout their elementary school careers. In contrast, the same studies showed that children whose language arts program failed to emphasize writing and wide reading remained significantly poorer spellers throughout their elementary school careers.

Research data relevant to children's growth in other aspects of mechanics come from Atkinson Academy (a public school, despite the name) in a rural area of New Hampshire. It is there that Donald Graves conducted an extensive investigation of children's writing processes and there that he and the researchers observing the classrooms have ultimately made a major difference in the way writing is taught in that school—and since then, across the nation and the English-speaking world.

Jason: Whole-Language Room

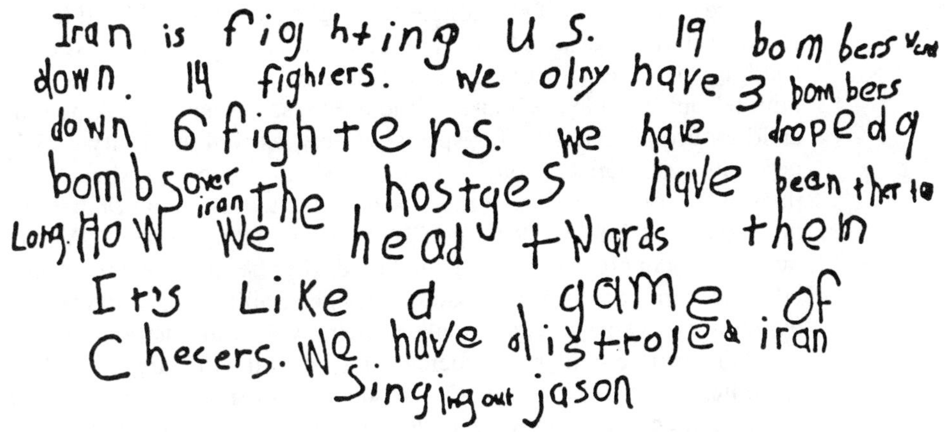

Iran is fighting US. 19 bombers went
down. 14 fighters. We olny have 3 bombers
down 6 fighters. we have droped 9
bombs over iran the hostyes have bean thr so
Long. How we head twards them
Its Like a game of
Checers. We have distroje iran
Singing out jason

FIGURE 7.13 *Typical writing of children in whole-language classroom (DeFord 1981)*

In a significant article titled "When Children Want to Punctuate: Basic Skills Belong in Context" (1980), researcher Lucy Calkins compared the approaches to learning punctuation that were adopted in two third grade classrooms. In one classroom, the teacher taught language mechanics through daily drills and workbook exercises.

"I start at the very beginning, teaching them simple sentences, periods, capitals," she [Ms West] explains. "Everything that is in the book, I do a whole lesson on it." Ms West writes sentences on the chalkboard and asks her children to insert the missing punctuation. She makes dittos on question marks and gives pre-tests and post-tests on periods. Her children rarely write.

In Ms. Hoban's class, the children didn't study punctuation from workbooks and dittos; they didn't do exercises on the chalkboard. Instead, they wrote: for an hour a day, three days a week.

The result? At the end of the year, Calkins interviewed all the children in each class to determine what they knew about punctuation. The children who studied punctuation day after day could explain, on the average, only 3.85 marks of punctuation. Most could explain the period and the question mark, and half explained the exclamation mark, typically by reciting the rules they'd learned. In contrast, the writing-only group explained, on the average, 8.66 marks of punctuation. More than half explained the period, question mark, exclamation mark, apostrophe, the paragraph sign and caret used in editing, the dash, quotation marks, and commas; nearly half could explain the colon, parentheses, and the asterisk. These children tended to explain such marks of punctuation not by reciting memorized rules, but by explaining or demonstrating how the marks are used in their own writing.

For example: Third grader Alan says, " 'If you want your story to make sense, you can't write without punctuation. . . . Punctuation tells people things—like if the sentence is asking, or if someone is talking, or if you should yell it out.' " According to another third grader, Chip, punctuation " 'lets you know where the sentence is heading, so otherwise one minute you'd be sledding down the hill and the next minute you're inside the house, without even stopping' " (Calkins 1980, p. 569). The children use punctuation for special effects, as well as clarity. " 'I keep putting in new kinds of punctuation,' " confides eight-year-old Andrea, " 'because I need them. Like sound effects—it takes weird punctuation to put *thud-thud* or *splat!* onto my paper' " (Calkins 1980, p. 571). Calkins summarizes: "When children need punctuation in order to be seen and heard, they become vacuum cleaners, sucking up odd bits from books, their classmates' papers, billboards, and magazines. They find punctuation everywhere, and make it their own" (Calkins 1980, pp. 572–73).

This study provides convincing evidence that skills are learned more effectively in context than in isolation. Or to put it another way, this investigation provides strong evidence that moving from the smallest bits of information (punctuation skills) towards larger chunks (someday the children may actually get to compose in writing) is not the most efficient way to teach even the so-called basics. This conclusion parallels our earlier observation that even if recognizing words in reading were our only goal, and comprehension were not an issue, teaching words out of context is not the most efficient way to achieve that limited goal.

In a similar vein, it is widely known that the direct teaching of grammar has little effect upon the grammar that children use in their writing or speaking (e.g., Weaver 1979, Hartwell 1985). Again, the active *use* of language seems to stimulate growth most effectively. For example: Using certain kinds of adjective clauses as data, Katharine Perera (1986) provides convincing evidence that at least some kinds of grammatical constructions are learned by *reading* extensively rather than by listening to adults' speech or studying grammar.

A personal anecdote further supports the notion that direct teaching of spelling, mechanics, and grammar may rarely be necessary in a program that encourages extensive reading and writing. Last year, when my son was in the tenth grade, his teacher asked the class to write a poem parallel in overall structure to William Stafford's "Fifteen." I was surprised to see that my son's poem contained three "absolute" constructions (near-sentences that can usually be made into full sentences by adding a word like *is* or *are*, *was* or *were*). Where had he learned to use those, I wondered? Stafford's poem didn't contain any absolutes, and they weren't discussed in any of the grammar and composition texts the school used, nor had any of his teachers taught them directly (I asked). When I asked my son where he thought he'd learned about them, he just shrugged and said, "Oh, all writers know how to use those." But most of my students don't use them spontaneously, as my son had. The obvious though unprovable conclusion was that he had simply absorbed them from his reading. This again supports the evidence that children learn to read and write by reading and writing, and that the two processes reinforce each other.

For the curious, my son's poem is reproduced on the next page, with the absolutes italicized:

A War Death

Shrapnel pounded into the dirt around me.
My buddies fell as the murderous pieces of metal embedded into their skin.
I ran. I tripped. I fell. I found myself in a ditch, *the foul smell of rotting corpses groping at my nostrils.*
I heard the screams of others as they fell beside me, *blood oozing from their mouths.*
I was dying.

I could smell the explosive powder in the air, *hand grenades whizzing overhead.*
Bombshells dropped like hailstones.
Men dropped to their knees and then to their deaths.
The death gases were now stinging my lungs.
I was dying.

A cold shiver shook my soul. I looked on as a hand grenade landed at my feet.
It exploded. I screamed. Blood more than trickled out of my legs, for they were only half attached. A numbness overswept my legs.
My eyelids let themselves slowly shut as a sense of peace overcame me.
I was dead.

Like the research studies cited, this anecdote gives further evidence that we may not need to teach directly many of the reading and writing "skills" that children need to learn. Wide reading and extensive writing appear to be the key.

In short, the bottom-up, part-to-whole, mechanistic paradigm is simply not the most effective in helping children learn to read and write—or in education generally. The greater effectiveness of an approach that focuses on the *whole* task of reading and writing shows up even in some standardized tests of children's ability to deal with smaller parts. This is again demonstrated at Atkinson Academy, where more and more teachers began to adopt a whole-language, integrative approach to writing and reading after seeing the success of the teachers who first began using such an approach. Calkins reports: "When children are involved, they learn more. At Atkinson school, achievement scores on the Iowa Test of Basic Skills have risen twenty points during the past seven years. This year the third graders scored in the 98th percentile on this test, according to national norms" (Calkins 1982, p. 46). While one can scarcely *prove* that this dramatic rise in scores is the result of shifting to a whole-language program where children take more responsibility for their own learning, the correlation between the change in program and the rise in test scores is so striking as to suggest more than mere coincidence.

Thus it seems that Emig's summary of the teaching-learning relationship is particularly applicable to the direct teaching of language skills: "That teachers teach and children learn no one will deny. But to believe that children learn *because* teachers teach and only what teachers explicitly teach is to engage in magical thinking" (Emig 1983, p. 135).

What, then, is the role of the teacher in teaching writing? If he or she is not to teach language skills directly to the whole class, how is the teacher to facilitate learning, to transact with children in ways that will enhance their own learning strategies?

One role of the teacher, of course, *is* simply to note and document the progress the individual children make—much as we note a child's progress in oral language acquisition, except that it is easier to note a child's writing progress because we can collect and if necessary solicit samples of the child's writing to analyze. Here are two ways of obtaining writing samples for this purpose:

1. Choose something that the child has already written and then have the child write the same thing at a later time; compare the two writing samples to determine progress in spelling and the mastery of other conventions of writing. Figure 7.14 shows Sandra's rendition of ''Humpty Dumpty'' in September of her first grade year; she had memorized the rhyme and was thus writing from memory. At the end of February, her teacher asked her to write the rhyme again, and she produced much more sophisticated results. Figure 7.15 shows the story another first grader wrote in September. When the story was dictated to her in June, the second version again showed considerable progress in mastering the conventions of written language (Fitzgerald 1984).

In late September, Sandra produced this rendition of ''Humpty Dumpty'':

In late February, she produced this rendition:

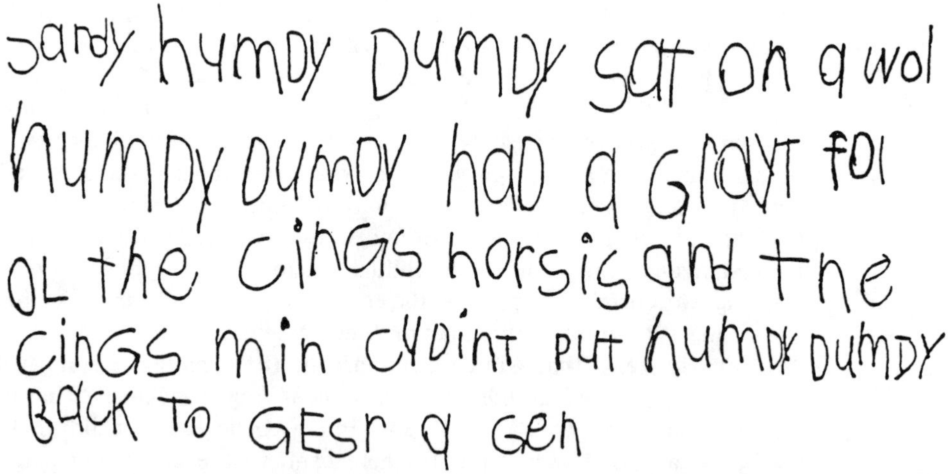

FIGURE 7.14 *A first grader's renditions of ''Humpty Dumpty''* (Fitzgerald 1984)

In September, a first grader wrote this story about her Barbie doll:

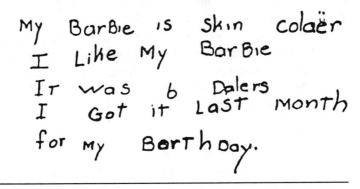

When the same story was dictated to her in June, she wrote this:

My BarBie is Skin colaër
I Like My BarBie
It was 6 Dolers
I Got it Last month
for my BerThDay.

FIGURE 7.15 *Two versions of a first grader's story about her doll (Cochrane, Cochrane, Scalena, and Buchanan 1984)*

2. Better yet, keep a folder of the child's daily writing. At regular intervals throughout the year, compare how the child has grown not only in spelling and mastery of mechanics but in such aspects of writing as development of story structure, completeness of information, vividness of details, effectiveness of "leads" (introductions) and conclusions.

Noting and documenting children's writing progress is crucial in an instructional setting, but of course the teacher can and should be much more active in facilitating that progress. Here are only a few of the ways in which the teacher might stimulate writing growth:

1. Model the writing process by composing on the chalkboard, on chart paper, or on the overhead, soliciting the children's help in shaping the writing.

2. Engage children in *shared writing* (McKenzie 1985); that is, guide the class or a group in composing, revising, and editing a piece together.

3. Help children generate their own ideas for topics.

4. Introduce children to a variety of written language forms (stories, folktales, "tall tales," fables, myths, poetry, interviews, plays, reports, various kinds of items found in newspapers, letters, invitations, and so forth).

5. Engage children in discovering the distinguishing features of such written language forms, and encourage children to write using such various forms.

6. Involve children in writing about literature they have read, perhaps in writing alternative endings, sequels, or brief book reviews.

7. Involve children in writing about topics in science and social studies.

8. Involve children in group discussions of their own writing, enabling them to learn effective writing techniques, such as "show, don't tell."

9. Encourage peer response to children's writing, in pairs and in small groups as well as with the whole class.

10. Conference with children individually during their writing, assisting them in developing their ideas more effectively.

11. Provide a broader audience for children's writing by displaying and publishing it, by encouraging children to write and send letters and invitations, etc.

12. Type young children's stories for them (perhaps one or two sentences per page), and help the children combine the pages into illustrated books, thus making the children feel like authors and at the same time modeling "correct" spelling and punctuation.

13. Facilitate children's development of mechanical skills by encouraging them to notice how the conventions of written language are used in printed texts and by making them responsible for gradually learning and applying such skills in their writing (see Figure 7.16).

These are but a few of the ways in which the teacher can foster children's writing growth. Many of these suggestions are typical of a "process" approach to writing, described in detail in such publications as Graves 1983, Calkins 1983 and 1986, and Newkirk and Atwell 1986. While fostering writing growth, one will of course be enhancing children's growth as readers also (see, for example, *Breaking Ground: Teachers Relate Reading and Writing in the Elementary School*, edited by Hansen, Newkirk, and Graves, 1985). When children try to imitate various kinds of written models, they gain a firmer understanding of writing forms, style, and structure: for example, children will gain a better understanding of the folktale if they have read some folktales, determined from their reading the elements that folktales typically have in common, then written folktales of their own. The reading and writing reinforce one another.

Encouraging children to write by spelling words as best they can will also assist them in reading. It is particularly important to encourage children to write as soon as they know a few letters of the alphabet by name—if not before. As they move into the early phonemic and letter-name stages, children are practicing what they know about letter/sound correspondences: they are using letters to represent sounds.

FIGURE 7.16 *First grader's list of editing skills. In their writing folders, Giacobbe's first graders keep a cumulative list of editing skills for which they can take responsibility. The child adds a new skill to the list when both teacher and child think the child is ready (Giacobbe 1984).*

Never mind that some of their letter choices are not yet the conventional ones; they have at least learned that there is some correlation between letters and sounds in English. This, of course, helps them grasp the grapho/phonemic cueing system in reading. In fact, the knowledge of letter/sound correspondences exhibited in their writing soon exceeds the knowledge that is called for by the phonics worksheets that the children often seemingly cannot do (Harste 1985, p. 8:27). As children begin to attend more to the visual aspects of printed words, they will begin to spell more and more conventionally, with some words correctly spelled and others showing the overgeneralization of patterns they have observed in print.

Thus writing stimulates reading, and reading in turn stimulates writing (e.g., King 1980). Perhaps this is in part because both processes involve repeated transactions between reader and text, and both involve the composition of meaning (see, for example, Shanklin 1982, Tierney and Pearson 1983, and Petersen, 1986).

LEARNING TO READ

Learning to read begins long before children are first exposed to formal instruction in school. It begins when children first start to notice print in their environment, and to recognize that such print stands for words. Before they know what those words say precisely, they know the gist of their meaning. While they may "correctly" read STOP on the octagonal red sign at the end of the street as *stop*, they may say that the red COLGATE on the white tube in the bathroom says *toothpaste*, or that CHICKEN NOODLE on the red-and-white can says *soup*. Like the child in the prephonemic stage of writing, they know that letters put together make words, even though they may not yet have grasped the fact that there is some relationship between letters and sounds.

It is widely understood that children who are read to from birth enjoy a tremendous advantage throughout their school years. Typically they learn to enjoy books and to love reading; many also learn to read before they enter school.

Children who learn to read in the home typically do so by going from whole to part, memorizing a familiar and favorite storybook (mine was *The Night Before Christmas*) and then gradually learning to identify more and more of the words and coming to grasp basic correspondences between letters and sounds.

Admittedly, it may be dangerous to talk about "stages" in learning to read, since there is by no means uniformity among children. But if we remember that not all children who learn to read "naturally" will exemplify this pattern, we might risk delineating some major phases that often occur. These phases or stages are in fact similar to the early stages discussed in Chall's *Stages of Reading Development* (1983):

1. *Schema emphasis.* The child turns the pages of the book, telling the story from memory or from the pictures more than from the print. Next the child may turn the pages at more or less appropriate times, reciting the memorized story. At this stage, the child is sometimes said to be "self-concepting" him/herself as a reader. That is, the child is engaging in reading-like behavior, even though not yet matching written words to spoken words. Rather, the child is relying on contextual cues and upon prior knowledge of the story—that is, upon his or her schemas. The child's attention is focused on using and getting meaning, on understanding the story (e.g., Dombey 1986).

2. *Early semantic/syntactic emphasis.* As the child begins to match his/her oral rendition with the language of the text, the child learns to pick out some individual words and letters, still using picture cues to supplement the print. Words read in one context may not be read in another; that is, the child's reading of words may depend on the situational context and/or on the semantic and syntactic cues in the text (remember my son's inability to recognize his own name "Weaver" when it occurred as the name of a bird in a museum).

3. *Later semantic/syntactic emphasis.* As the child's oral reading becomes increasingly tied to the print on the page, the child may nevertheless make many miscues that fit the context semantically and syntactically, but do not visually resemble the word on the page. That is, the child may make excellent use of the semantic and syntactic cueing systems but not yet correlate these with the grapho/phonemic. Reading "bird" for *canary* would be one example.

4. *Grapho/phonemic emphasis.* After a while, the child evidences more and more concern for reading exactly what is on the page. The child who was formerly

satisfied to read *canary* as "bird" may now struggle to sound the word out, perhaps even producing a non-word like "cainery" in the attempt. An important point to remember is that the child in this stage is typically getting the meaning, even when making miscues like "cainery." The seeming over-reliance upon the grapho/phonemic cueing system is simply a reflection of the child's attempt to master that cueing system *in addition* to the others.

5. *Simultaneous use.* Finally the child is able to use all three cueing systems simultaneously, using semantic and syntactic cues to predict what is coming next, sampling grapho/phonemic cues to confirm or correct that prediction and to make further predictions, and so forth. The child has become an independent reader.

These typical stages in reading development closely parallel the stages of spelling development outlined previously:

1. *Prephonemic stage in spelling, schema stage in reading.* The child has some understanding that written words correspond with spoken words and that letters are used to make words, but the child has not yet grasped the fact that there are correlations between letters and sounds and/or grasped specific letter/sound correspondences.
2. *Early phonemic stage, early semantic/syntactic stage.* The child understands that letters represent sounds (however imperfectly) but can make only minimal use of this understanding in writing or in reading. Substantial knowledge of letter/sound patterns has yet to develop.
3. *Letter-name (later phonemic) stage, later semantic/syntactic stage.* The child is gaining increasing knowledge of the correlations between letters and sounds, but still relies on the names of letters for spelling and semantic/syntactic cueing systems in reading. Attention to the visual aspects of words is increasing, but not yet fully developed.
4. *Transitional stage in spelling, grapho/phonemic stage in reading.* Both the child's spellings and the child's reading miscues show attention to the visual forms of words.
5. *Conventional spelling stage, simultaneous use stage in reading.* The ability to use all three language cueing systems simultaneously in reading seems to correlate with spelling that is becoming increasingly conventional, perhaps as the child becomes more able to attend simultaneously to message and form in writing and as more and more of the child's conventional spellings become automatic.

Seeing such stages helps us understand some of the natural phases that children may go through in learning to read and write, but of course day-to-day, child-by-child reality is much "messier." Figure 7.17 gives some sense of this, as it is a list of various "observations" regarding children's early literacy development. These authors have also organized their observations into stages (with somewhat different names), but the greater wealth of detail should give some sense of the potential variability among children (Cochrane, Cochrane, Scalena, and Buchanan 1984).

A. Pre-independent Reading Stages

1. Magical Stage

Displays an interest in handling books.

Sees the construction of meaning as magical or exterior to the print and imposed by others.

Listens to print read to him for extended periods of time.

Will play with letters or words.

Begins to notice print in environmental context (signs, labels).

Letters may appear in his drawings.

May mishandle books—observe them upside down. Damage them due to misunderstanding the purpose of books.

Likes to "name" the pictures found in book, e.g., "Lion," "rabbit."

2. Self Concepting Stage

Self concepts himself as a reader, i.e., engages in reading-like activities.

Tries to magically impose meaning on new print.

"Reads" or reconstructs content of familiar storybooks.

Recognizes his name and some other words in high environmental context (signs, labels).

His writing may display phonetic influence, i.e., wtbo = Wally, hr = her.

Can construct story meaning from pictorial clues.

Can not pick words out of print consistently.

Orally fills in many correct responses in oral cloze reading.

Rhymes words.

Increasing control over non-visual cueing systems.

Gives words orally that begin similarly.

Display increasing degree of book handling knowledge.

Is able to recall *key words*.

Begins to internalize story grammar, i.e., knows how stories go together, i.e., "Once upon a time," "They lived happily ever after."

3. Bridging Stage

Can write and read back his own writing.

Can pick out individual words and letters.

Can read familiar books or poems which could not be totally repeated without the print.

Uses picture clues to supplement the print.

Words read in one context may not be read in another.

Increasing control over visual cueing system.

Enjoys chants and poems chorally read.

Can match or pick out words of poems or chants that have been internalized.

FIGURE 7.17 *Observations for a reading development continuum (Cochrane, Cochrane, Scalena, and Buchanan 1984)*

B. Independent Reading Stages

1. Take-off Stage

Excitement about reading.

Wants to read to you often.

Realizes that print is the base for constructing meaning.

Can process (read) words in new (alternate) print situations.

Aware of and reads aloud much environmental print (signs, labels, etc.).

Can conserve print from one contextual environment to another.

May exhibit temporary tunnel vision (concentrates on words and letters).

Oral reading may be word-centered rather than meaning-centered.

Increasing control over the Reading Process.

2. Independent Reading

Characterized by comprehension of author's message by reader.

Reader's construction of meaning relies heavily on author's print or implied cues (schema).

Desire to read books to himself for pleasure.

Brings his own experiences (schemata) to the print.

Reads orally with meaning and expression.

Reads in word meaning clusters.

May see print as literal truth. What the print says is right (legalized).

Uses visual and non-visual cueing systems simultaneously (cyclically).

Has internalized several different print grammars, i.e., Fairy tales, general problem centered stories, simple expository.

3. Skilled Reader

Processes material further and further removed from his own experience.

Reading content and vocabulary become a part of his experience.

Can use a variety of print forms for pleasure.

Can discuss several aspects of a story.

Can read at varying and appropriate rates.

Can make inferences from print.

Challenges the validity of print content.

Can focus on or utilize the appropriate grammar or structuring of varying forms of print, e.g., Stories—science experiments—menus—diagrams—histories.

FIGURE 7.17 *Continued*

Given such "stages" in learning to read naturally, it is abundantly clear that learning progresses from whole to part rather than vice versa: from heavy use of the reader's schemas to increasing use of the semantic/syntactic cueing systems, then to increasing use of the grapho/phonemic cueing system, and finally to coordination of schemas with all the language cueing systems:

Schema stage	Almost exclusive use of schemas, along with pragmatic, situational context, and pictures
Early semantic/ syntactic stage	Use of schemas and situational context plus some use of semantic/syntactic cueing systems and minimal use of grapho/phonemic cueing systems
Later semantic/ syntactic stage	Use of schemas and situational context plus syntactic/ semantic cues plus increasing use of grapho/phonemic cues
Grapho/phonemic stage	Temporary overuse of grapho/phonemic cues, along with use of other cues
Simultaneous stage	Simultaneous coordination of schemas with situational context and all the language cueing systems

Of course, it is possible for children to get stuck in the semantic/syntactic stage, and not learn to make adequate use of the grapho/phonemic cueing system; this possibility is discussed in Chapter 11, where the concept of "dyslexia" is briefly addressed. The massive body of miscue research strongly suggests, however, that overuse of semantic/syntactic cues and underuse of grapho/phonemic is preferable to the opposite pattern, for at least such readers are often getting the essential meaning of the text. Far more damaging to comprehension and to the enjoyment of reading is getting stuck in the grapho/phonemic stage.

Some of the characteristics of such fixation in the grapho/phonemic stage are listed by Cochrane, Cochrane, Scalena, and Buchanan (1984, p. 47); in some cases, the wording is changed slightly for clarity:

Overemphasis on processing letters or words
Overdependence on grapho/phonemic cueing system
Sounding out words
Emphasis on word perfect reading
Underattention to nonvisual cueing systems
Poor comprehension of what has been read
Poor recall of what has been read
Reading or producing inappropriate words and not recognizing their inappropriateness; i.e.,

pin
"The bear climbed a pine tree."

I strongly suspect that a major reason why some children become stuck in this grapho/phonemic emphasis stage is that they have not fully experienced the preceding stages, either at home or at school. Not having learned that they should bring all of their knowledge and experience to bear in reading (or having been taught that their experience is irrelevant to school reading), not having learned to use semantic and syntactic cues, in short not already having learned to read for meaning, they focus just on the parts that are emphasized in the classroom: letter/sound correspondences and perhaps words, but often words taught in isolation. Without the prior background of working from top to bottom, from the known and essentially memorized story down toward words and letters/sounds, such children may find it very difficult to move from the grapho/phonemic emphasis stage to a stage where they are using all the cue systems simultaneously.

Instructionally, then, some implications seem clear: since many children will not already have experienced the earlier phases of reading development before entering school, teachers in kindergarten and the primary grades should provide the kinds of experiences necessary for children to progress from retelling a story while turning the pages of a book to coordinating all the language cueing systems with their own schemas and with situational cues. Of course the teacher does not directly *teach* such stages, any more than the parent teaches the preschooler increasingly more sophisticated rules for making sentences negative. Rather, the teacher encourages the children's individual development, though often through activities that involve the entire class. Such teaching that takes advantage of the natural learning strategies of the child is appropriate for virtually all children in grades K–2; each child will simply progress at his/her own rate.

For example, a teacher can engage children in a variety of activities that have come to be called *shared reading* (Holdaway 1979), which is a crucial part of a whole-language approach to literacy. The teacher chooses some material for the children to read as a group: perhaps a language experience story the children have dictated, perhaps a nursery rhyme or song, perhaps a patterned folktale or story—rhythmic and other patterned materials are especially good. The teacher uses or prepares a version of the material that is large enough for all the children to see: a big book or chart, typically, or something that can be shown with the overhead projector. Then the teacher and children learn the rhyme, song, or story by heart, repeating it as often as necessary. Finally they can "read" it together as a group, repeatedly for practice, as long as the children's interest is sustained. A variety of follow-up activities can help children move from whole to part. For example, children can be invited to locate and read certain lines—and later, certain words. The individual words can be written on pieces of tagboard and children can be invited to match a word on tagboard with the word in the selection they have learned. Much the same thing can be done to reinforce children's increasing grasp of letter/sound patterns. For example, the teacher can invite children to locate words beginning with a certain consonant or consonant blend, to locate words ending in the same way, and so forth.

It should be noted that both shared reading and shared writing involve the teacher first in *modeling* the activity to be done, then gradually withdrawing responsibility until the children can engage in the task individually. First, the teacher does the activity alone, or teacher and children do it together; then, the children engage in the activity in groups and in pairs; and finally, the children are able to perform the task alone. This procedure follows the developmental pattern articulated by Lev Vygotsky: "What a child can do in cooperation today, he can do alone tomorrow" (1962, p. 101; see also Vygotsky 1978, pp. 86–89). This gradual relinquishing of responsibility is illustrated in Figure 7.18.

Other ways to assist children in moving from whole to part are less obviously transactive, but ultimately perhaps even more effective (remember how children learn to talk: not by direct instruction!). The following are but three possibilities:

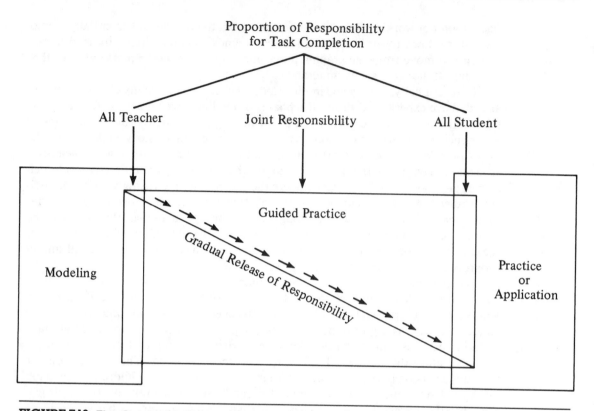

FIGURE 7.18 *The Gradual Release of Responsibility Model of Instruction (from Pearson 1985, after Campione 1981)*

1. As the teacher reads the selection, children can be invited to follow or read along in small, individual books or booklets (either teacher-made or commercially produced).

2. A tape recording of the selection can be made available for the children to listen to (either individually or in small groups) as they follow or read along in their small books.

3. Children can be invited to read in pairs, taking turns, each supporting the other as necessary.

Careful choice of materials that will interest the children and repeated use of these materials over a period of days and weeks will give children ample opportunity to progress through their own increasingly sophisticated approaches to reading.

There are an increasing number of commercially available materials for supporting this kind of teaching. The most common are the Big Book sets that originated in New Zealand. The Big Book itself is written in print large enough to be seen by a class grouped around the teacher; this, of course, is the book from which the teacher and class read together. Accompanying the Big Book are pupil-sized books and often a cassette tape of the selection; typically, these can be purchased either as a set (with about four to eight pupil-sized books) or as individual items. One of the best-known Big Books is Bill Martin's *Brown Bear, Brown Bear, What Do You See?* (Holt, Rinehart 1983). The pattern quickly becomes predictable. The book begins "Brown bear, brown bear, what do you see?" The bear replies, "I see a redbird looking at me." The second animal is then queried: "Redbird, redbird, what do you see?" By now, the pattern is set. Other especially predictable Big Books include *I Know an Old Lady, The Gingerbread Man, The Three Billy Goats Gruff*, and *The Magic Fish*. These and a number of others are available from Scholastic-TAB Publications in Canada. Other book-tape sets and sets of approximately 20 or so different predictable books are available from Scholastic-TAB for shared and individual reading in the primary grades. Scholastic in the U.S. now offers a number of such materials also. Reading Development Resources offers complete whole-language kits, as well as items that can be purchased separately. The Bill Martin Big Books from Holt, Rinehart come with eight child-sized Instant Readers plus a narrative and musical cassette featuring Bill Martin himself. Other companies which now import these kinds of materials from New Zealand include Richard C. Owen Publishers and The Wright Group. Rigby Education's list of Big Books includes some composed by children. See the "Lists of Useful Addresses," in Appendix B, for the addresses of these publishers.

By using such materials and emphasizing these and other shared reading materials in the classroom, the teacher facilitates the processes whereby most children can learn to read naturally. Consider this example of a girl who began to read at the age of 3 (Forester 1977, p. 164):

> She began by looking at storybooks (*The Wizard of Oz* was her first) and listening to the record which accompanied the book. The record signaled when she should turn the page and by listening over and over again she learned the story by heart while following the words in the book with her finger. From that beginning she learned to recognize words and by the time she was observed [at the age of four], it was apparent that she had derived the sound values of letters and used that knowledge to sound out unfamiliar words.

As noted, however, the teacher can be much more transactive than a record or a cassette tape in focusing children's attention explicitly on words and on letter/sound patterns. Of course, some children will need more direct assistance than others—when they are developmentally ready. Chapter 8 on whole language will discuss in more detail how the teacher can transact with children to facilitate and foster their natural learning strategies, and Chapter 11 will suggest how teachers can build on children's strengths and focus on their particular needs within a whole-language context. Meanwhile, in the process of discussing the report *Becoming a Nation of Readers*, we shall examine further the research basis for a whole-language approach to literacy.

BECOMING A NATION OF READERS

In 1985 a report called *Becoming a Nation of Readers* was published. Because the report has been widely cited as advocating phonics and denying the value of a whole-language approach, it seems wise to examine the report in some detail: who wrote it, what research they did and didn't consult, as well as what some of their assumptions and conclusions were.

The report was produced under the auspices of a group that calls itself the National Academy of Education, a group that established a Commission on Reading to produce a report under the sponsorship of the National Institute of Education. The National Academy of Education consists of about sixty members, many of whom have national reputations in education. Omitted from this select group, however, are equally notable educators. For example, neither Kenneth nor Yetta Goodman is a member of this Academy nor of its Commission on Reading, despite the fact that their work on miscue analysis and early literacy is known and respected worldwide, and that they have recently served as president of the largest professional organizations in their field, Ken as president of the International Reading Association and Yetta as president of the National Council of Teachers of English. Excluding educators of such stature, neither the self-styled National Academy of Education nor its Commission on Reading can claim to reflect a cross section of respected professional opinion on reading. As Carey (1985) has put it, "The vast majority of responsible scholars in reading were neither involved in nor consulted concerning the content of the report."

Comparing the 370 references cited in the report to the total number of articles on reading research published in the last two decades, Grundin (1985) estimates that the authors of the report cited approximately 7 percent of the potentially relevant research. This would not necessarily be bad, of course, if that research genuinely reflected the best that is known in the field. But in fact it does not adequately reflect the spectrum of opinion within the profession. In the Foreword, we are told that "the leading experts present their interpretations of our current knowledge of reading and the state of the art and practice in teaching reading" (p.v). But leading experts with conflicting views were excluded. Thus the report purports to reflect a concensus that, to put it bluntly, simply does not exist. Even many of the experts cited as consultants are *strongly* opposed to some of the major conclusions of the report!

Lest I seem to be debunking the entire report, let me hasten to add that it contains many conclusions and recommendations that would be applauded by virtually all reading experts, so far as I know. These recommendations, if implemented, could make a tremendous improvement in the way reading is taught. Thus the report deserves serious attention, but with one's critical faculties alert to the controversies that are being glossed over by such glib claims as Chall's statement in the Afterword, that the report is "a remarkable synthesis of the vast research on reading, which too often seems to have conflicting and controversial findings" (p. 123).

Such claims notwithstanding, controversy still remains. The major controversy that has simply been swept under the rug by the report is the controversy between those who advocate a phonics approach to the teaching of reading and those who advocate a whole-language approach. The authors accomplish this feat partly by assertion and partly by the research they have chosen to cite.

A Whole-Language Approach

The report has this to say about the whole-language approach:

> It is noteworthy that these approaches are used to teach children to read in New Zealand, the most literate country in the world, a country that experiences very low rates of reading failure. However, studies of whole language approaches in the United States have produced results that are best characterized as inconsistent. In the hands of very skillful teachers, the results can be excellent. But the average result is indifferent when compared to approaches typical in American classrooms, at least as gauged by performance on first- and second-grade standardized reading achievement tests. (p. 45)

One can readily question, of course, whether performance on first- and second-grade standardized tests is the best measure of how well children are learning to read. But unless one checks the footnote, one will not so readily realize that this comparison of approaches is based on research that is twenty years old—surely not the most up-to-date information available. Furthermore, the 1967 Bond and Dykstra study cited by the report does not even deal with whole-language approaches as that term is normally understood today! In fact, reanalyzing Bond and Dykstra's data, Grundin concludes that those approaches that come closest to being "whole language" actually produced the *best* results of the various approaches compared (Grundin 1985, p. 265). Thus the report's conclusions regarding the efficacy of whole-language approaches are by no means to be taken as definitive.

Like Chall (1983, p. 7), I too have found no definitive research that directly compares a whole-language approach with a skills or subskills approach. Nevertheless, some of the emerging research on the efficacy of a whole-language approach suggests a vastly different conclusion from that briefly stated in *Becoming a Nation of Readers*. Because available research still appears to be scarce, I have chosen to report in detail the results of a four-year informal research study conducted by teacher Margaret Phinney at Bridgetown Regional Elementary School in rural Nova Scotia—a school of average academic orientation, stable socioeconomic structure, and large classes of from 22 to 38 children, most commonly around 30 students per class. The research was carried out by Phinney and the project co-coordinator Judy Marshall, along with other school staff. Phinney describes the project and the results as follows (Phinney 1986):

> The project was to follow a class, from kindergarten through grade 3, that had been started out in kindergarten and grade 1 using the whole language approach to teaching reading and writing. The children were to be tested annually, using currently available commercial, norm-referenced tests. Previous and succeeding classes were also tested during the duration of the four-year project.

The children were tested at the end of their kindergarten and grade 1 years on the appropriate Gates-McGinitie tests, and at the beginning of each subsequent year using the Stanford Diagnostic Reading Test (SDRT). At the end of grade 3, they were tested on the Canadian Test of Basic Skills (CTBS), the standardized national achievement test—equivalent, I think, to the American Metropolitan Achievement Test. The test is administered annually to all grade 3 and grade 6 students in the district.

The children did extremely well at the end of kindergarten. At the end of the year, they were given the Gates-McGinitie Readiness Test. Of the 352 scores (8 subtests taken by 44 children), 4 (1%) were at Stanine 3 (below average), 13 (3.6%) at Stanine 4 (low average), and the remainder at Stanine 5 (average) or above. The majority, 228 subtest scores (65%), were at Stanine 8 or 9 (high end of the scale). In summary, 92% of all scores were average or above, with 65% at the high end of the scale (Stanine 8 and 9). Whole language definitely "prepared" the children in those terms. For four years we continued the end-of-year testing. The kindergarten teachers continued to use the whole language approach, and the results were similar every year—the children tested extremely well at the end of their kindergarten year. If the whole language approach were to be judged on the basis of that first year, it would have been deemed a miraculous cure.

In grade 1, the children continued to be exposed to the whole language approach in whole-group sessions. During instructional periods, those who were still in the emergent stage of reading remained in the whole language program until they were fully into the early reading stage. Those who entered grade 1 in the early reading stage were put in a basal program that was the most "holistic" we could find at the time. Most exercises and skills were taught in context and integrated with the story material.

At the end of grade 1, the grade 1 level of the Gates-McGinitie test was administered. Although 64% of the subtest scores were at or above Stanine 5, the children certainly did not do as well. We were close to a perfect bell curve, with a slight edge toward the high side, but with 8% of the scores at Stanine 1 and 2, where there had been none at this level the year before. In other words, the children performed acceptably, in terms of bell curves, but not exceptionally. The same pattern continued in succeeding years. Had the project ended there, it could have been said that whole language is fine for kindergarten, but it's no better than any other program once the children reach grade 1.

The results were similar for the Stanford Diagnostic Reading Test (SDRT) at the beginning of grade 2—the curve was slightly above average, but nowhere close to the astonishing results at the end of kindergarten.

But it was in grade 3 that the surprise came, and not from the SDRT results, which showed about as much improvement again as they had the previous year, but from the scores the children made on the CTBS, the Canadian Test of Basic Skills. In this region, the averages have traditionally been below national norms, with the top of the curve at Stanine 4 rather than 5. The year that our whole language group reached grade 3, the peak of our bell curve was, for the first time in anyone's knowledge, over Stanine 5. Further, our grade 3's had the highest scores overall in the county.

Phinney points out that she had no training in formal research at the time and that her informal study needs to be replicated properly, taking into account various factors that were not dealt with in this study—factors such as children repeating a grade or children entering from another school, or such "un-testables" as attitude, teacher satisfaction, increased independent reading, and the influence on and by writing. She also points out that she does not consider any of the currently available norm-referenced measures of reading evaluation to be valid evaluation tools:

> They simply do not tell us what we really want (and need) to know about the way a child processes written language. At this time, the only valid measures are miscue analysis and regular individual observation in informal settings (Yetta Goodman's "Kid-Watching"). I used standardized tests for this project to see whether, in the long run, the children in fact learned, through the whole language approach, those "skills" that the tests deem important, without having been directly taught them.

Obviously the children did learn those skills without direct teaching, and they learned those skills as well or better than children before them in the same school and as well or better than other children in the county, many or most of whom may have been taught these skills more directly.

Another interesting study that deserves mention was undertaken by Warwick Elley in the Fiji Islands of the South Pacific. Working with 9-to-11-year-old Class 4 and Class 5 students who did not speak English as their native language, Elley hypothesized that exposing these children to a wealth of storybooks written in English would not only stimulate their growth in reading but their growth in the acquisition of spoken English as well. The children in these grades were exposed to instruction in English only, but until that time had been typically exposed to English via oral drills rather than genuine communication, with errors being viewed as wrong responses rather than as necessary to natural language growth. As Elley puts it, "Exposure to the second language [English] is normally planned, restricted, gradual, and largely artificial" (Elley and Mangubhai 1983, p. 55). In short, the program in English as a second language fit squarely into what I have previously characterized as the mechanistic paradigm of teaching and learning.

To test his hypothesis, Elley randomly assigned the 380 children in his study to one of three "treatments": the Shared Book Experience group, where the teacher and children read together from Big Books and did other reading and reading-related activities, including reading in small groups and pairs and individually, along with role-playing, word study, artwork, and writing; a Sustained Silent Reading group, where the children simply read silently; and a control group using the traditional English language course described above. While the control group spent 20–30 minutes a day with the prescribed English language curriculum, the other two groups spent that amount of time with Shared Book or Silent Reading activities. Each of the two experimental classes was provided with 250 high-interest storybooks for the children to read.

The results on standardized tests demonstrated that after eight months of differential instruction, the experimental groups exposed to numerous stories progressed in reading and listening comprehension at twice the normal rate. The students were also tested on their ability to complete sentences calling for the use of syntactic structures explicitly taught to the control group but not directly taught to the Shared Book or Sustained Silent Reading group. While the differences were great enough to be statistically significant only with the Class 4 children, those differences favored the experimental groups. That is, the children who showed greatest command of these syntactic structures were the ones who read a lot, not the children to whom the structures were directly taught. A year later, the investigators gained access to the results of the Fijian pupils who took the Fiji Intermediate Examination for Class 6 pupils. This national examination provided results in English, mathematics, general studies, and Fijian language, each based on two hours of examination time. On this examination the Shared Book Experience and Sustained Silent Reading groups "demonstrated much greater progress in their English language growth, this time on all tests" (Elley and Mangubhai 1983, p. 63). While the Shared Book Experience group had shown greater gains than the Sustained Silent Reading group with the Class 4 students, these differences were not maintained over the two subsequent years.

While this study does not directly compare alternative methods of beginning reading instruction, it does strongly indicate the value of holistic approaches to reading and to language growth beyond the primary level. We shall see also in Chapter 11 some of the evidence for the value of whole-language programs in helping readers who have not developed or learned to effectively coordinate the skills and strategies crucial to reading with comprehension and enjoyment.

While hardly conclusive, such relatively recent research studies as these suggest that a whole-language approach may in fact be *more* effective than mechanistic methods in stimulating reading, writing, and thinking—even when these abilities are measured by limited and limiting standardized tests. At any rate, the brusque dismissal of this approach in *Becoming a Nation of Readers* is clearly not justified.

In the next section, we will deal with the second major area of controversy that is simply glossed over in that report: phonics.

Phonics

What, then, of the claims about phonics that are made in the report titled *Becoming a Nation of Readers*? First, it should be noted that even the authors of the report see phonics instruction as playing a very limited role in beginning reading instruction. The report issues such warnings as these (pp. 38–43):

1. The purpose of phonics instruction is to reveal the *alphabetic principle*, the fact that there is a relationship (however inexact) between letters and sounds in the English language.
2. Phonics instruction should teach only the most important and regular of letter/sound relationships.
3. Phonics can be expected to help children come up with only *approximate* pronunciations that must be checked against their knowledge of real words and against the context in which the words occur.
4. A number of reading programs try to teach too many letter/sound relationships; thus much of today's phonics instruction is probably unnecessary and unproductive.

5. It is not important that children be able to state the "rules" governing letter/sound relationships, but only that they have a working knowledge of the basic relationships.

Clearly these observations sound much like ones made in previous chapters of the present book.

Some of these cautions in the report are preserved in the U.S. Department of Education's *What Works: Research About Teaching and Learning* (1986), but the oversimplifications offered in the popular press are another matter. For example, an editorial in the Providence, Rhode Island, *Journal-Bulletin* ("Parents Should Be Concerned . . ." 1985) claimed that the report indicated phonics to be the most appropriate method for beginning reading instruction. This may seem a logical conclusion to the uniformed and the unwary, but it is not what the report said. Perhaps the report's strongest statement in favor of phonics is the following: "Thus, the issue is no longer, as it was several decades ago, whether children should be taught phonics. The issues now are specific ones of just how it should be done" (p. 37). Surrounding statements in the report, however, make it clear that phonics is not to be considered a *method* for teaching reading; rather, it is only *one* cue system used in identifying words, and should be taught as such. There is a vast difference between seeing phonics as one important component of a beginning reading program and seeing phonics as the most appropriate method for beginning reading instruction.

Besides the report's vulnerability to misinterpretation (something for which the report can scarcely be faulted), another difficulty with the report's discussion of phonics is that it assumes or asserts a greater degree of concensus than exists. Although all reading educators may agree that children need some knowledge of basic letter/sound correspondences, there is considerable disagreement regarding the degree to which this knowledge must be conscious rather than unconscious, and the degree to which it must be explicitly taught. Those with considerable understanding of language acquisition typically believe that most children can learn basic letter/sound correspondences through a whole-language approach, with little if any direct instruction.

What does the research say? As you have probably realized by now, it depends partly on whose research, and partly on how success in reading is measured. None of the aforementioned research on a whole-language approach was cited in the report's discussion of phonics or whole language. From the research that *was* cited, the report concludes as follows:

> Classroom research shows that, on the average, children who are taught phonics get off to a better start in learning to read than children who are not taught phonics. The advantage is most apparent in tests of word identification, though children in programs in which phonics gets a heavy stress also do better on tests of sentence and story comprehension, particularly in the early grades. (p. 37)

There are important questions that need to be asked about this kind of summary, among them these:

1. Does the summary include all of the relevant research? The answer clearly seems to be no, given not only Grundin's estimate that only about 7 percent of the overall research was consulted but also the conflicting research studies cited in this section of the chapter.

2. More specifically, did the cited studies compare the efficacy of phonics instruction in isolation versus instruction in using grapho/phonemic cues *along with* syntactic and semantic cues and the reader's schemas? All too often, studies which claim to show the superiority of phonics have tested it in comparison only with a sight word or "look-say" approach, not in comparison with a whole-language approach that focuses first on using schemas and syntactic/semantic cues and then *gradually* focuses more and more on using grapho/phonemic cues in conjunction with these. The issue is not a simple matter of phonics versus no-phonics but rather of phonics-in-isolation versus phonics-in-context, the latter being the approach of whole-language educators (see Harste 1985, p. 8:28).

3. What is really assessed in the so-called tests of sentence and story comprehension? To a great extent, such tests appear to measure the ability to read words in isolation (so as to complete a sentence) and/or the ability to locate answers to recall questions in a text they may not even understand, as we were able to do with the "corandic" and "blonke" passages.

4. Might there be more important goals than scoring higher on tests of word identification and on tests of so-called sentence and story comprehension? Yes, certainly.

About Tests . . . and Research . . .

The latter question above is a crucial one. Those who tout standardized test scores as appropriate measures of reading achievement are implicitly operating on assumptions like these, all of which are suspect:

1. Children's ability to identify words is an accurate measure of their reading ability. (But how can this be true, when words are easier to identify in context than in isolation?)

2. Children's ability to answer sentence-completion questions is an adequate measure of their reading ability. (But how can this be true, if such questions require children to identify a set of words in isolation in order to determine which best fits the blank?)

3. Children's ability to answer multiple-choice questions is an adequate measure of their reading ability. (But how can this be true, when it is so easy for many children to locate the "right" answer in the test passage, without necessarily understanding it? Or when children can tell us about what they've read, even though they are not very skilled at answering multiple-choice questions about their reading?)

In our understandable desire to make reading easier to teach and easier to test, we have drastically distorted the reading process and mistaken shadow for substance, children's ability to respond to bits and pieces of language for their ability to comprehend whole language used for real purposes. By mistaking shadow for substance, we overestimate the reading ability of many children but underestimate the ability of many others.

It is partly for this reason that many educators have come to distrust the *empirical* research that purports to demonstrate the efficacy of one approach over another—even when the favored approach is the one preferred by the investigator. Many of us are all too aware of the pitfalls of this kind of research.

Over the years, it has become increasingly obvious that the expectations of the researcher tend to affect the outcome of the research, and that any kind of special attention given to research subjects (in our situation, to schoolchildren) tends to have a positive effect on the outcome. The latter is called the "Hawthorne" effect, from an experiment conducted at the Hawthorne, Illinois, plant of the Western Electric Company: in an attempt to determine whether increasing the level of lighting would increase worker productivity, researchers discovered that decreasing the lighting level had an equally productive effect. It was finally concluded that almost any experimental manipulation, any extra attention, any apparent expectation of a change, could in fact stimulate the expected result. The mere knowledge that an experiment is being conducted is often enough to cause the experimental subjects to change.

This factor may explain the results of an experiment recently described to me by a colleague. At a conference on the use of computers in teaching writing, he had inquired about the results of another researcher's investigation, a few years ago, into the effectiveness of a computer program to assist students in "invention" (the generation of ideas) and in mechanics/grammar. Yes, the man reported, the computer group did better than the control group that received no special treatment, particularly with respect to mechanics/grammar. But, he confided, the experimenters had taken another group out to the basketball court and instructed them to practice shooting baskets, telling them that this would help their coordination in writing. You probably guessed it: the basketball-shooting group improved the most as writers, foiling the investigators' attempt to prove that the improved performance of the computer group could not be discounted as merely an instance of the Hawthorne effect. In fact, the experiment reinforced the observations at the Hawthorne plant: that giving special attention to workers (in this case, students) can have a positive effect on their work, regardless of whether the special attention seems in any way appropriate to the task!

Particularly well-documented is the "Pygmalion effect": in a classic experiment, 18 teachers in grades 1 through 6 were given the names of children in their classrooms who, in the following school year, would show dramatic intellectual growth; these children were roughly 20 percent of the students. The experimenters pretended that the predictions were made on the basis of an IQ test that had recently been administered to the children, but in fact the children labeled as potential "bloomers" were chosen by means of a table of random numbers. Thus the difference between the predicted "bloomers" and the other children was only in the minds of the teachers. When all the children were retested with the same IQ test at the end of the school year, the children labeled as "bloomers" were found to have gained significantly more than the other children in the same classes. Thus it appears that the teachers' expectations became self-fulfilling prophecies: the teachers expected the children to "bloom," and they did. The teachers' expectations, plus whatever differential treatment might have emanated from those expectations, had significant effects upon the children expected to show dramatic intellectual growth (Rosenthal and Jacobson 1968, pp. 174–82).

The effect of expectations is amply documented from the field of medicine as well, where it is known as the "placebo effect." Researchers have found that under certain conditions, giving patients so-called sugar pills or *placebos* can have as much of a positive effect on illness as giving them actual drugs. The placebo is particularly effective, of course, when the physician enthusiastically suggests to the patient that the "medication" will alleviate his or her condition. However, placebos also tend to have a high success rate in research studies where the patient does not know whether he or she is receiving an actual drug or a placebo. One explanation for this is the patient's knowledge that there's at least a strong chance that the medication is "real." Another potent factor is the belief of the physician. In studies where the *physician* has been led to believe that the real drug is the placebo and that the placebo is the real drug, patients taking the *placebo* have been known to do better! Such results can occur even in studies where the physicians or others administering the drug have tried to refrain from communicating their beliefs to the patients. In other words, medical personnel apparently communicate their expectations to patients in some subtle and not easily controlled way, with the result that patients tend to respond accordingly (see, for example, Englehardt, Margolis, Rudorfer, and Paley 1969, as discussed in Evans, 1985, p. 224).

As a result of studies such as these, many people are increasingly convinced that it is impossible to conduct empirical research without affecting the outcome (Weaver 1985; Harste, Woodward, and Burke, February 1984). Thus it seems futile to try to demonstrate the superiority of one teaching method over another by empirical research alone.

Fortunately, empirical research is not the only basis on which to determine the most appropriate instructional program—nor is it necessarily the best. Equally and perhaps more important considerations are:

1. What approach is most congruent with what we know about how people learn in general?
2. What approach is most congruent with what we know about how people naturally acquire language and literacy skills?
3. What approach is most congruent with what we know about the nature of the target behavior, in this case reading itself?
4. In which approach is the *means* of instruction and assessment most congruent with the desired *end*, in this case the ability to read, learn from, and enjoy a wide variety of printed materials?

Clearly a whole-language approach is favored in each case.

Determining the "Best" Approach

In light of the various possible criteria for determining which approach is the best, let us consider again the following statement from the *Becoming a Nation of Readers* report: "Classroom research shows that, on the average, children who are taught phonics get off to a better start in learning to read than children who are not taught phonics." Even if *all* the empirical research showed this, which it certainly doesn't, and even if empirical research weren't likely to be tainted by the expectations of those involved, which it is, would we necessarily be willing to agree that children who get the highest scores on word recognition tests and standardized tests are the ones who have gotten off to a better start in reading?

Given what is known about factors involved in human learning in general and language and literacy learning in particular, I think we might well suggest a different set of criteria for determining which children have gotten off to a "better start" in reading. We might suggest, for example, that those who have gotten off to a better start are the ones who have learned to read and enjoy various kinds of literature (folktales and fairy tales, nursery rhymes and songs, fantasy, realistic fiction, poetry, and so forth), those who have learned to express their comprehension of a story through a variety of means (oral explanation, writing, drawing/painting, drama), who have learned to read various kinds of informational print (signs, labels, notices, directions, informational articles), who have been encouraged to develop increasingly sophisticated reading strategies as they become ready, who have been encouraged to take risks and not been penalized for making "errors," and who have clearly been expected to succeed.

In short, one might argue that the children who have gotten off to a better start in reading are those who have developed confidence in their own ability to learn to read and to read independently, who have become motivated to read and learned to enjoy reading and sharing a wide variety of materials, even in the earliest years, regardless of their scores on standardized tests. Reducing the teaching of reading to phonics rules and flash cards and reducing instructional materials to severely limited and limiting reading fare can scarcely be justified on the grounds of a few percentage points.

Classroom teachers themselves tend to be impressed less by empirical (often laboratory) research than by naturalistic, *ethnographic* research, including case studies and extensive classroom observation that is not necessarily quantifiable—not to mention, of course, the teacher's own experience (e.g., Harste, Woodward, and Burke, both 1984 references; Moore 1983; Carey 1980). Such ethnographic research and experience strongly suggest that if we truly want a nation of readers, a nation of people who not only *can* read but *do* read—willingly—we need to develop reading programs that will acknowledge and build upon children's natural learning strategies and their strengths, in order to make them not only effective and efficient but eager readers. One might even suggest that only *if* children become eager readers are they likely to become highly efficient and effective as readers. More generally, as Bettelheim and Zelan warn (1981, p. 25), "A child's attitude toward reading is of such importance that, more often than not, it determines his scholastic fate. Moreover, his experiences in learning to read may decide how he will feel about learning in general, and even about himself as a person.'' It is imperative that our instructional paradigm and approach make children *want* to read and convince them that they *can* read.

THE CHAPTER IN REVIEW

The chapter began by exploring how children learn language, how they learn to speak, on the assumption that this understanding would guide us in developing appropriate programs for helping children learn to read and write. Some of the most crucial points are:

1. Adults do not, indeed cannot, teach the rules of language structure directly. Implication: Neither can we directly teach ''rules'' for reading and writing (or, we can teach rules, but they aren't necessarily learnable, nor necessarily the ones that children need to learn).
2. Rather, children internalize the rules for themselves, by transacting with a language-rich environment.
3. Children's focus of attention moves from the *whole*, the idea they are trying to communicate, to the *parts*; from meaning to form, from deep structure to greater and greater surface accuracy.
4. We expect children to succeed in learning to talk, and our expectation is reflected in the way we transact with them as they learn language.
5. Realizing that the process of learning a language is gradual, we do not expect surface structure perfection for several years—if ever.

One of the most crucial implications for the acquisition of literacy is that although we may ''teach'' rules and procedures for writing and reading, in fact nothing much is learned until and unless children internalize and develop writing and reading strategies by and for themselves. This is particularly clear when children who seem to have remained untouched by months of reading instruction suddenly become readers overnight. Learning occurs primarily from the inside out, and the most we can do is transact with children in ways that enhance their ability to learn.

This view emerging from research into the acquisition of language and literacy contrasts sharply, of course, with the popular view of education. Much of our classroom instruction is based upon a mechanistic view of reality, according to which everything can be built up from the smallest parts to increasingly larger wholes: hence a skills approach focusing first on letter/sound correspondences, then on other strategies for analyzing words, then on what are simplistically assumed to be increasingly more sophisticated comprehension skills. According to the mechanistic paradigm, the teacher is an active dispenser of information and the learner is a passive recipient. At the opposite extreme is the organic paradigm, according to which the teacher is a passive observer and the learner is active, formulating increasingly more sophisticated hypotheses about the world and integrating new knowledge with old. The transactional paradigm reflected in this book draws heavily upon the organic paradigm, as both emphasize the active role of the learner. However, a transactional view emphasizes the fact that the child does transact with the environment in order to learn; the child does not learn in a sensory-deprived environment. Furthermore, it emphasizes the role of the teacher as facilitator, someone who can create an environment that facilitates learning and who can provide classroom activities that encourage children's natural development, in particular the natural development of reading and writing strategies.

What patterns of development do seem to arise more or less naturally, in reading and writing? For simplicity, the discussion of writing development focused just on the phases children typically go through in learning to spell for themselves. Beyond the earliest scribble writing phase, four phases or "stages" that may occur during the preschool to primary years were discussed: a *prephonemic stage*, when the child uses letters to represent words, but these letters do not represent sounds; an *early phonemic stage*, when the child typically uses one or two letters to represent the most salient sounds in a word (often a first and last consonant); a *letter-name stage*, in which the child represents more of the sounds in a word, and it becomes increasingly clear that in trying to represent a sound, the child is choosing the letter whose *name* "makes" that sound; and a *transitional stage*, during which the child's spellings show the increasing influence of printed materials, including overgeneralizations of observed spelling patterns (like a final silent *e*). Last, of course, is a conventional spelling stage, when the majority of the child's spellings have become standard. Delineation of these stages led to a discussion of research suggesting that mastery of the *parts* in writing (spelling, punctuation, and so forth) is best achieved by first focusing on the *whole*, the process of writing to express oneself and to communicate. The teacher can best help the child master the parts by transacting with the child in the context of the child's own writing.

Closely paralleling the common patterns of development in learning to spell are related patterns in learning to read. To vastly oversimplify, children who learn to read naturally, in the home or at school, tend to go through several successive phases or "stages": a *schema stage*, when the child is relying on memory and pictures to "read" a printed book; early and later *semantic/syntactic stages*, when the child is partly reciting and partly reading, using mainly syntactic and semantic cues for dealing with unknown words; a *grapho/phonemic stage*, when the child focuses heavily on grapho/phonemic cues; and finally a *simultaneous stage*, when the child is integrating knowledge from his/her schemas and the situational context with information available from all three language cueing systems: semantic, syntactic, and grapho/phonemic. It is hypothesized that many children who get stuck in the grapho/phonemic stage, who persist in overusing grapho/phonemic cues at the expense of others, do so because they have not previously gone through phases where they relied primarily on their schemas and on semantic and syntactic cues. The recommendation: that teachers in kindergarten and the primary grades engage children in *shared reading*, a group of whole-language activities that will help the children progress from "reading" a remembered story to using all the knowledge and language resources available to them in reading new and unfamiliar material.

The last section on "Becoming a Nation of Readers" focused once again on the question of what method is the best for teaching children to read. Discussion dealt with two key issues in the report *Becoming a Nation of Readers*, in which it is asserted that classroom research shows on the one hand the whole-language approach to be not particularly effective, while on the other hand showing that children who are taught phonics generally get off to a better start in learning to read than children who are not taught phonics. Several points were made in rebuttal:

1. The research purporting to indicate that the whole-language approach is not particularly effective is not only severely outdated and incomplete, but in fact did not deal at all with what are today considered whole-language approaches.

2. The report clearly does not recommend phonics as a total approach to the teaching of reading, but merely suggests that important and regular letter/sound relationships be taught as a clarification of the alphabetic principle in English spelling and as one important cue to word recognition, in conjunction with schemas and context.

3. Other empirical research suggests the superiority of a whole-language approach over more limited skills approaches, such as those focusing on phonics.

4. Empirical research itself is, however, subject to severe limitations, partly because it may so readily be skewed by the experimenter's expectations and by the experimental subjects' tendency to respond favorably to *any* kind of change in conditions or treatment.

5. Instead of relying merely on empirical research to determine which instructional approach is most appropriate, we should look also at such questions as which approach is most congruent with what we know about how people learn, and how people learn language and become literate.

6. Instructional goals need not and should not be limited to what can be measured in percents and percentiles on standardized tests.

7. If we genuinely want to produce a nation of readers, people who not only can read but who do read voluntarily, then we cannot afford to focus first on "learning to read" (a skills approach) and postpone until later the pleasures of "reading to learn"; rather, reading must be made enjoyable and motivational from the very beginning.

It is to this topic that we shall turn in the next chapter: how to make children eager readers and *thereby* help them become effective and efficient readers.

ACTIVITIES AND PROJECTS FOR FURTHER EXPLORATION

1. For each group of questions below, try to determine the "rule" governing how they are formed. Then decide which rule you think would develop first, second, and third (Klima and Bellugi-Klima 1966; Dale 1972; Cazden 1972). How feasible would it be to *teach* children these rules?

a. What he can ride in?
How he can be a doctor?
Why he don't know how to pretend?
Where my spoon goed?

b. Where's his other eye?
Why are you thirsty?
What did you doed?

c. Who that?
What cowboy doing?
Where Ann pencil?
Where milk go?
Where horsie go?

2. The following conversation took place when a psychologist tried to correct an immaturity in her daughter's speech (McNeill 1966, p. 69):

> *Child*:　Nobody don't like me.
> *Mother*:　No, say "Nobody likes me."
> *Child*:　Nobody don't like me.
> 　　　　*(eight repetitions of this dialogue)*
> *Mother*:　No. Now listen carefully; say "Nobody likes me."
> *Child*:　Oh! Nobody don't likes me!

What does this incident suggest about the feasibility of deliberately trying to accelerate children's language development? What are some possible implications for teaching?

3. *a.* To enhance your understanding of the patterns typical of letter-name spellings, write the following words, spelling them in accordance with the letter-name patterns explained in Figure 7.6. This list could be used as a quick assessment of children's spelling development, too. If used in that way, it would be important to say the word, then use the word in a sentence, then repeat the word.

　　1. cat　　　　as in *Our cat purrs a lot.*
　　2. wet　　　　as in *The dog got all wet.*
　　3. make　　　as in *Let's make pizza.*
　　4. sent　　　as in *I sent her a birthday card.*
　　5. water　　　as in *Let's get a drink of water.*
　　6. why　　　　as in *Why did she do that?*
　　7. chip　　　as in *We baked some chocolate chip cookies.*
　　8. band　　　as in *Rob plays a trumpet in the band.*
　　9. clock　　　as in *Look at the clock to see what time it is.*
　　10. train　　　as in *Jimmy has a new electric train.*
　　11. once　　　as in *"Once upon a time . . ."*
　　12. city　　　as in *Molly lives in the city.*
　　13. dragon　　as in *It's a fire-breathing dragon.*
　　14. sheet　　　as in *May I have a sheet of paper?*
　　15. kind　　　as in *What kind of candy is it?*

    b. Choose five of the words in the list above and write each of them as you think they might be written in the *prephonemic, early phonemic*, and *transitional* stages. Explain the typical differences among the stages.

4. The following "stories" reflect the very first writing attempts of four first graders, with their spelling standardized. Which writings impress you the most? Which writers do you think were most concerned about spelling words "correctly," most afraid to take the risk of spelling words as best they could? (Cramer 1978, p. 43). Discuss.[1]

I play in the grass.
And I play with my friends.
And I play with Debbie.
        —Mary

My dad is nice.
My mom is nice.
My sisters are nice.
        —Danielle

Winnie the Pooh
One evening Winnie went
out to get some honey.
He climbed and climbed
for honey. He found honey.
        —John

I cracked my head. I fell
off the bed. My mom
took me to the hospital.
        —Nathalie

5. Realizing that they do not know the "correct" spelling for words, some first graders may hesitate to try writing. How could you help such children learn to spell words for themselves, assuming that they know at least the names of a few letters? Write a little dialogue in which you imagine yourself helping a child sound out and spell the word *hospital*. Remember that the early phonemic speller will typically represent only a few of the sounds (see Cramer 1978, p. 105).

6. Should teachers "correct" children's writing? Consider the following quote:

> Evidence is also clear on this point: Children who write frequently and receive no correction on their papers will write more, have more creative ideas, enjoy writing more, and—at worst—will make no more mechanical errors than do those who receive correction on their papers. According to most studies, those who do not receive corrections make even fewer errors in capitalization, punctuation, and spelling. (Hillerich 1977, p. 306; he cites several sources)

Considering your own experience (as student, parent, teacher), would you agree with this assertion? What better ways might there be to help students write "correctly"? Discuss how the issue of whether or not to correct children's writing reflects the two contrasting paradigms, mechanistic and transactional.

7. Patrick Hartwell has made some interesting comments on the issue of whether "formal" grammar (grammar isolated from other language activities, like writing and reading) should be taught in the schools. Read the following quote and consider whether much the same thing could be said about the issue of how children can best be taught to read. Discuss.

> Seventy-five years of experimental research has for all practical purposes told us nothing. . . . Studies are interpreted in terms of one's prior assumptions about the value of teaching grammar: their results seem not to change those assumptions. . . . It would seem unlikely, therefore, that further experimental research, in and of itself, will resolve the grammar issue. Any experimental design can be nitpicked, any experimental population can be criticized, and any experimental conclusion can be questioned or, more often, ignored. In fact, it may well be that the grammar question is not open to resolution by experimental research. (Hartwell 1985, pp. 106–7)

Do you think this is true of the teaching-to-read issue, that it is not open to resolution merely by experimental research? If you agree, then by what means do you think we should decide the nature of our beginning reading programs? Be sure to consider the conflicting paradigms that are involved.

8. Below are questions that administrators and/or parents might ask about introducing a whole-language program that encourages young children to write freely, using their own functional or "invented" spellings as needed, and not worrying about mechanics as they first compose. You might organize a "public meeting" for discussion, with one group representing doubters and another group representing enlightened teachers. Originally raised by my students, these questions are arbitrarily grouped into four categories, for discussion by four groups; thus there is some overlap in the questions.

   Goals/objectives—Rationale—Advantages
   a. What goals/objectives do you expect to accomplish by encouraging children to write freely, without worrying about correct spelling and mechanics?
   b. What are the principles upon which the approach is based?
   c. What are the advantages of encouraging functional spelling rather than insisting on correct spelling?

   Feared disadvantages—More on advantages
   d. Is there any evidence that this program won't succeed as well as a traditional approach to spelling and to mechanical correctness?
   e. Won't this procedure harm children by getting them in the habit of spelling words incorrectly?
   f. Is there any evidence that this approach will make children better writers? Better readers? Better spellers, and better in the use of other conventions of mechanics?

   Fostering "correctness"
   g. With this approach, how will children learn the rules for correct spelling, punctuation, and so forth?
   h. When, if ever, will you correct the children's spelling errors and other mechanical errors?
   i. How long do you recommend letting the children continue to use functional spelling, their own conventions of punctuation, and so forth?

Stimulating growth—Measuring progress—Introducing such a program

    j. How can you help children begin to use functional spelling? How do you help them use more sophisticated spellings?

    k. How can you determine whether or not the children are making progress in learning to spell, if they don't have to spell correctly? How can you determine if the children are making progress in learning to punctuate?

    l. Can you introduce this program without taking time away from other valuable activities? If so, how?

An outstanding book that deals with such issues is Lucy Calkins's *The Art of Teaching Writing* (Heinemann 1986). A very short and excellent book on spelling is Richard Gentry's *Spel . . . Is a Four-Letter Word* (Scholastic-TAB 1987). See also some of the other references within and at the end of this chapter.

  9. Pretending you are a primary grade teacher, write a letter to parents explaining "your" program for teaching reading and writing. Explain how it reflects what we know about how children initially acquire language and how it encourages children's natural reading and writing development. (You may want to read Chapter 8 on implementing a whole-language approach first.) Restrict the letter to two single-spaced pages or the equivalent, but be sure to enliven your discussion with examples of children's real reading and writing. Avoid technical terms and a formal, "stuffy" tone, but of course don't be *too* chatty, either.

10. Read the report *Becoming a Nation of Readers* (Anderson et al. 1985). Then do one or more of the following:

    a. Draw up a list of good points about basal reading programs and a list of bad points, based on the report. Add any other points you might think of. Be prepared to discuss.

    b. From the report, make a list of ten statements or recommendations that you think psycholinguists would agree with, and that also seem significant to you. Be prepared to discuss.

    c. From the report, make a list of half a dozen statements that you think would, for one reason or another, make psycholinguists uneasy. In several cases, many psycholinguists might agree with part of a sentence but be distressed about another part. Be prepared to explain why.

READINGS FOR FURTHER EXPLORATION

The following articles focus on language acquisition or on parallels between the acquisition of language and the acquisition of literacy; the last three focus on learning "skills" and dealing with "errors":

Slobin, Dan I. July 1972. They Learn the Same Way All Around the World. *Psychology Today* 6: 72–74, 82. Discusses possibly "universal" aspects of language acquisition that seem to reflect the nature of the human mind. An oldie-but-goodie.

Black, Janet K. May 1980. Those "Mistakes" Tell Us a Lot. *Language Arts* 57: 508–13. Suggests that we should view "errors" in reading and writing much the same as we view "errors" in language acquisition—namely, as evidence of the child's stage of development.

Calkins, Lucy McCormick. May 1980. When Children Want to Punctuate: Basic Skills Belong in Context. *Language Arts* 57: 567–73. Compares children's grasp of punctuation in two third-grade classrooms, one where students studied punctuation but did little writing and one where children wrote a lot but did not formally study punctuation.

Weaver, Constance. May 1982. Welcoming Errors as Signs of Growth. *Language Arts* 59: 438–44. Using sentence fragments as an example, demonstrates how errors become more sophisticated rather than simply diminishing in number, as writers mature.

The following articles deal with reading and the acquisition of literacy as a transactional process:

Dyson, Anne Haas. December 1984. "*N* Spell My Grandmama": Fostering Early Thinking About Print. *The Reading Teacher* 38: 262–71. Discusses children's early concepts about written symbols, explaining/demonstrating how, at first, children's understanding of written language is global and context-dependent, focused on meaning (the "whole") rather than details (the "parts"). Suggests that teachers determine where children are in their thinking about print, and build from there—a transactional view.

Smith, Frank. September 1981. Demonstrations, Engagement, and Sensitivity: The Choice Between People and Programs. *Language Arts* 58: 634–42. Defining "programs" as "sets of materials, workbooks, activity kits, guidelines, manuals, record sheets, objectives, television series, and computer-based instructional sequences," Smith argues that instruction should be guided not by such programs, but by people—the teachers and children engaged in the learning transaction. In effect, he argues for a transactional paradigm of teaching rather than a mechanistic one.

Harste, Jerome C., Virginia A. Woodward, and Carolyn L. Burke. February 1984. Examining Our Assumptions: A Transactional View of Literacy and Learning. *Research in the Teaching of English* 18: 84–108. Though somewhat challenging, this article presents an important delineation of the transactional paradigm.

Weaver, Constance. October 1985. Parallels Between New Paradigms in Science and in Reading and Literary Theories: An Essay Review. *Research in the Teaching of English* 19: 298–316. Also challenging, this article discusses the organic/transactional paradigm emerging in seemingly disparate fields.

The following articles focus on stages of spelling and writing development:

Heald-Taylor, B. Gail. October 1984. Scribble in First Grade Writing. *The Reading Teacher* 38: 4–8. This study of first-grade writing confirms the significance of scribble when it is an accepted language behavior in the classroom. Children learn many concepts of print even before they have precise knowledge of conventional orthography.

Kamii, Constance, and Marie Randazzo. February 1985. Social Interaction and Invented Spelling. *Language Arts* 62: 124–33. Reflecting Piaget's observation that knowledge is developed through the critical exchange of ideas, the authors show through extended examples how first graders can work cooperatively to spell and punctuate, a process that fosters their understanding of spelling and punctuation and stimulates cognitive growth.

Hall, Susan, and Chris Hall. December 1984. It Takes a Lot of Letters to Spell "erz." *Language Arts* 61: 822–27. Working with kindergarten children, these authors discovered that some children exhibit a spelling stage in between pre-phonemic and early phonemic. The authors discuss this stage and suggest that other stages may be discovered, if only we are alert enough to notice them.

Gentry, J. Richard. November 1982. An Analysis of Developmental Spelling in GNYS AT WRK. *The Reading Teacher* 36: 192–200. Details five stages of spelling development and provides guidelines for identifying these. Offers five suggestions for improving students' spelling competency.

In addition, the Summer 1980 issue of *Theory Into Practice* (Vol. 19, no. 3) contains a wealth of articles on writing and spelling development.

The following articles discuss early writing and reading:

Mayher, John S., and Rita S. Brause. March 1984. Learning Through Teaching: Lessons from a First Grade. *Language Arts* 61: 285–90. Discusses and illustrates some aspects of first graders' writing development.

Cohn, Margot. May 1981. Observations of Learning to Read and Write Naturally. *Language Arts* 58: 549–56. Using delightful examples from her three-year-old daughter and four-and-a-half-year-old son, the author illustrates some of the characteristics of emergent reading and writing behavior.

Estabrook, Iris W. October 1982. Talking about Writing—Developing Independent Writers. *Language Arts* 59: 696–706. A six-month case study illuminates the development of a student in a first/second grade classroom. Contains transcripts of writing conferences to outline the student's progress in critical writing skills.

Blackburn, Ellen. April 1984. Common Ground: Developing Relationships Between Reading and Writing. *Language Arts* 61: 367–75. Uses marvelous examples from children's reading and writing to illustrate the point that emerging reading and writing are highly similar processes that can best be encouraged in similar ways.

DeFord, Diane E. September 1981. Literacy: Reading, Writing, and Other Essentials. *Language Arts* 58: 652–58. Compares reading and writing in a phonics classroom, a skills classroom, and a whole-language classroom.

Sulzby, Elizabeth. Summer 1985. Children's Emergent Reading of Favorite Storybooks: A Developmental Study. *Reading Research Quarterly* 20: 458–81. A rather detailed but interesting article that delineates stages in learning to read naturally.

Chomsky, Carol. March 1976. After Decoding: What? *Language Arts* 53: 288–96, 314. Discusses how she used certain activities associated with a whole-language approach to move children beyond being stuck in a grapho/phonemic emphasis stage.

King, Dorothy F., and Dorothy J. Watson. 1983. Reading as Meaning Construction. *Integrating the Language Arts in the Elementary School*. Ed. B. A. Busching and J. I. Schwartz. Urbana, Ill.: National Council of Teachers of English, 70–77. Suggests that although most children will learn to read regardless of the approach, a whole-language approach is preferable for several reasons.

In addition, the May 1983 issue of *Language Arts* (Vol. 60, no. 5) contains excellent articles on reading and writing and the relationships between them.

And then, there's this:

Lindfors, Judith Wells. October 1981. How Children Learn Or How Teachers Teach? A Profound Conclusion. *Language Arts* 61: 600–606. Refers to four encounters involving a doctoral student, a primary-grade teacher, a child, and a sociolinguist. Concludes we must distinguish between instructional activities of teachers and the sense-making processes of children, in order to support children's learning. Interesting and persuasive.

8

How Can We Implement a Whole-Language Approach?

Dorothy Watson
Paul Crowley

This is what many teachers are learning again from children: keep language whole and involve children in using it functionally and purposefully to meet their own needs. That simple, very basic discovery is leading to some dramatic, exciting changes in schools. Put aside the carefully sequenced basal readers, spelling programs, and handwriting kits. Let the readiness materials, the workbooks, and the ditto masters gather dust on the shelves—or better yet, donate them to community paper drives. Instead, invite pupils to use language.

—Kenneth Goodman

QUESTIONS FOR JOURNALS AND DISCUSSION

1. What observations about how children learn underlie a whole-language approach to literacy? (You might review Chapter 7 and/or look ahead to the first major section of Chapter 11.)

2. What are some ways that teachers can observe children in order to learn about their lives and language, and to structure learning experiences and the learning environment accordingly?

3. What kinds of activities might one expect to find in a whole-language program that seeks to make children joyfully literate?

4. What are some kinds of strategy lessons a teacher can develop to meet the needs of individual students and small groups of children?

5. What are some of the ways that children can help other children learn to read and write?

6. How can teachers combine various aspects of a whole-language approach, organizing and managing the classroom so as to create a coherent whole?

7.   How can a teacher enlist parents' support for a whole-language approach, and what are some ways a teacher can involve parents in encouraging and assisting with children's literacy development?

8.   What are some ways, other than standardized tests, that teachers can assess children's needs and progress in becoming literate?

9.   How can whole-language teachers deal with basal reading systems? (See also the relevant section in Chapter 6.)

10.   How can whole-language teachers deal effectively with the concerns of other teachers, administrators, and the public?

INTRODUCTION

In this chapter we want to "paint a picture" of a whole-language classroom. Such a composition must reflect a complex arrangement and organization of people (students and teachers), materials, and activities, as well as the complete spectrum of language and life found in a classroom described as a whole-language classroom. We have chosen art as a metaphor for two reasons. First, learning and teaching remind us of the balance of textures, colors, perspective and aesthetics required in a quality painting. Second, we propose that whole-language teaching and learning are indeed quality works of art.

In order to provide depth for the whole-language picture, we will first present the basis for this student-centered program. In this discussion the term *whole language* will be defined.

Following clarification of the term, we will focus on a variety of whole-language pictures. Like any work of art, whole-language classrooms reflect the unique qualities of the individuals involved. In all our pictures you will see students and teachers engrossed in reading and writing activities that make sense, are satisfying, and are related to their worlds. You will also find teachers and students reflecting on the curriculum, their work within that curriculum, and on themselves as individuals and as members of groups.

We conclude the chapter with a discussion of issues in which the whole-language model is in conflict with the "commonsense" model—for example, evaluation and assessment, parent involvement, and teacher empowerment.

Integration of the Language Systems within the Lives of Learners

When one is painting-by-number, there is no attempt to integrate one section of a painting with another; the sections only superficially influence each other; the painter dutifully colors all the number 3s red, the number 5s blue, and so forth. By contrast, when an artist creates a picture, he or she considers the relationship of colors, of shadings, of depth; everything on the canvas influences everything else on the canvas. The analogy holds true for the use of language in the acts of creation through reading, writing, listening, and speaking. Language users do not read-by-number or write-by-number. That is, they don't isolate one aspect (system) of language and drill on it until it is thought to be mastered and then move on to another aspect of language. Rather, proficient readers and writers use *all* the systems of language in order to create meaning; they are whole-language users.

Now, what are these systems that language users keep whole? Think of language as having two major parts, linguistic and pragmatic; in real situations, when children are learning language, these are always kept whole and together (whole language). The linguistic part is made up of three major systems: semantic, syntactic, and grapho/phonemic. The semantic system gives language its life; it has to do with meaning, sense, ideas, and thoughts, and with the words we choose to express meaning, sense, ideas, and thoughts. The syntactic system is the frame, the grammatical structure that supports meaning. The grapho/phonemic system allows us to make the framed meaning available to others. The *grapho-* part of the system indicates the visual information that can be used: letters (graphemes), punctuation marks, underlinings, italics, upper and lower cases, even the white spaces between words. The *-phonemic* part of the system indicates the sounds (phonemes) that are available to language users. In a whole-language program these systems are kept whole and together.

The pragmatic system of language tells us about language in use. Think of pragmatics as having two major contributors, both of which are powerful aids when reading, writing, listening, and speaking. The first has to do with the off-the-page context (situation) in which the language is used. The second has to do with past experiences and knowledge—with schemas—that relate to the language event. For example, if on the first day of school you are seated at a desk in a college classroom, and someone who looks a great deal like a teacher hands everyone four or five typewritten pages, you can safely assume that you have in your hand material that has to do with the content and requirements of the course you are enrolled in. You know this because of the context of the situation and because of your prior experiences and knowledge of similar situations (your schema). You know with only a glance at the sheets of paper that you will find information about the class meetings, goals for the course, title of the text, requirements, and so on. The pragmatics of language help us realize the intention of the material to be read. In a whole-language program, pragmatics are used to the reader's advantage and never separated from the linguistic aspects of language.

In whole-language instruction, there are no pragmatic breaks in intention, such as being asked in "reading class" to circle medial consonants on a worksheet or during "writing time" to fill in the blanks. In whole-language instruction, there are no linguistic shocks that occur when language is torn apart in order to drill on one aspect of it. Children are never asked to do phonics drills in which their attention is focused on small and abstract units of language. Nor are students asked to master a set of flash cards in which their attention is directed to words out of situational context. They are not asked to look up ten words in the dictionary, write the meanings, give the diacritical markings, and use the words in written sentences. Students cannot bring past pragmatic information to bear on such activities; this is not the way language is used and learned in real situations, and therefore it is not the way language is presented in a whole-language classroom.

WHAT DO WE FIND IN A WHOLE-LANGUAGE PROGRAM?

If the activities mentioned above are not included in a whole-language reading program, what then can we expect to find? Based on our experiences of teaching classes and visiting classrooms, we know first of all that whole-language programs will reflect the individuality and creativity of the artists (students and teachers) in them; that is, we know that not every classroom will look the same. Differences are inevitable, welcome, and exciting.

But we also find similarities among whole-language classrooms, and among the teachers of these classrooms. In their own unique ways *all* whole-language teachers facilitate certain activities and procedures:

1. They find out about students' interests, abilities, and needs. And then they go an important step further—they use that information in planning curriculum.
2. They read to students or tell them stories every day.
3. They see to it that students have an opportunity to participate in authentic writing every day.
4. They see to it that students have an opportunity to read real literature every day.
5. They initiate discussions in which students consider the processes of reading and writing.
6. They know that kids can help other kids many times and in many ways that no one else can; therefore, they take advantage of the social nature of literacy (reading and writing) in order to promote it.

Whole-language teachers facilitate countless other experiences, but we will direct attention to these six important aspects from which other literacy events emerge naturally.

As these program components are discussed, we will present the rationale for each. Understanding the reasons for curriculum keeps us from feeling uncertain, uncomfortable, and not in charge, as if we were asked to color within the lines of a preformed drawing when we wanted to create our own images on the canvas.

Student-Centered Curriculum

Whole-language teachers find out about students' interests, abilities, and needs, and then use that information in curriculum planning and in instructional procedures.

How do teachers get information about their students? Primarily, whole-language teachers learn about their students in the same way they find out about people outside of the classroom—by showing interest in them as individuals and by giving each individual an opportunity to present himself or herself in the best possible light. Whole-language teachers take every opportunity to talk with students and to ask them questions that they really want to know the answers to. They have conversations with kids that may last no more than a few minutes but that are authentic exchanges in which the teacher and student are equal contributors. They let students know that they value their experiences, their interests, and their knowledge, and that they like them as individuals.

Following are literacy events that teachers and children have participated in that help them learn about each other as well as reflect on themselves as special individuals.

On the first day of school, teachers invite children to draw a picture of themselves and their family, including the family pet. Some of the children may want to talk about their drawings; teachers encourage classmates to comment and ask questions. At another time, they invite young children to write their names on a piece of paper of their own choosing (lined, unlined) and write all the words, letters, and numbers that they know. These are kept as data that all other writing can be compared to. Teachers use the information to find out what children know and feel about reading and writing: Are they linguistic risk-takers who write freely? Is their spelling standard, invented (functional), or do they refuse to spell if they aren't sure? Do they think of writing as composing or copying? Can they read what they have written?

For students of all ages, teachers might read Shel Silverstein's poem ''What's in the Sack?'' from *Where the Sidewalk Ends.* (For shared reading, which will be discussed later, write the poem on chartpaper.)

What's in the Sack?

What's in the sack? What's in the sack?
Is it some mushrooms or is it the moon?
Is it love letters or downy goosefeathers?
Or maybe the world's most enormous balloon?

What's in the sack? That's all they ask me.
Could it be popcorn or marbles or books?
Is it two years' worth of your dirty laundry,
Or the biggest ol' meatball that's ever been cooked?

Does anyone ask me, ''Hey, when is your birthday?''
''Can you play Monopoly?'' ''Do you like beans?''
''What is the capital of Yugoslavia?''
Or ''Who embroidered that rose on your jeans?''

No, what's in the sack? That's all they care about.
Is it a rock or a rolled-up giraffe?
Is it pickles or nickels or busted bicycles?
And if we guess it, will you give us half?

Do they ask where I've been, or how long I'll be stayin',
Where I'll be goin', or when I'll be back,
Or ''How do?'' or ''What's new?'' or ''Hey, why are you blue?''
No, all they keep asking is, ''What's in the sack?''
''What's in the sack?'' I'm blowin' my stack

At the next one who asks me, "What's in the sack?"
What?
Oh no. Not you, too!

From *Where the Sidewalk Ends*
by Shel Silverstein. Copyright
© 1974 by Snake Eye Music, Inc.
Reprinted by permission of
Harper & Row, Publishers, Inc.

After reading the poem, teachers bring out a sack in which they have placed three objects that tell something about their lives and interests. After sharing and encouraging children to ask questions, they invite one or two children each day to bring their "this-is-about-me sack." Before the students open their sacks, the teachers read Silverstein's poem with the children, or ask a trio, pair, or individual to read it. The teachers keep notes about individual and group interests.

The following questionnaires were compiled by a group of teachers who wanted to learn about their students' interests and their backgrounds in reading. Rather than asking children to write answers to all the questions, teachers select a few items that they feel will provide useful information. They think of interesting ways in which children can present their answers.

Getting to Know You—Part One
 1. What do you like to do on Saturday?
 2. Tell about your favorite TV program.
 3. Tell about your pets, if you have any.
 4. What is the best vacation you've ever taken?
 5. If you could be famous, what would you be famous for?
 6. Tell about the best gift you ever received.
 7. Tell about the best gift you ever gave.
 8. What would you like to do on your birthday?
 9. Tell about your collection, if you have one.
10. If you could start a new collection, what would it be? Why?
11. If you could do anything this weekend, what would it be?
12. What do you want to be doing ten years from now?
13. Tell about the sport you like best.
14. Tell about your hobby, if you have one. If you don't have one, what would you like to do as a hobby?
15. Tell about something you do very well.
16. What would you like to be able to do very well?
17. What would you like to have taught at school?
18. What person or place would you like to know more about?

19. Tell about the clubs or groups you belong to.

20. What do you do in your spare time?

Getting to Know You—Part Two

1. Do you like to read?

2. What is the best book you have ever read?

3. What kind of books do you like to read?

4. Do you like to talk with other people about what you (and they) have read?

5. Do you own any books? Tell about them.

6. How often do you read?

7. Do you read because you want to or because you have to?

8. Do you like to be read to?

9. Do you have trouble finding books that you like?

10. Did your parents read to you when you were younger? Do they read to you now?

11. Do you read to anyone?

12. Do you like to read alone or in a group?

13. How do you choose books to read?

14. Do you know a book or anything you would like to read?

15. Are you a good reader? Why do you think so?

16. Who is your favorite author?

17. Do you have a library card?

18. How often do you go to the school library? How often do you go to the public library?

19. Name a character you have read about and tell why you like or dislike him/her.

20. If someone were going to select something for you to read, what should that person keep in mind so that he/she will pick out the perfect thing for you?

A second-grade teacher, Diane Audsley, selected questions from Part Two that she thought would tell her something about her students' backgrounds in reading. She wrote the questions on paper "petals," leaving room for the student's answer. The children cut out the petals and placed them around a picture (school picture or drawing) of themselves. The children then drew a flowerpot on which they made a collage that represented their lives and interests, completing their "Personality Plant" (see Figure 8.1).

Students can help teachers find out about other students by interviewing each other and by presenting the subject of their interview to classmates and teacher. Many children have never experienced an interview and will need help in such procedures; these students will learn quickly through discussion and role-playing. Some students may be interested in making an audio- or videotape of an interview; such tapes will help inexperienced interviewers. Children may want to use items from the questionnaires above, or, better still, make up their own questions. After interviewing each other, students may want to interview faculty and staff members.

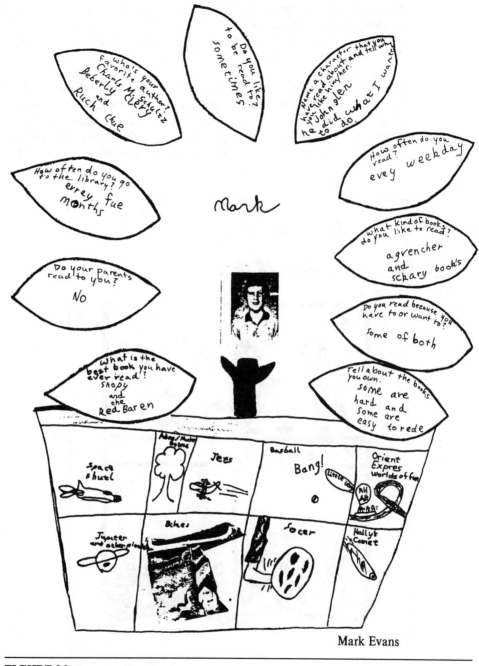

Mark Evans

FIGURE 8.1 *Personality plant*

A special bulletin board (Our Class, Student of the Week, and so on) can display the written report of interviews.

Another teacher, Sheryl McGruder, found out about her students by inviting them to make an *All About Me: My Family Banner* book. On the cover, in Space 1, the authors drew a picture of their family; in Space 2, they wrote their family's last name; in Space 3, they drew a picture of something they were good at doing, and in Space 4, they drew a picture of their family doing something together. On the second page of the book, the children wrote their name, address, phone number, and birthdate. On the following pages, they wrote about themselves by answering questions—those on the questionnaires or other questions thought of by the students.

Katy Graham

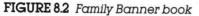

FIGURE 8.2 *Family Banner book*

Some questions took the form of unfinished sentences: At school I like to . . . , At school I would rather not . . . , Over the weekend I . . . , I would like to know how to . . . , I think it would be fun to learn about . . . , I wonder about . . . , I like it when my teacher . . . , Sometimes I have trouble . . . , and so forth (see Figure 8.2).

Students are invited to bring their favorite books and magazines to school and to talk about why they like them. When students discuss, draw, write, and respond, whole-language teachers participate in the activity right along with them. For example, the teacher brings his/her favorite book, shares an all-about-me sack, or makes an *All About Me* book. When teachers participate in such a way, they demonstrate and invite at the same time. Such *invitational demonstrations* indicate to children that the activity is valued and worthy of the efforts of both students and teacher.

There are countless interesting ways to learn about students. Simply by showing an interest, teachers not only promote in children feelings of belonging and worth, but they also gather information that can powerfully influence the curriculum and instructional procedures in the classroom. As students talk and write about themselves, teachers keep notes concerning individual and class interests, concerns, and needs. By using students as curricular informants (Harste, Woodward, and Burke 1984) teachers can, with confidence, suggest a special book for a particular student, encourage a topic for writing, or read a poem that will touch a life. Teachers along with their students can develop themes, select topics for genuine discussion and action, as well as collaborate on dramatic events, experiments, and purposeful projects.

Whole-language teachers start with what students know and are interested in—not with what they don't know and care nothing about. When children feel that they have something to say about the curriculum and with what is going on in the classroom, they feel good about themselves psychologically, socially, and academically. When this is the case, both students and teachers feel empowered—learning and teaching are harmonious and the classroom picture is compelling, comfortable, and appropriate for all learners.

Reading and Telling Stories to Students Every Day

Through the sharing of stories we celebrate and preserve our literary heritage, and we show children that literature is at the heart of their reading program. Whole-language teachers read to students or tell them stories every day as *an important part of the curriculum*. This activity is not offered as a reward for good behavior or for getting work completed, nor is it considered a time-filler or a way of getting students quiet. By reading to children or telling them stories every day, teachers make it very clear that oral and written stories hold a place of respect and importance in the curriculum. (The word *stories* is used to designate oral and written stories, poems, plays, books, articles from newspapers—language with meaning and intent.)

Children are encouraged to listen to stories in a relaxed, but active, way; they are invited to make ties to language they have heard before, to relate the messages, setting, and characters to their own lives, to learn from them, and to use the information gained to help them become better readers and writers.

More and more often we find whole-language teachers doing something that is not easy for everyone to do—telling stories to students. We know that before the advent of written language, storytelling was an important method of remembering human history and of passing it on from generation to generation. When children listen to stories told by good storytellers, history is relived, and children's imaginations are fired as they create in their heads pictures and images that can be used later when they read other stories or when they write and tell their own stories.

Teachers who know stories and can tell them well are empowered. Such strength can be passed on by teachers to students through the recurring invitational demonstration. Whole-language teachers *help children become storytellers* by sharing with them how they themselves came to love oral stories. Teachers help students find stories that they will want to be able to tell. They play story tapes, invite storytellers to the classroom, and help students locate in myths, fairy tales, and folk stories material suitable for storytelling. Teachers then encourage students to select several familiar stories that, read individually or in small groups, they can read, talk about in terms of content and structure, learn (not memorize), and finally present to classmates and children in other rooms or grades.

When children have had some experience with storyhearing and storytelling, teachers invite them to build a story. The teacher spins a bit of the tale, then asks, "Who wants to tell us what happens next?" The teacher or other students may weave in details, conflicts, twists, and turns. Together the teacher and students work out the problems and continue until the story is brought to a conclusion. If the story is tape recorded, the children listen to the tape, and then transcribe the finished story that will be added to their class book of group stories. Some students may want to write their own versions of the class story.

As teachers read or tell stories, they often pause in order to invite children to fill in the next word, phrase, or sentence, thus encouraging them to be linguistic risk-takers. Children begin to see that it is possible to fill in the next part of a story in a variety of ways, all of which make sense and sound like the language of the story. They also see that there are certain ideas and structures that would not be suitable.

Repetitious lines can be written on the board, such as "Alexander had a terrible, horrible, no good, very bad day" from the book of the same name by Judith Viorst, or "One pitch black, very dark night, right after Mom turned out the light . . ." from *It Didn't Frighten Me*, by Judy Goss and Jerry Harste. When the teacher comes to the repetitious or cumulative language, the children attend to the print as they read it with the teacher. In this activity, learners use all the systems of language (including symbol/sound relationships—grapho/phonemics) in order to read the predictable line.

In summary, by listening to stories, children can gain information that will help them in their own reading and writing. They can use what they know about how a story is put together (story grammar) to help them predict what might happen next, and they can use that story structure and other conventions (ways stories begin and end, development of characterization, and so on) to construct meaning when reading or writing on their own. Daily listening to stories read or told may be the first opportunity some children (especially those who have spent time in low reading groups) have had to hear language presented lovingly and well. Reading to students or telling them stories can provide background information for projects, experiments, and work in social studies, science, math—in *all* content areas. It also may be some children's entrance into the rich culture of other groups.

Students Writing Every Day

It may seem strange that in presenting a *reading* program we call attention to student writing even before calling attention to student reading. The reason for this is an important one: we believe that along with hearing stories, one of the most powerful influences in becoming a proficient and eager reader is writing stories. Children who hear many stories again and again, and are invited again and again to write, will do so. Children who write stories and are invited[1] to read stories will do so. The literacy cycle is strong and the parts of it are supportive: listening and responding, writing and reading make students better and avid listeners, speakers, writers, readers—and thinkers.

Don Graves (1981) tells us that children want to write. They come to school knowing something about the writing process: most of them have experimented with paper, crayon, or pencil; they have seen their parents use pencils, pens, markers, even chalk to write on stationery, backs of envelopes, message boards, in bankbooks, on birthday cards, on 3 × 5 cards, and on computers. Equally important, children know that adults write for a reason: to make a grocery list, leave a note, copy a recipe, keep score, write a letter, perhaps even to write a story or a poem. Children come to school knowing that real writing has intent and that it is always meant to be read, either by the author or by someone else. Children know that people don't write nonsense. They know that when they themselves decide to write it will be for a reason, it will be meaningful, and that either they or someone else will read what they have written.

In whole-language classrooms, children are invited on the first day of school to write something that makes sense. Kindergarten children, and other students for whom the activity is appropriate, are invited to draw a picture of themselves, write their name, and then write something about themselves. Teachers can immediately see which children are scribbling, using mock letters, using letters in their own names, copying letters from print in the environment, perhaps even using invented/functional spelling (see Chapter 7). They can also determine which children are linguistic risk-takers and which ones feel that they can't write because they can't spell or make the letters.

Authentic writing implies that students have their own ideas for writing; this is the beginning of being in charge. When very young children are invited to write, they usually have no problem generating many ideas, especially if they are encouraged to write every day and if their work is valued. For eager writers, it is only necessary to make sure that they have time and a conducive environment in which to create and compose—that is, to write.

As students get older, if they have not had the opportunity to write on a regular basis, they often feel hesitant about getting started. For these reluctant writers, teachers must facilitate the generation of ideas; they must convince such students that they have plenty to write about. Teachers who are good kid watchers (Goodman 1978) may be well aware of their students' abilities and interests and able to suggest topics to them: "Why don't you write about how you felt when you got your new bicycle?" "How about that trip you and your parents took to the zoo?" "Would you like to write about what made you so unhappy on the playground?" When children mention their interests, teachers often make a note of the subject and keep the information, or they ask students to add the idea to the list of topics kept in the front of their writing folders.

Most children who are asked to write in journals need guidance in doing so. Teachers who are willing to share their own journal writings issue invitational demonstrations to children. Teachers might leave their journal open during the day so that students can read it and even respond in writing; responses are written on a blank page or in the margins. By such sharing, teachers let their students know something about themselves and something about the writing process; they let their students know that they themselves sometimes write easily and sometimes have problems.

Journals can be used as reflections on things that have happened in school. Anne Shay Bayer (1987) suggests that children write about their content-area learning. At the end of a lesson, they write either to themselves or to their teacher about what they have learned. Then they ask questions about anything that may be confusing or bothering them (see Figure 8.3).

Prior to studying a particular topic, students might write in their journals (learning logs) everything they know about the subject. During or after the study, they reflect and then write about their new information; students discuss not only what they have learned, but how they learned it.

Students may respond in their journals about things happening to themselves outside of school or nonacademic happenings in school. Sometimes on Monday morning, students and teacher together make a list of topics students *may* want to write about during the week. Journal entries often spark ideas that can be used for more elaborate pieces of writing. Many students use their journals to respond to the books they are reading. Such literature response journals can be used during literature discussion groups.

Teachers and students need to work out a schedule for writing and responding in journals on a regular basis. Teachers usually can't write in all the students' journals every day, but can write in a few, perhaps on a rotating basis, thus seeing each student's journal twice a week. Teacher responses indicate to students that their work is important and is valued.

Students need to be invited to write on the first day of school; this includes kindergarten and special education students. To put off the first invitation until the second or third day, or to allow students to write only once a week, is making writing too distant and too difficult. When children know that they can return to their writing every day, they not only think about their creations but they talk with others about their stories even when they are not writing; they begin to think and act like

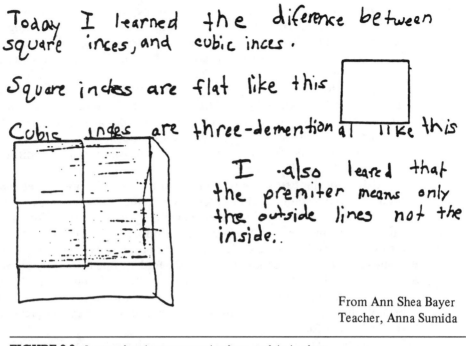

Today I learned the diference between square inces, and cubic inces.

Square inces are flat like this

Cubic inces are three-dementional like this

I also leared that the premiter means only the outside lines not the inside.

From Ann Shea Bayer
Teacher, Anna Sumida

FIGURE 8.3 *Journal entry: square inches, cubic inches*

authors. When children are asked to write only once or twice a week, they spend a great deal of valuable time reinventing the wheel—getting back into their stories, trying to remember what they were going to do next; sometimes they spend all their writing time trying to find their notes and papers.

Many teachers use a technique inspired by Don Graves to help students generate their own ideas for writing. Teachers ask students to close their eyes and think about something that has happened to them in the past that they would like to tell someone about. After a few minutes of reflection, students write or draw something on their papers that will remind them of the event. Depending on the age of the students, the teacher might ask them to do this same reflecting and writing one or two more times, thus generating one, two, or even three potential writing topics. The teacher next asks the children to turn to a partner and talk about the things they have jotted on their papers. The students ask each other questions and comment on all the possible topics. The teacher then asks the students to select one of the subjects and to write a "lead." After a few minutes, depending on their ages and writing experiences, the students are asked to write a second lead. After writing as many as three leads, the students are asked to close their eyes again and to picture in their minds one of the main characters in their story. They then write about him or her for a few minutes. A third reflection may be about the ending of the piece; the student is asked to spend a few minutes writing an ending. By the time students have experienced such a *guided reflection* and have rough drafts of three sections, they have confidence that they can write and they are eager to do so.

Once the hurdle of generating ideas is overcome, it is sometimes necessary to get past another: children must be convinced that writing means thinking and composing; that spelling, letter formation, and other conventions will be taken care of at a later time—during an editing conference. When children ask how to spell words as they are composing, teachers encourage them to do the best they can, to pretend they can spell it, to put something on paper that will help them remember what the word is, to spell it like a second grader (if the student is a second grader), to put the first letter(s) and a dash, to leave a blank—anything to make the students dependent on themselves, not the teacher. Teachers assure students that either they or a writing partner will help the students spell anything they want during the editing conference, if help is still needed at that time.

It is important to support children in the organization of their writing time. Students need a spiral notebook, loose leaf binder, or folder for their manuscripts. By making a habit of writing their name and the date on all of their work, and carefully putting away their manuscripts, students will find the process of getting into the writing becoming easier—there are no tears over lost or mutilated stories. Some teachers ask the children to keep two folders: one for in-process pieces and one for completed pieces. One kindergarten teacher, Jill Janes, staples together her students' writings, attaches a note, and sends the pieces home to parents every Friday. She makes a copy of any writings that show student progress and therefore should be kept for assessment purposes.

Why writing? Before suggesting other writing activities, it might be a good idea to restate clearly why writing is such an important part of the reading program.

1. Children know that the people they have seen writing do it for a reason, and that what they write makes sense. Therefore, when children begin to write, it will also be to communicate—to make sense; children will never on their own write nonsense. The carryover to reading: "Anything I am given to read or choose to read on my own was written by a real person and therefore it will make sense—I will be able to understand it." Of course, whole-language teachers avoid presenting children with written language that does not make sense.

2. When listening to and writing stories, children use and add to their knowledge of story language: conventions concerning beginnings and endings, characters and characterizations, events and plot, themes, humor and sorrow, and inferential language. The carryover to reading: such elements used in writing help students feel comfortable in making predictions as they read. Children also come to know that authors make assumptions about what readers know; therefore, it is necessary to bring off-the-page information from their own experiences to the on-the-page information presented by the author.

3. Children who appear to pay little attention to print when reading will learn that the author's meaning is presented to readers by way of written language. The carryover to reading: in order to construct meaning it is necessary not only to consider off-the-page information from life experiences, but it is also necessary to consider on-the-page information by sampling from print.

4. By observing children writing in authentic ways, a teacher can often see that students handle skills such as cause-effect relationships, following directions,

finding the main idea, and so forth. The carryover to reading: teachers can discard instructional procedures that drill such skills. For example, they can cease asking children to fill out worksheets and workbooks, on the grounds that such activities devalue and misrepresent the students' abilities.

5. Children draw upon and develop their knowledge of symbol/sound relationships when encoding their ideas in writing. The carryover to reading: the connections that children make between their perceptions of speech sounds and print support their control of the grapho/phonemic cues in reading. In other words, phonics skills are promoted when children write, even though the process of spelling is the reverse of the sounding-out skill of phonics.

6. To state the obvious: authors usually read, even reread, their own products, thus promoting the kind of practice that is meaningful and makes the reader stronger. Students who do not appear to read their own drafts need to be reminded that they must return to their pieces before those pieces are submitted to anyone else. Children learn to read by writing and by reading their own writings.

Other writing activities

The *Language Experience Approach* (LEA) to reading (Hall 1976; Van Allen 1976; and Stauffer 1970) has been adapted and used to some degree in whole-language classrooms. Basically, in such an approach, the students begin by having an experience worthy of writing about; they think about and discuss the experience; they decide how it is to take form; they dictate the story to a scribe (usually the teacher, but it could be an older student or a parent volunteer); and they reread and edit their story. Individual students, small groups, even entire classrooms can participate in this activity. It is, of course, an important and often-used procedure with students who for physical reasons cannot do their own writing. LEA is used with children who need to be shown that they have stories to tell even though they feel they cannot write them down, or who are in such a hurry to record their ideas that they need a secretary. It is also fun to work as a team writing a story: talking about how the parts of the story fit together and how the authors can make their audience understand what they have to say, and discussing suitable vocabulary and structures. Such group shaping of the writing is sometimes called ''shared writing'' (McKenzie 1985); see Chapter 7. In LEA, it is usual procedure for the teacher, after group discussion, to take dictation, writing the story on the board or on chart paper. When the story is completed, the children revise and edit. They may want to copy the story in their notebooks, or someone might write it on a master and duplicate it for all the authors and their friends. When a word processor is available, teachers can quickly type anything the students dictate, and then duplicate copies for all to read.

There are many advantages to LEA. Young children can dictate stories about their drawings and immediately feel the accomplishment of writing something that other people can read. Older students who have not been invited in the past to write and who feel that they can't compose, quickly see that they do indeed have stories in their heads. Writing as a group provides an opportunity to talk about both the writing and reading processes.

The Language Experience Approach is used—when the circumstances warrant—in a whole-language reading program, but it is never the predominant reading and writing activity. Children of all ages and in all classes need to be invited and expected to do their own writing. If students compose/write only when they have a teacher or older student to act as secretary, they may easily become dependent on someone else and refuse to write without outside help. Even before a teacher takes dictation from kindergartners, the children should be invited to try to do their own writing.

Extended Literature writing is a way of responding to literature by using professionally authored materials as an impetus for future writing. Probably the most basic way of extending literature is *patterning* after it—that is, using its format, its message, or both in order to create a personalized story. Bill Martin's *Brown Bear, Brown Bear, What Do You See?* may have the distinction of being the book most often used for this purpose. After children hear the highly predictable language of the book, they are eager to write their own versions. Such books are often referred to as *patterned books*. Other patterned books, such as Remy Charlip's *Fortunately*, will be discussed in the following section on early reading.

Children often *extend literature* by writing another episode or chapter to a story. Steven Kellogg's *Can I Keep Him?*, Margaret Wise Brown's *The Important Book*, and Patricia MacLachlan's *Sarah, Plain and Tall* lend themselves to children's responses through related writing. Raymond Briggs's *Jim and the Beanstalk* ends with the giant tossing Jim a giant gold coin that he can keep for himself. Some children may want to extend the literature by writing about what Jim did with his coin.

Wordless books are an open invitation for children to become authors. After discussing the story based on the pictures, individuals or small groups of children may want to write a story to accompany the illustrations. After the text is composed, the story can be paper-clipped to each page and read by the author and others. Such an *extension of literature* focuses attention on the elements of story that are paralleled in illustrations. Martha Alexander's *Bobo's Dream*, Ruth Carroll's *What Wiskers Did*, and Margaret Hartelius's *The Chicken's Child* are examples of wordless books for which children love to write texts.

Pen pal letters motivate children to do a great deal of personal reading and writing. Letters written to other children in faraway places are exciting, but it is often the case that very few letters are exchanged throughout the year. Many whole-language teachers partner their students with children in another school in the same city, with residents of a nearby home for the elderly, or with college students in reading education and language arts classes. Having pen (and picture) pals in the same school but in different grades can be very rewarding. For example, fifth graders and their first-grade pals not only write to each other, but they meet for special learning projects, go on field trips together, and celebrate special events such as Valentine's Day—when they can read their valentines to each other.

Similar to pen pal letters in that two authors are responding to each other, is an activity called *Written Conversations* (Burke 1985). In written conversations, a teacher and child or two students converse on paper (no talking allowed). The teacher usually begins by writing a sentence or two, hands the pen to the student,

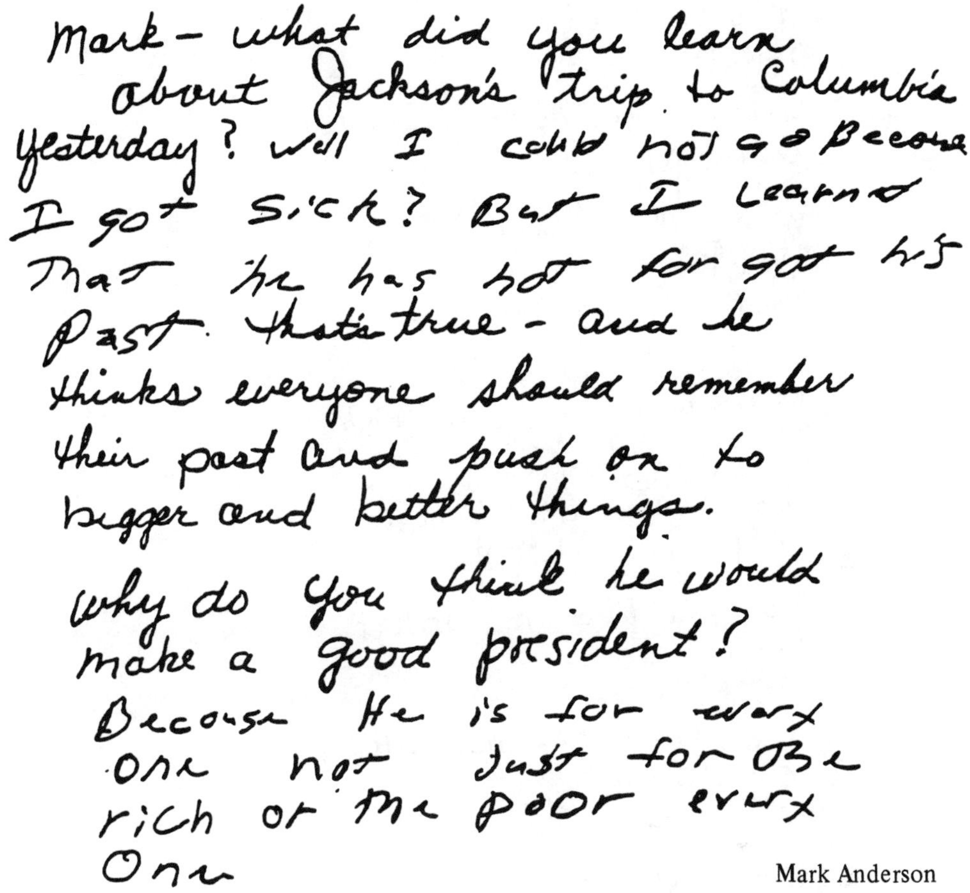

Mark - what did you learn
about Jackson's trip to Columbia
yesterday? Well I could not go because
I got sick? But I learned
that he has not forgot his
past. that's true - and he
thinks everyone should remember
their past and push on to
bigger and better things.
Why do you think he would
make a good president?
Because He is for every
one not just for the
rich or the poor every
One

Mark Anderson
and his teacher

FIGURE 8.4 *Mark's written conversation*

---

and waits for a reply. The transaction should be as close to an oral conversation as possible; the teacher doesn't interrogate the student, but rather encourages the student to make comments and to ask questions—in other words, to hold up his or her end of the conversation (see Figures 8.4 and 8.5).

We would be remiss if we did not mention poetry writing. In whole-language classrooms such writing is inevitable; students hear poetry every day, see it (special note of its form is made), select poetry to read to the group, copy favorite poems for their poetry board or poetry book, and naturally try their hand at expressing themselves through this special but familiar genre.

The possibilities for authentic writing in the classroom are numerous. Children keep notes about their experiments and projects, make charts and posters, write labels and captions for bulletin boards, take minutes of meetings, and write reports, letters, plays, poems, stories, and novels. In contrast, inauthentic writing includes

I like you
THAK YOU.

What will you be on Halloween?
A PRNSS

What will you wear?
A GRS

What color is the dress?
BLO

Where will you go that night?
TO MRGAMP

Where does Grandma live?
OKFU DRIV

Do you like to write?
YES

What book do you like?
SLEPG BUTE

I DONT NO

What would you like Santa to bring?
A STR WORS CLAKSHN

Who do you like best from Star Wars?
PRNS LA

Will you talk to me this way
again sometime?
YES

Good bye.
GOOD BYE

Heather and her mother
Nancy Watson

FIGURE 8.5 *Heather's written conversation*

making repetitious lines of letters or words, filling in blanks, copying for the sake of copying, and being asked to write on a topic for which there is no interest, need, or commitment.

Students Reading Every Day

Whole-language classrooms are replete with professionally authored and student authored literature. There are resource books, magazines, newspapers, games, maps and globes, and greeting cards; print from out-of-school-environments such as posters, brochures, menus, television schedules, baseball cards, cans, and cartons; and even photographs of street signs, bumper stickers, license plates, marquees, signs on buildings, banners, and print on clothing. In the words of Jerry Harste, the students' classroom should be "littered with literacy"—reading and writing that makes sense to those who live in that classroom.

Supportive language materials

Many of the items mentioned above can be read easily because of their familiarity and situational context (where the print is found, who has the print, who is wearing it, the contents of the can or carton, and so on). These off-the-page factors often make print highly predictable and therefore easy to read. Frank Smith (1973) says that teachers must make reading and learning to read easy—not hard. One of the first things children are able to read is the STOP sign. What could be more predictable? Every time the car comes to STOP, the driver does exactly what the sign says. The context of situation supports the print, and—what's more—the parent and child practice their reading; they say, "Stop." Reading made easy. In the classroom, the children (not the teacher) can label bulletin boards, shelves, boxes, drawers, and cabinets in which the contents support the labels. Seen in one sixth-grade classroom on a wastebasket was, not only the label, but a mandate: "Improve Your Aim—Hit the Basket!"

The notion of predictability in reading material (Rhodes 1981) is one that whole-language teachers are very familiar with, and take advantage of in selecting materials for all students, especially for those who are insecure or nonproficient readers. The reason for the use of predictable reading materials is straightforward: when language is predictable, it supports the writer's intentions and the reader's expectations, thereby making the text easier to read. Predictable language does not mean that the text is boring or old hat; rather it means that the text supports the reader in a variety of ways. Language is predictable and supportive when there are: repetitious lines (see, for example, *Drummer Hoff* by Barbara Emberley and *Millions of Cats* by Wanda Gag), cumulative lines (*The Gingerbread Boy*, a traditional folktale), rhyming or alliterative words (Dr. Seuss books), stories in which a picture or a word on one page indicates that a certain concept will appear on the next page (as in *Dinner Time* by Jan Piénkowski), and stories in which characters, settings, even plots are familiar (the Ramona series by Beverly Cleary, the Encyclopedia Brown series by Donald Sobol). Stories that children write themselves are supportive because the concepts are known; when children can't read their own writing, they are urged to reconstruct the text by thinking about what it was that caused them to write the piece in the first place.

Familiar poetry, chants, jump rope rhymes, fingerplays, or songs can be displayed on the board or on large chart paper and read as a group, trio, duo, or individually. The children may want to copy the text for their own or for the class poetry or jump rope book. Learning to read made easy; the language is supportive in that the children are familiar with it, the situational context supports it, and the text is predictable.

If the teacher believes that students need help on a blend, digraph, or other letters or combination of letters, attention can be called to grapho/phonemics easily, quickly, and naturally within the context of an entire chant or song. For example, either the poem or the jump rope jingle below can become a chant that the children enjoy by clapping the rhythm and by adding syncopation and movement. After becoming familiar with the poem, the children can *briefly* discuss the symbol/sound relationship of the letters and sounds such as *ck, ty, bl*, and *ea*.

The Pickety Fence

The pickety fence
The pickety fence
Give it a lick it's
The pickety fence
Give it a lick it's
A clickety fence
Give it a lick it's
A lickety fence
Give it a lick
Give it a lick
Give it a lick
With a rickety stick
Pickety
Pickety
Pickety
Pick
　　　David McCord

Mary Mac, Mac, Mac
Dressed in black, black, black
Had silver buttons, buttons, buttons
Down her back, back, back.
She loves coffee, coffee, coffee.
She loves tea, tea, tea.
She loves boys, boys, boys
And they love me, me, me.
　　　Jump Rope Jingle

In 1965, Don Holdaway and a group of experienced New Zealand teachers began an investigation into the backgrounds of proficient readers. They learned that all the successful readers came from homes in which family members shared written stories with them. Because of this finding, they devised a technique very similar to home reading; they called it *Shared Book Experience* (SBE). SBE involves books with rhymes, patterned language, interlocking structures, cumulative text, and other supportive text features that help children in their ability to predict. This enterprising group of professionals knew that wonderful books such as those listed above and *Are You My Mother?* by P.D. Eastman, *Henny Penny* by Paul Galdone, *Goodnight, Owl!* by Pat Hutchins and *Greedy Cat* by Joy Cowley would support the natural reading development and curiosity of children. SBE was a success, but there was one problem: when there was only one book available in the classroom, the children could not see the print. Undaunted, the teachers set about "blowing up" books, enlarging the pictures and stories so that they could be seen by all the children. These books are referred to as *Big Books* (Holdaway 1979).

These oversized books are usually used with young children to promote their early reading, but older, less successful readers can become teachers by preparing a *Big Book* to share with younger children, thus having an opportunity to practice their own reading. The usual procedure involves talking a bit about the book and urging the children to predict what it will be about. The teacher then reads the selection to the students, pointing out the illustrations and indicating the text (from top to bottom, left to right) as he or she reads. The teacher may stop once in a while to ask the children what they think will happen next. When appropriate, the students are invited to clap with the rhythm, make gestures, add sound effects with voice or instruments, and to read the refrain and anything else they can. Over time, children begin to read more and more of the text along with the teacher and other students. On subsequent readings, individuals or pairs may volunteer to read a page. The book is read together each day for the remainder of the week. Some children may make a tape of the book, or they may use the book in reading together in small groups.

Commercial *Big Books* are available from some publishers (such as Richard C. Owen Inc.; Scholastic and Scholastic-TAB; Holt, Rinehart & Winston; Wright Group; Rigby Education; and Reading Development Resources; see Appendix B for "Lists of Useful Addresses"). However, because such commercial books are rather expensive, teachers sometimes make books themselves, or even better, invite children to make them. In making *Big Books*, the children print the exact text of the story on either the top or bottom of a large page of light cardboard ($12'' \times 18''$ or 30 cm $\times$ 45 cm is a good size), talk about the pictures, and make decisions about who is going to illustrate each page. After the pictures are completed on another sheet of paper, they are cut out and glued on the *Big Book* pages. The *Big Book* is available for children to enjoy individually or in small groups (Heald-Taylor 1987).

Literature Groups

In whole-language classrooms, students are intensively and extensively involved in valued literature (R. Peterson 1987). Through *Literature Group* activities, children become involved in quality literature on both a personal and a group basis. The procedure for Literature Groups is somewhat the same for primary and upper grade children. Teachers select five or six titles they feel sure their students can relate to, make sense of, laugh or cry over—literature that can move children. The teacher briefly introduces the books, the children write the titles of their first and second choices, and then the children are placed in groups of five or six who have chosen the same book.

Literature Groups in primary grades are usually begun as the Shared Book Experience (SBE) described above. *Big Books* can be used in Literature Groups, but it is not necessary to do so; it is imperative, however, that all group members have their own regular size copy of the book. Having their own book promotes personal reading as well as assuring that every reader can attend to print. When Literature Groups are the major part of the primary grades' reading program, it takes about one week to read and reflect on one set of books. In addition to participating in group discussions, the children work together or individually to extend the literature by writing their own versions of the book; by making a poster, a mural, or book-marks advertising the book; and by making an audiotape of the book for the listening center or a videotape to share with other students and parents. The children explore books by the same author or books thematically related, and they reread not only the current Literature Group book, but past Literature Group books, thus becoming more familiar and reflective with the texts.

In upper elementary grades, after the books are chosen and the groups formed, the teacher and children decide on a certain number of pages to read before the group meets for its first discussion. The students read silently on their own. They are encouraged to write about their readings in journals. They might write their reactions to the book, what the story makes them think of in terms of ideas for their own written pieces, and comments about *how* they are reading, that is, where they moved along in the text as opposed to where they had trouble with the text. The groups typically meet twice a week. As a result, it usually takes two weeks to read and reflect on each book, in upper elementary grades.

The concepts of reflection and dialogue are at the heart of Literature Groups. After the children have read for personal meaning, for learning and enjoyment, they are encouraged to reflect on their readings by writing in their journals. They then come together as a group to reflect and enter into dialogue with others who have experienced, in their own unique ways, the same literature. The power of reflection and of authentic dialogue becomes evident as the children learn to take ownership of the discussion groups. Teachers often wait in silence for other group members to begin the discussion, or ask a student to lead the discussion, or do as Karen Smith (Harste 1986) does in her sixth-grade classroom—tell the children that she wants to take notes on their discussion and then move to the outside of the group. When teachers begin the discussion it is often by reading from their journal or by asking (never interrogating) a question that is an invitation to dialogue:

What do you think?
How are you different now from when you started this book?
What do you know or think about now that you didn't know or think about before you started this book?
Would you like to share something with us?
What would you like to ask the author, or someone in the group, about the book?

Does this book remind you of any other literature you know?
How did the author get you to think?
How did the author get you to feel happy, scared, sad?
Do you see any patterns—in the pictures or story?

Sustained Silent Reading

In most whole-language classrooms, there is a time set aside every day for SSR, *Sustained Silent Reading* (also known by names such as DEAR, Drop Everything and Read). During this time, the students and the teacher are reading something of their own choosing. The children are encouraged to have at least three pieces of reading material in their desks at all times to assure that every minute of the Sustained Silent Reading time is taken advantage of. This means that library visits are arranged in advance of SSR; the time is not spent searching for reading material, it is spent reading.

Teachers who have had a great deal of experience in a whole-language program do not find it necessary to set aside a time each day for SSR—simply because their students fill the entire day with reading and writing. Nevertheless, even these experienced and masterful teachers usually begin the year with a special time set aside for everyone to read, including the teacher. They often invite the principal or a parent into the classroom to read their own books during this special time. Some classes find it helpful to have a *Sustained Silent Writing* time immediately following the quiet reading time.

Assisted Reading

Assisted Reading (Hoskisson 1975) is used in whole-language classrooms with children who are having difficulties with beginning reading. This assisted reading experience is very much like that of parents and children reading together; the child is in a warm and accepting environment, involved in a book that is of interest, and is assisted into reading in a totally supportive way. The usual procedure involves the teacher and child reading together. The teacher sets a somewhat slower pace than that expected in oral reading, but in no way is the language of the text distorted by drawing out or sounding out each word. The teacher and child read together; usually the child chimes in slightly after the teacher. When the text is highly predictable, the child may move ahead of the teacher or read on his or her own. Careful selection of material is crucial; the content should be of interest and appropriate for the reader. It is important that the child attend to the text; this supports making the grapho/phonemic connection, the connection between letters and sounds.

Similar to, but less personal than reading with the teacher or with an older, more proficient partner, is *Read Along Booktapes*. Children listen individually (usually with headsets) to tape-recorded stories as they follow along in the written text. When the children feel that they have had enough assistance from the recorder, they can then read the book to their teacher, their reading partner, or to children in another room. Although there are many publishers of booktapes, teachers may want to make their own or invite children to make the tapes. Sound effects and background music can be added to classmade tapes.

Units, themes, and content areas

Whole-language teachers try to organize their classrooms in a way that will provide the best use of student and teacher time, materials, and resources—while continuing to promote reading and writing. They often organize around units and themes, using and integrating the areas of science, math, social studies, health, physical education, and so forth, while also employing other forms of expression such as music, art, drama, and dance. No matter if the unit or theme focuses on bears, the sea, transportation, or careers, literacy is an integral and integrating force in the whole-language classroom. Units and themes also invite students to meet information in a variety of genres, forms, and expressions; and they encourage reflection on both new and old knowledge in ways that promote seeing patterns and making connections.

Because a substantial amount of time is usually devoted to a unit or theme, it is important from the outset to decide on and organize the curriculum *with students*, using them as informants and resources. When the subject of the study has been agreed upon, the next step is to find out what the class members know and care about that subject. By brainstorming, the children reflect and talk not only about what they know, but also about what they don't know and want to find out; misconceptions are also explored. The students need to see their early ideas in print—perhaps on the board, or they can write a note in their logs or journals on what they know about the subject. By seeing their personal and collective knowledge on the board, they can begin to reflect on the topic(s) and draw some conclusions about their study. After the teacher and students set goals for themselves, they start bringing together all kinds of resources. If there is a textbook, it is only one source and is usually used after the students are into the study, or as a culmination of the study—seldom as the introduction. Students help find resources such as films, videos and filmstrips, articles from any likely source, fiction and nonfiction books, stories, and poems, and they interview and invite resource people into the classroom (see also Chapter 9 on reading in the content areas).

Specifically, reading materials can be found at many degrees of complexity and difficulty. Teachers often duplicate conceptually related materials from reference sources such as encyclopedias and other textbooks, or they actually tear up old out-of-adoption textbooks that have well-written and accurate sections that can easily be read by less proficient readers. Such materials are bound with construction paper; students have dubbed such materials "skinny books." As the students get into the study, they are invited to engage in research projects, review resources, create appropriate materials, and always to add information and questions to their log or journal. Children need an opportunity to present what they have learned; their creations, including writings, reports, and artistic endeavors, are celebrated.

Reflecting on the Processes of Reading and Writing

In most elementary school classrooms in the United States today, students receive reading instruction that involves basal readers; placement in a low, average, or high reading group; worksheets and workbooks. The purpose of these materials and the homogeneous grouping is to teach children the skills of reading (word identification, comprehension, interpretation, and so forth). In whole-language classrooms, these materials are used only when mandated or when the teacher feels that they contain stories and information that support learning to read by reading and writing, and by reflecting on these processes. Since grouping in a whole-language classroom is on the basis of interest and need, the groups last only as long as they are useful.

Bringing the reading process to a conscious level

Whole-language teachers do not teach skills in isolation; nevertheless, students learn all the skills needed to become successful readers by learning to read in the manner described in this chapter. It is important to remember, however, that whole-language teachers do talk about the reading process in both formal and informal ways with their students. They talk with students at the teachable moment—that is, when they need and can make immediate use of the information; furthermore, the teachers build on what readers are doing right, not what they are doing wrong. Additionally, teachers bring reading to the students' awareness by discussing strategies involved in real reading. According to Kenneth Goodman (1970), those strategies involve the reader's sampling from print, predicting on the basis of on-the-page and off-the-page information, confirming when the effort makes sense and sounds right, correcting when the effort results in nonsense or is garbled, and finally integrating new information with old. Instead of drilling on skills, children in whole-language classrooms are asked to reflect on the strategies they use. This can be done individually, in small groups, or with the entire class. The discussion rarely takes more than fifteen minutes (often a minute or two will do) and it is unnecessary (and harmful to self-esteem) to place the students in low, average, or high reading groups.

Bringing reading to a level of awareness so that a child can reflect on the process is a powerful teaching-learning experience. Fortunately, it is not difficult to do this because children are interested in language and how it works; that is, they are interested unless their curiosity is killed by skilling and drilling. Children want to know about *real* reading and writing.

The reading process can be brought to a conscious level on an individual basis through reading conferences. For example, Jarene has just finished reading a story to the teacher. The teacher asks Jarene to briefly retell the story. She then invites Jarene to reflect on her reading and to talk about how well she did. The teacher not only asks the student *what* she learned from the story, but *how she learned* from the story. After Jarene has an opportunity to tell about the things that went well, the teacher asks her to talk about the trouble spots, gently probing to get at the way Jarene was handling the text. She asks Jarene to look at the text and point out any places that gave her trouble; they discuss these and the teacher offers suggestions. The teacher asks Jarene about certain miscues—for example, why she substituted or omitted words, why she changed from reading ''cannery'' for *canary* to reading ''cardinal'' for *canary*. Jarene gets back into the text in order to talk about or reread a passage in which there was a great deal of miscue activity. Finally, Jarene is encouraged to comment on or ask about the story itself or about the way she read the story. Such conferences should last about five minutes. The teacher jots down notes to help in the total assessment of Jarene's reading.

In Literature Groups, children often talk about the reading process. Mynett asked the members of her group what they did when they came to the word *gargoyle* as they read Paula Fox's *One-Eyed Cat*. Billy said he hadn't even noticed the word because it was at an exciting part; apparently he skipped the word and went on. Gary said he didn't know how to pronounce it, but he knew it meant something ugly because it was talking about the housekeeper and she was "a real dog"; he substituted an idea (something ugly) and went on. Cory said that she didn't know how to pronounce it either, but if Mynett were still interested in the word she should look it up now; she confirmed Mynett's strategy of moving on in text, but trying to get information later. In this group, the children brought reading to a conscious level and talked about three possible ways of handling unfamiliar words—all used by successful readers.

The children can talk about the reading process as a total group. As they are reading during SSR, they make a pencil checkmark in the margin of the book at the spot that causes them trouble. At the close of the reading time, the students copy the troublesome text on a bookmark, underline the place where they had trouble, and then give the bookmarks to the teacher. If the students had no particular problem or the problem was resolved as they continued to read, they jot down a sentence or two about how the reading went during SSR and turn that information in on a bookmark. The teacher categorizes the information and spends a few minutes—either immediately or the next day—talking with the children about the reading process and suggesting productive reading strategies (Watson 1979).

Strategy lessons

Ken Goodman has identified *reading strategies* as what the reader does when the eye hits the page: the reader samples print, predicts what is coming, confirms those predictions, corrects if necessary, and integrates new with old information. Now we want to use the word *strategy* in another, but related way. Readers use certain strategies when they read, and some of these strategies are more effective than others. When a reader encounters an unfamiliar word, for example, there are choices to be made; these choices are strategies. When Mynett came to the word *gargoyle* in her story, she could have sounded out the word, broken it into syllables, related the word to a familiar word, looked it up in a dictionary, skipped it, stopped reading, or asked someone else. Mynett decided to use the strategy of asking someone else. Successful readers use various strategies at different times, depending on the context of text and context of situation.

We now want to discuss *strategy lessons*. These lessons are first of all whole language; that is, all the systems of language support the reader in the attempt to proficiently and efficiently sample, predict, correct if necessary, confirm, and integrate meaning—to read. Strategy lessons take advantage of the strengths of a reader, and they are often brief and always to the point. Equally important, they lead to a discussion of the reading process.

In order to introduce specific strategy lessons, we need to look at a specific learner. We will move from Gregg's reading below to a strategy lesson that will help him and other inefficient readers in their attempts to construct meaning.

Naming Strategy. Gregg read a story about an elephant named Sudana who was sick and needed to be given sulfa for her fever. The word *Sudana* appeared throughout the story and Gregg miscued on the word each time it appeared. These are some of his miscues:

Expected Response:	*Observed Response*
Sudana	1. (omitted "Sudana")
	2. S-
	Shadu
	Shadan, Shadan
	3. Sh-
	Shutten
	4. Shana
	5. Shoud
	6. Shata
	7. Shur
	8. Shadon
	9. Shana
Sudana's	10. hers
Sudana's	11. Shadon's
Sudana	12. Shadon

In the same story, Gregg also made repeated attempts on the word *sulfa*:

Expected Response:	*Observed Response*
Sulfa	1. s-
	shovel
	2. suchful
	3. shana
	4. shiffle
	(subvocalized:
	"or something")
	5. shum
	6. snafen
	serman
	(shook his book)
	7. surn
	8. surum
	9. surm
	10. surm

Gregg focused a great deal of attention on small, abstract units of language, particularly symbol/sound relationships. Multiple attempts on *Sudana* and *sulfa* exemplify a strategy that he used throughout this and other stories—a sounding-out process. Gregg took a long time to finish the story and his reading was hesitant and choppy. At one point, when he had a great deal of difficulty with the word *sulfa*, he shook the book in frustration. Nevertheless he was able to retell most of the story: Gregg knew that the main character was an elephant, female, and that her name was "Shana, or something"; and he was able to tell that the elephant was sick and that the doctor made numerous attempts to give her medicine and finally succeeded. In addition to these major propositions, Gregg remembered a number of details as well.

Gregg was an *effective* but *inefficient* reader: effective in that he could successfully retell the major propositions of the story, but inefficient in that his reading was slow and laborious.

What does this suggest for Gregg's reading program? Whole-language instruction always begins with what students are doing *right* and builds on these strengths. Successful readers take ownership of their own language and are empowered by an understanding of what they can do and where they are headed. Gregg needs to view language as a process he can comfortably and confidently direct by using strategies that will help him become more efficient.

Judged only on his oral performance, Gregg would probably be considered by many to be a poor reader. Analysis of his miscues (see Chapter 10) and his retelling, though, indicate a number of strengths. Consider Gregg's substitution of "her" for "Sudana's." These words have no graphic or sound similarity; at this point, Gregg abandoned the sounding out strategy and put in something that fit grammatically and semantically. Gregg probably wasn't aware that he deviated from the text; he had adjusted his focus to meaning and let the sense of the story he was constructing offer him the support that was lacking in the smaller cues. Gregg's previous reading instructional model would describe such a departure from the text as an "error" that needed to be corrected. On the contrary, Gregg should be made aware that what he did was linguistically sophisticated and positive because it made sense.

Gregg needs to move more fluently through a text in order to make reading less frustrating; he needs to *keep going*. "Keep going" strategies hold readers' attention to meaning and to cues that move them fluently through text. The two questions that successful readers have in the backs of their minds as they read are: Does this sound like language? Does this make sense? Gregg's miscues on *Sudana* indicate that he needs a "naming strategy" so that when he encounters a proper name, he will substitute for it whatever name he wants and then stick with that substitution throughout the text. The important concept is that it is a name, not how the name is pronounced. "Mr. Przybilski" becomes "Mr. P." Successful readers use this substitution strategy, allowing them to focus on meaning, not pronunciation. A lesson promoting this strategy involves the teacher briefly conferring with the student or talking with a group having similar needs about choices to be made when something unfamilar is encountered in a text. Reading is not an exact process, but Gregg's previous instruction indicated that it was, by focusing on exact oral reproduction of the text. Gregg must receive confirmation that it is acceptable to substitute a placeholder that makes sense.

Readers are flexible when they use a variety of strategies for handling a variety of texts; reading *instruction* involves engaging students in lessons that demonstrate the use of these strategies, and *reading itself* provides the opportunity to practice these strategies in the context of whole language.

For students who are bound to the text and will not move away from over-reliance on symbol/sound cues, the following strategy lesson helps them use both semantic and syntactic information.

Selected Deletions. When readers not only overuse *grapho/phonemic* information but also are reluctant to skip words that give them trouble or unwilling to substitute something that makes sense, words and phrases can be omitted from the text to encourage linguistic risk-taking. This "keep going" strategy lesson is a modified cloze procedure and referred to as *Selected Deletions*. It encourages readers to sample from *all* the available linguistic and pragmatic cues except the graphic information of the deleted text item.

The passages used for Selected Deletions can be professionally authored or teacher made; they must be cohesive and well organized. The teacher considers the reader as well as the text when selecting the items to be deleted. Deletions should be structurally and semantically unambiguous. The first sentence of the passage is kept intact to allow the reader to get enough information about the passage and to gain confidence. It is important to delete only highly predictable words, especially for reluctant readers, in order to move them fluently through the text. Some deletions can be replaced by a number of different possibilities. When this is done, the student sees that meaning is not altered by putting in something that makes sense, even if it is not the original text item.

Words can be deleted by whiting out the items or by omitting them when typing the text. Teachers should always try the activity themselves after all the deletions have been made; too many omissions or the omission of certain words can make this a difficult procedure, thereby defeating its purpose. After the words have been filled in by the students, the original text can be distributed for comparison and discussion about the process.

Gloria Crenshaw

Gloria was the first explorer to land on Jupiter. When she returned to
_____, she met with many important _____. One of these was the President _____ the United States. Gloria _____ the President talked a long _____.

"Congratulations, _____! Everyone is very, _____ proud of you."
"Thank _____, Mr. President."
"Are you happy to be back on _____?" asked the _____.
"Yes! I got very lonely on that _____ trip!"
"Do you _____ to go again?"
"I'd _____ any time you _____ me," said Gloria.
"What would _____ like to take with you on your next trip to Jupiter?" asked the President.
"Good _____ are always nice!" said Gloria.

Successful readers know that real authors will help them by building concepts from the unknown to the known. If, for example, the label (word) for a concept is unfamiliar to readers, the cues in well-written text will support readers in their attempts to make reasonable guesses at meaning; if there are no supportive cues, the word may not be important. When readers negotiate meaning with the author, they are learning from the text. In traditional classrooms, students are often advised to look up words in the dictionary before they have tried to make some guesses. But going to the dictionary not only interrupts the reading process, it often provides misleading definitions and keeps readers from gaining information; it is not what successful readers do. Proficient readers use the dictionary and other outside sources to *confirm* their predictions when there is sufficient ambiguity about an important concept, and when interest is high; vocabulary develops naturally during reading.

The following Selected Deletions text was developed for a boy who, upon seeing the title, decided that he could not read the selection because he did not know the word *sampan* (interestingly, though, he could pronounce it). He noticed that it occurred repeatedly through the text but his teacher could not convince him that he could read it, so she removed the word. It was not long into the reading that he inserted *raft*, then *boat*, and finally *houseboat* in the blanks.

Rain on the Sampan

Rain raised the river. Rain beat down on the _____ where it lay in a long row of _____ tied to the riverbank. Rain drummed down on the mats that were shaped in the form of an arched roof over the middle of the _____. It clattered hard on the four long oars lying on top of the roof of mats.

The rain found the bullethole in the roof of mats. Thick drops of water dripped through the bullethole onto the neck of the family pig, sleeping on the floor of the _____. The little pig twitched his neck every time a big, cold drop of water hit it, but he went on sleeping.

. . . .

Rain raised the river. The _____ swayed and bobbed on the rising water. Voices drifted from the other _____ in the long row of _____ and muttered among the drumming rain. Tien Pao closed his eyes and almost slept, and yet he didn't sleep. He sat sagged against the mats, dreamily remembering the hard days just past, the hard journey.

It had been a long journey. Tien Pao had lost count of all the days and nights. But all those nights when the horns of the new moon had stood dimly in the sky, Tien Pao and his father and mother had pushed the _____ on and on against the currents of the endless rivers.

From *The House of Sixty Fathers*
by Meindert DeJong

Proper names can also be deleted. In the previous strategy lesson, Gregg was encouraged to use a naming strategy to help him deal with the proper name, Sudana. If students are reluctant to use this strategy, the name can be deleted from the text.

This Selected Deletions strategy lesson helps students use context clues from text to determine the unknown words. The grammar of the sentence is the basic structural cue to draw upon. Texts also have *story grammars* that give readers information about meaning; *Schema Stories* is a strategy lesson that focuses on story grammar.

Schema Stories. Just as Selected Deletions require readers to supply omitted words in text based on meaning and *sentence* grammar, *Schema Stories* require readers to reconstruct the order of a text based on meaning and *story* grammar.

The choice of material for a Schema Story is important. It must have highly predictable structures such as "Once upon a time . . . ," "The *second* giant . . . ," or "*At last* he reached Grandmother's house." Directions for science experiments and other content area selections having predictable structures also work well as Schema Stories.

A Schema Story is divided (physically cut apart) into sections, each of sufficient length to allow students to consider meaning in the text. After the text is divided at clearly predictable cut-off points, each section is distributed to individuals within a group. As students read, they direct their attention to the cohesive features of the text, consider prior information, and predict subsequent text. The teacher invites the person who believes he or she has the first part of the story to read the section and to explain why it is the beginning. If everyone agrees, the procedure continues. If two people believe they have the subsequent section, both sections are read and a group decision is made.

There are at least two modifications of this strategy lesson. The first involves each student's receiving all sections of a story and reconstructing that story. The students then compare their constructions with those of the other students and discuss the process. Another alternative involves several groups. Each group receives a section or sections of the text and proceeds as a group through the procedure mentioned above.

Schema Stories provide the opportunity for talk about language and texts. Readers see not only that texts teach them, but that the meaning of text is supported by a structure that they can understand and use.

Determining Lessons. Whole language involves learning on the part of teachers as well as students. Teachers learn by reflecting on what they know about language and learning in light of what children do from day to day.

The purpose of *Determining Lessons* is to help the teacher reflect and search for patterns that make sense. For example, it may appear that a student needs to focus on an isolated skill. Before breaking language apart for instruction and drill on that skill, it is important for teachers to *determine*, in the context of continuous discourse (whole language), whether or not the skill needs to be studied in isolation. By giving the student whole language, teachers support the reader with all the cues that readers draw upon as they read. Consider Jan.

Jan, a fourth grader, was successful in school and considered herself a good reader. These views were shared by her teacher and parents. Jan and her mother were understandably concerned when she brought home the worksheet shown in Figure 8.6.

VOWEL DIGRAPH ea

The vowel digraph ea has three sounds: long e, short e, and long a. If a word is unfamiliar, try each of the three sounds. You should then recognize the word. Show the sound of ea on the line after each word. Show the sound of a short e with an unmarked e.

−14 (−41)

KEY: EACH ē   HEAD e   GREAT ā

1. TREATMENT ē
2. STEADIER a ✓
3. STEALTHY ✓
4. TEAK ā ✓
5. GREATEST ā
6. WREATH ē
7. DEALT e
8. CONGEAL ē
9. SHEATH ✓
10. CREASED ā ✓
11. MEASLES ē
12. BEACON ā ✓
13. BREAKNECK ā
14. HEATHEN e ✓
15. HEAVENLY e
16. EASEL ē
17. SWEAT ē ✓
18. UNHEALTHY e
19. SEASONING ē
20. CHESAPEAKE ✓
21. STREAMLINED ē
22. TREACHERY ē ✓
23. DEFEATED ē
24. PHEASANTS ē ✓

25. CREAKING ē
26. JEALOUSY ✓
27. APPEAL e ✓
28. DECREASE ē
29. BEEFSTEAK e
30. PEASANT e
31. PEACEABLE e ✓
32. REVEAL   *Finish*
33. WEAPON   *your*
34. CLEANSING   *work!*
35. BEAGLE   (−41)
36. SNEAKERS
37. FEATHERY
38. FEAT
39. FLEA
40. MEANWHILE
41. CEASE
42. HEAVILY
43. PEALED
44. WEASEL
45. DREAD
46. EATABLE
47. INCREASING
48. DEALER

49. TREACHEROUS
50. HEADQUARTERS
51. CLEANLINESS
52. MEANT
53. UNDERNEATH
54. BREAKTHROUGH
55. REPEAL
56. STREAKED
57. WEATHERED
58. MEANTIME
59. EAGERNESS
60. EAVES
61. THREATENED
62. LEASED
63. LEASH
64. BREAKWATER
65. DEAFEN
66. EASTERN
67. RETREATING
68. BLEACHERS
69. DEATHLESS
70. HEADACHE
71. LEAKY
72. SNEAKY

FIGURE 8.6 *Determining lesson, Part 1*

At first glance, it could be assumed that Jan is at fault: she doesn't have sufficient "readiness skills"; she isn't trying her best; she wasn't paying attention; she needs more work on the vowel digraph *ea*. Rather than operating on limited information, it is crucial to analyze Jan's performance; otherwise the "victim" may be blamed and punished.

The first requirement is to consider the task Jan is asked to do. It becomes immediately apparent that this worksheet has many problems. Even if a teacher believes strongly that isolated drill on the vowel digraph *ea* is important, the 72 items on this worksheet constitute excessive practice. Directions for any activity should be presented carefully and clearly. Consider the directions on this worksheet: "If a word is unfamiliar, try each of the three sounds. You should then recognize the word. Show the sound of *ea* on each line after each word.

KEY: Each ē   Head e   Great ā."

Because of her poor marks on the worksheet, Jan cried herself to sleep; her mother consulted a reading teacher. Rather than depending on the checkmarks and scanty numerical information on the worksheet, the reading teacher went to the informant—Jan. Jan followed the directions; she tried "each of the three sounds" (which she called "each e," "head e," and "great a") and when she recognized a familiar word, she wrote the symbol representing the sound of the familiar word: *Teak* became *take, beacon* became *bacon, sweat* became *sweet, heathen* (appearing before *heavenly*) became *heaven*, and *appeal* became *apple*. Many of the words were unfamiliar to Jan regardless of the particular sound of the *ea*. She was confused by *peaceable* because she didn't know which *ea* to mark. This student was not sloppy in her work; she struggled a great deal with each item, using her own linguistic knowledge and logic. What is ironic is that after encountering unknown words such as *stealthy, congeal*, and *sheath*, Jan did not expect this worksheet to make sense to her and consequently did not even recognize words with which she was familiar. For example, Jan's father and uncle went pheasant hunting regularly but she missed *pheasants* on the worksheet.

In order to determine whether Jan really had a problem with the vowel digraph *ea*, the reading teacher asked Jan to read the passage shown in Figure 8.7.

Does Jan have a problem with the vowel digraph *ea*? Obviously not. She omits *steady* when the word doesn't affect the meaning and occurs in an unfamiliar construction, *steady leash*. Later in the text, however, Jan reads *steady* in a more semantically predictable context, "Babe and Bingo's steady stream of barking. . . ." *Deafening* is the only other word with the *ea* digraph that Jan miscues on; she substitutes *deaf* and abandons it for the non-word *deefing*. Her explanation: "When two vowels go walking, the first one does the talking." With a sensible, predictable whole text, Jan becomes a much better reader. Rather than making reading hard by giving her a worksheet that raises her anxiety, wastes her time, and makes her feel stupid, her teacher should make reading easy by giving her good literature.

When language is stripped of its context and left with the bare bones of symbol/sound relationships, readers are in potential linguistic trouble. By relying on quality literature and maximizing the linguistic strengths of readers, teachers will find that the need to determine whether skills should be drilled in isolation will disappear.

ERRQ. *ERRQ (E*stimate, *R*ead, *R*espond, *Q*uestion) is a strategy lesson that helps reluctant readers make a commitment to a text and personalize their reading. When students think of themselves as poor readers, they tend to avoid reading. The focus of instruction at this point must be on helping them feel successful. By assisting readers in monitoring their pace and comprehension, this activity offers these readers an opportunity to prove to themselves that they do indeed have linguistic strengths and control of the reading process.

Readers begin by *estimating* how far they can read in the text with understanding in a given period of time; they make a checkmark at this point. This requires them to "stake their claim" and to make a decision about the text and themselves; the teacher doesn't make an assignment, the students do. Next, they *read*. The personal decision concerning the amount of reading to be done moves readers along and challenges them to go beyond.

Ⓡ When hunting season comes Uncle Bill is almost as eager

to head for the woods as Babe and Bingo are. Babe and Bingo

are beautiful beagles, but Uncle Bill calls them eager beavers

when it comes to pheasant hunting.

When Uncle Bill releases those dogs from their steady

leash, you should see them streak across the meadow at break-

neck speed. They can really work up a sweat!

Aunt Joan dreads hunting season. Babe and Bingo's

steady stream of barking is deafening and gives her headache.

She can't bear to think of one feather on a bird being harmed.

Uncle Bill gives the pheasants to a neighbor. Babe and Bingo

howl.

FIGURE 8.7 *Determining lesson, Part 2*

When students reach the place they've checked, they *respond*. The response should be brief and related to the reader's life and literary experiences, such as giving their opinion of a character, how they would feel in the same situation, or whether it reminds them of another piece of literature.

Finally, readers ask a *question* that can lead into a discussion or a written dialogue about the selection. This can be a question about something readers don't understand in the text, or a question that pulls the text beyond the page, as in raising issues concerning a character's motivation, for example. The teacher can ask readers a question, but this is optional.

Reading is neither "getting the author's meaning" nor an independent response of the reader; rather it is a transaction between the reader and the author's text. This strategy lesson capitalizes on the reading transaction and moves students to active, personal reading. In ERRQ, as in all whole-language strategy lessons, the reader is supported by the text, by the task, and by the teacher. Reading is made easy.

The Classroom Environment. We have mentioned earlier that the whole-language classroom is littered with literacy. Perhaps we should talk about the classroom environment as a strategy. Access to literacy and student ownership of the environment is crucial. The classroom is for everyone; teachers don't talk about *"my* room," *"my* pencils," *"my* rules"; rather they talk about "our room," "our pencils," "our rules." The bulletin boards are conceived, designed, and produced by students and teacher. Such boards often become idea-boards as well as sounding-boards; one student's product becomes another student's motivation to read and write. Tools, materials, references, and books are organized, but all over the classroom—wherever children might need them. The distribution and maintenance of materials is everyone's responsibility, and, at the end of a busy day, everyone restores and readies the environment for the next day. Whole-language teachers "read the environment" by looking at it from the children's point of view: Can students get materials? Are there places for quiet work? Are there places for groups to work that won't bother others? Are there places that invite trouble? Loughlin (1983) says that the outcome of a functional literacy environment assures self-growth, but that environment must be established.

Kids Helping Kids

It is probably no secret by now that a whole-language classroom gets its vitality not only from individual students and teachers and their personal involvement in reading and writing, but from the socialization of the members of the class. Lev Vygotsky's (1978) ideas about the influence of learners on each other are persuasive, and are confirmed constantly in whole-language classrooms: kids can make each other look better, do better, be better—at all learning enterprises, including reading.

From the very first day of class, children are encouraged to cooperate rather than compete. Whole-language teachers suggest that students read with a partner, talk over an idea with a friend, do research with someone who has similar interests, read a piece in a writer's circle, and then ask for revision and editing suggestions. Sometimes children applaud each other in quiet and unsuspecting ways: Gary exclaimed to the members of his Literature Group, "I wish I could write like Paula Fox. She makes me see everything!" Alon replied, "Gary, you're a good writer. You make me see a lot. You *do* write like Paula Fox." Later that morning when he offered his latest story to a visitor in the class, Gary commented, "Alon thinks you might like to read this story I just wrote." Without Alon's quiet and spontaneous comment, Gary might not have had the courage to share his writing with a visitor.

Children in whole-language classrooms are resource persons and teachers. They are consultants and guides to their reading and writing partners, and the help is reciprocal. Learners work in trios, collaborating on math and science problems and projects, making sure that all three members contribute and understand. As stated earlier, when students work in small or large groups, they are always grouped on the basis of need and interest. It is very likely that the most successful and the least successful readers are in the same group; many times it is difficult to tell one from the other; everyone contributes, and everyone's self-esteem is intact.

INFORMING AND INVOLVING PARENTS

Parents can appreciate the value of a whole-language program because it is based on natural language learning. Learning to read and write parallels oral language learning—something parents have been very close to. The experiences students have in a whole-language classroom are an extension of their family language experiences. Children enter school with language backgrounds that may or may not be similar to those of their teachers. Whole-language teachers involve parents in their programs in order to enrich the curriculum with the home language and to help students take what they learn in school back into their homes. Teachers, parents, and students engage in a cooperative learning venture.

Whole-language teachers invite parents at the beginning of the school year to learn about the teachers' reading and writing program. They collect and distribute articles that clearly define their position on theoretical and practical issues without overwhelming parents with technical jargon, and teachers support their position with samples of children's work. Sometimes a book, or a passage from a book, brings home a message that is otherwise difficult to articulate. For example, one teacher told about reading *Leo the Late Bloomer*, by Robert Kraus, to anxious parents who were concerned that their child was not progressing rapidly enough. They learned, as Leo's parents did, that development is an individual process to be nurtured and enjoyed.

Parents need to be aware of the kinds of papers their children will bring home. In whole-language classrooms, the students are working on the *processes* of reading and writing, and much of their written work is *in process*; it is important to discuss with parents the logic of functional spelling and why their children's work may come home with nonstandard grammar, nonstandard spelling, and scratching-out.

A whole-language teacher's enthusiasm about how children develop as language users is similar to the excitement of parents as they talk about their child's development. Parents are invited to tell their own stories about their children's language and logic, to keep track of these, and to share. These stories are more than "cute"; they catch our attention because they highlight children's logic in attempting to make sense of the world through language. Parents and teachers help each other become careful observers of children.

With guidance, parents can see the value of the reading and writing that their child has been involved with each day, such as grocery lists, mail, storybooks, and labels. The kind and amount of reading and writing varies from family to family; there are differences but not deficiencies. Written language serves different purposes for different people, and these varied purposes are the basis of the reading and writing program in school. Parents are invited to ask questions as well as to visit the classroom on a regular basis for both observation and participation.

Throughout the year, there are opportunities for parents and others to come into the classroom to share in special events such as plays, holiday parties, and book fairs. Parents can help in planning and organizing these activities. It is important to consider varied work schedules so that all parents have an opportunity to participate.

In addition to special events, parents can contribute to day-to-day classroom activities, sharing their expertise as well as finding out more about language and language learning. Parents can help make books, read aloud, talk about their hobbies and jobs, help with the class newsletter, publish student writing in the classroom, organize a play, and display student art. Another adult in the classroom opens up a number of possibilities.

For any number of reasons, some parents will not be able to spend time in the classroom. Therefore, information about the students and class must be sent home on a regular basis. Some children talk a lot about what they do in school, while others don't. Too often the only time parents hear about school is when the teacher calls with a bad report. Parents need to know about problems, but they also need to hear when things are going well. They are surprised and delighted when they receive a call or note about something special their child has done. Whole-language teachers tell parents not only about the big things, but also about the little things that make school a happy place, such as their child's recommending a book to a partner, generating an interesting writing topic, or telling a funny story.

A class newsletter includes information about weekly events, samples of children's art and writing, upcoming events, and reading and writing activities that parents can do with their children. If the newsletter is going to be a weekly activity, it need not be an involved process. On Friday morning, the students tell what they did in class that week and the teacher writes these things on the board; these notations are quickly duplicated and sent home to an appreciative audience.

An essential element of a whole-language program is bringing the life of the child into the classroom. Parent involvement affirms and extends the natural language development that begins in the home; it is a total (whole) language program in which parents, teachers, and students learn from one another.

EVALUATION

Whole-language teachers are learners. Every curricular endeavor—whether gathering materials, conferring with individuals or groups, presenting a mini-lesson, reading students' stories, or listening to children read—involves a component of finding out about (evaluating) language, learning, and students. Whole-language teachers direct their attention to the most reliable source of information—the child.

When children are used as informants—that is, when their use of language in real situations is the focus of assessment—teachers are less likely to impose labels such as "dyslexic," "behavior problem," or "nonreader." If a child does something that doesn't fit the teacher's expectations about language use and learning, a whole-language teacher takes the opportunity for authentic assessment, and then for using the information to make curricular decisions.

Whole-language teachers want to learn about students, not compare them to each other or to some standard score. Quantified information such as grade-level equivalents, percentile ranks, and test scores are not helpful to whole-language teachers. Such numbers can seem pristine or "scientific," but the truth is that at best they provide minimal information, and at worst they can be misleading and therefore damaging to students. Numbers can be manipulated but children can't.

When teachers attempt to translate what children do with language into levels or scores, they often distort and devalue the processes of learning to read and write—but that does not mean that the process and the products of language cannot be assessed. Evaluation suggests curriculum and enriches instruction by helping teachers learn how language works as they watch their students, describe what they see, and perceive patterns.

Whole-language teachers and their students are often evaluated on someone else's model. Standardized tests, end-of-the-level basal reader tests, and competency tests reflect a skills model of reading. They test isolated skills outside their context of use, and the resulting information is often reported in single scores. Reducing the complexity of language ability to a numerical designation may help in administrative record-keeping, but it doesn't help teachers teach. Unfortunately, mandated reading tests are a reality in most schools. This reality can be dealt with, though, without sacrificing a whole-language perspective.

Children know about authority; they understand about bed times, washing dishes, and other responsibilities. They can understand school responsibilities as well, including the required tests. Teachers can set the stage for a discussion of testing by reading Miriam Cohen's *First Grade Takes a Test*. This book tells an important story about a group of children that has a natural curiosity and sophisticated child logic (as all children have). When they use this logic and their extensive background information to make sense of a standardized test (that has a logic of its own), the children learn the hard way that tests cause problems, the greatest among them being self-doubt and low self-esteem. Teachers can follow the lead of the teacher in this book and tell students that tests yield very little information and that the things they know and value about each other will never be sacrificed for a test score.

It isn't necessary to skill and drill students in order to help them take tests. Children who are immersed in purposeful reading and writing experiences with sensible materials in a supportive environment do at least as well as students who drill on minute, abstract skills in the limited context of a worksheet (see, for example, Chapter 7). All students, though, in order to survive the politics of testing, must become test-wise. This does not mean that they study the test but that they are aware of the test *format*. Students in whole-language classrooms understand and use the skills of language, including symbol/sound relationships, because they use language; however, they may not be familiar with the symbol system on the test (such as "short u" and "long u" and their diacritical markings). These can be learned quickly and practiced by playing with language in the context of word games, jump rope rhymes, and poetry. The language of the test (circle the one that isn't a duck) may also present problems. Examples of such language will help prepare children for these experiences. Children are anxious on test days. One teacher reported that a fourth-grade student told her that she was very nervous about the Iowa Test because she knew "nothing about Iowa." Parents report that their children lose sleep, appetite, and confidence before major tests. One highly successful second grader was sure he would not be promoted to third grade because of the end-of-the-year tests. To relieve anxiety and pressure, the whole-language teacher not only talks to the children but tries to relieve the pressure by providing a special treat such as introducing a new book or game, singing songs, or even preparing and eating a snack.

Throughout this chapter, the instructional procedures presented indicate an inherent assessment component. Whole-language teachers use every instructional situation as an opportunity for assessment. Evaluation also involves more careful, organized data gathering, including information from the Burke Reading Interview (see p. 332) and miscue analysis (see Chapter 10). The "Getting to Know You" inventories illustrated earlier (see pp. 237–38) provide teachers with valuable information about students and suggest appropriate materials and activities. Inventories such as these can be re-administered later in the year in order to document changes in attitudes and interests.

Students in whole-language classrooms are aware of their own progress and set their own goals and directions. This kind of *self-evaluation* takes a variety of forms. In their writing folders, for example, students keep a running list of "Things I Can Do" and the date. The "things" may consist of poetry writing or using capital letters (see also Figure 7.16 on page 203). Students monitor their own learning because they are part of the curricular partnership. By presenting what they know and don't know, and what they want to find out, they are taking ownership of their learning.

Many whole-language teachers keep *journals* about their teaching and their students' learning. These records help teachers become more reflective about their own practices and their perceptions, in addition to documenting student learning. Students in whole-language classrooms learn language skills in the context of use, and therefore the sequence of their development varies. Teachers' records allow them to keep track of group as well as individual growth in all areas of language and at all rates of development.

Anecdotal records describe significant language events over time for each individual. Gary Kilarr and Gayle Jennings (from the New South Wales Department of Education, 1983) developed the following record:

Student: Yvonne	First Month	Fifth Month
READS	lacks confidence in SSR prefers to write	enjoys reading likes to share stories
TALKS	sometimes talks with friends	talks in conjunction with task and in groups
CONFERS	only with teacher	seeks help for self, helps others
DRAFTS	no	will start again
REVISES-SELF	no	during work

Student: Yvonne	First Month	Fifth Month
RE-READS	yes	yes
USES EXPERIENCE	very rarely	in group discussion and writing
TAKES RISKS	no	comes up with writing topics
		substitutes words that make sense for unfamiliar words when reading
SEEKS HELP TO SOLVE A PROBLEM	from teacher	from peers and classroom resources
SEEKS FEEDBACK	that he is working all right	that his work can be read
GENRE: (TOPICS)	interested in space and dinosaurs	science orientation
SPELLING	will attempt inventions, prefers to use resources to obtain conventional spelling	uses approximations, prefers to use resources rather than use too many nonconventional words
READING ATTITUDE	prefers to look in reference books	enjoys SSR and sharing, enjoys listening post, predictable books, rhyme books
WRITING ATTITUDE	would rather write than read	enjoys writing, realizes he is learning

Other inventories such as the "Literature Reading Behavior Inventory" (Haussler 1982) require only a checkmark in the "yes" column and the date as a way of recording information about a variety of early reading behaviors, including: "Turns pages in sequence from left to right, front to back; attempts to read by retelling a remembered text (attends to memory and pictures); recognizes where print ends on a page; accurately word matches a repetitive pattern in the story; uses a variety of cueing systems to read new material." These two inventories were developed by teachers who know about language and their students. Records such as these are very helpful, but teachers should use whatever system is the most useful and efficient for their own purposes.

BASAL READERS AND WHOLE LANGUAGE

The basal reader dominates reading programs in American classrooms today. Basal reader series usually include guidebooks containing objectives and instructions for each lesson, student books containing stories and activities, workbooks with drill and practice activities for various skills, and other materials such as charts, flash cards, and tests. Most basal reader programs are built on arbitrary skill sequences that divide language into parts for the purposes of instruction. Such programs, particularly for young readers, break language down into small, abstract units such as vowel digraphs and consonant blends. Stories limited to four or five words ("I will go. Will you go? I will not go" for example) and a few rebuses (picture reading) can hardly be called literature; such "stories" lack cohesion, coherence, and comprehensibility—to say nothing of interest. The most contrived texts tend to be offered to kindergarten and first-grade readers. What is the message? Reading is nonsense, or borders on it.

Many basal reader companies have begun excerpting chapters from quality children's literature to use in upper elementary books. This is a step in the right direction but there is a problem. When books are excerpted in this way, something is lost. Short stories are self-contained, but a chapter of a book loses something when it stands alone. Although reading a chapter out of a quality book is preferable to reading a contrived story developed by basal publishers, it is difficult to establish themes and trace character development with only a fragment of the total story.

Often the best and most meaningful experiences suggested in a basal reader lesson are the "enrichment" activities that follow the skills work. These activities often extend a narrow lesson into a broader context involving further research and additional reading. Most teachers who are tied to the guidebook find it impossible to do any of these activities because of time limitations; to complete the lesson takes precedence over in-depth study. Over-reliance on the guidebook has been labeled a "misuse" of the basal reader (Rosecky 1978).

If skill sheets *must* be used, whole-language teachers often turn them into games. If phonics *must* be taught directly, rhymes, riddles, or songs bring value and enjoyment where they would otherwise be lacking. Whole-language teachers find out how much of the material *must* be used and in what ways. Too often teachers believe that all of the activities in the guidebook need to be followed, but no research supports this practice. Sometimes teachers are required to use all of the stories in a basal reader, but not necessarily as specified in the guidebook or in the order in which they appear. The basal reader, if required, must never be thought of as the entire reading program. In an in-depth review of reading comprehension research, Jerry Harste and Phillip Harris (1985) have shown that *any* reading program that goes beyond the basal reader leads children to gains in comprehension.

Certainly there are activities and materials that are anomalous in whole-language teaching. Nevertheless, the mandate to use basal readers or any other skills materials will not break a whole-language teacher. When skills materials are required, whole-language teachers attempt to use them in holistic ways. A whole-language program involves an attitude about growth and development, language and learning, and the strengths of the learner—an attitude that goes beyond the issue of materials.

WHOLE-LANGUAGE TEACHERS AND REALITY

In complex technological societies, literacy is an empowering force. Those who read can find out what others know and those who write can share what they know;

written language is an effective vehicle for the exchange of information, beliefs, and values across time and space. Whether one is reading a recipe or reading a petition, writing a letter to a cousin or to the editor of the newspaper, written language helps get things done. In George Orwell's *1984*, Big Brother wanted people literate only to the extent that they could comprehend government slogans and propaganda on a literal level; writing was a heinous crime. Suppressive regimes carefully control access to information and the dissemination of ideas through print. On the other hand, democratic societies take pride in freedom of information and freedom of the press.

There is an implicit contract between the community and the school that children will learn to read and write so that they will be independent adults. People who leave school illiterate can receive negative national attention. It is no wonder that reading—and, more recently, writing—instruction is closely monitored within the school curriculum. There are pervasive influences affecting what happens in a public school classroom; one such influence has to do with accountability. Teachers are accountable to their principals, principals are accountable to their superintendents, superintendents are accountable to the school board and legislators, and the school board and legislators are accountable to parents/citizens. Other forces impacting on curriculum and teaching involve state mandates, district policies, departmental regulations, and expectations of principals and supervisors. The effects of these policies and expectations can be found in all classrooms.

Whole-language teachers do not sacrifice the needs of children for the sake of political issues; they do, however, use their knowledge and expertise to understand these influences and to use them for the benefit of students. Breakdowns in communication can lead to power struggles that teachers too often lose. Consider the following scenarios:

Scenario 1

A father is curious about what his first grader is doing in school and asks about her reading class. "We don't have reading class" is her answer. That evening he visits his neighbor, the school board member, inquiring as to the whereabouts of the "First R" in first grade. The next day when the teacher is called into the principal's office to explain why she is neglecting to teach the basic skill of reading, she is in a less than advantageous position.

Her explanation is good: every day the children are read to or told a story. The bookshelves are filled with a variety of children's literature, content texts, resource books, blank paper, and writing utensils. The children, from the first day of school, have been invited to read and write independently, and success is guaranteed. The children read for real purposes: for enjoyment, to find out about spiders, to find out what's for lunch, to read their friends' writing. There is no designated "reading class" because reading is a learning tool that is used all day, and when there is a need to talk about the process of reading, it is done individually or in small groups. The teacher explains that she doesn't view reading as an entity unto itself, but as a language process that is used to explore and express the content being studied.

Reading, in concert with writing, listening, and speaking, is not taught in isolation, but is learned and refined through use.

Reflection

People are uncomfortable with the unfamiliar. Parents, in particular, can become understandably concerned if they feel that their children's needs are not being met in school. The features of a whole-language program are sometimes unfamiliar to people who are accustomed to traditional reading instruction, but parents and administrators can understand the theory and the practice of whole language. If the parents had been invited to learn about the curriculum at the beginning of the year and if information had been sent home concerning reading and writing in this classroom, the miscommunication could have been avoided.

Scenario 2

A first-year third-grade teacher is dismayed by the spelling books ordered the previous year. The guidebook instructs the teacher to introduce a list of ten words on Monday, have the students write the words ten times each, use each in a sentence, look up their definitions in the dictionary, and copy these in the space provided. On Wednesday the children are tested on the words, and failed words are drilled on Thursday and retested on Friday.

The teacher knows that this is not the way spelling is learned. The prescribed words are often unfamiliar and unimportant to the student, and are chosen by the author of the spelling textbook. The activities can be completed with little or no thought; the teacher knows that the children are easily bored with such activities and can become uninvolved in their learning, often leading to passivity or behavior problems. But the teacher believes the spelling books must be used.

Reflection

Did the teacher ask if the books really had to be used? If so, how? Or how much time had to be spent on the books? Do the directions in the teacher's manual have to be the curriculum? Did the teacher propose alternatives, such as using the spelling books as reference books? Can pages be skipped? Can students substitute words they want to learn for those chosen by a publisher? Did the teacher explain to his or her supervisors how the teacher handles spelling in the curriculum? It is important for teachers to know what has to be done and where they have freedom and autonomy. Administrators and supervisors respect professionals who can articulate their beliefs and knowledge, who have confidence in what they know, and who show a genuine concern for the needs and welfare of their students.

Scenario 3

The second-grade teacher walks into the teacher's lounge during lunch complaining to the faculty about how terrible her students' writing is. They have drilled on correct formation of the lower case "k" for a week now and there are still children who can't do it. They just need more drill. The language arts consultant is annoyed because by "writing," this teacher means "handwriting." The consultant tells her not to worry about such a trivial matter: writing is generating ideas, learning through language use, and expressing inner thoughts and feelings. She has the undivided attention of the teacher and all of her colleagues. Later, she's the only member of the faculty not invited to that teacher's yearly Christmas party.

Reflection

Teachers must afford their colleagues the same consideration that they expect and that they give their students. When teachers are empowered by their beliefs, they want everyone to share their excitement. But others have their own beliefs and they too are seeking acknowledgment. People are less likely to change when their practices are attacked or when they are told that they should do things differently; individuals change because they see value in something else.

The well-meaning consultant embarrassed her colleague and questioned her expertise. Rather than taking an adversarial role with the other teacher, she might have simply shared student writings. This would have provided an opportunity to offer what she knew and to present children in a positive light, both in an unassuming manner.

Reflecting on Reflections

The problem common to these three scenarios is poor communication. Teachers must be open about what they know, and they need to find out what others are doing—really doing, if there is to be hope for positive communication. Teachers need to talk to parents, administrators, and other teachers in order to support each other's endeavors, always maintaining the child at the center.

Teachers need support. How frequently does someone come into the classroom to talk with teachers or to discuss curricular matters? Teachers often close their doors, hoping to be left alone. Whole-language teachers have found it necessary to metaphorically "open their doors" to other whole-language teachers who can share their successes and problems. Throughout Canada and the United States, whole-language teachers are meeting together for the purpose of encouraging and informing each other. These groups are known by names such as: TAWL (*T*eachers *A*pplying *W*hole *L*anguage), CAWL (*C*hildren *A*nd *W*hole *L*anguage), and CEL (*C*hild-centered, *E*xperience-based *L*earning). The group activities consist not only of sharing ideas, professional writings, and samples of children's work, but also of presenting the teachers' own expertise through conferences and writings.

A FINAL WORD

In truth, we can never put the finishing touches on a whole-language picture. That artistic endeavor is up to individual teachers and their students. As you read this chapter we hope that you made sketches in your own mind about children you know, literature you love, and all you believe about good language teaching. That's the exciting and authentic beginning of your whole-language picture.

ACTIVITIES AND PROJECTS FOR FURTHER EXPLORATION

1. Think about how you learned to read and write, and how you were taught to read and write in school. What are some of the negative experiences you would want to avoid in your own teaching? What are some of the positive experiences that you would want to provide for the children you teach? How might you build upon these good memories to create a more humane learning environment? Discuss.

2. Draw on paper how you might design the physical aspects of your classroom. How would you arrange the students' desks and/or tables? Where would your own desk be? Would you have a carpeted area where children can come to be read to, to share their writings, and so forth? A class library? Centers for writing, for listening to taped stories, for social studies and science activities? Would you have plants? These are only some of the major aspects that you might consider in designing your classroom.

3. Think further about the children you want to teach and the situation and classroom in which you want to teach. Describe the first day/week those children might have in your whole-language classroom.

4. Find at least three stories that you would like to read to children and a story that you would like to tell to them. Practice these, and present them to a study partner or to the class.

5. Choose a favorite children's literature book. How would you invite students to "extend" this work of literature?

6. How would you help a first-grade reluctant reader become a confident and joyful reader? How would you help a fifth-grade unsuccessful reader become a confident reader? Discuss.

7. What is happening in schools today that stands in the way of whole-language teaching? What suggestions do you have for coping with these situations and solving the problems? Discuss.

8. What materials are required for reading instruction in your school district? Collect samples of materials such as basal readers. Critique these samples in light of what you know about language and learning.

9. Develop a newsletter that might form the basis of one you would actually send to parents early in the school year. Briefly explain and illustrate how children can learn to read and write "naturally," as they learned to talk. Convince parents that a whole-language approach will be the best for their children.

10. Develop a list of ways that you could involve parents in the curricular as well as the social aspects of the classroom (for example, by taking dictation from individual children).

READINGS FOR FURTHER EXPLORATION

Goodman, Yetta, and Kenneth Goodman. March 1981. Twenty Questions About Teaching Language. *Educational Leadership* 38: 437–42. Examines, from a scientific base, common beliefs and misconceptions about language and language learning.

Goodman, Yetta. June 1978. Kid Watching: An Alternative to Testing. *National Elementary School Principal* 57: 41–45. This landmark article indicates how teachers can assess children's level of development and progress through observation rather than through formal testing.

Rich, Sharon. November 1985. Restoring Power to Teachers: The Impact of "Whole Language." *Language Arts* 62: 717–24. This inspirational article demonstrates how teachers and children are beginning once again to take charge of their own classrooms.

King, Dorothy F., and Dorothy J. Watson. 1984. Reading as Meaning Construction. *Integrating the Language Arts in the Elementary School.* Ed. B. A. Busching and J. I. Schwartz. Urbana, Ill.: National Council of Teachers of English, 70–77. Demonstrates how children learn language in meaningful, useful contexts, and develop strategies for constructing meaning by drawing upon all of the cueing systems available.

Smith, Frank. January 1981. Demonstrations, Engagement, and Sensitivity: A Revised Approach to Language Learning. *Language Arts* 58: 103–12. Defines learning as a natural product of *demonstrations* indicating how something is done, the learner's *engagement* with the task, and the learner's *sensitivity*: "the absence of any expectation that learning will not take place, or that it will be difficult." Smith relates this concept of learning to the acquisition of literacy.

Edelsky, Carol, and Karen Smith. January 1984. Is That Writing—Or Are Those Marks Just a Figment of Your Curriculum? *Language Arts* 61: 24–32. Demonstrates the importance of having children engage in authentic writing rather than many of the writing tasks traditionally assigned in school.

Barrett, Frank L. 1982. *A Teacher's Guide to Shared Reading.* Richmond Hill, Ontario: Scholastic-TAB. This little booklet offers a brief overview of shared reading activities and how to conduct them.

McCracken, Robert A. May 1971. Initiating Sustained Silent Reading. *Journal of Reading* 14: 521–24, 582–83. This landmark article on sustained silent reading was followed with an article by Robert and Marlene McCracken. Modeling Is the Key to Sustained Silent Reading. *The Reading Teacher.* January 1978. 31: 406–8.

Hoskisson, Kenneth. March 1975. The Many Facets of Assisted Reading. *Elementary English* 52: 312–15. Discusses various methods of "assisted reading."

Norton, Donna E. April 1982. Using a Webbing Process to Develop Children's Literature Units. *Language Arts* 59: 348–56. Shows how thematic units can be developed to teach science and social studies topics, drawing upon children's literature as a major resource.

Fitzgerald, Jill. December 1983. Helping Readers Gain Self-Control Over Reading Comprehension. *The Reading Teacher* 37: 249–53. Discusses monitoring one's comprehension, or "metacomprehension," which she defines as follows: "You know when you know (and when you don't)." Provides guidelines for teaching the process of monitoring one's comprehension.

Atwell, Margaret A., and Lynn K. Rhodes. May 1984. Strategy Lessons as Alternatives to Skills Lessons in Reading. *Journal of Reading* 27: 700–705. Valuable in suggesting how to teach strategy lessons instead of skills lessons.

Goodman, Kenneth. April 1986. Basal Readers: A Call for Action. *Language Arts* 63: 358–63. The knowledge gap between reading research and basal readers is discussed, and publishers are challenged to close the gap by using real literature and abandoning meaningless workbook drills in basals.

Langer, Judith A., and Gordon M. Pradl. November 1984. Standarized Testing: A Call for Action. *Language Arts* 61: 764–67. Examines the over-reliance on the results of standardized tests in making curricular decisions in language arts. Educators are encouraged to speak out against the misuse of standardized tests.

Goodman, Kenneth. 1986. *What's Whole in Whole Language*? Richmond Hill, Ontario: Scholastic-TAB. This booklet provides an overview of a whole-language philosophy and approach.

The following booklets are useful in implementing a whole-language approach:

Lynch, Priscilla. 1986. *Using Big Books and Predictable Books*. Richmond Hill, Ontario: Scholastic-TAB. Provides practical suggestions for using *Big Books* and predictable books in the classroom.

Peetoom, Adrian. 1986. *Shared Reading: Safe Risks with Whole Books*. Richmond Hill, Ontario: Scholastic-TAB. Provides practical suggestions for enabling slower, less confident readers to tackle whole books appropriate for their interest level.

Useful resource books include the following:

Goodman, Yetta, Dorothy Watson, and Carolyn Burke. 1987. Miscue Analysis and Curriculum Development. *Reading Miscue Inventory: Alternative Procedures*. New York: Richard C. Owen. This section of the book shows how teachers can develop an individualized reading program based upon the findings of miscue analysis.

Goodman, Yetta M., and Carolyn Burke. 1980. *Reading Strategies: Focus on Comprehension*. New York: Richard C. Owen. Presents theoretically based strategy lessons that facilitate various components of the reading process.

Watson, Dorothy J., ed. 1987. *Ideas with Insights: Language Arts K–6*. Urbana, Ill.: National Council of Teachers of English.

Baskwill, Jane, and Paulette Whitman. 1986. *Whole Language Sourcebook*. Richmond Hill, Ontario: Scholastic-TAB. Presents sample thematic units and discusses materials, organization, scheduling, curriculum requirements, and teaching strategies.

For a variety of books valuable in implementing a whole-language approach to literacy, see the list titled "Teaching Reading and Writing in a Whole-Language Perspective" in the "Suggested Readings" section of the bibliography.

9

How Can We Teach Reading in the Content Areas?

Marilyn Wilson

Teaching skills for the sake of skills is as purposeless as teaching ancient history in a vacuum. It's all Greek to students. When it comes to reading, then, a content teacher's job is not to teach skills per se but to show students how to use reading effectively to comprehend and learn from text materials. Therein lies the real value of content area reading instruction.

—Richard and Jo Anne Vacca

QUESTIONS FOR JOURNALS AND DISCUSSION

1. What are the elements that create optimal conditions for reading comprehension in the content area classroom?

2. How can teachers motivate students to read content material, and how can they activate and build readers' schemas for reading?

3. What strategies for fostering metacomprehension are available to the content area teacher?

4. What are the limitations of a taxonomy or hierarchy of questions for discussion after reading? How can better questioning techniques aid readers' comprehension?

5. What are some response-centered activities that can be used successfully after reading?

6. How can readers be encouraged to read critically within and beyond the text?

7. What is the role of writing in the comprehension process? How can writing be used both as preparation for and as response to reading?

8. How can a greater awareness of the organizational patterns of texts aid readers' comprehension of the content?

9. What are the limitations of readability formulas for determining text comprehensibility and for the writing of texts? What are some alternative means of text assessment and selection?

10. How can the content area classroom teacher incorporate reading beyond the text to help sustain the content material and readers' interest in it?

CONTENT AREA READING: A CONTRAST

Scene One: Middlebury Middle School, eighth-grade social studies class. Mr. Randolf, the teacher, has just assigned chapter eight in the text, allotting the rest of the period for the students to read. During the reading of the chapter "Rebellion in the Colonies" (*American Spirit: A History of the United States*, Follett Publishing Company, 1982), the teacher stresses the need to discover reasons why the colonists rebelled. The students begin reading the text with interest and with sufficient reading ability to deal with it because the text material is appropriate to their reading level. Furthermore, the students bring adequate background knowledge to the task to handle the concepts, having seen a short film on major figures and events leading to the conflict. They are relatively confident, independent readers whose self-monitoring strategies enable them to take corrective action if meaning and comprehension break down. They read until the end of the hour, and Mr. Randolf can be reasonably satisfied that the discussion of the material will go well the following day.

Scene Two: Ashton Middle School, eighth-grade social studies class. Like Mr. Randolf, Ms. Smith has also assigned the chapter to her class to be read by the following day. The class begins the reading, but with varying degrees of success. Jeff reads the text with considerable ease and when finished, recaps the main points of the chapter with excellent comprehension, as he has been instructed to do. Sarah, too, appears to read the text with ease but has difficulty recapping the main points and eventually doesn't bother, as she says to herself, "I just don't get it." Betsy, on the other hand, reads with some difficulty but has good comprehension, while Sam reads with great difficulty and appears to have little text comprehension. In addition, there's Marie, who *can* read, but rarely chooses to, particularly when the assignment is from the textbook, and today, as usual, she chooses not to.

Our first mythical classroom highlights the optimal conditions for reading: texts that are readable and interesting, closely matched to students' reading levels; readers whose backgrounds are sufficient to handle the conceptual difficulty of the text; high student interest in the material; and confident readers who know what to do when the reading becomes difficult. But rare are the classrooms where these optimal conditions occur naturally and without effort. In fact, many teachers would have difficulty pointing to any one student for whom the optimal conditions occur with any regularity.

Our second classroom, of course, is much more typical: those five students represent the wide range of abilities one finds in a typical classroom, the range of background knowledge and experience that students bring to the material, and the wide range of interest and motivation to read and to learn the course material. Add to this, textbooks that rarely match the range of reading abilities represented by the students in this class, that sometimes inadequately explain complex concepts, or that in an attempt to simplify the language may omit many of the connecting words that clarify the relationship between ideas. To round off the scene, we add to it a teacher who probably knows her subject very well and loves it dearly, who finds herself frustrated that her students don't necessarily share those same interests, and who finds it difficult to recall the experience of learning and struggling with new concepts in a subject that she has long since mastered. This scene describes a classroom with a high probability of frustration for students and teacher alike. Recognizing the difference between the ideal and the real, teachers may be tempted to look at readers' shortcomings and resign themselves to either providing more information through lecture rather than through the reading, or making the same reading assignments in the same way but giving fewer passing grades. If the students can't read the text, or won't, many teachers see these as their only alternatives.

Few teachers would argue then, with the need for more and better comprehension instruction, given Durkin's far-reaching and widely publicized study (1978–79) of the kinds and extent of comprehension instruction occurring in grades 3 to 6. She found that, in those classrooms studied, less than *1 percent* of class time was devoted to instruction about comprehension during the study of reading and social studies. If this is the state of the art in elementary classrooms, is it any wonder that secondary teachers feel even greater reluctance and uncertainty about comprehension instruction in their content areas, where it isn't even part of the stated curriculum?

This chapter suggests ways of helping classroom teachers in various content areas, and at various levels, readjust materials and approaches to reading to more closely reach those optimal reading conditions where comprehension will occur. Classroom teachers have little control over the kinds of students coming into their classrooms, but they can change the conditions under which students read and learn. The chapter focuses on strategies to *increase readers' motivation* to read and learn, to help *build conceptual background* to enable readers to comprehend more easily, to *provide purposes* and a focus for reading, to help readers *build and integrate meaning* more successfully as reading occurs, to help readers *monitor their own comprehension* while reading, and to *create a greater awareness of text structure and rhetorical devices* to make the process of comprehension easier.

READER, TEXT, AND CONTEXT FOR READING

It is common in content area reading to focus on *text*: its organization and rhetorical structure, its concepts, and its linguistic patterns, on the assumption that if the reader understands the text structure, the reader will more easily be able to read it. While text considerations are important, they are by no means sufficient. Reading comprehension is equally dependent on the contributions of the *reader* to the process of reading, as discussed in earlier chapters. Sarah, our Ashton Middle School reader who seems to read with ease but with little comprehension, may be proficient in processing the surface structure of the text but may have insufficient background knowledge of the causes of the Revolutionary War to read with comprehension. And Marie, capable of reading, is simply not motivated to do so. Teachers in the content areas must consider the reader a primary focal point and provide ways of bridging the gap between the reader's background, experience, and motivation and the text itself. A third consideration, then, is necessarily the *context* for reading—the environment and the conditions under which the reading will occur. Bridging the gap between reader and text involves structuring the context in such a way that the reader feels more capable of reading, has built up a sufficient background for the reading, and is motivated to do it. The strategies for reading comprehension that follow focus on the dynamic relationship existing among these three elements, and ways in which this relationship can be exploited to its fullest for comprehension to occur easily and productively.

If comprehension can be increased by adjusting any of the elements in this triad, our definition of comprehension must be expanded to account for its fluid, dynamic nature. Comprehension is not simply an end product of the reading process. It is a condition for reading, a driving force that guides the reading, and a result of the reading that allows for full integration of meaning. The reader does not merely reconstruct the author's meaning but instead builds his or her own meaning; the process is constructive, not merely reconstructive. It is not simply bottom-up or text-based, nor exclusively top-down or concept-based, but rather transactive, with the reader using both knowledge of the linguistic elements of the text as well as knowledge of the larger meanings generated by the reader's schemas. The text, Langer (1982, p. 41) says, is:

> . . . merely a blueprint using a linguistic code; readers must use the blueprint to stimulate their own ideas and create their own meanings. This is not to suggest that readers go off into an idiosyncratic world of fanciful meaning but that they alone have the power to create meaning—their meaning that is closer to or further from the meaning that the author intended, but reader-generated nonetheless.

A text has meaning potential that is realized only by the individual reader constructing his or her own personal meaning.

Chapter 2 discusses the dynamic relationship between the reader, the text, and the ''poem'' as described by Rosenblatt (1978): the reader transacts with the text—the print on the page—to create the ''poem,'' the meaning that emerges from the transaction. The critical element is the reader, who acts upon the text to create meaning. An expansion of this view of text is offered by Devine (1986), who sees the existence of three texts during the reading process: (1) the text in the mind of the writer before and during the writing; (2) the text the writer actually creates, that exists in print (Rosenblatt's ''text''), which is likely to be an inadequate relection of the first text; and (3) the text that exists in the reader's mind (Rosenblatt's ''poem'') during and after the reading, as determined by the reader's linguistic capabilities, background knowledge, cognitive abilities, and expectations for the text. These latter factors will undoubtedly create for readers meanings that differ in varying degrees from either text one or text two.

This transactional view of reading in which readers create their own meaning through application of their general and specific schemas to the linguistic cues in the text is compatible with current research on the brain. Recent studies (Weaver 1986) suggest that the left hemisphere is not the exclusive domain of linguistic capabilities. While the left hemisphere largely controls speech production and literal comprehension of words and phrases, the right hemisphere appears to be involved in visual and spatial perception of words and in the comprehension of larger wholes. These studies suggest that reading involves a coordination of right and left hemispheric processing and as such is a whole-brain process that incorporates the bottom-up and top-down processing that reading theorists have postulated. If reading comprehension is a whole-brain function involving a complex relationship between textual linguistic elements and meaning brought to the reading through the reader's schemas, the context for reading must incorporate a variety of strategies that put the reader's background knowledge into full play in order for a comprehension-based reading experience to occur.

Creating optimal conditions for reading involves techniques and strategies that are based, as well, on the following assumptions:

1. The skills necessary for proficient reading are not separate, discrete, identifiable skills that can be easily sequenced for instruction; they develop through the act and practice of reading whole, meaningful, relevant materials, and they develop over long experience with reading materials that encourage and support the building of those skills. Teachers can create optimal conditions that will nurture their development, but they cannot "teach" them through a sequential series of skills lessons.

2. Content area reading involves active, interested, motivated readers who willingly engage with the text, emotionally as well as intellectually. A transaction with the text occurs more readily when readers feel some personal commitment to the reading and see its relevance to their own interests and experiences. Content area classrooms can foster such experiences by allowing and encouraging personal reading to occur. Reading *Johnny Tremain* (Forbes 1943) in an American history class, for example, can spark readers' interest in the history text as well as encourage readers to see the connections between classroom reading, literature, and the world at large. Reading beyond the text can enhance the experience of reading the text itself.

3. Writing and reading are reciprocal and mutually supportive processes, and as such, both should be integral in classroom activities. Considerable evidence demonstrates the powerful effect of writing on reading comprehension when the reader writes about, and in response to, the reading. (See Julie Jensen, ed., *Composing and Comprehending*. NCTE, 1984, for relevant articles on reading/writing relationships and classroom implications.) Using language, either through talk or writing, allows readers to comprehend, to clarify previous experience and knowledge, and to integrate new information with old. Verbalizing information and concepts is integral to internalizing and integrating new concepts. Writing and talking about the reading in personally relevant and interesting ways should be an important component of every classroom.

4. American educational institutions have traditionally viewed learning as a highly individual, personal event, a primarily solitary activity. There is considerable evidence, however, that learning is immeasurably enhanced by group interaction and inquiry. Comprehension and learning are strengthened when they occur as collaborative efforts (Kraft 1985), and reading comprehension and enjoyment are increased when students share their reading with one another (Manning and

Manning 1984). Content area classrooms can create optimal reading experiences by fostering peer interaction and collaboration.

PRE-READING STRATEGIES

Capitalizing on students' curiosity and innate interest in learning is critical to learning, though often neglected in assignment-making. Simply giving students assigned pages and chapters in the text does little to stimulate interest or to help students make connections between the content and their own experiences. Pre-reading strategies are designed to accomplish the following goals: (1) to motivate students to want to do the reading; (2) to help them set purposes and find a focus for their reading; (3) to bridge the gap between students' conceptual backgrounds and the concepts being presented in the reading; and (4) to activate and build on readers' existing schemas for making the material more comprehensible. In fact, the latter two goals strongly increase readers' motivation to read: when readers recognize that they already know something about the topic, that the topic is relevant, the reading will more likely occur with greater interest and sharper focus.

Particularly useful for introducing new units of study are films and videotapes, records, related fiction or nonfiction, and demonstrations and experiments. A unit on the American Revolution, for example, can be introduced with famous quotes from American men of letters: Patrick Henry's cry of "Give me liberty or give me death!" in his speech to the Virginia convention, or Thomas Paine's stirring words in the opening of *Common Sense*. A recording of Revolutionary songs like "Yankee Doodle" or "The Liberty Song" can create interest in the political situations giving rise to their creation. A study of America's expansion and its effect on native Americans might be introduced with a painting like Robert Lindneux's *Trail of Tears*, depicting the forced removal of the Cherokee Nation from Georgia to Oklahoma and the hardships and indignities the people endured. The study of a country might be introduced with recordings of their music or pictures of native dress. Teachers can introduce pioneer life with the concept of buttermaking, demonstrated by the students in the classroom shaking cream in a jar until it turns to butter. A study of insects in science can be introduced by looking at various kinds of beetles that the students themselves bring to class. A prism can initiate the study of the color spectrum.

Wagner (1983) suggests a less common but equally valuable way of arousing interest and helping students relate the matter to be studied to their own lives and understanding: the use of role-playing and dramatization in the content area classroom. Wagner and a colleague introduced a group of eight- and nine-year-olds to a social studies unit on Brazil and a science unit on water by having students dramatize and role-play events that occurred when a team of Brazilian engineers built a dam down river from the valley that for generations had been the home of the Moqui Indian tribe (Wagner 1983, p. 156). Students played the parts of the tribespeople as well as the engineers, working through several imaginary dramatic episodes as the Indians were forced to leave their homeland for another area.

After the drama was ended, the children were encouraged to make lists of questions that they wanted to find out about, such as what the Moqui eat, whether or not they plant crops, what their homes are like, and so on. The children's urge to learn, to find out, to read, had been fanned by the drama, Wagner says (p. 161); the drama had stimulated their thinking and their curiosity to learn more. Children, claims Wagner, "will not likely hear or read what they have not first seen and touched . . ." (p. 162). Students come to the reading with a sharper focus, a heightened curiosity, and a more personal investment in the reading when they have had the opportunity to explore issues of controversy from different points of view *before* they read.

Developing Purposes for Reading

Motivating students to read is, of course, a primary objective of the activities just described. But an added benefit is that students also develop specific purposes for reading through these activities. In fact, when students put themselves into role-playing situations before they do the reading, they not only imagine how they would respond to the situation but they establish for themselves a more personally relevant purpose for reading. An unfortunate consequence of reading assignments made with little or no introduction to the material is unfocused reading. Readers approaching the task without a guided framework sometimes assume that reading the text simply means identifying words and processing the surface of the printed page; in other cases they don't know how to focus because they don't know what to look for: all facts and ideas seem equally important or equally irrelevant, as the case might be. Proficient readers, on the other hand, read with a set of questions in mind, and they read to get those questions answered (F. Smith 1975). They are reading for a specific purpose.

How we read—the approach we take or the strategy we use—will largely depend on our purpose(s) for reading. We do not read poetry the same way we read novels and short stories, nor do we read nonfiction the same way we read fiction. Textbook reading is somewhat different from newspaper and magazine reading. Students, then, need to learn to vary their reading rate and approach in accordance with what they are reading, and with what their purposes are for reading it.

Readers approaching the same text may use somewhat different strategies. But the effective and *efficient* reader will in some cases have adopted strategies for scanning and skimming. When looking for particular information, the reader may look initially just at the first sentence of every paragraph; another reader may look for key words or phrases. Such strategies help a reader determine which part(s) of a text will need to be read more carefully in order to find the desired information.

Our overall approach also depends, to some extent, on what we intend to *do* with the information and ideas once they have been located. Do we merely want to know how a particular court case was decided, or do we want to understand the Court's position and be able to explain its reasoning? Do we want to be able to savor the language and the style of the novel we are reading, or are we so eager to find out the perpetrator of the crime in the who-done-it novel that we ignore stylistic nuances in order to concentrate on plot details? Do we merely want to comprehend, in general, why the American colonies broke with Great Britain, or do we instead want to be able to apply this understanding in some way? And if the latter, then which details do we need to extract from the passage? And how will we store these details: in our heads, on note cards, or what?

It is clear, then, that there is no single way to read. Our approach will depend on our external and internal reasons for reading, the nature of the text itself, the particular kinds of information or understanding we want to gain from the material, and how we want to use the knowledge gained. Still another factor influencing our reading strategy is the relevant knowledge and experience we bring to the reading task, information that is within the reader rather than in the text itself.

It is often not enough that students have some implicit knowledge of the topic before they read—that knowledge needs to be activated. Class discussions prior to reading help students begin to use their schemas by taking stock of what they already know. Such discussions may encourage readers to make predictions about the text and enlarge their own schemas by learning from one another. This approach is illustrated by the following hypothetical discussion, intended to prepare students to read a selection about the construction of the first continental railroad (Pearson and Johnson 1978, pp. 189–91):[1]

Instructor:	Tell me what you know about the Union Pacific Railroad. (No response.) Well, when was it built? (No response.) Before the Civil War? After? During?
Student 1:	Before!
Student 2:	After!
Instructor:	Now, why do you say before?
Student 1:	Just seems right to me. Maybe it had something to do with the Gold Rush?
Student 2:	No, it was after!
Instructor:	You're sure about that?
Student 2:	Pretty sure. There's something about a Golden Spike out West in Utah, or Nevada, or Wyoming, and that country wasn't even settled by the time of the Civil War.
Instructor:	Didn't they have railroads before the Civil War?
Student 3:	Sure the railroads came as early as 1820 or 1830. Right after the steam engine.
Student 4:	But they were mostly in the Eastern United States.
Instructor:	So no one is sure when it was built. Anyone want to guess about a date (several are offered ranging from 1840 to 1910)? Okay, where did it start and where did it end? (No responses.) Did it start over here on the East Coast, say Pittsburgh? Did it start up here, say Minneapolis? Did it start here, say St. Louis? Where?
Student 4:	I think it was St. Joseph. Something started there.
Student 5:	Omaha sounds right to me.
Student 3:	St. Louis rings a bell for me.
Instructor:	(Who has been jotting down guesses all along.) Well, we have three candidates. I'm not sure either. But we'll find out. Where did it end? Here, in Los Angeles? Here, in San Francisco? Here, in Seattle? Here, in Utah? Where?

Student 6:   San Francisco, because Los Angeles was just a small town then.

Student 7:   I seem to remember that it was not one railroad but two that built the first transcontinental railroad.

Student 8:   That's right. It was a contest.

Instructor: So, when the railroad across the country was built it wasn't from East to West?

Student 8:   No, it wasn't! One company started from the East and the other started from the West.

Instructor: I think you're right. The first transcontinental railroad was built from both ends toward the middle. What do you need to build a railroad?

Student 5:   Rails.

Student 4:   Railroad ties.

Student 1:   Workers.

Instructor: Okay. For the company that went from East to West, I can see how they got their materials.

Student 3:   Yeah, they just loaded them onto railroad cars and hauled them to the end of the line.

Instructor: But how did they get their materials on the West Coast?

Student 5:   Same way.

Student 7:   Not then. No iron ore out there. But they could get ties.

Instructor: I think you're right. I think Pittsburgh was the center of steel production then. It still is, I guess. Well, let's assume they had to transport the rails. How could they do it? Overland Stage?

Student 6:   No! Rails would have been too heavy for the wagons. And if they only took one or two it would have taken forever to haul the rails.

Instructor: Pony Express?

Student 6:   No! By boat.

Instructor: (Pointing to map.) You mean they went from Pittsburgh to New York then around through the Panama Canal and up to San Francisco? (lots of nos.) Why not, that's about the shortest way.

Student 3:   The Panama Canal wasn't built yet. They had to go around South America.

Instructor: How do you know that? We haven't even established when the railroad was built. Maybe the Panama Canal was already finished.

Student 4:   No!

Instructor: Did they have to go from Pittsburgh to New York to get a ship? Could they have gone another way?

Student 5:   Maybe they went by barge down the Ohio River to the Mississippi, then to New Orleans.

Instructor: Could they? Does the Ohio River go through Pittsburgh?

Student 6:   I'm not sure but I bet some river did that eventually went into the Mississippi.

Instructor: What about the ties? Do you think they just got those out in California and Nevada as they went along? Or do you think they hauled those from the Midwest or the East?

Student 7:   There's a lot of timber in California, in the mountains.

Instructor: But is it the right kind? Can you make ties out of redwood or pine or fir?

Student 4:   You could probably use fir, but not redwood or pine. They're too soft.

Instructor:	I'm not sure myself. As a matter of fact, I'm not sure about much of this at all. Let's just review what we're not sure about at this point. (Instructor jots down the following points.) When was it built? Where did it start? Where did it end? Where and how did they get the rails and ties? Oh, one other thing—who were the workers?
Student 9:	Coolies. Chinese coolies.
Student 7:	On the West Coast. But from the East it was the Irish.
Instructor:	Why the Irish and the Chinese?
Student 9:	They brought in the Chinese just to work on the railroad because they were cheap.
Student 7:	The Irish were new immigrants. They were cheap, too. It was the only kind of job they could get. There were discriminated against then.
Instructor:	That's one more thing to look for—who built the railroad? And there's one other thing that's always puzzled me. Why did they build it from both ends toward the middle? It would seem to me to make more sense just to go from the East to the West. Then they wouldn't have had to worry about transporting materials by boat or whatever. Well, that's enough to look for. Here's an article about the railroad. Let's read it to see whether or not we were right about any of this.

A discussion like the one just quoted serves several valuable functions. It demonstrates to students that they already know something about the topic they are going to read about. Even with relatively unfamiliar material, the teacher can usually find some way of relating the unknown to something already known. Moreover, such a discussion enables students to pool their prior knowledge. For some, the discussion will add to existing knowledge and fine-tune it; for others it may modify inexact schemas. In addition, such discussion arouses students' curiosity and encourages them to set *their own purposes* for reading. To be sure, providing questions for students to consider as they read, or asking them to read the questions at the end of the chapter before they do the reading, will help them focus their reading, but the kind of discussion quoted above does much more to activate their own knowledge and bring it into play as they read the text.

Reader-Based Pre-Reading Strategies

As the previous discussion illustrated, it is important to help students generate their own questions, to make them less teacher-dependent in setting purposes for reading. To get students to initiate rather than to merely respond, teachers need to develop strategies that will foster reader independence in forming questions and in making predictions about the reading. ''What questions do *you* have about the first transcontinental railroad?'' may begin to stimulate student-generated questions. Listing students' questions on the chalkboard then gives more validity to them and demonstrates for other students the kinds of thinking students are engaged in as they prepare to do the reading.

Several other activities, as well, encourage students to find a focus growing out of their own questioning and predicting, while simultaneously activating their prior knowledge. Singer (1978) recommends teacher-modeling of the question-asking process that can then be transferred to the students. The three stages of the modeling process include (1) the teacher's formulating questions about the reading to be done, (2) the phasing-in of student-generated questions with some guidance from the teacher, and (3) the final stage of active comprehension, when students begin formulating and searching for answers to their own questions as they read the text. The modeling of the process can begin with the teacher's asking questions from pictures, titles, and subtitles in the text. With an article entitled "Safe from Enemies" in a third-grade science text (*Science*, Harcourt Brace Jovanovich, 1985), for example, the teacher models the "thinking-aloud" process based on the title and the two accompanying pictures, one a picture of a group of prairie dogs standing beside their burrow, and the other a picture of a coyote: "I wonder what this will be about? The title says, 'Safe from Enemies,' and the pictures are of some prairie dogs, I think, and an animal that looks like a wolf or a coyote. Maybe this is going to be about how smaller animals keep themselves safe from larger ones. I wonder how prairie dogs protect themselves when an enemy comes along. Maybe this article will tell me." The teacher and students together can make predictions based on similar reading selections, and eventually students can continue with the process independently.

This process is similar to the ReQuest procedure designed by Manzo (1969) in which an individual student and teacher silently read sections of the text and then take turns asking and answering each other's questions. The procedure allows modeling, guidance, and feedback by the teacher.[2]

A more detailed form of this process is SQ3R, developed by Robinson (1962) and modified by other researchers in a variety of ways. The acronym represents the five major stages of the process, Survey, Question, Read, Recite, and Review, a process that helps readers survey an assignment and develop a conceptual framework to guide their reading. Surveying a reading assignment involves examining the major headings, the highlighted items, questions within or at the end of the selection, visual aids, and introductory and concluding paragraphs. Questioning involves turning the headings into questions, usually section by section. This process establishes text-determined purposes for reading, while at the same time encouraging student-generated questions. The three remaining steps involve during-reading and post-reading stages of the process. The students read the selection to find out answers to the previously formulated questions, in an active search for meaning. They then recite, by answering in their own words the questions they posed, and using the text to develop the answer where necessary. Finally, they review by looking over any notes taken in the process, looking over the text material, and consciously articulating the major points and supporting evidence provided in the text. Like the predicting/questioning techniques recommended above, SQ3R needs to be modeled by the teacher and guided carefully as students first attempt it. Students also need to practice the technique and use it with some regularity if it is to be a useful, ongoing strategy for reading and learning the material.

In preparation for reading, Hammond (1986) recommends having students, in pairs, jot down everything they know about the topic to be read. For example, in the article on glaciers from a sixth-grade science text (*Science*, Addison-Wesley, 1980), students can be asked to list as many things as they can about glaciers. As students work, the teacher may be able to go from group to group providing additional questions to get them on their way: Where do glaciers exist? How big are they? What are they made of? How do they move? Students can put checks beside those they are sure of and question marks beside those they are not. After they have completed their lists, students can read the article. Hammond (1982) proposes that teachers ask the following five questions after the completion of the reading:

1. *Did you find answers to your questions?* This lets students know that the teacher assumes that they *had* questions, that proficient reading is a directed search for meaning, not something done without direction or focus.

2. *Which questions are still unanswered?* This suggests that most texts do not provide all the information one might want or need, and that readers might need to go to other sources for further information. In fact, this activity can lead to further research if the reader is so inclined. A related question is: "What new questions do you have on this topic?"

3. *What information was provided that you didn't have a question for?* Students might share those sections of the reading or summarize the information provided. This question suggests to readers that the teacher expects them to find additional information as well. A considerable amount of information is acquired through incidental learning. For example, many students may not realize until they read the text that glaciers contain, in addition to ice, stone and rock ranging from small pebbles to large boulders.

4. *What was most surprising or interesting to you?* This question acknowledges that it is important to put values on reading—that reading content material doesn't have to be dull. In fact, my experience in using this strategy, even with college students, is that the reading comes alive for them as they match their knowledge against the information provided in the text. Their reading and their response to the reading is animated and intense as they discover information they had speculated about.

5. *What have you learned by reading this?* This question forces students to integrate information and clarify concepts by composing their own versions of the reading. This form of retelling or rehearsal helps readers to interpret the reading and to understand its significance. It also provides closure for the activity.

Hammond's strategy suggests that interest drives comprehension, that previous knowledge must be activated for increased comprehension, and that self-generated questions allow a more personal engagement with the text than do teacher-generated ones. Activities such as this demonstrate that comprehension is a nurturable process.[3]

Langer (1981) presents a Pre-Reading Plan (PReP) that involves a three-stage process for building background knowledge and formulating questions prior to reading. The first stage is eliciting from students their initial associations with the concept to be studied. Using the chapter "Rebellion in the Colonies" from a junior high text (Ver Steeg, *American Spirit: A History of the United States*, Follett, Publishing Company, 1982), the teacher might begin by saying, "Tell me anything that comes to mind when you hear the words 'The Revolutionary War.' " As students give their responses, the teacher records them on the chalkboard. This stage helps them make connections between the concept to be studied and their own prior knowledge. Their responses may range from "It reminds me of the Boston Tea Party" to "I think somebody said, 'Give me liberty or give me death.' "

The second stage involves asking the students questions like "What made you think of the Boston Tea Party?" to which the student might respond, "I just remember something about some guys dressed up like Indians who threw tea into the ocean, and the King of England didn't like it." This stage allows students to become more aware of their own network of associations and at the same time to develop new or different associations as they listen to the responses of others. They may also begin to reject or modify their earlier associations as they learn more from the class interaction.

The third stage is one of reformulation, where the teacher asks, "Based on our discussion, and before we read the text, have you any new ideas about the Revolutionary War or what caused it?" As in the first two stages, the teacher records student responses on the board. The responses are often more refined in this stage than in the first because the students have filtered their original associations through the information presented in the ensuing discussion. Langer sees this strategy not only as a way of building schemas for readers and making predictions but as a way of assessing the depth and breadth of knowledge the students have about the topic. Instruction can be tailored to reflect the students' knowledge.

Still another technique for predicting major points in the reading is to select major words or phrases from the selection and give them to students before they read, asking them to work together in small groups to try to arrange the phrases into a unified sentence or two that will capture their predicted meaning of the passage. For example, from a short selection on Florence Nightingale in a world history text (*The Human Experience: A World History*, Charles E. Merrill Publishing Co., 1985), the teacher might give students the following list of phrases:

> Florence Nightingale
> Crimean War
> reduction of death rate
> battle zone
> hospitals
> appalling conditions
> International Red Cross

After coming up with their sentence(s) using these phrases, each group can share them with the class. One group, for example, might write: "Florence Nightingale was a nurse in the Crimean War, where she was sent by the International Red Cross to the hospitals in the battle zone. She found appalling conditions there but was able to reduce the death rate." Group members share their own knowledge and predictions with one another in an attempt to come to a consensus about what the passage might mean; each group in turn shares its best knowledge with the rest of the class. Students now have a specific purpose for reading the passage, a reading that they will more actively engage in as a result of the pre-reading predictions. As they read, their predictions will be modified or confirmed: one group will discover, for example, that Florence Nightingale helped to found the International Red Cross after her service in the Crimean War. Wrong predictions facilitate comprehension as well as accurate ones; readers, in fact, may remember more easily the information in the text after having made an inaccurate prediction about it.

Anticipation guides (Herber 1978, Nelson-Herber 1985) can be used to activate students' prior knowledge and establish a focus for reading by having students respond to a number of statements related to key issues discussed in the text. Students are asked to respond to the statements by first checking those statements they agree with, and then, after reading the selection, checking those statements they feel the author agrees with. If carefully written, the statements can stimulate students' curiosity about the topic by challenging their prior knowledge. Students are encouraged to work in small groups to complete the activity (see Figure 9.1).

Anticipation guides work best with material that is not purely factual, that is even perhaps controversial, and about which there may reasonably be differences of opinion. They also work well with students whose opinions may in some instances be misconceptions that will be challenged by other opinions expressed during the

---

Directions: Please read each of the statements below; before each one you agree with, place a check. When each group member has completed the list, share your responses with other participants in the group, justifying your opinions and supporting them.

Then read the selection in the text, "Breakthroughs in Biology: Effects of Maternal Alcohol Consumption on the Fetus." After reading it, place a check in the second column next to those statements that you feel the author agrees with. You may work together as a group to complete the second set of responses.

You	*Author*	
1. _____	_____	When it comes to women and their unborn babies, the saying, "Eating for two," can also be translated to "Drinking for two."
2. _____	_____	While even small amounts of substances like drugs can be harmful to fetuses, only large amounts of alcohol consumed by the mother seriously affect fetuses.
3. _____	_____	Alcohol consumption during pregnancy can result in both miscarriage and severe abnormalities in the infants.
4. _____	_____	Much of the damage to the fetus results from a lack of oxygen.
5. _____	_____	Studies conclusively prove that lack of oxygen causes the collapse of the umbilical cord in women who consume large amounts of alcohol.
6. _____	_____	Pregnant women should avoid even small amounts of alcohol.

FIGURE 9.1 *Anticipation guide. Based on Slesnick, et al.,* Biology. *Glenview, Ill.: Scott, Foresman and Company, 1985.*

discussion and in the reading that follows. As in the case with most of the activities discussed here, the class interaction generated by the activity before reading even occurs is the major benefit. When preparing an anticipation guide, the teacher should identify the major concepts in the reading that deserve attention and that will support or challenge existing beliefs, and then build the statements around them. Some of the statements should be debatable; the value of the activity lies in students' attempts to justify their own opinions before they do the reading and to justify their interpretations of the author's intended meaning after the reading.

Semantic mapping of various kinds can also introduce new material to students before reading (for various uses and examples of semantic maps, see Heimlich and Pittelman 1986). One type can be developed by teacher and students together as they brainstorm about the kinds of information a text chapter might contain, based on illustrations, chapter headings, and so on, or the map might reflect the kinds of questions students have about the topic. The semantic map in Figure 9.2 represents the kinds of questions generated by the students about the chapter on glaciers. As students read, they can rearrange, add to, or delete elements from the map as the chapter unfolds.

A more detailed kind of map, alternatively referred to as a graphic organizer or structured overview, can be presented to the students as a scheme for visualizing the information in the reading they will do. It provides a view of the "whole" and the relationship of the elements within the whole. The teacher can talk students through the map, discussing major relationships and ties among the elements, thereby providing an overview of major concepts and vocabulary. Although there is no one

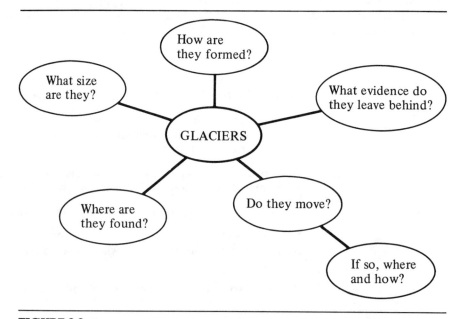

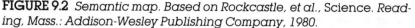

FIGURE 9.2 *Semantic map. Based on Rockcastle, et al., Science. Reading, Mass.: Addison-Wesley Publishing Company, 1980.*

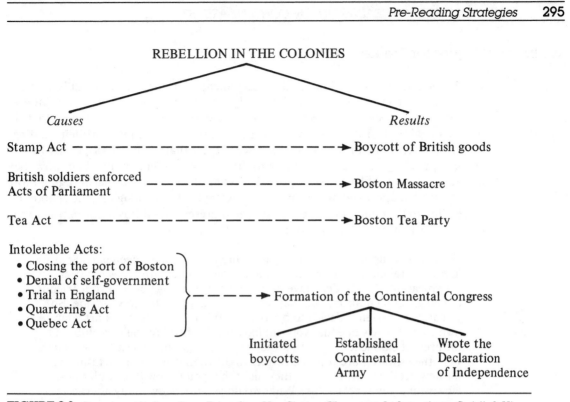

REBELLION IN THE COLONIES

Causes   *Results*

Stamp Act — — — — — — — — — — — — — → Boycott of British goods

British soldiers enforced
Acts of Parliament — — — — — — — — — — → Boston Massacre

Tea Act — — — — — — — — — — — — — — → Boston Tea Party

Intolerable Acts:
  • Closing the port of Boston
  • Denial of self-government
  • Trial in England   — — — — → Formation of the Continental Congress
  • Quartering Act
  • Quebec Act

Initiated   Established   Wrote the
boycotts   Continental   Declaration
                 Army   of Independence

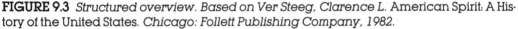

FIGURE 9.3 *Structured overview. Based on Ver Steeg, Clarence L.* American Spirit: A History of the United States. *Chicago: Follett Publishing Company, 1982.*

right way to construct a structured overview—there are many variations—overviews whose very form graphically reflects the text's organizational pattern may be most helpful. The structured overview in Figure 9.3, based on the American history chapter, was developed to reflect the cause-effect structure of the reading. The overview helps students comprehend the text, not just because it indicates major concepts and their relationship to each other but because its structure highlights the cause-effect patterns established in the text.

Different kinds of graphic organizers can be used for different content areas: time lines in history, diagrams in biology and the other sciences, charts and graphs as they are appropriate to any content area. Overviews are equally useful for reviewing material after reading, and students can add to some of these diagrams and charts *as* they read.

Pre-reading strategies that demonstrate their success most conclusively in empirical studies are those that involve interaction between teachers and students (Vaughan 1982), those that are modeled and monitored regularly over a substantial period of time. Merely introducing students to the techniques of SQ3R or to an overview does not guarantee their success; students and teachers working together, discussing each part of the strategy after applying it, and sharing reasons why it does or does not work, will more likely result in a successful reading experience.

Writing Strategies for Pre-Reading

Writing activities often follow reading assignments, but they can be equally or more useful when used to activate prior knowledge and set purposes for reading. Moore, Readence, and Rickelman (1982) recommend a problem-solving activity to help students deal with situations similar to those they will encounter in their reading. While they recommend that students discuss the situation in small groups before doing the reading, it would be equally useful to have students write about how they would solve the problem first, *before* discussing it, as a way of encouraging more student participation and involvement. For example, before assigning the chapter on "Rebellion in the Colonies," the teacher could present the following situation to the students for writing and discussion:

> You and a group of friends belong to a club that you have been participating in for several months. Recently, though, your participation has not been very pleasant. The leaders have been unjustly accusing you and your friends of being troublemakers, and they seem unwilling to listen to your side. So you and your friends decide to break away from the group and start your own club. You assume that you will have total control of the new club, but the present club leaders feel that they have the right to govern the new one as well; they still require you to pay dues to them, they insist on dictating who the new president will be, and they insist that you follow their club rules. How would you react to this? What would you do? How many alternatives can you think of?

Although not all the details in the hypothetical situation are parallel to the historical event, students may be better prepared to deal with the issues of colonial rebellion because they have a more personal involvement in the issues.

Journal writing offers interesting possibilities as well. Although traditionally considered the domain of the English teacher, journals have been used successfully by content area teachers to encourage students to focus on specific ideas and to relate concepts to their own experiences (Fulwiler 1982). One science teacher has her students keep science logs in which they speculate about the results of an experiment they are about to perform; another has his students periodically write short entries about what they already know about the topic coming up in the reading. Social studies teachers can encourage students to write comments on current events as these relate to course content, or speculate about cause-effect events in a period of history the students are about to study. Regardless of format or focus, the students involve themselves, Fulwiler says (1982, p. 19), "because they have committed themselves, through their own language, to at least a tentative exploration of an idea."

Summary writing is often used as a post-reading activity, but Devine (1986) recommends that students write summaries, growing out of their predictions of the reading, *before they do the reading*, based on headings, subheadings, illustrations, and so on. Students can then share their summaries with each other to get different perspectives. Teachers who use this activity report it as not only a valuable writing experience but a way of increasing students' desire to read; they are eager to compare the text with their own predictions about it.

The pre-reading strategies described here foster successful reading experiences. When content is familiar and when readers can make connections from their own experience and knowledge to the concepts in the reading, motivation to read increases, and the reading occurs with a sharper focus. Schemas for reading are generated and activated and students' curiosity is aroused. As Vacca and Vacca (1986) suggest, students read to resolve conflicts arising from problem situations, from taking different perspectives, and from examining values and attitudes. Thinking about the issues, making predictions, discussing and writing about them, prepare students for the issues they will encounter in the reading.

A related benefit from the use of these activities is that, in many cases, major concepts presented for discussion before reading will make unfamiliar vocabulary more understandable during the reading. When readers are in control of the concepts, the otherwise potentially difficult vocabulary will be much less of a problem. Lindberg and Smith (1976, p. 440) argue that students do not need to be pre-taught particular vocabulary words so much as they need to be "equipped with flexible meaning-gathering strategies for dealing with unfamiliar language." The strategies provided in this discussion encourage teachers to deal with the major concepts/ vocabulary before reading occurs, in ways that will build bridges between the new information and the information already existing in the readers' schemas. Vocabulary taught directly, out of context, and unrelated to students' prior knowledge and experience, is in danger of being ignored and remaining largely unlearned.

Which of the preceding pre-reading activities will be used for a particular assignment will, of course, be determined by the teacher's objectives and the nature of the assignment, but enough variety in pre-reading activities is presented here that teachers can avoid the daily grind of repeating just one activity. Furthermore, activities are designed as learning experiences, not as tests of students' comprehension or knowledge; as such they should reduce anxiety about the reading because they help readers anticipate meaning. They are aids to reading, not tests of reading proficiency. Above all, they encourage students to value the topic because they begin to see a greater relevance to their own experiences.

DURING-READING STRATEGIES

Proficient reading and comprehending involve not only preparation for reading but active involvement during reading and the ability to monitor one's own progress. This monitoring system, referred to as metacomprehension, is described by Langer (1982) as having two separate components: (1) awareness of the goal of the reading assignment, what is known about the topic, what needs to be known, and the strategies that can be used to facilitate comprehension; and (2) self-regulatory actions that readers engage in as a response to their self-monitoring—what they do, in other words, when things go wrong. Poor readers are less aware than good readers of their reading strategies and less aware of when the process breaks down. "What this means to the classroom teacher," says Langer (1982, p. 45), "is that we cannot expect students to 'read more carefully,' 'figure things out for themselves,' 'look it up,' or 'ask someone for help' when so often the student is unaware that something has 'gone wrong' in the first place.''

To facilitate metacomprehension, teachers need to help students develop those self-reflective processes that will increase their comprehension. Carefully designed and implemented, during-reading activities can do that. One activity is the study guide, which might simply call students' attention to text features and important information:

Top of p. 53:	Study this graph carefully.
Middle of p. 54:	Be sure you understand what impact the Stamp Act had on . . .
Bottom of p. 55:	Note the cause-effect pattern here; be able to explain the three main reasons why the colonists organized the boycott of British goods . . .

And so on. Study guides might also include speculative questions to be answered on the guide itself or in an academic journal that all students keep. (See the section ''Organizational Patterns of Texts'' for other examples of reading guides.)

Applying the middle three steps of SQ3R, ''Question, Read, and Recite,'' as discussed earlier, encourages readers to search for answers to the questions asked prior to reading and to rehearse those answers with or without going back to the text for further support.

Another commonly used strategy is Stauffer's Directed Reading-Thinking Activity (Stauffer 1969) which moves students from prediction to verification or modification. The purpose of DRTA is to promote active comprehension by having students predict, based on titles, headings, and illustrations, and then read the designated portion of the text to check the accuracy of their predictions. They are asked to provide proof of their predictions, and if evidence arises to contradict earlier predictions, to make new ones. The process continues for each segment of the text. DRTA is applicable to all kinds of written material—fiction, nonfiction, and textbook material.

The ''click or clunk'' strategy for self-monitoring[4] urges readers at the end of each paragraph or section read, to ask themselves if the meaning or message ''clicks'' for them or if it goes ''clunk.'' If it clunks, what is wrong? What can the reader do to make sense of it? This is a delightfully simple yet very effective way of getting readers to stop their reading and rethink rather than continuing to read without comprehension.

While these strategies all help readers focus more carefully on the reading and on their evolving comprehension, some students may need more help in discovering the sources available for finding answers to their questions. Pearson and Johnson's comprehension taxonomy (1978) helps teachers understand what kinds of information readers can draw upon in answering questions about a text. The taxonomy suggests the following classification of questions: *text explicit* if the question has an answer stated in the text; *text implicit* if the answer can be inferred from text information that requires some integration of meaning; and *script implicit* (schema-based) if the answer must come from the reader's background knowledge. The following paragraph and questions illustrate the concept (Pearson and Johnson 1978, p. 157):

Will Wends His Way

Right after the Civil War, many distraught soldiers made their way West to find fame and fortune. Some could not go home because there were no homes to go to. The war had devastated them. One young man, Will Good-lad, made his fortune in the hills of Colorado. He found gold in a little river near Grand Junction. His fortune was short-lived, however. In 1875, he declared bankruptcy and returned to the land of his birth—the Piedmont of South Carolina.

1. When did Will Goodlad declare bankruptcy?
2. Where did Will Goodlad discover gold?
3. When did Will Goodlad discover gold?

The answer to the first question is stated directly in the text, so it is considered a text-explicit question. The second is similar; its answer is stated directly as a little river near Grand Junction. The third is textually implicit because the text implies that he discovered gold between the end of the Civil War and 1875. If, however, the reader said between 1865 and 1875 in response to the third question, the reader would be using information that was only script implicit, part of his or her schemas or internalized "script" about the Civil War. Thus we can see that it is possible for readers to come up with different sources of information—for example, from the reader's head rather than just from the text, despite the intent of the question. Some students may need help in using these various sources to respond to questions—and teachers need to be aware that in answering questions, students may legitimately use sources of information other than what the teacher anticipated.

Finding sources of information for questions can be aided by Raphael's Question Answer Relationship (QAR) strategy (1984). She suggests providing students with experience in using these three sources of information by describing them as (1) *Right There*—where the answers are explicitly stated in the text; (2) *Think and Search*—where the answer is in the text but not stated directly (text implicit); and (3) *On My Own*—where the reader needs to search his or her own knowledge for the answer (script/schema implicit). Students are encouraged to think about the questions and the source of the answers as a way of building their sensitivity to the kinds of questions and sources of information available to them. It is important to help students learn not only to use information that is "right there" and to "think and search" for answers, but to bring their own knowledge and experience to the process of making meaning.

Techniques such as this are more effective if modeled by the teacher. "Talking through" one's own thought processes during the act of reading can demonstrate to young or inexperienced readers how to generate questions and how to find answers, particularly by tapping into their own knowledge. "On my own" questions such as: "Why do you think Will Goodlad's fortune was so short-lived?" answered by the teacher can demonstrate the process of using one's prior knowledge. As readers become more conscious of the thinking processes involved in reading, they will increase their ability to read inferentially, and to read beyond the text.

POST-READING STRATEGIES

Our definition of comprehension and the strategies recommended to increase it underscore reading as a thinking process, with the assumption that proficient reading is synonymous with critical thinking. We don't see critical thinking as a *kind* of comprehension; we see it rather as part of the process of comprehension, a factor that enables comprehension to occur. It is functional within the process, not simply an end result of the process. Anything short of critical thinking during reading results in processing surface structure only—reading passively rather than actively—with mechanical participation rather than transactional. Not all reading instruction, of course, operates with this definition of reading. In fact, it is common to see instruction labeled "successful" with the mere attainment of "basic skills": word identification, sufficient decoding skills, and recall of literal information. Reading just well enough to survive in a highly technological society falls far short of the definition of comprehension described here.

Several commissions on education call for higher standards in educational institutions. The Commission on Excellence in Education, in *A Nation at Risk* (1983), for example, suggests that higher standards can be achieved, in part, by administering more standardized tests at major transition points. While it is true that quantifiable data are most expediently achieved through standardized measures, such expediency has its price: the very nature of such tests, rather than helping to uphold standards, may, in fact, be contributing to their decline (Wilson 1985). The problem is suggested in the results of the National Assessment of Educational Progress (Petrosky 1982) that show that high-school students do not read sufficiently in depth, have difficulty with some types of inferences, and find it difficult to use the text to support their interpretations. Petrosky suggests that students' apparent inability to examine adequately the ideas they take away from their reading and their inability to find support in the text may reflect current practices in testing and instruction:

> When multiple-choice testing and quick easy discussion dominate the curriculum, how can we expect anything but the most basic performance from students? When reading and writing are separated in the curriculum and when students are not encouraged to discuss or write about their reading in any extended, reasoned way, is it such a surprise that they then lack the most comprehensive thinking and analytic skills? (1983, p. 16)

Checking students' comprehension through testing, multiple-choice or otherwise, doesn't provide the kinds of opportunities Petrosky suggests are necessary for full, complete comprehension of ideas. Readers need to discuss, write about, argue about, and grapple with the ideas and concepts they are confronted with, and they need to be able to support their opinions from the text and from their own experiences. Testing provides minimal experience for this kind of critical reading and responding. The transaction of reading occurs only when opportunities for response, interpretation, and evaluation of the reading experience are made possible (Rosenblatt 1978).

In assessing student performance, Langer and Pradl (1984) urge educators to use data from multiple sources, both formal and informal, with particular emphasis on teacher judgments as the key factor. Given the complexities of the processes of comprehending and learning, no single factor like a multiple-choice test, for example, can provide adequate evaluation of readers' comprehension strengths and weaknesses.

Equally popular to the testing of reading is the teacher-directed questioning session that often follows reading. But just as multiple-choice testing has limited utility for critical thinking, so do many of the typical teacher-directed questioning sessions. In fact, question-asking can be counterproductive if students feel that they are being put on the spot, if the game is to try to guess what is in the teacher's head, or if the questioning is primarily at the literal level as a check on whether or not the reading has been done (Vacca and Vacca 1986).

In general, if literal recall questions are used, they should lead to more challenging questions such as those that focus on the major concepts; those that involve students in evaluating the results, conclusions, and outcomes presented in the text; and those that invite students to project themselves into the issues discussed in the text. Questions like: "Do you think that John Adams's decision was a wise one?" or "How do you think *you* would have felt if . . . ?" involve students more personally with the issues, and because they have no "wrong" or "right" answers, may serve to stimulate students to contribute to the discussion. (For a more detailed discussion of levels of questioning and questioning techniques, see Chapter 6.)

The ultimate goal of questioning is to promote thinking, but while questioning is a time-honored activity in most classrooms, a number of other activities can be used as well. The activities that are discussed in this section provide opportunities for readers to transact with the text and to respond to, interpret, and evaluate their reading experiences. And as a critical element of the reading experience, they also provide closure to the reading activity; otherwise, reading without response and evaluation may result in comprehension that is tentative, vague, and unclarified.

The obvious, although not always utilized strategy for post-reading is to follow up on the pre-reading and during-reading activities. Initial predictions can be confirmed, disconfirmed, or modified; semantic maps or graphic organizers can be completed or modified as new information becomes integrated with prior knowledge; the fifth step of SQ3R, "Review," can occur either individually, in small groups, or with the whole class; responses to anticipation guides can be discussed, supported, and evaluated; films, videotapes, or experiments used to introduce the reading can be used in the discussion that follows the reading.

Retellings of a wide variety are useful for understanding the significance of the reading. They can consist of recapping main points, recalling major events or causes and effects, or retelling the chronological events in a narrative. They allow readers to construct their knowledge of the material and to integrate new information into their schemas. But besides building one's own meaning, retellings allow readers to hear responses and reflections from other students (Y. Goodman 1982). Both teller and listeners benefit from students pretending to be TV reporters who must "sum up" a story in two minutes, or from demonstrations of how a union-management negotiating team operates, or how an opinion poll is conducted (Devine 1986). Dolan (1986) has developed a strategy called "Life Styles of the Literary" with her high school literature students in which they sign up to become one character, author, or historical personage. Each character or personage gives a two-to-three-minute presentation about himself or herself to the other class members without revealing names, and the class members then guess who the presenters are. An activity like this would be equally effective in a social studies unit, for it would require students to construct a description of their personage that would reflect historical facts and related issues accurately.

Alvermann (1986) recommends a strategy focusing on the relevancy and synthesis of information as a way of fostering critical thinking. After students read a selection, they are provided with lists of words/concepts from the reading and are asked to delete the irrelevant word/concept from each list. After studying the remaining three, the students are to suggest a term that synthesizes those three. For example, with a fourth-grade social studies chapter, "State and Local Governments" (*HBJ Social Studies: States and Regions*, Harcourt Brace Jovanovich, 1985), the teacher can present the following lists to students:

List One	*List Two*
legislature	city manager
governor	municipal court
state courts	council
mayor	state representatives

Students would then identify "mayor" and "state representatives" from the respective lists as the irrelevant items, and their terms synthesizing the remaining three might be "parts of state government" and "parts of city government." This activity requires categorizing and synthesizing skills and helps students see important relationships.

A technique for getting students back into the text for more critical analysis is the Group Reading for Different Purposes (GRDP), adapted from Dolan et al. (1979).[5] After the class has read the assignment, they divide into groups. Each group is given one card with one of the following sets of directions:

Card 1:   Go back to the reading assignment to find three *facts* and three *opinions* expressed by the author. Try to come to an agreement as a group about which are facts and which are opinions. Be able to defend your decisions.

Card 2:   Go back to the reading assignment. The author provides several solutions to the problem posed in the reading. Try to come up with an *alternative solution* to the problem. Or be able to defend one of the author's solutions as the best one.

Card 3:   Go back to the reading assignment and decide as a group what the author's main point is. Then find *other sources* in the classroom—newspapers, encyclopedias, other texts, or supplementary material—that can verify the main point made in the text.

Card 4:   Go back to the reading assignment and develop three to five good *questions* that you can ask other class members that would stimulate thought about the reading.

After students have had sufficient time to complete the assignments, one member of each group reports to the class as a whole. The group with Card 4 can ask the class questions posed by the group and evaluate the responses. Instructions on the cards can be modified to deal with specific kinds of content or with different ages of students. As the strategy is repeated from time to time, it is useful to ensure that students get different cards, in order to build variety for them and to provide different critical thinking tasks. The value of the activity is in its ability to get readers back into the text for further exploration of ideas through group collaboration. Students who may initially have some difficulty comprehending the text have another chance to reread with a more specific focus, which will make the reading task easier. They also have the advantage of hearing opinions expressed by other students as they begin to integrate the information for themselves.

Writing in Response to Reading

While the discussion activities described above are excellent for encouraging critical thinking, it is also useful to have students assimilate new information by writing about it. Writing allows more time to ponder, reread, synthesize, and organize. A review of research on reading-writing relationships shows that almost all studies that used writing activities to improve reading comprehension found significant gains, varying from better recall of specific material read to improved scores on standardized reading tests or achievement tests in academic areas (Stotsky 1984).

Several researchers recommend précis writing, summarizing, and paraphrasing as good "retelling" techniques that enable readers to assimilate and integrate the information (Bromley and McKeveny 1986; Shugarman and Hurst 1986). Devine (1986) suggests written summaries using the format of *Reader's Digest*-type "condensations"—summaries that can be duplicated and shared, or newspaper stories using the Who, What, Where, When, Why, and How format. The chapter "Rebellion in the Colonies," for example, lends itself well to collaborative writing of newspaper articles on several sections within the chapter: "Stirrings of Discontent," "The Coming Crisis," and "The Final Break." A class newspaper could be published with the final results, and duplicated copies could be shared with class members or students in other history classes.

Tchudi and Huerta (1983) recommend various discourse forms that can be used in content area writing in response to reading. Third-grade science students reading about animals' protection from their enemies might make a class magazine using additional information gathered from other sources: from other reading, from a talk given by a naturalist, or from observations they have made at a wildlife preserve. Social studies students might be encouraged to write conversations taking place between Paul Revere and his wife the night before his historic ride, between George Mason and the British envoy concerning the Stamp Act, or between Patrick Henry and a colonist who wants to avoid war at any cost. Debates can be organized between groups of students taking opposite viewpoints on the controversial issues discussed in their reading.

Sixth graders reading the chapter on glaciers might write imaginary scenes of what their own regional area may have been like during the glacial age; they can write prophecies and predictions of future ice ages or prepare a mini-documentary on glaciers to be presented to other classes. Students at various levels can write biographical sketches of famous people, using some little-known facts they have uncovered in their reading. They can write imaginary journals and diaries of other historical figures, or imaginary letters from George to Martha, from Florence Nightingale to her family during the Crimean War, from King George III to the rebellious American colonists. Such events can be turned into TV scenarios and scripts, short stories, interviews, and dramatizations. The possibilities and benefits are endless if students become engaged in the task, and thereby assimilate new information as they write for publication or performance. These activities encourage a more personal engagement with the reading that leads to greater comprehension. Asking students to participate in activities that require emotional as well as intellectual involvement enhances the reading experience. Furthermore, because many of the activities involve group inquiry and collaborative problem-solving, students benefit from one another's thinking. Students take control of their own learning, with the teacher serving as facilitator.

Writing in response to reading can also include note-taking in a variety of forms, one of which is the typical form of taking running notes, similar to lecture notes, which are clear and usable for later review. Rather than assuming that students know intuitively how to take notes, the teacher may need to model and monitor the process in class. A technique that may help is to have students take notes only on notebook paper with a lined margin, and after taking notes, to add in the margin phrases or questions that will serve as cues to the notes themselves.

Even more important, students often need to be shown how to indent and space their notes to indicate coordinate and subordinate relationships. For example:

Main idea	Main idea
Subordinate idea	Subordinate idea
Main idea	Supporting detail
Subordinate idea	Supporting detail

Of course, students will need guided practice in such note-taking because they do not always find it easy to distinguish between main ideas and details, to determine which ideas are coordinate and which are subordinate. Thus guided practice in note-taking will actually be much-needed practice in determining how information and ideas are related.

Note-taking can also take other forms. If students have approached their reading with some sort of graphic organizer, semantic map, time-line, and so on, then note-taking may involve primarily expanding upon the organizer: adding branches to hierarchical trees, cells to charts, labels to diagrams, bars to graphs, points to the time-line, and so on. These visual modes of representation are in many ways more useful as study tools than the more traditional notes, because they have most likely been used to build readers' schemas even before the reading began. It is abundantly clear that note-taking of any kind is significantly easier when students have sufficient background knowledge for both the reading and the writing that follows. In fact, being able to tell which ideas are coordinate and which are subordinate results from sufficient knowledge of the subject; it is not, initially, a means to accomplish that end. Efficient, useful note-taking, regardless of type, will occur only when readers have sufficient control of the subject.

ORGANIZATIONAL PATTERNS OF TEXTS

While our focus has been primarily on the reader and on the context of reading up to this point, we now want to turn our attention to the third element of the triad of reader, context, and text. The content of a piece of writing and the organizational patterns used to convey it are, of course, intimately connected. A text's internal organization is determined in large part by the nature and type of content. Comprehension of material may be greatly enhanced by a reader's conscious or unconscious recognition of the text's organization. Several studies suggest that the careful organization of a passage for presenting the content plays a crucial role in the interpretability of a passage (Meyer 1982). Major rhetorical patterns include cause-effect, comparison-contrast, listing or enumeration, chronological order, generalization with supporting evidence, description, and question and answer. Obviously there is overlap between some of these patterns, and few writers, if any, use one pattern exclusively in extended discourse.

Meyer (1982) suggests that students need to be made aware of writers' organizational plans so that they can utilize the information in both their reading and their writing. She studied five different patterns and their effect on reading comprehension. When ninth graders provided written recalls of what they had read, those who organized their recalls according to the author's organizational pattern remembered far more content, including both main ideas and supporting details, than those readers not using the author's plan. A subsequent study in which one group of ninth graders was given a week of training in identifying and using the author's plans remembered twice as much content from the texts than they could before the training, and they performed nearly twice as well as those in the control group who received no training.

Teachers must be careful, however, if teaching writers' patterns directly, not to oversimplify by implying that a selection will make use of only one plan to the exclusion of others or that plans are always easily discernible and identifiable. Using samples as illustrations runs the risk of oversimplifying patterns, which will make difficult the transfer of pattern recognition to more complex material.

One could also argue that discerning a plan is much easier when the concepts themselves are more accessible; identifying a cause-effect pattern in a history text will be less difficult when the reader already knows something about the events leading up to the Revolutionary War. Building students' background knowledge for the concepts they will be reading about is still the best preparation. Being able to recognize the pattern may enhance comprehension of the material but cannot re-place one's conceptual framework for the reading, and may, in fact, be partially a result of the comprehension process rather than a cause.

Perhaps more helpful than teaching rhetorical patterns directly is having students generate these structures themselves, in discussion or in writing. Students, for example, might compare and contrast rock music with jazz or classical music, or Ted Nugent with Bruce Springsteen. The teacher can write the points of similarity and difference on the board, illustrating the technique of using comparison and contrast structures for organizing the writing. Helping students understand cause and effect might be accomplished by having them discuss or write reasons for the food wastage in the cafeteria, or possible results of a stricter dress code as school policy. For chronological sequencing, they can list major events in their own lives, or write a how-to paper on making a pizza, changing the oil in a car, or building a tree house. The transfer from studying rhetorical patterns to identifying and using them to comprehend other texts occurs more easily when the students have themselves been involved in creating the patterns.

Hennings (1982) proposes a six-step strategy for helping students handle complex ideas in texts by learning how to organize informational content for writing: (1) *"Factstorming"* occurs after students have some information about the topic, through reading, discussion, viewing filmstrips, or taking a field trip. Students brainstorm by randomly calling out phrases that come to mind on the topic while someone records these ideas on paper or on the chalkboard. (2) Students *categorize facts* by organizing the ideas listed into related groups. A list of facts about the Revolutionary War may be categorized into causes and effects, for example, or into categories ranging from famous colonial revolutionaries to major battles, from political acts to personal acts of bravery. The remaining steps include (3) the collaborative *drafting of paragraphs* based on the categories established earlier; (4) *sequencing paragraphs* into an interrelated whole; (5) *drafting introductions and conclusions*; and (6) *interpreting similar pieces* of discourse. The last step involves the application of the students' understanding of informational content from their own writing experiences with it. From composing an informational text themselves, students develop an understanding of how similar content is usually structured. This activity can be used with students of all ages, including elementary-age students; Hennings, in fact, used it with third graders very successfully.

Olson and Longnion (1982) recommend the use of simple-to-construct pattern guides that allow readers to use the organizational pattern of the text as a way of focusing on the content of the material. After the essential concepts in the passage are identified, along with the organizational pattern used by the author, the concepts and the pattern can be integrated in the development of the guide. Depending on the degree of difficulty of the reading and the ability of the readers, teachers can provide as much or as little help as is necessary in the guide itself. In some cases specifying page numbers is useful, in others not. Teachers are cautioned to provide clear and concise directions and to keep the guide relatively simple so that students are not overwhelmed with a task too detailed or too extensive.

The three guides in Figures 9.4, 9.5, and 9.6, based on Olson and Longnion's suggestions (1982), are structured around comparison-contrast, cause-effect, and

Directions: Read pages 318–320 in the textbook. Then list the three major branches of state government in the left column and the three major branches of local government in the right.

State Government	Local Government
1.	1.
2.	2.
3.	3.

In the left column below, list three things that state laws are concerned with, and in the right column list three things that local laws are concerned with.

1.	1.
2.	2.
3.	3.

FIGURE 9.4 *Comparison-contrast guide—fourth grade. Based on States and Regions. Chicago: Harcourt Brace Jovanovich, Publishers, 1985.*

Directions: Read the chapter on glaciers, pp. 208–215. In this chapter look for cause-effect relationships in the situations mentioned below. If a cause is listed in the left column, list the effect of that cause in the right. If the effect is provided, list the cause in the left column.

Cause	Effect
1. Several layers of snow accumulate over several years without melting.	1.
2.	2. The glacier flows and slides.
3. Glacial ice melts and evaporates.	3.
4.	4. Granite boulders are sometimes found in areas where the bedrock is limestone.
5.	5. Drumlins, eskers, and kettles remain as evidence.

FIGURE 9.5 *Cause-effect guide—sixth grade. Based on Rockcastle, et al., Science. Reading, Mass.: Addison-Wesley Publishing Company, 1980.*

Directions: Read p. 381, "History and People: Florence Nightingale." Then arrange the events randomly listed below in the order in which they occurred by placing a 1 before the first event, a 2 before the second, etc.

_____ The International Red Cross was organized.

_____ Improvements were made in the conditions in British army hospitals.

_____ Nursing became a respected profession for women.

_____ Florence Nightingale was asked to lead a group of nurses to the Crimean War.

_____ Florence Nightingale was the director of a women's hospital in London.

_____ The death rate in British hospitals was sharply reduced.

_____ Florence Nightingale published *Notes on Hospitals* which revolutionized hospital management.

FIGURE 9.6 *Chronological order guide. Based on Farah, et al., The Human Experience: A World History. Columbus, Ohio: Charles E. Merrill Publishing Company, 1985.*

chronological sequencing. (For more detailed and complex pattern guides, see Herber 1978.)

The chronological pattern guide (Figure 9.6) would perhaps be more useful with more difficult material, but we offer this as an example of what can be done. Pattern guides in general have greater utility when students may have some difficulty with the material and when comprehension can be facilitated by using the structure to focus on the major concepts.

As Olson and Longnion (1982) present them, these pattern guides occur as post-reading activities. Atwell and Rhodes (1984) recommend using a guide like the one on chronological order as a *pre*-reading activity in which the teacher first asks readers to predict what the content of the article is—based on title, subtitles, illustrations, and so on—and then to make predictions about the sequence of events. Students can work in small groups on this activity, pooling their knowledge and trying to come to a consensus. Then they can read the text to evaluate their initial predictions. The reading itself is likely to be more active and animated as a result of the discussion preceding it.

Providing a selection cut into separate paragraphs and asking students to order them in a logical sequence also helps students deal with organizational structure. This activity can also highlight the kinds of phrases that signal particular functions in the text: comparison-contrast signaled by words like *however, but, nevertheless, on the other hand, in contrast*; cause-effect signaled by words like *because, in order that, unless, since, as a result, consequently, therefore*; and sequence signaled by *next, meanwhile, then, finally*, and so on.

When the concepts in the text are comprehensible, these signal words present little difficulty, for in most cases the context and meaning will clarify the function of the word or phrase. In the following sentences most readers would probably supply either *because* or *since* in the blanks, assuming their experiential backgrounds were adequate (Weaver 1980, p. 244):

> Their boots squeaked in the cold and their voices sounded far away, _____ the temperature was far below zero.

> The fox's brown fur of summer was splotched with white patches, reminding Miyax again that winter was coming, _____ the fur of the fox changes each season to match the color of the land.

> From Julie of the Wolves
by Jean Craighead George

When students see that they can supply a function word that makes sense in the context of the passage, they may be introduced to the word that was actually used in the original text: *for*. Because we seldom use this word in oral language for this function, students may need some help learning to recognize its use in written language. We can use implicit information in the text to understand and recognize explicit signals, Weaver adds, without teaching a grammatical label for this use of *for*: "What matters is not that it is a subordinating conjunction, but that it is roughly equivalent to *because*" (1980, p. 245).

Students may also need guidance in handling relationships implicitly suggested in texts rather than explicitly stated. Meyer's study (1982) found that the use of signal words was particularly important for average ability readers, who were able to recall more information from the text used in the study when the signal words were present, than they were able to recall from a text when the signal words were deleted. The deletions apparently had little effect on recall ability for very good readers, who were able to handle the text regardless, or for poor readers, who were unable to handle the text with or without the existence of the signal words. Meyer's study suggests that for large numbers of students, providing experience with and understanding of signal words clearly increases their ability to comprehend.

We would like to caution, however, that *guided practice* in understanding textually explicit and implicit information, rather than workbooks and worksheets, will benefit students most. Workbooks do little to teach; rather students learn from the teacher and from peers as they work through lessons together, discussing the text and how it can be comprehended.

READABILITY OF TEXTS

Readers' comprehension difficulties have a number of potential sources, as is clear from the preceding discussion: the reader's inadequate knowledge base, the reader's lack of motivation, the abstractness or difficulty of concepts or concepts that are too densely packed, difficult text organization, and syntactic complexity, among others. Teachers and textbook publishers have long been concerned with the readability of texts and with the process of matching books and students. Obviously the considerations are many and the factors too complex for any simple way of finding the appropriate text for a particular class. Teachers have often used readability formulas to determine the readability of texts under consideration for adoption as a simple, "objective" measure of text difficulty. And publishers have obligingly provided figures for text readability based on one or more of the standard formulas. Those that are commonly used—Dale-Chall, SMOG, Fry, Flesch, among others—use two factors primarily in determining degree of text difficulty: length of sentence and difficulty of vocabulary. The former is usually expressed as an average in a sample of a book's text, and the latter as an average in number of unfamiliar words or number of syllables (*Becoming a Nation of Readers* 1984).

Such text-based formulas,[6] relatively simple to use and apply, are nevertheless equally simple in the information they provide—grade level equivalencies based almost exclusively on two linguistic features among a multitude of factors that actually determine comprehensibility. Even more problematic is the fact that sentences that are short are not necessarily easier to comprehend than those that are longer or more complex, nor is a word of two or more syllables necessarily more difficult than a monosyllabic one (see, in Chapter 4, Weaver's example of a child being able to read *helium* when he had not been able to read *gas* correctly). Further, the tendency of publishers and authors to write to fit the formula often results in prose that is choppy, language that is unnatural, and syntax that may obscure complex ideas and relationships rather than clarify them (Davison and Kantor 1982; Cullinan and Fitzgerald 1984). Complex ideas cannot be written in the prose style dictated by readability formulas without violating the intended meaning or creating additional obscurities. For example, consider the following two sentences:

Some insects are hard for birds to find. Insects often have protective coloring.

While these sentences may fit the formula for syntactic simplicity, the cause-effect relationship is only implied, not stated explicitly as it would be if the second sentence were preceded by the cause-effect signal:

Some insects are hard for birds to find *because* insects often have protective coloring.

The more syntactically complex sentence would clarify the meaning. In fact, writing to formula is a use of readability formulas never intended by their developers (*Becoming a Nation of Readers* 1984). The practice has resulted in what some educators have labeled the "dumbing down" of study materials for U.S. classrooms ("A Debate over 'Dumbing Down,'" *Time*, 1985). Textbooks are written simplistically, and readers get watered-down versions that distort and obscure rather than clarify and explain.

Considering the importance of the reader's contributions to the comprehensibility of a text, any technique for determining text readability that ignores the reader's background knowledge, interests, and motivations falls far short. As Robinson (1983, p. 134) says, "The material can be labeled 'more readable' based on the standards of a given readability formula but certainly not on the basis of comprehensibility to the reader."

One technique for determining readability that is more reader-based in its ability to consider the reader is Bormuth's Cloze Readability procedure (Bormuth 1968). It is designed as a way of determining the degree to which students are able to cope with the text or other reading material assigned in class. Readers are asked to supply the words that have been deleted from the passage, on the assumption that they can use their schemas and their knowledge of the syntactic-semantic relationships in the passage for making their decisions. Directions for setting up a cloze readability are as follows:

1. Using a selection from the text approximately 250 words long, leave the first sentence and the last sentence of the passage intact. Then delete every fifth word, leaving a blank about 1 ½ inches long. Fifty blanks are needed.
2. Distribute copies of the paragraph to the class and instruct students to fill in the blanks, one word per blank, by guessing from context. There is no time limit.
3. When students have completed this task, their cloze passages can be scored by giving 2 points for each word that exactly matches the one in the original text. (Research by Bormuth indicates that when cloze tests are used for readability, you get more valid scores if you don't count synonyms.) Incorrectly spelled words should not be marked wrong since spelling doesn't count.
4. Interpretation of the scores is as follows:

44%–57%	Instructional reading level—material is at a suitable reading level with help from the teacher.
58%–100%	Independent reading level—material is suitable for independent work.
0%–43%	Frustration level—the student will not be able to deal adequately with the material. Now check these very low scores for synonyms. If the student used many acceptable synonyms, he or she may be able to use the material. For those students who couldn't achieve a score of at least 44 percent despite allowances for synonyms, either an easier text or an alternative method of instruction should be provided.

Based on the assumption that reading is a transactional, constructive process, cloze allows readers to use their knowledge of syntax and their content schemas to make sense out of the text. The degree to which readers are able to complete the cloze passage reflects their understanding of the syntactic-semantic relationships expressed in the text and suggests the appropriateness of the text for these students. It should be emphasized that, although synonyms aren't counted in determining the readability of texts, they *are* to be encouraged when using the cloze procedure for instructional purposes.

Still another valuable technique for more accurately assessing the readability of texts is miscue analysis, described in Chapter 10 and discussed more fully in *Reading Miscue Inventory: Alternative Procedures* (Y. Goodman, Watson, and Burke 1987). Teachers can use a particular selection with a number of readers representative of those who may be using the text. The information miscue analysis provides can help textbook writers and users alike determine factors that might cause difficulty for students: sentence structure, inadequately developed or overly sophisticated concepts, unhelpful text structure, and so forth. The readability of proposed materials for the Scott Foresman Reading Unlimited Reading Systems published from 1970 to 1975 was, in fact, determined this way, with changes made in the materials in response to the recurring patterns of miscues and students' ability—or inability—to explain the material adequately after reading (Smith and Lindberg 1973). Miscue analysis is even better than the cloze procedure in taking into account not only the text but the reader in determining text difficulty.

Cullinan and Fitzgerald (1984) suggest that educators and publishers use approaches other than simple formulas for measuring text difficulty, including:

1. Teacher evaluation of proposed texts, based on the teachers' knowledge of their students' prior information and experiences, and their reading ability and interests.
2. Teacher observations of students using proposed texts in instructional settings, in order to evaluate the effectiveness of the material.
3. Checklists for evaluating the readability of the proposed materials, involving attention to such variables as student interests, text graphics, the number and difficulty of ideas and concepts in the material, the length of lines in the text, and the many other factors that contribute to relative difficulty of text material. (For an excellent checklist, see Irwin and Davis 1980.)

Vacca and Vacca (1986, p. 59) summarize, in general, the three major factors to consider: "*understandability* (how likely are my students to comprehend this text?); *usability* (is this text coherent, unified and structured enough to be usable with my class?); and *interestability* (will features of this text have appeal for my students?)."

READING BEYOND THE TEXT

Supplementary reading materials should become a part of every content area classroom. Given the wide range of reading abilities represented in any one classroom, it is evident that using one text for all students is far from ideal. Creating optimal environments for active reading may require the use of nontext materials to supplement the text, and perhaps for some students, to replace it. Unless students are given materials at their level of ability and interest, some of the assigned text reading is going to go unread, despite attempts to motivate students and prepare them for the reading.

As old textbooks are being discarded, teachers may be able to salvage good chapters for placement in folders as supplementary reading on topics inadequately covered in the new text. Equally useful are chapters on the same topic but written for younger readers and therefore easier for the less proficient readers in the class. In fact, it's useful when introducing a new topic in class to bring in a variety of materials on the topic for student perusal; some students may appreciate a magazine or newspaper article that briefly introduces the concepts to be discussed in more depth in the text. Calkins (1983) describes a fourth-grade classroom in which the teacher introduced the topic of bird migration as a possible topic for research by showing them a variety of materials, including an encyclopedia article and a primary-level book on the topic. Children were encouraged to read the simpler books first to gain a grasp of the subject before they tackled the denser texts, a useful suggestion for older as well as younger students, for the more experienced readers as well as the less experienced. Using a variety of materials on the same topic, from easier to more difficult, will enable readers to find materials at their own reading level. Assimilating concepts comes only when readers have transacted with the ideas—as Calkins (1983) suggests, when they have put the ideas into their own words and made the concepts their own. And this kind of assimilation of concepts will occur most easily when the reading material is accessible and comprehensible.

Magazines and newspapers, unfortunately underused in content area classrooms, provide a wealth of resources on a wide variety of topics. Science sections in daily newspapers can be clipped, used for individual projects, or copied for use with the entire class when the topics relate to course content; current events become an integral part of any social studies class when the newspaper becomes regular reading fare. *Scientific American, Omni*, and *Discover* can supplement the science classroom, while *National Geographic* and *National Geographic World* might play a major role in the geography class.

The newspaper, in particular, provides positive reading experiences because it is "adult" reading, it offers a variety of high-interest topics, it is current and relevant to students' worlds, and it can be used in a variety of ways, for different purposes. Furthermore, it is relatively inexpensive to use and encourages lifelong readership (Kossack 1986).

Strongly recommended in social studies classrooms is the use of fiction, autobiographies, biographies, and diaries as a way of bringing history to life on a more personal level. Students can experience history through literature more dramatically, and can often have a more in-depth transaction with the subject, when it deals with characters "who were there." A particularly useful historical novel with a Revolutionary War setting is Esther Forbes's *Johnny Tremain*. Caudell, DeVries, Garthe, and Wilson (1980) compiled a variety of activities for use with this novel, several of which would be particularly appropriate in a history class. The following are samples of their suggestions:

1. In Chapter 6, do some research to find out what happened to the famous men who were members of the "Boston Observers." What did they do after the Revolution? What was their role during the actual fighting? Or pretend you are one of the young boys involved in the Boston Tea Party. Write a poem or a short story telling how you are dressed, how you feel, what your assignment is, how you are going to carry it out, and so on.

2. In Chapter 7, discuss some different ways that the British government could have handled the Boston Tea Party. Why do you think they handled it as they did? How would you have handled it? How would you have felt if you were a British citizen in England at the time?

3. Write a headline story for the *Boston Observer* about the British and Boston conflict.

4. The King of England ordered the Port of Boston closed. No ships could enter, other than His Majesty's warships and transports, until the tea was paid for. This had an effect on everyone in Boston. The hundreds of sailors, ropemakers, dockhands, and wharfingers were out of work. Long Wharf was quiet and empty. Write a poem or a short story about how you felt living in Boston during that time. Assume that you were one of the following: a young boy or girl of sixteen, a merchant or tradesman, a fisherman, a mother of a large family, or someone else.

5. Do some research into the background of the generals sent over from England— Generals Gage, Howe, Clinton, and Burgoyne. What part did they play in the Revolution?

6. Have the class participate in a daily news broadcast, reporting on such events in the book as Johnny's accident, the trial involving Johnny's alleged theft of the silver cup, the tea tax, the Sons of Liberty, Paul Revere's ride, and so on.

7. Publish a class newspaper dealing with events prior to and during the Revolutionary War. Have the students write the articles, do the illustrations, and so on.

8. Set up a debate within the classroom between the British and the Americans. Research the feelings of each side so as to argue convincingly for your viewpoint.

9. Dress up according to the time period and do a demonstration speech about an occupation in the 1700s. For example, you might be a silversmith, nurse, soldier, or merchant. Tell how you live, what you do, how much money you make, your contribution to society, and if your occupation changed because of the war.

10. Write a letter to Johnny Tremain, Paul Revere, John Adams, or another American patriot, praising the person for his or her part in winning the war.

Similar activities can be devised for use with a wide variety of fiction and nonfiction related to social studies. (See "Suggested Readings" in the final bibliography for a listing of related reading material.)

DIRECTED INDIVIDUALIZED READING

We know that readers develop reading proficiency by reading a wide variety of materials, but we've traditionally relegated the responsibility for developing and enhancing reading skills to the English/language arts classroom. In fact, that is where most Sustained Silent Reading programs operate. Reading for its own sake, not necessarily for the purpose of "learning" content material, usually occurs in a free reading format within the bounds of a language arts curriculum. SSR has long been considered a way of increasing reading proficiency and sustaining an interest in reading that will lead to lifelong reading habits. Schools need to provide opportunities for students to read freely and widely beyond textbook material, and not just in language arts classes, if good reading habits are going to be extended beyond the school years.

SSR programs occur in different forms. Some elementary school educators who recognize the intellectual and emotional benefits of wide, self-selected reading have developed SSR across all classrooms, where, for a 20-minute or 30-minute period of time all other activity ceases and everyone reads, from administrators and secretaries to teachers and students. When a schoolwide SSR policy is difficult to implement, individual teachers can set aside SSR time in their own classrooms.

A critical element for success in SSR programs is the modeling done by the teacher. McCracken and McCracken (1978) argue that only when the teacher reads along with the students do they begin to value the activity and take it seriously. Manning and Manning (1984) discovered in their study that SSR is even more effective when readers interact with their peers about their reading. Readers in the peer interaction group had significantly higher scores on a measure of attitude toward reading and on a measure of reading achievement than did students in regular SSR programs and in programs where readers participated in teacher conferences about the reading. Teacher conferences, however, produced better results than did the basic SSR program. Clearly, SSR programs in which students interact with one another and share their reading have high potential for success.

Several excellent references are available to help in the selection of appropriate and interesting reading in individualized reading programs. Each of the following references contains annotations of fiction and nonfiction books, organized by topics and categories:

Elementary:	*Adventuring with Books*. 1985. Ed. D. L. Monson. Urbana, Illinois: National Council of Teachers of English.
Middle School:	*Your Reading*. 1983. Ed. J. Christensen. Urbana, Illinois: National Council of Teachers of English.
Senior High:	*Books for You*. 1985. Ed. D. R. Gallo. Urbana, Illinois: National Council of Teachers of English.
All Levels:	*Reading Ladders for Human Relations*. 1983. Ed. E. Tway. Urbana, Illinois: National Council of Teachers of English.

What impact do individualized reading programs have on content area teachers? Emphasis has been shifting from the traditional assumption that only English/ language arts teachers need be concerned with the development of reading proficiency to the assumption that all teachers need to take more responsibility for fostering good reading habits, both in class assignments and in recreational reading beyond the text. While content area teachers perhaps have no direct obligation to foster independent reading habits, they do have an opportunity to enhance their own class reading assignments directly and indirectly.

Bishop (1981) recommends "starter shelves" of paperback books related to the particular content area in every classroom, because books on a wide variety of subjects are readily available and teachers can serve as links between student interests and appropriate sources. Teachers also can demonstrate for students that they value reading that extends beyond the limits of the textbook. Furthermore, this kind of reading can increase readers' reading proficiency in general and possibly create reading habits that last long after formal schooling is completed.

Teachers can introduce the books to students by reading brief synopses of them, connecting book topics to student experiences or class topics, and reading interesting passages to stimulate interest and independent reading. It should be stressed that these books are to be read voluntarily, so that some class time should be devoted to self-selected reading from the starter shelf. After some reading has been done, students might be encouraged to give short book talks for stimulating further reading interest, or they might jot down their impressions on a 3 × 5 card to keep on file for further reference and recommendation. Teachers should be cautioned not to require any formal reporting on the books, unless by student choice, because the purpose is not to "test" students on their reading but to encourage wide reading beyond the text.

Bishop (1981) goes on to say that once students begin to use the starter shelves freely, teachers can develop other activities to capitalize on their interest through greater involvement with the books, including creative ways of having students share books, memberships in student book clubs, and making connections between the books and TV productions such as the Jacques Cousteau series, "Nova," and National Geographic specials, as well as the increasingly popular historical docu-dramas.

Books on starter shelves should be regularly updated, and after they have become successfully integrated into classroom activities, they may be used for further assigned reading, reporting, or researching, as the situation allows. The original goal of self-selected, individualized reading should always remain paramount, however.

As the starter shelves get updated, teachers may want periodically to do a "book-pass" (Carter and Rashkis 1980), a procedure to provide as much exposure to the books as possible. For one class period or portion thereof once a month, once every other month, or whatever frequency is most useful, the teacher distributes one book to each student and gives students five minutes to look the book over, reading the title and as much of the book's beginning as the time allows. Each student fills out a simple response sheet with author, title, and an indication of whether he or she would like to read the book. At the end of five minutes, each student passes his or her book on to someone else and the process is repeated. Each student gets to see a new book every five minutes, and during the course of one class period, each has a chance to look over 10 or 12 books, one or more of which may generate interest for further reading. The activity gets several books into the hands of all the students in a short amount of time.

QUESTING: READING AND WRITING INTEGRATED IN THE CONTENT AREA CLASSROOM

The wide variety of resources that content area classrooms should have available—books, magazines, newspapers, and other supplementary materials—can also serve as resources for researching topics that students want to develop. The QUEST is an approach to learning, reading, and writing developed by Stephen N. Tchudi (1986) for use in all levels of content area classrooms, elementary through college. When groups or classes as a whole have selected a topic they want to investigate, the first step is formulating questions about the topic. The topic can be listed in the center of the chalkboard, and as students brainstorm questions about the topic, the questions are arranged around the topic, similar to a mapping activity. When several questions have been generated, students can divide into interest groups related to the questions and can then do a more detailed webbing based on their particular subtopic. After several sessions of question formation and discussion, each student takes a specific question related to the more general subtopic to investigate further.

To illustrate, the web in Figure 9.7 represents a sample of the questioning process undertaken from a high-school class considering the general topic of nuclear energy. One group decided to focus on nuclear weapons as their subtopic, and during the questioning process, they generated the topics/questions in Figure 9.7.

The second stage is finding resources—nonprint as well as print. Resources may include people, institutions like museums, newspapers, businesses, and industries. Students may need to write letters, interview people, or gather information by telephone; reading, writing, listening, and speaking are all language skills that will be employed in gathering information about the topic.

The final stage is the reporting back that can be accomplished in a variety of ways, depending on the nature of the QUEST: fiction, drama, TV reports, newscasts, position papers, children's books, posters, demonstrations, and so forth. Questing is a natural way of involving students in research growing out of course content. It is particularly useful in its emphasis on a wide variety of resources and reporting formats. As Tchudi (1986, p. 66) explains, the QUEST "is a model of learning . . . with its phases of questioning, finding answers, and reporting to others. It is also fundamentally linked to language use, in general, and to writing in

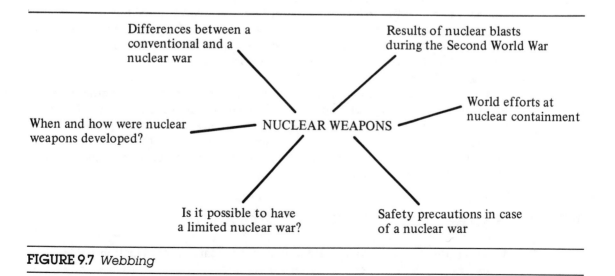

FIGURE 9.7 *Webbing*

the content areas, in particular.'' Built on researching topics of personal interest from self-generated questions, the process encourages students' transactions with text—those they read and those they write and share with other class members.

CONTENT AREA READING IN REVIEW

We have provided a number of strategies in this chapter that can be modified and adapted to students of varying ages and with varying reading abilities, strategies that can be used separately or in conjunction with one another. While some are designed specifically as pre-reading, during-reading, or post-reading, the majority in actuality span all three phases of the reading process: journal writing, graphic organizers, anticipation guides, and DRTAs can be used throughout the reading, initially to get students to think about the topic and build their schemas for reading, and finally to help them integrate and assimilate new information and to respond to the reading from both emotional and intellectual perspectives.

Reading in the content area is essentially no different from other kinds of reading. It demands active participation in the process; readers bring their background knowledge and experience to bear on the meaning they construct. Their comprehension is their own creation, the result of a transactional process, not a mechanistic one.

But while meaning is relative and individual, based largely on the readers' schemas, meaning is constantly being modified through a variety of experiences with other readers. Reading is not the be-all and end-all of the content area classroom, it is one part of learning—a part that will facilitate learning, to be sure, but also one that is immeasurably enhanced by other aspects of transactional learning occurring in the classroom: the transaction of readers with various kinds of texts, the transaction of readers with their own writing and with the writing of their peers, and the transaction of peers with one another as they grapple with ideas and concepts, old and new. Creating optimal conditions for learning involves providing a context for learning where these kinds of transactions can occur, as Haggard (1985) suggests, in a safe, cooperative environment. Reading, writing, thinking, learning are not sequential steps in a mechanistic process—they are interrelated, almost indistinguishable ingredients in the comprehension process.

Given this view of reading and the strategies that support it, the Sarahs and the Sams in our classrooms who struggle with reading now have a greater chance of success. And the Maries who often refuse to read may find new compelling reasons for engaging with print. There are no guarantees, of course, but there is reason to hope that more content area classrooms will become the centers of inquiry and exploration they are intended to be.

ACTIVITIES AND PROJECTS FOR FURTHER EXPLORATION

1. Select a textbook in your content area and prepare an anticipation guide for a selection in the text. Be sure to find a selection that lends itself to this kind of pre-reading activity.

2. Select a chapter from a text in your content area and prepare a pattern guide for use with a class. Develop the guide, using the basic rhetorical organization of the selection as an integral part of the guide.

3. Investigate paperback books that would be useful to include in a starter shelf for your content area. Select five to seven books that you think students would enjoy reading. Then prepare three activities that could be used with the books for student projects.

4. Select a chapter or a topic related to your content area and list as many writing activities as you can that would be useful for this topic. You may want to categorize them as pre-reading, during-reading, or post-reading activities that incorporate writing.

5. Find two or three texts, junior high or senior high level, in your content area, and analyze them according to their comprehensibility, using the checklist provided by Irwin and Davis, Assessing Readability: The Checklist Approach, *Journal of Reading* 24 (November 1980): 124–30.

6. Make a list of at least ten creative ways for a student to "report" on something he or she has read.

READINGS FOR FURTHER EXPLORATION

Cooper, Charles R., and Anthony R. Petrosky. December 1976. A Psycholinguistic View of the Fluent Reading Process. *Journal of Reading* 20: 184–207. An outstanding article that outlines a reading program for secondary students and includes an especially valuable bibliography.

Davison, Alice, and Robert N. Kantor. 1982. On the Failure of Readability Formulas to Define Readable Texts: A Case Study from Adaptations. *Reading Research Quarterly* 17, ii: 187–209. Though the article itself is not easy to read, it contains marvelous examples of how "simplifying" children's literature for inclusion in basal reading series can actually make the literature harder to comprehend.

Bishop, David M. 1981. Motivating Adolescent Readers via Starter Shelves in Content Area Classes. *Motivating Reluctant Readers*. Ed. A. J. Ciani. Newark, Delaware: International Reading Association, 44–70. Contains excellent bibliographies of supplementary reading materials for students in several content areas.

Haggard, Martha Rapp. December 1985. An Interactive Strategies Approach to Content Reading. *Journal of Reading* 29: 204–10. This article demonstrates reading strategies in which content and process interact, encouraging critical thinking and learning.

Heimlich, Joan E., and Susan D. Pittelman. 1986. *Semantic Mapping: Classroom Applications*. Newark, Delaware: International Reading Association. Includes ten classroom applications of the semantic mapping procedure in a variety of content areas.

Hennings, Dorothy Grant. January 1982. Writing Approach to Reading Comprehension—Schema Theory in Action. *Language Arts* 59: 8–17. Suggests ways of helping students organize informational content for writing as a way of helping them refine their ability to comprehend this kind of content.

Kraft, Robert G. 1985. Group Inquiry Turns Passive Students Active. *College Teaching* 33, iv: 149–54. Outlines a procedure that, through group collaboration, asks students to problem-solve ideas and issues presented in their reading of literature. As a means of responding to, and critically evaluating, their reading, the technique can be adapted for other content areas as well.

Robinson, H. Alan. 1983. *Teaching Reading, Writing, and Study Strategies: The Content Areas.* 3rd ed. Boston: Allyn and Bacon. The chapter on readability assessment, pp. 133–43, is particularly relevant. It contains an excellent checklist for assessing the appropriateness of texts.

Wagner, Betty J. 1983. The Expanding Circle of Informal Classroom Drama. *Integrating the Language Arts in the Elementary School.* Ed. B. A. Busching and J. I. Schwartz. Urbana, Ill.: National Council of Teachers of English, 155–63. Demonstrates through excellent examples how to move from improvised drama to writing and then on to reading.

10

How Can We Assess Readers' Strengths and Begin to Determine Their Instructional Needs?

Only two basic uses of reading tests are legitimate. They are as follows: (1) To measure the effectiveness with which any person uses reading to comprehend written language. . . . (2) To diagnose the strengths and weaknesses of readers as an aid to planning instruction which will help to make them more effective.

—Kenneth Goodman

QUESTIONS FOR JOURNALS AND DISCUSSION

1. Why is a so-called Informal Reading Inventory generally not the best means of assessing a reader's strengths and weaknesses?

2. What are some of the principles that should underlie any procedure used to assess readers' strengths and needs?

3. Why does a miscue analysis need to be balanced by an assessment of the reader's retelling?

4. Why might the assessment of someone's comprehension after oral reading need to be balanced by an assessment of comprehension after silent reading?

5. In deciding whether the reader needs focused instructional help, why is it important to take into account not only the quality of the reader's miscues and the frequency with which they occur, but also the retelling?

6. How might we help a reader learn to monitor his/her own comprehension, continually asking him/herself "Does this sound like language?" and "Does this make sense?"

ASSESSING THE INFORMAL READING INVENTORY

As everyone knows, reading can be assessed in a variety of ways, and for a variety of purposes. Perhaps most common is the *standardized test*, commercially prepared and machine scored. One obvious purpose of such tests is to measure students, classes, and schools in contrast to one another. In recent years, however, some standardized tests have purported to measure students' specific strengths and weaknesses as well. A major difficulty with this attempt is that reading is reduced to skills or subskills, with such aspects as comprehension and phonics knowledge typically being measured by no more than five questions each. Clearly this is an inadequate measure of a student's ability to comprehend or of the student's ability to use grapho/phonemic knowledge in real reading. Furthermore, standardized reading tests cannot tell us what strategies a person uses as he or she reads.

Recent standardized cloze tests are somewhat better in the latter regard, as we *could*, potentially, analyze each response to see how it fits the context, thus gaining some insight into how well the reader uses syntactic and semantic cues to predict and confirm/correct. Far better, however, is to observe the reading process in action. In order to do this, we must listen to the person read aloud.

Recognizing this necessity, many teachers and reading specialists have come to use what is often called an *Informal Reading Inventory* (IRI). The examiner actually listens to a person read and analyzes the reader's miscues or "errors," as they are still sometimes called.

Used flexibly, the informal reading inventory may be an acceptable way of tentatively deciding where to place a child within a basal reading series. The teacher begins by having the child read from a basal reader that is likely to be quite easy for him or her, and ends when the child has progressed through other readers to one that is obviously too difficult. The wise teacher determines the child's placement through a variety of factors, such as the quality of the child's miscues, the child's comprehension, and the child's fluency and confidence. Often these factors cannot (or at least should not) be weighted in any simple, numerical way. For example, suppose that Mary and Sally both read from the same text and both make good miscues, about the same number overall. Suppose further that they both show good comprehension of what they have read. Does this mean that they should both be placed at the same level of reading materials? Not necessarily. One child may read the text fluently and with confidence, while the other may read the same text slowly, choppily, and with obvious discomfort and frustration. The wise teacher will take such differences into account in deciding what instructional materials to use with a given child.

Unfortunately, teachers' good judgment tends to be thwarted by the more rigid procedures often recommended for administering and scoring an informal reading inventory. The word "administering" is itself a key to the current state of affairs, for the teacher may merely be using any of several informal reading inventories now commercially available, either separately or as part of a basal reading package (see, for example, Johns et al. 1977, p. 36). Even in textbooks for prospective teachers, the recommended procedure tends to be excessively rigid. Remember, for example, the ofttimes misleading recommendation that when a person miscues on more than ten words out of one hundred, the reading selection is probably too difficult for instructional use with that person (see Chapter 5, p. 115).

In addition to rigidity, there are other problems with the informal reading inventory as it is often advocated and structured. One problem is presented by the various word recognition and word analysis tests that often accompany an informal reading inventory. Another problem is that even in analyzing the reader's miscues, teachers are subtly encouraged to consider quantity rather than quality.

Let us consider the tests that assess a reader's sight vocabulary or ability to apply phonics rules and other skills for analyzing words. By now the reason for worry about such tests should be obvious. Some readers are good at recognizing words on sight, but not very good at getting meaning from connected text. Other readers are good at getting meaning, but not particularly good at recognizing or analyzing isolated words. In either case, such tests do not tell us very much about a reader's ability to comprehend a written text. This is perhaps most distressing when as a result of such tests, we underestimate someone's reading ability.

Indeed, this is true for most methods of assessing an individual's reading "errors": they generally assume that reading is an exact process, requiring word-for-word accuracy. When readers make miscues, it is assumed that they need instructional help. The only question is, what kind of help? To answer this question, teachers are encouraged to determine the kind(s) of miscues that the reader commonly makes.

Typically, the teacher is directed to tabulate the number of insertions, omissions, substitutions, reversals, and so forth, as if these were obviously and always a sign of reading weakness. Even repetitions and regressions are sometimes counted against the reader, though we know that *good* readers tend to regress and repeat words to correct any miscue that does not make sense in context. Many methods of analysis actually penalize the use of good reading strategies.

Although those who advocate an informal reading inventory are often aware that miscues should be analyzed in context rather than as if they occurred in isolation, the various charts and schemes tend to take on a life and character quite distinct from that originally intended. Let us look at one version of the informal reading inventory and see what kinds of inappropriate conclusions might easily be drawn. In *To Help Children Read* (1978, p. 156), May and Eliot provide a checklist for analyzing a child's oral reading. The checklist itself invites teachers to make various kinds of observations, as the child reads from increasingly higher level basals. That is, the teacher is directed to look for such things as whole-word omissions, whole-word insertions, acceptable substitutions, nonsemantic substitutions, and nongrammatical substitutions (a considerable improvement over the 1973 version, which had just one "substitution" category). After recording whatever observations seem appropriate, the teacher is directed to make inferences about the reader's problems. The checklist suggests these areas of possible difficulty:

1. Basic irregular sight words not known
2. Weak in phonic analysis skills
3. Weak in structural analysis skills
4. Nonstandard dialect
5. Weak in contextual analysis: semantic clues
6. Weak in contextual analysis: grammatical clues
7. Comprehension poor

8. Punctuation not understood

9. Needs help on phrasing

Obviously the checklist is directed toward helping teachers pinpoint children's reading weaknesses, rather than both their strengths and their weaknesses. And that, indeed, is one serious objection to such a scheme. A further objection is that such a scheme can all too easily encourage teachers to find weaknesses that do not exist.

To see how this might happen, let us focus upon some of the inferences that an examiner is invited to make. Much of the discussion is from Weaver and Smith (1979).

"Basic Irregular Sight Words Not Known"

Observing a child sometimes substitute one basic sight word for another or omit basic sight words, one might conclude that the child does not know these words. But the child may simply be reading for deep structure rather than for surface structure. Function words and pronouns are often among the "basic sight words," and we have already seen that good readers are likely to make miscues involving such words. They tend to substitute one pronoun or function word for another, and to omit or insert optional function words. The following are examples (some from K. S. Goodman 1973, *Theoretically Based Studies*):

their
White men came from the cities.

It
That took us about an hour.

might
"You may be right."

She made her own paints from ⟨the⟩ roots.

. . . but after a month we saw ⟨that⟩ nothing was growing.

Mr. Tully beat me more often and more cruelly than Mr.
   Coffin had ⟨done⟩

the
Billy feasted on ∧ roast corn. . . .

up
. . . it was enough to wake ∧ the dead.

that
They told him ∧ he had been foolish to plant sesame. . . .

In each of the foregoing examples, the meaning is preserved even though the surface structure is altered. The child made *good* miscues, and we are not justified in assuming that the child did not know the word printed in the text. Instead, we should assume that the child is reading for meaning rather than for accurate reproduction of all the words. And since the getting of meaning is supposedly the goal of reading and of reading instruction, we would do well not to lead the child away from this goal by insisting that every detail of the text be rigorously preserved.

In the 1973 edition of *To Help Children Read*, one possibility the teacher was to consider is that the reader might be "guessing at words" (May 1973, p. 130). Observing that a child sometimes replaces the text word with a word that looks and sounds radically different, one might indeed conclude that the child is guessing at words. Again, however, we must look at the quality of the "guess." We know that the good reader makes educated guesses or *predictions* about what is to come next, and that such predictions sometimes result in miscues. But if these resulting miscues preserve the essential meaning of the text, or if they fail to fit with following context but are subsequently corrected by the reader, then the teacher has little or no reason for concern. Examples of such good miscues might be "roof" for *house*, "baby" for *child*, and "bird" for *canary* (depending, of course, on the context). Note also the following example, where the child made a miscue at the end of a line, then corrected her miscue when the next line revealed the error of her prediction:

> *saw*
> I first saw Claribel when I was
>
> working in my office.

The miscue "saw" for *was* is not a habitual association for this girl, nor was it merely a random guess: it was a logical prediction, given the preceding grammar and meaning, and it reflected minimal attention to grapho/phonemic cues. When the following line failed to confirm the appropriateness of "saw," the girl corrected it to "was." A similar miscue from the same student is the following (both are from Y. Goodman and Burke's *RMI Practice Analysis Manual*, 1972):

> Instead, there was a
>
> *heard*
> lovely song. I looked up and had
>
> my first view of Claribel.

The miscue "heard" was again logical, given the preceding grammar and meaning. And it too reflected minimal attention to grapho/phonemic cues. Such miscues suggest that this reader does not merely guess at words; rather, she makes good use of predicting and sampling strategies.

Note that if we were to look at these last substitutions without reference to context, we might indeed assume that the child was guessing—or, in the case of "saw" for *was*, that the child might have a tendency to confuse the two words or to reverse letters. By examining these words in context, however, we can see that they are good quality miscues, stemming from productive reading strategies.

"Weak in Phonic Analysis Skills"

Observing a child sometimes sound out words but end up with the wrong word or a nonword, one might conclude that the child is weak in phonic analysis skills. Examples we have seen that might lead to such a conclusion are the following miscues made by one child:

beaches
the children sat on little benches in front of the teacher

expert
Every day except Friday,

souts
The sandy shore rang with the happy shouts and cries of
    the village boys and girls.

ramped
the boys repeated everything the teacher said

Seeing such miscues, one might be tempted to conclude that the child needs more work with phonics. Examining the words in context, however, we see that the problem may be *too much* phonics, or rather phonics with too little else. The miscue "beaches" makes reasonable sense in the total context, but the miscue "expert" for *except* does not. The nonwords "souts" and "ramped" show that the child is attending to grammar (the plural *-s* and the past tense *-ed*), but they show no concern for meaning.

As we saw in Chapter 3, an extensive study revealed 211 letter/sound correspondences in just the one-syllable and two-syllable words typically understood by six- to nine-year-olds. Of this total, 166 were considered "rules" because they occurred in ten or more words (Berdiansky et al. 1959, as reported in F. Smith 1973). Thus even if it were possible for beginning readers to master all 166 rules, how would they know whether any given case represented a rule or an exception? Clearly phonics can supply only a clue, an approximation to how the word is pronounced. The child who made the foregoing miscues needs to learn to predict what is coming next, then use his knowledge of letter/sound correspondences to produce a word that makes sense in context. *More* phonics instruction will simply make the child an even poorer reader than he already is, because it will force him to pay even closer attention to small details and lead him away from a concern for meaning. Indeed, at the junior high and high school levels, the poorest readers are often those whose miscues show the *closest* letter/sound correspondence to the text word (K. Goodman 1973, *The-*

oretically Based Studies, pp. 51, 53). Such readers come close to sounding out the word, but because they are using grapho/phonemics almost exclusively, they get neither the word itself nor the essential meaning of the material being read.

In contrast, the same series of studies suggest that 50 percent of the substitution miscues of proficient readers have little or no grapho/phonemic similarity to the text word. Such readers are going for deep structure rather than surface structure, for meaning rather than for precise word identification.

We must be cautious, then, about concluding that a reader does not know basic sight words, or that a reader merely guesses at words, or that a reader is weak in phonic analysis skills. If inappropriately drawn, such conclusions could lead to instruction that is not merely unnecessary, but damaging. The reader may be led to focus too much upon words and parts of words, and too little upon meaning.

Since I wrote the above discussion of informal reading inventories for *Psycholinguistics and Reading*, some IRIs have been published with much more sensible directions for analyzing miscues. Johns, for example, recommends counting as errors only those miscues that change meaning (Johns 1981). Still, there are several drawbacks to most IRIs, as pointed out by Harris and Niles (1982, p. 161):

1. Generally the passages are too short to give the reader a chance to demonstrate his/her reading ability under more realistic sustained silent reading conditions. Of the twelve IRIs analyzed by Harris and Niles, only three have passages more than 225 words long. Yet we saw earlier that the nature of readers' miscues often changes after the first 200 words (Menosky 1971).

2. Comprehension questions can often be answered on the basis of prior knowledge, or else the topics are unknown and totally unfamiliar to the reader, thus preventing the reader from making normal use of his/her schemas to read and understand. I would add that comprehension questions can often be answered simply by manipulating the language of the text, if the reader is allowed to look at the passage again. This we saw clearly with the "blonke" and "corandic" passages in earlier chapters.

3. In order to devise an adequate number of comprehension questions on such short passages, the test-maker may be virtually forced to include mostly questions that focus on detail and recall of fact, rather than the more sophisticated kinds of questions that stimulate comprehension of the whole.

Given these typical limitations, even most of today's IRIs are far from ideal for determining readers' strengths and needs.

What can teachers do instead? I would suggest that instead of struggling to use an informal reading inventory, with its typical limitations, we might better adopt a procedure that more adequately reflects what is known about proficient reading. Such a procedure should involve whole texts with natural language, and should have the following characteristics:

1. It should take into account the fact that no two readers (for example, teacher and student) will ever read or understand the same selection in exactly the same way.

2. It should implicitly recognize that getting meaning is more important than reproducing surface detail.

3. It should help us determine a reader's strengths as well as his or her weaknesses.

4. It should examine miscues in context, distinguishing between those that are appropriate in context and those that are not.

5. It should in effect reward the correction of miscues that are not appropriate in context.

6. It should provide insight into a reader's strategies, particularly into how well the reader uses context to predict what is coming next and to correct those miscues that do not make sense in context.

7. It should suggest, in general terms, what kind(s) of strategy lessons the reader might need, if any.

8. It should provide an opportunity for considering the reader's miscues in light of the reader's apparent comprehension of the material read.

Such characteristics are embodied in the total procedure known as "miscue analysis," as discussed below. Miscue analysis actually includes not only an analysis of the reader's miscues themselves but a comparison of the miscue data with an assessment of the reader's ability to discuss or "retell" what was read.

ASSESSING READING STRATEGIES AND COMPREHENSION: MISCUE ANALYSIS PROCEDURES

Kenneth Goodman inaugurated not only a new way of thinking about reading "errors," but also an insightful way of analyzing them. His Taxonomy of Reading Miscues has been widely used in research. The 1973 version has been readily available in Allen and Watson's *Findings of Research in Miscue Analysis: Classroom Implications* (1976) and is now available in Y. Goodman, Watson, and Burke's *Reading Miscue Inventory: Alternative Procedures* (1987). However, this taxonomy is far too complicated for the day-to-day needs of classroom teachers and reading specialists.

To meet the ordinary needs of teacher and specialist, Yetta Goodman and Carolyn Burke prepared a *Reading Miscue Inventory Manual* (1972), which explains their simpler procedure for analyzing a reader's strengths and weaknesses. In the newer *Reading Miscue Inventory: Alternative Procedures* (Y. Goodman, Watson, and Burke 1987), the authors offer four procedures for analyzing miscues, the first similar to that in the original *Reading Miscue Inventory Manual* and the others progressively simpler. The discussion below draws heavily on both of these manuals as well as on my own experience, and I am particularly grateful to the authors and to Richard Owen, the publisher of the newer manual, for allowing me to read it in manuscript form. Henceforth, I shall refer to the first of these manuals as the *RMI Manual* and to the second as *RMI Alternatives*.

Like the authors of the *RMI Alternatives*, I consider the most important use of miscue analysis to be helping teachers gain insight into the reading process. As those authors express it, "Once professionals concerned with reading have developed miscue analysis techniques they will never again listen to readers in the way they did in the past" (Y. Goodman, Watson, and Burke 1987, p.4). This, then, is my first and primary aim: to help you gain appreciation for reading as a unique transaction between reader and text, to help you learn to perceive the productive reading strategies that often cause readers to make miscues, to help you understand that there is not always a close correlation between miscues and comprehension, and so forth. In order to gain such insights, it is important to begin by analyzing miscues in some detail: later, when you have learned to listen to readers in a new way, you can use simpler procedures for analyzing the reading strengths and needs of students with whom you work.

The procedures below are essentially those recommended in the *RMI Manual* and the *RMI Alternatives*, but the form is in many respects my own. As you become more familiar with miscue analysis, you may find it useful to experiment with variations in procedure and form.

It is important to remember that people may read more effectively when they read silently: for many of us, the task of reading aloud interferes with comprehension. However, if we are to determine a reader's strategies for dealing with print by analyzing the reader's miscues, we must of course have the person read aloud. But collecting and analyzing miscues is only part of the procedure: we need to have the reader retell what he or she recalls and understands from the material read. This retelling provides an important check on our miscue analysis. Some readers are good at reproducing surface structure, but not very good at getting meaning. Others get most of the meaning, even though they have made a number of miscues that did not seem to preserve meaning and that they did not overtly correct. Besides providing a balanced view, an examination of both the miscues and the retelling provides us with two different measures of comprehension: a measure of how well the reader seemed to comprehend while in the process of reading, and a measure of what the reader remembered and understood after reading the selection. Both, of course, will be influenced by the reader's pre-existing schemas as well as by the reader's perception of the situation and the task. If the reader recalls little of what has been read, it is important to try other alternatives before drawing absolute conclusions about the reader's ability to understand and/or recall written text. You might have the reader assist you in choosing material of greater interest, perhaps, and/or have the reader read silently and then tell you about the selection. In short, it is crucial to give the reader other opportunities to demonstrate his or her reading strengths.

When you try the following procedure for yourself, you will doubtless have some questions that are not answered by this brief discussion. Do not be afraid to use your own good judgment in deciding what to do. However, it would also be wise to consult someone more experienced in such matters or to consult the *RMI Manual* or the *RMI Alternatives*. Although these resources need not be construed as ultimate authorities, they are based on years of experience with miscue analysis and therefore provide useful guidelines and valuable insights that go considerably beyond what is presented here.

Preparing for the Reading Session

First, you will need to select material appropriate to the individual whose reading ability you are analyzing. The material must be difficult enough to cause the reader to make miscues, but not so difficult as to cause extreme frustration and distress. Keep in mind that you will need to analyze 25 or more consecutive miscues, preferably from the same reading selection. Research has demonstrated that the quality of miscues tends to change beyond the first 200 words of text, as the reader begins to get a sense of the developing meaning (Menosky 1971). Therefore, it is best to collect enough miscues so that you can ignore, for purposes of analysis, the miscues on the early part of the text. This is important in order to give the reader a "fair deal," so to speak. But for your own learning, it can be quite valuable to compare the reader's miscues on the introductory parts of the text with the miscues on the middle and the end (see, for example, Betsey's miscues in activity 1 at the end of this chapter).

Here are some further suggestions and guidelines:

1. Generally, a good rule of thumb is to begin with material one grade level above what the reader usually deals with in class. For beginning and/or poorer readers, however, it may be better to choose something only a little beyond what they are presently reading in class. When my students go to do miscue analysis in an unfamiliar classroom with children they do not know, I usually ask the classroom teacher to choose material appropriate for each child, using the guidelines here. If you yourself must choose material for a child you have never met, it may be best to choose something further along in the child's basal reader, being sure to avoid something with stilted language that impedes fluent reading. Ideally, it would be best to select materials that you know the individual reader will be interested in. If time permits, you might invite the reader to join with you in selecting something on the basis of the title and pictures. Again ideally, it is best to have two or three selections of different difficulty available for use, because you will need to try another selection if the reader is not making many miscues or if the selection is producing *extreme* distress. If you use miscue analysis frequently in your own classroom, you would be well advised to create a collection of materials that can be used for this purpose, perhaps a combination of trade books, stories from basal readers, articles, and other appropriate materials.

2. The passages selected for reading should rarely be less than 500 words; use two or three short selections if absolutely necessary, in order to provide enough text for the reader to make a sufficient number of miscues for analysis. The selections provided with an informal reading inventory are usually too brief to allow the reader to develop the sense of an emerging whole. What's needed is something that is complete in itself: a story, a self-contained chapter in a book, an article or section of a textbook—something that has a sense of wholeness. If you select a story, it should ordinarily have a strong plot (usually centering around some problem or conflict), as well as a theme (an underlying idea). The language should be "natural"—that is, it should not sound like the stilted, contrived language of some basal readers. If you select an informational piece, it too should have natural language, and it should involve concepts that are clearly stated and not too complex. *The selection must be entirely new to the reader*, but the content

should be something that he or she can understand and relate to. Not surprisingly, miscue research shows that the more personally involved readers become in their reading, the more proficiently they read (*RMI Alternatives*, Ch. 6). *The entire selection must be read in order for the retelling to have much significance.*

Second, you will need to gather and prepare the materials needed while working with the reader. You will need:

1. A tape recorder to record the session for later playback.
2. The material that the student is to read (see above). The reader should read from the original printed material (book, or whatever).
3. Your own copy of the selection(s) for marking the reader's miscues. It is a good idea to have this copy ready in advance of the reading session, so that you can make notes concerning any behavior that will not be apparent from the tape recording. If there is enough room to write between the lines of the original text, you can simply make a photocopy for your use. Otherwise, you will need to prepare a typed copy for marking the reader's miscues. This typed copy should be double-spaced or triple-spaced, so that there is enough room to indicate the reader's miscues above the lines. Be sure to retain the line divisions of the original, and indicate all page divisions. Be careful to be completely accurate in retyping the selection.
4. Notes on the selection, to use in asking questions to elicit more of what the reader recalls, after you have encouraged him or her to tell you about the selection without specific prompting.

With regard to the fourth item, I suggest that you first read the selection aloud yourself and jot down what you recall: for example, if the selection is a story, jot down what seems important about the characters, events and plot, theme, and perhaps setting. If possible, have someone else do the same and compare notes, so that you thereby get not only a sense of what might be centrally important in the story but also a sense of how idiosyncratic we are in deciding what's most important. If you and a group of people did this with regard to the ''Petronella'' story (Appendix A) as one of the activities in Chapter 1, you should already have a strong appreciation of the fact that what a reader comprehends and recalls is very much affected by the reader's prior knowledge, beliefs, thoughts, emotions, and feelings— including, in the case of reading assessment, the reader's feelings about the situation, the assessor, the task, and the reader's perception of his or her ability to succeed in the assessment task.

Keeping all of this in mind, be judicious in your selection of what you think the reader ''should'' remember about the selection. Because it is easy to forget everything you planned to ask about, you should prepare careful notes on the selection(s) you have chosen. If it is a story, for example, prepare an outline or list dealing with characters, events, plot, theme, and perhaps setting:

Characters: Which characters might the reader reasonably be expected to recall? What might the reader be likely to remember about each of these characters? This could include such aspects as physical appearance (particularly if important to the plot), attitudes and feelings, behavior, relationship with other characters, problems or conflicts, and so forth.

Events: What events might the reader reasonably be expected to recall? What should the reader remember about the sequence of events?

Plot: What might the reader reasonably be expected to tell about the central conflict or problem of the story?

Theme: If there seems to be a theme, an underlying idea, what might be some alternative ways of expressing it?

Setting: If the setting is important to the story, what might the reader reasonably be expected to tell about the setting?

It is also wise to note along with your outline the kinds of questions you might ask to elicit more information from the reader (see p. 334).

In addition to the four previously mentioned items and materials, you may want to prepare another:

5. A list of questions to elicit the reader's views about reading and about himself or herself as a reader. These questions might be the same or similar to those in activity 2 at the end of Chapter 1 (mostly from Burke 1980, as reported in the *RMI Alternatives*, Ch. 7):

    1. What do you think reading is? What do people do when they read something?
    2. When you are reading and come to something you don't know, what do you do? (After receiving a response, you might ask a follow-up question: Do you ever do anything else?)
    3. Who is a good reader you know?
    4. What makes _____ a good reader?
    5. Do you think _____ ever comes to something he/she doesn't know? (After receiving a response, ask: Suppose _____ does come to something he/she doesn't know. What do you think _____ would do?)
    6. If you knew someone was having trouble reading, how would you help that person?
    7. What would a/your teacher do to help that person?
    8. How did you learn to read?
    9. What would you like to do better as a reader?
    10. Do you think you are a good reader? Why?

Conducting the Reading Session: An Overview

You will need to make certain that you have all the aforementioned materials:

1. A tape recorder—and, of course, a tape.
2. The selection(s) for the student to read.

3. Your own copy of the selection(s).

4. Notes on the selection(s), to use in asking questions.

5. Perhaps questions to elicit the reader's views on reading and about himself or herself as a reader.

Here are some additional guidelines:

1. It is helpful to let the reader briefly talk into the tape recorder and then play it back, to lessen any concern about being recorded. You might invite the reader to state his or her name and add other identifying information, such as the name of the teacher and the school, the reader's age and grade, and the date. Explain that you will be recording the entire session, both the reading and the retelling (and, if pertinent, the interview).

2. If you are sure you will still have enough time for the reading and the retelling, you might begin by asking the reader some or all of the interview questions. Or you could save them until the end, or ask some now and some later.

3. Tell the reader that he or she is expected to read the *entire* selection aloud and that it is important to try to understand the material being read, because afterwards you will ask the reader to pretend you've never read the selection and to tell you all about it. You might encourage the reader to flip through the pages of the text to get some idea of the length of the selection, too.

4. Tell the reader that when encountering a problem word, the reader should do whatever he or she usually does in such situations, when there's no one around to help. You might explain that the reason you can't help is that you're trying to find out what readers do when they must solve reading problems for themselves.

5. If the reader stops over a problem word, wait . . . and wait some more. If necessary, remind the reader to do whatever he or she would ordinarily do when reading alone, and reassure the reader that anything he or she chooses to do is all right.

6. Stop the reader if he or she is making scarcely any miscues, and turn to a more challenging selection. Do not, however, be quick to stop a reader who is having difficulty: hesitations, long pauses, and repetitions are not in themselves sufficient justification for deciding that the selection is too difficult. In fact, readers may often surprise themselves (and everyone else) by gleaning meaning from a text that *seems* too difficult.

7. While the reader is reading, jot down notes on your copy of the selection(s) and, if appropriate, on another sheet of paper. It is particularly important to jot down things the reader says that you think you might not later be able to hear on the tape, or aspects of the situation and the reader's nonverbal behavior that seem particularly important. Usually a reader quickly becomes oblivious to such jottings. Both during the session and later in marking the worksheet and coding sheets, be sure to use PENCIL. You'll need to be able to erase and revise.

8. Follow the guidelines below in conducting the retelling session.

9. Ask the remaining interview questions, if desired.

10. Remember to end by making the reader feel good about himself or herself.

Guiding the Retelling

After the reader has finished the selection, ask the reader to close the book, pretend you've never read the selection, and tell you everything he or she can about it. *It is important that you not interrupt or ask any questions during this initial retelling.*

Some readers will tell you absolutely everything about what they have read. Others will volunteer very little, even though they may remember a great deal. This is why you should be prepared to ask questions that will encourage the reader to expand upon the retelling. As you listen to the unaided retelling, you can check off mentioned items on your notes or outline, provided you do so unobtrusively. Then when the reader has finished the unaided retelling, you can ask questions. Here are some useful guidelines:

1. During the retelling session, be careful not to respond in such a way as to confirm or disconfirm the accuracy of what the reader is saying. Just be friendly and encouraging.
2. In formulating your questions, be sure to retain any mispronunciations or name changes that the reader used. At the end of the retelling session, you can ask about such words: for example, if the reader said "typeical baby" for *typical baby*, you can ask "What is a 'typeical baby,' anyway?"
3. In asking questions, be careful not to supply any information that the reader has not already given you. And try not to suggest insights that the reader has not acquired on his or her own.
4. Avoid questions that the reader can answer with a simple "yes" or "no." Instead, mostly use questions that begin with the so-called WH-words. Often, you can introduce these questions by referring to information the reader has already given you, as do the following examples keyed to the basic elements of a story:

Characters:	What else can you tell me about so-and-so?
	Who else was in the story besides the characters you've mentioned?
Events:	What else happened in the story?
	What happened after such-and-such?
	Where/when did such-and-such happen?
	How did such-and-such happen?
Plot:	Why do you think such-and-such happened?
	What was so-and-so's main problem?
Theme:	How did you feel when such-and-such happened?
	What do you think the author might have been trying to tell us in this story?
Setting:	Where/when did the story take place?
	How was this important to the story?

It is important to focus your questions on crucial aspects of the story, not on relatively insignificant details. Remember, too, that there may be legitimate difference of opinion as to what is important in the story! On the other hand, try not to accept "I don't know" as an answer. If you think the matter is important, try to rephrase the question to get at the information in another way.

5. You might ask questions that elicit the reader's responses to the story. Here are some possibilities:

> How did you feel when _____?
> Why do you think so-and-so did such-and-such? Would you have done that? Why (or why not)?
> Have you ever been in a similar situation? What did you do?
> Do you think the story ended the way it should? Why (or why not)? If not, how would you have ended it?

6. You might ask questions designed to stimulate what Piaget called "formal operational thought." Such questions are appropriate for virtually all elementary-level children as well as for older students:

> *Questions that invite readers to think about abstract ideas and concepts, and to apply such concepts to their reading*:
> What is a true friend? Do you think so-and-so was being a true friend when he or she . . .? Why/why not?"
>
> *Questions that invite readers to reason hypothetically*:
> "If so-and-so had done this, then what might have happened?"
>
> *Questions that invite readers to systematically consider multiple causes/ explanations/factors and weigh their relative importance*:
> "You said you think there are three reasons why so-and-so did such-and-such. Which reason seems most important to you? Why?"

7. You might ask questions related directly to the reading event (most are from the *RMI Alternatives*, p. 48):

> Is there anything you'd like to ask me about this story?
> Were there any (concepts, ideas, sentences, words) that gave you trouble? What were they?
> Why did you leave this word out?
> Do you know what this word means, now?
> Were there times when you weren't understanding the story? Show me where. Tell me about those times.
> Remember when you said the kid was a "typeical baby"? What is a "typeical baby"? (Ask about key words that were mispronounced or otherwise miscued, to see if the reader got the concept despite the miscue.)

Other questions should occur to you in response to the individual student's reading. Time permitting, you might play back the tape of a particular portion of the reading and discuss it with the reader.

Analyzing and Evaluating the Retelling

You will need to replay the tape so that you can make thorough notes on the retelling. Depending on your purposes and expectations, you might begin by preparing a verbatim transcript of the retelling session, writing in dialogue format exactly what each of you said in turn. Then using your original notes or outline of what you thought the reader might reasonably be expected to recall and understand, you might simply check off those items that the reader dealt with adequately, cross out items that the reader did not deal with at all, and add additional information that the reader provided. When the reader misremembered or misunderstood something, you will need to make specific annotations on your outline. Once you have done this preliminary work, you are ready to evaluate the retelling.

As you prepare to evaluate, remember that a retelling can *never* adequately reflect a reader's understanding of a text, and that the "story" the reader has created will *never* be exactly the same as the one you have created. Something else to consider is the possibility that remembering a lot of details may be a sign that the reader is reading more to meet the typical demands of school and tests than to understand or appreciate the selection read. This is why, to get away from this focus on minutiae, I have recommended above that you ask questions only about "important" information and that you ask questions designed to elicit the reader's personal and critical response to the selection.

One way to evaluate the retelling is to assign a predetermined number of points to various aspects of the selection and then evaluate the retelling accordingly. In the original *RMI Manual*, Goodman and Burke recommend assigning 30 points to character recall and development; 30 points to events; 20 to plot, and 20 to theme (p. 24). In the newer *RMI Alternatives*, the authors recommend focusing just on character (40 points) and events (60 points), without attending to plot, to theme, or—as I have suggested—to setting. Obviously you will have to determine what's appropriate based on the particular story you have used. It's also possible that after using a selection a time or two, you will reconsider what is appropriate for a reader to recall.

I find in my own assessment of retellings (and of essay exams), that if I rigidly determine point values in advance of receiving students' work, I inevitably end up with scores that contradict my experienced professional judgment: more often than not, such predetermined point values leave no opportunity to appreciate and reward the unique insights of the individual and thus underestimate the individual's knowledge. Therefore I tend to favor a holistic scoring procedure. As "subjective" as it may appear, I am convinced that with experience, teachers can actually make fairer and in some respects more "objective" assessments this way. In the new *RMI Alternatives*, Y. Goodman, Watson, and Burke also recommend a holistic scoring procedure for all but the first of their four miscue analysis procedures (Chapter 6). They suggest using either an even-numbered scale (such as 1–4) so that there will be no average category, or an odd-numbered scale (such as 1–5) in order to provide a midpoint. In *Psycholinguistics and Reading*, I suggested an odd-numbered, seven-point scale:

1	2	3	4	5	6	7
poor		adequate		good		excellent

Notice that ''adequate'' is not the midpoint, as might have been expected. My labeling of the scale thus encourages finer distinctions at the upper end of the range. In my opinion, a holistic scoring procedure such as this is preferable to a more rigid one, because it is more in line with our understanding that reading is a unique transaction between a reader and a text. Assigning a certain number of points to various aspects of a selection tends more to reflect the notion that everyone should remember and understand a text in exactly the same way.

With experience, I think you may find that a ''subjective,'' holistic evaluation procedure may actually produce more consistent and more comparable results as you compare one reader with others or as you compare one reader with himself or herself at different times and/or on different kinds of reading materials.

Some reminders may be in order. Unfortunately, some readers will do less well than others at retelling and discussing a story, simply because they have rarely been encouraged to engage in this kind of response. Some readers may understand a selection well, yet do a relatively poor job of retelling the material, simply because they see no need to retell it. As my son used to say, ''I know what it's about and so do you, so why do I need to tell you?'' Other readers may do relatively poorly with a reading selection simply because they are not interested in it, or because the concepts are too difficult, despite one's best intentions in selecting materials. In that case, a reassessment with different material is in order. Some readers comprehend relatively little when they read aloud, yet comprehend well when reading silently. For such readers, the oral reading session is still important, because it enables you to determine the reader's strategies. But if the subsequent retelling is less successful than the reading led you to expect, you should check the reader's comprehension after silent reading. That is, you should have the person read a different but equally difficult selection silently, and then conduct another retelling session.

Preparing the Miscue Worksheet

Before you can analyze or evaluate the reader's miscues, you must of course mark them on your copy of the selection(s) read; this copy is known as the *worksheet*. When the reader has said a nonword, or ''nonsense'' word, you should use as much of the spelling of the original as possible in representing the reader's pronunciation. Suppose, for example, that the text word is *psychology*, and the reader has said /SI•ko'•lo'•gi/. Write this as *psykology*, not as *sikology*. If the text word is *wrapped* and the reader has said /rāpt/, write the word as *wrāpped* or *wrāped*, not as *rāpt* or *rāped*.

The following examples indicate the markings most commonly used in miscue analysis:

Substitution   ''Blow your nose ᵂⁱᵗʰ̲ into the Kleenex.''
       (The substitution is simply written over the text.)

Omission   ''I will make you some ⟨hot⟩ tea.''

(Sometimes intonation suggests that the reader realizes he or she is uttering only part of a word. On the worksheet, use a hyphen to indicate what seems to be a *partial word*. Later it will be coded as an omission because usually the partial does not provide enough information for us to answer questions about it. Thus you might want to circle the partial to remind you to code it as an omission.)

re-

With these (reservations) out of the way . . .

Insertion

on

"You should just suck cough drops."

Reversal

"No, no," Boris said.

Correction

©   *saw*

I first saw Claribel when I was working in my office.

(The underlining attached to the © indicates what part of the text was repeated as the reader made the correction.)

Unsuccessful attempt at correction

2 putty
uc 1 pondly

His mother . . . scrubbed and pounded the clothes . . .

Abandoning a correct response

Ac

He left home to make his fortune.

(The reader first said "his fortune," then abandoned this response and said "his future.")

Repeating

®

"Why don't you do my work some day?"

(When the reader repeats a word or phrase not for the purpose of correcting but apparently for the purpose of reflecting or of getting a running start on what comes next, this can be marked as above, with the underlining indicating what part was repeated.)

The last three markings are sometimes considered optional, and in fact have not been used in the examples in this text. If other symbols are needed, you can devise your own (but provide a key to the symbols if someone else will be reading your analysis). For unusual kinds of miscues, sometimes it is easiest just to write brief explanations in the margins. You might also consult the original *RMI Manual* or the new *RMI Alternatives*. Three of the above examples are from Chapter 3 of the latter source; one, previously cited, is from Goodman and Burke's *RMI Practice Analysis Manual* (1972).

Once you have marked the miscues on your copy of the reading selection, it is time to number those miscues that are to be analyzed. As noted before, if you have collected more than 25 miscues, it is usually a good idea to discard the miscues on approximately the first 200 words of text (if, of course, this leaves at least 25 miscues). In most cases, 25 consecutive miscues will provide a representative sample of the reader's strategies. Rarely is it necessary to code more than 50 miscues, except perhaps for research.

The following procedures are recommended in numbering the miscues for analysis:

1. If the reader omits most or all of a line of text (or more), you need not number the miscue for later analysis, though you should make note of such omissions, if they occur at all frequently. Or, you may code the omission as a single, complex miscue (see item 5 below).

2. Ordinarily, it is not considered necessary to number and analyze miscues that merely reflect the sound system of a reader's dialect. For example, if a reader normally says "hep" for *help* or "picher" for *picture*, miscues such as these should not be coded. On the other hand, miscues that reflect the reader's own grammatical or semantic system are ordinarily coded and analyzed, but considered completely acceptable: "We was" for *We were*, for example, or "further" for *farther*. (See the next section on analyzing miscues.)

3. Do not consider a partial attempt at a word as a miscue to be numbered and analyzed, if the partial is corrected. For example, if the text says *psychology* and the reader says "psy-" and then "psychology," mark it on the worksheet but don't number it for coding. On the other hand, if a partial word is not corrected, code it as an omission, since a partial word ordinarily provides too little information to make coding decisions about how it fits with context.

4. If a reader more than once makes *exactly the same substitution* for a *content* word, number and analyze only the first occurrence. The implication is that each *new* substitution for a content word, and each substitution for a function word (new or not) should be coded. However, there are times when this should not be done. For example: In reading "A Camel in the Sea," Betsey (activity 1 at the end of this chapter) made so many miscues on the proper names that listing each "new" pronunciation would mean that a large percentage of the 25 coded miscues would be miscues on proper names. Since this would give a very distorted picture of Betsey's miscues and reading strategies, I chose not to number the various substitutions for names. Such repeated attempts should be noted at the bottom of the worksheet, however, or on a separate record sheet.

5. If one particular miscue seems to have caused one or more others, it may be best to consider them together as a single complex miscue. Here is one such example:

Ain't ever heard (anybody)

(call) her (a) beauty.

Instead of three omissions and one insertion, what we seem to have is a longer substitution miscue: "much about her beauty," instead of *anybody call her a beauty*. Regardless of how we first marked these miscues on the worksheet, it is easiest to number and analyze them as a single miscue. (On the other hand, it can be reasonably argued that coding these as one complex miscue obscures rather than highlights the fact that additional miscues may result from readers accommodating following text to previous miscues, as in this example.)

As you become more experienced at analyzing reading miscues, you will probably add some other guidelines for determining how miscues should be selected and numbered for analysis.

Analyzing the Miscues

When you prepare to analyze the miscues, again keep in mind that you bring your own schemas to your reading of the text as well as to your analysis and evaluation of the reader's miscues. The meaning is not "in" the text but rather is created by each reader uniquely. Thus "it is best to avoid the common sense notion that what the reader was supposed to have read was printed in the text" (*RMI Alternatives*, Ch. 4). If this seems appallingly subjective, remember that machine-scored standardized tests only *appear* to provide an objective measure of students' reading ability. As a test-taker, I'd rather have a human being subjectively trying to understand my subjective responses than a computer providing a numerical score without any ability to analyze or understand what good reasons I might have had for doing what I did.

Before analyzing and coding the miscues, it helps to read the completed worksheet once or twice, reproducing all the miscues made by the reader. This should give you a better "feel" for the reader's strategies. Then you will be ready to transfer the miscue data to the coding form. This form can be simple or complex, depending on the kinds of information you want to obtain. The form in Figure 10.1 (see page 347) is somewhere in between the extremes: simple enough to be used by most teachers, but thorough enough to help you gain a better understanding of the reading process and thorough enough to suggest what kind of instructional help readers might need.

For each miscue numbered for analysis, you will first need to indicate what the text itself said, and what the reader said. This information should be entered in the "Text" and "Reader" columns, respectively. Then, for each miscue, you can ask the following questions. *Keep in mind that if the miscue is grammatically and semantically appropriate for the reader's dialect, it should be coded as entirely acceptable* (checked under *yes* in columns 1, 2, 3, and 5).

1. *Did the miscue go with the preceding context?* If the answer is a simple yes, put a check in the *yes* column. *Consider the miscue acceptable if it resulted in a meaningful sentence, even if the meaning is clearly changed;* question 3 asks you specifically to look at whether or not the intended meaning seems to have been altered significantly, but questions 1 and 2 are designed to give credit for meaningful sentences, even if that meaning appears not to be "the same" meaning. If the miscue fits with the preceding grammar but not with the preceding meaning (or vice versa), put a check in the column labeled *partially*; or put a G to indicate that it fits with the grammar and an M to indicate that it fits with meaning, if you want more precise data. If the miscue was not at all acceptable with preceding

context, put a check in the *no* column. In trying to decide whether the miscue fits with the preceding context, read the preceding part of the sentence the way it finally ended up, perhaps with some miscues uncorrected but others corrected.

2. *Did the miscue go with the following context?* Follow essentially the same procedure as explained immediately above, but this time examine only the miscue and what follows it in the sentence.

3. *Did the miscue preserve essential meaning?* This is clearly the most subjective of the questions. Some teachers steeped in the notion that good reading must be word-perfect reading want to code *any* departure from the text as changing essential meaning. However, this is contrary to the whole purpose and spirit of miscue analysis. At the other extreme, some teachers are inclined to ask merely whether the miscue might have affected the reader's understanding of major elements in the story, such as major characters, significant events, plot, and so forth. It is instructive to look at miscues this way, for you will often find that few miscues seem likely to have a major effect upon understanding. For the purposes of this text, however, I have chosen in my examples to consider *whether or not the miscue seems to have preserved the essential meaning of the sentence.* This is a narrower question and one about which it is much easier to obtain consensus, even though the meaning of ''essential'' still invites negotiation among coders working together. If you must, you can put a check on the borderline between the *yes* column and the *no* column to indicate that a miscue *partially* preserved essential meaning.

   Notice that the advantage of construing question 3 conservatively is that you will obtain a clearer picture of the reader's ability to make sense of a text at the sentence level. On the other hand, construing question 3 more liberally gives you a greater appreciation for the reader's ability to grasp the essential meaning of a text despite numerous miscues that seem not to preserve the meaning of individual sentences. Important insights are obtained either way, so it is valuable to try both procedures.

4. *Was the miscue corrected?* If so, put a check in the *yes* column. If not, put a check under *no*. If you marked unsuccessful attempts at correction on the coding sheet, you might want to put a check on the borderline between the two columns, indicating that the reader at least attempted to correct.

5. *Was the miscue either meaning-preserving or corrected?* The point here is that if the miscue preserved essential meaning (column 3), there was no need for the miscue to be corrected. On the other hand, if the miscue didn't preserve meaning but was corrected (column 4), that too means that ultimately the miscue reflected no essential loss of meaning. In other words, check *yes* in column 5 if the miscue received a *yes* in either column 3 or 4; otherwise, check the *no* column. (If you marked some miscues as partially acceptable in column 3, you can again check them on the borderline between *yes* and *no* in column 5, unless they were corrected; in that case, they automatically receive a *yes* in column 5.) In effect, the *yes* column here indicates which miscues initially or ultimately resulted in *no significant loss of comprehension* (at the sentence level, if that's the way you looked at the question in column 3, or at the text level, if that's the way you viewed that question).

Interpreting the Miscue Analysis

Once you have answered these five questions for each miscue, calculate the percentage of responses for each column. If you have coded 25 miscues in the column, simply count the number of checks and multiply by 4.

To interpret the data, it is crucial to consider it in a larger perspective. For example:

1. How *frequent* are the miscues? If the reader has miscued relatively infrequently, then even a preponderance of miscues showing a loss of comprehension (''no'' in column 5) may be of little concern.
2. How does the miscue analysis compare with the retelling? Again, if the retelling has been excellent, then there may be little reason to be concerned about a preponderance of miscues showing a seeming loss of comprehension.

Keep in mind such considerations in deciding how seriously to view the data from the miscue analysis itself.

Remembering this, it may be helpful to know that in general, proficient readers usually produce miscues that are semantically and syntactically acceptable with the preceding and following context at least 70 percent of the time. When they do produce miscues that reflect a loss of meaning, most proficient readers will correct these, most of the time—especially if they consider the miscue significant to the developing meaning. On the other hand, the less proficient readers may produce contextually acceptable miscues as infrequently as 30 percent or 40 percent of the time (K. Goodman, *Theoretically Based Studies* . . . , 1973). Thus keeping in mind that the miscue data does not tell the whole story, we can tentatively suggest the following interpretations, keyed to the questions on my miscue form:

1. *Did the miscue go with the preceding context?* If fewer than 60 percent of the reader's miscues rated a *yes* answer to this question, that probably means that the reader is making inadequate use of preceding grammar and/or meaning to *predict* what is coming next. If in the *partially* column you put G for miscues that went only with the preceding grammar and M for miscues that went only with the preceding meaning, this may give you additional insight into the reader's strategies. Often, readers are much better at predicting a word that fits with the preceding grammar than at predicting a word that fits with the preceding meaning.
2. *Did the miscue go with the following context?* If fewer than 60 percent of the reader's miscues rated a *yes* answer *and if most of these miscues were left uncorrected* (see column 4), this may mean that the reader is making inadequate use of following context to *confirm/correct* his or her predictions and sampling of the text. Remember, however, that some readers tend to correct silently, so that failure to correct disruptive miscues may not adequately reflect the reader's correction, much less his or her actual comprehension. Consider the frequency of the miscues and the adequacy of the retelling before deciding how seriously to take the data from this column.

3. *Did the miscue preserve essential meaning?* Again, if fewer than 60 percent of the reader's miscues rated a *yes* and *if most of these miscues were left uncorrected* (see column 4), this may mean that the reader is making inadequate use of context, perhaps both preceding and following context (compare with columns 1 and 2). Again, however, consider the frequency of the miscues and the adequacy of the retelling before drawing firm conclusions from this data.

4. *Was the miscue corrected?* If fewer than 30 percent of the miscues were corrected, this may be a matter for concern, *unless most of these uncorrected miscues preserved essential meaning*. Once again, however, we should consider this data in light of the frequency of miscues and the adequacy of the retelling, as well as any other obviously relevant information.

5. *Was the miscue either meaning-preserving in context, or else corrected?* Again, if fewer than 60 percent of the miscues rated a *yes* response, this may be a matter for concern, for this column indicates the percentage of miscues that *ultimately* reflected no loss of comprehension: either because they were meaning-preserving in the first place, or because they were corrected. (The *no* column will then indicate the percentage of miscues that ultimately reflected partial or complete loss of comprehension.) Again, though—need I say it?—we must consider this data in light of other relevant factors, such as the frequency of the miscues and the adequacy of the retelling.

In short, though these percentages may provide useful guidelines, they cannot be interpreted in isolation from other relevant data. Just as reading itself is a holistic act, so too is the analysis and assessment of a reader's strategies, strengths, and needs.

What, then, can be learned from the miscue analysis and the retelling? Both kinds of data are important. The miscue questions give some indication of how well the reader seems to comprehend during the actual process of reading; this is sometimes called the *comprehending score*. The retelling provides us with an estimate of how well the reader can remember and interpret what he or she has read; this is sometimes called the *comprehension score*. The comprehending score reflects the *process* of reading, while the comprehension score reflects the *product*.

More specifically, the miscue questions help us understand how the reader goes about the task of reading. The questions on context, preservation of essential meaning, and correction suggest whether or not the reader is making good use of preceding context to predict what will come next and good use of following context to confirm or overtly correct. If miscues showing lack of predicting and/or correcting strategies occur *frequently*, and/or if they seem seriously disruptive of meaning, as reflected in the retelling, then the reader may need guided practice in developing these strategies.

Using the Miscue and Retelling Information to Assist the Reader

You surely have noticed that I tend to be very cautious about too quickly assuming that the reader needs explicit reading strategy lessons to encourage more effective use of predicting and confirming/correcting strategies. This is because many readers who make numerous seemingly disruptive miscues nevertheless grasp the essentials of much of what they read—provided, of course, that the material is interesting to them and the concepts are within their grasp. Often, what such readers need most is plenty of opportunities to read a variety of interesting and meaningful materials, at least some of which they themselves can choose. In conjunction with this, they need to be encouraged to read for meaning and not to worry overmuch about their miscues, to be encouraged to perceive themselves as competent readers who *can*, in fact, comprehend what they read.

For those whose retelling and miscue patterns together suggest they need help in learning to predict and/or confirm/correct more effectively, many of the kinds of reading strategy lessons suggested in Chapter 8 will be appropriate. In addition, two excellent sources of ideas for reading strategy lessons are the following:

Goodman, Yetta M., and Carolyn Burke. 1980. *Reading Strategies: Focus on Comprehension*. New York: Richard C. Owen.

Gilles, Carol, et al., eds. In press. 1987. *Whole Language Strategies for Secondary Students*. New York: Richard C. Owen.

However, what may be most useful for readers who need direct assistance are "mini-lessons" during and after an individual conference with the student. Here are some strategies you might try—not every time the student reads aloud to you, but occasionally, when you and the student have agreed that this is to be an instructional session:

1. Have the reader read a paragraph, and then ask the reader to go back and point out any trouble spots. Discuss, being sure to ask the reader if the meaning became clear(er) as he or she read further. Help the reader use predicting and/or confirming/correcting strategies, along with grapho/phonemic cues, as appropriate. (If necessary, *you* can call attention to apparent trouble spots, but first try to get the reader to do so.)

2. If trying this procedure several times (perhaps over a period of days or weeks) has not resulted in the reader making noticeably better use of the needed strategies, you might try interrupting the reader when he or she has finished a sentence but left uncorrected one or more miscues that cause serious disruption to the meaning of the evolving story. Discuss, again trying to help the reader see that he or she needs to continually ask "Does that sound like language?" and "Does that make sense here?" and to rethink and reread accordingly—or to read ahead, consciously looking for clarification. You shouldn't use this procedure with every problem sentence, of course, because the reader might quickly become frustrated. In general, use the technique sparingly, for it may serve to convince the reader that you really are looking for word-perfect reading rather than expecting the reader to concentrate on the meaning.

3. You can tape record a reading session and play it back, listening together for trouble spots and proceeding from there to discuss and model or "teach" effective strategies.

4. When the reader has become more proficient at using the needed strategies, you can have the reader tape record his or her own reading, play it back, and try again to create sentences that sound like language and make sense in the context of the selection.

Of course, these suggested teaching strategies are subject to modification as the need arises. With practice, you will surely develop alternative procedures of your own.

MISCUE ANALYSIS IN ACTION

Miscue analysis is an invaluable way of determining a reader's use of language cues and reading strategies. But we must remember that miscue analysis does not give us a complete or necessarily accurate picture of a reader's ability to comprehend what he or she reads. A miscue analysis must be balanced by a more direct measure of comprehension, an analysis of the reader's ability to remember and explain what has been read. We need both the *comprehending score* (the percentage of miscues which show no loss of comprehension) and the *comprehension score* (as determined from an analysis of the retelling).

This need for balance should be kept in mind, even though here we are examining just the *miscues* of two readers, Jay and Tony. In both cases, we have fewer than 25 miscues in the available sample, and no detailed retelling data. Unfortunately, I let the retelling transcripts slip through my hands at a time when I did not yet fully appreciate the importance of the retelling. However, the miscues of Jay and Tony are still some of the most interesting and illuminating that I have. Thus, as so often in everyday experience, we will make do with what we have.

Let us begin by looking once again at Jay's miscues on a passage from "Jimmy Hayes and Muriel":

>   *around* ①
> After a hearty supper Hayes joined the smokers about
>
>   *at all* ②
> the fire. His appearance did not ∧ settle all the questions in
>
>   ③
> the minds of his brother rangers. They saw ⌐simply a loose,
>
> ©*young* ④
> lank⌐youth with tow-colored sunburned hair and a berry-
>
>   *ingenious* ⑤
> brown, ingenuous face that wore a quizzical, good-natured
>
> smile.
>
> "Fellows," said the new ranger, "I'm goin' to interduce

⑥ much about ⑦

you to a lady friend of mine. Ain't ever heard anybody

⑦   a⑧

call her a beauty, but you'll all admit she's got some fine

points about her. Come along, Muriel!"

He held open the front of his blue flannel shirt. Out of ⑨

⑨   toad ⑩

it crawled a horned frog. A bright red ribbon was tied

the ⑪

jauntily around its spiky neck. It crawled to its owner's

it ⑫

knee and sat there motionless.

's ⑬

"This here Muriel," said Hayes, with an oratorical wave

⑬. She's ⑬

of his hand, "has got qualities. She never talks back, she

⑭

always stays at home, and she's satisfied with one red

dress for everyday and Sunday, too."

d ⑮

"Look at that blame insect!" said one of the rangers

toads ⑯

with a grin. "I've seen plenty of them horny frogs, but I

c   ⑰

never knew anybody to have one for a side partner. Does

the blame thing know you from anybody else?"

her ⑱

"Take it over there and see," said Hayes.

We hardly need to analyze these miscues in order to see that Jay uses good reading strategies. Jay's miscues are a good starting point, for this very reason: they are relatively easy to analyze. It would be a good idea to photocopy the blank miscue analysis form (Figure 10.1) and try to analyze the miscues yourself, before reading

Reader's name _____

Date _____

Reading selection _____

TEXT	DID THE MISCUE GO WITH THE PRECEDING CONTEXT? 1			DID THE MISCUE GO WITH THE FOLLOWING CONTEXT? 2			DID THE MISCUE PRESERVE ESSENTIAL MEANING? 3		WAS THE MISCUE CORRECTED? 4		WAS THE MISCUE EITHER MEANING-PRESERVING OR CORRECTED? 5 (columns 3&4)	
READER	Yes	Partially	No	Yes	Partially	No	Yes	No	Yes	No	Yes	No
1.												
2.												
3.												
4.												
5.												
6.												
7.												
8.												
9.												
10.												
11.												
12.												
13.												
14.												
15.												
16.												
17.												
18.												
19.												
20.												
21.												
22.												
23.												
24.												
25.												
TOTALS												
PERCENTS												

FIGURE 10.1 Miscue analysis form. From Constance Weaver, Reading Process and Practice: From Socio-Psycho-linguistics to Whole Language (Portsmouth, N.H.: Heinemann, 1988). © 1988 by Constance Weaver.

Reader's name __Jay__
Date __April 1977__
Reading selection __"Jimmy Hayes and Muriel"__

TEXT	READER	DID THE MISCUE GO WITH THE PRECEDING CONTEXT? 1			DID THE MISCUE GO WITH THE FOLLOWING CONTEXT? 2			DID THE MISCUE PRESERVE ESSENTIAL MEANING? 3		WAS THE MISCUE CORRECTED? 4		WAS THE MISCUE EITHER MEANING-PRESERVING OR CORRECTED? 5 (columns 3&4)	
		Yes	Partially	No	Yes	Partially	No	Yes	No	Yes	No	Yes	No
1. about	around	✓			✓			✓			✓	✓	
2.	at all	✓			✓			✓			✓	✓	
3. saw simply	simply saw	✓			✓			✓		✓		✓	
4. youth	young	✓				✓		✓			✓	✓	
5. ingenuous	ingenious	✓				✓			✓		✓		✓
6. ever		✓						✓		✓		✓	
7. anybody about beauty	much about beauty	✓			✓			✓			✓	✓	
8. some	a	✓			✓			✓		✓		✓	
9. out of it crawled	out crawled	✓					✓	✓			✓	✓	
10. frog	toad	✓			✓			✓			✓	✓	
11. its	the	✓			✓			✓			✓	✓	
12. it	it	✓			✓			✓			✓	✓	
13. "This does Muriel--"	"She's got qualities--"	✓			✓			✓			✓	✓	
14. at	at	✓			✓			✓			✓	✓	
15. blame	blamed	✓			✓			✓			✓	✓	
16. frogs	toads	✓			✓			✓		✓		✓	
17. size	her	✓						✓			✓	✓	
18. it	her	✓											
19.													
20.													
21.													
22.													
23.													
24.													
25.													
TOTALS		18	0	0	15	2	1	17	1	3	15	17	1
PERCENTS		100%	0%	0%	83%	11%	6%	95%	5%	17%	83%	95%	5%

FIGURE 10.2 Analysis of Jay's miscues

further. Figure 10.2 reflects my own analysis of Jay's miscues. As always with miscue analysis, I have made a few idiosyncratic and perhaps arbitrary decisions. In most cases, however, we should agree on responses to the miscue questions.

The following summary of Jay's miscues should hardly be surprising:

100% fit completely with the preceding context
83% fit completely with the following context
95% preserved the essential meaning of the sentence
17% were corrected
95% were entirely acceptable in context or were corrected

In short, it appears that Jay is a highly effective reader, one who is well able to predict what is coming next and to correct those miscues that do not fit with the following context. His low percentage of correction is not a matter for concern, since most of his miscues were originally acceptable in context. His 95 percent comprehending score suggests that he understands what he reads, and this was confirmed by his excellent job of retelling the story.

Tony, however, is another matter, as we see in this sample of his miscues from *A Camel in the Sea*. Again, it would be a good idea to first try to analyze the miscues yourself.

Mo – ①
Mohamed (mo-hah′med) loved to go swimming in the sea.

2 Sammon ②
1 Sam –   *③*
How lucky he was to live in a Somali (so-mah′lee) (village)

ran ④
right on the Indian Ocean! The sandy shore rang with the happy

souts ⑤   *⑥*
shouts and cries of the (village) boys and girls. They liked

high ⑦
to race one another into the surf, splashing ^ and spraying

drase ⑧
the water into a white dancing foam before they dove into the

Mola ⑨   *yŭng ⑩*   *Asla ⑪*
waves. Mohamed and his young sister, Āsha (ie′shuh),

(spent all the time they could in the cool, clean) sea,

swimming and playing water games. They were good swimmers

because their mother had taught them.

expert (12)   Holda (13)

Every day except Friday, Mohamed went to school with the

(14)nother viner (15)

other village boys. The class was outdoors, and the children

beaches (16) frose (17)   shape (18)

sat on little benches in front of the teacher in the shade

of a tall palm tree. They did not have books, so the boys

ramped (19)

repeated everything the teacher said, over and over, until

other classrooms hurt. (20)   vengil (21)

they knew their lessons by heart. The girls of the village

did not go to school, for the people thought that school was

imprentice (22)   to (23)

not as important for girls as it was for boys.

In analyzing Tony's miscues (Figure 10.3), I have made certain assumptions, partly on the basis of his retelling session (which, as mentioned, I unfortunately did not keep a record of). First, I have assumed that his nonword miscues on the proper names reflect no essential loss of meaning—even from the very beginning, I am assuming that by the time Tony got to the second word, *loved*, he must have realized that "Mo-" was a proper name. It seems clear that Tony at least knows that these are the names of people and places, and that "Mola/Molda" is a boy and "Asla" is his sister. I have also assumed that Tony's other nonwords are *grammatically* acceptable with both preceding and following context. This seems reasonably clear with miscues like "souts" for *shouts* and "ramped" for *repeated*, where Tony appears to have retained the grammatical ending of the original. It is admittedly less clear with miscues like "imprentice" for *important* and "viner" or "vengil" for *village*, so there is indeed room for difference of opinion here. In part, the original investigator used Tony's intonation as an indication that these nonwords were grammatically appropriate. Except for the proper names, these other nonword miscues showed no evidence of preserving meaning at the sentence level, as far as I could see, so I coded them all as not semantically acceptable with the preceding or following context. Thus, all of these nonword miscues except for the proper names are listed in the *partially* column for questions 1 and 2, and coded as *not* preserving essential meaning. You might try to see if you can grasp the reasoning behind my other coding decisions, especially those with which you do not initially agree.

Even with some variations in coding from person to person, Tony's miscues reflect certain strengths. If at first he does not get a word, he does not merely give up: he makes several attempts at the word *village*, for example, after initially omitting it. Some of his miscues clearly show a concern for meaning, as when he

Reader's name Tony
Date April 1974
Reading selection excerpt from "A Camel in the Sea"

TEXT	READER	DID THE MISCUE GO WITH THE PRECEDING CONTEXT? 1			DID THE MISCUE GO WITH THE FOLLOWING CONTEXT? 2			DID THE MISCUE PRESERVE ESSENTIAL MEANING? 3		WAS THE MISCUE CORRECTED? 4		WAS THE MISCUE EITHER MEANING-PRESERVING OR CORRECTED? 5 (columns 3&4)	
		Yes	Partially	No	Yes	Partially	No	Yes	No	Yes	No	Yes	No
1. Mohamed	Ho —	✓			✓		✓	✓			✓	✓	
2. Somali	Sammon	✓						✓			✓	✓	
3. village	village		✓	✓							✓		✓
4. rang	ran	✓									✓		✓
5. shouts	souts		✓			✓			✓		✓		✓
6. village	village	✓	✓		✓			✓			✓	✓	
7. —	high	✓			✓			✓			✓	✓	
8. dancing	avase	✓	✓			✓			✓		✓		✓
9. Mohamed	Hola	✓			✓		✓	✓			✓	✓	
10. young	yang	✓			✓				✓		✓		✓
11. Asha	Asla	✓							✓		✓		✓
12. except	expert		✓		✓		✓	✓			✓	✓	
13. Mohamed	Holda	✓			✓				✓		✓		✓
14. other	nother		✓ ✓			✓			✓		✓		✓
15. village	viner				✓		✓		✓		✓		✓
16. benches	beaches	✓			✓				✓		✓		✓
17. front	frose					✓			✓		✓		✓
18. shade	shape	✓			✓				✓		✓		✓
19. repeated	ramped	✓	✓			✓			✓		✓		✓
20. their lessons by heard	other classrooms back	✓							✓		✓		✓
21. village	venal	✓	✓			✓			✓		✓		✓
22. important	imprentice		✓						✓		✓		✓
23. it	to			✓			✓		✓		✓		✓
24.													
25.													
TOTALS		10	10	2	8	10	4	7	16	0	23	7	16
PERCENTS		45%	45%	10%	36%	45%	19%	30%	70%	0%	100%	30%	70%

FIGURE 10.3 Analysis of Tony's miscues

351

inserts "high" in "splashing *high* and spraying the water." He makes good use of grapho/phonemic cues, especially at the beginnings and ends of words. And even some of his nonword miscues strongly suggest that he is preserving the grammar of the original, resulting in a high percentage of miscues analyzed as partially acceptable with the preceding and following context. Note, however, his other percentages, which would not change even if some of my "partially acceptable" codings on the nonwords were coded as unacceptable:

45% fit completely with the preceding context
36% fit completely with the following context
30% preserved the essential meaning of the sentence
 0% were corrected
30% were meaning-preserving in context or were corrected

His miscues suggest that he needs help in predicting something that makes sense with what comes before and in correcting whatever does not make sense with what comes after. His comprehending score, the last percentage listed, suggests that his use of reading strategies is only somewhat effective.

Despite this initial picture of Tony, we might have found that he comprehended the story moderately or even extremely well: sometimes readers who make numerous low-quality miscues do, in fact, have good comprehension. But in Tony's case, the retelling was unfortunately no more encouraging than the miscue analysis: it was clear that he needed to read for meaning, and to more effectively use semantic as well as syntactic and grapho/phonemic cues in order to predict and to confirm and correct.

Obviously the original retelling data and the miscue form itself did not supply us with all of these conclusions. Rather, the insights came from the *analysis* that was necessary in order to respond to the questions about each miscue. This, of course, will always be true: at best, a form does nothing more than help us get our analysis together.

For analyzing Tony's miscues, a slightly different form might have been more helpful. Instead of the two questions about context, we might better have had two questions like the following (see Figure 10.4): *Did the miscue create a grammatical sentence? Did the miscue create a meaningful sentence* (whether or not it was "the same" meaning)? These new questions for columns 1 and 2 would quickly have pinpointed Tony's basic strength and his basic weakness: he uses syntactic cues, but seems to make little use of semantic cues when the going gets tough (see Figure 10.5). This conclusion is confirmed by his correction pattern: he has corrected none of the miscues that fail to preserve meaning. And while he *might* have corrected silently rather than overtly, his weak retelling suggests that he probably did not.

SELECTING AND DEVISING MISCUE ANALYSIS FORMS

Clearly my basic miscue analysis form has both advantages and disadvantages: on the one hand, it is easy to draw tentative conclusions from the form as to whether the reader might need assistance in using syntactic and semantic cues more effectively to

Reader's name _____
Date _____
Reading selection _____

TEXT	READER	DID THE MISCUE PRESERVE GRAMMAR? 1			DID THE MISCUE PRESERVE MEANING? 2			DID THE MISCUE PRESERVE ESSENTIAL MEANING? 3		WAS THE MISCUE CORRECTED? 4		WAS THE MISCUE EITHER MEANING-PRESERVING OR CORRECTED? 5 (columns 3&4)	
		Yes	Partially	No	Yes	Partially	No	Yes	No	Yes	No	Yes	No
1.													
2.													
3.													
4.													
5.													
6.													
7.													
8.													
9.													
10.													
11.													
12.													
13.													
14.													
15.													
16.													
17.													
18.													
19.													
20.													
21.													
22.													
23.													
24.													
25.													
TOTALS													
PERCENTS													

FIGURE 10.4 Alternative miscue analysis form. From Constance Weaver. Reading Process and Practice: From Socio-Psycholinguistics to Whole Language (Portsmouth, N.H.: Heinemann, 1988). © 1988 by Constance Weaver.

Reader's name _Tony_

Date _April 1974_

Reading selection _excerpt from "A Camel in the Sea"_

TEXT	READER	DID THE MISCUE PRESERVE GRAMMAR? 1			DID THE MISCUE PRESERVE MEANING? 2			DID THE MISCUE PRESERVE ESSENTIAL MEANING? 3		WAS THE MISCUE CORRECTED? 4		WAS THE MISCUE EITHER MEANING-PRESERVING OR CORRECTED? 5 (columns 3&4)	
		Yes	Partially	No	Yes	Partially	No	Yes	No	Yes	No	Yes	No
1. Mohamed	Ho —	✓					✓	✓			✓	✓	
2. Somali	Sammon	✓			✓			✓			✓	✓	
3. village	van			✓			✓		✓		✓		✓
4. rang	ran	✓					✓		✓		✓		✓
5. shouts	souts	✓					✓		✓		✓		✓
6. village	high	✓					✓		✓		✓		✓
7.		✓			✓			✓			✓	✓	
8. dancing	arase	✓			✓			✓			✓	✓	
9. Mohamed	Hola	✓					✓		✓		✓		✓
10. young	yung	✓			✓			✓			✓	✓	
11. Asha	Asla	✓					✓		✓		✓		✓
12. except	expert	✓					✓		✓		✓		✓
13. Mohamed	Holda	✓			✓			✓			✓	✓	
14. other	nother	✓					✓		✓		✓		✓
15. village	viner	✓					✓		✓		✓		✓
16. benches	beaches	✓			✓				✓		✓		✓
17. front	frose	✓			✓				✓		✓		✓
18. shade	shape	✓					✓		✓		✓		✓
19. repeated	ramped	✓					✓		✓		✓		✓
20. their knees by heart	their class rooms hurt	✓					✓		✓		✓		✓
21. village	venail	✓					✓		✓		✓		✓
22. important	imp/ventire	✓					✓		✓		✓		✓
23. it	to	✓					✓		✓		✓		✓
24.													
25.													
TOTALS		21	0	1	9	0	14	7	16	0	23	7	16
PERCENTS		95%	0%	5%	39%	0%	61%	30%	70%	0%	100%	30%	70%

FIGURE 10.5 _Alternative analysis of Tony's miscues_

354

predict and/or confirm and correct. On the other hand, the form is in some ways both too complicated and too simple: too complicated for day-to-day use with whole classes of students, and yet not detailed and sophisticated enough for some kinds of research, or for studying in depth some of the more interesting students one might encounter in the classroom.

One obvious shortcoming is that the form provides no systematic way for examining the reader's use of grapho/phonemic cues in relationship to his or her use of syntactic and semantic cues. We know from years of miscue research that the best readers typically make miscues which show less grapho/phonemic similarity to the text word than the miscues of poorer readers (for example, see p. 326). Less proficient readers tend to make less effective use of syntactic and especially semantic cues: often they read to identify words and use sounding-out as their major conscious strategy for dealing with words not immediately recognized on sight. But to confirm or disprove this in a particular case, it would be useful to compare a reader's use of grapho/phonemic cues with his or her use of syntactic and semantic cues.

The most detailed and sophisticated form for obtaining such information is Kenneth Goodman's Taxonomy of Reading Miscues, included as an appendix in the *RMI Alternatives*. The miscue analysis form in the original *RMI Manual* asks questions dealing with the extent to which substitution miscues resemble the text word graphically and phonemically, as do the first two of the forms in the newer *RMI Alternatives*.

What most classroom teachers need, however, is not more detailed forms and procedures but simpler ones that will be less time-consuming to use, yet still sophisticated enough to yield information useful in planning instruction. Once you have gained some experience with analyzing readers' miscues, you should be able to choose or devise simpler forms that will be adequate for classroom assessment and record-keeping. For example, as you listen to a student read, you might simply keep a running tally of your responses to one crucial question about each miscue:

Was the miscue either meaning-preserving in context or corrected?

If the reader has made a large number of miscues that are neither meaning-preserving nor corrected, and if the retelling is also sketchy, there is good reason to assume that the reader may need help in reading for meaning.

Although impressionistic responses without prior tabulation of data are obviously risky, with experience you might be able to listen to a student read, or at least to replay a tape recording of a reading session, and respond appropriately to questions like these:

	seldom		sometimes		usually
1. Does the reader use preceding context to predict what is coming next?	1	2	3	4	5
2. Do the reader's miscues make sense in context?	1	2	3	4	5

		seldom		sometimes		usually
3. Does the reader correct those miscues that do not make sense in context?		1	2	3	4	5
4. Are the reader's miscues either meaning-preserving in context or corrected?		1	2	3	4	5
5. Does the reader pay too much attention to grapho/phonemic cues and too little attention to syntactic and/or semantic cues (or vice versa)?		1	2	3	4	5

Of course it is best to use such an impressionistic checklist only after you have developed substantial experience listening to and analyzing readers' miscues.

The last three alternative forms offered in the *Reading Miscue Inventory: Alternative Procedures* differ from all the previously mentioned forms in one major way: they focus on whole sentences rather than on individual miscues (Y. Goodman, Watson, and Burke 1987, Ch. 6). Thus the most thorough of the alternative procedures offers questions such as these:

Is the sentence syntactically (grammatically) acceptable in the reader's dialect and within the context of the entire passage?

Is the sentence semantically acceptable in the reader's dialect and within the context of the entire story?

Does the sentence, as finally produced by the reader, change the meaning of the story?

In addition, there are questions asking the degree to which substitution miscues look like the text item and sound like the expected response. The third of the proffered RMI procedures is similar to this second one, except that the miscues are both marked and coded on the worksheet; there is no separate coding sheet. The fourth and simplest procedure does not even involve tape recording the session, though of course you *could* tape record and replay the reading until you have gained enough confidence to analyze miscues on-the-spot. This procedure involves asking just one question of each sentence:

Does the sentence, as the reader left it, make sense within the context of the selection?

Sentences are coded *yes* if they are totally acceptable semantically within the context of the entire selection, and/or if they are corrected. Otherwise, they are coded *no*.

Obviously this procedure is to be used only when one has had sufficient experience with miscue analysis to be able to make assessments quickly and reliably. Before using such simplified procedures, it would be best to do several detailed analyses first and to consult the *Reading Miscue Inventory: Alternative Procedures* (Y. Goodman, Watson, and Burke 1987) for detailed suggestions on how to use the alternative procedures.

As I see it, then, miscue analysis is valuable in several ways. First and most important, it gives teachers invaluable insight into the nature of the reading process and a greater appreciation for readers' strengths. It can give teachers added insight into how students perceive the reading process—their ideas of what reading is and how it is done. It can help teachers avoid overrelying on the ofttimes misleading results of standardized tests and also help them avoid the often erroneous assumption that few miscues indicate good comprehension and numerous miscues indicate poor comprehension. In addition, it can provide useful information as to the kinds of instructional help that individual students might need, provided that the teacher looks not just at the miscues themselves but at the relative frequency of the miscues and the quality of the retelling.

Fortunately, miscue analysis is almost as variable as it is invaluable. Different forms and different procedures can be adopted or developed, depending on your particular needs and resources. What's crucial is not any one particular miscue analysis form or procedure, but the underlying philosophy. As suggested earlier, a ''psycholinguistic'' form of assessment will use selections of sufficient length for the reader to develop a sense of an emerging whole, and these selections will be written in natural language, with both language and concepts being appropriate to the individual reader. In addition, the adopted forms and procedures should reflect the fact that no two readers will ever read or understand a given selection in the same way; emphasize the fact that getting meaning is more important than reproducing surface structure; help identify a reader's strengths as well as his or her weaknesses; examine miscues in the context of the whole sentence and whole selection; reward the correction of miscues that do not fit the context; provide insight into a reader's use of language cues and reading strategies; suggest, in general terms, what kinds of strategy lessons a reader might need; and provide retelling data that enables teachers to interpret the miscue data within a larger perspective.

In the next chapter, we will discuss the use and effectiveness of such reading strategy lessons within the context of a whole-language approach to helping readers with particular needs.

ACTIVITIES AND PROJECTS FOR FURTHER EXPLORATION

1. To gain practice in analyzing and evaluating miscues, you might begin by analyzing David's (pp. 5–6) or Anne's (p. 114) or Billy's (pp. 128–29). Use one of the more detailed forms suggested here (p. 347 or p. 353), or else devise a similar form. Then, to gain further practice, analyze Betsey's miscues as illustrated below. You should begin by reading the passage as she read it, complete with all

her miscues. As you will see, her miscues improve as she gets further and further into the story. Decide which consecutive stretch of 25 miscues to analyze, and again use one of the more detailed forms. Judging by your examination and analysis of Betsey's miscues, what are her reading strengths? What are her weaknesses? What kind of reading instruction and assistance do you think she needs? Discuss your conclusions and recommendations.

   The reading selection is adapted from Lee Garrett Goetz, *A Camel in the Sea* (1966, pp. 11–30). Again, the line divisions reflect the way the material was presented to the reader. To give a more balanced picture of the reader's strategies, this time I have numbered only the first substitution for each of the proper names, even though the subsequent substitutions are not always the same.

Mahoad ① *s* ② *-minging* ③
Mohamed loved to go swimming in the sea. How lucky he was

island ④   ⑤
to live in a Somali village right on the Indian Ocean! The sandy

shore rang with the happy (shouts and cries of the village boys)

                               ⑥ *2 surfy*   *sp* ⑦
(and girls.) They liked to race one another into the surf, splash-   *1 surfing*

                                        form ⑧   *the* ⑨
ing and spraying the water into a white dancing foam before they

                    Mohema   *2 Ala* ⑩
dove into the waves. Mohamed and his young sister, Asha, spent   *1 Almea*

all the time they could in the cool, clean sea swimming and play-

ing water games. They were good swimmers because their mother

had taught them.

         especially ⑪ *Mohema*   ⑫
Every day except Friday, Mohamed went to (the) school with

another ⑬
the other village boys. The class was outdoors, and the children

      a ⑭   ⑮   *and* ⑯ *2 shell* ⑰
sat on little benches in front of the teacher in the shade of   *1 sand*

⑱ *the*
a (tall palm tree. They did not have books, so the) boys repeated

everything the teacher said, over and over, until they knew their
~~were learned~~ (20) (19)

~~it~~ (21)   (22)
lessons by heart. The girl~~s~~of the village did not go to school,

(C) ~~taught~~ (23)   s (C) ~~were~~ (24)
for the people thought that school was not as important for girls

as it was for boys.

Sunday (25)   Madoona
On sunny days, as soon as school was over, Mohamed went with

Ashes (C) wa — (26)   's (27)
his mother and Asha to wash the family clothes. His mother stood
the 2 putty (28)
i pondy

in the water and scrubbed and pounded the clothes until they were
(C) had (29)   2 Madoona   Ash
1 Madoo

clean. Then she handed them to Mohamed and Asha, who took them
agreed (30)
and arranged them on the beach to dry.

Madoona   (31) ed
Mohamed had helped his mother and (Asha) wash the clothes ever

since he could remember. He was very much surprised, therefore,

one day not long before his tenth birthday, when his mother told

(32)
him not to come with her and (Asha.)
(C) don't (33)   2 Madoona
1 Madoosa
"I do not want you to help us any more, Mohamed," his mother

Ashes
said. "It is time that Asha had more work to do around the

(34)   taught (35)
house. Beside~~s~~ in two more years you will be thought of as a

troubles (36)   (37)
man by our tribe, and it is not fitting that people see you

will (38)
always doing women's work. From now on, you help your father in

ship (39)   we (40)
the shop and Asha will help me at home."

Madoona　　　　　　　　*suprised* ㊶
That first day, Mohamed felt quite grown-up and superior

Azza
when he saw his mother and Asha carrying a heavy basket to the

beach. But this feeling did not last long. He had no one to

had Azza ㊷
play with! He and Asha had played together for so long that the

other children were used to his not playing with them.

①*Ma doona*
⓪*Madoosa*
Mohamed stood and watched the other boys play "kick the ㊸

the ㊹　　　　　　　㊺
ball" and "hunt for robber" and "water tag." When no one

the ㊻
called him for a game, he turned and walked down the beach,　㊿

㊼ *a* ㊽　　　　　　　*tried* ㊾ *thoughtful*
kicking up the sand with one foot, and trying to look as though

©*did* ㊿¹　　　*ed* ㊿²
he really didn't care or want to play.

Hamasam ㊾³
Finally, he decided to take his problem to his father, Hassan.

's 54
"Mother doesn't want me to help wash the family clothes any more,

Madooha　　　　　*Ashes*
Father," Mohamed told his father. "Asha has her work and her

friends, but now I have no one to play with."

Probably 55　　　　*Madooha*
"Perhaps your mother is right, Mohamed," his father said,

©*help* 56
and he put down the piece of board that he held in his hand.

ship
"It is time that you should learn to help me in the shop."

© *when* 57
Hassan was a builder of fishing boats that went out to sea

every morning and returned to the shore every evening. His

ship

small shop was right on the beach.

                                                Madooha

    "When you come home from school each day, Mohamed," said

                                trouble (58)

his father, "I will show you the beginning of your trade. You

will be a builder of boats like me."

                                          Madooha

    "But father, when will I have time for games?" Mohamed asked.

    "You help me a little, and I shall see that you have plenty

                 Hansa   *slowly* (59)

of time to yourself," Hassan promised. He laughed softly. "I

do remember that boys need to have time to think and play. You

shall have it, my son."

                    desert (60)

    That summer was the driest one that anyone—even the oldest

  Madooha's (61)

people in Mohamed's village—could recall. It did not rain at

all. Each day the people would look up at the sky to see if they

could see any rain clouds. But each day the sun shone brightly.

                      (2)*hiding* (62)
                      (1)*hidden*   (63)

There was not even one cloud to hide the sun's face for a while.

Soon all the leaves of the trees started to turn brown. The

    dropped (64) (65)

flowers drooped lower and lower on their stems. Finally they

became dry as paper. When the wind blew the dry leaves, they

                      's (66)

made a noise like a snake slipping through the sand.

Day after day the sun beat down, and there was no shade from

leaves ⑥⑦ *Jane* ⑥⑧ *Julie*

the leafless trees. June and July came and went without rain.

August was nearly over and still no rain.

2. After you have practiced analyzing some miscues that have already been recorded and numbered, it is time to try the whole procedure discussed in this chapter: everything from preparing for the reading session to analyzing and evaluating the retelling and the reader's miscues, and finally to interpreting the results and making recommendations for reading instruction. As a valuable learning experience, I would recommend that you try one of the following:

a. Compare a good reader (someone who usually comprehends) with a poor reader (someone who usually has trouble comprehending). Pay attention to the differences in their miscues. It should be interesting to have both persons read the same material. But in order to do this, you may have to select students from different grade levels: for example, a good third-grade reader and a relatively poor fourth-grade or fifth-grade reader. After you have collected and analyzed the data from each reader, compare the results. Do the two readers seem to use the same reading strategies? Discuss this question in detail.

b. If you know of two teachers who have widely differing views of reading and/ or methods of reading instruction, choose one of the poorer readers from each class, and compare them. Do they seem to use the same reading strategies? In each case, does there seem to be any relation between the teacher's views or methods, and the student's approach to reading? Discuss in detail.

3. Once you have become fairly comfortable with miscue analysis, try to use one of the short, impressionistic forms on pp. 355–56. At first, it is a good idea to tape record the person's reading, so that you can listen to the miscues two or three times if necessary. Then, record your overall impressions on the short form. If at all possible, compare your analysis with that of someone who is more experienced in miscue analysis.

READINGS FOR FURTHER EXPLORATION

Harris, Larry A., and Jerome A. Niles. Spring 1982. An Analysis of Published Informal Reading Inventories. *Reading Horizons* 22: 159–74. Provides a useful analysis of IRIs, with various factors considered.

D'Angelo, Karen, and Marc Mahlios, April 1983. Insertion and Omission Miscues of Good and Poor Readers. *The Reading Teacher* 36: 778–82. Concludes that the insertion and omission miscues made by both good and poor readers at "instruction'' or ''frustration'' levels cause very little syntactic or semantic distortion, and recommends that therefore, miscue analysis should focus on only substitutions and corrected substitutions.

Smith, Laura, and Constance Weaver. Fall 1978. A Psycholinguistic Look at the Informal Reading Inventory, Part I: Looking at the Quality of Readers' Miscues: A Rationale and an Easy Method. *Reading Horizons* 19: 12–22. Presents another form for analyzing miscues and determining instructional needs.

Taylor, Jo Ellyn. September 1977. Making Sense: The Basic Skill in Reading. *Language Arts* 54: 668–72. Presents an easy way to assess readers' concern for meaning, with a particularly interesting discussion of self-taught readers.

Goodman, Yetta, Dorothy Watson, and Carolyn Burke. 1987. *Reading Miscue Inventory: Alternative Procedures*. New York: Richard C. Owen. This manual discusses in much more depth four major ways to assess readers' miscues and retellings. In addition, it demonstrates what kind of instructional program and reading strategy lessons the authors would recommend for one of the children whose reading is discussed in depth.

Goodman, Yetta, and Carolyn Burke. 1980. *Reading Strategies: Focus on Comprehension*. New York: Richard C. Owen. This book is invaluable in offering strategy lessons designed to help readers with particular needs.

Gilles, Carol, Mary Bixby, Paul Crowley, Shirley Crenshaw, Margaret Henrichs, Frances Reynolds, and Donelle Pyle. In press. *Whole Language Strategies for Secondary Students*. New York: Richard C. Owen. This book offers valuable strategies for use with secondary students.

11

How Can We Help Those with Reading Difficulties?

Students must have time to read. . . . We suggest that 70–80% of the time allotted to reading instruction be devoted to real reading and writing, with 20–30% of the time spent in working on instructional strategy lessons that include thinking and talking about reading and writing.

—Yetta Goodman, Dorothy
Watson, and Carolyn Burke

QUESTIONS FOR JOURNALS AND DISCUSSION

1. How can we determine students' preferred reading styles and adjust instruction accordingly, so as to prevent or at least minimize reading difficulties?

2. Why should reading strategy lessons constitute only a small part of the total reading program for those who are having difficulty reading?

3. How might we assess beginning readers' awareness of the conventions of print and of the terminology used in reading instruction?

4. How might we design a whole-language reading recovery program for young readers who appear to be "at risk" as readers?

5. In general, how can reading strategy lessons be incorporated into a whole-language lesson?

6. What kinds of evidence suggest the wisdom of this kind of approach to helping readers with particular difficulties?

7. What is "dyslexia"?

8. How might different kinds of reading difficulties be related to different kinds of hemispheric processing in the brain?

9. Why might a whole-language reading recovery program be the best for addressing various kinds of reading difficulties, and specifically what kinds of activities might be most effective?

10.   How can inappropriate reading instruction actually help to create readers who become progressively poorer—or at least not better?

11.   How might we develop a whole-language, whole-brain, whole-curriculum approach to educating the whole child?

PREVENTING OR MINIMIZING READING DIFFICULTIES: MATCHING STUDENTS' READING STYLES

Before discussing how to help those with reading difficulties, it seems appropriate to consider additional ways of preventing or minimizing such difficulties. To begin, let me ask some questions about the conditions under which you prefer to read. When you read a book for sheer enjoyment, do you

prefer to sit in a straight chair or prefer to sit on a comfortable chair or couch—or even to lie in bed?

prefer to munch and/or drink something while you read or prefer not to eat or drink?

prefer quiet, prefer to listen to music or prefer to hear talking in the background?

prefer to read in bright light or in dim or subdued lighting?

prefer to read by yourself or with others?

As an adult, you can often choose the conditions under which you read for pleasure—or you can choose not to read. Possibly one reason so many adults do not think of reading as pleasurable is that as schoolchildren, they rarely or never had the opportunity to read under conditions that made reading pleasurable for them. This is one of the reasonable inferences that might be drawn from research into students' learning styles. It may explain in large part why, in addition to the millions of adults who cannot read even functionally, there are millions and millions more who can read but choose not to.

What Are Some Factors Involved in Different Reading Styles?

The foremost researcher on reading styles is Marie Carbo, whose work draws upon the earlier and more general learning styles research by Rita and Kenneth Dunn. In determining a person's learning and reading style, these researchers examine a variety of environmental, emotional, sociological, physical, and psychological factors, including those mentioned above (see Figure 11.1.).

For reading and learning to read, some of the most crucial factors seem to be the following:

Whether the person is global and/or analytic in the processing of information or strong in both styles, and whether the reading methods match the reader's style(s).

I. **Environmental Stimuli** *Does the student prefer to read:*

Sound with music, with talking, in silence?
Light in bright or dim light?
Temperature in a warm or cool temperature?
Design in a formal design (hard chair at a desk) or an informal design (soft chair, rug, floor)?

II. **Emotional Stimuli** *When reading, is the student:*

Motivation self-motivated, not self-motivated, motivated by peers, motivated by adults?

Does the student:

Persistence complete reading tasks?
Responsibility do the reading work agreed upon or assigned?
Structure prefer: little or much direction when reading?
  many or few choices of reading materials?
  reading work checked immediately or seldom?
  reading work checked by peers, adults, self?

III. **Sociological Stimuli** *Does the student prefer to read:*

Peers with five or six students?
Self alone?
Pair with one student?
Teacher with a teacher?
Varied with a teacher and students?

IV. **Physical Stimuli** *Does the student read best:*

Perceptual when taught through his/her visual modality, auditory modality, tactual modality, kinesthetic modality, and/or with a multisensory approach?

Does the student prefer to read:

Intake when permitted to eat and drink?
Time in the morning, early afternoon, late afternoon, evening?
Mobility when permitted to move?

FIGURE 11.1 *Elements of reading style. From the* Reading Style Inventory Manual *by Marie Carbo, 1981, p. 2.*

Whether the person learns best through kinesthetic and/or tactile and/or visual and/or auditory modes, and whether the reading method matches the reader's modality strengths.

Whether the reader's strongest needs are met in terms of environmental, emotional, sociological, and physical factors.

Preferences in the latter areas vary, of course, from child to child, and certain of the child's preferences may change as he or she gets older. Young children, for example, overwhelmingly express a preference for reading in pairs rather than reading alone or in small groups, such as the traditional reading group. As they move into the intermediate grades, more and more children express a preference for reading alone. Another age-related difference is that younger children tend to prefer structure, to be told fairly precisely what they should do. As children get older, they more and more express a preference for less structure. The age factor intersects in this case with a competence factor: poor readers generally prefer structure, but they prefer less structure when they become more competent. Many poor readers also express a preference for an informal and comfortable reading environment, such as that created by rugs and carpet squares, pillows, and beanbag chairs. They often prefer dim lighting, and they often prefer to read in the late morning rather than in the early morning or afternoon. They may have high mobility needs, a high need to move around. And they may have high intake needs—that is, a high need to eat or drink while reading. Allowing them to munch on healthful snacks like carrot and celery sticks, raw broccoli and cauliflower pieces, tends to reduce their need for mobility, as does creating an informal and comfortable environment in which they can read.

Providing a reading environment that accommodates the strongest of a student's preferences in such environmental, emotional, sociological, and psychological areas can significantly increase students' reading achievement (Carbo, Dunn, and Dunn 1986, pp. 26–29, 46–48; also Carbo 1983). However, the factors that are probably most crucial for initially learning to read are the reader's overall processing style, global and/or analytic, and the reader's preferred learning modalities: kinesthetic and/or tactile and/or visual and/or auditory.

What distinguishes global and analytic learning styles? In general, people who are strongly global tend to

1. Learn things as wholes, or by moving from whole to part.
2. Learn things better in a meaningful context.
3. Need to be emotionally involved in order to learn.
4. Be more interested in the feelings generated by a story than in factual recall of details.
5. Be less interested in tasks that require analysis, such as phonics.
6. Find it easier to learn to recognize content words and emotionally charged words like "elephant" and "love" than supposedly simple words like "a" and "the" or phonically regular sets of words like "cat," "fat," "hat."

In contrast, people who are strongly analytic tend to

1. Learn and do things sequentially and logically, step-by-step.
2. Be more able than globals to learn things just for the sake of learning them, whether or not they're presented in a meaningful context.
3. Have a lesser need than globals to be emotionally involved in order to learn.
4. Be more able than globals to learn facts, such as the literal details of a story, or dates, names, and such in social studies.
5. Have an easy time with and enjoy tasks that require analysis, such as phonics.
6. Find it easier than globals to learn to recognize words that have no emotional content and/or words that are phonically regular, like "cat," "fat," "hat."

Some people, both children and adults, are strong in only one of these kinds of processing, while others are strong in both. Children who are both global and analytic tend to be good readers, probably in part because any reading program is bound to have matched one or the other of their strengths.

There appears to be a correlation between processing styles and preferred modalities. People who are strongly analytic tend to be more auditory, while those who are strongly global tend to be kinesthetic and tactile and/or visual, as is suggested more visually below:

$$
\text{Globals—tend to be} \left\{ \begin{array}{l} \text{Kinesthetic and tactile} \\ \textit{and/or} \\ \text{Visual} \end{array} \right.
$$

Analytics—tend to be   Auditory

However, it should be remembered that these are only tendencies, not invariants.

Perhaps some of these modalities need somewhat more explanation. A person who has a strong *auditory* preference is one who learns readily by listening. An "auditory learner" can be defined as one who recalls at least 75 percent of what is discussed in a normal 40 to 45 minute period. The younger children are, the less likely they are to be auditory (Carbo, Dunn, and Dunn 1986, p. 13). However, even for adults, auditory is typically the *least* preferred mode. Thus even with the majority of adults, lecturing is not the most effective method of teaching! However, Carbo claims that students who are both analytic and auditory will typically find phonics both easy and fun to learn. As Carbo defines it, a child who is more auditory than visual learns to read best by focusing on letter/sound correspondences rather than on larger units.

Someone who has a strong *visual* preference is one who learns easily by viewing, watching, and observing. Children typically become more visual as they mature, and the visual modality is the strongest preference for many adults. (One wonders to what extent this preference might be due to the influence of television.) As Carbo defines it, a child who is more visual than auditory learns to read best by initially focusing on whole words (or, I'd say, even larger units), rather than on letter/sound correspondences.

A *tactile* learner is one who learns easily by touching, manipulating, and handling. For example: A tactile learner is likely to assemble a child's bicycle or a set of bookshelves by handling the parts and trying to figure out how they go together, rather than by reading the instructions. This is particularly likely if the person is global rather than analytic. Reading-related activities which can help tactile learners are writing independently, tracing letters in the air, tracing plastic blocks or letters, tracing letters in sand or salt, tracing letters made of clay, and so forth. Running a finger over the letters helps the child remember the letter and the word.

A *kinesthetic* learner is one who learns easily by doing and experiencing, someone who learns best when emotionally involved. Actions are the external manifestation of a kinesthetic learner, while feelings are the internal manifestation. Kinesthetic learners need both to do and to feel. For such children, it is particularly important to introduce new concepts and information through field trips, cooking and baking, drawing and sculpting, creative drama and other activities that involve experiencing and feeling.

How Important Is It to Match Reading Styles with Reading Methods?

The research that is beginning to accumulate strongly demonstrates the importance of matching reading styles with reading methods. Carbo summarizes in ''Reading Styles Research: 'What Works' Isn't Always Phonics,'' 1987:

> The research on reading styles makes one thing clear: reading achievement generally depends on how well the instructional program accommodates a given youngster's natural reading style. During our four years of matching instructional approaches to children's reading styles, my colleagues and I saw students make better-than-average gains in reading, enjoy learning to read, and develop better self-concepts—even though these youngsters had previously been labeled ''emotionally disturbed,'' ''learning disabled,'' or ''poor readers.''

These claims are documented in more detail in Carbo 1983, February 1983, April 1983, and in Carbo, Dunn, and Dunn 1986.

Of particular note is a study by Lois LaShell. After determining the reading styles of her handicapped students and matching instruction to their styles, LaShell was able to mainstream 37 of the 40 students the following year; she had mainstreamed only 2 of 40 the previous year. In a doctoral study, LaShell then studied the reading achievement of 90 learning disabled students in grades 2–6. The control group was taught with a strong phonics program, while the individual reading styles of the experimental group were matched with appropriate materials and procedures. Most of the students in the experimental group were tactile/kinesthetic/global students who needed ''hands-on'' materials and who learned well with holistic reading approaches, not with phonics. After ten months, the control group had advanced only 3.9 months in reading achievement, while the experimental group gained 1.4 years. Perhaps most remarkable is the fact that the previous year, with the same teachers and a great deal of phonics instruction, the experimental group had progressed only 4 months in reading achievement (Carbo, "Reading Styles Research: 'What Works' Isn't Always Phonics," 1987; LaShell 1986).

Research with older disabled readers has produced equally impressive gains. For example, Helene Hodges worked with twice-retained fifteen-year-olds in Harlem, young people who were reading from three to five years below grade level. These students averaged overall reading gains of 1.9 years in one school year, when they learned through their reading style strengths (Carbo, "Reading Styles Seminar," 1986).

In another notable doctoral study, Mary Sudzina compared the reading achievement of 213 second graders in three different basal reading programs, one with a strong phonics emphasis, one with a whole-word emphasis, and one with mixed phonic and whole-word emphases. No attempt had been made to match the children's learning styles with the methods. Within each of the three groups, the children who were matched by chance with an appropriate method made better progress in reading than the mismatched youngsters (Carbo, "Reading Styles Research: 'What Works' Isn't Always Phonics," 1987).

How Can We Determine Students' Reading Styles?

One way to determine students' reading styles is to observe them in their daily activities. Another, faster way is by asking them. The *Reading Styles Inventory* developed by Carbo is precisely that: a way of asking students about their reading style preferences. Students respond to 52 statements that enable a teacher to determine with considerable reliability the student's preferred learning modality or modalities, and preferences with respect to various environmental, emotional, sociological, and physical factors (see again Figure 11.1). The inventory can be taken with paper and pencil and the data later transferred to a computer diskette, or the inventory can be taken directly on a computer. With appropriate adjustments, the inventory can be used with children in grades 2 to 12, and with a few children able to understand the questions toward the end of first grade.

With younger children, one can use observational checklists. The factors that Carbo has found statistically most significant in distinguishing global and analytic styles are listed in Figure 11.2, while those most significant in determining strengths in the kinesthetic, tactile, visual, and auditory modalities are listed in Figures 11.3 through 11.6 (Carbo, Dunn, and Dunn 1986, pp. 58–62). Additional checklists can be devised for the other kinds of factors involved in reading style preferences.

In order to obtain more information regarding Carbo's *Reading Style Inventory* and the various resources available to enable you to use it profitably, write to: Learning Research Associates, Inc., P.O. Box 39, Roslyn Heights, New York 11577. The available resources include, among others, the book *Teaching Students to Read Through Their Individual Learning Styles* (Carbo, Dunn, and Dunn 1986), Carbo's *Reading Style Inventory Manual* (1981) and *Reading Style Inventory Research Sup-*

Global Reading Style

Global students often:

1. concentrate and learn when information is presented as a gestalt or whole
2. respond to emotional appeals
3. tend to like fantasy and humor
4. get "wrapped up" in a story and do not concentrate on the facts
5. process information subjectively and in patterns
6. easily can identify the main ideas in a story
7. dislike memorizing facts such as dates, names or specifics
8. learn easily through stories
9. use story context often to figure out unknown words

Analytic Reading Style

Analytic students often:

1. concentrate and learn when information is presented in small, logical steps
2. respond to appeals of logic
3. solve problems systematically
4. process information sequentially and logically
5. enjoy doing puzzles (e.g., crossword, jigsaw)
6. like putting things together by following specific directions (e.g., mechanical toys, objects with parts)
7. pay close attention to exact directions, such as measurements in a recipe or explanations for assembling an object
8. enjoy learning facts such as dates, names, and other specifics
9. learn phonics easily
10. understand and apply phonic rules
11. are critical and analytic when reading
12. can identify the details in a story

FIGURE 11.2 *Global and analytic reading styles (Carbo, Dunn, and Dunn 1986, pp. 61–62)*

---

plement (1983), various specimen sets of materials, and computer diskettes for recording and analyzing the data from individuals and groups. The diskettes for producing *group* profiles might be most valuable to many teachers who are interested in matching students' reading styles with reading methods, but initially concerned about adjusting to such variety. The group profiles will suggest how just a few changes in one's reading program—major though they may be—may go a long way toward meeting the individual needs of most learners.

Identifying Kinesthetic Strengths

10–12 = Excellent

7–9 = Good

4–6 = Moderate

0–3 = Poor to Fair

The student can:

_____ 1. run, walk, catch a ball, and so on, in a rhythmical, smooth fashion

_____ 2. concentrate for fifteen to thirty minutes during kinesthetic activities that require whole-body movement

_____ 3. recall dances, games, sports, and/or directions after performing them a few times

_____ 4. move his/her body easily and freely when acting in a play

_____ 5. remember words seen on posters and signs when on a trip

_____ 6. memorize a script more easily when actually performing in a play

_____ 7. understand concepts after "experiencing" them in some way (e.g., going on a trip, acting in a play, caring for pets, performing experiments, and so on)

_____ 8. remember words after "experiencing" them (e.g., looking at the word "apple" while eating an apple or pretending to be an elephant while learning the word "elephant")

_____ 9. recall words used in a floor game after playing the game a few times

_____ 10. remember facts, poetry, lines in a play more easily when he/she is walking and/or running, rather than standing still

_____ 11. recall a letter of the alphabet after forming it with his/her entire body

_____ 12. remember the "feeling" of a story better than the details

FIGURE 11.3 *Checklist for identifying kinesthetic strengths.* © *Marie Carbo 1976.* (*Carbo, Dunn, and Dunn 1986, p. 60.*)

In advocating Carbo's Reading Style Inventory, I want, however, to comment upon certain of her recommendations:

1. For students who are strongly analytic and auditory, the two major methods Carbo recommends are the "linguistic" method, and the phonic method. The linguistic method, as explained here in Chapter 2, is based on the assumption that children need to be exposed to regularly patterned words, so that they can induce the patterns for themselves. Thus the linguistic method uses materials that show less concern for story content than for presenting certain letter clusters, patterns, or "word families"—the "Nan can fan Dan" sort of fare. What is particularly noteworthy is not Carbo's definition of the linguistic approach (essentially the same as mine), but her delineation of the phonic approach. She explains:

Identifying Tactile Strengths

11–13 = Excellent

8–10 = Good

5–7 = Moderate

0–4 = Poor to Fair

The student can:

_____   1. draw and color pictures

_____   2. perform crafts such as sewing, weaving, and/or making models

_____   3. remember a phone number after dialing it a few times

_____   4. concentrate on a tactile task for 15 to 30 minutes

_____   5. hold a pen or pencil correctly

_____   6. write legible letters of the alphabet appropriate in size for his/her age

_____   7. write with correct spacing

_____   8. recall words after tracing over clay or sandpaper letters that form the words

_____   9. remember words after writing them a few times

_____   10. recall words after playing a game containing those words, such as bingo or dominoes

_____   11. recall the names of objects after touching them a few times

_____   12. write words correctly after tracing over them with his/her finger

_____   13. recall words after typing them a few times

FIGURE 11.4 *Checklist for identifying tactile strengths.* © *Marie Carbo 1976. (Carbo, Dunn, and Dunn 1986, p. 59.)*

> Generally, the child is taught isolated letter sounds in a prescribed sequence. After a youngster has mastered the sounds of a few letters, those letters are blended to form words. Then the child learns additional letter sounds and learns to decode new and more complex words. That procedure continues until the student masters all the sounds of individual letters and some letter groups. (Carbo, Dunn, and Dunn 1986, p. 67)

Notice, however, that Carbo makes no mention of learning phonics rules of the sort discussed in Chapter 3. More emphatically, she has indicated in personal correspondence (December 12, 1986) that ''The recommendation of phonic or linguistic instruction on the RSI profiles is *not* a recommendation for the teaching of phonic rules.'' Furthermore, students who *can* learn well through a phonics or linguistics approach may nevertheless not need to. For example, in working with some third graders recently, my students found a few for whom a phonics or linguistics approach was recommended by the RSI. However, the children's pattern of *miscues* suggested that they no longer needed (if they ever did) instructional focus on grapho/phonemic cues.

Identifying Visual Strengths

11–13 = Excellent

8–10 = Good

5–7 = Moderate

0–4 = Poor to Fair

The student can:

_____   1. follow a simple direction that is written and/or drawn

_____   2. place four to six pictures in proper story sequence

_____   3. recall a phone number after seeing it a few times

_____   4. concentrate on a visual activity for 15 to 30 minutes

_____   5. concentrate on a visual task when a visual distraction is presented

_____   6. work on a visual task without looking away or rubbing his/her eyes

_____   7. recall words after seeing them a few times

_____   8. remember and understand words accompanied by a pictorial representation

_____   9. read words without confusing the order of the letters (e.g., reading "spot" for "stop")

_____ 10. discriminate between/among letters that look alike (e.g., as "m" and "n" or "c," "e," and "o")

_____ 11. discriminate between/among words that look alike (e.g., "fill" and "full" or "that" and "what")

FIGURE 11.5 *Checklist for identifying visual strengths. © Marie Carbo 1976. (Carbo, Dunn, and Dunn 1986, pp. 58–59.)*

---

2. A second important point is that when Carbo recommends holistic methods such as language experience, recorded book, and individualized reading as most appropriate for students who are global and kinesthetic/tactile (e.g., " 'What Works' Isn't Always Phonics," 1987), she does not intend to discredit or discount a whole-language approach. On the contrary, she strongly advocates such an approach, which potentially includes all the aforementioned components—and more. As Carbo has indicated in personal conversation, had she been acquainted with "whole language" as an approach at the time of writing *Teaching Students to Read Through Their Individual Learning Styles* (Carbo, Dunn, and Dunn 1986), she would certainly have included whole language as an approach that is particularly appropriate for global and kinesthetic/tactile learners—which includes most young children and, nowadays, many if not most older students who have difficulty with reading.

3. A third point concerns the importance of manipulative games for students who are highly kinesthetic and tactile. While whole-language teachers generally believe that engaging in "real" reading and writing stimulates the acquisition of literacy more effectively than most manipulative materials and games, Carbo points out that such manipulative materials can be particularly important for

Identifying Auditory Strengths

12–14 = Excellent

9–11 = Good

5–8 = Moderate

0–4 = Poor to Fair

The student can:

_____   1. follow a short verbal direction

_____   2. repeat simple sentences of eight to twelve words

_____   3. remember a phone number after hearing it a few times

_____   4. recall simple math facts or a few lines of poetry after hearing them several times

_____   5. understand long sentences

_____   6. remember and sequence events discussed

_____   7. use appropriate vocabulary and sentence structure

_____   8. pay attention to a story or lecture for 15 to 30 minutes

_____   9. concentrate on an auditory task even when an auditory distraction is presented

_____   10. identify and recall the sounds of individual letters

_____   11. discriminate between/among words that sound alike (e.g., "leaf" and "leave" or "cot" and "cat")

_____   12. discriminate between/among letters that sound alike (e.g., "sh" and "ch" or "a" and "o")

_____   13. blend letters quickly to form words

_____   14. sound out words and still retain the storyline

FIGURE 11.6 *Checklist for identifying auditory strengths.* © *Marie Carbo 1976.* *(Carbo, Dunn, and Dunn 1986, p. 58.)*

children who have already been turned off to reading, who have learned to view themselves as poor readers, and who do not like to read. Such games can most effectively be based upon the stories in children's reading materials, including stories they themselves have dictated or written. This makes the games more meaningful, thus meeting global children's need for materials that are personally relevant.

Are There Typical Patterns in Reading Styles?

To give teachers a "feel" for the pattern that is typical of many young children and of older underachieving readers as well, Carbo uses the following case study of Jimmy in her Reading Styles Seminar. As you read the case study, jot down your observations regarding his learning style, modalities, and preferences regarding environment, mobility, intake (food or drink), and whatever else seems noteworthy. The case study is from Carbo's Reading Styles Seminar, 1986.

Case Study of Jimmy

Kindergarten

"Mommy, what's that word?" Jimmy asked as he shifted from foot to foot. Jimmy's mother was reading a storybook to him and, as usual, he interrupted her on every page to ask questions about the words. He would fidget, lean, and stretch in his chair while he nibbled on a cookie or a piece of fruit.

Jimmy loved to go to the library and choose books for his mother to read to him. He was able to read many words already—words on signs, in books and on television. Jimmy loved exciting stories and he was looking forward to first grade.

In his kindergarten class, Jimmy enjoyed playing with a couple of buddies on a little rug in the block corner. He particularly liked to create clay animals and then tell fantastic stories about them. Jimmy had an excellent imagination and vocabulary. He was a great favorite with his peers.

First Grade

"Jimmy, please sit down. We're ready to work," repeated Mrs. Jeremy. "Put away that snack and sit down, dear. You can talk to Paul later. Sit down now. Is everyone ready now? Good. Let's see if you remember what I taught you yesterday.

"Everyone sit up nice and straight. That's better. We are working on the 'm' sound. Now, Jimmy where do you hear the 'm' sound in the word 'family?' In the beginning, the middle, or at the end of the word?"

Jimmy shrugged his shoulders hoping that Mrs. Jeremy would ask another student. But she didn't.

"Jimmy, *listen* very carefully. You're a bright boy. I *know* you can do it if you just try a little harder. That's good. Sit up now."

Mrs. Jeremy knew that Jimmy had a high I.Q., but she could not understand why his skills were so weak. Immaturity was her guess. Even if he could read some words, Mrs. Jeremy wanted to give Jimmy a good phonics foundation before he left first grade. She went on.

"Do you hear the 'm' sound in the beginning, the middle or the end . . . 'fa - mi - ly,'" Mrs. Jeremy said more slowly.

A few of the students turned to watch Jimmy. He felt more and more uncomfortable. Tears were about to well in his eyes. He fought them back. The kids would make fun of him if he cried. Jimmy decided to guess. "At the end?" he asked.

"No Jimmy, please listen," said Mrs. Jeremy. "Sit up, dear. You can think better if you're sitting up. There now."

Jimmy couldn't understand why he couldn't do the work. Mrs. Jeremy was trying so hard. Everyone was staring now. Jimmy felt he would burst. Suddenly, he got up from his chair and ran out into the hall.

© 1981 Marie Carbo

From this sketch, the following are some of my own observations about Jimmy:

He is global, and not analytic.

He is kinesthetic and tactile, and at least somewhat visual; he is definitely not strongly auditory.

He tends to prefer an informal learning environment, to have high mobility and intake needs, to enjoy working with peers, and to enjoy making his own book choices.

According to Carbo, this pattern is typical of many young children, up to about the age of eight. They tend to be highly kinesthetic and tactile, somewhat visual, and low in ability to process information auditorily. Beginning around the age of eight, some children become more strongly analytic and auditory (Carbo, ''Reading Styles Change . . .'' 1983). These children, and the ones who are both global and analytic, visual and auditory, generally learn to read with little difficulty in our phonics and skills-emphasis programs. The more global children do not need the phonics or necessarily benefit from it, but if they are analytic and auditory also, they will usually succeed. The ones who have most difficulty in today's typical classrooms are generally those who remain global, highly kinesthetic and tactile, and moderately visual, but who are low in both analytic and auditory abilities. Thus underachieving older readers tend to have the same pattern of reading styles, modalities, and preferences as younger children. In addition to being highly global, highly kinesthetic and tactile, and only moderately visual, they tend to have strong preferences for an informal learning environment, strong needs for mobility and intake, and strong preferences for working with peers and for making reading choices—though until they gain increased self-confidence, they may need a fairly structured program, with strong direction from the teacher (see, for example, Carbo, Dunn, and Dunn 1986, pp. 18, 30–31).

Remembering that it is important to determine each student's reading style and to match instruction to it as closely as possible, we can nevertheless generalize, then, about the kind of instruction and instructional environment that is likely to benefit *the majority* of beginning readers and older underachieving readers. That instruction will be:

1. Global, focusing on wholes rather than the analysis of parts.
2. Highly kinesthetic and tactile, and more visual than auditory.
3. Provided in a comfortable, informal environment where students are allowed to interact with peers, to move about somewhat, and to munch on healthful snacks as they read and work.
4. Structured, but allowing the students to choose much of their own reading material.

Using the Reading Style Inventory to determine each student's reading preference will, of course, provide teachers with information for determining which students will benefit from all or most of the features of such an instructional program and environment and those who will benefit most from considerably different features. Thus, if the majority of the children exhibited the pattern indicated above and instruction were provided accordingly, adjustments would then need to be made for those children who are strongly analytic and/or auditory, those who prefer to read alone, and so forth.

Is There Any One Reading Approach That's Best?

Of course the message of reading styles research is that there isn't any one "best" method—that children have differing styles, abilities, and needs, and the most effective instruction will be that which best matches each child's strengths and preferences. Given this caveat, I am nevertheless convinced that the so-called whole-language approach is by far the best for the greatest number of children. I say this for three reasons:

1. It nicely matches the global processing style and the kinesthetic/tactile and—to a lesser degree, visual—style typical of most beginning readers and of most older underachieving readers.
2. The environment of a typical whole-language classroom also matches the learning preferences of many beginning and underachieving readers.
3. It has the flexibility to adapt to the needs of those who do not learn best by its primary methods.

To explain: a whole-language approach is global, in that it focuses on wholes (whole stories, songs, rhymes, and whole words) and moves from whole to part. However, it can readily incorporate auditory and analytic elements as well. For example, teachers can draw upon language experience stories that children have dictated, or songs they have learned, and focus not only upon key vocabulary words but also upon important letter/sound correspondences. Having children spell words the best they can is another way of focusing on analytic/auditory abilities. For children whose analytic and auditory abilities suggest they would benefit from and enjoy more intensive focus on letter/sound patterns, the teacher could call attention to patterns in interesting books like Dr. Seuss's *Green Eggs and Ham, The Cat in the Hat, Yertle the Turtle,* and *The Lorax.* Thus although primarily global, and much more visual than auditory, whole-language activities do involve some use of analytic and auditory skills. And more analytic and/or auditory activities can be added for those who are or who might become strong in those abilities.

A second feature of a whole-language approach is that it is highly kinesthetic, in several ways. First, a whole-language approach to literacy typically involves learning by doing—learning about books by being an author, for example, and learning about plays by writing them and then acting them out. A major feature of the philosophy is that language and literacy activities are integrated with social studies and science, thus perhaps involving children in improvised drama to understand social studies and science concepts (see Chapter 9). In a whole-language classroom, children may learn certain science concepts by raising animals and growing plants—and by going on a field trip to a science museum. Along with all of this, it is typical to integrate the so-called creative arts—drawing, painting, working in clay, music, and dance, as well as creative drama and guided visualization (for an example of the latter, see the activity accompanying the "Petronella" story in Appendix A). These kinds of activities are "kinesthetic" in two ways: they involve the learners in both doing and feeling. That is, most involve physical as well as intellectual activity, and most tend to stimulate high emotional involvement.

For children who are highly tactile, various activities could be added. For example, children might manipulate blocks or plastic letters to make words, use a typewriter or word processor to compose, or trace words in a variety of ways—by tracing over words written in crayon, tracing words in sand or salt, and so forth. Obviously *writing*, in one way or another, is a key here. Engaging in "real" reading and writing is particularly important for children who are highly kinesthetic and tactile, as is engaging in creative movement and drama, guided visualization, music, and art. Highly kinesthetic/tactile children can also be given manipulative materials and language games based upon the stories they are reading, if they seem to enjoy such materials and need them to help develop a repertoire of sight words, for example. A limited number of such materials have, in fact, been used in some of the "reading recovery" programs described in subsequent sections. However, whole-language teachers use such materials sparingly, if at all, withdrawing them as children's interest and confidence in reading increases.

In short, I see a whole-language approach as basically global, but able to accommodate the child who is strongly analytic; as basically visual and highly kinesthetic and moderately tactile, but able to accommodate the child who is highly auditory. The chart below further explains what modalities are involved in various activities that are frequently associated with a whole-language approach; the parentheses indicate modalities that seem to be involved in a minor or optional way rather than centrally. Figure 11.7 provides a succinct summary.

Whole Language: A Global Method That Can Incorporate Analytic Features

Modalities	*Method or Technique*
K (T) V (A)	*Language Experience*—as defined in this text, language experience involves children in dictating, individually or as a group, to a teacher or other scribe, who writes down what the children dictate. Teacher and children then read what's been dictated.
	Obviously global and visual; usually kinesthetic in involving high emotional investment.
	Can involve auditory/analytic skills if teacher incorporates not only activities in recognizing phrases and words, but activities focusing on letter/sound correspondences.
	Can involve kinesthetic elements not only through high emotional involvement, but also through language games that might be created from the dictated materials.

Modalities	Method or Technique

Modalities   *Method or Technique*

Can involve tactile elements if the teacher writes the "story" in heavy crayon that the children can trace, or glues sand or salt to the letters or script.

K (T) V (A)   *Shared Writing*—teacher does not merely take dictation, but rather helps the children develop and shape the writing, so as to guide them in composing, revising, and editing. Teacher and children then read.

Obviously global, visual, and kinesthetic, like the language experience approach.

Can involve auditory/analytic skills if teacher has children work together to sound words out and accepts the spellings that the group decides upon.

Can involve auditory/analytic skills in follow-up activities; kinesthetic elements in follow-up language games; and tactile elements in other follow-up activities (see under "language experience").

K T (V) (A)   *Individual Writing*—the child writes individually, spelling words as best he or she can. The child reads the writing—to teacher, to peers; peers read each other's writings.

Global in starting with child's intent to mean; kinesthetic in having high emotional investment; obviously tactile.

Can be auditory/analytic if the child is spelling phonetically (early phonemic, phonemic, letter-name stages).

Can be visual if the child is spelling words based on memory (often inaccurate) of how they look in print (transitional stage).

K (T) V (A)   *Big Books*—involves teacher initially reading to and then with students, using large, class-sized books or charts. Obviously global and visual; kinesthetic if the materials are highly interesting.

Follow-up activities can focus on auditory/analytic skills and/or use of tactile and kinesthetic modalities (see under "language experience").

K (T) V (A)   *Songs and Rhymes*—involves children in first learning to sing songs, chant rhymes, then learning to associate the oral words with the written.

Obviously global and visual; kinesthetic if emotional investment is high.

The rhythm and (often) rhyme involved in songs and rhymes provides another kinesthetic element that is particularly beneficial for the global child.

Can include movement accompanying the singing or chanting, thus incorporating yet another kinesthetic element.

Modalities	*Method or Technique*
	Follow-up activities can focus on auditory/analytic skills and/or use of tactile and kinesthetic modalities (see under ''language experience'').

K (T) V (A)   *Recorded Books*—involves following along in a book while listening to a cassette or tape recording of the book and thus gradually learning to read the book.

Obviously global and visual; kinesthetic if emotional investment is high.

The rhythm and feeling of the recorded voice provide another strong kinesthetic element.

Follow-up activities can focus on auditory/analytic skills and/or use of tactile and kinesthetic modalities (see under ''language experience'').

K   V   *Individualized Reading*—involves children in selecting many of the materials that they read, from a wide variety of high-quality children's literature, informational books, magazines, and other print materials.

Obviously global, visual, and highly kinesthetic because of the personal choice involved.

Follow-up activities, if any, would typically include a variety of ''creative'' options with potentially high kinesthetic elements, both because the child is actively involved in ''doing'' something (e.g., writing a play based on the story) and because of the potentially high emotional investment in the doing.

Sustained silent reading can be considered a form of individualized reading, but it is also a group activity in that everyone in the classroom (or school) is participating simultaneously, each person silently reading the material of his/her own choice.

(K) (T) (V) (A)   *Reading Strategy Lessons*—involves working on whatever strategies will benefit the child. From a reading styles perspective, this means working on the kinds of strategies that the child has the potential for using most effectively, not the strategies for which he/she has little aptitude.

Thus global children might, for example, be helped in using context (syntactic and semantic cues) to predict and/or to confirm and correct.

Analytic children with strong auditory skills might be helped in using grapho/phonemic cues to sample text—if their miscues suggest a need for such help.

Thus the individualized or small group lessons can be global or analytic; they can also be visual or auditory, and can incorporate tactile and kinesthetic elements as needed.

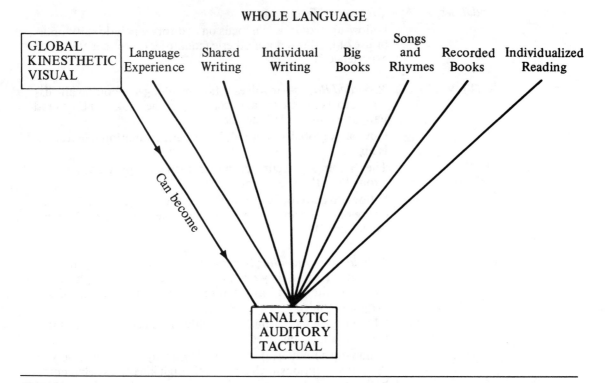

FIGURE 11.7 *Accommodating various learning styles through a whole-language approach*

How Can One Begin to Modify Instruction to Adapt to Students' Reading Styles?

Of course, it is best to administer a Reading Styles Inventory to the children in your class and to modify instruction accordingly. Given that the reading styles of young children and older underachieving readers are not well met by the typical classroom, however, there may be a number of helpful things you can do, even without detailed information on each child:

1. If you have to use a basal reading series, at least eliminate dull, boring stories. Then use the highly interesting stories as a jumping-off point for a variety of creative activities, perhaps involving not only reading and writing and speaking but creative drama, art, music—whatever seems most appropriate.
2. Allow children to choose more of their own reading materials.
3. Eliminate worksheets, dittos, and workbooks as much as possible, especially with those students for whom they are clearly least effective.

4. Also eliminate most of the literal recall questions that follow the stories in the basal reader, substituting discussion questions that focus on the motivation and feelings of the characters and on the feelings of the children as they imagine themselves in the same or similar circumstances.

5. Vary your story introductions by sometimes reading aloud the first few pages of the story while students follow along in their own books, thus arousing students' interest and building their confidence.

6. Tape record at least portions of stories in the basal reader. Allow students to listen to the recorded portion *before* reading or discussing it, to increase confidence and comprehension.

7. Use guided visualizations (like that accompanying the ''Petronella'' story in Appendix A) and creative drama activities (like that described on pp. 285–86), both as preparation for reading and as follow-up. When possible, incorporate the other arts—song, dance, and creating through various media such as clay and paint.

8. When you teach a lesson directly, begin in a manner that would be appropriate for the global and kinesthetic/tactile students, particularly if the lesson ultimately focuses on the kinds of tasks that the more analytic and/or auditory children do best.

9. Eliminate most activities focusing on letter/sound relationships, except for highly analytic and auditory children who seem to need and enjoy them.

10. In interpreting standardized tests, ignore low decoding scores when children are comprehending well.

11. Incorporate more and more whole-language activities, so that reading and writing become personally rewarding and meaningful.

12. Create one or more informal areas in the classroom, so that children may read while sitting on rugs or carpeting, on pillows, in beanbag chairs—or even, if they like, on carpet squares under their desks!

13. Allow children to munch on healthful snacks while they are reading. Though at first *all* the children may want to eat while reading, soon only those who really need to eat will do so.

14. Permit children to move about somewhat during the time they are reading. (Children with high mobility needs often have high intake needs as well, and allowing them to eat will typically lessen this need for mobility).

15. Experiment with lighting and sound: for example, turn off half or a third of the lights, and allow children to choose where to sit. Provide music for children to listen to through headphones, if this is possible. In short, be alert for other ways in which children's reading preferences can be accommodated.

Doubtless you can think of other, related changes that will help to accommodate the learning styles of students in your classroom. Such efforts will surely go a long way toward preventing and alleviating many reading difficulties. See, for example, Carbo's ''How to Start Your Own Super Reading Styles Program!'' (1984) and ''Five Schools Try Reading Styles Programs . . .'' (1984).

The research in matching reading approaches with reading styles clearly indicates the wisdom of teaching children to read through their *strengths* rather than trying to remediate their weaknesses, the former being all too rarely attempted in working with underachievers in any area. The following sections document the use of a whole-language approach in dealing with ''poor'' or ''disabled'' readers. I have focused on this approach because in recent years it has been the global and highly kinesthetic/tactile readers whose reading instruction has been most in conflict with their reading styles. The instruction has tended to be highly analytic and auditory, focusing on phonics and other ''skills.'' With a whole-language approach, on the other hand, children who are analytic and highly auditory might well need additional instructional help in the areas of their strengths.

It is with these reminders that we turn to a discussion of how to identify and help those readers most in need of additional assistance.

READING RECOVERY

In the early 1960s, New Zealand educator Marie Clay began investigating emergent reading behavior. She concluded that after only a year of instruction—typically by the age of 6, in New Zealand schools—children could be identified as progressing normally or as being ''at risk'' with regard to reading: that is, after a year of instruction, about 10 percent or so of the children with whom she worked seemed to have developed inappropriate reading strategies, or not to have developed important ones, or simply not yet to have developed the ability to coordinate different strategies into a workable system for reading effectively. Given this assessment, Clay devised a program for ''reading recovery'': an early intervention program that has had considerable success in helping such ''at risk'' readers make normal progress in reading. Clay reports her assessment procedures, teaching procedures, and results in *The Early Detection of Reading Difficulties*, now in its third edition (1985).

This section will discuss Clay's and others' procedures for assessing young children's book handling knowledge and concepts about print, briefly discuss her program for teaching needed concepts and strategies within a whole-language approach, and then discuss a sampling of other ''reading recovery'' programs in various places and with various levels and populations of students. Finally, the chapter will conclude with a discussion of so-called ''dyslexia,'' with suggestions as to how it might be viewed and approached within a socio-psycholinguistic, whole-language perspective.

Assessing Emergent Reading

In order to determine young children's understanding of the nature of books and how books are read, Clay developed a ''Concepts About Print'' test and two small books to use with them, *Sand* (Clay 1972) and *Stones* (Clay 1979). The books are unusual in that some pages are printed upside down and in other unusual ways, to determine children's knowledge about print (see directions for administering and scoring the test in Clay's *Early Detection of Reading Difficulties* 1985, pp. 27–30). Building on the work of Clay and of David Doake, Yetta Goodman and B. Attwerger (n.d.) have devised a similar test of "Pre-Schoolers' Book Handling Knowledge," to be used with "normal" books. Such individually administered tests aim to determine whether the child knows such things as the following:

1. That a book is called a book.
2. What do you do with a book, and what's inside it.
3. Where you begin reading a book and a page.
4. That you read from left to right and return down left for the next line.
5. What a word is and what a letter is.
6. Where to find the first letter in a word, and the last letter.

As Clay points out (*Early Detection* 1985, p. 27), most five-year-olds enjoy this task and have little difficulty with it, but for a few children, confusions about the vocabulary used in reading instruction and some of the arbitrary conventions about print in the English language tend to persist. These are among the children for whom Clay provides individualized instruction beginning with their second year of schooling.

Before examining the essential features of Clay's reading recovery program, however, let us look at one more means of assessing young children's emergent reading behavior: a Concept of Word (Reading) test developed by Darrell Morris. This assessment can be made while carrying out some of the activities characteristic of a whole-language classroom. The teacher introduces a favorite rhyme or song to a group of children, until they have essentially memorized it. Then the rhyme or song (for example, "Humpty Dumpty") is put on the chalkboard or on chart paper, with the teacher pointing to each word as he or she reads the rhyme, being careful to preserve a natural rhythm. Finally, after the children have read the rhyme or song several times together, the children take turns at reading and finger-pointing to each word. As Morris puts it (1981, p. 660), "By noting the following behaviors as individual children begin to read the rhyme, the knowledgeable teacher can assess the presence, absence, or fledgling development of the concept of word":

1. Do they point to each word correctly as they read across the line?
2. If they err in their pointing, mismatching spoken word to written word, are they able to self-correct without teacher assistance, and continue with the reading?
3. Having read the entire rhyme, can the children identify individual words scattered throughout the five lines when the teacher points to the words in a random order? Do they identify the target words immediately or must they go back to the beginning of the line—even the beginning of the rhyme—and use contextual support for the identification?
4. After going back and re-reading a given line in the rhyme (e.g. "Humpty Dumpty had a great fall"), can the children identify a target word in the line (e.g. *great*)? Is the identification immediate or does it require a word by word contextual strategy? (Morris 1981, pp. 660–61)

Each of these behaviors gives evidence of the child's emerging grasp of the concept of "word." Therefore, such an observational test as this could be used as one measure of emergent reading, presumably with children slightly more advanced than those with whom one would use the aforementioned print awareness tests. Morris's test, too, could be used to help determine which children might benefit from early intervention in a reading recovery program of the kind that Clay has developed.

Clay's Reading Recovery Program

Clay's "Concepts About Print" test is only one of a group of individually administered tests used to determine young children's understanding of books and print, their understanding of reading and writing, and their ability to read and write. Assessment of both reading and writing is important, for together they provide a much more complete picture of the extent to which a child has acquired appropriate concepts about the written word. Given such observational assessments, one might find such needs as the following:

1. Some children may need help in understanding how books are read and/or in understanding the terminology used in reading instruction, terms such as *word, letter, sound.*
2. Some children may need help in using the most salient graphic cues, such as the first letter(s) and the last letter(s).
3. Some children may need help in hearing the separate sounds in words and/or in blending sounds together, when they try to make use of grapho/phonemic cues.
4. Some children may need help in using semantic and syntactic cues to predict and to confirm/correct, particularly if they have not gone through the stages of "reading" a book virtually from memory, and then reading by using more and more of the syntactic and semantic cues within the text.
5. Some children may be ready for and need help with integrating all of the language cues into a workable system.

Children's particular needs will depend a great deal upon their prior reading experiences, including their reading instruction. Children involved in a whole-language program may be more likely to need individualized help in using grapho/phonemic cues than children in phonics-oriented programs, while children in programs with a heavy phonics emphasis are of course much more likely to need individualized help in using syntactic and semantic cues. And for each child, the pattern of strengths and needs will be unique.

In Clay's reading recovery program, the tutor focuses on the child's particular skill and strategy needs within the context of an individually tailored whole-language program that involves both reading and writing. The typical session might include the following (Clay 1985, p. 56):

> Rereading of two or more familiar books
> Rereading of previous day's new book (while the tutor does a running tabulation and analysis of the reader's miscues)

Working with the particular skills or strategies the reader needs to develop
Writing a story
Introducing a new book, which the reader attempts to read

Obviously the work on particular skills or strategies is only a part of the total program. As Clay points out, too much focus on detail seriously threatens the child's progress (p. 53). Clay also reminds us that only a small proportion of children will need such focused lessons: "Most children (80 to 90 percent) do NOT require these detailed, meticulous and special reading recovery procedures *or any modification of them*. They will learn to read more pleasurably without them" (1985, p. 47).

For those children with such special needs, however, early intervention may well be the answer, though one must guard as much as possible against the potentially damaging effects of singling children out for special instruction. Clay found generally quite encouraging results with her reading recovery program, not only at the end of the year when the children had special tutoring but also three years later. She points out the degree of challenge inherent in the program: the children chosen for the reading recovery program were those with the very poorest performance in reading and writing at the age of 6; the group included bicultural Maori children, bilingual Pacific Island children, children with handicaps, and children awaiting Special Class placements. Despite the fact that major gains with such a group could scarcely be expected in both reading and writing with even daily tutoring over only a 13-to-14-week period, the children typically left the program with average levels of performance in three to six months, and many still retained those average levels of performance three years later (Clay 1985, p. 105).

In a more recent paper on reading recovery, Clay reports that since the program was first introduced in New Zealand, hundreds of teachers in New Zealand, in Victoria, Australia, and in Columbus, Ohio have now brought thousands of low-achieving children up to average levels of reading. The Ohio project, begun by teacher educators at Ohio State University, has now been extended to the entire state of Ohio; see, for example, Pinnell 1985 and various documents available from Ohio State University's Department of Educational Theory and Practice. As Clay explains it, the children are "taught to discover things about reading and writing for themselves. They were [are] trained to be independent and were [are] able to survive as learners back in their classrooms" (Clay 1986). This has been accomplished with daily lessons like those outlined above: 30-minute individual lessons supplementing regular classroom instruction for only 12 to 20 weeks. Children who are not responding to the program after four to six months maximum are transferred to a reading specialist. However, these have typically constituted only 1 percent of the total number of students of that age!

Other "Reading Recovery" Programs

Using the term "reading recovery" generically to refer to any program focusing on helping children achieve expected reading skills and strategies within a whole language context, we can say that there have been a variety of such successful programs both before the publication of Clay's work and since, with both young readers and older, and in various locales. The following is but a small sampling of earlier and more recent research, all of which suggests that focusing on specific needs through a whole-language approach is effective for a wide variety of readers considered in need of "remedial" assistance.

In an article titled "After Decoding: What?" Carol Chomsky reports on her work with five eight-year-olds. She describes the children at the outset of the tutoring program (1976, p. 288):

> These children were not nonreaders. They had received a great deal of phonics training and had acquired many phonetic skills. They met regularly with the remedial reading teacher with whom they had worked intensively since first grade. After much effort, they could "decode," albeit slowly and painfully. What was so frustrating was their inability to put any of this training to use, their failure to progress to even the beginnings of fluent reading. . . . In spite of their hard-won "decoding skills," they couldn't so much as read a page of simple material to me. The attempt to do so was almost painful, a word-by-word struggle, long silences, eyes eventually drifting around the room in an attempt to escape the humiliation and frustration of the all too familiar, hated situation.

What Chomsky succeeded in using with these children was, in effect, a whole-language program, with skills and strategies taught in context as needed. She obtained for the children two dozen picture books, recorded on tape, from which the children were to make their own selections. The task was to listen to the tape while following along in the text, until the children had become familiar enough with the book to read it fluently. In effect, they would be first memorizing the book and then learning to read it, attending to the whole and then to parts as necessary.

Chomsky explains her rationale (1976, p. 289):

> When it comes to memorizing a book, these 8 year olds are in a very different position from the pre-reader. They have already had two years of drill in word analysis, long and short vowels, word endings, blending, and so on. They can sound out words and have a fair sight vocabulary. They are beyond needing introduction to the alphabetic nature of the English writing system. What they need is to shift their focus from the individual word to connected discourse and to integrate their fragmented knowledge. It is the larger picture that they need help with, in learning to attend to the semantics and syntax of a written passage, and in developing reliance on using contextual clues from the sentence or even longer passages as they read.

Using pages that the children could already "read" fluently in semi-rote fashion, Chomsky and her graduate assistant supplemented the reading itself with game-like activities involving mostly word recognition and analysis. In addition, the children did substantial writing connected with their reading: for example, they wrote stories, question-and-answer sequences, and sentences using words from the stories.

Progress at first was slow: it took four of the five children about a month to learn to read their first book fluently. After that slow beginning the pace increased, and subsequent books took less and less time, so that when the children were on their fourth or fifth book they were able to finish it in a week. Soon there seemed less and less need for the analytical work; after a while, the tutoring sessions became times for simply reading the books and discussing the story, doing some writing, or discussing some stories the children had written. Those children who progressed the most improved in both reading and writing—not a surprising outcome, given the holistic nature of the approach. In general, the children improved dramatically, not only in fluency but also in their attitude toward reading. They began reading TV commercials, cereal boxes, magazines in the home. They began picking up books to read instead of avoiding reading at all costs. In short, they began to feel and act like readers.

In Nova Scotia, David Doake developed a reading recovery program for thirteen students, ages 11–12. Ten of the children had been retained a grade at some stage of their schooling, all were in the lowest reading group in their classroom, and most had had some "specialist" individually based tutoring. Though they had been classified on a variety of tests as being of "average ability," they were making little or no progress in learning to read and write; on the Gates-McGinitie reading test, for example, their scores ranged from a grade level of 2.1 to 3.2. Doake characterizes their previous reading and writing instruction as follows (Doake 1985, Appendix D):

Highly structured:
a. teacher controlled
b. teacher the evaluating agent

Reading program: Basal type
a. controlled vocabulary
b. heavy emphasis on learning word "attack" skills
  phonics
  little words in big words
  syllabication
c. more time spent on workbook exercises than on reading
d. daily oral circle reading
e. word accuracy emphasis rather than meaning emphasis
f. seldom read to in school or at home

Writing program:
a. accuracy oriented
  spelling
  grammar
  punctuation
b. little or no choice on what to write
c. teacher the only audience

Handwriting
a. daily
b. standard script drill aimed at perfection

In contrast, the reading recovery program included the following whole-language activities (Doake 1985, Appendix H):

Shared Reading (Big Books)
Read-Along with a listening post

Story reading to students (extensive)

Sustained Silent Reading (SSR)

Reading at home to and with parents

Individualized reading (conferences and sharing books)

Reading in the content areas related particularly to thematic studies

Creating plays and dramatizing them

Learning songs, rhymes and poems from enlarged print

Reading to younger children from predictable books

Thematic reading and writing resulting from initial brainstorming sessions on a topic; commenced with whole class projects and moved to individual studies

Environmental written language used initially

Language Experience charts and individual books made

Board News composed daily and used

Dialogue Journals used regularly

Story writing, initially modelling stories read

Story writing using wordless picture story books

Writing directions

Regular reading and writing conferences

Books made from stories written (given library cards)

Follow-up activities from reading (writing own ending to a story; constructing a game; rewriting the story as a play and acting it out; etc.)

During the two years they were enrolled in this literacy recovery program, the students' progress was dramatic. In the year prior to their enrolling in the program, the students' average (mean) scores on the Gates-McGinitie went from approximately grade 2.2 to 2.4, an increase of only two months. In the first year of the program, the scores rose from an average of 2.4 to 3.8, an increase of one year, four months. In the third year, the scores on the Gates-McGinitie rose from an average of 3.8 to over 5.2, again an average increase of approximately one year, four months. And yet these standardized scores, which should be convincing to those concerned about educational "accountability," tell only part of the story. As in Chomsky's small-scale reading recovery program, the most significant gains were in the students' attitude toward reading and writing. As Doake says, "These students received no formal instruction in reading and writing, nor did they experience any correction in their efforts to learn to read and write—and yet they have become readers and writers. They now enjoy these activities and engage in them frequently of their own volition" (Doake 1985, pp. 5–6).

To those who work directly with children, such observations are worth far more than the impressive statistical gains on standardized tests. For this reason, I think it worth presenting sketches of some individual students who have become—and learned to think of themselves as—readers and writers through a whole-language approach.

Crowley (in Gilles et al. 1987) reports the case of John:

As a seventh grader, John was enrolled in the typical junior high curriculum, with one exception: he was not in an English class, but rather in a special education class for students labeled "learning disabled." This label was not new to John. He had been singled out early in his educational career, particularly for his lack of success in writing and reading. Descriptions such as "perceptual motor difficulties" and "processing deficit" were used to describe John's problems in school.

Like most junior high students, John did not want to be identified as different; from the first day he made this clear to his L.D. teacher. John frequently said that he didn't need the class, he came in late each day so that no one would see him enter "that room," he made sure that the door was closed for the duration of his stay and he skirted out quickly when the bell rang.

John's teacher hated the label as much as John did, but for different reasons. As a whole language teacher, he was comfortable concentrating on students' linguistic strengths, not their difficulties. Instead of lumping kids into ill-defined categories, he accepted the abilities of language users as a starting point. Instead of describing the class of four boys as "Learning Disabled," the teacher gave them the name "Unlabeled Gifted."

Instead of giving the students workbook pages to complete or drilling the students on specific reading skills, the teacher gave them whole texts. Instead of giving them fine motor exercises, he gave them a pen and paper to write. "Reading, writing, speaking, and listening were the curriculum, whether John was studying fighter planes, working on a social studies assignment, reading about motorcycles or learning about the circulatory system."

By ninth grade, John had enough confidence in his reading and writing to take a regular English class, but he took the "Unlabeled Gifted" class as well, using it as a workshop to pursue new interests. He began reading an adventure series, typically reading two to five books a week. Then he decided to read George Orwell's *1984*. He kept a response log while reading the book: after reaching a logical stopping point, he would write what he was thinking about. Instead of writing a book report, he raised questions, explored ambiguous ideas, offered interpretations, and recorded his feelings and attitudes. He noticed intriguing parallels between *1984* and *Romeo and Juliet*, which he was reading in his regular English class. "On the last day of 9th grade John gave his teacher a beautifully written expository essay discussing the themes that John gleaned from *1984*. He thought his teacher 'might like it.'" Crowley closes his sketch of John by saying "John has not decided where he wants to go for college, but he is sure that he wants to go to the University of Michigan for his master's degree." What a transformation wrought by Crowley's whole-language approach to "remedial" instruction for "learning disabled" students!

Perhaps an even more remarkable success story is reported in Rigg and Taylor's "A Twenty-One-Year-Old Begins to Read" (1979). The authors worked with a young woman named Renee, who was diagnosed as mentally retarded at the age of six, due to the effects of cerebral palsy, and who had been placed in a program for retarded children for the next 14 years. Then she had been retested and rediagnosed as having a normal IQ, after which she was placed in another program where the teacher taught her the alphabet and fifteen sight words. Little wonder, then, that at the age of 21 she conceived of herself as a nonreader: not merely someone who did not read, but someone who could not learn to read.

Rigg and Taylor devised a whole-language reading recovery program designed to give Renee confidence in her ability to read. Into each hour of tutoring, they tried to incorporate at least three of the following components, and ideally all five:

1. Sustained silent reading, with both Renee and the tutor silently reading materials of their own choice;

2. Language experience, with Renee dictating or writing stories and then reading and discussing them;

3. Retelling what was read, to focus on comprehension rather than on "word-calling";

4. Rereading, to develop fluency and confidence;

5. Assisted reading, with the tutor reading and pointing at the words and Renee chiming in, which enabled and encouraged Renee to attempt stories that she might not have had the confidence to try on her own.

During the semester, Renee created twelve language experience stories, and read three short novels and eight stories—all in about twenty hours of instructional time. Like John's instructor, Renee's tutors didn't work at all on reading or writing "skills." Believing that she could and would read if given materials of interest to her and that used "whole natural language," they structured their tutoring program accordingly. From the very first meeting, Renee was immediately able to read whole, connected text because she was reading stories that she herself had created. Because her attention was focused on getting meaning rather than on identifying words, she began to think of herself as a reader rather than a nonreader.

Rigg and Taylor sum up the results of their whole-language reading recovery tutoring program (1979, p. 56):

> After fifteen years of formal instruction, Renee was convinced that she could not read, and she did not read. In twenty hours of tutoring, she became convinced that she could read, and she did read. We asked Renee to do what evidently she had seldom or never been asked to do in school: We asked her to read, and then we got out of her way and let her do it.

Such reports of success should again make us suspect that much of our "skills" instruction with beginning readers as well as "remedial" readers is not only unnecessary but actually detrimental to the goal of literacy.

"DYSLEXIA"

But, people will ask, what of children who are "dyslexic"? Don't they need a much more narrowly focused program of individualized instruction? Before attempting to address this question, we need to examine, insofar as possible, the nature of so-called "dyslexia."

Defining "Dyslexia"

The term "dyslexia" has come to designate severe reading difficulty in people "who are otherwise normal intellectually, emotionally, and medically" (Witelson 1977, p. 16), people who have severe difficulty in reading even though they have no identifiable physical, psychological, intellectual, or environmental deficits (Karlin 1980, p. 103). Thus the term "dyslexia" or "specific reading disability" typically means that for some *un*specifiable reason, the person so labeled has severe difficulty in reading. As Harris and Hodges point out, the term "dyslexia" has become little more than a fancy word for a reading problem (1981, p. 95). Because of the uncertainty as to what "dyslexia" really means, it is perhaps not surprising that some authorities estimate that about 3 percent of the schoolage population suffers from dyslexia, while others place the estimate as high as 15 percent.

To put it mildly, it can be extremely detrimental to label people with severe reading difficulties as "dyslexics" and treat them as if they have some sort of congenital or acquired disease. This can lead all too readily to "blaming the victim," instead of giving adequate consideration to instructional and environmental factors that might have contributed to the difficulty. It can (and typically does) also lead to an inappropriately narrow medical model of diagnosis and remediation, a model stemming from the mechanistic paradigm. Historically, however, this connotation of "dyslexia" is understandable, since the term originally came from the medical community.

The concept of "dyslexia" was popularized by a neurologist named Samuel Orton. In 1937, he proposed that severe reading difficulty with no obvious physical, mental, or environmental cause might in fact be caused by poorly established hemispheric dominance in the brain. While the left cerebral hemisphere is dominant for many aspects of language processing in most right handers and many left handers, and the right hemisphere is dominant for most other left handers, Orton hypothesized that for the people termed "dyslexic," neither hemisphere was dominant. He based this hypothesis largely on his observation that many such readers and writers seemed to reverse visual images, reading and writing *b* as *d, was* as *saw,* and so forth. Orton hypothesized that this apparent misperception stemmed from the brain receiving images from both the left and the right cerebral hemisphere simultaneously, rather than from just one dominant hemisphere. This, he reasoned, might be responsible for the apparent perception of words and letters as mirror images of one another (see Monaghan 1980 for a more thorough discussion of the history of "dyslexia").

As a result of Orton's early hypothesis, many people think of "dyslexia" as being characterized by reversals of letters and words. However, there are several things to keep in mind regarding reversals like *b* for *d* and *was* for *saw* in reading and writing. First, many people with severe reading problems show little or no tendency toward reversals. Second, many children misperceive such isolated elements of language during the early stages of reading; this is a normal part of language development, and most children outgrow it with no difficulty or need for special instruction. Third, some children do not outgrow it naturally, but persist in having problems with reversals, particularly in writing; they may, for example, typically write a word completely backwards, from the last letter to the first. Such children may need specialized help as well as sympathetic understanding on the part of parents and teachers. However, it is all too seldom recognized that children who need help overcoming "reversals" in reading can often overcome the difficulty when they are helped to view the troublesome elements within a larger context. How many times do you need to focus on *b* and *d* or *was* and *saw* as isolated elements, except in the classroom? Instead of focusing on isolated elements, instructional assistance should involve using the troublesome letters in words and the words in highly predictable sentences, thus focusing the reader's attention on *meaning* (see activity 6 at the end of Chapter 4). The reader who has difficulty distinguishing between *b* and *d* in isolation will not long read *b* as *d* in a context like "Let's get a shovel and *dig* here," when the reader's attention is focused on meaning rather than on distinguishing one letter from another.

What, then, of Orton's hypothesis that otherwise unexplained severe reading difficulty may be characterized by the two cerebral hemispheres producing conflicting "mirror images"? Today this particular hypothesis is accepted by almost no one, perhaps partly because few people with severe reading difficulties persist with such reversals (especially if taught to focus on meaning), but also because there appears to be no evidence for his hypothesis in the rapidly accelerating body of brain research. Nevertheless, some of today's brain specialists think that severe reading difficulty may often result from a deficiency in the functioning of one cerebral hemisphere, from the abnormal dominance of one hemisphere, and/or from inadequate integration of the two hemispheres (see, for example, Zaidel 1979 and Hynd and Hynd 1984). There are three major lines of research that converge to support this hypothesis: research into the functioning of the brain hemispheres, correlated with research into the nature of the reading process and with research into the nature of severe reading difficulties. We shall turn, then, to a discussion of this evidence for the broad hypothesis that "dyslexia" may result from lopsided hemispheric processing.

Reading as a Whole Brain Process

Recent studies of hemispheric functioning in normal, healthy brains clearly indicate that reading, writing, and other complex processes involve both the right and the left hemisphere. This is shown by studies of blood flow on the surface of the brain and by studies that map the electrical activity on the surface of the hemispheres. Though in most people the left hemisphere is more involved than the right, clearly widespread areas of both hemispheres are involved in reading (see, for instance, Lassen, Ingvar, and Skinhoj 1978; McKean 1981; and Duffy et al., 1980 and 1984).

Research into damaged brains at first seemed to indicate that the left hemisphere was dominant for virtually all kinds of language processing, in most right-handed people and a sizeable majority of left-handed people. However, the accumulating body of research suggests that this is an oversimplification. It is not a matter of language being processed by the left hemisphere and visual images being processed by the right, as was originally hypothesized, but more a matter of certain kinds of language and visual processes being handled by each hemisphere. In the normal brain of about 90 percent of right-handed people and about 70 percent of left-handed people (Sinatra and Stahl-Gemake 1983, p. 4), the left hemisphere apparently engages in sequential, linear, step-by-step processing; it is analytical, focusing on detail, "the parts." The right hemisphere seems more to engage in simultaneous, holistic processing; it synthesizes, seeks closure, looks for the gestalt, the pattern. While the left hemisphere focuses on parts, the right hemisphere apparently seeks the whole that is more than merely the sum of the parts.

More specifically, in most people the left hemisphere seems to be heavily involved in the linear processing of grapho/phonemics and syntax, and in literal comprehension of words and phrases. But the right hemisphere seems to be involved in visual and spatial perception of words and in comprehension, particularly of larger wholes. The latter function of the right hemisphere is strongly suggested by certain studies of right-hemisphere-damaged individuals. Using primarily their left hemispheres for language processing, such people are often very literal-minded, unable to determine the significance of details in a story, and unable to integrate details into a coherent whole. Thus it looks as if the right hemisphere typically plays a significant role in what we think of as higher levels of comprehension (see Weaver 1986 for a variety of references).

The accumulating evidence is summarized by Levy (1985, pp. 43–44):

When a person reads a story, the right hemisphere may play a special role in decoding visual information, maintaining an integrated story structure, appreciating humor and emotional content, deriving meaning from past associations and understanding metaphor. At the same time, the left hemisphere plays a special role in understanding syntax, translating written words into their phonetic representations and deriving meaning from complex relations among word concepts and syntax. But there is no activity in which only one hemisphere is involved or to which only one hemisphere makes a contribution.

Clearly both hemispheres are involved in normal reading—and indeed, in all but perhaps the very simplest of mental processes.

Also relevant for understanding reading and reading difficulties, however, is the observation that the two hemispheres seem to specialize in different functions. Given the gestalt-seeking function currently attributed to the right hemisphere, perhaps it typically comes into play first, initiating the active search for meaning and drawing upon the reader's schemas in that search (at present, this suggestion is no more than a hypothesis). But as the act of reading progresses, there is complementary interplay between the two kinds of processing: the linear, element-by-element processing attributed to the left hemisphere, and the simultaneous, pattern-seeking processing attributed to the right. These are the two kinds of processing characteristic of what I have called the mechanistic and the organic paradigm, respectively (see Chapter 7).

Now what if one hemisphere predominated over the other—if one kind of processing predominated, or if the two kinds were not integrated into a smoothly functioning whole? Clearly we might expect to find the kind of reading that is characteristic of beginning readers and of those who have severe reading difficulty. Let us look, then, at some of the research on "dyslexia," to see whether so-called dyslexics seem to have the kinds of difficulties that would be predicted if one kind of processing predominated and/or the two kinds were not well coordinated.

Characterizing "Dyslexia"

One thing that emerges clearly from the research on dyslexia is the observation that no two individuals exhibit exactly the same configuration of reading difficulties. Thus we must be wary of too readily categorizing individuals as having this kind of problem or that kind, and thereby overlooking the person's unique strengths and needs. On the other hand, one may gain a deeper understanding of typical reading difficulties if one looks at some of the recurring patterns.

So far, much of the dyslexic research purports to test reading comprehension by focusing on students' ability to identify single words—a procedure that psycholinguists consider hopelessly inadequate. Nevertheless, the results of such assessment suggest lopsided hemispheric processing in many cases. In a widely cited article, for example, Boder (1973) characterizes two major types of "dyslexia." Of the 107 "dyslexic" students in her study, approximately 9 percent had a poor memory for visual patterns and tended to read analytically, "'by ear,' through a process of phonetic analysis and synthesis, sounding out familiar as well as unfamiliar combinations of letters, rather than by whole-word visual gestalts" (Boder 1973, p. 670). They read "laboriously, as if . . . seeing each word for the first time" (p. 670). Such readers tend to spell the way they read: phonetically. That is, the misspellings resemble the way words "should" be spelled if there were one-to-one correspondences between letters and sounds in English. These readers typically have a much lower sight vocabulary than those in the major group, whose sight vocabulary was itself characterized as "limited."

In contrast were "dyslexic" readers who read words globally as instantaneous visual gestalts, rather than analytically. Lacking word-analysis skills, they are unable to sound out and blend the letters and syllables of a word. While such readers may make substitutions based primarily on visual resemblance and apparently grammar ("horse" for *house*, "monkey" for *money*, "stop" for *step*), their most striking substitutions, according to Boder, are words closely related conceptually but not phonetically to the original word. Examples are "funny" for *laugh*, "chicken" or "quack" for *duck*, "answer" for *ask*, "stairs" for *step*, "airplane" for *train*, "person" for *human*, "planet" for *moon*, and "Los Angeles" for *city* (Boder 1973, p. 670). Interestingly, such substitutions occur when words are presented in isolation, lending further support to the observation that the general sense of a word can be understood even when the word itself is not identified or identifiable (see Chapter 3, p. 62). Boder indicates that the largest percentage of dyslexics in her study, approximately two-thirds, exhibited this pattern. As noted, 9 percent read words analytically rather than globally, while the rest (22 percent) exhibited both patterns (Boder 1973, p. 676). According to Boder, these proportions seem to be typical of other studies as well.

It appears, then, that when left hemispheric processing predominates, we may get word-for-word reading with little comprehension, or letter-by-letter processing that because of inattention to meaning results in frequent nonwords, such as Tony's "souts" for *shouts* and "ramped" for *repeated*. Some researchers have called such readers "surface dyslexics," since they attend mainly to the superficial, surface features of the text rather than to meaning (Hynd and Hynd 1984, pp. 493–94). On the other hand, when right hemispheric processing predominates, we may get renditions that sometimes bear little visual or auditory resemblance to the actual words on the page, such as Jay's "toad" for *frog* or Anne's "went" for *ran*, both of which made eminently good sense in context (see pp. 98 and 114 respectively). Such readers may be called "deep dyslexics" because they attend primarily to deep structure, to meaning (see Coltheart, Patterson, and Marshall 1980 for various articles on "deep dyslexia").

However one chooses to label them (and I confess I find the various labels confusing), clearly there appear to be some readers who make insufficient use of the global, meaning-seeking strategies attributed to the right hemisphere, and other readers who make insufficient use of the linear, analytical strategies attributed to the left. This is roughly equivalent to saying that some people make insufficient use of semantic cues to glean non-literal and global meaning, while others make insufficient use of grapho/phonemic cues.

According to Boder and others, the largest share of dyslexics are those who make insufficient use of grapho/phonemic cues. *But I cannot help suspecting that many of these so-called "dyslexics" might be considered adequate-to-good readers if meaning and not word identification were the goal.* Remember on the one hand that word recognition was tested in isolation (as in many, if not most, of the studies on dyslexia), and that even then, most of the miscues of the larger group of "dyslexics" bear syntactic and semantic resemblance to the stimulus word. If such readers were to read connected text, might we not find some of them exhibiting the patterns of good readers like Jay and Anne? Thus I suspect that some of the readers typically called "dyslexic" are viewed as such because the examiners define reading as first and foremost a matter of identifying words "correctly" and because they are looking for readers' weaknesses in identifying words rather than their strengths in gaining meaning. Given a psycholinguistic perspective of the reading process, many students considered "dyslexic" might be viewed and treated much differently.

Reducing "Dyslexia"

The foregoing discussion begins to suggest, then, that there may be many factors contributing to what appear to be severe reading difficulties, or "dyslexia." One factor may simply be an inappropriate definition of reading, an inadequate understanding of what constitutes effective reading strategies. Another factor may be a developmental one: some children may be developing normally, but at a slower rate than most of their peers, so that they are less advanced in their use and integration of reading strategies than most of those peers. Other children may have had little opportunity to see the value of reading, either at home or in school, so that they have little desire to learn to read; this can be particularly true if they have not read or been read to prior to entering school, and if reading instruction in school emphasizes sounding out and/or identifying words correctly rather than reading for meaning and enjoyment. Thus their reading difficulties may be more a matter of not seeing any value in reading and/or not understanding that reading is an active search for meaning. Other children may have severe reading difficulties because of problems at home and/or problems adjusting to school, problems in getting along with their peers, and so forth. In short, the most appropriate way to help many children may be to consider their reading in light of what we know about effective reading, simply to encourage their natural development, to find ways to make reading meaningful, and/or to help them overcome personal problems, insofar as a teacher can.

But how best to help students with reading difficulties that cannot be dealt with in such ways? How, for example, to help those who still seem to need assistance in using the linear, analytic strategies attributed to the left hemisphere—particularly the use of grapho/phonemic cues to help them identify words? How to help those who still seem to need assistance in using the global, pattern-seeking strategies attributed to the right hemisphere—particularly the use of semantic cues to grasp subtleties of meaning? Even when we have reconsidered the way we look at students' miscues and when we have considered other factors, it is clear that there are students at all levels of schooling who would benefit from help in developing one or the other kind of strategy—or both. But how best to help them?

Most methods of "remediation" recognize that there are strong, reinforcing links between reading and writing, but there are still vast differences among approaches. Perhaps the most widely used approach is that originated by Samuel Orton and further developed by his associate, Anna Gillingham: the so-called Orton-Gillingham method. Seemingly designed for those "dyslexics" who need further help in mastering letter/sound correspondences, the procedures in the program are specifically designed to:

a. overcome the tendency to reverse symbols and to transpose letters within syllables and words;
b. strengthen and ensure visual-auditory association for alphabetic symbols through a kinesthetic linkage;
c. establish the necessary left-to-right sequential process for reading, spelling, and writing;
d. strengthen mnemonic processes [processes for remembering things];
e. provide a phonetic and syllabic basis for the building of an accurate and sufficiently extensive reading vocabulary. (Ansara 1982, pp. 418–19).

Notice that basically this is a bottom-up approach, working from smaller units to larger—an approach that seems to assume once words are identified, meaning will take care of itself. By isolating what at least *seem* to be the problem units—letters and words—the method focuses on readers' weaknesses while preventing them from using what might be their strengths, perhaps the ability to use syntactic and semantic cues to get meaning.

Various kinds of research suggest, however, that is it more effective to focus on learners' strengths and to address the weaknesses or needs in the context of those strengths, and/or simply to minimize the weaknesses—in this case, perhaps not to burden readers with the expectation of word-perfect reading or burden writers with the expectation of word-perfect spelling, so long as meaning is obtained and conveyed. In the new *Reading Miscue Inventory: Alternative Procedures* (Y. Goodman, Watson, and Burke 1987, Ch. 8), the authors nicely exemplify this general view in making recommendations for Betsey, the young reader whose miscues and comprehension they have discussed in detail. They predict that "Strategies that inhibit and interfere with her reading progress will diminish as Betsey becomes more proficient at what she is already doing well and as her successful reading strategies are brought to a conscious awareness through strategy lessons and discussions about her reading." In order to capitalize upon Betsey's strengths and minimize her weaknesses, they suggest she and readers like her spend 70 percent to 80 percent of the time allotted to reading instruction in real reading and writing, with only 20 percent to 30 percent of the time spent working on "instructional strategy lessons that include thinking and talking about reading and writing." In other words, they suggest a whole-language program with focused strategy lessons being only a part of that program. The parts are dealt with in the context of the whole.

Which approach is more effective, a part-to-whole approach like that of Orton and Gillingham, or a whole-to-part approach like that recommended here? Unfortunately, comparative research is virtually nonexistent. Only a few years ago, Ansara reported the following in her sympathetic account of the Orton-Gillingham approach (1982, p. 426):

> After half a century of practice in clinics and schools where, according to numerous accounts, tutors and teachers have successfully used the Orton-Gillingham Approach, we should expect to be able to cite studies comparing it with other approaches. This is not the case, however, although there are many anecdotal descriptions of clinic and school programs, as there are case reports, demonstrating the effectiveness of this approach to selected populations of dyslexic children, adolescents, and adults. Yet good research reports remain few, for the Orton-Gillingham approach as well as for others equally or even better known.

With a whole-language approach to lessening reading difficulties, there are likewise anecdotal reports, like the success stories of John and Renee. There are reports comparing children's progress in a regular reading and remediation program with their later progress under a whole-language approach, such as Doake's research in Nova Scotia. And there are reports demonstrating the effectiveness of whole-language reading recovery program with beginning readers who appear to be "at risk" with respect to reading, as in Clay's study. But to date, I know of no research directly comparing the Orton-Gillingham approach itself to an approach that makes specific reading strategy lessons only a small part of a whole-language approach to helping readers with particular difficulties.

As with beginning reading, then, I think we must not just look for comparative studies upon which to base our choice of methodology. Rather, we should consider which approach is based upon the soundest knowledge regarding how people learn in general, how they acquire language and literacy, and how proficient readers actually read. The vast bulk of this evidence supports a whole-to-part approach, rather than a part-to-whole approach like phonics. For most children, even letter/sound patterns themselves can best be learned through involvement in real reading and writing. Figure 11.8 summarizes major lines of evidence supporting the development of phonics knowledge through a whole-language approach. Figure 11.9 further develops each of these lines of evidence.

One reason a whole-language approach is more effective in learning to read for meaning is that with a phonics approach, the *means* (a knowledge of letter/sound relationships) runs the risk of becoming the *end*, taught for as well as by itself. Unfortunately, standardized testing strongly reinforces this tendency. With a whole-language approach, on the other hand, the means and the end are the same: comprehension. In order to attain this end when instruction focuses on the means, readers have to intuitively go beyond what is taught in part-to-whole instruction like that provided in a phonics-oriented subskills approach, or even a basal reader skills approach.

Fortunately many children just naturally read for meaning, predicting and confirming/correcting from context without being told to do so. Unfortunately, some children do not intuitively use these strategies very effectively. From a three-year program in which British secondary school English teachers worked intensively one-on-one with readers in difficulty, Margaret Meek shares the following observation (1983, p. 214):

> We confirmed our conviction that reading has to be taught as the thing that it is, holistically. To break it down into piecemeal activities for pseudo-systematic instruction is to block the individual, idiosyncratic moves that pupils of this age make to interact with a text and to teach themselves how to *make it mean*. When we began, our pupils had one reading strategy. They held it in common because they had all been taught it when they first had reading lessons in school. They were efficient sounders and blenders and decipherers of initial consonants; so efficient, indeed, that words they could have recognized "at sight" were subjected to the same decoding as those they had never seen or heard before.

What they could not do effectively was use their grapho/phonemic knowledge and sampling skills effectively in a coherent approach to constructing meaning from a text.

The teachers working with these students tried focusing on the students' apparent needs, based in part on an analysis of their miscues. What proved most effective, however, was adopting a "language experience" approach. The teachers became scribes for each student, writing to the student's dictation, inviting the student to reread the evolving text to see if he or she had said what was wanted, then writing and discussing some more, and finally providing opportunities for the student to read the finished text to an appreciative audience. *That* did more than anything else to affect the students' view of themselves as readers and to increase their competence.

It seems to me that assisting students in actually writing down parts of stories they themselves are composing may also be one of the best ways to help students who

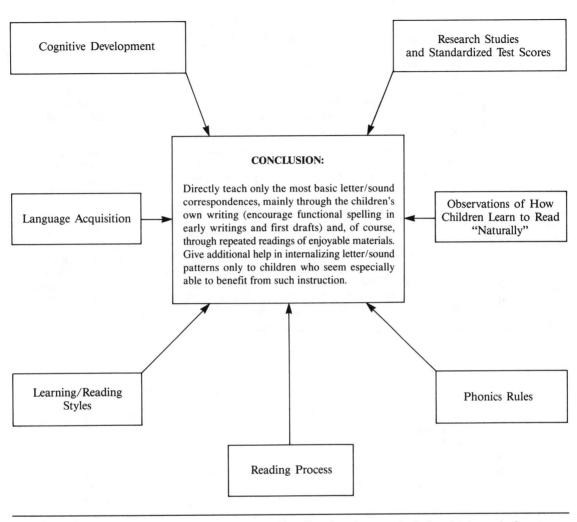

Cognitive Development

Research Studies
and Standardized Test Scores

Language Acquisition

CONCLUSION:

Directly teach only the most basic letter/sound correspondences, mainly through the children's own writing (encourage functional spelling in early writings and first drafts) and, of course, through repeated readings of enjoyable materials. Give additional help in internalizing letter/sound patterns only to children who seem especially able to benefit from such instruction.

Observations of How
Children Learn to Read
"Naturally"

Learning/Reading
Styles

Phonics Rules

Reading Process

FIGURE 11.8 *Various lines of evidence supporting the development of phonics knowledge through a whole-language approach*

need to gain greater mastery of letter/sound correspondences. Just as one might help a beginning writer in the phonemic stage, so one might help an older writer/reader sound out words, teaching basic letter/sound patterns in the process. The older writer/reader need not write out the entire story this way, for that might become a laborious process that would inhibit composition and the sense of satisfaction that would otherwise come from having created a longer and more adult story. However, guided assistance in hearing and writing the sounds in words could greatly facilitate the acquisition of basic grapho/phonemic knowledge needed for reading, just as it does for beginning readers. In both cases, however, one must remember that a

CONCLUSION:

Directly teach only the most basic letter/sound correspondences, mainly through the children's own writing (encourage functional spelling in early writings and first drafts) and, of course, through repeated readings of enjoyable materials. Give additional help in internalizing letter/sound patterns only to children who seem especially able to benefit from such instruction.

THIS CONCLUSION IS SUPPORTED BY EVIDENCE FROM

COGNITIVE DEVELOPMENT—e.g., Piaget

Children must be active in their own learning—which means, in part, that they learn best when they are engrossed in what they are doing, when it has personal meaning for them. Also, learning must be concrete, rather than abstract—and phonics is abstract. Since young children tend to center their attention on one aspect of something at a time, they will tend to center on sounding-out as their only conscious reading strategy, if phonics is emphasized.

LANGUAGE ACQUISITION—naturalistic observations of how children learn to speak

We do not directly teach children the rules for putting sounds together to make words and putting words together to make sentences. Rather, our youngsters induce the rules for themselves, creating more and more sophisticated rules as they mature.

We assist children in learning language by modeling adult language, in somewhat simplified form; by making explicit connections between words and the real world; by responding positively to their attempts to communicate (rather than by correcting immature forms); and by expecting success.

LEARNING/READING STYLES—styles and modalities through which children learn best

Most primary grade children are not very analytic (as we know also from Piaget's research), and even "synthetic" phonics requires analytic skills as well. Most primary children are not very auditory, either. They tend to be somewhat more visual, but highly kinesthetic and tactual—which means that they learn best through active involvement, both physical and emotional. Though relatively "kinesthetic" phonics programs have been developed, children tend to be even more engaged in writing and reading their own books and stories, and in reading other material that is intrinsically interesting: songs, rhymes, stories, and print in the environment.

FIGURE 11.9 *Various lines of evidence supporting the development of phonics knowledge through a whole-language approach.*

READING PROCESS—how proficient readers read (whether they're age 6 or 60)

Letter/sound patterns are only one of the language cues available to readers. If they already know that reading is for enjoyment and information, even beginning readers can and do use grammar and meaning to predict what's coming next, and then use subsequent grammar and meaning to confirm or correct their tentative identification of words. Wh-n w-rds -cc-r -n - m--n-ngf-l c-nt-xt, w- h-rdl- n--d t- s-- th- v-w-ls -n -rd-r t- r--d th- s-l-ct--n. Even word identfication suffers when readers use sounding-out as their only conscious strategy; comprehension, of course, suffers even more.

PHONICS RULES—i.e., rules for sounding-out words

There are various problems with phonics rules themselves, and with teaching them:

1. Relatively few phonics rules are consistent *and* comprehensive—that is, applicable to enough words to make them worth teaching.
2. If children have been taught rules that are fairly inconsistent, they are likely to apply the rules when it is inappropriate to do so.
3. The majority of phonics rules deal with vowels, which are fairly predictable from the consonants and from context. In real reading, readers rarely need to concentrate on vowels.
4. Most children can induce the major letter/sound patterns merely from doing lots of reading and writing—just as they induced the patterns of oral language from doing lots of listening and talking. Most of our country's middle generations (including many teachers) had little or no phonics instruction as children, yet they can sound out words as well as anyone else.

OBSERVATIONS OF HOW CHILDREN LEARN TO READ NATURALLY—
in the home, with assistance but without direct instruction

Children who learn to read naturally do so from whole to part: by first learning the gist of favorite stories, next by memorizing them, and then by gradually making associations between spoken words and written words. Gradually these children become conscious of letter/sound relationships as well.

SUCCESS OF A WHOLE-LANGUAGE APPROACH—teacher observations

Teachers who have used a whole-language approach report that more children become proficient readers and writers with an approach that moves from whole to part, focusing first on writing and reading whole stories (songs, rhymes, and so forth) and gradually on recognizing words and grasping basic letter/sound patterns. Teachers who have switched from a more direct approach to teaching the parts (e.g. emphasis on phonics or sight words, in reading; emphasis on spelling and mechanical correctness, in writing) generally report that, paradoxically, children exposed to a whole-to-part approach tend to master the parts of language *better* through such an indirect approach. Furthermore, the children are engrossed in real writing and real reading.

FIGURE 11.9 *Continued*

RESEARCH STUDIES, STANDARDIZED TEST SCORES—

Despite the claims in *Becoming a Nation of Readers*, there is by no means consensus among the leading reading educators regarding the direct teaching of phonics. The oft-cited summaries of research that support the direct teaching of phonics are themselves approximately twenty years old; the research studies themselves are, of course, older. In her 1967 book *Learning to Read: The Great Debate*, the widely known study that concluded in favor of phonics, Jeanne Chall admitted that many of the research studies she was summarizing were not well constructed or well conducted. In her 1983 update of this book, Chall also admitted that other scholars who had examined many of the same studies had drawn different conclusions. Similarly, the report *Becoming a Nation of Readers* indicates that whole-language approaches are used to teach children to read in New Zealand, "the most literate country in the world, a country that experiences very low rates of reading failure" (p. 45). The report goes on to say that the results of these approaches in the United States have produced results that are "indifferent when compared to approaches typical in American classrooms," but again cites as the only evidence for this conclusion a research summary from twenty years ago—long, long before the development of approaches that are characterized as "whole language" by teachers today.

Given the outdatedness and unreliability of the aforementioned summaries that claim superiority for the direct teaching of phonics, it should come as no surprise that the evidence from standardized test scores is mixed. There is an accumulating body of evidence that whole-language approaches produce better results on standardized tests, both with beginning readers and with those receiving remedial instruction. However, many of these research studies also tend not to be rigorously designed. Both those who advocate a part-to-whole approach such as phonics and those who advocate a whole-to-part approach such as whole language agree that there appear to be no research studies that adequately compare the approaches or conclusively decide the issue.

In the absence of clear-cut statistical evidence, it seems all the more imperative that we consider other lines of evidence, most if not all of which seem to support a whole-to-part approach to phonics knowledge, with more of an emphasis on indirect learning than on direct teaching.

START OVER AGAIN AT "CONCLUSION"

FIGURE 11.9 *Continued*

reasonable "phonetic" spelling is the aim, not "correct" spelling. Emphasis on correct spelling would defeat the purpose for having the writer sound out and write words for him or herself.

Do students with radically different kinds of reading difficulties need, then, radically different kinds of individual assistance? I think not. A whole-language approach by its very nature capitalizes upon a reader's strengths while minimizing the reader's weaknesses, which seems the best approach for everyone. Within the whole-language context, teachers and tutors can focus as needed on helping readers develop whatever abilities they can best develop, whether those be the kinds of analytic strategies attributed to the left hemisphere or the kinds of global strategies attributed to the right. Regardless of students' preferred processing styles and modality strengths, they can be accommodated in a whole-language approach.

Since our typical subskills and skills approaches are so left-hemisphere oriented, however, we might give particular thought to developing strategies that build upon the strengths of those students who are strongly right-hemispheric in their approach to learning—and who therefore may have most difficulty in acquiring left-hemispheric skills. For example, those who are strongly right-hemispheric seem to learn especially well through music, drama and movement, visual patterns and pictures, and even color. The following are just a few of the possible implications for reaching such students more effectively—and the approaches tend to enhance learning for more "left-brained" students as well. Most of the suggestions are appropriate for teaching beginning readers, working with developmental readers who have particular difficulties, and teaching "content" and the reading of "content area" texts:

1. Teach students first to sing and then to read songs. Choose songs that incorporate both rhythm and rhyme, and that invite rhythmic movement.

2. Read a story that invites visualization of the characters and events; invite students to visualize as they listen, and then to draw a picture representing some scene from the story. Finally, invite students to read the story on their own.

3. Write out a guided visualization relating to a story students are to read and/or a unit they will be studying in social studies or science. Lead students through the guided visualization so that they can experience what's being described, using in their imaginations as many of the senses as you can reasonably incorporate into the guided visualization. Use this visualization trip as a preparation for reading. (See as an example the guided visualization included in the appendix on "Petronella.")

4. Have students role-play a situation they are to read about, whether the reading is to be fiction or nonfiction—if the latter, perhaps something related to social studies. Or show a film that will activate students' schemas. All techniques of this sort will make reading easier.

5. Invite students who have difficulty reading aloud to visualize their favorite color and concentrate on that visualization as they read orally. (Barbara Vitale, 1985, reported amazing results with even virtual non-readers, using this technique. Many readers showed several years' improvement on standardized tests of reading with less than two hours' practice in reading while visualizing their favorite color!)

Obviously these suggestions are only a beginning. I recommend you consult the sources under "The Whole Curriculum, the Whole Child" in the end-of-book "Selected Readings" and, of course, brainstorm for your own ideas on facilitating reading.

Other ideas for enhancing learning in general seem, of course, worth exploring in the teaching of reading. For example, there is considerable evidence that a relaxed state facilitates learning. We can encourage relaxation in a variety of ways: by leading students through the kinds of relaxation exercises recommended in books on stress management; by playing relaxing music (baroque music at about 55–60 beats a minute is helpful, as is much of the dreamy "New Age" music); by providing a classroom environment that encourages relaxation through its use of color, space, furniture, and such; and of course by the way we conduct class and structure classroom activities. The suggestions are equally appropriate for working with students in individual tutoring sessions. All deserve the best that teachers have to offer.

"Dyslexia" . . . or Dyspedagogia?

There are a variety of reasons, of course, why students do *not* in fact always receive the best that teachers have to offer: inappropriate pressures for teaching to the standardized tests, overcrowded classrooms, an inordinate amount of time that must be spent in record-keeping; the list could go on and on. Many of these are situations over which the teacher has little control. However, it is important to consider the degree to which teachers can prevent or reduce reading difficulties just by changing that over which they do have control. Hence the title of this section: dyslexia . . . or dyspedagogia. In many ways, I think, "dyslexics"—people with severe reading difficulties—are created, not born.

Robert Hillerich begins an article titled "Let's Pretend" with the following question: "What would happen if you pretended in your classroom that the poor readers were actually good readers?" His answer: "We have enough research evidence to suggest that your expectation would be fulfilled—they would actually become much more successful" (1985, p. 15). Good readers, of whatever age, typically see reading as having to do with getting meaning. Poor readers typically see reading as a matter of pronouncing or understanding words, a view obviously less conducive to grasping the meaning of the whole. How do readers acquire such a detrimental view of reading? Probably from the kind of reading instruction that focuses on identifying words. How do they maintain such a view over years of instruction? Hillerich summarizes a variety of research studies indicating that students perceived as poor readers are treated in ways that tend to perpetuate this unproductive and inaccurate view of reading. The following are some examples, with Hillerich's sources listed as appropriate:

1. Poor readers spend approximately 75 percent of their time in oral reading—in trying to say the words correctly while the teacher listens and corrects. Good readers, in contrast, spend about 75 percent of their time reading silently, for meaning (Allington 1983).

2. When good readers make a miscue, teachers typically ignore the miscue, but when poor readers make a miscue, teachers typically stop them and often call attention to the grapho/phonemic cues exclusively. Again, for the poorer reader, attention is focused on getting the words rather than on getting the meaning.

3. Poorer readers receive much more drill on isolated words than do good readers. It is the poor readers who are drilled on word lists and flash cards, the ones who take home word lists to study instead of stories to read (Hiebert 1983).

4. Poorer readers are often given inadequate guidance in reading a text to comprehend it. Worse yet, some teachers assume that poorer readers can be expected to answer only "literal" comprehension questions and not the more interesting inferential, interpretive, and evaluative kinds of questions. Again, literal questions focus students' attention on details, often minute details, and away from an understanding and appreciation of the whole.

5. Various studies show that teachers typically allow students far too little time to formulate a response to their questions. But which students are allotted the least time? The poorer readers, of course.

6. Poorer readers are often kept busy with workbooks, dittos, and other kinds of drills, while better readers are enjoying library books and participating in role playing, dramatization, and other "creative" ways to enhance and express comprehension of what's been read. Thus poorer readers again have less opportunity to learn through experience what reading is supposed to be all about.

With such teaching practices being all too typical, is it any wonder that children who do not quickly "take off" as readers become, if anything, poorer and less motivated readers as time goes on? As Margaret Meek notes, "once readers are thought to be poor, even the best teachers may expect too little rather than too much" (1983, p. 212). And in such an environment, students may conclude, as did those with whom Meek and her teachers worked, that they cannot be successful as readers, no matter what they do.

To prevent readers from gaining such detrimental views of reading and such disastrous views of themselves as readers, I suggest that we try in every way possible to implement a whole-language, whole-brain, whole-curriculum approach to the whole learner. Add to this a whole-language reading recovery program for young children who appear to be "at risk" with regard to reading, and perhaps we too can reduce the number of children who might be considered "dyslexic" to a mere 1 percent of the school-age population. Our children deserve no less.

ACTIVITIES AND PROJECTS FOR FURTHER EXPLORATION

1. If you did activity 1 in Chapter 6, you should be well prepared to do this activity after also reading the present chapter: make a list of twelve easy ways to create poor readers and another list of twelve (possibly difficult) ways to create good readers. For the latter, consider how you would like to have been taught—or how

you would like someone to teach any children you may have, now or later. Be prepared to discuss.

You may find it valuable to read the following two articles first, if you have not already done so:

Smith, Frank. 1973. Twelve Easy Ways to Make Learning to Read Difficult, and One Difficult Way to Make It Easy. *Psycholinguistics and Reading.* Ed. F. Smith. New York: Holt, Rinehart and Winston, 183–196.

Estes, Thomas H., and Julie P. Johnstone. November/December 1977. Twelve Easy Ways to Make Readers Hate Reading (and One Difficult Way to Make Them Love It). *Language Arts* 54: 891–97.

2. Brainstorm for additional ways to teach reading and content-through-reading to children who learn less readily through the written word than through music, drama and movement, visual patterns and pictures. You might focus on a particular grade level or even use a particular novel, social studies unit, or science unit as the focal point for such brainstorming. For example: the novel *Across Five Aprils*, by Irene Hunt, is an excellent junior novel to integrate with the study of the Civil War, from upper elementary level through high school. You might brainstorm for ideas to facilitate the reading of the novel in particular and the study of the Civil War in general. Or you might choose a science unit, such as the solar system, and brainstorm ideas for facilitating reading about and understanding the solar system. See Chapter 9 for other techniques you might incorporate into this brainstorming. Time permitting, this brainstorming might form the basis for a lesson plan or even a unit plan. For ideas you might consult some of the suggested readings in the final bibliography under the heading of ''The Whole Curriculum, the Whole Child.''

3. Below is a selection from the reading material given to an eleven-year-old boy in a special education classroom, with his miscues marked. Examine the miscues to determine his apparent reading strengths and needs. Then discuss what kind of reading recovery program *you* might design for this boy. Be as specific as possible.

Sail

                 light   ②*bake*
                                          ①*mim*
Gail and Ben can not get home. The lake is wide. "I can make

             You Gail   *Gail*
a boat," said Ben. "Use the pail," said Gail. "The pail is big,"

        ②*not*
  is   ①*Pete boat* *pail*   *Ben they said boat boat*
said Ben. "A nut can make a fine boat." "Nail the sail to the pole,"

             sailed   *I we*
said Gail. Gail and Ben set sail in the boat. "It is wet in the

                is   *to*   *is*
boat," said Gail. "The boat has a hole in it." "Take the cap," said

and eat   *Gail*   *pail*   *said*

Ben. ʌ "Use it to bail." Gail did bail, but the hole is big. "I see

       sail mad   *pail*   *is*

rain," said Gail. The rain came. "The sail is in the lake," said

Tom   *Pete*

Gail. Tim is in the lake. ("Wait,") said Ben. "Save us," (said) Gail.

Tom   *lake*   *Tim Nut is*

Tim came up to the boat. "Tim can save us," said Ben. "Take his

         Nut is   *ride Tim*

tail," said Gail. "Get on top," said Tim. Gail and Ben rode on top

        is   *is*

of Tim. "Tim got us home," said Gail. "Tim is a fine boat," said

Tim

Ben.

The reader made some corrections, but most were prompted by the teacher. Since she did not indicate which were prompted and which were not, I have not marked any of the miscues as corrected.

4. If appropriate, design a whole-language reading recovery program for students with whom you are working.

READINGS FOR FURTHER EXPLORATION

Carbo, Marie. May 1984. Why Most Reading Tests Aren't Fair. *Early Years K–8*: 73–75. Explains why most reading tests are particularly inappropriate for global learners, thus leading to a disproportionate number of them being considered poor readers.

———. April 1983. Research in Reading and Learning Style: Implications for Exceptional Children. *Exceptional Children* 49: 486–94. Provides evidence that "poor readers tend to be tactile-kinesthetic learners with a biased arousal of the right hemisphere," and recommends teaching poor readers through their learning style strengths.

Morris, Darrell. September 1981. Concept of Word: A Developmental Phenomenon in the Beginning Reading and Writing Processes. *Language Arts* 58: (September) 659–68. Discusses Morris's methods for assessing emergent readers' concepts of word in both reading and writing.

Rigg, Pat, and Liz Taylor. March 1979. A Twenty-One-Year-Old Begins to Read. *English Journal* 68: 52–56. This article details the whole-language reading recovery program used with Renee, as mentioned in the chapter.

Wagner, Betty J. 1983. The Expanding Circle of Informal Classroom Drama. *Integrating the Language Arts in the Elementary School.* Ed. Beverly A. Busching and Judith I. Schwartz. Urbana, Illinois: National Council of Teachers of English, 155–63. Provides a marvelous extended example of using creative drama to facilitate first writing and later reading about a social studies unit on Brazil and a science unit on water.

Steinley, Gary. April 1983. Left Brain/Right Brain: More of the Same? *Language Arts* 60: 459–62. Suggests various "right brain" activities to enhance students' experience of literature in the classroom.

Shook, Ronald. October 1986. The Two-Brain Theory: A Critique. *English Education* 18: 173–183. The author argues that popular notions to the contrary, there are actually very few aspects of mental functioning that can be attributed to the left hemisphere or to the right. He specifically criticizes Steinley's article (above), among others, and suggests that even thinking of left-hemispheric and right-hemispheric capacities in a metaphorical fashion may be harmful educationally, as it leads to labeling of students that may limit their self-concept and their growth. A timely warning, as the profession is looking more and more toward meeting the needs of the "right-brained," "global" learners.

Hillerich, Robert L. Summer 1985. Let's Pretend. *Michigan Reading Journal* 18: 15–18, 20. This is a must-read article; as discussed in the chapter, it summarizes many of the ways that teachers treat good and poor readers differently, thus contributing to the poor readers' difficulties and lack of interest in reading.

Altwerger, Bess, and Lois Bird. January 1982. Disabled: The Learner or the Curriculum? *Topics in Learning and Learning Disabilities* 1: 69–78. This is another must-read article. It shows through journal entries and interviews with two college students how repeated skills-oriented instruction can create and maintain "disabled" readers—and how those same students can learn to read and write effectively with a whole-language approach that emphasizes reading and writing as communicative processes and that values and builds upon the strengths of the learners.

Goodman, Kenneth S. January 1982. Revaluing Readers and Reading. *Topics in Learning and Learning Disabilities* 1: 87–93. In a similar vein, Goodman discusses the importance of revaluing readers in trouble, and of helping them learn to revalue themselves as readers. Goodman also discusses some methods and materials for revaluing.

Rhodes, Lynn K., and Joy L. Shannon. January 1982. Psycholinguistic Principles in Operation in a Primary Learning Disabilities Classroom. *Topics in Learning and Learning Disabilities* 1: 1–10. Dismayed by her relative lack of success during 11 years of typical LD teaching, the second author studied recent work in oral and written language development. Abandoning the kind of "mechanistic" paradigm described here in Chapter 7 for the kind of paradigm underlying a whole-language approach, Shannon began implementing the latter in her LD classroom. The article demonstrates the value of persisting in such an approach, even though the children are initially inattentive, disruptive, and inclined to reply to every request with "I can't." After a while, that attitude declines and disappears, as children willingly and spontaneously engage in reading and writing activities.

Hasselriis, Peter. January 1982. IEPs and a Whole-Language Model of Language Arts. *Topics in Learning and Learning Disabilities* 1: 17–21. Clarifying the point that the law requiring IEPs (Individualized Educational Programs) for all "handicapped" students does not in fact require readily measurable skills-oriented testing and instruction, Hasselriis then provides examples of three IEPs in which the assessment consists primarily of interviews, observations, and reading miscue analysis, and the short-term objectives consist of various "whole-language" activities that are appropriate, given the assessment of each student and the annual goal determined from that assessment.

As the last four entries suggest, the entire January 1982 issue of *Topics in Learning and Learning Disabilities* is highly relevant to the concerns of this chapter and this book.

12

Coming Whole Circle

Dorothy Watson

"Snip, snap, snout, our tale's told out." Well, almost. In this book, we have attempted to present a point of view about reading that is both personal and social, and that is based in research. We have taken this theoretically sound socio-psycho-linguistic view an important step farther—we have suggested many ways in which teachers can implement, or begin to implement, this view in the classroom. In Chapter 6, for example, we have suggested some ways that a basal reader lesson can be modified to better reflect what is known about how people read and comprehend. In Chapter 9, we have offered a multitude of research-based suggestions for helping students read content area texts more effectively and more appreciatively. In Chapter 10, we have described a way of assessing reading that reflects the primacy of comprehension, and that focuses more on readers' strengths than on their weaknesses. In Chapter 11, we have demonstrated ways of matching instruction with students' individual reading styles, and indicated effective ways of helping students who experience reading difficulties.

All of the aforementioned chapters suggest valuable ways of moving toward the approach for which the rationale is provided in Chapter 7: a whole-language approach, described in detail in Chapter 8. Such a program, we feel, is based upon the best that is known about how children become literate. It is an approach that places teacher and children at the center of the curriculum. And thus at the end of the book we come "whole circle" in more ways than one: back to a whole-language approach, and back to our initial emphasis on the importance of the *teacher* to effective instruction.

We know, however, that if we want teachers to create whole-language classrooms, what we have written simply isn't enough. We have heard teachers expressing their fears: The upper grade teacher think a whole-language program is for primary classes, while the first-grade teacher thinks it's for fifth graders. The special education teacher is convinced it's for the academically successful kids, and the teachers of self-contained classrooms believe it is just right for the Learning Disabled kids. And everyone says, "I don't know how to begin."

412

We have seen students learn to read and write and love doing so in kindergarten, special education classes including Educable Mentally Impaired, and of course, the typical self-contained classes. If this is the case, why then won't teachers who appear to accept the new information about learning to read and write move smoothly and painlessly into a whole-language program? In their own words—"I don't know where and when and how to begin." Specifically, then, what might the first day look like?

Of course, we invite teachers to take a pedagogical risk—right now, in their own classroom, to whatever extent they feel relatively comfortable. You notice that we say *relatively comfortable*: teachers may have to enter a temporary discomfort zone in order to make literacy learning easy for students. For example, teachers may have to wait longer for children to take the initiative than these teachers are accustomed to, or they may find themselves seeking help from other whole-language teachers when they and their textbook have sufficed in the past. To survive the discomfort zones, teachers must trust themselves, their new knowledge, and their students. Because we are painfully aware that becoming a whole-language teacher is easier said than done, we will attempt pedagogically to practice what we preach by offering (long distance) an invitational demonstration. The demonstration is actually a description of a first-grade classroom on the first day of school. We believe that our description is invitational because it is within the designing and modifying capabilities of potential whole-language teachers.

The teacher we want to describe is Kittye Copeland, who for ten years on the first day of school passed out worksheets, workbooks, basals, and other texts, and then spent the year trying to get her students to master all the first-grade information. Kittye loved teaching, but what she had done for ten years could only be described as routine; she was nearing burnout. This dedicated teacher decided to try once again; she spent the summer studying socio-psycholinguistic research and theory, including miscue analysis, and she began to develop a whole-language alternative to her traditional reading program.

Kittye's eleventh year of teaching started as no other year had. The first major difference was attitudinal; Kittye focused on what her students did *right* rather than what they did *wrong*; she truly respected their efforts. This enlightened observer of children developed literacy across the curriculum based on the strengths of her students. She valued the individual and the group, and she promoted both.

On the first day of school, the children were surrounded with meaningful print. They chose their nametag off the bulletin board and helped other children who had trouble reading their own name. There were letters from Kittye in their class mailbox, and on that first day they wrote back to their teacher. The children were constantly encouraged to take linguistic risks (with reading, "Put in something that makes sense"; with writing, "What would you like to tell us through writing?"; with spelling, "Spell it the best you can—think how it looks, sounds, feels in your mouth").

On the first day of school, the children listened to stories, read by themselves and with partners, wrote letters, and dictated a finger play ("Eensey Weensy Spider") to their teacher. On their own initiative they acted out "Eensey Weensy Spider"—learning concepts and labels such as *water spout/faucet*. Interest in spiders led to some research in the science corner reference books. "Eensy Weensy Spider" became a chant that all the children easily read as a group and individually.

As the children moved from a large-group sharing of the highly predictable book, *The Bus Ride*, to reading the book with their partner, the rhythm of the class began to emerge—even on that first day. The children knew that they could consult with other students; they knew that if they needed to try out an idea, or get help and encouragement from others, it was permissible to do so.

The classroom and materials were arranged for the students. There were large and small group work areas as well as spots where children could find a quiet place if one were needed. Unexpected events, such as a note from the cafeteria manager, were turned into literacy events in which the children shared in both receiving a message and replying to it.

At the end of the day, 26 first graders left their classroom eager and happy—not one tear, not one squabble, not one deflated and defeated learner. These children did not take home a handful of worksheets and memories of a disappointing school day. Rather, they proudly presented their parents with a copy of their finger play, a real book, a letter from their teacher, and the unshaken notion that they happily were readers and writers.

Appendix A

PETRONELLA

* * * * *

Jay Williams

In the kingdom of Skyclear Mountain, three princes were always born to the king and queen.

* * * * *

The oldest prince was always called Michael, the middle prince was always called George, and the youngest was always called Peter. When they were grown, they always went out to seek their fortunes. What happened to the oldest prince and the middle prince no one ever knew. But the youngest prince always rescued a princess, brought her home, and in time ruled over the kingdom. That was the way it had always been. And so far as anyone knew, that was the way it would always be.

* * * * *

Until now.

* * * * *

Now was the time of King Peter the twenty-sixth and Queen Blossom. An oldest prince was born, and a middle prince. But the youngest prince turned out to be a girl.

* * * * *

"Well," said the king gloomily, "we can't call her Peter. We'll have to call her Petronella. And what's to be done about it, I'm sure I don't know."

Note: Asterisks are used throughout this story to suggest appropriate places to stop and predict what's coming next.

There was nothing to be done. The years passed, and the time came for the princes to go out and seek their fortunes. Michael and George said goodbye to the king and queen and mounted their horses. Then out came Petronella. She was dressed in traveling clothes, with her bag packed and a sword by her side.

*   *   *   *   *

"If you think," she said, "that I'm going to sit at home, you are mistaken. I'm going to seek my fortune too."

"Impossible!" said the king.

"What will people say?" cried the queen.

"Look," said Prince Michael, "be reasonable, Pet. Stay home. Sooner or later a prince will turn up here."

Petronella smiled. She was a tall, handsome girl with flaming red hair, and when she smiled in that particular way it meant she was trying to keep her temper.

"I'm going with you," she said. "I'll find a prince if I have to rescue one from something myself. And that's that."

*   *   *   *   *

The grooms brought out her horse, she said good-bye to her parents, and away she went behind her two brothers.

They traveled into the flatlands below Skyclear Mountain. After many days, they entered a great dark forest. They came to a place where the road divided into three, and there at the fork sat a little, wrinkled old man covered with dust and spiderwebs.

Prince Michael said haughtily, "Where do these roads go, old man?"

"The road on the right goes to the city of Gratz," the man replied. "The road in the center goes to the castle of Blitz. The road on the left goes to the house of Albion the enchanter. And that's one."

"What do you mean by 'And that's one'?" asked Prince George.

"I mean," said the old man, "that I am forced to sit on this spot without stirring, and that I must answer one question from each person who passes by. And that's two."

*   *   *   *   *

Petronella's kind heart was touched. "Is there anything I can do to help you?" she asked.

The old man sprang to his feet. The dust fell from him in clouds.

"You have already done so," he said. "For that question is the one which releases me. I have sat here for sixty-two years waiting for someone to ask me that." He snapped his fingers with joy. "In return, I will tell you anything you wish to know."

"Where can I find a prince?" Petronella said promptly.

"There is one in the house of Albion the enchanter," the old man answered.

"Ah," said Petronella, "then that is where I am going."

"In that case I will leave you," said her oldest brother. "For I am going to the castle of Blitz to see if I can find my fortune there."

"Good luck," said Prince George. "For I am going to the city of Gratz. I have a feeling my fortune is there."

They embraced her and rode away.

Petronella looked thoughtfully at the old man, who was combing spiderwebs and dust out of his beard. "May I ask you something else?" she said.

"Of course. Anything."

"Suppose I wanted to rescue that prince from the enchanter. How would I go about it? I haven't any experience in such things, you see."

The old man chewed a piece of his beard. "I do not know everything," he said, after a moment. "I know that there are three magical secrets which, if you can get them from him, will help you."

"How can I get them?" asked Petronella.

"Offer to work for him. He will set you three tasks, and if you can do them you may demand a reward for each. You must ask him for a comb for your hair, a mirror to look into, and a ring for your finger."

"And then?"

"I do not know. I only know that when you rescue the prince, you can use these things to escape from the enchanter."

"It doesn't sound easy," sighed Petronella.

"Nothing we really want is easy," said the old man. "Look at me—I have wanted my freedom, and I've had to wait sixty-two years for it."

Petronella said good-bye to him. She mounted her horse and galloped along the third road.

*   *   *   *   *

It ended at a low, rambling house with a red roof. It was a comfortable-looking house, surrounded by gardens and stables and trees heavy with fruit.

On the lawn, in an armchair, sat a handsome young man with his eyes closed and his face turned to the sky.

Petronella tied her horse to the gate and walked across the lawn.

"Is this the house of Albion the enchanter?" she said.

The young man blinked up at her in surprise.

"I think so," he said. "Yes, I'm sure it is."

"And who are you?"

The young man yawned and stretched. "I am Prince Ferdinand of Firebright," he replied. "Would you mind stepping aside? I'm trying to get a suntan and you're standing in the way."

Petronella snorted. "You don't sound like much of a prince," she said.

"That's funny," said the young man, closing his eyes. "That's what my father always says."

*   *   *   *   *

At that moment the door of the house opened. Out came a man dressed all in black and silver. He was tall and thin, and as sinister as a cloud full of thunder. His face was stern, but full of wisdom. Petronella knew at once that he must be the enchanter.

He bowed to her politely. "What can I do for you?"

"I wish to work for you," said Petronella boldly.

Albion nodded. "I cannot refuse you," he said. "But I warn you, it will be dangerous. Tonight I will give you a task. If you do it, I will reward you. If you fail, you must die."

Petronella glanced at the prince and sighed. "If I must, I must," she said. "Very well."

*   *   *   *   *

That evening they all had dinner together in the enchanter's cozy kitchen. Then Albion took Petronella out to a stone building and unbolted its door. Inside were seven huge black dogs.

"You must watch my hounds all night," said he.

Petronella went in, and Albion closed and locked the door.

*   *   *   *   *

At once the hounds began to snarl and bark. They showed their teeth at her. But Petronella was a real princess. She plucked up her courage. Instead of backing away, she went toward the dogs. She began to speak to them in a quiet voice. They stopped snarling and sniffed at her. She patted their heads.

"I see what it is," she said. "You are lonely here. I will keep you company."

And so all night long, she sat on the floor and talked to the hounds and stroked them. They lay close to her, panting.

In the morning Albion came and let her out. "Ah," said he, "I see that you are brave. If you had run from the dogs, they would have torn you to pieces. Now you may ask for what you want."

"I want a comb for my hair," said Petronella.

The enchanter gave her a comb carved from a piece of black wood.

Prince Ferdinand was sunning himself and working at a crossword puzzle. Petronella said to him in a low voice, "I am doing this for you."

"That's nice," said the prince. "What's 'selfish' in nine letters?"

"You are," snapped Petronella. She went to the enchanter. "I will work for you once more," she said.

That night Albion led her to a stable. Inside were seven huge horses.

"Tonight," he said, "you must watch my steeds."

He went out and locked the door. At once the horses began to rear and neigh. They pawed at her with their iron hoofs.

*   *   *   *   *

But Petronella was a real princess. She looked closely at them and saw that their coats were rough and their manes and tails full of burrs.

"I see what it is," she said. "You are hungry and dirty."

She brought them as much hay as they could eat, and began to brush them. All night long she fed them and groomed them, and they stood quietly in their stalls.

In the morning Albion let her out. "You are as kind as you are brave," said he. "If you had run from them, they would have trampled you under their hoofs. What will you have as a reward?"

"I want a mirror to look into," said Petronella.

The enchanter gave her a mirror made of gray silver.

She looked across the lawn at Prince Ferdinand. He was doing setting-up exercises. He was certainly handsome. She said to the enchanter, "I will work for you once more."

That night Albion led her to a loft above the stables. There, on perches, were seven great hawks.

"Tonight," said he, "you must watch my falcons."

As soon as Petronella was locked in, the hawks began to beat their wings and scream at her.

*   *   *   *   *

Petronella laughed. "That is not how birds sing," she said. "Listen."

She began to sing in a sweet voice. The hawks fell silent. All night long she sang to them, and they sat like feathered statues on their perches, listening.

In the morning, Albion said, "You are as talented as you are kind and brave. If you had run from them, they would have pecked and clawed you without mercy. What do you want now?"

"I want a ring for my finger," said Petronella.

*   *   *   *   *

The enchanter gave her a ring made from a single diamond.

All that day and all that night Petronella slept, for she was very tired. But early the next morning, she crept into Prince Ferdinand's room. He was sound asleep, wearing purple pajamas.

"Wake up," whispered Petronella. "I am going to rescue you."

*   *   *   *   *

Ferdinand awoke and stared sleepily at her. "What time is it?"

"Never mind that," said Petronella. "Come on!"

"But I'm sleepy," Ferdinand objected. "And it's so pleasant here."

Petronella shook her head. "You're not much of a prince," she said grimly. "But you're the best I can do."

She grabbed him by the wrist and dragged him out of bed. She hauled him down the stairs. His horse and hers were in a separate stable, and she saddled them quickly. She gave the prince a shove, and he mounted. She jumped on her own horse, seized the prince's reins, and away they went like the wind.

*   *   *   *   *

They had not gone far when they heard a tremendous thumping. Petronella looked back. A dark cloud rose behind them, and beneath it she saw the enchanter. He was running with great strides, faster than the horses could go.

Petronella desperately pulled out the comb. "The old man said this would help me!" she said. And because she didn't know what else to do with it, she threw the comb on the ground.

At once a forest rose up. The trees were so thick that no one could get between them.

Away went Petronella and the prince. But the enchanter turned himself into an ax and began to chop. Right and left he chopped, flashing, and the trees fell before him.

Soon he was through the wood, and once again Petronella heard his footsteps thumping behind.

She reined in the horses. She took out the mirror and threw it on the ground. At once a wide lake spread out behind them, gray and glittering.

Off they went again. But the enchanter sprang into the water, turning himself into a salmon as he did so. He swam across the lake and leaped out of the water on to the other bank. Petronella heard him coming—*thump! thump!*—behind them again.

This time she threw down the ring. It didn't turn into anything, but lay shining on the ground.

The enchanter came running up. And as he jumped over the ring, it opened wide and then snapped up around him. It held his arms tight to his body, in a magical grip from which he could not escape.

"Well," said Prince Ferdinand, "that's the end of him."

Petronella looked at him in annoyance. Then she looked at the enchanter, held fast in the ring.

*   *   *   *   *

"Bother!" she said. "I can't just leave him here. He'll starve to death."

She got off her horse and went up to him. "If I release you," she said, "will you promise to let the prince go free?"

Albion stared at her in astonishment. "Let him go free?" he said. "What are you talking about? I'm glad to get rid of him."

It was Petronella's turn to look surprised. "I don't understand," she said. "Weren't you holding him prisoner?"

"Certainly not," said Albion. "He came to visit me for a weekend. At the end of it, he said, 'It's so pleasant here, do you mind if I stay on for another day or two?' I'm very polite and I said, 'Of course.' He stayed on, and on, and on. I didn't like to be rude to a guest and I couldn't just kick him out. I don't know what I'd have done if you hadn't dragged him away."

*   *   *   *   *

"But then—" said Petronella, "but then—why did you come running after him this way?"

"I wasn't chasing him," said the enchanter. "I was chasing *you*. You are just the girl I've been looking for. You are brave and kind and talented, and beautiful as well."

"Oh," said Petronella.

"I see," she said.

"Hmm," said she. "How do I get this ring off you?"

"Give me a kiss."

She did so. The ring vanished from around Albion and reappeared on Petronella's finger.

"I don't know what my parents will say when I come home with you instead of a prince," she said.

"Let's go and find out, shall we?" said the enchanter cheerfully.

He mounted one horse and Petronella the other. And off they trotted, side by side, leaving Prince Ferdinand of Firebright to walk home as best he could.

*   *   *   *   *

GUIDED VISUALIZATION BASED ON PETRONELLA'S TASKS

Preparation

The teacher would first get children into a relaxed, receptive state. He or she might tell them to settle into a comfortable position, sitting straight but relaxed, with their hands on their desk, their eyes closed. Then the teacher might have them take a few deep breaths, breathing slowly in and out, then give them directions for progressively relaxing each part of the body, beginning with the toes and working upwards. It can be particularly effective to imagine a warm liquid flowing down the arms and out to the fingertips. It may also help to have students imagine riding an escalator down and down, deeper and deeper into relaxation. This accomplished, the teacher could begin slowly reading the guided visualization, pausing at appropriate points while the students experience what has been described. The teacher must remember to later bring students out of the guided visualization slowly, perhaps saying that they are to ride back up the escalator and awaken gradually as he or she counts to five and telling them that they will return to the classroom alert and refreshed; the teacher would then count to five very slowly.

Guided visualization

Now let yourself become Petronella, the daughter of King Peter the twenty-sixth and Queen Blossom. You are *there*, in the kingdom of Skyclear Mountain. You have left your brothers at the crossroads and gone on a quest to find a prince. At the home of Albion the enchanter you have found a prince, Prince Michael. He is sitting in the sun, trying to get a suntan. How do you feel about him? . . . Clearly he is selfish and lazy, but you are determined to carry through with your quest and "rescue" him from Albion.

   In order to free the prince, you have offered to work for Albion. Now it is dark. . . . Albion leads you outside toward a stone building. He hasn't told you what task you must perform, but he *has* said that if you fail at the task, you will die. How do you feel, alone with Albion, being led through the dark night to goodness-only-knows what? . . . Now you have reached the building. The stone is cold and clammy as you lean up against it. . . . From around the door comes the smell of rotting straw, and you sense the presence of animals within. . . . How do you feel? . . . Do you and Albion say anthing to each other? If so, what do you say? . . . Now Albion unbolts and opens the door. Inside are seven *huge* black dogs, larger than any you have ever seen or imagined. . . . "You must watch my hounds all night," Albion says. He closes and locks the door behind you. . . . Your eyes have scarcely begun to adjust to the dimmed light when the hounds begin to snarl and bark menacingly, showing their teeth. How do you feel? . . . What are you thinking? . . .

You remember that you are, after all, a real princess. . . . You screw up your courage and walk toward the dogs. You speak to them in a quiet voice. What do you say? Speak to them. . . . They stop snarling and sniff at your hands. Slowly, you reach forward and pat the head of the dog nearest you. He licks your hand. How do you feel now? . . . You pet the others in turn, letting them nudge you with their cold noses and lick your hands and face. They are lonely, you realize. Finally you sit down on the floor. Two of the hounds put their heads in your lap; the others snuggle up as close as they can get. Now how do you feel? . . . You sit and stroke their short, smooth fur, talking to them softly, and singing lullabies. What do you say to them? Talk to them, sing to them, in your imagination. . . .

Hours have now passed. Just as you are about to fall asleep exhausted, the sun streams through the cracks around the door. It is morning, and you know that you have succeeded at the task. How do you feel now? . . .

B

Appendix B

LISTS OF USEFUL ADDRESSES

Professional Organizations and Publishers of Professional Books and "Big Books" for Whole-Class Use

Boynton/Cook Publishers, Inc.
70 Court Street
Portsmouth, New Hampshire 03801

Publishes outstanding books for teachers and students, many focusing on writing. Emphasis is on junior high through college teaching.

Good Apple
Box 299
Carthage, Illinois 62321

Provides creative and stimulating resources for teaching in language arts and self-concept development, as well as social studies, science, and math.

Heinemann Educational Books, Inc.
70 Court Street
Portsmouth, New Hampshire 03801

Heinemann offers an outstanding collection of professional books on reading, writing, and whole-language teaching. In Canada, Heinemann books are distributed by Irwin Publishing, listed below.

International Reading Association
800 Barksdale Road
P.O. Box 8139
Newark, Delaware 19711

Offers a wide variety of publications on reading, in addition to professional journals for teachers. The latter include *The Reading Teacher*, for elementary teachers; *Journal of Reading*, for secondary teachers; and *Reading Research Quarterly*, for scholars and researchers.

Irwin Publishing, Inc.
180 West Beaver Creek Road
Richmond Hill, Ontario
Canada L4B 1B4

Irwin publishes and distributes a variety of high-quality professional books on language arts and literacy education, including books originally published by Heinemann (above). In addition, Irwin publishes literature for classroom use.

LINK
The Language Company
1895 Dudley Street
Lakewood, Colorado 80215

This growing company offers packets of instructional activities and ideas to accompany children's literature books.

National Council of Teachers
of English
1111 Kenyon Road
Urbana, Illinois 61801

The NCTE offers an impressive variety of high-quality professional resources on the teaching of English and the language arts, in addition to professional journals for teachers. The latter include *Language Arts*, for elementary teachers; *English Journal*, for secondary teachers; and *Research in the Teaching of English*, for scholars and researchers.

Reading Development Resources, Ltd.
P.O. Box 36391
Louisville, Kentucky 40232

Authors Elizabeth and Hans Grundin offer sets of classroom materials—big Books, small books, cassettes, games. These "3L" materials focus on language, literacy, and literature.

Richard C. Owen, Publisher
P.O. Box 819
New York, New York 10085

Publishes and distributes several excellent "psycholinguistic" and "whole-language" books for teachers, films and videos demonstrating a whole-language approach in action, plus some Big Books for use with children. Also publishes a whole-language newsletter, *Teachers Networking*.

Rigby Education
454 S. Virginia Street
Crystal Lake, Illinois 60014

Offers a wide selection of Big Books, most with accompanying small books and some with cassettes. Some of the books have been composed by children; others focus on topics in the content areas; many are from traditional or modern literature.

Scholastic Inc.
Box 7502
Jefferson City, Missouri 65102

Scholastic offers a wealth of high-quality paperbacks for children K–12, for both whole class and individual use. Many of the selections for younger children have predictable structures, such as those in the "easy to read" folktales. Scholastic also offers a selection of Big Books, most of which are available with accompanying sets of small books and cassette tapes. In addition, Scholastic offers regular-sized predictable books, some of which are accompanied by cassette tapes.

Scholastic–TAB Publications
123 Newkirk Road
Richmond Hill, Ontario L4C 3G5
Canada

In addition to a wide selection of high quality paperbacks for young people, Scholastic–TAB offers a variety of resources particularly valuable for whole-language teaching. These include Big Books, many with accompanying sets of small books, plus a cassette tape of the selection; classroom sets of predictable books; and other book/cassette sets for shared reading. Also publishes *Whole Language Newsletter*; see below.

TAWL (Teachers Applying Whole Language)
c/o Debra Goodman
20020 Renfrew
Detroit, Michigan 48221

This grass roots organization of whole-language teachers is a valuable resource for establishing your own teacher support group. See also *Teacher's Networking* below.

Teachers & Writers Collaborative
5 Union Square West
New York, New York 10003

The Teachers & Writers Collaborative publishes a variety of creative books on writing and the teaching of writing, plus the journal called *Teachers & Writers Magazine*.

Teachers Networking
c/o Richard C. Owen, Publisher
P.O. Box 819
New York, New York 10085

This whole-language newsletter includes articles, practical suggestions for teachers, book reviews, and a column by one of the major whole-language teacher networks (see TAWL, above).

Weston Woods
Weston, Connecticut 06883

Weston Woods offers a large selection of high-quality children's literature in the audio-visual media: filmstrips (including nonverbal filmstrips); sets of filmstrips, cassettes, and books; and sets of books and cassettes. All of their films are also available in videocassette form.

Whole Language Consultants
140 Malcana Street
Winnipeg, Manitoba R2G 2S9
Canada

This group of teachers has published excellent professional books for teachers and some delightful resources for use with children in a whole-language classroom.

Whole Language Newsletter
c/o Adrian Peetoom
Scholastic–TAB Publications
123 Newkirk Road
Richmond Hill, Ontario L4C 3G5

This newsletter offers success stories and practical suggestions for the whole-language teacher.

The Wright Group
10949 Technology Place
San Diego, California 92127

Their catalog of whole-language resources offers Big Books and other delightful materials for shared reading and language experience and reading recovery.

The Writing Company
10,000 Culver Blvd.
Dept. E2, P.O. Box 802
Culver City, California 90230

The Writing Company distributes a wide variety of materials on writing, both books for teaching and resources to use with students.

Zephr Press
430 South Essex Lane
Tucson, Arizona 85711

Zephr offers books and instructional kits on language arts, whole-brain learning, self-awareness, thinking and problem solving, and educating the gifted, plus learning packets on anthropology and science that involve "reading, writing, building, creating, imagining, thinking and reacting."

Publishers of "Whole-Language" Basals

Holt, Rinehart and Winston
383 Madison Avenue
New York, New York 10017

Holt published the famed *Sounds of Language* series, by Bill Martin with Peggy Brogan, in the early 1970s. The series is now out of print, but well worth trying to locate if you can. It's currently the only American "whole-language" series not encumbered with lots of supplemental paraphernalia.

Holt, Rinehart and Winston of
   Canada, Ltd.
55 Horner Avenue
Toronto, Ontario M8Z 4X6

Holt, Rinehart and Winston of Canada has more recently (1984) published a "whole-language" series titled *Impressions*. This series is available through the U.S. office of Holt, Rinehart.

McGraw-Hill Ryerson Limited
330 Progress Avenue
Scarborough, Ontario M1P 2Z5

The mid-1980s "whole-language" series published by this company is called *Unicorn: A Reading and Language Series*. As of this printing, it was not yet available through the U.S. office of McGraw-Hill.

Nelson Canada
1120 Birchmount Road
Scarborough, Ontario M1K 5G4

Nelson's mid-1980s "whole-language" series is *Networks*, with John McInnes as senior author. Again, not yet available in the U.S.

Schofield & Sims Ltd.
Dogley Mill
Fenay Bridge
Huddersfield
England HD8 0NQ

The 1986 *Journeys into Literacy* series is designed for 5- to 9-year-olds. The Teacher's Manual, by Moira McKenzie, contains many wonderful suggestions for using the books with children.

Publishers of High-Quality Paperbacks for Children

Dell Publishing Company
1 Dag Hammarskjold Plaza
245 E. 47th St.
New York, New York 10017
  (Banbury, Delta, Laurel Leaf,
    Standish, & Yearling books)

Dial Books for Young Readers
E.P. Dutton Publishing Co.
2 Park Avenue
New York, New York 10016
  (Pied Piper books)

Harper & Row
10 E. 53rd St.
New York, New York 10022
  (Trophy books)

Holt, Rinehart and Winston
383 Madison Avenue
New York, New York 10017
  (Owlet books)

Penguin
40 W. 23rd St.
New York, New York 10010
  (Puffin books)

Scholastic Inc.
Box 7502
Jefferson City, Missouri 65102

Scholastic–TAB Publications
123 Newkirk Road
Richmond Hill, Ontario
Canada L4C 3G5

Resources for Locating High-Quality Children's Literature

American Library Association
50 East Huron Street
Chicago, Illinois 60611

The association for Library Services to Children and the Young Adult Services of this group publishes *The Top of the News*, which contains articles on children's literature and articles by and about children's authors, as well as reviews.

Children's Book Council
67 Irving Place
New York, New York 10003

The Council is headquarters for National Children's Book Week and a center for children's book promotion. It publishes *The Calendar*, a bulletin with bibliographies appropriate for each month of the year, articles on books and authors, and materials available for book promotion (twice a year; no charge).

Council on Interracial Books
  for Children
Racism/Sexism Resource Center
1841 Broadway
New York, New York 10023–7648

Offers a variety of books and audio-visual educational materials to combat racism and sexism in school and society.

Great Books Foundation
40 East Huron Street
Chicago, Illinois 60611

This foundation has developed a series of Junior Great Books for grades 2 through 9. Though designed for a supplemental program, these books could also be used in the classroom. The selections are designed to stimulate divergent thinking.

The Horn Book
Park Square Building
31 St. James Square
Boston, Massachusetts 02116

A bi-monthly journal of articles on and reviews of children's books. One of the most respected resources in the field.

International Reading Association
800 Barksdale Road
P.O. Box 8139
Newark, Deleware 19714–8139

Among the IRA's useful resources on children's literature is a publication titled *Books About Children's Books.*

National Council of Teachers of
    English
1111 Kenyon Road
Urbana, Illinois 61801

Among the NCTE's annotated booklists are: *Adventuring with Books: A Booklist for Pre-K–Grade 6; Books for You: A Booklist for Senior High Students; Your Reading: A Booklist for Junior High and Middle School Students;* and *High Interest-Easy Reading: For Junior and Senior High School Students.*

*   *   *   *   *

Bulletin of the Center for
    Children's Books
University of Chicago Press
Journals Division
P.O. Box 37005
Chicago, Illinois 60637

Published monthly, except in August, this gives detailed reviews of new titles with specific recommendations or condemnations.

The Children's Catalog. 14th ed.
Wilson, 1981.

A selected catalog of children's fiction and non-fiction, classified by Dewey system and revised every five years, with annual supplements between editions.

The Junior High School Library Catalog, 5th ed.,
Wilson, 1985.

Revised every five years, with annual supplements.
This and the *Children's Catalog* are invaluable aids to librarians.

Notes

Chapter 1

1. Function words are the "little words" that glue the content words together. The main types of function words are as follows: noun determiners (like *the*, and like *this* in *this boy*); verb auxiliaries (like *will* in *will win*); prepositions (like *by* in *by the lake*); and conjunctions (like *because* and *and*). For a more thorough discussion of these and other "parts of speech" (grammatical categories), see Chapter 2.

Chapter 2

1. I am grateful to my colleague Jim Burns for introducing me to a similar activity and to the book from which these "lost words" are taken (Susan Kelz Sperling. 1977. *Poplollies and Bellibones: A Celebration of Lost Words*. New York: Clarkson N. Potter). Given the brevity of Sperling's definitions, it is possible that some words may have been misused in my story. In any case, here are her definitions:

> *Bellytimber*—Food, provisions
>
> *Blonke*—A large, powerful horse
>
> *Blore*—To cry out or bleat and bray like an animal
>
> *Crinet*—A hair
>
> *Drumly*—Cloudy, sluggish
>
> *Fairney cloots*—Small horny substances above the hoofs of horses, sheep, and goats
>
> *Flosh*—A swamp or stagnant pool overgrown with weeds
>
> *Givel*—To heap up
>
> *Icchen*—To move, stir
>
> *Kexy*—Dry, juiceless
>
> *Lennow*—Flappy, limp
>
> *Maily*—Speckled
>
> *Quetch*—To moan and twitch in pain, shake

Samded—Half-dead

Shawk— Smell

Sparple—To scatter, spread about

Spiss—Thick, dense

Venenate—To poison

Wam—A scar, cicatrix

Wong—Meadowlands, commons

Yerd—To beat with a rod

2. This transactional model of the reading process emphasizes the top-down processing and the irreducible complexity of the reading process more than most so-called "interactive" models of reading. See, for example, Rumelhart 1977; Stanovitch 1980; and Lesgold & Perfetti 1981.

Chapter 3

1. It seems to me that the terms *perception, identification*, and *recognition* are nearly synonymous; hence I use them more or less interchangeably. My particular choice in any given instance is dictated by connotation rather than denotation: it seems to me that "perception" more readily includes the possibility of error, that "identification" and "recognition" imply *accurate* perception. Note, however, that all three of these words indicate a decision on the part of the *brain*.

2. The words, in order of occurrence, are: *could, short, about, voice, trust, scarf, drank, ghost, which, stand*. For a similar list of mutilated words, see Anderson and Dearborn 1952, p. 189; they reproduced the words by permission from a test constructed by L. L. Thurstone.

3. One interesting example of such experiments involved the reversal of two letters at the beginning or the middle or the end of a word, as with *vaiation, avitaion*, and *aviatino* for the word *aviation*. The words were hardest to identify when the reversal occurred at the beginning, and easiest to identify when the reversal occurred in the middle; thus the experiment suggests that beginnings are most important in word perception and middles are least important (Bruner and O'Dowd 1958).

Chapter 4

1. The omitted words are: (1) aren't, (2) Most, (3) three, (4) and, (5) 40, (6) of, (7) most, (8) is, (9) as, (10) Beavers, (11) dams, (12) They, (13) paws, (14) their, (15) tree, (16) pointed, (17) beaver, (18) tree, (19) about.

2. To see this for yourself, try a brief experiment with someone you know to be a reasonably proficient reader. First, locate a book that the person has not read, but that will not be especially difficult for him or her. Have the person begin reading a page aloud, and after a few lines stop the person's reading by suddenly turning out the light (if it is dark) or by putting your hand over the part being

read. Then ask the person to tell you what words he or she saw beyond the word last focused upon. If you repeat this procedure several times, you will probably find that the person can report, on the average, about four additional words. This is the person's *eye-voice span*, or *EVS*: the number of words the eye is ahead of the voice. In silent reading, of course, one has a similar *eye-memory span*, or *EMS*: the number of words the eye is ahead of the word being focused upon (Dechant 1970, p. 18; see Anderson and Dearborn 1952, pp. 127–36). The EVS and the EMS indicate the number of following words *seen* during one eye fixation, in addition to the word being identified. These additional words may, of course, be used in identifying the word being focused upon.

3. *Kalamazoo Gazette*, August 1, 1978, p. A-1. The article was a UPI tidbit originating in Chicago.

4. *Structural analysis* involves identifying prefixes, suffixes, and bases as cues to word recognition.

5. I like the word *sneakers* best here, because its connotation seems to fit best with the description of the passage. Other good possibilities are *tennis shoes* and *gym shoes*. Check Bradbury to see which word he chose!

6. This nonsense word comes from an article by Robert Hillerich (1977, p. 301). Hillerich explains that "To arrive at the spelling, one could consider *n* as the most likely beginning letter, although the other reasonable possibilities are *kn (know)*, *gn (gnaw)*, *pn (pneumonia)*, and *mn (mnemonic)*. The $/\bar{e}/$ in medial position could be spelled *ae (aegis), e (between), ea (meat), ee (meet), ei (neither), ie (chief), eo (people), ey (keynote)*, or *oe (amoeba)*; /d/ is easy—it is *d* or *dd;* /ər/ could be *ar (liar), er (term), ir (first), or (worm), ur (turn), ear (learn), our (journey), eur (chauffeur)*, or *yr (myrtle)*; /1/ again is easy as either *1* or *11*, but final $/\bar{e}/$ could be *ay (quay), i (ski), ee (see), ey (key), y (baby), e (be)*, or *ois (chamois)*. In fact, we have demonstrated that the nonsense word could be spelled in 5 x 9 x 2 x 9 x 2 x 7 or 11,340 different ways. Of course, if one were unfamiliar with the influence of position, seventeen different spellings of $/\bar{e}/$ would have to be considered for both occurrences, increasing the possibilities to 52,020!''

Chapter 5

1. Two amusing books capitalizing upon this kind of misconception are Fred Gwynne's *The King Who Rained* and *Chocolate Moose* (New York: Windmill-Dutton, 1970 and 1979 respectively).

2. Conclusions such as those discussed here are suggested by studies of perception, studies of language acquisition and use, and studies concerning the relation between the syntax children use and the syntax they can readily comprehend in reading. See, for example, Fodor, Bever, and Garrett 1974, pp. 326, 356–58; Menyuk 1969, pp. 16, 95, and 100–101; O'Donnell, Griffin, and Norris 1967, pp. 90–93; Coleman 1965, pp. 334–35; Ruddell 1965, pp. 272–73; Tatham 1970, p. 418; Reid 1958, p. 297; Wm. Smith 1971, p. 55; and Peltz 1973–74, esp. pp. 615 and 618.

3. Here is the discussion I originally read, from Carton 1976, pp. 61–62:

Russian investigators (Mallitskaya cited by Slobin, 1966) have done some fascinating studies of how children learn names of things when an experimenter attempts to teach them. It seems reasonable to conclude from some of these studies that sheer repetition is not very effective, particularly if the child is paying attention to something else. Children who were allowed to hold dolls and toys and were free to play with them and move them about during the study did not learn the names of objects in their hands even if the name was repeated 1500 times! On the other hand, children who had been trained to play a game where the experimenter showed them pictures on the sides of blocks and told them the names for the pictures, showed a kind of "orienting behavior" (that is, a readiness to look and listen) when they later encountered pictures on these blocks for which they did not know the name. Under these circumstances names were learned in one to three trials.

4. When I tried to locate "Jimmy Hayes and Muriel" through a short story index, the entry under "Frogs, horned" referred me to an entry for horned *toads*. I have since discovered that so-called horned frogs do exist, though.

5. Here is the original passage:

The crack of the rifle volley cut the suddenly still air. It appeared to go on, as a solid volley, for perhaps a full minute or a little longer.

Some of the students dived to the ground, crawling on the grass in terror. Others stood shocked or half crouched, apparently believing the troops were firing into the air. Some of the rifle barrels were pointing upward.

Near the top of the hill at the corner of Taylor Hall, a student crumpled over, spun sideways and fell to the ground, shot in the head.

When the firing stopped, a slim girl, wearing a cowboy shirt and faded jeans, was lying face down on the road at the edge of the parking lot, blood pouring out onto the macadam, about 10 feet from this reporter.

6. My opinion supported the position of the family. The definitions in some of our major dictionaries suggested that the word *passenger* at least *could* be taken to include the operator of a vehicle. Ultimately, however, the Michigan Supreme Court ruled in support of the insurance company's interpretation, arguing that the "ordinary man" would not consider the operator of a vehicle to be one of its passengers (Kinnavy v. Traill, 1976).

7. One important point about such "grammatical" miscues is that they are not all grammatical in nature. Their origin may be phonological, as is the apparent omission of the past tense marker by speakers of Black English. The past tense marker is absent from Black English primarily when the base word is a regular verb ending in a consonant other than /t/ or /d/. In such cases, addition of the past tense ending results in a consonant cluster (the examples are mostly from Fasold and Wolfram 1970, p. 45):

stopped	/pt/	rubbed	/bd/
looked	/kt/	hugged	/gd/

laughed	/ft/	loved	/vd/
unearthed	/θt/	seethed	/ðd/
missed	/st/	raised	/zd/
watched	/čt/	judged	/jd/
finished	/št/		
		named	/md/
		rained	/nd/
		hanged	/ŋd/
		called	/ld/
		cured	/rd/

In each case, the past tense ending is represented by /t/ or /d/. Word-final consonant clusters are especially likely to be simplified when they end in a /t/ or /d/, and virtually all speakers of English show some tendency to omit the final /t/ or /d/ when it does not represent a tense marker. Such omission is particularly common when the word in question is followed by a word that begins with a consonant, as in *She* just *left* or *I'll* find *the book*. Speakers of so-called standard English occasionally omit even a past tense /t/ or /d/ when the following word begins with a consonant, as in *I* missed *Mike* and *He* lived *near me*. Speakers of Black English simply carry this tendency somewhat further, so that they are often perceived as consistently omitting past tense markers although in reality their usage varies, as it does for all of us. The same is true for other dialect features.

8. Note that in this approximation of Black English, pastness is not always indicated by the verb form itself, even for verbs which express pastness by some means other than the mere addition of /t/ or /d/.

Chapter 6

1. A historical note may be of interest. In the 1948 edition of *On Their Own in Reading*, William Gray suggested five major aids to word perception. "Meaning clues from the context" was listed first (p. 41). In the 1960 edition of his book, "memory of word form" came first, and "context clues" came second (p. 16). Now, context seems to have fallen to third position, after memory for word form and the use of phonic and structural analysis skills.

2. Of the cues available in the text itself, context seems to have become a last resort. However, the dictionary is often recommended, when even context proves insufficient.

3. Michigan Department of Education, "Reading Position," no date. A draft copy was obtained in 1978 from Robert Trezise, then Coordinator for Communication Skills. Used by permission.

Chapter 7

1. Here are the "stories" with the children's original spellings: (Cramer 1978, p. 44):

I play in the grass
And I play with my frads
And I play with Debbie.
                    —Mary

Wane the poho

Wan evng wane wt
iut to get some hane
he kalimd and kalimd
for hane he fnd hane.
                    —John

My Dad is nice
My Mom is nice
My sistrss is nice
                    —Danielle

I kak My had I fel
off the bed My Mom
Tok Me to the hsptl.
                    —Nathalie

Chapter 8

1. Whole-language *instructional invitations* are well thought-through and compelling suggestions that are made with assurance that the suggestions have to do with the life, interests, and needs of the learner. They are offered from a whole-language model of literacy, and are made with confidence that they will be accepted, but with the realization that they might be modified or rejected depending on the state of the learner.

Chapter 9

1. Pearson and Johnson are in turn indebted to W. Dorsey Hammond of Oakland University, who is indebted to Russell Stauffer for the example.

2. For a full description of the process, see Tierney, Robert J., Readence, John E., and Dishner, Ernest K. 1980. *Reading Strategies and Practices: Guide for Improving Instruction*. Boston: Allyn and Bacon, Inc.

3. See Goodman, Yetta M., and Burke, Carolyn. 1980. *Reading Strategies: Focus on Comprehension*. New York: Holt, Rinehart and Winston, for further examples of strategies to use when teaching reading for information.

4. This strategy is developed in *Developing Metacognitive Skills: The Key to Success in Reading and Learning*, for the MERIT, Chapter 2 Project, The School District of Philadelphia, Hilda K. Carr, MERIT Supervisor, 1986.

5. These adaptations were presented by Alvermann, Donna. 17 March 1986. "It's the Thought That Counts: Critical Reading in the Classroom," paper presented at the 30th Annual Michigan Reading Association Conference, Grand Rapids, Michigan.

6. For a description of several formulas and how to apply them, see Vacca, Richard T., and Vacca, JoAnne L. 1986. *Content Area Reading*. 2nd ed. Boston: Little, Brown and Company.

Bibliography

The following bibliography is divided, somewhat arbitrarily, into two major sections: "References" and "Suggested Readings." Of necessity, many items are listed in both sections. The brief bibliographies at the end of each chapter are designed primarily for those just beginning a study of psycholinguistics and reading. In contrast, the following bibliographies are designed more for those who want to pursue such study in greater depth and detail.

When there is more than one entry for a given author, those entries are listed chronologically.

REFERENCES

The following section includes not all of the references I consulted, but at least most of the ones that helped shape my own views on the nature of the reading process. Most of these references are cited in the text. Almost all of the others were cited in an earlier version, and are retained here because they may be relevant to those with a scholarly interest in the reading process and related matters. Particularly useful articles and chapters are often listed separately, even when they are printed in one of the books cited. Many such articles and chapters are appropriate for a wide audience, as their titles will suggest.

Abrams, Kenneth, and Thomas G. Bever. August 1969. Syntactic Structure Modifies Attention during Speech Perception and Recognition. *Quarterly Journal of Experimental Psychology* 21: 280–90.

Adams, Marilyn Jager, and Allan Collins. 1979. A Schema-Theoretic View of Reading. *New Directions in Discourse Processing*. Ed. Roy O. Freedle. Norwood, N.J.: ABLEX, 1–22.

Aitchison, Jean. 1976, 1983. *The Articulate Mammal: An Introduction to Psycholinguistics*. New York: Universe Books.

Alexander, Martha. 1970. *Bobo's Dream*. New York: Dial Press.

Allen, Jobeth. Fall 1985. Inferential Comprehension: The Effects of Text Source, Decoding Ability, and Mode. *Reading Research Quarterly* 20: 603–15.

Allen, P. David. 1976. Implications for Reading Instruction. *Findings of Research in Miscue Analysis: Classroom Implications.* Ed. P. David Allen and Dorothy J. Watson. Urbana, Ill.: ERIC Clearinghouse on Reading and Communication Skills and the National Council of Teachers of English, 107–12.

Allen, P. David, and Dorothy J. Watson, eds. 1976. *Findings of Research in Miscue Analysis: Classroom Implications.* Urbana, Ill.: ERIC Clearinghouse on Reading and Communication Skills and the National Council of Teachers of English.

Allington, Richard L. May 1983. The Reading Instruction Provided Readers of Differing Reading Abilities. *The Elementary School Journal* 83: 548–59.

Allington, Richard L., and Anne McGill-Franzen. April 1980. Word Identification Errors in Isolation and in Context: Apples vs. Oranges. *The Reading Teacher* 33: 795–800.

Altwerger, Bess, and Lois Bird. January 1982. Disabled: The Learner or the Curriculum? *Topics in Learning and Learning Disabilities* 1: 69–78.

Alvermann, Donna. 17 March 1986. It's the Thought That Counts: Critical Reading in the Classroom. Paper presented at the 30th Annual Michigan Reading Association Conference, Grand Rapids, Michigan.

Anderson, Billie V., and John G Barnitz. November 1984. Cross-Cultural Schemata and Reading Comprehension Instruction. *Journal of Reading* 28: 102–8.

Anderson, Irving H., and Walter F. Dearborn. 1952. *The Psychology of Teaching Reading.* New York: Ronald Press.

Anderson, Richard C., Richard J. Spiro, and M. C. Anderson. 1977. *Schemata as Scaffolding for the Representation of Meaning in Connected Discourse.* Tech. Rep. no. 24. Urbana, Ill.: University of Illinois, Center for the Study of Reading. ERIC Document Reproduction Service, no. ED 136-236.

Anderson, Richard C., Elfrieda H. Hiebert, Judith A. Scott, and Ian A. G. Wilkinson. 1985. *Becoming a Nation of Readers: The Report of the Commission on Reading.* Champaign, Ill.: Center for the Study of Reading.

Anisfeld, Moshe. 1968. Language and Cognition in the Young Child. *The Psycholinguistic Nature of the Reading Process.* Ed. Kenneth S. Goodman. Detroit: Wayne State University Press, 169–83.

The Ann Arbor Decision: Memorandum Opinion and Order and the Educational Plan. 1979. Arlington, Va.: Center for Applied Linguistics.

Ansara, Alice. 1982. The Orton-Gillingham Approach to Remediation in Developmental Dyslexia. *Reading Disorders: Varieties and Treatments.* Ed. R. N. Malatesha and P. G. Aaron. New York: Academic Press, 409–33.

Arno, Ed. 1967. *The Gingerbread Man.* New York: Scholastic.

Artley, A. Sterl. February 1977. Phonics Revisited. *Language Arts* 54: 121–26.

Atwell, Margaret A., and Lynn K. Rhodes. May 1984. Strategy Lessons as Alternatives to Skills Lessons in Reading. *Journal of Reading* 27: 700–705.

Bailey, Mildred H. 1967. The Utility of Phonic Generalizations in Grades One through Six. *The Reading Teacher* 20: 413–18.

Ball, Zachary. 1962. *Bristle Face.* New York: Holiday House.

Baratz, Joan C. 1969. Teaching Reading in an Urban Negro School System. *Teaching Black Children to Read*. Ed. Joan C. Baratz and Roger W. Shuy. Washington, D.C.: Center for Applied Linguistics, 102–16.

Baratz, Joan, and William Stewart. 1970. *Friends*. Washington, D.C.: Education Study Center.

Barr, Jene. 1949. *Little Circus Dog*. Chicago: Albert Whitman.

Barr, Rebecca. January 1975. Processes Underlying the Learning of Printed Words. *Elementary School Journal* 75: 258–68.

Barrett, Frank L. 1982. *A Teacher's Guide to Shared Reading*. Richmond Hill, Ontario: Scholastic-TAB.

Baskwill, Jane, and Paulette Whitman. 1986. *Whole Language Sourcebook*. Richmond Hill, Ontario: Scholastic-TAB.

Bateman, Barbara D. April 1974. Educational Implications of Minimal Brain Dysfunction. *Reading Teacher* 27: 662–68.

Bayer, Ann Shea. 1987. Learning Logs Across the Curriculum. *Ideas with Insights: Language Arts K–6*. Ed. Dorothy Watson. Urbana, Ill.: National Council of Teachers of English.

Becoming a Nation of Readers: The Report of the Commission on Reading. 1984. Washington, D.C.: The National Institute of Education. Available from the National Council of Teachers of English.

Berdiansky, Betty, B. Cronnell, and J. Koehler. 1969. *Spelling-Sound Relations and Primary Form-Class Descriptions for Speech-Comprehension Vocabularies of 6–9 Year-Olds*. Inglewood, Calif.: Southwest Regional Laboratory for Educational Research and Development, Technical Report no. 15.

Berko, Jean. 1958. "The Child's Learning of English Morphology." *Word* 14: 150–77.

Bettelheim, Bruno, and Karen Zelan. November 1981. Why Children Don't Like to Read. *Atlantic Monthly*: 25–31.

Betts, Emmett A. 1946. *Foundations of Reading Instruction*. New York: American Book Company.

Bever, T. G., and T. G. Bower. January 1966. How to Read Without Listening. *Project Literacy Reports no. 6*, Educational Resources Information Center, no. ED 010 312: 13–25.

Bever, T. G., J. R. Lackner, and R. Kirk. 1969. The Underlying Structures of Sentences are the Primary Units of Immediate Speech Processing. *Perception & Psychophysics* 5: 225–34.

Biemiller, Andrew. Fall 1970. The Development of the Use of Graphic and Contextual Information as Children Learn to Read. *Reading Research Quarterly* 1: 77–96.

Bishop, David M. 1981. Motivating Adolescent Readers via Starter Shelves in Content Area Classes. *Motivating Reluctant Readers*. Ed. Alfred J. Ciani. Newark, Del.: International Reading Association, 44–70.

Bissex, Glenda. 1980. *Gnys at Wrk: A Child Learns to Write and Read*. Cambridge: Harvard University Press.

Blachówicz, Camille L. Z. 1977–1978. Semantic Constructivity in Children's Comprehension. *Reading Research Quarterly* 13, ii: 188–99.

Black, Janet K. May 1980. Those "Mistakes" Tell Us a Lot. *Language Arts* 57: 508–13.

Blackburn, Ellen. April 1984. Common Ground: Developing Relationships Between Reading and Writing. *Language Arts* 61: 367–75.

Blatt, Gloria T. February 1978. Playing with Language. *The Reading Teacher* 31: 487–93.

Bleich, David. 1975. *Readings and Feelings: An Introduction to Subjective Criticism*. Urbana, Ill.: National Council of Teachers of English.

Bloome, David. February 1985. Reading as a Social Process. *Language Arts* 62: 134–42.

Bloome, David, and Judith Green. 1985. Looking at Reading Instruction: Sociolinguistic and Ethnographic Approaches. *Contexts of Reading*. Ed. Carolyn N. Hedley and Anthony N. Baratta. Norwood, N.J.: ABLEX, 167–84.

Bloomfield, Leonard. April 1942 and May 1942. Linguistics and Reading. *The Elementary English Review* 19: 125–30, 183–86.

Bloomfield, Leonard, and Clarence L. Barnhart. 1961. *Let's Read: A Linguistic Approach*. Detroit: Wayne State University Press.

Boatner, Maxine Tull, and John Edward Gates. 1975. *A Dictionary of American Idioms*, updated by Adam Makkai. Rev. ed. Woodbury, N.Y.: Barron's Educational Series.

Boder, Elena. 1973. Developmental Dyslexia: A Diagnostic Approach Based on Three Atypical Reading-Spelling Patterns. *Developmental Medicine and Child Neurology* 15: 663–87.

Bond, Guy L., and Robert Dykstra. Summer 1967. The Cooperative Research Program in First-Grade Reading Instruction. *Reading Research Quarterly* 2: 5–142.

Bormuth, John R., ed. 1968. *Readability in 1968*. Urbana, Ill.: National Council of Teachers of English.

_____. April 1968. The Cloze Readability Procedure. *Elementary English* 45: 429–36. Reprinted in *Readability in 1968*. Ed. J. Bormuth. Urbana, Ill.: National Council of Teachers of English, 40–47.

_____. 1975. Literacy in the Classroom. *Help for the Reading Teacher: New Directions in Research*. Ed. William D. Page. Urbana, Ill.: National Council of Teachers of English, 60–89.

Bortnick, Robert, and Genevieve S. Lopardo. January 1973. An Instructional Application of the Cloze Procedure. *Journal of Reading* 16: 296–300.

Bowen, Ezra. 5 May 1986. Losing the War of Letters. *Time*.

Bower, Thomas G. R. 1970. Reading by Eye. *Basic Studies on Reading*. Ed. Harry Levin and Joanna P. Williams. New York: Basic Books, 134–146.

Bradbury, Ray. 1957. *Dandelion Wine*. Garden City, N.Y.: Doubleday.

Bransford, John D., and Jeffrey J. Franks. October 1971. The Abstraction of Linguistic Ideas. *Cognitive Psychology* 2: 331–50.

Bransford, John D., and Nancy S. McCarrell. 1974. A Sketch of a Cognitive Approach to Comprehension: Some Thoughts about Understanding What It Means to Comprehend. *Cognition and the Symbolic Processes*. Ed. Walter B. Wiemer and David S. Palermo. Hillsdale, N.J.: Erlbaum, 189–229.

Brause, Rita S. Spring 1977. Developmental Aspects of the Ability to Understand Semantic Ambiguity, with Implications for Teachers. *Research in the Teaching of English* 11: 39–48.

Briggs, Raymond. 1970. *Jim and the Beanstalk*. New York: Coward-McCann.

Bromley, Karen D'Angelo, and Laurie McKeveny. February 1986. Précis Writing: Suggestions for Instruction in Summarizing. *Journal of Reading* 29: 392–95.

Brown, Claude. 1965. *Manchild in the Promised Land*. New York: Macmillan.

Brown, Margaret Wise. 1949. *The Important Book*. Ill. Leonard Weisgard. New York: Harper & Row.

Brown, Roger. 1970. Psychology and Reading: Commentary on Chapters 5 to 10. *Basic Studies on Reading*. Ed. Harry Levin and Joanna P. Williams. New York: Basic Books, 164–87.

Brown, Roger, and David McNeill. August 1966. The "Tip of the Tongue" Phenomenon. *Journal of Verbal Learning and Verbal Behavior* 5: 325–37.

Bruce, D. J. 1958. The Effects of Listeners' Anticipations on the Intelligibility of Heard Speech. *Language and Speech* 1: 79–97.

Bruner, Jerome S. 1960. *The Process of Education*. Cambridge, Mass.: Harvard University Press.

Bruner, Jerome S., and Donald O'Dowd. 1958. A Note on the Informativeness of Parts of Words. *Language and Speech* 1: 98–101.

Burgess, Anthony. 1963. *A Clockwork Orange*. New York: Norton.

Burke, Carolyn. 1973. Preparing Elementary Teachers to Teach Reading. *Miscue Analysis: Applications to Reading Instruction*. Ed. Kenneth S. Goodman. Urbana, Ill.: National Council of Teachers of English, 15–29.

_____. 1980. The Reading Interview: 1977. *Reading Comprehension: Resource Guide*. Ed. B. P. Farr and D. J. Strickler. Bloomington: School of Education, Indiana University.

_____. 1985. Written Conversations. *The Authoring Cycle: A Viewing Guide*. Ed. Jerome Harste, Kathryn Pierce, and Trevor Cairney. Portsmouth, N.H.: Heinemann.

Burling, Robbins. 1973. *English in Black and White*. New York: Holt, Rinehart and Winston.

Burmeister, Lou E. January 1968. Usefulness of Phonic Generalizations. *The Reading Teacher* 21: 349–56, 360.

Buswell, Guy Thomas. 1945. *Non-Oral Reading: A Study of Its Use in the Chicago Public Schools*. Supplementary Educational Monographs, no. 60. Chicago: University of Chicago Press.

Butler, Andrea, and J. Turbill. 1984. *Towards a Reading-Writing Classroom*. Portsmouth, N.H.: Heinemann.

Cajon Valley Union School District. 1974. Psycholinguistic Approach to Reading (PAR). El Cajon, Calif. Available from the Educational Resources Information Center, no. ED 108-150.

Calkins, Lucy McCormick. May 1980. When Children Want to Punctuate: Basic Skills Belong in Context. *Language Arts* 57: 567–73. Repr. *Donald Graves in Australia*. Ed. R. D. Walshe. Portsmouth, N.H.: Heinemann, 89–96.

———. 1982. Writing Taps a New Energy Source: The Child. *Donald Graves in Australia*. Ed. R. D. Walshe. Portsmouth, N.H.: Heinemann, 45–54. Based on an earlier article: Work in Progress: One School's Writing Program. June 1980. *National Elementary Principal* 59: 34–38.

———. 1983. *Lessons from a Child*. Portsmouth, N.H.: Heinemann.

———. 1986. *The Art of Teaching Writing*. Portsmouth, N.H.: Heinemann.

Campione, Joseph. April 1981. Learning, Academic Achievement, and Instruction. Paper presented at the second annual conference on reading research of the Center for the Study of Reading, New Orleans.

Canney, George. Fall 1977. Reading Problems—Prevention Rather Than Cure. *Reading Horizons* 18: 7–12.

Caplan, David. 1972. Clause Boundaries and Recognition Latencies for Words in Sentences. *Perception and Psychophysics* 12: 73–76.

Carbo, Marie. December 1978. Teaching Reading with Talking Books. *The Reading Teacher* 32: 267–73.

———. 1981. *Reading Style Inventory Manual*. Roslyn Heights, N.Y.: Learning Research Associates.

———. 1983. *Reading Style Inventory Research Supplement*. Roslyn Heights, N.Y.: Learning Research Associates.

———. February 1983. Reading Styles Change Between Second and Eighth Grade. *Educational Leadership*: 56–59.

———. April 1983. Research in Reading and Learning Style: Implications for Exceptional Children. *Exceptional Children* 49: 486–94.

———. May 1984. Why Most Reading Tests Aren't Fair. *Early Years K/8*: 73–75.

———. August/September 1984. Five Schools Try Reading Styles Programs . . . And See How Their Kids Have Grown! *Early Years K/8*: 52, 57–61.

———. 30 October 1986. Reading Styles Seminar. Kalamazoo, Mich.

———. February 1987. Reading Style Research: "What Works" Isn't Always Phonics. *Phi Delta Kappan* 68: 431–35.

———. March 1987. Ten Myths About Teaching Reading. *Teaching K/8*: 77–80.

Carbo, Marie, Rita Dunn, and Kenneth Dunn. 1986. *Teaching Students to Read Through Their Individual Learning Styles*. Reston, Va.: Prentice-Hall.

Carey, Robert F. Summer 1980. Empirical vs. Naturalistic Research? *Reading Research Quarterly* 3: 412–15.

———. 17 September 1985. Reading Something Too Simple into the Complicated Process of Reading. *Providence Journal-Bulletin*: A-14.

_____. ed. Forthcoming. *Findings of Research in Miscue Analysis: 10 Years Later*. Urbana, Ill.: ERIC and the National Council of Teachers of English.

Carey, Robert F., Jerome C. Harste, and Sharon L. Smith. 1981. Contextual Constraints and Discourse Processes: A Replication Study. *Reading Research Quarterly* 16, ii: 201–12.

Carroll, John B., The Nature of the Reading Process. 1970. *Theoretical Models and Processes of Reading*. Ed. Harry Singer and Robert B. Ruddell. Newark, Del.: International Reading Association, 292–303.

Carroll, Ruth. 1932. *What Whiskers Did*. New York: Macmillan.

Carter, Candy, and Zora M. Rashkis. 1980. *Ideas for Teaching English in the Junior High and Middle School*. Urbana, Ill.: National Council of Teachers of English.

Carton, Aaron S. 1976. *Orientation to Reading*. Rowley, Mass.: Newbury House.

Caudell, Jan, Denise DeVries, Peggy Garthe, and Jeane Wilson. 1980. Experiencing History Through Literature: Integrated Activities for *Johnny Tremain*. *Another Day, Another Pineapple* 1. Ed. Jan Caudell and Constance Weaver. Kalamazoo, Mich.: Western Michigan University Department of English, 32–39.

Cazden, Courtney B. 1972. *Child Language and Education*. New York: Holt, Rinehart and Winston.

Chall, Jeanne. 1967. *Learning to Read: The Great Debate*. New York: McGraw-Hill.

_____. 1983a. *Learning to Read: The Great Debate*. Updated edition. New York: McGraw-Hill.

_____. 1983b. *Stages of Reading Development*. New York: McGraw-Hill.

Charlip, Remy. 1964. *Fortunately*. New York: Four Winds Press.

Chomsky, Carol. 1971a. Invented Spelling in the Open Classroom. *Word* 27: 499–518.

_____. 1971b. Write First, Read Later. *Childhood Education* 47: 296–99.

_____. March 1976. After Decoding: What? *Language Arts* 53: 288–96, 314.

_____. 1979. Approaching Reading Through Invented Spelling. *Theory and Practice of Early Reading*. Ed. Lauren B. Resnick and Phyllis A. Weaver. Hillsdale, N.J.: Erlbaum, 2: 43–65.

Chomsky, Noam. 1965. *Aspects of the Theory of Syntax*. Cambridge, Mass.: M.I.T. Press.

_____. 1968. *Language and Mind*. New York: Harcourt Brace Jovanovich.

Clark, Herbert H., and Eve V. Clark. 1977. *Psychology and Language: An Introduction to Psycholinguistics*. New York: Harcourt Brace Jovanovich.

Clark, Mae Knight. 1965a. *A Magic Box*. New York: Macmillan.

_____. 1965b. *Opening Doors*. New York: Macmillan.

Clay, Marie M. 1972. *Sand: The Concepts About Print Test*. Portsmouth, N.H.: Heinemann.

_____. 1975. *What Did I Write?* Portsmouth, N.H.: Heinemann.

_____. 1979. *Stones: The Concepts About Print Test*. Portsmouth, N.H.: Heinemann.

_____. 1985. *The Early Detection of Reading Difficulties*. 3rd ed. Portsmouth, N.H.: Heinemann.

_____. 4–5 February 1986. Why Reading Recovery Is the Way It Is. Paper presented at the Reading Recovery Conference, Ohio Department of Education, Columbus, Ohio. *Proceedings from the First Reading Recovery Conference*, Ohio Department of Education, Columbus, Ohio. Forthcoming.

Cleland, Donald L. 1971. Vocalism in Silent Reading. *Teaching Reading—Not by Decoding Alone*. Ed. Joseph P. Kender. Danville, Ill.: Interstate Printers and Publishers, 131–44.

Clymer, Theodore L. 1963. The Utility of Phonic Generalizations in the Primary Grades. *The Reading Teacher* 16: 252–58.

Cochrane, Orin, Donna Cochrane, Sharen Scalena, and Ethel Buchanan. 1984. *Reading, Writing and Caring*. Winnipeg: Whole Language Consultants. Also available from Richard C. Owen, New York.

Cohen, Miriam. 1980. *First Grade Takes a Test*. Ill. Lillian Hoban. New York: Dell.

Cohn, Margot. May 1981. Observations of Learning to Read and Write Naturally. *Language Arts* 58: 549–56.

Coleman, E. B. October 1965. Learning of Prose Written in Four Grammatical Transformations. *Journal of Applied Psychology* 49: 332–41.

Coltheart, M., K. Patterson, and J. C. Marshall, eds. 1980. *Deep Dyslexia*. Boston: Routledge & Kegan Paul.

Conrad, R. 1972. Speech and Reading. *Language by Ear and by Eye*. Ed. James F. Kavanagh and Ignatius G. Mattingly. Cambridge, Mass.: MIT Press, 205–40.

Cook, Doris M. 1986. *A Guide to Curriculum Planning in Reading*. Madison, Wisc.: Wisconson Department of Public Instruction.

Cooper, Charles R., and Anthony R. Petrosky. December 1976. A Psycholinguistic View of the Fluent Reading Process. *Journal of Reading* 20: 184–207.

Corcoran, D. W. J. May 1966. An Acoustic Factor in Letter Cancellation. *Nature* 210: 658.

_____. May 1967. Acoustic Factor in Proof Reading. *Nature* 214: 851–52.

Cowley, Joy. 1986. *Greedy Cat*. Ill. Robyn Belton. New York: Richard C. Owen.

Cramer, Ronald L. 1978. *Children's Writing and Language Growth*. Columbus, Ohio: Charles Merrill.

Culhane, Joseph. February 1970. Cloze Procedures and Comprehension. *Reading Teacher* 23: 410–13, 464.

Cullinan, Bernice, and Sheila Fitzgerald. 1984. Background Information Bulletin on the Use of Readability Formulae. International Reading Association and National Council of Teachers of English. (Mimeographed)

Cunningham, Patricia M. Summer 1977. Teachers' Correction Responses to Black Dialect Miscues Which are Non-Meaning Changing. *Reading Research Quarterly* 12: 637–53.

D'Angelo, Karen. January 1982. Correction Behavior: Implications for Reading Instruction. *The Reading Teacher* 35: 395–98.

D'Angelo, Karen, and Marc Mahlios. April 1983. Insertion and Omission Miscues of Good and Poor Readers. *The Reading Teacher* 36: 778–82.

Dahl, Patricia R., and S. Jay Samuels. March 1977. Teaching Children to Read Using Hypothesis/Test Strategies. *The Reading Teacher* 30: 603–6.

Dahl, Roald. 1950. *Someone Like You*. New York: Knopf.

Dale, Philip S. 1972. *Language Development: Structure and Function*. Hinsdale, Ill.: Dryden Press.

Davison, Alice, and Robert N. Kantor. 1982. On the Failure of Readability Formulas to Define Readable Texts: A Case Study from Adaptations. *Reading Research Quarterly* 17, ii: 187–209.

Dawkins, John. 1975. *Syntax and Readability*. Newark, Del.: International Reading Association.

A Debate over "Dumbing Down." 3 December 1985. *Time*: 68.

Dechant, Emerald V. 1970. *Improving the Teaching of Reading*. 2nd ed. Englewood Cliffs, N.J.: Prentice-Hall.

DeFord, Diane E. September 1981. Literacy: Reading, Writing, and Other Essentials. *Language Arts* 58: 652–58.

_____. Spring 1985. Validating the Construct of Theoretical Orientation in Reading Instruction. *Reading Research Quarterly* 20: 351–67.

DeFord, Diane E., and Jerome C. Harste. September 1982. Child Language Research and Curriculum. *Language Arts* 59: 590–600.

DeJong, Meindert. 1956. *The House of Sixty Fathers*. Ill. Maurice Sendak. New York: Harper & Row.

Devine, Thomas G. 1986. *Teaching Reading Comprehension: From Theory to Practice*. Boston: Allyn & Bacon.

Dewey, John, and Arthur F. Bentley. 1949. *Knowing and the Known*. Boston: Beacon.

Diack, Hunter. 1965. *The Teaching of Reading in Spite of the Alphabet*. New York: Philosophical Library.

Diebold, A. Richard. 1965. A Survey of Psycholinguistic Research, 1954–1964. *Psycholinguistics: A Survey of Theory and Research Problems*. Ed. Charles E. Osgood and Thomas A. Sebeok. Bloomington, Ind.: Indiana University Press, 205–91.

Doake, David. 1985. *Whole Language Principles and Practices in Reading Development with Special Emphasis on Reading Recovery*. Viewing guide accompanying videotape, filmed at the 1985 Reading for the Love of It conference in Toronto. Richmond Hill, Ontario: Scholastic-TAB.

Dobson, Lee. 15 May 1986. Emergent Writers in a Grade One Classroom. Paper presented at the Fourth International Conference on the Teaching of English, Ottawa, Ontario.

_____. Fall 1986. Emergent Writers in a Grade One Classroom. *Reading-Canada-Lecture* 4: 149–56.

Dolan, Martha Walsh. December 1986. Advanced Placement (Literature and Composition) Course Outline. Paper presented at English Education Seminar, East Lansing, Michigan.

Dolan, Terry, Elizabeth Dolan, Vic Taylor, John Shoreland, and Colin Harrison. 1979. Improving Reading through Group Discussion Activities. *The Effective Use of Reading*. Ed. Eric Lunzer and Keith Gardner. London: Heinemann Educational Books for the Schools Council, 228–66.

Dombey, Henrietta. 17 May 1986. A Three Year Old Making Sense of Narrative Through Conversation. Paper presented at the Fourth International Conference on the Teaching of English, Ottawa.

Donaldson, Margaret. 1978. *Children's Minds*. New York: Norton.

Downing, John. 1969. How Children Think about Reading. *The Reading Teacher* 23: 217–30.

Duffy, Frank H., Martha B. Denckla, Peter H. Bartels, Givlio Sandini, and Louise S. Keissling. May 1980. Dyslexia: Automated Diagnosis by Computerized Classification of Brain Electrical Activity. *Annals of Neurology* 7: 421–28.

Duffy, Frank H., G. B. McAnulty, and S. C. Schachter. 1984. Brain Electrical Activity Mapping. *Cerebral Dominance: The Biological Foundations*. Ed. N. Geschwind and A. M. Galaburda. Cambridge: Harvard University Press, 53–74.

Durkin, Dolores. January 1961. Children Who Read before Grade One. *The Reading Teacher* 14, iii: 163–66.

_____. 1966. *Children Who Read Early*. New York: Teachers College Press, Columbia University.

_____. 1974–1975. A Six Year Study of Children Who Learned to Read in School at the Age of Four. *Reading Research Quarterly* 10, i: 9–61.

_____. 1976. *Teaching Young Children to Read*. 2nd ed. Boston: Allyn & Bacon.

_____. 1978–1979. What Classroom Observations Reveal About Reading Comprehension Instruction. *Reading Research Quarterly* 14, iv: 481–553.

_____. 1981. Reading Comprehension Instruction in Five Basal Reading Series. *Reading Research Quarterly* 16, iv: 515–44.

Dykstra, Robert. October 1968. The Effectiveness of Code- and Meaning-Emphasis Beginning Reading Programs. *The Reading Teacher* 22: 17–23.

_____. Fall 1968. Summary of the Second-Grade Phase of the Cooperative Research Program in Primary Reading. *Reading Research Quarterly* 4: 49–70.

_____. 1974. Phonics and Beginning Reading Instruction. In *Teaching Reading: A Phonic/Linguistic Approach to Developmental Reading*, by Charles Child Walcutt, Joan Lamport, and Glenn McCracken. New York: Macmillan, 373–97.

Dyson, Anne Haas. 1984. "*N* Spell My Grandmama": Fostering Early Thinking About Print. *The Reading Teacher* 38: 262–71.

Eastman, P. D. 1960. *Are You My Mother?* New York: Random House.

Edelsky, Carol, Kelly Draper, and Karen Smith. Winter 1983. Hookin' Em in at the Start of School in a "Whole Language" Classroom. *Anthropology and Education Quarterly* 14: 257–81.

Edelsky, Carol, and Karen Smith. January 1984. "Is that Writing—or Are those Marks Just a Figment of Your Curriculum?" *Language Arts* 61: 24–32.

Edfeldt, Ake W. 1960. *Silent Speech and Silent Reading*. Chicago: University of Chicago Press.

Ehri, Linnea C., and Lee S. Wilce. 1980. Do Beginners Learn to Read Function Words Better in Sentences or in Lists? *Reading Research Quarterly* 15, iv: 451–76.

Elley, Warwick B., and Francis Mangubhai. Fall 1983. The Impact of Reading on Second Language Learning. *Reading Research Quarterly* 19: 53–67.

Emans, Robert. 1967. The Usefulness of Phonic Generalizations above the Primary Grades. *The Reading Teacher* 20: 419–25.

Emberley, Barbara. 1967. *Drummer Hoff*. Ill. Ed Emberley. Englewood Cliffs, N.J.: Prentice-Hall.

Emig, Janet. 1983. Non-Magical Thinking: Presenting Writing Developmentally in Schools. *The Web of Meaning: Essays on Writing, Teaching, Learning, and Thinking*. Upper Montclair, N.J.: Boynton/Cook, 135–44. (First published in *Writing: The Nature, Development, and Teaching of Written Communication*, Vol. 2. Ed. Marcia Farr Whiteman. Hillsdale, N.J.: Erlbaum. 1982.)

Endicott, A. L. 1973. A Proposed Scale for Syntactic Complexity. *Research in the Teaching of English* 7: 5–12.

Englehardt, D. M., R. A. Margolis, L. Rudorfer, and H. M. Paley. 1969. Physician Bias and the Double-blind. *Archives of General Psychiatry* 20: 315–20.

English Language Curriculum Services Unit. 1985. *National Early Literacy Inservice Course*. (Address: Wattle Park Teachers Centre, 424 Kensington Road, Wattle Park, South Australia 5066.)

Epstein, William. 1961. The Influence of Syntactical Structure on Learning. *American Journal of Psychology* 74: 80–85.

Erdmann, B., and R. Dodge. 1898. Psychologische Untersuchungen uber das Lesen, auf Experimenteller Grundlage. Halle. As cited in Edmund Burke Huey. 1908. *The Psychology and Pedagogy of Reading*. Rep. 1968. Cambridge, Mass.: MIT Press.

Estabrook, Iris W. October 1982. Talking About Writing—Developing Independent Writers. *Language Arts* 59: 696–706.

Estes, Thomas H., and Julie P. Johnstone. November/December 1977. Twelve Easy Ways to Make Readers Hate Reading (and One Difficult Way to Make Them Love It). *Language Arts* 54: 891–97.

Evans Frederick J. 1985. Expectancy, Therapeutic Instructions, and the Placebo Response. *Placebo: Theory, Research, and Mechanisms*. Ed. Leonard White, Bernard Tursky, and Gary E. Schwartz. New York: The Guilford Press, 215–28.

Fagan, William T., C. R. Cooper, and J. M. Jensen. 1975. *Measures for Research and Evaluation in the English Language Arts*. Urbana, Ill.: National Council of Teachers of English.

Farnes, N. C. 1973. *Reading Purposes, Comprehension and the Use of Context*. Bletchley, Buckinghamshire, England: The Open University Press.

Farrar, Mary Thomas. October 1984. Asking Better Questions. *The Reading Teacher* 38: 10–15.

Fasold, Ralph W., and Walt Wolfram. 1970. Some Linguistic Features of Negro Dialect. *Teaching Standard English in the Inner City*. Ed. Ralph W. Fasold and Roger W. Shuy. Arlington, Va.: Center for Applied Linguistics, 41–86.

Feldman, David, and Brian Feldman. 4–8 April 1983. The Responses to Written Language by Elementary Level Learning Disabled Students. Paper presented at the Annual International Convention of the Council for Exceptional Children, Detroit. Educational Documents Reproduction Service, no. ED 242 128.

Ferreiro, Emilia, and Ana Teberosky. 1982. *Literacy Before Schooling*. Tr. Karen Goodman Castro. Portsmouth, N.H.: Heinemann.

Fish, Stanley. 1980. *Is There a Text in This Class? The Authority of Interpretive Communities*. Cambridge, Mass.: Harvard University Press.

Fitzgerald, Jill. December 1983. Helping Readers Gain Self-Control Over Reading Comprehension. *The Reading Teacher* 37: 249–53.

Fitzgerald, Sheila. Spring 1984. Beginning Reading and Writing through Singing: A Natural Approach. *Highway One* 7, ii: 6–12.

Flesch, Rudolf. 1955. *Why Johnny Can't Read*. New York: Harper & Row.

———. 1 November 1979. Why Johnny *Still* Can't Read. *Family Circle*, 26, 44, 46.

———. 1981. *Why Johnny* Still *Can't Read*. New York: Harper & Row.

Fodor, J. A., T. G. Bever, and M. F. Garrett. 1974. *The Psychology of Language*. New York: McGraw-Hill.

Fodor, J., and M. Garrett. 1966. Some Reflections on Competence and Performance. *Psycholinguistic Papers*. Ed. J. Lyons and R. J. Wales. Edinburgh: Edinburgh University Press, 135–54.

Forbes, Esther. 1943. *Johnny Tremain*. Boston: Houghton Mifflin.

Forester, Anne D. November 1977. What Teachers Can Learn from "Natural Readers." *The Reading Teacher* 31: 160–66.

Forster, Kenneth I., and Leonie A. Ryder. June 1971. Perceiving the Structure and Meaning of Sentences. *Journal of Verbal Learning and Verbal Behavior* 10: 285–96.

Fox, Paula. 1984. *One-Eyed Cat*. New York: Bradbury Press.

Fries, Charles C. *Linguistics and Reading*. 1963. New York: Holt, Rinehart and Winston.

Fulwiler, Toby. 1982. The Personal Connection: Journal Writing across the Curriculum. *Language Connections: Writing and Reading Across the Curriculum*. Ed. Toby Fulwiler and Art Young. Urbana, Ill.: National Council of Teachers of English, 13–31.

Gag, Wanda. 1928. *Millions of Cats*. New York: Coward-McCann.

Galdone, Paul. 1968. *Henny Penny*. London: Seabury.

Gates, Arthur I. 1949. Character and Purposes of the Yearbook. *Reading in the Elementary School*. Part II of *The Forty-eighth Yearbook of the National Society for the Study of Education*. Chicago: University of Chicago Press, 1–9.

———. 1962. *Teaching Reading: What Research Says to the Teacher*. 2nd ed. Washington, D.C.: National Education Association.

Gates, Arthur I., and Eloise Boeker. November 1923. A Study of Initial Stages in Reading by Pre-school Children. *Teachers College Record* 24: 469–88.

Geertz, Clifford. 1983. *Local Knowledge*. New York: Seabury.

Geissal, Mary Ann, and June D. Knafle. November 1977. A Linguistic View of Auditory Discrimination Tests and Exercises. *The Reading Teacher* 31: 134–40.

Genishi, Celia, and Anne Dyson. 1984. *Language Assessment in the Early Years*. Norwood, N.J.: ABLEX.

Gentry, J. Richard. November 1982. An Analysis of Developmental Spelling in GYNS AT WRK. *The Reading Teacher* 36: 192–200.

Gentry, Richard R. 1987. *Spel . . . Is a Four-Letter Word*. Richmond Hill, Ontario: Scholastic-TAB.

Giacobbe, Mary Ellen. 1984. Helping Children Become More Responsible for Their Own Writing. *LiveWire*. Urbana, Ill.: National Council of Teachers of English 11: 7–9.

Gibson, Eleanor J. 1972. Reading for Some Purpose. *Language by Ear and by Eye*. Ed. James F. Kavanagh and Ignatius G. Mattingly. Cambridge, Mass.: MIT Press, 3–19.

Gibson, Eleanor J., and Harry Levin. 1975. *The Psychology of Reading*. Cambridge, Mass: MIT Press.

Gibson, Eleanor J., Arthur Shurcliff, and Albert Yonas. 1970. Utilization of Spelling Patterns by Deaf and Hearing Subjects. *Basic Studies on Reading*. Ed. Harry Levin and Joanna P. Williams. New York: Basic Books, 57–73.

Gilles, Carol, Mary Bixby, Paul Crowley, Shirley Crenshaw, Margaret Henrichs, Frances Reynolds, and Donelle Pyle. In press. *Whole Language Strategies for Secondary Students*. New York: Richard C. Owen.

Glazer, Susan Mandel. February 1974. Is Sentence Length a Valid Measure of Difficulty in Readability Formulas? *The Reading Teacher* 27: 464–67.

Goetz, Lee Garrett. 1966. *A Camel in the Sea*. New York: McGraw-Hill.

Goodman, Kenneth S. October 1965. A Linguistic Study of Cues and Miscues in Reading. *Elementary English* 42: 639–43.

_____. ed. 1968, 1973. *The Psycholinguistic Nature of the Reading Process*. Detroit: Wayne State University Press.

_____. May 1967. Reading: A Psycholinguistic Guessing Game. *Journal of the Reading Specialist* 6: 126–35.

_____. 1970. Behind the Eye: What Happens in Reading. *Reading: Process and Program*. Kenneth S. Goodman and Olive S. Niles. Urbana, Ill.: National Council of Teachers of English, 3–38.

_____. December 1972. Orthography in a Theory of Reading Instruction. *Elementary English* 49: 1254–61.

_____. ed. 1973a. *Miscue Analysis: Applications to Reading Instruction*. Urbana, Ill.: National Council of Teachers of English.

_____. 1973b. Testing in Reading: A General Critique. *Accountability and Reading Instruction*. Ed. Robert B. Ruddell. Urbana, Ill.: National Council of Teachers of English, 21–33.

_____. 1973c. *Theoretically Based Studies of Patterns of Miscues in Oral Reading Performance*. Detroit: Wayne State University. Available from the Educational Resources Information Center, no. ED 079 708.

_____. September 1974. Effective Teachers of Reading Know Language and Kids. *Elementary English* 51: 823–28.

_____. 1975. *Strategies for Increasing Comprehension in Reading*. Glenview, Ill.: Scott, Foresman.

_____. 1976. What We Know about Reading. *Findings of Research in Miscue Analysis: Classroom Implications*. Ed. P. David Allen and Dorothy J. Watson. Urbana, Ill.: ERIC Clearinghouse on Reading and Communications Skills and the National Council of Teachers of English, 57–70.

_____. September 1979. The Know-More and the Know-Nothing Movements in Reading: A Personal Response. *Language Arts* 56: 657–63.

_____. January 1982. Revaluing Readers and Reading. *Topics in Learning and Learning Disabilities* 1: 87–93.

_____. April 1986. Basal Readers: A Call for Action. *Language Arts* 63: 358–63.

_____. 1986. *What's Whole in Whole Language?* Richmond Hill, Ontario: Scholastic-TAB. Available in the U.S. from Heinemann.

_____. 1987a. Reading and Writing: A Psycholinguistic View. Kenneth Goodman, E. Brooks Smith, Robert Meredith, and Yetta Goodman. *Language and Thinking in School: A Whole-Language Curriculum*. 3rd ed. New York: Richard C. Owen, 265–83.

_____. 1987b. Learning and Teaching Reading: Strategies for Comprehension. Kenneth Goodman, E. Brooks Smith, Robert Meredith and Yetta Goodman. *Language and Thinking in School: A Whole-Language Curriculum*. 3rd ed. New York: Richard C. Owen, 284–302.

Goodman, Kenneth, and Catherine Buck. October 1973. Dialect Barriers to Reading Comprehension Revisited. *The Reading Teacher* 27: 6–12.

Goodman, Kenneth S., and Yetta M. Goodman. August 1978. *Reading of American Children Whose Language is a Stable Rural Dialect of English or a Language Other than English*. U.S. Dept. of HEW, Project NIE-C-00-3-0087, Final Report.

_____. 1979. Learning to Read is Natural. *Theory and Practice of Early Reading*. Ed. Lauren B. Resnick and Phyllis A. Weaver. Hillsdale, N.J.: Erlbaum, 1: 137–54.

_____. 1981. A Whole-Language, Comprehension-Centered Reading Program. Program in Language and Literacy Occasional Paper Number 1. University of Arizona. Educational Resources Information Center, no. ED 210 630.

Goodman, Kenneth S., E. Brooks Smith, Robert Meredith, and Yetta Goodman. 1987. *Language and Thinking in School: A Whole-Language Curriculum*. New York: Richard C. Owen.

Goodman, Yetta. 1973. Miscue Analysis for In-Service Reading Teachers. *Miscue Analysis: Applications to Reading Instruction*. Ed. Kenneth S. Goodman. Urbana, Ill.: National Council of Teachers of English, 49–64.

_____. November 1974. "I Never Read Such a Long Story Before." *English Journal* 63: 65–71.

_____. 1975. Reading Strategy Lessons: Expanding Reading Effectiveness. *Help for the Reading Teacher: New Directions in Research*. Ed. William D. Page. Urbana, Ill.: National Conference on Research in English and the National Council of Teachers of English, 34–41.

_____. 1976a. Developing Reading Proficiency. *Findings of Research in Miscue Analysis: Classroom Implications*. Ed. P. David Allen and Dorothy J. Watson. Urbana, Ill.: ERIC Clearinghouse on Reading and Communication Skills and the National Council of Teachers of English, 113–28.

_____. 1976b. Strategies for Comprehension. *Findings of Research in Miscue Analysis: Classroom Implications*. Ed. P. David Allen and Dorothy J. Watson. Urbana, Ill.: ERIC Clearinghouse on Reading and Communication Skills and the National Council of Teachers of English, 94–102.

_____. June 1978. Kid Watching: An Alternative to Testing. *National Elementary School Principal* 57: 41–45.

_____. 1982. Retellings of Literature and the Comprehension Process. *Theory into Practice* 21: 301–7.

Goodman, Yetta, and Bess Attwerger. n.d. Pre-Schoolers' Book Handling Knowledge. Unpublished paper, University of Arizona, Tucson.

Goodman, Yetta M., and Carolyn L. Burke. 1972a. *Reading Miscue Inventory Complete Kit: Procedure for Diagnosis and Evaluation*. New York: Macmillan.

_____. 1972b. *Reading Miscue Inventory Manual: Procedure for Diagnosis and Evaluation*. New York: Macmillan.

_____. 1972c. *Reading Miscue Inventory Practice Analysis Manual*. New York: Macmillan.

_____. 1980. *Reading Strategies: Focus on Comprehension*. New York: Richard C. Owen.

Goodman, Yetta, and Jennifer Greene. 1977. Grammar and Reading in the Classroom. *Linguistic Theory: What Can It Say about Reading*? Ed. Roger W. Shuy. Newark, Del.: International Reading Association, 18–30.

Goodman, Yetta, and Dorothy J. Watson. November/December 1977. A Reading Program to Live With: Focus on Comprehension. *Language Arts* 54: 868–79.

Goodman, Yetta M., Dorothy J. Watson, and Carolyn L. Burke. 1987. *Reading Miscue Inventory: Alternative Procedures*. New York: Richard C. Owen.

Gorman, Richard M. 1972. *Discovering Piaget: A Guide for Teachers*. Columbus, Ohio: Charles E. Merrill.

Goss, Janet, and Jerome Harste. 1981. *It Didn't Frighten Me*. Ill. Steve Romney. School Book Fairs, Inc.

Gough, Philip. 1972. One Second of Reading. *Language by Ear and by Eye*. Ed. James F. Kavanagh and Ignatius G. Mattingly. Cambridge, Mass.: MIT Press, 331–58.

Graves, Donald. 1981. Patterns of Child Control of the Writing Process. *Donald Graves in Australia*. Ed. R. D. Walshe. Portsmouth, N.H.: Heinemann, 17–28.

Graves, Donald H. 1983. *Writing: Teachers and Children at Work*. Portsmouth, N.H.: Heinemann.

Gray, William S. 1948. *On Their Own in Reading: How to Give Children Independence in Attacking New Words*. Glenview, Ill.: Scott, Foresmann.

_____.1960. *On Their Own in Reading: How to Give Children Independence in Analyzing New Words*. Rev. ed. Glenview, Ill.: Scott, Foresman.

Greene, Graham. 1940. *The Power and the Glory*. New York: Viking Press.

Grundin, Hans U. December 1985. A Commission of Selective Readers: A Critique of *Becoming a Nation of Readers*. *The Reading Teacher* 39: 262–66.

Guthrie, John T., ed. 1976. *Aspects of Reading Acquisition*. Baltimore: The John Hopkins University Press.

Gwynne, Fred. 1970. *The King Who Rained*. New York: Windmill Books and E. P. Dutton.

_____. 1979. *Chocolate Moose*. New York: Windmill Books and E. P. Dutton.

Haggard, Martha Rapp. December 1985. An Interactive Strategies Approach to Content Reading. *Journal of Reading* 29: 204–10.

Hall, MaryAnne. 1976. *Teaching Reading as a Language Experience*. 2nd ed. Columbus, Ohio: Charles E. Merrill.

_____. 1981. *The Language Experience Approach for Teaching Reading: A Research Perspective*. 3rd ed. Newark, Del.: ERIC Clearinghouse on Reading and Communication Skills and the International Reading Association.

Hall, Robert A., Jr. 1961. *Sound and Spelling in English*. New York: Chilton.

Hall, Susan, and Chris Hall. December 1984. It Takes a Lot of Letters to Spell "erz." *Language Arts* 61: 822–27.

Halliday, M. A. K. 1975. *Learning How to Mean: Explorations in the Development of Language*. London: Edward Arnold.

_____. 1978. *Language as Social Semiotic*. Baltimore: University Park Press.

Hammond, Dorsey. November 1982. "Language Across the Curriculum, Across the Grades." Paper presented at National Council of Teachers of English Conference, Washington, D.C.

_____. 1986. Common Questions on Reading Comprehension. *Learning 86* 14: 49-51.

Hansen, Jane, Tom Newkirk, and Donald M. Graves, eds. 1985. *Breaking Ground: Teachers Relate Reading and Writing in the Elementary School*. Portsmouth, N.H.: Heinemann.

Harber, Jean R. 1981. The Effect of Cultural and Linguistic Differences on Reading Performance. *The Social Psychology of Reading*. Ed. John R. Edwards. Silver Springs, Md.: Institute of Modern Languages, 1: 173–92.

Harper, Robert J., and Gary Kilarr. November/December 1977. The Law and Reading Instruction. *Language Arts* 54: 913–19.

Harris, Larry A., and Jerome A. Niles. Spring 1982. An Analysis of Published Informal Reading Inventories. *Reading Horizons* 22: 159–74.

Harris, T. L., and R. W. Hodges, eds. 1981. *A Dictionary of Reading and Related Terms*. Newark, Del.: International Reading Association.

Harste, Jerome C. Fall 1977. Understanding the Hypothesis, It's the Teacher That Makes the Difference: Part I. *Reading Horizons* 18: 32–43.

———. Winter 1978. Understanding the Hypothesis, It's the Teacher That Makes the Difference: Part II. *Reading Horizons* 18: 89–98.

———. 1985. Becoming a Nation of Language Learners: Beyond Risk. *Toward Practical Theory: A State of Practice Assessment of Reading Comprehension Instruction*. Ed. Jerome C. Harste and Diane Stephens. Bloomington, Ind.: Indiana University, 8:1–122. USDE-C-300-83-0130.

———. 1986. Toward Practical Theory: Becoming a Reflexive Profession of Language Learners. Bloomington, Ind.: Unpublished paper.

Harste, Jerome C., and Carolyn L. Burke. July 1978. Toward a Socio-Psycholinguistic Model of Reading Comprehension. *Viewpoints in Teaching and Learning* 54: 9–34.

Harste, Jerome, and Philip Harris. 1985. *Landscapes: A State-of-the-Art Assessment of Reading Comprehension Research 1974–1984*. Bloomington, Ind.: Indiana University. U.S. Department of Education Project USDE-C-300-83-01320.

Harste, Jerome C., Cathy G. Short, Carolyn L. Burke, et al. Forthcoming. *Reading, Writing, Reasoning: The Authoring Cycle at Work in Classrooms*. Portsmouth, N.H.: Heinemann.

Harste, Jerome C., Virginia A. Woodward, and Carolyn L. Burke. February 1984. Examining Our Assumptions: A Transactional View of Literacy and Learning. *Research in the Teaching of English* 18: 84–108.

———. 1984. *Language Stories and Literacy Lessons*. Portsmouth, N.H.: Heinemann.

Hartelius, Margaret A. 1975. *The Chicken's Child*. Garden City, N.Y.: Doubleday.

Hartwell, Patrick. February 1985. Grammar, Grammars, and the Teaching of Grammar. *College English* 47: 105–27.

Hasselriis, Peter. January 1982. IEPs and a Whole-Language Model of Language Arts. *Topics in Learning and Learning Disabilities* 1: 17–21.

Haussler, Myna. 1982. Transitions into Literacy: A Psycholinguistic Analysis of Beginning Reading in Kindergarten and First-Grade Children. Doctoral diss., University of Arizona, Tucson.

Heald-Taylor, B. Gail. October 1984. Scribble in First Grade. *The Reading Teacher* 38: 4–8.

———. 1987. Big Books. *Ideas with Insights: Language Arts K–6*. Ed. Dorothy Watson. Urbana, Ill.: National Council of Teachers of English.

Heckleman, R. G. Summer 1969. A Neurological-Impress Method of Remedial Reading Instruction. *Academic Therapy* 4: 277–82.

Heilman, Arthur W. 1972. *Principles and Practices of Teaching Reading*. Columbus, Ohio: Charles E. Merrill. (5th ed., 1981).

Heimlich, Joan E., and Susan D. Pittelman. 1986. *Semantic Mapping: Classroom Applications*. Newark, Del.: International Reading Association.

Henderson, Edmund H., and James W. Beers, eds. 1980. *Developmental and Cognitive Aspects of Learning to Spell*. Newark, Del.: International Reading Association.

Hennings, Dorothy Grant. January 1982. A Writing Approach to Reading Comprehension—Schema Theory in Action. *Language Arts* 59: 8–17.

Herber, Harold L. 1978. *Teaching Reading in Content Areas*. 2nd ed. Englewood Cliffs, N.J.: Prentice-Hall.

Hiebert, E. Winter 1983. An Examination of Ability Grouping for Reading Instruction. *Reading Research Quarterly* 18: 231–55.

Hillerich, Robert L. March 1977. Let's Teach Spelling—Not Phonetic Misspelling. *Language Arts* 54: 301–7.

_____. Summer 1985. Let's Pretend. *Michigan Reading Journal* 18: 15–18, 20.

Hochberg, Julian. 1970. Components of Literacy: Speculations and Exploratory Research. *Basic Studies on Reading*. Ed. Harry Levin and Joanna P. Williams. New York: Basic Books, 74–89.

Holdaway, Don. 1979. *The Foundations of Literacy*. Sydney: Ashton-Scholastic. Also available from Heinemann and, in Canada, from Scholastic-TAB.

Hollingsworth, Paul M. March 1978. An Experimental Approach to the Impress Method of Teaching Reading. *The Reading Teacher* 31: 624–26.

Hoskisson, Kenneth. March 1975. The Many Facets of Assisted Reading. *Elementary English* 52: 312–15.

Hoskisson, Kenneth, and Bernadette Krohm. September 1974. Reading by Immersion: Assisted Reading. *Elementary English* 51: 832–36.

Huey, Edmund Burke. 1908, 1968. *The Psychology and Pedagogy of Reading*. Reprint, Cambridge, Mass.: MIT Press.

Hunt, Barbara Carey. 1974–1975. Black Dialect and Third and Fourth Graders' Performance on the Gray Oral Reading Test. *Reading Research Quarterly* 10, i: 103–23.

Hunt, Kellogg W. 1970. *Syntactic Maturity in Schoolchildren and Adults*. Monographs of the Society for Research in Child Development, no. 134. Chicago: University of Chicago Press.

Hutchins, Pat. 1972. *Goodnight, Owl!* New York: Macmillan.

Hynd, George W., and Cynthia R. Hynd. Summer 1984. Dyslexia: Neuroanatomical/Neurolinguistic Perspectives. *Reading Research Quarterly* 19: 482–98.

Iran-Nejad, Asghar. 1980. *The Schema: A Structural or a Functional Pattern*. Tech. Rep. no. 159. Urbana, Ill.: University of Illinois, Center for the Study of Reading. Also in *Understanding Readers' Understanding*, Ed. R. J. Tierney, P. Anders, and J. N. Mitchell. Hillsdale, N.J.: Erlbaum, in press.

Iran-Nejad, Asghar, and Andrew Ortony. Spring 1984. A Biofunctional Model of

Distributed Mental Content, Mental Structures, Awareness, and Attention. *The Journal of Mind and Behavior* 5: 171–210.

Irwin, Judith W. and Carol A. Davis. November 1980. Assessing Readability: The Checklist Approach. *Journal of Reading* 24: 124–30.

Iveson, Margaret L., ed. 1982. *Senior High Language Arts Curriculum Guide*, 1982. Edmonton: Alberta Education.

Jensen, Julie M., ed. 1984. *Composing and Comprehending*. Urbana, Ill.: National Conference on Research in English and ERIC Clearinghouse on Reading and Communication Skills.

Jewell, Margaret Greer, and Miles V. Zintz. 1986. *Learning to Read Naturally*. Dubuque: Kendall/Hunt.

Johns, Jerry, et al. 1977. *Assessing Reading Behavior: Informal Reading Inventories, An Annotated Bibliography*. Newark, Del.: International Reading Association.

Johns, Jerry. 1981. *Basic Reading Inventory*. Dubuque: Kendall/Hunt.

_____. 1986. Students' Perceptions of Reading: Thirty Years of Inquiry. *Metalinguistic Awareness and Beginning Literacy*. Ed. David B. Yaden, Jr., and Shane Templeton. Portsmouth, N.H.: Heinemann, 31–40.

Johns, Jerry L., and DiAnn Waksul Ellis. December 1976. Reading: Children Tell It Like It Is. *Reading World* 16: 115–28.

Jongsma, Eugene. 1971. *The Cloze Procedure as a Teaching Technique*. Newark, Del.: International Reading Association.

_____. 1980. *Cloze Instruction Research: A Second Look*. Newark, Del.: International Reading Association.

Kamii, Constance, and Marie Randazzo. 1985. Social Interaction and Invented Spelling. *Language Arts* 62: 124–33.

Karlin, Robert. 1980. Learning Disability and Reading: Theory or Fact? *Inchworm, Inchworm: Persistent Problems in Reading Education*. Ed. Constance McCullough. Newark, Del.: International Reading Association, 102–10.

Kellogg, Steven. 1971. *Can I Keep Him?* New York: Dial Press.

Kennedy, Delores Kessler, and Paul Weener. Summer 1973. Visual and Auditory Training with the Cloze Procedure to Improve Reading and Listening Comprehension. *Reading Research Quarterly* 8: 524–41.

Kess, Joseph. 1976. *Psycholinguistics: Introductory Perspectives*. New York: Academic Press.

King, Dorothy F., and Dorothy J. Watson. 1983. Reading as Meaning Construction. *Integrating the Language Arts in the Elementary School*. Ed. Beverly A. Busching and Judith I. Schwartz. Urbana, Ill.: National Council of Teachers of English, 70–77.

King, Martha L. Summer 1980. Learning How to Mean in Written Language. *Theory Into Practice* 19: 163–69.

Klima, E. S., and Ursula Bellugi-Klima. 1966. Syntactic Regularities in the Speech of Children. *Psycholinguistics Papers*. Ed. J. Lyons and R. J. Wales. Edinburgh: Edinburgh University Press, 183–208.

Koestler, Arthur. 1969. Beyond Atomism and Holism—The Concept of the Holon. *Beyond Reductionism*. Ed. A. Koestler and J. R. Smythies. New York: Macmillan, 192–227.

Kohler, Ivo. May 1962. Experiments with Goggles. *Scientific American* 206: 62–72.

Kolers, Paul A. 1969. Reading Is Only Incidentally Visual. *Psycholinguistics and the Teaching of Reading*. Ed. Kenneth S. Goodman and James T. Fleming. Newark, Del.: International Reading Association, 8–16.

_____. 1973. Three Stages of Reading. *Psycholinguistics and Reading*. Ed. Frank Smith. New York: Holt, Rinehart and Winston, 28–49.

Kossack, Sharon. May 1986. Realism: The Newspaper and the Older Learner. *Journal of Reading* 29: 768–69.

Kraft, Robert G. 1985. Group-Inquiry Turns Passive Students Active. *College Teaching* 33, iv: 149–54.

Kraus, Robert. 1971. *Leo the Late Bloomer*. Ill. José Aruego. New York: Young Readers Press.

Langer, Judith A. November 1981. From Theory to Practice: A Prereading Plan. *Journal of Reading* 25: 152–56.

_____. 1982. The Reading Process. *Secondary School Reading: What Research Reveals for Classroom Practice*. Ed. Allen Berger and H. Alan Robinson. Urbana, Ill.: National Conference on Research in English and ERIC Clearinghouse on Reading and Communication Skills, 38–51.

_____. Summer 1984. Examining Background Knowledge and Text Comprehension. *Reading Research Quarterly* 19: 468–81.

Langer, Judith A., and Gordon Pradl. November 1984. Standardized Testing: A Call for Action. *Language Arts* 61: 764–67.

Larrick, Nancy. May 1976. Wordless Picture Books and the Teaching of Reading. *The Reading Teacher* 29: 743–46.

La Shell, Lois. Spring/Summer 1986. Matching Reading Styles Triples Reading Achievement of Learning Disabled Students. *The Clearinghouse Bulletin on Learning/Teaching Styles and Brain Behavior* 1, i:4.

Lassen, Niels A., David H. Ingvar, and Erik Skinhoj. October 1978. Brain Function and Blood Flow. *Scientific American* 239, iv: 62–71.

Lefevre, Carl A. 1962. *Linguistics and the Teaching of Reading*. New York: McGraw-Hill.

Lesgold, Alan M., and Charles C. Perfetti, eds. 1981. *Interactive Processes in Reading*. Hillsdale, N.J.: Erlbaum.

Levin, Harry, and Eleanor L. Kaplan. 1970. Grammatical Structure and Reading. *Basic Studies on Reading*. Ed. Harry Levin and Joanna P. Williams. New York: Basic Books, 119–33.

Levy, J. May 1985. Right Brain, Left Brain: Fact and Fiction. *Psychology Today*, 38–44.

Lindberg, Margaret, and Laura A. Smith. 1976. Teaching Vocabulary as an Introduction to New Material: Is It Worthwhile? *Current Topics in Language*. Ed. Nancy Ainsworth Johnson. Cambridge, Mass.: Winthrop, 436–42.

Lindfors, Judith W. 1980. *Children's Language and Learning*. Englewood Cliffs, N.J.: Prentice-Hall.

_____. October 1984. How Children Learn or How Teachers Teach? A Profound Conclusion. *Language Arts* 61: 600–6.

Locke, John L., and Fred S. Fehr. 1970. Subvocal Rehearsal as a Form of Speech. *Journal of Verbal Learning and Verbal Behavior* 9: 495–98.

Loughlin, C. E. November 1983. *Reflecting Literacy in the Environment*. Center for Teaching and Learning, University of North Dakota, Grand Forks, 16, no. 3.

Lynch Priscilla. 1986. *Using Big Books and Predictable Books*. Richmond Hill, Ontario: Scholastic-TAB.

McCord, David. 1952. The Pickety Fence. *Far and Few, Rhymes of Never Was and Always Is*. Ill. Henry B. Kane. Cambridge, Mass.: Little, Brown and Company.

McCracken, Glenn, and Charles C. Walcutt. 1970. *Lippincott's Basic Reading*. 2nd ed. Philadelphia: Lippincott.

McCracken, Robert A. May 1971. Initiating Sustained Silent Reading. *Journal of Reading* 14: 521–24, 582–83.

McCracken, Robert A., and Marlene J. McCracken. 1972. *Reading Is Only the Tiger's Tail*. San Raphael, Calif.: Leswing Press.

_____. January 1978. Modeling Is the Key to Sustained Silent Reading. *The Reading Teacher* 31: 406–8.

McCullough, Constance M. 1972, 1985. What Should the Reading Teacher Know about Language and Thinking? *Language and Learning to Read: What Teachers Should Know About Language*. Ed. Richard E. Hodges and E. Hugh Rudorf. Boston: Houghton Mifflin, 202–15. Reprint, University Press of America.

McDonell, Gloria M., and E. Bess Osburn. January 1978. New Thoughts about Reading Readiness. *Language Arts* 55: 26–29.

McIntosh, Margaret E. April 1985. What Do Practitioners Need to Know about Current Inference Research? *The Reading Teacher* 38: 755–61.

McKean, Kevin. December 1981. Beaming New Light on the Brain. *Discover* 2: 30–33.

_____. February 1985. In Search of the Unconscious Mind. *Discover* 6: 12–14, 16, 18.

McKee, Paul. 1975. *Primer for Parents*. 3rd ed. Boston: Houghton Mifflin.

McKenna, Michael, and Richard D. Robinson. 1980. *An Introduction to the Cloze Procedure*. Newark, Del.: International Reading Association.

McKenzie, Gary R., and Elaine D. Fowler. April 1973. A Recipe for Producing Student Discovery of Language Arts Generalizations. *Elementary English* 50: 593–98.

McKenzie, Moira, ed. 1985. *Shared Writing*. (Nos. 1 and 2 of *Language Matters*.) London: ILEA Centre for Language in Primary Education.

McLaughlin, G. Harry. March 1969. Reading at "Impossible" Speeds. *Journal of Reading* 12: 449–54, 502–10.

McNeill, David. 1966. Developmental Psycholinguistics. *The Genesis of Language: A Psycholinguistic Approach*. Ed. Frank Smith and George A. Miller. Cambridge, Mass.: MIT Press, 15–84.

Mallitskaya, M. K. 1960. K Metodike Ispol'zovania dl'a Razvitiya Ponimaniya Rechi u Detei v Kontse Pervogo i na Vtorom Godu Zhizni (A Method for Using Pictures to Develop Speech Comprehension in Children at the End of the First and in the Second Year of Life). *Voprosy Psikhol* 3: 122–126.

Malmstrom, Jean, et al. 1965. *Course Book for English Language*. Kalamazoo, Mich.: Western Michigan University.

Manning, Gary L., and Maryann Manning. May 1984. What Models of Recreational Reading Make a Difference? *Reading World* 23: 375–80.

Manzo, A. V. 1969. The ReQuest Procedure. *Journal of Reading* 13: 123–26.

Marchbanks, Gabrielle, and Harry Levin. 1965. Cues by Which Children Recognize Words. *Journal of Educational Psychology* 56: 57–61.

Marcus, A. 1970. The Development of a Diagnostic Test of Syntactic Meaning Clues in Reading. *Diagnostic Viewpoints in Reading*. Ed. R. E. Leibert. Newark, Del.: International Reading Association.

Marks, Lawrence E., and George A. Miller. February 1964. The Role of Semantic and Syntactic Constraints in the Memorization of English Sentences. *Journal of Verbal Learning and Verbal Behavior* 3: 1–5.

Martin, Bill, Jr. 1983. *Brown Bear, Brown Bear, What Do You See?* New York: Holt, Rinehart and Winston.

Martin, Bill, Jr., with Peggy Brogan. 1972–1974. *Sounds of Language* Readers. New York: Holt, Rinehart and Winston.

Mathews, Mitford M. 1966. *Learning to Read: Historically Considered*. Chicago: University of Chicago Press.

Max, Louis William. October 1937. Experimental Study of the Motor Theory of Consciousness: IV. Action-Current Responses in the Deaf during Awakening, Kinaesthetic Imagery and Abstract Thinking. *Journal of Comparative Psychology* 24: 301–44.

May, Frank B. 1973. *To Help Children Read: Mastery Performance Modules for Teachers in Training*. Columbus, Ohio: Charles E. Merrill.

May, Frank B., and Susan B. Eliot. 1978. *To Help Children Read: Mastery Performance Modules for Teachers in Training*. 2nd ed. Columbus, Ohio: Charles E. Merrill.

Mayher, John S., and Rita S. Brause. March 1984. Learning Through Teaching: Lessons from a First Grade. *Language Arts* 61: 285–90.

Meek, Margaret. 1983. *Awakening to Literacy*. London: Routledge & Kegan Paul.

Mehler, Jacques. November 1963. Some Effects of Grammatical Transformation on the Recall of English Sentences. *Journal of Verbal Learning and Verbal Behavior* 2: 346–51.

Menosky, Dorothy M. 1971. A Psycholinguistic Description of Oral Reading Miscues Generated during the Reading of Varying Portions of Text by Selected Readers from Grades Two, Four, Six and Eight. Doctoral diss., Wayne State University.

Menyuk, Paula. 1969. *Sentences Children Use*. Cambridge, Mass.: MIT Press.

MERIT: Developing Metacognitive Skills: The Key to Success in Reading and Learning. 1986. MERIT, Chapter 2 Project, the School District of Philadelphia, Hilda K. Carr, MERIT Supervisor.

Meyer, Bonnie J. F. February 1982. Reading Research and the Composition Teacher: The Importance of Plans. *College Composition and Communication* 33: 37–49.

Miller, George A. 1956. The Magical Number Seven, Plus or Minus Two: Some Limits on Our Capacity for Processing Information. *Psychological Review* 63: 81–97.

———. 1962. Some Psychological Studies of Grammar. *American Psychologist* 17: 748–62.

———. July 1964. The Psycholinguists. *Encounter* 23: 29–37.

Miller, George A., Jerome S. Bruner, and Leo Postman. 1954. Familiarity of Letter Sequences and Tachistoscopic Identification. *Journal of General Psychology* 50: 129–39.

Miller, George A., and Noam Chomsky. 1963. Finitary Models of Language Users. *Handbook of Mathematical Psychology* 2. Ed. Robert D. Luce, Robert R. Bush, and Eugene Galanter. New York: John Wiley, 420–91.

Miller, George A., and Stephen Isard. 1964. Free Recall of Self-Embedded English Sentences. *Information and Control* 7: 292–303.

Monaghan, E. Jennifer. 1980. A History of the Syndrome of Dyslexia with Implications for its Treatment. *Inchworm, Inchworm: Persistent Problems in Reading Education*. Ed. Constance McCullough. Newark, Del.: International Reading Association, 87–101.

Moore, David W. November/December 1983. A Case for Naturalistic Assessment of Reading Comprehension. *Language Arts* 60: 957–69.

Moore, David W., John E. Readence, and Robert J. Rickelman. 1982. *Pre-Reading Activities for Content Area Reading and Learning*. Newark, Del.: International Reading Association.

Morris, Darrell. September 1981. Concept of Word: A Developmental Phenomenon in the Beginning Reading and Writing Processes. *Language Arts* 58: 659–68.

Murphy, Sandra. Spring 1986. Children's Comprehension of Deictic Categories in Oral and Written Language. *Reading Research Quarterly* 21:118–31.

National Commission on Excellence in Education. 1983. *A Nation at Risk: The Imperative for Educational Reform*. Washington, D.C.: U.S. Department of Education.

National Council of Teachers of English, Commission on the English Curriculum. 1952. *The English Language Arts*. New York: Appleton-Century-Crofts, Inc.

Nelson-Herber, Joan. 1985. Anticipation and Prediction in Reading Comprehension. *Reading, Thinking, and Concept Development*. Ed. Theodore L. Harris and Eric J. Cooper. New York: College Entrance Examination Board, 89–103.

Newkirk, Thomas, and Nancie Atwell. 1986. *Understanding Writing*. 2nd ed. Chelmsford, Mass.: Northeast Regional Exchange, Inc.

Newman, Judith M., ed. 1985. *Whole Language: Theory in Use*. Portsmouth, N.H.: Heinemann.

News from the Professional Studies and Standards Committee: Department of Education Definition of Reading. Spring 1977. *The Michigan Reading Journal* 11, ii: 35–36.

Nix, D., and M. Schwarz. 1979. Toward a Phenomenology of Reading Comprehension. *New Directions in Discourse Processing*. Ed. Roy O. Freedle. Norwood, N.J.: ABLEX.

Norton, Donna E. April 1982. Using a Webbing Process to Develop Children's Literature Units. *Language Arts* 59: 348–56.

O'Donnell, Roy C., William J. Griffin, and Raymond C. Norris. 1967. *Syntax of Kindergarten and Elementary School Children: A Transformational Analysis*. Research report no. 8. Urbana, Ill.: National Council of Teachers of English.

O'Donnell, Roy C., and F. J. King. Winter 1974. An Exploration of Deep Structure Recovery and Reading Comprehension Skills. *Research in the Teaching of English* 8: 327–38.

Olsen, Hans C., Jr. 1968. Linguistics and Materials for Beginning Reading Instruction. *The Psycholinguistic Nature of the Reading Process*. Ed. Kenneth S. Goodman. Detroit: Wayne State University Press, 273–87.

Olson, Mary W., and Bonnie Longnion. May 1982. Pattern Guides: A Workable Alternative for Content Teachers. *Journal of Reading* 25: 736–41.

Page, William D., ed. 1975. *Help for the Reading Teacher: New Directions in Research*. Urbana, Ill.: National Conference on Research in English and the National Council of Teachers of English.

Palermo, David S. 1978. *Psychology of Language*. Glenview, Ill.: Scott, Foresman.

Palermo, David S., and Dennis L. Molfese. December 1972. Language Acquisition from Age Five Onward. *Psychological Bulletin* 78: 409–28.

Parents Should Be Concerned with How Kids Learn to Read. 3 September 1985. *Providence Journal-Bulletin*, A-10.

Pearson, P. David. 1974–1975. Effects of Grammatical Complexity on Children's Comprehension, Recall, and Conception of Certain Semantic Relations. *Reading Research Quarterly* 10, ii: 155–92.

———. April 1985. Changing the Face of Reading Comprehension Instruction. *The Reading Teacher* 38: 724–38.

Pearson, P. David, and Dale D. Johnson. 1978. *Teaching Reading Comprehension*. New York: Holt, Rinehart and Winston.

Peetoom, Adrian. 1986. *Shared Reading: Safe Risks with Whole Books*. Richmond Hill, Ontario: Scholastic-TAB.

Peltz, Fillmore Kenneth. 1973–1974. The Effect upon Comprehension of Repatterning Based on Students' Writing Patterns. *Reading Research Quarterly* 9, iv: 603–21.

Perera, Katharine. 13 May 1986. Language Acquisition as a Continuing Process—The Role of the English Teacher. Paper presented at the Fourth International Conference on the Teaching of English, Ottawa.

Perfetti, Charles A., and T. Hogaboam. August 1975. Relationship between Single

Word Decoding and Reading Comprehension Skill. *Journal of Educational Psychology* 67: 461-69.

Perkins, Al. 1969. *Hand, Hand, Fingers, Thumb.* Bright and Early Book series. New York: Random House.

Petersen, Bruce T., ed. 1986. *Convergences: Transactions in Reading and Writing.* Urbana, Ill.: National Council of Teachers of English.

Peterson, Mary. Spring 1987. A Ghostly Evening. *The Michigan Reading Journal* 20: 9–23.

Peterson, Ralph. 1987. Literature Groups: Intensive and Extensive Reading. *Ideas with Insights: Language Arts K–6.* Ed. Dorothy Watson. Urbana, Ill.: National Council of Teachers of English.

Petrosky, Anthony R. 1982. Reading Achievement. *Secondary School Reading: What Research Reveals for Classroom Practice.* Ed. Alan Berger and H. Alan Robinson. Urbana, Ill.: National Conference on Research in English and ERIC Clearinghouse on Reading and Communication Skills, 7–19.

Phinney, Margaret. 19 April 1986. Personal communication.

Piénkowski, Jan. 1981. *Dinner Time.* Text by Anne Carler. London: Gallery Five, Ltd.

Pikulski, John. November 1974. A Critical Review: Informal Reading Inventories. *Reading Teacher* 28: 141–51.

_____. February 1978. Readiness for Reading: A Practical Approach. *Language Arts* 55: 192–97.

Pinnell, Gay Su. Spring 1985. Helping Teachers Help Children at Risk: Insights from the Reading Recovery Program. *Peabody Journal of Education* 62: 70–85.

Porter, William S. 1936. *The Complete Works of O. Henry.* Garden City, N.Y.: Doubleday, Doran.

Poulton, E. G. 1962. Peripheral Vision, Refractoriness and Eye Movements in Fast Oral Reading. *British Journal of Psychology* 53: 409–19.

Prigogine, Ilya, and Isabelle Stengers. 1984. *Order out of Chaos: Man's New Dialogue with Nature.* New York: Bantam.

Raphael, Taffy E. January 1984. Teaching Learners about Sources of Information for Answering Comprehension Questions. *Journal of Reading* 27: 303–11.

Read, Charles. 1971. Pre-school Children's Knowledge of English Phonology. *Harvard Educational Review* 41: 1–34.

_____. 1975. *Children's Categorization of Speech Sounds in English.* Research report no. 17. Urbana, Ill.: National Council of Teachers of English.

Reading Redefined: A Michigan Reading Association Position Paper. Winter 1984. *Michigan Reading Journal* 17: 4–7.

Reid, Jessie F. 1958. An Investigation of Thirteen Beginners in Reading. *Acta Psychologica* 14, iv: 295–313.

_____. 1966. Learning to Think about Reading. *Educational Research* 9: 56–62.

Reynolds, Ralph E., Marsha A. Taylor, Margaret S. Steffensen, Larry L. Shirey, and Richard C. Anderson. 1982. Cultural Schemata and Reading Comprehension. *Reading Research Quarterly* 17, iii: 353–66.

Rhodes, Lynn K. February 1981. I Can Read! Predictable Books as Resources for Reading and Writing Instruction. *The Reading Teacher* 34: 511–18.

Rhodes, Lynn K., and Joy L. Shannon. January 1982. Psycholinguistic Principles in Operation in a Primary Learning Disabilities Classroom. *Topics in Learning and Learning Disabilities* 1: 1–10.

Rich, Sharon J. November 1985. Restoring Power to Teachers: The Impact of "Whole Language." *Language Arts* 62: 717–24.

Rigg, Pat. March 1978. Dialect and/in/for Reading. *Language Arts* 55: 285–90.

Rigg, Pat, and Liz Taylor. March 1979. A Twenty-One-Year-Old Begins to Read. *English Journal* 68: 52–56.

Robinson, Francis P. 1962. *Effective Reading*. New York: Harper and Brothers.

Robinson, H. Alan. 1983. *Teaching Reading, Writing, and Study Strategies: The Content Areas*. 3rd ed. Boston: Allyn & Bacon.

Rode, Sara S. 1974–1975. Development of Phrase and Clause Boundary Reading in Children. *Reading Research Quarterly* 10, i: 124–42.

Roseckyk, Marion. January 1978. Are Teachers Selective When Using Basal Guidebooks? *The Reading Teacher* 31: 381–84.

Rosenblatt, Louise M. 1938. *Literature as Exploration*. New York: D. Appleton-Century.

———. 1964. The Poem as Event. *College English* 26: 123–28.

———. 1978. *The Reader, the Text, the Poem: The Transactional Theory of the Literary Work*. Carbondale, Ill.: Southern Illinois University Press.

Rosenthal, Robert, and Lenore Jacobson. 1968. *Pygmalion in the Classroom*. New York: Holt, Rinehart and Winston.

Ruddell, Robert B. 1965. The Effect of Oral and Written Patterns of Language Structure on Reading Comprehension. *Reading Teacher* 18: 270–75.

———. 1969. Psycholinguistic Implications for a Systems of Communication Model. *Psycholinguistics and the Teaching of Reading*. Ed. Kenneth S. Goodman and James T. Fleming. Newark, Del.: International Reading Association, 61–78.

———. 1970. Language Acquisition and the Reading Process. *Theoretical Models and Processes of Reading*. Ed. Harry Singer and Robert B. Ruddell. Newark, Del.: International Reading Association, 1–19.

Rumelhart, David E. 1977. Toward an Interactive Model of Reading. *Attention and Performance VI*. Ed. Stanislov Dornic. Hillsdale, N.J.: Erlbaum, 573–603.

———. 1980. Schemata: The Building Blocks of Cognition. *Theoretical Issues in Reading Comprehension*. Ed. R. J. Spiro, B. C. Bruce, and W. F. Brewer. Hillsdale, N.J.: Erlbaum, 33–58.

Rupley, William H., and Carol Robeck. February 1978. ERIC/RCS: Black Dialect and Reading Achievement. *The Reading Teacher* 31: 598–601.

Samuels, S. Jay. 1970. Modes of Word Recognition. *Theoretical Models and Processes of Reading*. Ed. Harry Singer and Robert B. Ruddell. Newark, Del.: International Reading Association, 23–37.

_____. 1980. The Age-Old Controversy between Holistic and Subskill Approaches to Beginning Reading Instruction Revisited. *Inchworm, Inchworm: Persistent Problems in Reading Education*. Ed. Constance M. McCullough. Newark, Del.: International Reading Association, 202–21.

Santa, Carol Minnick. 1981. Children's Reading Comprehension; A Final Word. *Children's Prose Comprehension: Research and Practice*. Ed. Carol M. Santa and Bernard L. Hayes. Newark, Del.: International Reading Association, 157–70.

Saporta, Sol, ed. 1962. *Psycholinguistics: A Book of Readings*. New York: Holt, Rinehart and Winston.

Savin, Harris B. 1972. What the Child Knows about Speech When He Starts to Learn to Read. *Language by Ear and by Eye*. Ed. James F. Kavanagh and Ignatius G. Mattingly. Cambridge, Mass.: MIT Press, 319–26.

Savin, Harris B., and Ellen Perchonock. October 1965. Grammatical Structure and the Immediate Recall of English Sentences. *Journal of Verbal Learning and Verbal Behavior* 4: 348–53.

Schneyer, J. Wesley. December 1965. Use of the Cloze Procedure for Improving Reading Comprehension. *The Reading Teacher* 19: 174–79.

Sebasta, Sam. May 1981. Why Rudolph Can't Read. *Language Arts* 58: 545–48.

Shanklin, Nancy. 1982. *Relating Reading and Writing: Developing a Transactional Model of the Writing Process*. Bloomington, Ind.: Monographs in Teaching and Learning, Indiana University School of Education.

Shannon, Claude E. 1948. A Mathematical Theory of Information. *Bell System Technical Journal* 27: 379–423, 623–56.

Sharp, Stanley L. 1981. *The REAL Reason Why Johnnie Still Can't Read*. Pompano Beach, Fla.: Exposition Press of Florida.

Shook, Ronald. October 1986. The Two-Brain Theory: A Critique. *English Education* 18: 173–83.

Shugarman, Sherrie L., and Joe B. Hurst. February 1986. Purposeful Paraphrasing: Promoting a Nontrivial Pursuit for Meaning. *Journal of Reading* 29: 396–99.

Silverstein, Shel. 1974. What's in the Sack? *Where the Sidewalk Ends*. New York: Harper & Row.

Sinatra, R., and J. Stahl-Gemake. *Using the Right Brain in the Language Arts*. Springfield, Ill.: Charles C. Thomas, 1983.

Singer, Harry. 1978. Active Comprehension: From Answering to Asking Questions. *Reading Teacher* 31: 901–8.

Singer, Harry, Jay Samuels, and Jean Spiroff. 1973–1974. The Effect of Pictures and Contextual Conditions on Learning Responses to Printed Words. *Reading Research Quarterly* 9, iv: 555–67.

Slaughter, Judith Pollard. April 1983. Big Books for Little Kids: Another Fad or a New Approach for Teaching Beginning Reading? *The Reading Teacher* 36: 758–61.

Slobin, Dan I. 1971. *Psycholinguistics*. Glenview, Ill.: Scott, Foresman.

_____. July 1972. They Learn the Same Way All Around the World. *Psychology Today* 6: 72–74, 82.

Smith, E. Brooks, Kenneth S. Goodman, and Robert Meredith. 1970, 1972. *Language and Thinking in the Elementary School*. New York: Holt, Rinehart and Winston.

Smith, Frank. 1971, 1978, 1982. *Understanding Reading*. Hillsdale, N.J.: Erlbaum.

_____. ed. 1973. *Psycholinguistics and Reading*. New York: Holt, Rinehart and Winston.

_____. 1975. *Comprehension and Learning: A Conceptual Framework for Teachers*. New York: Richard C. Owen.

_____. March 1975. The Role of Prediction in Reading. *Elementary English* 52: 305–11.

_____. 1978, 1985. *Reading Without Nonsense*. New York: Teachers College Press.

_____. 1979. Conflicting Approaches to Reading Research and Instruction. *Theory and Practice of Early Reading* 2. Ed. Lauren B. Resnick and Phyllis A. Weaver. Hillsdale, N.J.: Erlbaum, 31–42.

_____. September 1981. Demonstrations, Engagement, and Sensitivity: The Choice Between People and Programs. *Language Arts* 58: 634–42.

_____. January 1981. Demonstrations, Engagement, and Sensitivity: A Revised Approach to Language Learning. *Language Arts* 58: 103–12.

Smith, Frank, with Deborah Lott Holmes. 1973. The Independence of Letter, Word, and Meaning Identification in Reading. *Psycholinguistics and Reading*. Ed. Frank Smith. New York: Holt, Rinehart and Winston, 50–69.

Smith, Laura A., and Margaret Lindberg. 1973. Building Instructional Materials. *Miscue Analysis: Applications to Reading Instruction*. Ed. Kenneth S. Goodman. Urbana, Ill.: National Council of Teachers of English, 77–90.

Smith, Laura, and Constance Weaver. Fall 1978. A Psycholinguistic Look at the Informal Reading Inventory, Part I: Looking at the Quality of Readers' Miscues: A Rationale and an Easy Method. *Reading Horizons* 19: 12–22.

Smith, Nila Banton. 1965. *American Reading Instruction: Its Development and Its Significance in Gaining a Perspective on Current Practices in Reading*. Newark, Del.: International Reading Association.

Smith, Richard J., and Thomas C. Barrett. 1974. *Teaching Reading in the Middle Grades*. Reading, Mass.: Addison-Wesley.

Smith, William L. 1971. The Effect of Transformed Syntactic Structures on Reading. *Language, Reading, and the Communication Process*. Ed. Carl Braun. Newark, Del.: International Reading Association, 52–62.

Soffietti, James P. 1955. Why Children Fail to Read: A Linguistic Analysis. *Harvard Education Review* 25: 63–84.

Stanovich, Keith E. 1980. Toward an Interactive-Compensatory Model of Individual Differences in the Development of Reading Fluency. *Reading Research Quarterly* 16, i: 32–71.

Stauffer, Russell G. February 1960. Productive Reading-Thinking at the First Grade Level. *The Reading Teacher* 13: 183–87.

_____. 1969. *Directing Reading Maturity as a Cognitive Process*. New York: Harper & Row.

_____. 1970. *The Language-Experience Approach to the Teaching of Reading*. New York: Harper & Row.

Stauffer, Russell G., and Ronald Cramer. 1968. *Teaching Critical Reading at the Primary Level*. Newark, Del.: International Reading Association.

Steiner, R., M. Weiner, and W. Cromer. 1971. Comprehension Training and Identification of Good and Poor Readers. *Journal of Educational Psychology* 62: 506–13.

Steinley, Gary. April 1983. Left Brain/Right Brain: More of the Same? *Language Arts* 60: 459–62.

Stewig, John Warren. January 1978. Alphabet Books: A Neglected Genre. *Language Arts* 55: 6–11.

Stotsky, Sandra. 1984. Research on Reading/Writing Relationships: A Synthesis and Suggested Directions. *Composing and Comprehending*. Ed. Julie M. Jensen. Urbana, Ill.: National Conference on Research in English and ERIC Clearinghouse on Reading and Communication Skills, 7–22.

Strickland, Ruth G. January 1964. *The Contribution of Structural Linguistics to the Teaching of Reading, Writing, and Grammar in the Elementary School*. Bloomington, Ind.: Indiana University, *Bulletin of the School of Education* 40, i.

Sudzina, Mary. 1986. An Investigation of the Relationships Between the Reading Styles of Second Graders and their Achievement in Three Different Basal Reader Programs. Doctoral diss., Temple University.

Sulzby, Elizabeth. Summer 1985. Children's Emergent Reading of Favorite Storybooks: A Developmental Study. *Reading Research Quarterly* 20: 458–81.

Tatham, Susan Masland. Spring 1970. Reading Comprehension of Materials Written with Select Oral Language Patterns: A Study at Grades Two and Four. *Reading Research Quarterly* 5: 402–26.

Taylor, Insup. 1976. *Introduction to Psycholinguistics*. New York: Holt, Rinehart and Winston.

Taylor, Jo Ellyn. September 1977. Making Sense: The Basic Skill in Reading. *Language Arts* 54: 668–72.

Taylor, Stanford E., Helen Frackenpohl, and James L. Pettee. 1960. *Grade Level Norms for the Components of the Fundamental Reading Skill*. Huntington, N.Y.: Educational Developmental Laboratories, Bulletin no. 3.

Tchudi, Stephen N. 1986. *Teaching Writing in the Content Areas: College Level*. National Education Association of the United States. Distributed by the National Council of Teachers of English.

Tchudi, Stephen N., and Margie C. Huerta. 1983. *Teaching Writing in the Content Areas: Middle School/Junior High*. National Education Association of the United States. Distributed by the National Council of Teachers of English.

Teach Reading Old-Fashioned Way? 19 April 1982. *U.S. News and World Report*: 69–70.

Teale, William H. September 1982. Toward a Theory of How Children Learn to Read and Write Naturally. *Language Arts* 59: 550–70.

Temple, Charles, and John Burns. 12 May 1986. The Meaning of a Basal Reader Story. Presentation at the Fourth International Conference on the Teaching of English, Ottawa.

Temple, Charles A., Ruth G. Nathan, and Nancy A. Burris. 1982. *The Beginnings of Writing*. Boston: Allyn & Bacon.

Terman, Sibyl, and Charles C. Walcutt. 1958. *Reading: Chaos and Cure*. New York: McGraw-Hill.

Tierney, Robert J., and P. David Pearson. May 1983. Toward a Composing Model of Reading. *Language Arts* 60: 568–80.

Tierney, Robert J., John E. Readence, and Ernest K. Dishner. 1980. *Reading Strategies and Practices: Guide for Improving Instruction*. Boston: Allyn & Bacon.

Tovey, Duane R. Summer 1979. Teacher's Perceptions of Children's Reading Miscues. *Reading Horizons* 19: 302–7.

_____. January 1980. Children's Grasp of Phonics Terms vs. Sound-Symbol Relationships. *The Reading Teacher* 33: 431–37.

Troutman, Denise E., and Julia S. Falk. 1982. Speaking Black English and Reading—Is There a Problem of Interference? *Journal of Negro Education* 51, ii: 123–32.

Tulving, Endel, and Cecille Gold. October 1963. Stimulus Information and Contextual Information as Determinants of Tachistoscopic Recognition of Words. *Journal of Experimental Psychology* 66: 319–27.

U.S. Department of Education. 1986. *What Works: Research About Teaching and Learning*. Washington, D.C.: U.S. Department of Education.

Vacca, Richard T., and JoAnne L. Vacca. 1986. *Content Area Reading*. 2nd ed. Boston: Little, Brown and Company.

Van Allen, Roach. 1976. *Language Experiences in Communication*. Boston: Houghton Mifflin.

Vaughan, Joseph L., Jr. 1982. Instructional Strategies. *Secondary School Reading: What Research Reveals for Classroom Practice*. Ed. Alan Berger and H. Alan Robinson. Urbana, Ill.: National Conference on Research in English and ERIC Clearinghouse on Reading and Communication Skills, 67–84.

Venezky, Richard L. 1967. English Orthography: Its Graphical Structure and Its Relation to Sound. *Reading Research Quarterly* 2: 75–106.

_____. 1970a. Regularity in Reading and Spelling. *Basic Studies on Reading*. Ed. Harry Levin and Joanna P. Williams. New York: Basic Books, 30–42.

_____. 1970b. *The Structure of English Orthography*. The Hague: Mouton.

Venezky, Richard L., and Robert C. Calfee. 1970. The Reading Competency Model. *Theoretical Models and Processes of Reading*. Ed. Harry Singer and Robert B. Ruddell. Newark, Del.: International Reading Association, 273–91.

Viorst, Judith. 1972. *Alexander and the Terrible, Horrible, No Good, Very Bad Day*. Ill. Ray Cruz. New York: Atheneum.

Vitale, Barbara Meister. 1982. *Unicorns Are Real: A Right-Brained Approach to Learning*. Rolling Hills Estates, Calif.: Jalmar Press.

_____. 17 April 1985. Right-Brained Approach to Learning. Presentation for Kalamazoo Intermediate School District, Kalamazoo, Michigan.

Vygotsky, Lev S. 1978. *Mind in Society: the Development of Higher Psychological Processes*. Ed. Michael Cole, Vera John-Steiner, Sylvia Scribner, and Ellen Souberman. Cambridge, Mass.: Harvard University Press.

_____. 1982. *Thought and Language*. Trans. E. Hanfmann and G. Vakar. Cambridge, Mass.: MIT Press.

Wagner, Betty J. 1983. The Expanding Circle of Informal Classroom Drama. *Integrating the Language Arts in the Elementary School*. Ed. Beverly A. Busching and Judith I. Schwartz. Urbana, Ill.: National Council of Teachers of English, 155–63.

Walcutt, Charles Child. 1961. *Tomorrow's Illiterates: The State of Reading Instruction Today*. Boston: Little, Brown and Company.

Walcutt, Charles Child, Joan Lamport, and Glenn McCracken. 1974. *Teaching Reading: A Phonic/Linguistic Approach to Developmental Reading*. New York: Macmillan.

Walshe, R. D., ed. 1982. *Donald Graves in Australia*. Portsmouth, N.H.: Heinemann.

Wardhaugh, Ronald. 1969a. *Reading: A Linguistic Perspective*. New York: Harcourt Brace Jovanovich.

_____. 1969b. The Teaching of Phonics and Comprehension: A Linguistic Evaluation. *Psycholinguistics and the Teaching of Reading*. Ed. Kenneth S. Goodman and James T. Fleming. Newark, Del.: International Reading Association, 79–90.

Watson, Dorothy J. 1973. Helping the Reader: From Miscue Analysis to Strategy Lessons. *Miscue Analysis: Applications to Reading Instruction*. Ed. Kenneth S. Goodman. Urbana, Ill.: National Council of Teachers of English, 103–15.

_____. December 1979. Reader-Selected Miscues: Getting More from Sustained Silent Reading. *English Education* 10: 75–85.

_____., ed. 1987. *Ideas with Insights: Language Arts K–6*. Urbana, Ill.: National Council of Teachers of English.

Weaver, Constance. November/December 1977. Using Context: Before or After? *Language Arts* 54:880–86.

_____. 1979. *Grammar for Teachers: Perspectives and Definitions*. Urbana, Ill.: National Council of Teachers of English.

_____. 1980. *Psycholinguistics and Reading: From Process to Practice*. Cambridge, Mass.: Winthrop Publishers, Inc.

_____. 1982. Reading in the Content Areas. Kalamazoo, Mich.: Western Michigan University. Mimeo.

_____. May 1982. Welcoming Errors as Signs of Growth. *Language Arts* 59: 438–44.

_____. October 1985. Parallels Between New Paradigms in Science and in Reading and Literary Theories: An Essay Review. *Research in the Teaching of English* 19: 298–316.

_____. 11 May 1986. Reading as a Whole-Brain Process: Both Reality and Metaphor. Paper presented at the Fourth International Conference on the Teaching of English, Ottawa. Educational Resources Information Center, no. ED 273 926.

Weaver, Constance, and Laura Smith. Winter 1979. A Psycholinguistic Look at the Informal Reading Inventory, Part II: Inappropriate Inferences from an Informal Reading Inventory. *Reading Horizons* 19: 103–11.

Weber, Rose-Marie. 1970. First-Graders' Use of Grammatical Context in Reading. *Basic Studies on Reading*. Ed. Harry Levin and Joanna P. Williams. New York: Basic Books, 147–163.

_____. 1973. Linguistics and Reading. *Psychological Factors in the Teaching of Reading*. Compiled by Eldon Ekwall. Columbus, Ohio: Charles E. Merrill, 268–291.

Weinstein, Rhona, and M. Sam Rabinovitch. February 1971. Sentence Structure and Retention in Good and Poor Readers. *Journal of Educational Psychology* 62: 25–30.

Wells, Gordon. 1986. *The Meaning Makers: Children Learning Language and Using Language to Learn*. Portsmouth, N.H.: Heinemann.

White, Leonard, Bernard Tursky, and Gary E. Schwartz, eds. 1985. *Placebo: Theory, Research, and Mechanisms*. New York: The Guilford Press.

Williams, Joanna P. 1970. Reactions to Modes of Word Recognition. *Theoretical Models and Processes of Reading*. Ed. Harry Singer and Robert B. Ruddell. Newark, Del.: International Reading Association, 38–46.

Williamson, Joanne. 1961. *The Glorious Conspiracy*. New York: Knopf.

Wilson, Marilyn. 1985. Testing and Literacy: A Contradiction in Terms? *Testing in the English Language Arts: Uses and Abuses*. Ed. John Beard and Scott McNabb. Michigan Council of Teachers of English, 12–16.

Wisemann, Bernard. 1978. *Morris Has a Cold*. New York: Dodd, Mead.

Witelson, Sandra F. 1977. Neural and Cognitive Correlates of Developmental Dyslexia: Age and Sex Differences. *Psychopathology and Brain Dysfunction*. Ed. C. Shagass, S. Gershon, and A. J. Friedhoff. New York: Raven Press, 15–49.

Wolfram, Walter A., and Ralph W. Fasold. 1969. Toward Reading Materials for Speakers of Black English: Three Linguistically Appropriate Passages. *Teaching Black Children to Read*. Ed. Joan C. Baratz and Roger W. Shuy. Arlington, Va.: Center for Applied Linguistics, 138–55.

Woodworth, Robert S. 1938. *Experimental Psychology*. New York: Holt, Rinehart and Winston.

Yngve, Victor H. June 1962. Computer Programs for Translation. *Scientific American* 206: 68–76.

Zaidel, E. 1979. The Split and Half Brains as Models of Congenital Language Disability. *The Neurological Bases of Language Disorders in Children: Methods and*

Directions for Research. Ed. Christy L. Ludlow and Mary Ellen Doran-Quine. NINCDS Monograph no. 22. Bethesda, Md.: U.S. Dept. of Health, Education, & Welfare, 55–89.

SUGGESTED READINGS

In some sections, an asterisk indicates one book particularly recommended as a starting point for further exploration.

The Teaching of Reading: History and Controversies

Chall, Jeanne. 1967, 1983. *Learning to Read: The Great Debate*. New York: McGraw-Hill.

Diack, Hunter. 1965. *The Teaching of Reading in Spite of the Alphabet*. New York: Philosophical Library.

Downing, John. 1967. *Evaluating the Initial Teaching Alphabet*. London: Cassell.

Flesch, Rudolf. 1955. *Why Johnny Can't Read*. New York: Harper & Row.

———. 1981. *Why Johnny Still Can't Read*. New York: Harper & Row.

Gray, William S. 1948. *On Their Own in Reading: How to Give Children Independence in Attacking New Words*. Glenview, Ill.: Scott, Foresman.

———. 1960. *On Their Own in Reading: How to Give Children Independence in Analyzing New Words*. Glenview, Ill.: Scott, Foresman.

———. 1984. *Reading: A Research Retrospective, 1881–1941*. Ed. John T. Guthrie. Newark, Del.: International Reading Association.

Harrison, Maurice. 1964. *The Story of the Initial Teaching Alphabet*. New York: Pitman.

*Mathews, Mitford M. 1966. *Teaching to Read, Historically Considered*. Chicago: University of Chicago Press.

Sharp, Stanley L. 1981. *The REAL Reason Why Johnnie Still Can't Read*. Pompano Beach, Fla.: Exposition Press of Florida.

Smith, Nila Banton. 1965. *American Reading Instruction: Its Development and Its Significance in Gaining a Perspective on Current Practices in Reading*. Newark, Del.: International Reading Association.

Staiger, Ralph C., ed. 1973. *The Teaching of Reading*. Paris: UNESCO, and Lexington, Mass.: Ginn.

Walcutt, Charles Child, Joan Lamport, and Glenn McCracken. 1974. *Teaching Reading: A Phonic/Linguistic Approach to Developmental Reading*. New York: Macmillan.

The Nature of the Reading Process: A Psycholinguistic and Sociolinguistic Perspective

Carton, Aaron S. 1976. *Orientation to Reading*. Rowley, Mass.: Newbury House.

Clay, Marie. 1980. *Reading: The Patterning of Complex Behaviour*. 2nd ed. Portsmouth, N.H.: Heinemann.

Gibson, Eleanor J., and Harry Levin. 1975. *The Psychology of Reading*. Cambridge, Mass.: MIT Press.

Goodman, Kenneth S., ed. 1968, 1973. *The Psycholinguistic Nature of the Reading Process*. Detroit: Wayne State University Press.

Hedley, Carolyn N., and Anthony N. Baratta, eds. 1985. *Contexts of Reading*. Norwood, N.J.: ABLEX.

Huey, Edmund Burke. 1908, 1968. *The Psychology and Pedagogy of Reading*. Repr. Cambridge, Mass.: MIT Press.

Pearson, P. David, ed. 1984. *Handbook of Reading Research*. Newark, Del.: International Reading Association.

Raphael, Taffy E., ed. 1986. *The Contexts of School-Based Literacy*. New York: Random House.

Resnick, Lauren B., and Phyllis A. Weaver, eds. 1979. *Theory and Practice of Early Reading*. 3 vols. Hillsdale, N.J.: Erlbaum.

Rosenblatt, Louise M. 1978. *The Reader, the Text, the Poem: The Transactional Theory of the Literary Work*. Carbondale, Ill.: Southern Illinois University Press.

Singer, Harry, and Robert B. Ruddell, eds. 1985. *Theoretical Models and Processes of Reading*. 3rd ed. Newark, Del.: International Reading Association.

Smith, Frank, ed. 1973. *Psycholinguistics and Reading*. New York: Holt, Rinehart and Winston.

_____. 1975. *Comprehension and Learning: A Conceptual Framework for Teachers*. New York: Richard C. Owen.

_____. 1982. *Understanding Reading*. 3rd ed. Hillsdale, N.J.: Erlbaum.

*_____. 1985. *Reading Without Nonsense*. 2nd ed. New York: Teachers College Press.

Tierney, R. J., P. Anders, and J. Mitchell, eds. In press. *Understanding Readers' Understanding*. Hillsdale, N.J.: Erlbaum.

Miscue Research and Its Implications and Applications

Allen, P. David, and Dorothy J. Watson, eds. 1976. *Findings of Research in Miscue Analysis: Classroom Implications*. Urbana, Ill.: ERIC Clearinghouse on Reading and Communication Skills and the National Council of Teachers of English.

Carey, Robert F., ed. 1987. *Findings of Research in Miscue Analysis: 10 Years Later*. Urbana, Ill.: ERIC and the National Council of Teachers of English.

Goodman, Kenneth S., ed. 1973. *Miscue Analysis: Applications to Reading Instruction*. Urbana, Ill.: National Council of Teachers of English.

_____. 1973. *Theoretically Based Studies of Patterns of Miscues in Oral Reading Performance*. Detroit: Wayne State University. Available from the Educational Resources Information Center, no. ED 079 708.

Goodman, Yetta M., and Carolyn L. Burke. 1972. *Reading Miscue Inventory Manual: Procedure for Diagnosis and Evaluation*. New York: Macmillan.

*Goodman, Yetta, Dorothy Watson, and Carolyn Burke. 1987. *Reading Miscue Inventory: Alternative Procedures*. New York: Richard C. Owen.

Page, William D., ed. 1975. *Help for the Reading Teacher: New Directions in Research*. Urbana, Ill.: National Conference on Research in English and the National Council of Teachers of English.

The Development of Language and Literacy

Bissex, Glenda. 1980. *Gnys at Wrk: A Child Learns to Write & Read*. Cambridge, Mass.: Harvard University Press.

Butler, Dorothy, and Marie Clay. 1979. *Reading Begins at Home*. Portsmouth, N.H.: Heinemann. (booklet for parents)

Ferreiro, Emilia, and Ana Teberosky. 1982. *Literacy Before Schooling*. Translated by Karen Goodman Castro. Portsmouth, N.H.: Heinemann.

Genishi, Celia, and Anne Dyson. 1984. *Language Assessment in the Early Years*. Norwood, N.J.: ABLEX.

Gentry, Richard R. 1987. *Spel . . . Is a Four-Letter Word*. Richmond Hill, Ontario: Scholastic-TAB.

Goelman, Hillel, Antoinette Oberg, and Frank Smith, eds. 1984. *Awakening to Literacy*. Portsmouth, N.H.: Heinemann.

Harste, Jerome C., Virginia Woodward, and Carolyn L. Burke. 1984. *Language Stories and Literacy Lessons*. Portsmouth, N.H.: Heinemann.

Henderson, Edmund H., and James W. Beers, eds. 1980. *Developmental and Cognitive Aspects of Learning to Spell*. Newark, Del.: International Reading Association.

Jaggar, Angela, and M. Trika Smith-Burke, eds. 1985. *Observing the Language Learner*. Newark, Del.: International Reading Association. Co-published by the National Council of Teachers of English.

Lindfors, Judith W. 1980. *Children's Language and Learning*. Englewood Cliffs, N.J.: Prentice-Hall.

Meek, Margaret. 1982. *Learning to Read*. Portsmouth, N.H.: Heinemann.

Smith, Frank. 1983. *Essays into Literacy*. Portsmouth, N.H.: Heinemann.

Taylor, Denny. 1983. *Family Literacy: Young Children Learning to Read and Write*. Portsmouth, N.H.: Heinemann.

Taylor, Denny, and Dorothy S. Strickland. 1986. *Family Storybook Reading*. Portsmouth, N.H.: Heinemann.

Temple, Charles A., Ruth G. Nathan, and Nancy A. Burris. 1982. *The Beginnings of Writing*. Boston: Allyn & Bacon. 2nd ed., forthcoming.

Wells, Gordon. 1986. *The Meaning Makers; Children Learning Language and Using Language to Learn*. Portsmouth, N.H.: Heinemann.

White, Dorothy. 1984. *Books Before Five*. Portsmouth, N.H.: Heinemann.

Yaden, David B., Jr., and Shane Templeton, eds. 1986. *Metalinguistic Awareness and Beginning Literacy: Conceptualizing What It Means to Read and Write*. Portsmouth, N.H.: Heinemann.

Teaching Reading and Writing from a Whole-Language Perspective

Anderson, Gordon S. 1984. *A Whole Language Approach to Reading*. Lanham, Md.: University Press of America.

Barrett, Frank. 1982. *Teacher's Guide to Shared Reading*. Richmond Hill, Ontario: Scholastic-TAB.

Baskwill, Jane, and Paulette Whitman. 1986. *Whole Language Sourcebook*. Richmond Hill, Ontario: Scholastic-TAB.

Butler, Andrea, and Jan Turbill. 1984. *Towards a Reading-Writing Classroom*. Portsmouth, N.H.: Heinemann.

Calkins, Lucy McCormick. 1983. *Lessons from a Child*. Portsmouth, N.H.: Heinemann.

_____. 1986. *The Art of Teaching Writing*. Portsmouth, N.H.: Heinemann.

Clay, Marie M. 1985. *The Early Detection of Reading Difficulties*. 3rd. ed. Portsmouth, N.H.: Heinemann.

Cochrane, Orin, Donna Cochrane, Sharen Scalena, and Ethel Buchanan. 1984. *Reading, Writing and Caring*. Winnepeg: Whole Language Consultants. Also available from Richard C. Owen, New York.

Gentry, Richard R. *Spel . . . Is a Four-Letter Word*. 1987. Richmond Hill, Ontario: Scholastic-TAB.

*Goodman, Ken. 1986. *What's Whole in Whole Language?* Richmond Hill, Ontario: Scholastic-TAB. Available from Heinemann in the U.S.

Goodman, Kenneth S., E. Brooks Smith, Robert Meredith, and Yetta Goodman. 1987. 3rd ed. *Language and Thinking in School: A Whole-Language Curriculum*. New York: Richard C. Owen.

Goodman, Yetta M., and Carolyn L. Burke. 1980. *Reading Strategies: Focus on Comprehension*. New York: Richard C. Owen.

Graves, Donald H. 1983. *Writing: Teachers and Children at Work*. Portsmouth, N.H.: Heinemann.

Hansen, Jane, Tom Newkirk, and Donald M. Graves, eds. 1985. *Breaking Ground: Teachers Relate Reading and Writing in the Elementary School*. Portsmouth, N.H.: Heinemann.

Heald-Taylor, Gail, 1986. *Whole Language Strategies for ESL Students*. Toronto: OISE Press.

Henderson, Edmund. 1985. *Teaching Spelling*. Boston: Houghton Mifflin.

Hittleman, Daniel R. 1983. *Developmental Reading K–8: Teaching from a Psycholinguistic Perspective*. 2nd ed. Boston: Houghton Mifflin.

Holdaway, Don. 1979. *The Foundations of Literacy*. New York: Ashton Scholastic. Available from Heinemann in the U.S.

_____. 1980. *Independence in Reading*. 2nd ed. Portsmouth, N.H.: Heinemann.

_____. 1984. *Stability and Change in Literacy Learning*. Portsmouth, N.H.: Heinemann.

Jewell, Margaret Greer, and Miles V. Zintz. 1986. *Learning to Read Naturally*. Dubuque: Kendall/Hunt.

Lynch, Priscilla. 1986. *Using Big Books and Predictable Books*. Richmond Hill, Ontario: Scholastic-TAB.

McCracken, Robert A., and Marlene J. McCracken. 1986. *Stories, Songs, and Poetry for Teaching Reading and Writing*. New York: Teachers College Press.

Newkirk, Thomas, and Nancie Atwell, eds. 1986. *Understanding Writing: Ways of Observing, Learning, & Teaching*. 2nd ed. Portsmouth, N.H.: Heinemann.

Newman, Judith. 1985. *The Craft of Children's Writing*. Portsmouth, N.H.: Heinemann.

_____. ed. 1985. *Whole Language: Theory in Use*. Portsmouth, N.H.: Heinemann.

Peetoom, Adrian. 1986. *Shared Reading: Safe Risks with Whole Books*. Richmond Hill, Ontario: Scholastic-TAB.

Rhodes, Lynn K., and C. Dudley-Marling. Forthcoming. *Teaching and Learning Reading and Writing*: *Remedial and Learning Disabled Students*. Portsmouth, N.H.: Heinemann.

Ringler, Lenore H., and Carol K. Weber. 1984. *A Language-Thinking Approach to Reading*. New York: Harcourt Brace Jovanovich.

Smith, Frank. 1982. *Writing and the Writer*. New York: Holt, Rinehart and Winston.

Taylor, Denny, and Dorothy S. Strickland. 1986. *Family Storybook Reading*. Portsmouth, N.H.: Heinemann.

Trelease, Jim. 1985. *The Read-Aloud Handbook*. 3rd ed. New York: Penguin.

Walshe, R. D., ed. 1981. *Donald Graves in Australia—"Children Want to Write. . . ."* Portsmouth, N.H.: Heinemann.

Watson, Dorothy J., ed. 1987. *Ideas with Insights: Language Arts K–6*. Urbana, Ill.: National Council of Teachers of English.

The Whole Curriculum, the Whole Child

Blatt, Gloria T., and Jean Cunningham. 1981. *It's Your Move: Expressive Movement Activities for the Language Arts Class*. New York: Teachers College Press.

Busching, Beverly A., and Judith I. Schwartz, eds. 1983. *Integrating the Language Arts in the Elementary School*. Urbana, Ill.: National Council of Teachers of English.

Canfield, Jack, and Harold C. Wells. 1976. *100 Ways to Enhance Self-Concept in the Classroom*. Englewood Cliffs, N.J.: Prentice-Hall.

Chenfeld, Mimi Brodsky. 1986. *Teaching Language Arts Creatively*. 2nd ed. New York: Harcourt Brace Jovanovich.

Cottrell, June S. 1984. *Teaching with Creative Dramatics*. Lincolnwood, Ill.: National Textbook Company.

_____. 1987. *Creative Drama in the Classroom—Grades 1–3*. Lincolnwood, Ill.: National Textbook Company.

_____. 1987. *Creative Drama in the Classroom—Grades 4–6*. Lincolnwood, Ill.: National Textbook Company.

Cowen, John W., ed. 1983. *Teaching Reading Through the Arts*. Newark, Del.: International Reading Association.

Fox, Mem. 1986. *Teaching Drama to Young Children*. Portsmouth, N.H.: Heinemann.

Heinig, Ruth Beall, and Lyda Stillwell. 1981. *Creative Drama for the Classroom Teacher*. 2nd ed. Englewood Cliffs, N.J.: Prentice-Hall. 3rd ed. forthcoming, 1988.

Heinig, Ruth Beall. 1987. *Creative Drama Resource Book for Kindergarten through Grade 3*. Englewood Cliffs, N.J.: Prentice-Hall.

_____. 1987. *Creative Drama Resource Book for Grades Four through Six*. Englewood Cliffs, N.J.: Prentice-Hall.

Lipson, Greta B., and Baxter Morrison. 1977. *Fact, Fantasy, and Folklore*. Carthage, Ill.: Good Apple.

Vitale, Barbara Meister. 1982. *Unicorns Are Real: A Right-Brained Approach to Learning*. Rolling Hills Estates, Calif.: Jalmar Press.

A Psycholinguistic Approach to Teaching Reading and Writing in the Content Areas

Berger, Allen, and H. Alan Robinson, eds. 1982. *Secondary School Reading: What Research Reveals for Classroom Practice*. Urbana, Ill.: National Conference on Research in English and ERIC Clearinghouse on Reading and Communication Skills. National Council of Teachers of English.

*Devine, Thomas G. 1986. *Teaching Reading Comprehension: From Theory to Practice*. Boston: Allyn & Bacon.

Harris, Theodore L., and Eric J. Cooper, eds. 1985. *Reading, Thinking, and Concept Development*. New York: College Entrance Examination Board.

Herber, Harold L. 1978. *Teaching Reading in the Content Areas*. 2nd ed. Englewood Cliffs, N.J.: Prentice-Hall.

Fulwiler, Toby, and Art Young, eds. 1982. *Writing and Reading Across the Curriculum*. Urbana, Ill.: National Council of Teachers of English.

Hittleman, Daniel R., and Carol Hittleman. 1983. *Developmental Reading, K–8: Teaching from a Psycholinguistic Perspective*. Boston: Houghton Mifflin.

Jensen, Julie M., ed. 1984. *Composing and Comprehending*. Urbana, Ill.: National Council of Teachers of English. Originally issued by National Conference on Research in English and ERIC Clearinghouse on Reading and Communication Skills.

McNeil, John D. 1987. 2nd ed. *Reading Comprehension: New Directions for Classroom Practice*. Glenview, Ill.: Scott, Foresman.

Moore, David W., John E. Readence, and Robert J. Rickelman. 1982. *Pre-Reading Activities for Content Area Reading and Learning*. Newark, Del.: International Reading Association.

Pearson, P. David, and Dale D. Johnson. 1978. *Teaching Reading Comprehension*. New York: Holt, Rinehart and Winston.

Readence, John E., Thomas W. Bean, and R. Scott Baldwin. 1981. *Content Area Reading: An Integrated Approach*. Dubuque: Kendall/Hunt.

Robinson, H. Alan. 1983. *Teaching Reading, Writing, and Study Strategies: The Content Areas*. 3rd ed. Boston: Allyn & Bacon.

Tchudi, Stephen N. 1986. *Teaching Writing in the Content Areas: College Level*. National Education Association of the United States. Distributed by the National Council of Teachers of English.

Tchudi, Stephen N., and Margie C. Huerta. 1983. *Teaching Writing in the Content Areas: Middle School/Junior High*. National Education Association of the United States. Distributed by the National Council of Teachers of English.

Tchudi, Stephen N., and Susan J. Tchudi. 1983. *Teaching Writing in the Content Areas: Elementary*. National Education Association of the United States. Distributed by the National Council of Teachers of English.

Tchudi, Stephen N., and Joanne Yates. 1983. *Teaching Writing in the Content Areas: Senior High School*. Urbana, Ill.: National Education Association of the United States. Distributed by the National Council of Teachers of English.

Tierney, Robert J., John E. Readence, and Ernest K. Dishner. 1980. *Reading Strategies and Practices: Guide for Improving Instruction*. Boston: Allyn & Bacon.

Vacca, Richard T., and JoAnne L. Vacca. 1986. *Content Area Reading*. 2nd ed. Boston: Little, Brown and Company.

Vaughan, Joseph L., and Thomas H. Estes. 1986. *Reading and Reasoning Beyond the Primary Grades*. Boston: Allyn & Bacon.

Selecting and Using Books for Children and Young People

Agee, Hugh, 1984. *High Interest—Easy Reading: For Junior and Senior High School School Students*. 4th ed. Urbana, Ill.: National Council of Teachers of English.

Christensen, Jane, ed. 1983. *Your Reading*. Urbana, Ill.: National Council of Teachers of English.

Gallo, Donald R., ed. 1985. *Books for You*. Urbana, Ill.: National Council of Teachers of English.

Lipson, Greta B., and Baxter Morrison. 1977. *Fact, Fantasy, and Folklore: Expanding Language Arts and Critical Thinking Skills*. Carthage, Ill.: Good Apple.

Monson, Dianne L., ed. 1985. *Adventuring with Books*. Urbana, Ill.: National Council of Teachers of English.

Nilsen, Alleen Pace, and Kenneth L. Donelson. 1985. *Literature for Today's Young Adults*. 2nd ed. Glenview, Ill.: Scott, Foresman.

Speigel, Dixie Lee. 1981. *Reading for Pleasure: Guidelines*. Newark, Del.: International Reading Association.

Stewig, John Warren. 1980. *Children and Literature*. Boston: Houghton Mifflin.

Tway, Eileen, ed. 1983. *Reading Ladders for Human Relations*. Urbana, Ill.: National Council of Teachers of English.

Tiedt, Iris M. 1979. *Exploring Books with Children*. Boston: Houghton Mifflin.

Historical Fiction and Nonfiction for Social Studies

Suggested Readings for World History

Titles and annotations provided by Leah Graham, Language Arts Consultant, Lansing Public Schools, Lansing, Mich.

Atkinson, Linda. 1985. *In Kindling Flame: The Story of Hannah Senesh*. New York: Lothrop. The story of the courageous life of one young woman who dedicates herself to saving others from the Nazis.

Beatty, John and Patricia. 1974. *Master Rosalind*. New York: Morrow. Rosalind rebels against lady-like training and disguises herself as a boy. Her adventures lead her through the underworld of crime, Shakespeare's Globe, and the court of Elizabeth I.

_____. 1968. *Witchdog*. New York: Morrow. Boye, the poodle belonging to Prince Rupert, who led Charles I's forces in the English civil wars, was thought to have supernatural powers.

Burton, Hester. 1975. *Kate Ryder*. New York: T. Y. Crowell. A family in mid-seventeenth century England is split by the Civil War. Kate Ryder opposes her brother on the king's side.

de la Trevino, Elizabeth. 1986. *I, Juan de Pareja*. New York: Farrar, Straus and Giroux. A slave, owned by court painter Velasquez, discovers his own creative abilities and finally gains his freedom.

DeJong, Meindert. 1956. *The House of Sixty Fathers*. New York: Harper & Row, Tien Pao is separated from his family during the Japanese occupation of China in World War II. This novel tells the true story of his efforts to be reunited with his family.

Innocenti, Roberto. 1985. *Rose Blanche*. Mankata, Minn.: Creative Education. Picture book dealing with a child's experience in World War II. The text is simple, but there is much to discuss.

O'Dell, Scott. 1979. *The Captive*. Boston: Houghton Mifflin.

———. 1982. *The Feathered Serpent*. Boston: Houghton Mifflin.

———. 1983. *The Amethyst Ring*. Boston: Houghton Mifflin. A trilogy dealing with European intrusion into Mayan culture in the sixteenth century.

Speare, Elizabeth. 1973. *The Bronze Bow*. Boston: Houghton Mifflin. This story is told about a boy in Israel battling the Romans at the time of Jesus.

Stewart, Mary. 1979. *Hollow Hills*. New York: Fawcett.

———. 1984. *Crystal Cave*. New York: Fawcett.

———. 1984. *Last Enchantment*. New York: Fawcett.

———. 1984. *Wicked Day*. New York. Fawcett. A four-book series dealing with Arthurian Britain and the legend of Merlin.

Sutcliff, Rosemary. 1978. *Sun Horse, Moon Horse*. New York: Dutton. A chieftain's son develops his gift as a talented artist in pre-Roman Britain.

———. 1981. *The Lantern Bearers*. New York: Dutton. This story of Roman soldiers in Britain is for mature readers.

Treece, Henry. 1979. *Man with a Sword*. New York: Oxford University Press. Adventures in England at the time of William the Conqueror.

Selected Readings for American History

Recommended by Iris Tiedt. 1979. *Exploring Books With Children*. Boston: Houghton Mifflin.

Dahlstedt, Marden. 1972. *The Terrible Wave*. New York: Coward, McCann and Geoghegan. This book focuses on the famous Johnstown Flood in Pennsylvania in 1889. The two main characters help people cope with this disaster as they search for their own families.

Fleishman, Sid. 1963. *By the Great Horn Spoon!* Boston: Little, Brown and Company. The adventures of Jack and his butler who stow away on a boat in order to get to California and who get involved with the forty-niners.

Frazier, Neta Lohnes. 1973. *Stout-hearted Seven*. Boston: Houghton Mifflin. Based on historical documents, this novel describes the problems encountered by early settlers who traveled the Oregon Trail.

Hamilton, Virginia. 1968. *The House of Dies Drear*. New York: Macmillan. A thirteen-year-old and his family move to Ohio and rent a haunted house once belonging to Dies Drear, an active abolitionist.

Recommended by John Warren Stewig. 1980. *Children and Literature*. Boston: Houghton Mifflin.

de Angeli, Marguerite. 1949. *Thee, Hannah*. New York: Doubleday. The appealing story of a small girl who despises her plain Quaker garb until she finds it has unexpected advantages during the Civil War.

Fox, Paula. 1973. *The Slave Dancer*. New York: Bradbury. A gripping drama of Jessie, 13 years old and white, who was abducted to a slave ship to provide fife music for "dancing the slaves," a common practice to prevent atrophied muscles during the long trip to America.

Gauch, Patricia. 1974. *This Time, Tempe Wick?* New York: Coward, McCann and Geoghegan. A Revolutionary War story set in New Jersey that tells of a surprising girl who singlehandedly prevented disillusioned Pennsylvania soldiers from robbing her.

Levitin, Sonia. 1973. *Roanoke*. New York: Atheneum Publishers. A Roanoke settler learns to adjust to his new environment in the new world and establishes a genuine friendship with a native American who teaches him many survival skills.

Monjo, F. N. 1970. *The Drinking Gourd*. New York: Harper & Row. A fictionalized account of the factual escape of thousands of slaves north to freedom on the underground railroad.

Speare, Elizabeth. 1958. *The Witch of Blackbird Pond*. Boston: Houghton Mifflin. The story of Kate, accused of witchcraft because, among other things, she could swim.

Index